PENGUIN ((P)) CLASSICS

THE LIGHT OF TRUTH

IDA B. WELLS was born a slave in Holly Springs, Mississippi, in 1862. After beginning a teaching career to support her orphaned siblings, she moved to Memphis to become a journalist. There, she eschewed pressure to confine herself to writing women's interest pieces in favor of reporting on major social and political issues. In 1883, she was arrested for refusing to give up her seat on a train, an experience that she chronicled in her first published piece. Though Wells achieved success as a writer, editor, and even co-owner of a newspaper, her greatest accomplishments came after the lynching of a close friend in 1892 spurred her into a lifelong anti-lynching campaign. She published powerful diatribes against lynching, leading to death threats and forced exile in the North. In her work, she exposed and publicized the myths by which Southerners justified lynching. Wells devoted the rest of her life to civil rights, publishing widely and delivering impassioned speeches throughout the Northern states and Great Britain advocating for African Americans' and women's rights. A cofounder of the NAACP, she continued to fight for social justice late into her life. Wells died in 1931 in Chicago.

MIA BAY is a professor of history at Rutgers University and director of the Rutgers Center for Race and Ethnicity. A 2010 Alphonse Fletcher Sr. Fellow and 2009 National Humanities Fellow, she is the author of two books on African American history and a biography of Ida B. Wells entitled *To Tell the Truth Freely: The Life of Ida B. Wells.*

HENRY LOUIS GATES JR. is the Alphonse Fletcher University Professor and founding director of the Hutchins Center for African and African American Research at Harvard University. He is editor in chief of the Oxford African American Studies C
TheRoot.com, and creator of the
The African Americans: Many
for a Penguin Classics series of

IDA B. WELLS

The Light of Truth

Writings of an Anti-Lynching Crusader

Edited with an Introduction and Notes by
MIA BAY

General Editor
HENRY LOUIS GATES JR.

PENGUIN BOOKS

PENGUIN BOOKS
Published by the Penguin Group
Penguin Group (USA) LLC
375 Hudson Street
New York, New York 10014

USA | Canada | UK | Ireland | Australia | New Zealand | India | South Africa | China
penguin.com
A Penguin Random House Company

First published in Penguin Books 2014

ISBN 978-014-310682-1
Printed in the United States of America
7 9 10 8 6
Set in Sabon

Contents

What Is an African
American Classic?

I have long nurtured a deep and abiding affection for the Penguin
Classics, at least since I was an undergraduate at Yale. I used to
imagine that my attraction for these books—grouped together,
as a set, in some independent bookstores when I was a student,
and perhaps even in some today—stemmed from the fact that my
first-grade classmates, for some reason that I can't recall, were
required to dress as penguins in our annual all-school pageant,
and perform a collective side-to-side motion that our misguided
teacher thought she could choreograph into something meant to
pass for a "dance." Piedmont, West Virginia, in 1956, was a very
long way from Penguin Nation, wherever that was supposed to
be! But penguins we were determined to be, and we did our level
best to avoid wounding each other with our orange-colored card-
board beaks while stomping out of rhythm in our matching or-
ange, veined webbed feet. The whole scene was madness, one
never to be repeated at the Davis Free School. But I never stopped
loving penguins. And I have never stopped loving the very audac-
ity of the idea of the Penguin Classics, an affordable, accessible
library of the most important and compelling texts in the history of civilization, their black-and-white spines and covers and
uniform type giving each text a comfortable, familiar feel, as if
we have encountered it, or its cousins, before. I think of the
Penguin Classics as the very best and most compelling in human
thought, an Alexandrian library in paperback, enclosed in black
and white.

I still gravitate to the Penguin Classics when killing time in
an airport bookstore, deferring the slow torture of the security
lines. Sometimes I even purchase two or three, fantasizing that I
can speed-read one of the shorter titles, then make a dent in the
longer one, vainly attempting to fill the holes in the liberal arts

education that our degrees suggest we have, over the course of a plane ride! Mark Twain once quipped that a classic is "something that everybody wants to have read and nobody wants to read," and perhaps that applies to my airport purchasing habits. For my generation, these titles in the Penguin Classics form the canon—the canon of the texts that a truly well-educated person should have read, and read carefully and closely, at least once. For years I rued the absence of texts by black authors in this series, and longed to be able to make even a small contribution to the diversification of this astonishingly universal list. I watched with great pleasure as titles by African American and African authors began to appear, some two dozen over the past several years. So when Elda Rotor approached me about editing a series of African American classics and collections for Penguin's Portable Series, I eagerly accepted.

Thinking about the titles appropriate for inclusion in these series led me, inevitably, to think about what, for me, constitutes a "classic." And thinking about this led me, in turn, to the wealth of reflections on what defines a work of literature or philosophy somehow speaking to the human condition beyond time and place, a work somehow endlessly compelling, generation upon generation, a work whose author we don't have to look like to identify with, to feel at one with, as we find ourselves transported through the magic of a textual time machine; a work that refracts the image of ourselves that we project onto it, regardless of our ethnicity, our gender, our time, our place. This is what centuries of scholars and writers have meant when they use the word *classic*, and—despite all that we know about the complex intersubjectivity of the production of meaning in the wondrous exchange between a reader and a text—it remains true that classic texts, even in the most conventional, conservative sense of the word *classic*, do exist, and these books will continue to be read long after the generation the text reflects and defines, the generation of readers contemporary with the text's author, is dead and gone. Classic texts speak from their authors' graves, in their names, in their voices. As Italo Calvino once remarked, "A classic is a book that has never finished saying what it has to say."

Faulkner put this idea in an interesting way: "The aim of every artist is to arrest motion, which is life, by artificial means, and hold it fixed so that a hundred years later, when a stranger looks at it, it moves again since it is life." That, I am certain, must be the desire of every writer. But what about the reader? What makes a book a classic to a reader? Here, perhaps, Hemingway said it best: "All good books are alike in that they are truer than if they had really happened and after you are finished reading one you will feel that all that happened to you, and afterwards it belongs to you, the good and the bad, the ecstasy, the remorse and sorrow, the people and the places and how the weather was."

I have been reading black literature since I was fifteen, yanked into the dark discursive universe by an Episcopal priest at a church camp near my home in West Virginia in August 1965, during the terrifying days of the Watts Riots in Los Angeles. Eventually, by fits and starts, studying the literature written by black authors became my avocation; ultimately, it has become my vocation. And, in my own way, I have tried to be an evangelist for it, to a readership larger than my own people, people who, as it were, look like these texts. Here, I am reminded of something W. S. Merwin said about the books he most loved: "Perhaps a classic is a work that one imagines should be common knowledge, but more and more often isn't." I would say, of African and African American literature, that perhaps classic works by black writers are works that one imagines should be common knowledge among the broadest possible readership but that less and less are, as the teaching of reading to understand how words can create the worlds into which books can transport us yields to classroom instruction geared toward passing a state-authorized standardized exam. All literary texts suffer from this wrongheaded approach to teaching, mind you; but it especially affects texts by people of color, and texts by women—texts still struggling, despite enormous gains over the last twenty years, to gain a solid foothold in anthologies and syllabi. For every anthology, every syllabus, every publishing series such as the Penguin Classics constitutes a distinct "canon," an implicit definition of all that is essential for a truly educated person to read.

James Baldwin, who has pride of place in my personal canon of African American authors since it was one of his books that that Episcopal priest gave me to read in that dreadful summer of 1965, argued that "the responsibility of a writer is to excavate the experience of the people who produced him." But surely Baldwin

would have agreed with E. M. Forster that the books that we remember, the books that have truly influenced us, are those that
"have gone a little further down our particular path than we
have yet ourselves." Excavating the known is a worthy goal of
the writer as cultural archaeologist; yet, at the same time, so is
unveiling the unknown, the unarticulated yet shared experience
of the colorless things that make us human: "something we have
always known (or thought we knew)," as Calvino puts it, "but
without knowing that this author said it first." We might think of
the difference between Forster and Baldwin, on the one hand,
and Calvino, on the other, as the difference between an author
representing what has happened (Forster, Baldwin) in the history
of a people whose stories, whose very history itself, has long been
suppressed, and what could have happened (Calvino) in the atem-
poral realm of art. This is an important distinction when thinking about the nature of an African American classic—rather,
when thinking about the nature of the texts that constitute the
African American literary tradition or, for that matter, the texts
in any under-read tradition.

One of James Baldwin's most memorable essays, a subtle meditation on sexual preference, race, and gender, is entitled "Here
Be Dragons." So much of traditional African American literature, even fiction and poetry—ostensibly at least once removed
from direct statement—was meant to deal a fatal blow to the
dragon of racism. For black writers since the eighteenth-century
beginnings of the tradition, literature has been one more weapon—
a very important weapon, mind you, but still one weapon among
many—in the arsenal black people have drawn upon to fight
against antiblack racism and for their equal rights before the law.
Ted Joans, the black surrealist poet, called this sort of literature
from the sixties' Black Arts movement "hand grenade poems."
Of what possible use are the niceties of figuration when one must
slay a dragon? I can hear you say, give me the blunt weapon any-
time! Problem is, it is more difficult than some writers seem to
think to slay a dragon with a poem or a novel. Social problems
persist; literature too tied to addressing those social problems
tends to enter the historical archives, leaving the realm of the literary. Let me state bluntly what should be obvious: Writers are
read for how they write, not what they write about.

Frederick Douglass—for this generation of readers one of the most widely read writers—reflected on this matter even in the midst of one of his most fiery speeches addressing the ironies of the sons and daughters of slaves celebrating the Fourth of July while slavery continued unabated. In his now-classic essay "What Is to the Slave the Fourth of July" (1852), Douglass argued that an immediate, almost transparent form of discourse was demanded of black writers by the heated temper of the times, a discourse with an immediate end in mind: "At a time like this, scorching irony, not convincing argument, is needed. . . . a fiery stream of biting ridicule, blasting reproach, withering sarcasm, and stern rebuke. For it is not light that is needed, but fire; it is not the gentle shower, but thunder. We need the storm, the whirlwind, and the earthquake." Above all else, Douglass concludes, the rhetoric of the literature created by African Americans must, of necessity, be a purposeful rhetoric, its ends targeted at attacking the evils that afflict black people: "The feeling of the nation must be quickened; the conscience of the nation must be roused; the propriety of the nation must be startled; the hypocrisy of the nation must be exposed; and its crimes against God and man must be proclaimed and denounced." And perhaps this was so; nevertheless, we read Douglass's writings today in literature classes not so much for their content but to understand, and marvel at, his sublime mastery of words, words—to paraphrase Calvino—that never finish saying what it is they have to say, not because of their "message," but because of the language in which that message is inextricably enfolded.

There are as many ways to define a classic in the African American tradition as there are in any other tradition, and these ways are legion. So many essays have been published entitled "What Is a Classic?" that they could fill several large anthologies. And while no one can say explicitly why generations of readers return to read certain texts, just about everyone can agree that making a best-seller list in one's lifetime is most certainly not an index of fame or influence over time; the longevity of one's readership—of books about which one says, "I am rereading," as Calvino puts it—on the other hand, most certainly is. So, the size of one's readership (through library use, Internet access, and sales) cumulatively is an interesting factor to consider; and because of series such as the Penguin Classics, we can gain a sense, for our purposes, of those texts written by authors in previous generations that have sustained sales—mostly for classroom use—long after their authors were dead.

There can be little doubt that *Narrative of the Life of Frederick Douglass* (1845), *The Souls of Black Folk* (1903), by W. E. B. Du Bois, and *Their Eyes Were Watching God* (1937), by Zora Neale Hurston, are the three most classic of the black classics—again, as measured by consumption—while Langston Hughes's poetry, though not purchased as books in these large numbers, is accessed through the Internet as frequently as that of any other American poet, and indeed profoundly more so than most. Within Penguin's Portable Series list, the most popular individual titles, excluding Douglass's first slave narrative and Du Bois's *Souls*, are:

Up from Slavery (1903), Booker T. Washington
The Autobiography of an Ex-Coloured Man (1912), James
   Weldon Johnson
God's Trombones (1926), James Weldon Johnson
Passing (1929), Nella Larsen
The Marrow of Tradition (1898), Charles W. Chesnutt
Incidents in the Life of a Slave Girl (1861), Harriet Jacobs
The Interesting Narrative (1789), Olaudah Equiano
The House Behind the Cedars (1900), Charles W. Chesnutt
My Bondage and My Freedom (1855), Frederick Douglass
Quicksand (1928), Nella Larsen

These titles form a canon of classics of African American literature, judged by classroom readership. If we add Jean Toomer's novel *Cane* (1922), arguably the first work of African American modernism, along with Douglass's first narrative, Du Bois's *The Souls*, and Hurston's *Their Eyes*, we would most certainly have included many of the touchstones of black literature published before 1940, when Richard Wright published *Native Son*.

Every teacher's syllabus constitutes a canon of sorts, and I teach these texts and a few others as the classics of the black canon. Why these particular texts? I can think of two reasons: First, these texts signify or riff upon each other, repeating, borrowing, and extending metaphors book to book, generation to generation. To take just a few examples, Equiano's eighteenth-century use of the trope of the talking book (an image found, remarkably, in five slave narratives published between 1770 and 1811) becomes, with Frederick Douglass, the representation of the quest for freedom as, necessarily, the quest for literacy, for a freedom larger than physical manumission; we might think of this as the representation of metaphysical manumission, of freedom and literacy—the literacy of great literature—inextricably intertwined. Douglass transformed the metaphor of the talking book into the trope of chiasmus, a repetition with a stinging reversal: "You have seen how a man becomes a slave, you will see how a slave becomes a man." Du Bois, with Douglass very much on his mind, transmuted chiasmus a half century later into the metaphor of duality or double consciousness, a necessary condition of living one's life, as he memorably put it, behind a "veil."

Du Bois's metaphor has a powerful legacy in twentieth-century black fiction: James Weldon Johnson, in *Ex-Coloured Man*, literalizes the trope of double consciousness by depicting as his protagonist a man who, at will, can occupy two distinct racial spaces, one black, one white, and who moves seamlessly, if ruefully, between them; Toomer's *Cane* takes Du Bois's metaphor of duality for the inevitably split consciousness that every Negro must feel living in a country in which her or his status as a citizen is liminal at best, or has been erased at worst, and makes of this the metaphor for the human condition itself under modernity, a tellingly bold rhetorical gesture—one designed to make the Negro the metaphor of the human condition. And Hurston, in *Their Eyes*, extends Toomer's revision even further, depicting a character who can gain her voice only once she can name this condition of duality or double consciousness and then glide gracefully and lyrically between her two selves, an "inside" self and an "outside" one.

More recently, Alice Walker, in *The Color Purple*, signifies upon two aspects of the narrative strategy of *Their Eyes*: First, she revisits the theme of a young black woman finding her voice, depicting a protagonist who writes herself into being through letters addressed to God and to her sister, Nettie—letters that grow ever more sophisticated in their syntax and grammar and imagery as she comes to consciousness before our very eyes, letter to letter; and second, Walker riffs on Hurston's use of a vernacular-inflected free indirect discourse to show that black English has the capacity to serve as the medium for narrating a novel through the black dialect that forms a most pliable and expansive language in Celie's letters. Ralph Ellison makes Du Bois's metaphor of the veil a trope of blindness and life underground for his protagonist in *Invisible Man*, a protagonist who, as he types the story of his life from a hole underground, writes himself into being in the first person (in contradistinction to Richard Wright's protagonist, Bigger Thomas, whose reactive tale of fear and flight is told in the third person). Walker's novel also riffs on Ellison's claim for the revolutionary possibilities of writing the self into being, whereas Hurston's protagonist, Janie, speaks herself into being. Ellison himself signified multiply upon Richard Wright's *Native Son*, from the title to the use of the first-person bildungsroman to chart the coming to consciousness of a sensitive protagonist moving from blindness and an inability to do little more than react to his environment, to the insight gained by wresting control of his identity from social forces and strong individuals that would circumscribe and confine his life choices. Toni Morrison, master supernaturalist and perhaps the greatest black novelist of all, trumps Ellison's trope of blindness by returning over and over to the possibilities and limits of insight within worlds confined or circumscribed not by supraforces (à la Wright) but by the confines of the imagination and the ironies of individual and family history, signifying upon Faulkner, Woolf, and Márquez in the process. And Ishmael Reed, the father of black postmodernism and what we might think of as the hip-hop novel, the tradition's master parodist, signifies upon everybody and everything in the black literary tradition, from the slave narratives to the Harlem Renaissance to black nationalism and feminism.

This sort of literary signifying is what makes a literary tradition, well, a "tradition," rather than a simple list of books whose authors happen to have been born in the same country, share the same gender, or would be identified by their peers as belonging to this ethnic group or that. What makes these books special— "classic"—however, is something else. Each text has the uncanny capacity to take the seemingly mundane details of the day-to-day African American experience of its time and transmute those details and the characters' actions into something that transcends its ostensible subject's time and place, its specificity. These texts reveal the human universal through the African American particular: All true art, all classics, do this; this is what "art" is, a revelation of that which makes each of us sublimely human, rendered in the minute details of the actions and thoughts and feelings of a compelling character embedded in a time and place. But as soon as we find ourselves turning to a text for its anthropological or sociological data, we have left the realm of art; we have reduced the complexity of fiction or poetry to an essay, and this is not what imaginative literature is for. Richard Wright, at his best, did this, as did his signifying disciple Ralph Ellison; Louis Armstrong and Duke Ellington, Bessie Smith and Billie Holiday achieved this effect in music; Jacob Lawrence and Romare Bearden achieved it in the visual arts. And this is what Wole Soyinka does in his tragedies, what Toni Morrison does in her novels, what Derek Walcott does in his poetry. And while it is risky to name one's contemporaries in a list such as this, I think that Rita Dove and Jamaica Kincaid achieve this effect as well, as do Colson Whitehead and Edwidge Danticat, in a younger generation. (There are other writers whom I would include in this group had I the space.) By delving ever so deeply into the particularity of the African and African American experience, these authors manage, somehow, to come out the other side, making the race or the gender of their characters almost translucent, less important than the fact that they stand as aspects of ourselves beyond race or gender or time or place, precisely in the same magical way that Hamlet never remains for long stuck as a prince in a court in Denmark.

Each classic black text reveals to us, uncannily, subtly, how the Black Experience is inscribed, inextricably and indelibly, in the human experience, and how the human experience takes one of its myriad forms in blackface, as it were. Together, such texts also demonstrate, implicitly, that African American culture is one of the world's truly great and eternal cultures, as noble and as resplendent as any. And it is to publish such texts, written by African and African American authors, that Penguin has created this new series, which I have the pleasure of editing.

HENRY LOUIS GATES JR.

Introduction

"The way to right wrongs is to turn the light of truth upon them."

This book brings together the writings of Ida B. Wells, a remarkable African American journalist, reformer, and social critic. Born a slave in Holly Springs, Mississippi, in 1862, Wells arrived in the world only a few months before the Emancipation Proclamation, and grew up to be a prominent member of a vast generation of African Americans whose lives were forever changed not only by the Confederacy's defeat but also by the turbulent postemancipation decades that followed. The nation's great Reconstruction era experiment in racial democracy shaped Wells's childhood, while the South's turn toward disenfranchisement, Jim Crow, and vigilante violence was the scourge of her adult life and the major subject of her writing. Her work inspired death threats that drove her out of the South in 1892 and she ultimately resettled in Chicago, where she lived until her death in 1931.

Wells's writings remain fascinating today because she was far more than a spectator to her changing times. Raised by ex-slave parents who taught her to do something when confronted with injustice, Wells confronted injustice daily, and wrote to expose the exploitation, discrimination, disenfranchisement, and racial violence that African Americans were subject to during her lifetime. Best known for her tireless crusade against lynching, Wells took on all forms of social injustice, and understood her anti-lynching campaign as an all-out assault on white supremacy.

Toward the end of her life, she wrote an unfinished autobiography in which she described her life as a "crusade for justice," and the articles and pamphlets collected here document the uncompromising brilliance she brought to her crusade.[2]

Who was Ida B. Wells? And what inspired her crusade for justice? The first of Elizabeth and James Wells's eight children, Wells came into the world as slavery was coming to an end. Her parents welcomed emancipation with open arms, abandoning their former owner (who was also Jim Wells's father) in favor of setting up their own household. Both parents were fortunate enough to emerge from slavery with marketable skills: Jim Wells was a carpenter and Elizabeth Wells was a cook, and together the couple were soon prosperous enough to entertain high ambitions for both themselves and their children.

Jim Wells was among the Reconstruction era's black Republicans who managed to elect African American officials to both their state legislatures and the Congress, despite bitter opposition from the South's white Democrats. He braved the vigilante violence to which the black voters in Mississippi, and most other Southern states, were often subjected when they attended political meetings, despite the anxieties such activities inspired in his wife. Lizzie Wells, as Elizabeth Wells was known, seems to have been supportive of her husband's political commitments, but she was also understandably worried whenever he attended such meetings. Accordingly, Ida's childhood memories included watching her mother anxiously "walking the floor at night when my father was out at a political meeting."[3]

The Wellses sought education and autonomy for their family, as well as a brighter political future. They enrolled their children in a local missionary school, which Lizzie Wells herself also attended until she had learned to read the Bible. In addition, Lizzie Wells supplemented her children's education at home, enriching their schoolwork with lessons in morals, manners, and housework, which made an enduring impression on Ida, who admired her mother for bringing up eight children "with strict discipline that many mothers with educational advantages could not have exceeded."[4]

Sadly, Ida Wells would put such lessons to the test all too early. Her parents died in the yellow fever epidemic that swept the

Mississippi Valley in the summer of 1878, which also killed her youngest brother, Stanley. Only sixteen at the time, Ida was visiting her grandparents in rural Mississippi when she heard the tragic news. She rushed back to Holly Springs to find that Jim Wells's Masonic brothers were planning to tend to the Wellses' orphaned children by splitting them up among several different families. Ida would not have it. "My parents [would] turn in their graves to know their children had been scattered," she told them, volunteering to take care of the children herself, if the Masons would help her find work.[5]

That fall, Ida, who had been a "butterfly school girl" before her parents' death, had her "dresses lengthened" and took a job teaching elementary school.[6] Too young for the job, Ida found it challenging. She had not even finished normal school (as high school was then known) and had no work experience other than teaching Sunday School, so the only jobs she could get as she began her teaching career were positions teaching elementary school in isolated rural areas, to which she traveled by mule, returning home only on the weekend.

Ida would always remember herself as feeling wholly inadequate during her years teaching in country schools. Still a teenager, she scrambled to prepare lessons and complete her own education by reading at night, and questioned whether she could meet the needs of the rural freedpeople in the communities where she taught. Not only the children she taught, she quickly realized, but their parents too "needed the guidance of everyday life and that the leaders, the preachers were not giving them this help. They would come to me with their problems because I, as their teacher, should have been their leader. But I knew nothing of life but what I had read."[7]

Ida would never like teaching, perhaps because she found this early experience so daunting. But she made the best of it, polishing her skills and eventually taking a test that would allow her to get a more lucrative teaching job in the city schools of Memphis, Tennessee. Moreover, once she moved to Memphis with her two youngest sisters in tow—her brothers having grown old enough to support themselves—she was also able to put her self-education to more satisfying use, by writing for local newspapers.

In journalism, Wells found her vocation. Writing allowed her to address her race not as a poorly qualified elementary schoolteacher

but as herself: an opinionated young black woman. She wrote
under the pen name Iola, choosing a name with a rural twang to
reflect her origins in small-town Mississippi, and wrote for an
audience not unlike the rural black communities in which she
had so recently taught. As Iola, she dedicated herself to writing
"in a plain common sense way on the things which concerned
our people."[8]

Included in chapter I of this volume, her early writings show
that Wells believed African Americans had a wide range of concerns. Writing in an age when female journalists often wrote primarily on subjects of special interest to women—and often
published their articles within the confines of their newspaper's
"Women's Department"—Wells acknowledged no such limita-
tions in her choice of subjects. Single and in her twenties, Wells
was interested in women's issues and aspirations, and wrote about
them in articles with titles such as "Woman's Mission," "The
Model Woman: A Pen Picture of the Typical Southern Girl," and
"Our Women." But women were not Wells's primary subject.
Most of her articles took up the major political and social questions of her day, presenting her thoughts on black leadership,
party politics, segregation laws, African emigration, and racial
violence. Highly opinionated and committed to racial justice,
Wells was a crusading journalist from the start. Her very first
article, a now-lost piece that appeared in a local Baptist newspaper, the *Living Way*, chronicled her experience of being thrown
out of the "ladies' car" on the Chesapeake, Ohio and Southwestern
Railroad in September 1883.

Her ill-fated journey took place at a time when the segregated
world of the Jim Crow South was still taking shape, and the railroad's best accommodations were still set aside for ladies rather
than "whites only." These cars were a legacy of the slavery era,
when free black travelers were neither common nor assertive
enough to make claims on the ladies' cars, which typically accommodated white women travelers and their families. Southern
railroad regulations would have to change before they could successfully confine middle-class black women such as Wells to the
substandard accommodations typically offered to blacks. By
1883, such changes were under way. Tennessee had adopted a
separate-coach law mandating colored cars for blacks, and while
there was no designated colored car on Wells's train, its conduc-

tor felt she had no place in the ladies' car, and told her to move to the train's smoking car. Wells resisted, hanging on to her seat and biting the conductor's hand when he tried to force the issue. And she remained in her seat until the conductor came back with two other men, who picked her up and carried her out of the car, at which point Wells got off the train rather than accepting a seat in the smoking car. Disheveled but still defiant, she rode home by wagon and promptly sued the railroad. Wells won her initial suit, but her quest to ride in the ladies' car was ultimately rebuffed in Tennessee's Supreme Court, which challenged Wells's unladylike "persistence."[9]

Discouraged but not deterred, Wells continued to publicly protest transportation segregation and other forms of racial discrimination. She received no compensation for her early articles for the *Living Way*, but by the late 1880s, Wells was writing for pay, and publishing what she wrote in black newspapers across the country. Moreover, her spirited editorials and articles were widely reprinted and earned her the nickname "Iola, the Princess of the Press." By 1889, her growing reputation allowed her to move into the news business full time, becoming editor and publisher as well as writer. That year, she became co-owner of the *Memphis Free Speech and Headlight*, the city's black newspaper. But in the decades to come it was Wells's career as a journalist and activist, rather than her impressive accomplishments as a businesswoman, that brought her to worldwide attention.

WELLS'S ANTI-LYNCHING CAMPAIGN

The early 1890s saw Wells's willingness to take on racial violence, and her brilliant analysis of the social functions of racial violence, propel her to national and international renown. Like her move toward journalism, Wells's anti-lynching campaign took shape around events she experienced personally: namely, a brutal lynching that rocked black Memphis not long after she took the helm at *Free Speech*. In the second week of March 1892, three black businessmen, including a man named Thomas Moss who was one of Wells's closest friends, were first arrested and then dragged out of the county jail and shot. Their arrest followed a series of altercations between blacks and whites in a

mixed neighborhood known as the Curve. First, a group of black
and white boys squabbled over a game of marbles. Later, their
parents joined in—after the father of one of the white boys personally whipped a victorious black player, and black men gathered to protest the whipping. Eventually, the dispute moved into
People's Grocery Store, an African American–owned joint-stock
grocery store where Memphis blacks congregated. That night, a
group of armed white men stormed the store and were met with
gunfire from black men who had assembled to guard the place.
Three white men were wounded before the store's protectors and
patrons fled. Spurred by reports of a massive black uprising, a
white mob gathered the next day, looted the store, terrorized the
black inhabitants of the Curve, and dragged more than thirty
black men off to jail.

   Among them were the three men who were taken out of the jail
and lynched four days later. Two of the men, Thomas Moss and
Calvin McDowell, were proprietors of People's Grocery Store,
while Will Stewart worked there as a clerk. All three were otherwise largely blameless in the conflict. None had fired shots; indeed,
Thomas Moss was not even present during the shootout in the
store. Rather, his offense, and those of McDowell and Stewart,
seems to have been the success of the store, which competed directly with a white-owned store across the street.

   The "lynching at the Curve," as Wells called it, was the first
lynching to occur in Memphis, and it made an indelible impression on her. In Natchez selling subscriptions to *Free Speech* when
the lynching occurred, Wells witnessed none of the violence. But
she returned to find her dear friend Tommie Moss dead and
blacks fleeing Memphis. For her, the events in Memphis were not
only her first personal experience of the realities of white violence
in the post-Reconstruction South but a revelation into the logic
of white supremacy. Prior to the murders in Memphis, Wells, like
"many another person who had read of lynching in the South," had
not questioned conventional accounts of lynching. She had thought
that "although lynching was irregular and contrary to law and
order," the motives behind it were defensible—"unreasoning
anger over the terrible crime of rape led to lynching . . . perhaps
the brute deserved death anyhow and the mob was justified in
taking his life." But events in Memphis opened her "eyes to what
lynching really was."[10] The Memphis victims were not accused of

rape or any other crime, and their deaths made Wells suspect that lynching might be little more than "an excuse to get rid of Negroes who were acquiring wealth and property and thus keep the race terrorized and 'the nigger down.' "[11]

Wells's suspicions were confirmed when she began to research every lynching that she read about. What happened in Memphis was not unusual, she found: fully two-thirds of the victims of lynch mobs were never even accused of rape. Moreover, of those who were, they often accused on the flimsiest of evidence. Wells's discoveries about lynching enraged her, inspiring her to run a series of anti-lynching editorials in *Free Speech* castigating white Memphis.

Writing at a time when rape was supposedly on the rise in the South—*Harper's Weekly* labeled it the "new Negro Crime"—Wells took on the charge that white Southerners most often invoked rape as unassailable justification for lynching.[12] Not only had her research revealed to her that most lynchings occurred in the absence of any accusations of rape, it also called into question many of the cases in which rape was alleged. All too often, the black men accused of rape were guilty of no other crime than having a sexual relationship with a white woman. Many of the cries of rape came only after clandestine interracial relationships were exposed. Wells was not the first African American to doubt the allegations of rape that accompanied many lynchings, but she was one of the very first to voice her doubts publicly. Writing in a May 21, 1892, editorial in *Free Speech*, she challenged white Southern interpretations of lynching in no uncertain terms. "Nobody in this section of the country believes the threadbare old lie that Negroes rape white women," she wrote. "If Southern men are not careful, they will over reach themselves and public sentiment will have a reaction; a conclusion will be reached which will then be very damaging to the moral reputation of their women."[13]

Wells was away when her editorial came out, which turned out to be fortunate. With its publication, a white mob descended on the offices of *Free Speech*, shutting it down permanently. Although Wells was not immediately identified as the author of the editorial, which was not signed, its author was threatened with death and dismemberment. The editors of one white Memphis paper, who assumed the author of the editorial was a man, threatened to tie "the wretch who has uttered these calumnies to a stake at the intersection of Main and Madison Sts., brand him with a hot iron, and perform on him a surgical operation with a pair of shears." Wells's gender did not protect her once her authorship became known. Instead, local whites renewed and revised this threat by letting Wells know that if she returned "they would bleed my face and hang me in front of the court house."[14]

Such threats kept Wells from ever returning to Memphis, but they did not silence her. Exiled from the South, Wells devoted herself to exposing the truth about lynching. Becoming a public speaker for the first time, she toured the Northern United States and Great Britain testifying about her experiences in Memphis, and the facts she had gathered about lynching. A poised and attractive young woman who sometimes spoke through tears, Wells was a powerful speaker. She testified on the events that led her to exile, including heart-wrenching details such as a description of the loss suffered by the "baby daughter of Tom Moss," who although "too young to express how she misses her father, toddles to the wardrobe, seizes the legs of his letter-carrier uniform, hugs and kisses them with evident delight and stretches her little hands to be taken up into arms that will nevermore clasp his daughter's form."[15] But, while Wells sought the sympathy of her audience, she did not confine herself to pathos.

Instead, she expanded on the accusations in her editorial, exposing the rape myth that white Southerners used to justify lynching by challenging the connection between the two. Naming specific white women, and specific cases, she documented the consensual nature of interracial liaisons for which black men had been lynched, concluding "white men lynch the offending Afro-American, not because he is a despoiler of women, but because he succumbs to the smiles of white women."[16] She also presented evidence on the many lynchings for which rape was not even invoked as justification and underscored that Southern whites victimized black women as well as men by imposing no punishment whatsoever on white men who assaulted black women.

By exposing the rape myth used to justify lynching, Wells recast lynching as "a lesson of subordination" that had little to do with sex or sexual assaults. A terrifying and extralegal form of racial subjugation, it supplemented the disenfranchisement, legal disabilities, and economic exploitation that white Southerners used to enforce "their oft-repeated slogan: 'This is a white man's country, and the white man must rule.' "[17]

Wells's incisive analysis of lynching turned her anti-lynching crusade into an attack on the color line. In addition to demystifying the rape myth, her 1890s lectures and writings contained a stinging critique of conditions in the South. A witness to the collapse of Reconstruction, Wells deplored the repeal of the Reconstruction-era civil rights acts, and the disenfranchisement of African Americans that followed. She also decried the passage of "separate car" state laws requiring segregated coaches on the railroads, and advised Southern blacks to boycott Jim Crow travel in an effort to force the repeal of these laws. Lynching, she emphasized, was a product of social and legal disabilities that white Southerners imposed on blacks, and would not be eradicated until black Southerners gained their rights.

Wells's anti-lynching campaign made her a celebrity and defined anti-lynching as a cause. In addition to speaking before packed houses in both America and England, Wells published her anti-lynching lectures in the pamphlets *Southern Horrors: The Lynch Law in All Its Phases* (1892) and *A Red Record* (1894), which are included in this volume.

Wells's writings and lectures were generally well received among blacks, who tended to endorse her analysis of lynching. Her African American supporters included black America's senior statesman, Frederick Douglass, who wrote prefaces for a number of her anti-lynching pamphlets, and a broad cross section of African American women, who attended her lectures and lent their support to her cause.

Some of New York's most influential and elite black women organized and attended her first public lecture, which took place in New York in the spring of 1892, and her work was subsequently feted at black women's clubs across the Northeast. In 1895, her supporters rallied together, forming the National Association of Colored Women (NACW), after Wells was the subject of a defamatory public letter written by a white Mississippi editor. The insult inspired club women across the nation to come together to defend Wells and all their members from the "base aspersions . . . [that] blight and dwarf the spirit of Negro women."[18]

Whites, by contrast, were far more mixed in their responses to Wells. In the South, she continued to receive viciously negative press long after she left the region—coverage that publicized, though certainly did not promote, her anti-lynching campaign. But she encountered more sympathetic whites in the North, and especially in Britain, where she lectured on two separate visits in 1893 and 1894. There she found allies among the British reform communities that had once supported the abolition of slavery, and were troubled by Wells's account of the South.

Her activities in Britain are chronicled in chapter III of this volume, which contains a selection of the articles she published during her second, more extended visit to Britain. Her first visit had been cut short by a falling-out between her English backers, Catherine Impey and Isabella Fyvie Mayo. But when she returned to England in 1894, Wells managed to mobilize an anti-lynching movement among several influential British reformers, who founded and staffed an Anti-Lynching Committee that investigated and condemned lynchings, and even sponsored her fact-finding tour of the United States in 1895.

Lynching continued, but never as unopposed as it had been before Wells's campaign. Wells and British reformers helped generate a more critical attitude in the North toward lynching, as well as some organized opposition. Moreover, anti-lynching became one of the central platforms of the black civil rights organizations that formed around the turn of the century, as did the fact-finding techniques that Wells pioneered to expose the truth about lynching. Organizations like the NAACP (1909) and the Urban League (1915) followed the lead established in Wells's anti-lynching pamphlets of the 1890s, which investigated the facts behind lynching cases, and compiled detailed statistics on the incidence of lynching.

Other links between Wells and early civil rights organizations are not difficult to find. Wells was a founding member of the NAACP, as well as several other less-successful civil rights ventures that preceded it, such as the Niagara Movement and the Afro-American Council. However, Wells did not last long at the NAACP or any of the other major black organizations. Part of it might have been personal. In 1895, Wells married Ferdinand Barnett, a Chicago lawyer, and subsequently had four children with him. Thereafter, the challenges of marriage and children made it more difficult for Wells-Barnett (as she renamed herself) to sustain an activist life. Still, marriage brought no end to Wells-

Barnett's activism. Far from traditional in his gender politics, Ferdinand Barnett supported his wife's work and did not expect her to stay at home. Instead, he hired household help and even took on the chore of preparing the family's meals himself—having grown up cooking alongside his father, who was a chef. As a married woman, Wells-Barnett continued to work, write, and move in and out of political and social organizations.

A mother to two young sons by 1899, Wells-Barnett still managed to protest the lynching of Sam Hose in Georgia, even coming up with a fact-finding exposé despite the fact that her children kept her close to home, a feat that she achieved by hiring the services of a detective whose research exonerated Hose. Moreover, she also used the white-authored papers the *Atlanta Journal* and *Atlanta Constitution* to further illuminate *Lynch Law in Georgia* (1899). Both papers reported the deaths of Hose and the other black men in enthusiastic, almost pornographic detail, making Wells-Barnett's case against mob violence for her. A year later, when Robert Charles was brutally lynched in New Orleans, Wells-Barnett was no freer to travel, and had no money to hire a detective. But she still managed to write a brilliant analysis of the events in New Orleans by once again mining the work of local white journalists for details about the case.

Moreover, events in Atlanta also inspired Wells-Barnett to publicly denounce Booker T. Washington, who was then widely celebrated by whites as the leader of black America. Wells-Barnett was an admirer of Washington's self-help philosophy, but had long been troubled by his accommodationist stance on black civil rights and racial violence, and became more so in the aftermath of the Hose lynching. Traveling abroad when the violence took place, Washington was slow to issue any public statement on events in Georgia, and when he finally did so months later, it took the form of a mild-mannered letter that deplored lynchings as bad for both blacks and whites and counseled African Americans to repudiate the Negro rapist as a "beast in human form."[19] Outraged, Wells-Barnett denounced Washington in a "sassy" letter to the *New York Age*, which Washington's friend T. Thomas Fortune refused to publish.[20] That letter has not survived, but Wells-Barnett's critique of Washington can be found in her 1904 essay "Booker T. Washington and His Critics" (in chapter V).

By 1904, Wells-Barnett was a mother of four young children, and had ever-fewer opportunities to travel or write. But she remained a tireless activist. Operating from Chicago after her marriage, she continued to monitor lynchings and other forms of racial injustice. She published anti-lynching articles in a number of mainstream national publications, such as the *Arena* and the *Independent*, and worked with radical black journalist William Monroe Trotter to revive the National Equal Rights League— a civil rights organization with Reconstruction-era roots that Wells-Barnett and Trotter envisioned as a radical alternative to the NAACP. But much of her twentieth-century activism had a distinctly local focus.

A lifelong supporter of voting rights for women, Wells-Barnett was an influential participant in the Illinois women's suffrage movement, and helped organize Chicago's female voters. After 1908, she also began working to provide jobs, guidance, and living accommodations for Chicago's growing population of black Southern migrants, who were unwelcome at many of the city's social service agencies. That year, she founded an organization called the Negro Fellowship League to support such migrants, which she led for more than a decade. During this time, she also worked as one the state's first probation officers for several years, and used the league as a source of support and guidance for the parolees she supervised.

The World War I era, however, saw her venture out on fact-finding missions again. Her children were all but grown up, and Wells-Barnett was appalled by the wave of racial violence triggered by the war. She traveled to St. Louis to investigate the race riot there in 1917; she snuck into an Arkansas jail in 1919 to secure testimony from the seventy-nine black sharecroppers imprisoned in Helena, Arkansas, after they defended themselves against a group of armed white men who stormed their union meeting.

The East St. Louis Race Riot: The Greatest Outrage of the Century (1917) and *The Arkansas Race Riot* (1920), which are both included in this volume, were Wells-Barnett's last pamphlet-length publications. The Negro Fellowship League folded in 1919, leaving Wells-Barnett with no organization to support her investigative publications. She spent the last decade of her life seeking new platforms for her work at a time when civil rights organization staffers were beginning to take over the jobs once performed by activist reformers such as Wells-Barnett.

The anti-lynching movement that Wells-Barnett founded remained very much alive, but it was led by the NAACP, which assembled black organizations across the country in an energetic but unsuccessful campaign to pass federal anti-lynching legislation in the early 1920s. Wells-Barnett lent her support to the campaign, but largely from the sidelines. James Weldon Johnson, general counsel for the NAACP, was feted for his organization's "agitation" against lynching, while Wells-Barnett's crusade was largely forgotten. Moreover, she was likewise marginal to the National Association of Colored Women's Clubs, which she was convinced had become little more than "a tail to the kite of the NAACP."[21] In 1924, she attempted to reassert her influence in the organization whose founding her own work had helped inspire by running for the presidency of the NACW. But with little record of recent activity in the organization, she was trounced by longtime club woman Mary McLeod Bethune, who won 658 of the 700 delegates' votes.

Wells-Barnett's last attempt to find a new organizational base for her leadership resulted in another landslide defeat. In 1930, she campaigned for a Senate seat in Illinois's Third Senatorial District. Virtually unfunded, Wells-Barnett attracted few endorsements, and never made it past the primary, garnering only 752 of the more than 10,000 votes cast.

She died the following year, on March 14, 1931. After a brief illness, she succumbed quite suddenly to "uremic poisoning"—or what we would today call kidney failure. Sixty-eight years old, she remained an activist until the end, and left behind an autobiography that she never found the time to finish. Published by her daughter Alfreda Duster long after Wells-Barnett's death, *Crusade for Justice* does not record her life past the year 1927. Instead, it ends, quite fittingly, in the middle of a chapter entitled "Eternal Vigilance Is the Price of Liberty."

Note on the Text

Although Wells was a prolific writer, many of her publications have not survived. A house fire in Chicago destroyed many of her personal papers, and there are no known copies of some of the nineteenth-century newspapers, such as the *Living Way*, that published some of her earliest articles. Moreover, Wells's own paper, the *Memphis Free Speech and Headlight*, is also lost in the historical record. Its office and presses were destroyed by the white mob that descended on the *Free Press* in 1892, and no copies of Wells's newspaper have ever been located. However, copies of all of Wells's pamphlets still exist, as do copies of her publications in white-owned magazines such as the *Independent* and the *Arena*, as well as the articles she published in prominent black newspapers such as the *New York Age* and the *Chicago Defender*. In addition, even some of Wells's early writings for the *Free Speech* and other small newspapers have survived, because they were reprinted in other, larger newspapers such as the *New York Age*.

Scattered in different newspapers, church magazines, and collections of pamphlets, Wells's writings have been impossible to read in anything approaching their entirety until now. This book offers a comprehensive collection of her surviving articles and pamphlets. I have omitted the purely informational notices that Wells posted in various newspapers regarding meetings of her Negro Fellowship League and other organizational matters; I have also left out a number of Wells's published letters to the editors of various newspapers, which tend to contain somewhat abbreviated explanations of the current events they discuss, and can therefore be difficult for modern readers to follow. In addition, I have also made no attempt to include Wells's surviving diaries, which have already been published in Miriam DeCosta-Willis's splendid book *The Memphis Diary of Ida. B. Wells* (1995), nor her posthumous autobiography, *Crusade for Justice: The Autobiography of Ida B. Wells* (1991), which is also widely available.[1]

Readers of this text will notice that Wells recycled some of her writings, sometimes republishing identical chunks of text in two or more publications. The product of an era in which such recycling was common among journalists, Wells was more consistently focused on her message than on its format. Her work often contains lengthy excerpts from the writings of other journalists, and *Lynch Law in Georgia* (1899) features the full text of the report that Pinkerton detective Louis Lavin wrote on the Sam Hose lynching. I have retained Wells's repetitions, as well as her pastiches of supporting documents, throughout this collection because they are characteristic of her work, and give careful readers insights into Wells's one-woman protest tradition.

Suggestions for Further Reading

Bay, Mia. *To Tell the Truth Freely: The Life of Ida B. Wells.* New York: Hill and Wang, 2010.

Bederman, Gail. "Civilization, the Decline of Middle-Class Manliness, and Ida B. Wells's Anti-Lynching Campaign (1892–94)." *Radical History Review*, no. 52 (December 21, 1992): 5–30.

Carby, Hazel V. "'On the Threshold of Woman's Era': Lynching, Empire, and Sexuality in Black Feminist Theory." *Critical Inquiry* 12, no. 1 (October 1, 1985): 262–77.

Davidson, James West. *"They Say": Ida B. Wells and the Reconstruction of Race.* New York: Oxford University Press, 2007.

Davis, Simone W. "The 'Weak Race' and the Winchester: Political Voices in the Pamphlets of Ida B. Wells-Barnett. *Legacy: A Journal of American Women Writers* 12.2 (1995): 77–97.

DeCosta-Willis, Miriam, ed. *The Memphis Diary of Ida B. Wells.* Boston: Beacon Press, 1995.

Giddings, Paula J. *Ida: A Sword Among Lions: Ida B. Wells and the Campaign Against Lynching.* Reprint. New York: Harper Paperbacks, 2009.

Goldsby, Jacqueline. *A Spectacular Secret: Lynching in American Life and Literature.* Chicago: University of Chicago Press, 2006.

Karcher, Carolyn. "Ida B. Wells and Her Allies Against Lynching: A Transnational Perspective." *Comparative American Studies* 3, no. 2 (June 1, 2005): 131–51.

McMurry, Linda O. *To Keep the Waters Troubled: The Life of Ida B. Wells.* New York: Oxford University Press, 2000.

Schechter, Patricia A. *Ida B. Wells-Barnett and American*

Reform, 1880–1930. Chapel Hill: University of North Carolina Press, 2000.

Silkey, Sarah L. "Redirecting the Tide of White Imperialism: The Impact of Ida B. Wells's Transatlantic Antilynching Campaign on British Conceptions of American Race Relations," in *Women Shaping the South: Creating and Confronting Change.* Edited by Angela Boswell and Judith N. McArthur. Columbia, MO: University of Missouri Press, 2006.

Thompson, Mildred I. *Ida B. Wells-Barnett: An Exploratory Study of an American Black Woman, 1893–1930.* New York: Carlson Publishing, 1990.

Wells, Ida B. *Crusade for Justice: The Autobiography of Ida B. Wells.* Edited by Alfreda M. Duster. Chicago: University of Chicago Press, 1991.

The Light of Truth

CHAPTER I

"Iola, the Princess of the Press": Wells's Early Writings

Ida B. Wells's earliest newspaper articles date back to 1884, when she published an account of her legal challenge to railroad segregation in the *Living Way*, a black Baptist weekly published in Memphis. A full-time schoolteacher, she wrote her early articles on a volunteer basis, publishing in both the *Living Way* and the *Evening Star*, a publication of the Memphis Lyceum, a literary society that Wells joined in 1885. Sadly, no copies of either of these publications exist, so we cannot retrace Wells's first steps toward journalism. However, we do know that Wells's concise, well-written articles soon attracted the attention of black newspaper editors across the country, who began republishing them and soliciting additional contributions. Elected editor of the *Evening Star* in 1886, Wells also secured her first paying assignment that year, becoming a regular correspondent for the *American Baptist*, a national publication that paid her "the lavish sum of one dollar weekly."[1]

The network of publications that solicited and featured her work increased steadily thereafter, and soon included the *A.M.E. Church Review*, the *Indianapolis World*, the *Kansas City Dispatch*, and *Chicago Conservator*. By the late 1880s, Wells was one of the most prolific and well-known black female journalists of her day. She wrote under the pen name Iola, a name she selected because its rural twang expressed the ambitions that shaped her journalism. Raised in a small town, Ida considered herself a country girl and addressed her writings to the rural black Southerners who formed the vast majority of the region's black community. She was all too aware that the farm families whose children she taught during her years as a country schoolteacher were in desperate need of guidance and education, and wrote in a simple and direct style designed to communicate with this audience.

Her efforts earned her the title "Iola, the Princess of the Press," and a fan base large enough to allow her to shift from teaching to full-time journalism—a shift that became a necessity in the winter of 1891 when she published a scathing critique of the conditions of Memphis's colored schools. She was fired, probably not for complaining that the schools occupied "few and utterly inadequate buildings" but rather because she also noted that some of the teachers "had little to recommend them save an illicit relationship with a member of the school board."[2] Wells's accusation referenced a not-so-clandestine affair between a black schoolteacher and a young white lawyer who worked for the school board, who had been instrumental in securing the teacher's job, which she considered a "glaring evil."[3] But she might have also been ready to leave. In 1889, she had purchased a one-third interest in the black newspaper the *Memphis Free Speech and Headlight*, and by 1892, she was the half owner and full-time editor of *Free Speech*. Once she left teaching behind, Wells built up the paper's business by using her railroad press pass to traverse the Delta selling subscriptions. Soon *Free Speech*'s circulation all but tripled, providing Wells with "an income nearly as large" as the salary she had earned while teaching.[4]

Republished here, Wells's surviving early works demonstrate her talent for addressing a range of issues. Writing at a time when female journalists were still relatively scarce and wrote largely on women's issues, Wells took a genuine interest in subjects such as "Woman's Mission" and "The Model Woman." Still in her twenties, and dating a variety of eligible men, Wells hoped to achieve the "ladylike refinement" she extolled in her discussions of these topics, although she often rued her own "tempestuous, rebellious hard-headed willfulness."[5]

But at the same time, Wells was also fascinated by many of the same political and social issues that preoccupied her male journalist colleagues. Like them, she was concerned with the rising tide of racial discrimination that was relegating African Americans to segregated railroad cars and separate organizations. She protested racial segregation in articles such as "The Jim Crow Car," and "'Iola' on Discrimination"—which also critiqued black self-segregation. Moreover, she was also bitterly aware of the legal and political developments that had helped erode African American civil rights. She mourned the repeal of the Civil Rights Bill of 1875, which was declared unconstitutional in 1883, and condemned the Republican Party for abandoning any further support for black civil rights. A political independent, like her mentor Thomas Fortune, she was convinced that blacks owed little loyalty to either party, and advocated "Freedom of Political Action."

And finally, Wells was also concerned about racial violence and lynching. Although nowhere near as preoccupied with these subjects as she would become after the lynching that rocked Memphis in 1892, Wells published a controversial article in *Free Speech* in 1891, the text of which has not survived. But its contents are described in a brief editorial that Wells wrote for the *New York Age*, which is preserved in her papers, and also included here. In it, Wells defends her paper's praise for the residents of Georgetown, Kentucky, who took "revenge for the lynching" of a member of their community. "Two wrongs do not make a right," the Memphis *Commercial Appeal* told the *Free Speech*'s outspoken editor, while the Jackson (Mississippi) *Tribune and Sun* suggested that Memphis whites should get together and "muzzle the '*Free Speech.*'"[6] This suggestion would prove prophetic less than a year later, when the *Free Speech*'s fearless female editor finally went too far.

"STICK TO THE RACE"

In the years following Reconstruction, African Americans received little support from the Republican Party, which inspired some black thinkers to question their race's tradition of loyalty to the party. Among them was Wells's mentor, black journalist T. Thomas Fortune,[7] who believed that African Americans ought to abandon party loyalties in favor of pressing their case with both parties. His position was unpopular with most black editors, who charged him with trying to solicit political appointments from the Democrats. But Wells supported Fortune. In this article, she defends Fortune's loyalties as a race man, and argues that no other publication was as outspoken and worthy of support as the *Freeman*.

SOURCE: "Stick to the Race," *Living Way*, reprinted in the *New York Freeman*, February 7, 1885.

STICK TO THE RACE

A Word Concerning Southern Editors

FROM THE LIVING WAY

As Mr. Fortune, in THE FREEMAN says, so pointedly: "It is noticeable that these self-same editors who attempt to confuse, ridicule and abuse the author of this article, and bemoan that the Negro would, under these circumstances, assume social equality, are the very ones, who a few short weeks ago, were assuring the Negro he would be more safe, and have more of his rights accorded him than

ever before." Such a ridiculous farce as they are attempting! Such il-
logical deductions as they make! Such sorry shams as they are anyway! They excite the contempt and anger of every fair-minded
person. One good result of the late political revolution[8] is already
apparent; it has aroused the mass of colored people as never before
since the war. Every paper contains a protest, a gem of its kind from
some one who voices the sentiment of a long-suffering people. From
all over the land comes this cry, the ranks of which are being swelled
by the voices of other nations. May it continue to swell until the
public opinion, like Banquo's ghost[9] will not down a Southern editor's (caterers to a minority's will) bidding. May you continue to let
such articles, with just such headings, concerning the unjust treatment of the railroads, stand in your papers until every wrong is
righted!

Of the 100 (according to THE FREEMAN) newspapers in existence, devoted to the interests of the race, I know of none more
fearless, outspoken, more ready to sound the alarm of coming
danger, or present situation, none more worthy of support than
THE FREEMAN itself. Yet, strange to say, it has enemies of its
race, who claim that it has been disloyal to the Republican party.
Mr. Fortune has always claimed to be working in the interests of
the race, which he holds to be superior to those of any party, and
not for party favors or interests; and his position is right, the
true one.   IOLA

"FUNCTIONS OF LEADERSHIP"

Wells was a consistent critic of the elite and wealthy race leaders, who used their wealth to shelter themselves from discrimination but failed to employ their power and resources to help other African Americans. A lifelong advocate of racial uplift, she was impatient with African American leaders who distanced themselves from the masses. In many ways, this article is typical of Wells's acerbic style—she was known for her bold choice of targets and cutting wit.

SOURCE: "Functions of Leadership," *Living Way*, reprinted in the *New York Freeman*, August 8, 1885.

FUNCTIONS OF LEADERSHIP

"Iola" States some Facts about Leadership which may Make Somebody Wince

---

FROM THE MEMPHIS (TENN.) LIVING WAY

I came across a letter last week in the Detroit *Plaindealer*,[10] from Washington, signed S. S. R., in which he gave a whole string of names, of men who are famous as orators, politicians, office-holders, teachers, lawyers, congressmen, and an ex-senator—from whom to choose a leader or leaders of the race. "Let me see," mused I, "these men have acquired fame and wealth in their several callings, they have and are now declaring themselves devoted to the interests of the people, and are thereby looked upon as

leaders, have unimpeachable characters, are justly called representatives of the race—but since they have by individual energy,
gotten the well earned laurels of fame, wealth, individual recognition and influence—how many of them are exerting their talents and wealth for the benefit or amelioration of the condition of
the masses?" I look around among those I know, and read up the
histories of those I do not know, and it seems to me the interest
ceases after self has been provided for. Of those who are amassing, or have wealth I can not call to mind a single one who has
expended or laid out any of his capital for the purpose of opening
business establishments, or backing those that are opened by
those of limited means; none of them have opened such establishments where the young colored men and women who have been
educated can find employment, and yet complain that there is no
opening for the young people.

The whites have the young people of their own race to employ,
and it is hardly to be wondered at that they do not do for the
Negro what his leaders have not done for him; if those who have
capital to employ in establishing such enterprises as are needed
why—the—the leaders are leaving a great field, whereby their
leadership can be strengthened, undeveloped. The ambition
seems to be to get all they can for their own use, and the rest may
shift for themselves; some of them do not wish, after getting
wealth for themselves, to be longer identified with the people to
whom they owe their political preferment; if no more. They are
able to pay for berths and seats in Pullman cars,[11] and consequently can report that—"railroad officials don't bother me, in
traveling;" and give entertainments that have but a single representative of their own race present, can see and hear of indignities and insults offered their people because of individual
preservation from such, can look and listen unmoved saying, "if
it were my wife or daughter or relative I would do so and so," so
what real benefit are they to their race any way? "Their example
is beneficial, by inspiring others to follow in their footsteps with
a hope of similar success," did some one say? True, I had almost
forgotten that; example is a great thing, but all of us can not be
millionaires, orators, lawyers, doctors; what then must become
of the minority, the middle and lower classes that are found in all
races? It is easier to say "go thou and do likewise," than do it. I

would like very much for S. S. R. to tell me what material benefit
is a "leader" if he does not, to some extent, devote his time, talent and wealth to the alleviation of the poverty and misery, and
elevation of his people?

IOLA

"FREEDOM OF
POLITICAL ACTION"

Here, Wells endorses T. Thomas Fortune's suggestion that African Americans support neither the Democratic nor Republican parties, but instead remain politically independent.

SOURCE: "Freedom of Political Action," *Living Way*, reprinted in the *New York Freeman*, November 7, 1885.

FREEDOM OF POLITICAL ACTION

A Woman's Magnificent Definition of the Political Situation

"RENDER UNTO CAESAR THE THINGS THAT ARE CAESAR'S"—MR. FORTUNE'S STATEMENT OF THE SOLUTION OF THE SOUTHERN QUESTION A PUZZLER

To the Editor of THE NEW YORK FREEMAN:

There is an old saying that advises to "give the devil his due," and after reading your editorial on "Mr. Cleveland and the Colored People," I was forcibly struck with the thought, that so few people are willing to admit that he has any "due." Evidently there is very little reasoning powers among those who need such a plain rehearsal of historical facts. According to their logic the side they espouse is all good, the opposite—all bad; the one, the Republican party, can do no wrong—however often they use colored men for tools; the other, the Democratic side, can do no good—whatever the profession—because of past history. More could not be expected of ignorant, unthinking men than to be incapable of giving one credit for honest difference of opinion. It is considered a sign of narrow, bigoted mind to be unable to listen to a diverse argument without intolerance and passion, yet how few among so-called "leaders," editors (moulders of public opinion) but are guilty of this same fault, are ready to cry "stop thief" to those who dare to step out of the beaten political track and maintain honest opinions and independent convictions of their own? It seems strange—well nigh impossible to me—that a highminded soul would refuse to credit even his bitterest foe for an honorable action. If the Democratic party had continued its past attitude in all its rigor toward the Negro, is not Mr. Cleveland to be commended for his attitude and expressions? Is it an inconsistency to commend the qualities that call forth admiration without endorsing all an opponent's traits and party too? And yet to read some editorials one would think so.

Of course such sentiments as these make me a Democrat, according to some creeds, notwithstanding the following definition of my position: I am not a Democrat, because the Democrats considered me a chattel and possibly might have always so considered me, because their record from the beginning has been inimical to my interests; because they had become notorious in their hatred of the Negro as a man, have refused him the ballot, have murdered, beaten and outraged him and refused him his rights. I am not a Republican, because, after they—as a party measure and an inevitable result of the war—had "given the Negro his freedom" and the ballot box following, all through their reign—while advocating the doctrine of the Federal Government's right to protecting her citizens—they suffered the crimes against the Negro, that have made the South notorious, to go unpunished and almost unnoticed, and turned them over to the tender mercies of the South entirely, as a matter of barter in '76,[12] to secure the Presidency; because after securing the Negro vote in full—from a slavish sense of gratitude a Republican Supreme Court revoked a law of a Republican Congress and sent the Negro back home for injustice to those whom the Republican party had taught the Negro to fear and hate. Because they care no more for the Negro than the Democrats do, and because even now, and since their defeat last November, the Republican head(?) and the New York Republican Convention are giving to utterances and passing resolutions recommending State rights, and the taking from the Negro—for the reason his vote is not counted, but represented in the Electoral College, that they claim his gratitude for giving—the ballot.

This being my position I can see very plainly how one can sanction some particular phase of each party without being able to endorse either as a whole and thus be independent—and because that is my position. I naturally wonder that others do not "see as I do." I do not think with the *Plaindealer* that independence is evinced by studiously avoiding reference to politics that would be indirect acknowledgment of subserviency. Colored men have been ostracized for joining the ranks of the Democracy—in obedience to a time-worn tradition that no Negro could conscientiously be a Democrat; that he who so voted did so because of being bought, and therefore deserving the contempt of all honest men. But in view of the foregoing synopsis of the history of the Republican party; in view of the declaration made by John Sherman,[13] in 1894, in a recently published letter to some Martin, a Louisiana friend, that he did not care a rap for the "nigger," and would not have troubled them in their slave rights, if they had not raised hands against the Union; in view of his "Bloody Shirt"[14] cry in 1885 to secure his own re-election; in view of the fact that almost the only argument used by stump-speakers for the g.o.p. now is—"colored men have a chance for office"—and almost the only regret and fear, when Cleveland was elected, by the office holders was concerning their offices; in view of all this and their willingness to retain them under a Democratic Administration and remain "mum" about the g.o.p., it would seem to a disinterested observer that the Republican party was being served as much for the "loaves and fishes" within its gift as from principle, and "what is sauce for the goose, etc."

It is not in favor, nor against the interest of either party that I write this. Let a man be Democrat, Republican or Independent as his judgment dictates, if he is obeying honest and intelligent convictions. It is the spirit of intolerance and narrow mindedness among colored men of intelligence that is censured and detested. This is a free country and among other things it boasts the privilege of free speech and personal opinion. If you are a man worthy the name, you should not become a scoundrel, a "time-server" in my estimation because you differ from me in politics or otherwise—for intelligent reasons. I can respect your views without endorsing them and still believe you to be honest, nor will I stop my paper on that account.

There is (as all are having a pick at you for your Lynchburg sayings and doings) one question I would like to ask. It has puzzled me and I come to the fountain head for a solution. In consideration of the fact of the unjust treatment of the Negro in the South; of the outrages and discriminations to which he is and has been a victim, as is well, very well known to yourself, do you really and candidly believe your assertion that if appealed to in honesty the white people of the South "could not and would not refuse us justice?" I don't believe it, because they have been notably deaf to our calls of justice heretofore, as well as to the persuasions, in our behalf, of their own people. What I see every day and what you know of the case caused surprise at the assertion. I don't believe, however, it was done for effect, for I don't believe you are a toady. If I did the matter would be easily explained.

IOLA

MEMPHIS, TENN., OCT. 19

"WOMAN'S MISSION"

Wells wrote this early article for T. Thomas Fortune, who added its sweeping subtitle, "A Beautiful Christmas Essay on the Duty of Woman in the World's Economy." A discussion of the male and female spheres ordained in the Bible, Wells's piece stresses that women have a "supreme influence for good" that makes them as powerful as men. She also encourages African American women to better cultivate their influence.

SOURCE: "Woman's Mission," *New York Freeman*, December 26, 1885.

WOMAN'S MISSION

A Beautiful Christmas Essay on The Duty of Woman in the World's Economy

PREPARED FOR THE FREEMAN BY "IOLA"

After this planet had been thrown in space and chaos resolved into land and water, the earth was prepared for the habitation of the various animal creation, and man was given dominion over them.

Adam, not satisfied with being ruler of all living things and monarch of all he surveyed, still felt a void in his heart. In the vast solitude of the garden of Eden, as far as the eye could reach, could be seen the cattle on a thousand hills, the creeping things of the earth, air and water—all subservient to his will and owning him as master. In all this vast expanse there was no one to dispute his authority or question his sway; still he was not satisfied, for he was alone. Aye, though surrounded by all that was fairest and wonderful in animal and vegetable life, throughout the countless swarm there was no other soul; thus he was alone, for there was no one to share his glory, exult in his magnificence, nor praise his handiwork.

The Grand Architect of the Universe created a being to fill this void, to be the kindred spirit, to help in the work of tending and dressing the garden; in short, to be a companion and helpmeet to man; and when Adam awoke and found this living soul created alike, and yet differently, beside him, he called her woman, and ever since by that name has this being been known. Truly—

> "The world was sad, the garden was a wild.
> The man, the Hermit sighed, till woman smiled."[15]

In all histories, biblical and political, ancient and modern, among the names of those who have won laurels for themselves as philanthropists, statesmen, leaders of armies, rulers of empires— we find here and there the name of woman. She has gradually ascended the scale of human progress as men have become more enlightened, until in this 19th century there are few positions she may not aspire to. In colleges she has nobly vindicated her right of equality; in the professions essayed she has borne herself with credit and honor; in positions of trust she has proven her ability and faithfulness.

What is, or should be, woman? Not merely a bundle of flesh and bones, nor a fashion plate, a frivolous inanity, a soulless doll, a heartless coquette—but a strong, bright presence, thoroughly imbued with a sense of her mission on earth and a desire to fill it; an earnest, soulful being, laboring to fit herself for life's duties and burdens, and bearing them faithfully when they do come; but a womanly woman for all that, upholding the banner and striving for the goal of pure, bright womanhood through all vicissitudes and temptations. Her influence is boundless. Only the ages of eternity will serve to show the results of woman's influence. A woman's influence gave a new continent to the world. A woman's influence caused man to sin and entailed a curse on all succeeding generations. Woman's influence has been the making of great men, the marring of many more; the inspiration of poets, students and artists, the bane of others. Woman's influence, through "Uncle Tom's Cabin,"[16] was indirectly one of the causes of the abolition of slavery. But it is not queens, conscious of power and security [illegible] and yet the many workers and artists who minister to their love of the truthful and beautiful, that most possess this influence for good; of whom men speak with supreme admiration and revere with tender love; but woman as embodied in the various characters of daughter, sister, wife, mother. While hallowed associations cluster around all these, no earthly name is so potent to move men's hearts, is sweeter or dearer than that of mother. No other blessing can compensate the loss of a good mother. Speak to the hardened criminal of his mother and he is subdued; his defiant look is replaced by one of unutterable longing for the time in the long ago when he was a white-souled child, with no conception of the world outside his home and no pastime without his mother's face as the central picture.

The masses of the women of our race have not awakened to a true sense of the responsibilities that devolve on them, of the influence they exert; they have not yet realized the necessity for erecting a standard of earnest, thoughtful, pure, noble womanhood, rather than one of fashion, idleness and uselessness. A standard bearing these lines:

> "A perfect woman, nobly planned
> To warn, to comfort and command;
> With something of an angel's light
> And yet, a spirit still and bright."[17]

The world labored under a burden of a curse four thousand years, the consequence of one woman's sin. But a promise was given that redemption should come at the hands of a woman, and in the year 4004 there came to a Jewish virgin an angel of the Lord and delivered unto her the tidings that she of all women had been chosen to bear to the world the promised Messiah. Eighteen hundred years ago, as the shepherds watched their flocks by night, came the fulfillment of this prophecy. Suddenly on the astonished eyes of the affrighted shepherds, broke the vision of angels proclaiming "Peace on earth, good will to men!"[18] And this Son born of woman, whose birthnight we celebrate, is owned the world over; and wherever the Christ child is recognized, nations this night join in worship and adoration.

O, woman, woman! thine is a noble heritage! how tenderly He speaks for thee, when others censure thee for thy service of love and denial! How cheering His invitation to thee to lay thy burdens at His feet! And when thou wast reviled, scorned, outcast, and in danger of being stoned by the multitude, He had only words of pity for thy weaknesses, compassion, pardon and peace. Thou was last at His cross and first at His tomb; in his dying agony thy welfare was His expiring thought. Continue in the good offices that first won His approval; make a living reality of the herald's good tidings of great joy and help men to know this Savior of mankind; to feel that there is a better, higher life and a purer, nobler, more fitting way of celebrating this anniversary of His birth, than in drunken debauchery and midnight carousals; recall to their minds the poor and needy, the halt and blind that are always with us and who stand in need of Christmas cheer. Teach them this better way of honoring Him who made visible to the world that "by woman came sin and death into the world— by woman, also, came redemption."[19]

IOLA
CHRISTMAS, 1885

"A STORY OF 1900"

Although Wells would make her career as a journalist, she loved
fiction, and dreamed of being a novelist. In practice, however, fiction does not seem to have come easily to Wells, who was otherwise prolific. Published in the *Fisk Herald* in 1886, "The Story of
1900" is among the few fictional pieces that Wells ever produced.
Clearly autobiographical, and stronger on message than on plot,
it looks to the future to underscore the importance higher education had in racial uplift and reflects on how black teachers might
best serve their students.

SOURCE: "A Story of 1900," *Fisk Herald*, 1886.

A STORY OF 1900

Twenty years ago a young girl went from one of the many colleges of our Southland to teach among her people. While she
taught for a livelihood she performed her duty conscientiously
with a desire to carry the light of education to those who dwelt in
darkness, by faithfully instructing her charges in their text-books
and grounding them firmly in the rudiments. She was born,
reared and educated in the South, consequently the sentiments
regarding, and the treatment of, the Negro were not unknown to
her. Justice compelled her to acknowledge sadly that his moral
and temporal status had not kept pace with the intellectual, and
while reluctantly admitting this fact that was so often so exul-
tantly and contemptuously cited against him she wondered if
there were no remedy for a state of things that she knew was not
irremediable. Since it had been amply proven that education

alone would not be the salvation of the race, that his religion generally, was wholly emotional and had no bearing on his everyday
life she thought that if the many ministers of the gospel, public
and professional men of the race would exert their influence
specifically—by precept and example—that they might do much
to erase the stigma from the name. She never thought of the opportunities she possessed to mould high moral characters by—as
the Episcopalians do their religion—instilling elevated thoughts,
race pride and ambition with their daily lessons. One day a gentleman visited the school and mentioned a promising youth, 18
years old, who had attended that school, as being sentenced to
the penitentiary the day before for three years for stealing a suit
of clothes; he concluded his recital by sorrowfully saying: "That's
all our boys go to school for, they get enough education to send
them to the penitentiary and the girls do worse." It flashed on her
while he was talking that the real want was proper home and
moral training combined with mental that would avert a too frequent repetition of this sad case and that the duty of Negro teachers was to supplement this lack, as none had greater opportunities.
There came over her such a desire to make the case in point an
impressive lesson that school-work was suspended while she related the story and for half an hour earnestly exhorted them to
cultivate honest, moral habits, to lay a foundation for a noble
character that would convince the world that worth and not
color made the man. From that time forth, whenever a case in
point came up, she would tell them to illustrate that the way of
the transgressor is hard; also that every such case only helped to
confirm the discreditable opinion already entertained for the
Negro. These casual earnest talks made a deep impression, her
pupils became thoughtful and earnest, a deeper meaning was
given to study; school-life began to be viewed in a new light; as a
means to an end; they learned, through her, that there was a
work out in the world waiting for them to come and take hold,
and these lessons sunk deep in their minds.

Their quiet deportment and manly independence as they grew
older was noticeable. This teacher who had just awakened to a
true sense of her mission did not stop here; she visited the homes,
those where squalor and moral uncleanness walked hand in hand
with poverty, as well as the better ones and talked earnestly with
the parents on these themes, of laboring to be self-respecting so

they might be respected; of a practical Christianity, of setting a pure example in cleanliness and morals before their children. Before, she viewed their sins with loathing and disgust; now she was animated by a lofty purpose and earnest aim and the Son of Righteousness sustained her. She spent her life in the school-room and one visiting the communities to-day in which she labored will say when observing the intelligent happy homes and families, the advanced state of moral and temporal elevation of her one time pupils—that she has not lived in vain, that the world is infinitely better for her having in one corner of the earth endeavored to make it bloom with wheat, useful grain or beautiful flowers instead of allowing cruel thorns, or rank and poisonous thistles to flourish unmolested.

Some may ask, why we have been thus premature in recording a history of twenty years hence. The answer is short and simple that the many teachers of the race may not be content simply to earn a salary, but may also use their opportunity and influence. Finally gentle reader, that you and I "may go and do likewise."

IOLA

MEMPHIS, TENN., FEB. 19TH, 1886

"OUR WOMEN"

In this article, Wells defends black women, whose morality and womanly virtues were often questioned by nineteenth-century white commentators. Under slavery, Wells points out, black women suffered an "involuntary . . . and enforced poverty, ignorance, and immorality" from which they had only recently escaped. Moreover, she also notes that despite these hardships, many African American women in Memphis and throughout the South managed to achieve "true, noble, and refining womanhood."

SOURCE: "Our Women," *New York Freeman*, January 1, 1887.

OUR WOMEN

The Brilliant "Iola" Defends Them

FROM THE MEMPHIS SCIMITER

Among the many things that have transpired to dishearten the Negroes in their effort to attain a level in the status of civilized races, has been the wholesale contemptuous defamation of their women.

Unmindful of the fact that our enslavement with all the evils attendant thereon, was involuntary and that enforced poverty ignorance and immorality was our only dower at its close, there are writers who have nothing to give the world in their disquisitions on the Negroes, save a rehearsal of their worthlessness, immorality, etc.

While all these accusations, allowed as we usually are, no op-

portunity to refute them, are hurtful to and resented by us, none
sting so deeply and keenly as the taunt of immorality; the jest and
sneer with which our women are spoken of, and the utter incapacity or refusal to believe there are among us mothers, wives
and maidens who have attained a true, noble, and refining womanhood. There are many such all over this Southland of ours,
and in our own city they abound. It is this class who, learning of
the eloquent plea in defense of, and the glowing tribute paid
Negro womanhood, by G. P. M. Turner[20] in the speech he delivered in the Bewden case, return him their heartfelt thanks and
assure him that their gratitude and appreciation of him as a gentleman, a lawyer and a far seeing economist is inexpressible. Our
race is no exception to the rest of humanity, in its susceptibility to
weakness, nor is it any consolation for us to know that the nobility of England and the aristocratic circles of our own country
furnish parallel examples of immorality. We only wish to be
given the same credit for our virtues that others receive, and once
the idea gains ground that worth is respected, from whatever
source it may originate, a great incentive to good morals will
have been given. For what you have done in that respect accept
the sincere thanks of the virtuous colored women of this city.

IOLA

" 'IOLA' ON DISCRIMINATION"

In December 1886, Wells attended a meeting of the Knights of Labor Union. Her experience there inspired her to ponder the merits of integration versus voluntary segregation. In this article, Wells expresses a largely negative view of voluntary segregation, and suggests that African Americans should avoid self-segregation. She believed that blacks helped "keep prejudice alive" when they held their own meetings of the Knights of Labor, provided separate seating for whites who attended black events, or created separate schools for black children.

SOURCE: " 'Iola' on Discrimination," *New York Freeman*, January 15, 1887.

"IOLA" ON DISCRIMINATION

FROM THE AMERICAN BAPTIST

We howl about the discrimination exercised by other races, unmindful that we are guilty of the same thing. The spirit that keeps Negroes out of the colleges and places him by himself, is the same that drives him in the smoking car; the spirit that makes colored men run excursions with "a separate car for our white friends," etc., provides separate seats for them when they visit our concerts, exhibitions, etc., is the same that sends the Negro to theatre and church galleries and second class waiting rooms; the feeling that prompts colored barbers, hotel keepers and the like to refuse accommodation to their own color is the momentum that sends a Negro right about when he presents himself at any similar first-class establishment run by white men; the short-sightedness that insists on separate Knights of Labor[21] Assemblies for colored men, is the same power that forces them into separate Masonic and Odd Fellow lodges.[22] Consciously and unconsciously we do as much to widen the breach already existing and to keep prejudice alive as the other race. There was not a separate school in the State of California until the colored people asked for it. To say we wish to be to ourselves is a tacit acknowledgment of the inferiority that they take for granted anyway. The ignorant man who is so shortsighted has some excuse, but the man or men who deliberately yield or barter the birthright of the race for money, position, self-aggrandizement in any form, deserve and will receive the contumely of a race made wise by experience.

IOLA

MEMPHIS, TENN., DEC. 28, 1886

"THE MODEL WOMAN"

In this article, Wells reflects on the nineteenth-century cult of true womanhood, which defined morality and piety as distinctly female virtues, and assigned women a central role in advancing the moral character of their race. Wells agrees, and also suggests that black women have a special duty to uplift and provide an example for the race's lower classes.

SOURCE: "The Model Woman," *New York Freeman*, February 18, 1888.

THE MODEL WOMAN

A Pen Picture of the Typical Southern Girl

FROM CHATTANOOGA (TENN.) JUSTICE

Although there may be girls in our sunny southland to whom the definition in the preceding article may apply, they are not the ideal type. Whatever else she may be, "the typical Southern girl" of to-day is not without refinement, is not coarse and rude in her manners, nor loud and fast in her deportment.

Nor is the stiff, formal, haughty girl the ideal. The field is too broad and the work too great, our people are at once too hospitable and resentful to yield such one much room in their hearts.

The typical girl's only wealth, in most cases, is her character; and her first consideration is to preserve that character in spotless purity.

As a miser hoards and guards his gold, so does she guard her virtue and good name. For the sake of the noble womanhood to which she aspires, and the race whose name bears the stigma of immorality—her soul scorns each temptation to sin and guilt. She counts no sacrifice too great for the preservation of honor. She knows that our people, as a whole, are charged with immorality and vice; that it depends largely on the woman of to-day to refute such charges by her stainless life.

In the typical girl this jewel of character is enriched and beautified by the setting of womanly modesty, dignity of deportment, and refinement of manners; and the whole enveloped in a casket of a sweetness of disposition, and amiability of temper that makes it a pleasure to be near her. She is like the girl of fairy tales, who was said to drop pearls from her mouth as she talked, for her language is elegant from its simplicity and chastity; even though not always in accordance with rules of syntax, is beautiful because of absence of slang.

She is as far above mean, petty acts and venomous, slanderous gossip of her own sex as the moon—which sails serenely in the heavens—is above the earth. Her bearing toward the opposite sex, while cordial and free, is of such nature as increases their respect for and admiration of her sex, and her influence is wholly for good. She strives to encourage in them all things honest, noble and manly. She regards all honest toil as noble, because it is ordained of God that man should earn his bread by the sweat of his brow. She does not think a girl has anything of which to be proud in not knowing how to work, and esteems it among her best accomplishments that she can cook, wash, iron, sew and "keep house" thoroughly and well.

This type of Negro girl may not be found so often as she might, but she is the pattern after which all others copy.

To those who recognize in this pen picture the true woman, and desire to model after her, I send this beautiful gem of an acrostic, written by a friend for a young lady's album. In its five lines is epitomized all of the above. If young girls would commit and engrave them on their hearts, they would bear with them everywhere a true inspiration and guide:

> "Lucile! Since all the world's a stage—
> Upon which, we, the actors
> Come and go in every age,

In each act needful factors,—
Live nobly, grandly, aim afar!
Live nobly, grandly, aim afar!
E'er onward, skyward—be a star!"

IOLA
MEMPHIS, TENN

"ALL THINGS
CONSIDERED . . ."

Published in the *A.M.E. Church Review* (April 1891), this essay takes on the antiblack sentiments expressed by Frances E. Willard, president of the National Woman's Christian Temperance Union. Whereas Willard maintained that black men were especially prone to intemperance, and dangerous to white women while drunk, Wells countered that intemperance was no greater a problem among African Americans than within any other race. She also pointed out that "in his wildest moments [the black man] seldom molests others than his own, and this article is a protest against such wholesale self-injury." A temperance supporter herself, Wells clearly thought temperance was a matter of class rather than race. Her article calls upon the lower classes to live virtuous, temperate lives, and the higher classes to aid in their progress.

SOURCE: "All Things Considered . . . ," *A.M.E. Church Review*, April 1891.

ALL THINGS CONSIDERED . . .

All things considered, our race is probably not more intemperate than other races. By reason, though, of poverty, ignorance, and consequent degradation *as a mass*, we are behind in general advancement. We can, therefore, less afford to equal other races in that which still further debases, degrades and impoverishes, when we lack so much of being their equals in noble manhood and womanhood (intellectual, moral, and physical), in houses, lands, gold and most things whatsoever which tend to elevate and ennoble a people. Hence the present treatment of the temperance question will be from a race and economic standpoint.

Races, as individuals, make name and place for themselves by emulating the virtues of those who have made themselves great and powerful. The history of such nations teaches us that temperance is one of the cardinal virtues necessary to success. What headway are we making in cultivating this virtue?

Miss Frances E. Willard,[23] president of the National Woman's Christian Temperance Union, lately told the world that the center of power of the race is the saloon; that white men for this reason are afraid to leave their homes; that the Negro, in the late Prohibition campaign, sold his vote for twenty-five cents, etc.

Miss Willard's statements possess the small pro rata of truth of all such sweeping statements. It is well known that the Negro's greatest injury is done to himself.

In his wildest moments he seldom molests others than his own, and this article is a protest against such wholesale self-injury.

Our color stands as a synonym for weakness, poverty and ignorance. It says to other nationalities: "This man belongs to a race possessing little of the power or influence which comes through riches, intellect, or even organization. We may proscribe, insult, ignore and oppress him as we please; he cannot help himself."

The Anglo-Saxon in every avenue of life puts in practice this line of reasoning; and as intemperance is one of the strongest foes to intellectual, material, and moral advancement, it is like playing with fire to take that in the mouth which steals away the brains, and thus gives judges and juries the excuse for filling the convict camps[24] of Georgia alone with fifteen hundred Negroes, out of the sixteen hundred convicts in them, most of whom are young men—the flower of the race, physically speaking.

At the close of the year, when farmers receive pay for the year's work, thousands of dollars, which might flow into honorable channels of trade and build up race enterprises, are spent for liquor to inflame the blood and incite to evil deeds. That which is not directly spent for liquor is lost or wasted; and thus, year in and out, one of the most useful factors in race progress—the farmer—is kept at a dead level, without money, without ambition, and consequently at the mercy of the landholder.

The belief is widespread that our people will patronize the saloon as they do no other enterprise. Desiring to secure some of the enormous profits flowing into Anglo-Saxon coffers, many of our young men are entering the nefarious traffic for the money it brings, and thus every year sacrificing to the Moloch[25] of intemperance hundreds of our young men. Intemperance is general and organized. In the cities it beguiles from every street corner and is found in many homes.

What shall be done to neutralize this power which tempts our young manhood and robs us of their time, talents, labor and money? Throughout the length and breadth of our land there exists little organized effort among ourselves against it. What can we do?

The convention of Educators of Colored Youth in Atlanta, Ga., last December, in discussing the relative mortality of the race, took the ground that intemperance was chiefly the cause of our alarming mortality. The presidents of the schools and colleges in that convention assembled represented thousands of students who are to be the teachers of the race. The subject of temperance and her twin sister, frugality, should not be left for them to touch upon as an abstract matter, or in an incidental or spasmodic manner. An earnest, constant, systematic course of instruction from an economic standpoint in these schools, on this subject, which the students are in turn to impart to the people, is of vital importance, would be far-reaching and beneficial in its results; that association can wield a great power for the spread of temperance.

The National Press Association (representing over one hundred newspapers) which met in Cincinnati last month, speaking weekly to a constituency of perhaps a million readers, as an organized body can revolutionize public sentiment by showing how intemperance is sapping our physical and financial resources. The writer knows one secular journal which has lost many dollars by refusing to advertise saloons. That is the action of one sheet. There is needed, however, harmonious and consistent combination of agitation and effort from the entire body.

Nor must the ministers of the gospel, the most potent agents, who directly reach the masses, cease to preach temperance in their lives and pulpits, line upon line, and precept upon precept.

The Negro's greatest lack is his seeming incapacity for organization for his own protection and elevation. Yet every reader of

these lines, who loves his race and feels the force of these statements, can make himself a committee of one to influence some
one else. One person does not make a race, but the nation is made
up of a multiplicity of units. Not one grain of sand, but countless
millions of them, *side by side*, make the ocean bed. A single
stream does not form the "Father of Waters," but the conjunctive
force of a hundred streams in the bottom of the Mississippi Basin,
swells into the broad artery of commerce, which courses the
length of this continent, and sweeps with resistless current to the
sea. So, too, an organized combination of all these agencies for
humanity's good will sweep the country with a wave of public
sentiment which shall make the liquor traffic unprofitable and
dishonorable, and remove one of the principal stumbling blocks
to race progress.

MEMPHIS, TENN

"THE JIM CROW CAR"

Founded by T. Thomas Fortune in 1890, the National Afro-American League was one of the nation's earliest civil rights organizations. Its second annual meeting, which was held in Knoxville, Tennessee, was well attended by black Southerners but attracted few Northerners or Westerners, whose absence was widely attributed to Tennessee's separate-car laws. At the meeting, the league passed a number of resolutions, including a denunciation of segregated transportation. Wells pushed the league to adopt a more aggressive plan of action regarding separate-car laws, which were becoming ubiquitous throughout the South, but the meeting did not produce anything concrete. This article, which originated in a private letter that Wells wrote to Fortune, condemns Jim Crow cars and expresses Wells's frustration with the Afro-American League's moderate leadership.

SOURCE: "The Jim Crow Car," *New York Age*, August 8, 1891.

THE JIM CROW CAR

A Woman's Opinion of the Infamous Thing

In a personal letter to our Mr. Fortune, Miss Ida B. Wells of the Memphis *Free Speech*, dated Memphis, Tenn., July 25, has the following to say on "The Jim Crow Car:"

I am glad you express determination to do some fighting on the separate car question. It's the League's[26] work and it should never have adjourned without adopting that as its immediate work. We cannot and should not wait for the support of the masses before we begin the work but trust to the inherent drawing power of the eternal principles of right. Since we haven't a national organization in the strict sense of the term, we should and must depend for success upon earnest zeal and hard work to spread the truth of our cause and insure its success. The history of the abolitionists shows that they did it, and kept it up with tireless zeal, until that handful of men and women made themselves heard and people began to think. Surely we can do as much to make their work complete, as they did to begin with. But the right steps were not taken at Knoxville and the pity of it all was there seemed no time to find or agree upon the right steps. Certainly none were taken.

As to my journey to Chattanooga, I rode (as I anticipated) in the Jim Crow car; I waited (as I had to) in the Negro waiting-room, with a score or more of the men of my race looking on with indifferent eyes. Yes, we'll have to fight, but the beginning of the fight must be with our own people. So long as the majority of them are not educated to the point of proper self-respect, so long our condition here will be hopeless. One of the gravest questions of that convention should have been—How to do it? What steps should be taken to unite our people into a real working force—a unit, powerful and complete?

I had not intended to write so much, but, I feel deeply on the subject, as my paper this week shows. Unless something is done in this way, we lose with our own as well as other people.

"THE LYNCHERS WINCE"

Wells also used *Free Speech* to publicize and protest the racial violence suffered by blacks. In 1891, Wells's militant response to the violent clash between blacks and whites in Georgetown, Kentucky, outraged the editors of several nearby white newspapers, who seem to have kept a close eye on the opinions expressed in *Free Speech*. The Wells editorial that inspired their outrage has not survived, but evidently it expressed support for "retaliatory measures" taken by black citizens of Georgetown after a member of their community was lynched. In a second editorial, featured below, Wells responds to the Memphis *Commercial Appeal* and the Jackson (Mississippi) *Tribune and Sun*'s criticisms of her work.

SOURCE: "The Lynchers Wince," Ida B. Wells Papers (Box 8, Folder 8, Item 3), Special Collections Research Center, University of Chicago Library.

Editorial N. Y. Age Sept. 19, 1891

THE LYNCHERS WINCE

The Jackson (Miss) Tribune and Sun, and the Memphis (Tenn) Daily Commercial Appeal are squirming in great shape over the outspoken sentiments of the "Memphis Free Speech" commending the retaliatory measures adopted by the Afro Americans of Georgetown, Ky., in revenge for the lynching of one of its members. The Sun insists that the people of Memphis should proceed to muzzle the "Free Speech", and the Commercial Appeal drops into philosophy and declares that two wrongs do not make one right; and that while white people should stick to the law, if they do not do so, the blacks can hope for nothing but extermination if they attempt to defend themselves.

This is a cowardly argument. Fundamentally men have an inherent right to defend themselves when lawful authority refuses to do it for them; and when a whole community makes itself responsible for a crime it should be held responsible . . . The way to prevent retaliation is to prevent the lynching. Human nature is human nature.

"THE REQUISITES OF TRUE LEADERSHIP"

Speaking before the American Association of Colored Educators in 1891, Wells discussed "true leadership" as a quality that would be crucial to the future progress of African Americans. Her speech anticipates Du Bois's call, in *The Souls of Black Folk* (1903), for the development of an African American "talented tenth" who could guide their race. However, unlike Du Bois, who maintained that this talented tenth would be led by "exceptional men," Wells envisioned a leadership class made up of both men and women.

SOURCE: Ida B. Wells, "The Requisites of True Leadership," *Journal of the Proceedings of the American Association of Colored Educators. The Session of 1891, Held in Nashville Tennessee, December 29th to 31st, 1891* (Winston, NC: Stewarts' Printing House, 1892).

"THE REQUISITES OF TRUE LEADERSHIP"

BY MISS IDA B. WELLS, EDITOR OF *FREE SPEECH*, MEMPHIS, TENN

———

Mr. President:—I do not know how the subject which has been given me is to harmonize with aims of this Association, unless it be that it recognizes that the race whose youth we are engaged in teaching is without the one great essential of elevation and progress—True Leadership—and that from the schools and colleges here represented must come the true leaders of the people.

Humanity in all ages has been a disorganized mass of power until driven by some great molecular force into cohesion in church and State—a human Solar System which some human sun draws with centripetal force towards itself—a gigantic body requiring a head to complete its symmetry of figure and direct its movement.

Indeed all organized effort betokens leadership, and upon the world's leadership the seal of history has set the stamp, and by that seal we know that leadership is true or false in proportion as it has been true to God, humanity and self.

The world is familiar with the history of the race whose youth we represent, and it is therefore not necessary to rehearse how we became a ship suddenly cut loose from its mooring and borne far out upon life's ocean by the tempest of war without a rudder, chart or compass; whose crew have largely been unscrupulous politicians, and ministers and teachers of limited education.

Brushing aside the cobwebs of self-complacency and the veil of sentiment about what this race of ours has already accomplished, the plain naked truth confronts us that except in education centers, and then largely in individual cases, the masses of the people are making too little progress in the things which make a nation strong and great, namely: Education, Character, Wealth and Unity; and that the proscription, injustice and outrage of which we complain is due to this condition of affairs; that if we would slay the Hydra-headed monster prejudice there must be earnest, persistent efforts along these lines.

The Negro is the backbone of the South; his labor has cleared the forest, drained the swamps, tilled the soil, built the railroads and dotted the wilderness with cities. He is the preferred laborer of the section of the country and he needs to be taught how to utilize that power for his own benefit. He needs to be taught also that he holds the solution of the problem in his own hand, and that solution lies in saving his money that with it he may educate himself and children, buy a home, and go into business and build for himself individually and collectively, a good character. If we travel abroad with our eyes open we know that the better class of our people are yet a handful as compared with the thousands who yet grope in darkness; waste their money, squander their time, and undermine health—many knowing nothing of race pride and others caring not even when they know. They need to be taught that it is absolutely necessary to save money, combine their earnings and enter the commercial and financial world if they would have employment for their sons and daughters after education.

For the dissemination of these truths among the thousands are needed true leaders who themselves possess an intelligent grasp of the situation, and consecration to the work. It is a work in which all members of the race so fitted should engage: for until this leaven is thoroughly mixed among the masses and they have risen in the scale, the most intellectual, refined and wealthy among us must suffer proscription and be deprived many advantages because of race connection. Withdrawing one's self from one's race does not hasten the glad and happy time when this class shall be in the majority, and ignorance, poverty and immorality, the minority.

The individual suffers because of the general race condition. Too well is it known that we are representatives of a race possessing no collective power or strength in commerce, politics, intellect or character; and our treatment, however unjust or unchristian, is but an expression of scorn and contempt that such a condition obtains among us.

Truly it is a condition tangible and real, and not a theory which confronts us. Yet how few of our hundreds of graduates with all their learning have gone into the world with a true conception of the work before them.

Their aspirations were high to do valiant work for the race; but they lacked the strength which comes from knowledge of the situation, and too often, like the seed which fell among thorns these aspirations are choked by worldly cares and disappointments, or wither away under the fierce sun of persecution.

They go forth armed with their diplomas, honestly believing that armour invincible and that their talents will batter down the walls of prejudice and secure individual recognition and employment. They find in reality that it does not lift them above general race conditions—that the race is not financially, politically nor intellectually able to help either itself or him and that he must battle with and for his people. Too often he fails to realize the promise of his young manhood, becomes discouraged, gives up the struggle in disgust and rusts away his life as a drone in the hive, or else confines himself to selfish pursuits caring naught save for his individual welfare. Neither his home nor school life prepared him for life in its reality—for the real leadership expected of him, and his ignorance of these things, however great his knowledge of classics and abstract sciences, causes him to fall by the wayside.

The united training of its youth by the home, school and State, in patriotism, fortitude and frugality made one nation so celebrated that the name of Sparta has become a synonym for heroism and endurance. Rome easily commanded the world because of her youth, trained from the cradle as soldiers, presented a front of matchless discipline to the combined armies of the world.

A race situated as peculiarly as our own, along with its book-learning, calls for instruction for its youth (who are our embryo leaders) adapted to its peculiar needs, and training which will meet existing and not imaginary conditions. They should not only go out from these institutions with trained intellects, skilled hands, refined tastes, noble aspirations of the civilizing and Christianizing influences thrown around them in these schools, but they should be taught in some concrete systematic way that the masses of his people are literally "children of a larger growth" who are just learning the rudiments of self-government and to whom, by reason of his superior intelligence, he is to be a leader; that they are poverty stricken, ignorant and superstitious and the whole race suffers from proscription and injustice because of it and that it requires his active, honest, earnest leadership to bring them to the required standard. Send them forth as missionaries; even as the teachers of the North came South to teach us, we must go forth to others.

The main requisites of such leadership are first, devotion to principle or courage of conviction. No great reform in the world's history has ever been successful or far-reaching in its influence without an earnest, steadfast devotion which so takes hold of its leaders that they willingly brave the world's censure—aye, even death itself in its defense. So perished the Apostles and counted the world well lost,—the sacrifice of life glorious; so died the early Christian in Rome's amphitheater and at her stakes until, as has been said of Thomas Crammer, that his death at the stake lighted a torch which has shone round the world; so Leonidas and his immortal three hundred gave up their lives in defense of country. Owen Lovejoy died in defense of the freedom of the press, and brave old John Brown's blood was shed at Harper's Ferry in advocacy of liberty, of whom his son truly says: "He gave noble life for a mighty sentiment." Their deaths were not in vain; they not only wrote their names in the highest niche in the temple of fame but added impetus to the cause of liberty and Christianity which shall roll on gathering new strength while time shall last, and men are left to exclaim, "As Christ died to make men holy, so they died to make men free."

This devotion to principle does not always call for life, but it always means sacrifice of some kind. No man does great things without great sacrifice. Said Lady Henry Somerset in a sermon at Tremont Temple in Boston, recently: "If I were asked to summarize that which I believe condensed the whole secret of every great leader's history, I would go straight to these words, for in them I find the whole inspiration of every life that has been called to lead humanity—self-sacrifice, suffering and pain. Right through the ages this principle has come down to us, even from the time when it was breathed in the old legend, which tells how Curtius leaped into the dark chasm which closed on the flashing form of horse and rider, and we realize that the divine in the human heart, struggling in the twilight of the world, had grasped, as it must always grasp—as it did when Father Damien went to the Leper Island—the sublime, God-given principle that one must die—nay, better, one must be *willing* to die for the people.

When the great light of the beacon fire of Calvary illuminated that black darkness around, it seemed for a time but to kindle the flames of the fagots on which the martyrs died; but that light lit the great heathen world of Rome, and dispelled the darkness of mythology, until the temples of Jupiter and Venus rang out with the glorious Te Deums with the worship of Jesus Christ.

No cause was ever victorious against evil for which men and women have not lived and suffered and died, and the secret of true power for sacrifice has been that they dared to look beyond the paltry, visible surroundings of that cause."

It was this devotion to principle which dragged William Lloyd Garrison through the streets of Boston at the heels of a howling mob. No one is a true leader who to save himself in position fears to speak in defence of right no matter what its apparent cost.

He does not know that all the forces of nature are friends to the friend of God. And his is a base motive who cannot trust these forces to sustain him—which as servants of the Most High are more unerring than weak human foresight. The spirit of earnest devotion in pulpit, school-room, and work-shop is absolutely necessary in leading the people to elevation.

Perseverance is the next great element entering into true leadership. "No man having put his hand to the plow and looking back is fit for the kingdom of God," or capable of true leadership. Patient, persistent, intelligent effort brings all things to pass, as shown by the success of the abolition movement, temperance and other reforms, which were scoffed and jeered in the outset. It is this which has given us the cable, steam engine, electric motors, cotton gin, sewing machine and other inventions in the material world, the result of tireless persistent activity. And this constant effort will wear away the barriers which impede race progress.

I will denominate self-control as the third requisite of true leadership, "Better is he that ruleth his spirit than he that taketh a city." Only the man who holds the forces of his physical, intellectual and moral nature in subjection to a firm and intelligent will, can ever hope to lead or control others. A pure example is better than much preaching. There is no stronger illustration of the truths we would teach, the paths we would have mankind follow than that our own lives represent the standards of sobriety, virtue and honor and stand a silent yet forceful exponent for all we would have the race become; that self-control which restrains from hasty or intemperate action, degrading habits or immoral practices.

The greatest test of character is the ability to stand prosperity. In moments of success which come to earnest devoted souls, comes also the temptation to use power and influence for selfish ambition or turning aside from the paths of virtue.

Charles Stewart Parnell, the most magnificent leader of modern times, met the English Parliament on its own grounds and steadily, persistently and by their own methods forced concessions and won more splendid victories in the cause of home rule than ever before. He united Ireland, kept the British lion at bay and aroused the admiration of the civilized world for his matchless leadership. In an evil hour he forgot to be true to himself and exert in his own behalf the moral strength, the possession of which he had given such splendid evidence, and he went down in the wreck occasioned by one grave instance of his lack of self-control, and not all his former prestige and power could restore him; and the cause for which he fought so grandly and had brought so near to victory has been indefinitely retarded.

Our would-be leaders need especially to cultivate and practice self-control.

And while devotion to principle or courage of conviction, perseverance and patience, and self-control are the predominating requisites of true leadership, over and above them all—embodying the truest leadership—is a deep abiding love for humanity.

It is this which inspires devotion to principle; ennobles perseverance; gives the divine patience and tenderness so necessary in dealing with ignorance, superstition and envy; and strengthens and encourages self-control. The world has never witnessed a sublime example of love for humanity than that of our blessed Savior whose life on earth was spent in doing good. We cannot hope to equal the infinite love, tenderness and patience with which He taught and served fallen humanity, but we can approximate it. Only in proportion as we do so is our leadership true. The reward of such love is expressed in the following beautiful poem:

> "Abou Ben Adhem (may his tribe increase)
> Awoke one night from a dream of peace,
> And saw, within the moonlight in his room,
> Making it rich, and like a lily in bloom,
> An angel writing in a book of gold:—
> Exceeding peace had Ben Adhem bold,
> And to the presence in the room he said:
> 'What writest thou?'—The vision raised its head,
> And with a look made all of sweet accord,
> Answer'd, 'The names of those who love the Lord.'
> 'And is mine one?' said Abou. 'Nay, not so,'
> Replied the angel. Abou spoke more low
> But cheerily still; and said 'I pray thee then
> "Write me as one that loves his fellow men.' "
> The angel wrote, and vanished. The next night
> It came again with a great awakening light,
> And show'd the names whom love of God had bless'd
> And lo! Ben Adhem's name led all the rest."

—IDA B. WELLS-BARNETT

CHAPTER II

To Call a Thing by Its True Name: Wells's Crusade Against Lynching

By 1892, Wells was happily settled in Memphis. Now a full-time journalist, she "thoroughly enjoyed" producing and promoting the paper, and felt that she had "at last found my real vocation." Moreover, *Free Speech* was flourishing, largely as a result of her efforts. Wells used her press pass to travel "up and down the Delta spur of the Illinois Central Railroad" gathering news and selling subscriptions to *Free Speech*. Written in clear and direct prose, the paper soon became popular even among uneducated black Southerners, "who could not read for themselves." They brought it home so they could listen as their children, or other literate members of their community, read its news aloud, and formed a large enough share of the paper's audience that Wells and her co-owner, John Fleming, began to have *Free Speech* printed on pink paper, so that even nonreaders could get the *Free Speech* by "asking for the pink paper."[1]

But the paper's success was soon cut short by the brutal triple lynching that rocked black Memphis on March 9, 1892. Out of town selling subscriptions when the violence took place, Wells came home to find one of her friends—Tommie Moss—dead, and blacks fleeing Memphis. Moreover, she found herself thinking of joining them. "We are outnumbered and without arms," she told *Free Speech*'s readers in an editorial published shortly after she returned. "The white mob could help itself to ammunition without pay, but the order was rigidly enforced against the selling of guns to Negroes. There is . . . only one thing left that we can do; save our money and leave a town that will not protect our lives or our property."[2] But even as a fearful Wells began to speak out for black emigration from the U.S. South for the first time in articles such as "Afro-Americans and Africa," she also felt compelled to protest the murders of Moss, McDowell, and Stewart. She published a series of editorials discussing both their deaths and lynching in general. Few of these editorials have survived because Wells's analysis of lynching was nothing short of incendiary and led to the destruction of her newspaper.

In a fateful May 21 editorial in *Free Speech*, Wells contended that lynching had nothing to do with rape or the defense of white women, whose relationships with black men were often consensual. Instead, it was a form racial terrorism designed to reinforce white political and economic power in the South, and usually targeted blameless victims such as Moss, McDowell, and Stewart. "Eight Negroes lynched since the last issue of *Free Speech*," she wrote, in a laconic style complete with a disbelieving question mark designed to underscore the routine and socially accepted nature of the violence—"one at Little Rock, Ark., last Saturday morning where the citizens broke (?) into the penitentiary and got their man; three near Anniston, Ala., one near New Orleans; and three at Clarksville, Ga., the last three for killing a white man, and five on the same old racket—the new alarm about raping white women. The same programme of hanging, then shooting bullets into the lifeless bodies was carried out to the letter."

With the publication of the editorial, Wells's career in Memphis came to abrupt end. Not only did an outraged white mob respond to her charges by destroying her paper, but Wells herself, once her authorship of the editorial became known, was subject to very pointed death threats that prevented her from ever returning to Memphis. On the East Coast when she received word of the destruction of her paper and the threats against her life, Wells stayed there, taking a job with T. Thomas Fortune's *New York Age*.

But she did not abandon her "fight against lynching and lynchers." Instead, she arrived in New York convinced that she "owed it to myself and my race to tell the whole truth now that I was where I could do so freely" and began lecturing and publishing articles designed to expose what "lynching really was."[3] She made her debut in the *New York Age* in June 1892 with a series of articles that were later reprinted as *Southern Horrors*, which expanded on the analysis of lynching that she had offered in *Free Speech*. In them, she challenged the rape myth by stressing that most lynchings had nothing to do with rape, and also by exposing an underworld of black/white sexual interactions that were criminal only under the South's Jim Crow statutes. Pathbreaking for their frank discussion of such liaisons, her lectures and writings also contained a sweeping critique of Southern race relations, which linked lynching to other forms of racial injustice, such as segregation and disenfranchisement.

Southern Horrors won Wells accolades from black America's elder statesman, Frederick Douglass, who found her work to be a "revelation," as well as the admiration of a broad cross section of elite black women in New York and Brooklyn, who sponsored its publication.[4] But not all black leaders seemed to have gotten her message. In "Bishop Tanner's 'Ray of Light,'" Wells takes on Benjamin Tucker Tanner, the editor of the *A.M.E. Church Review*, for his overly optimistic view of lynching as a punishment largely reserved for criminals; and in "The Requirements of Southern Journalism," Wells urges other black journalists not to ignore racial violence.

Moreover, Wells faced still greater challenges when it came to getting through to white audiences. She delivered "Lynch Law in All Its Phases" to an audience at the Tremont Temple in Boston—a city where the white South was regarded with suspicion and the abolitionist movement was still revered. But she had trouble attracting white audiences anywhere else. So in 1893, she traveled to both Britain and the World's Columbian Exposition in Chicago in search of a broader audience. Her British trip was sponsored by two British reformers: Catherine Impey, a forty-five-year-old Quaker reformer from an antislavery family, who was the founder and editor of an anti-imperialist journal, *Anti Caste* (1888–95); and Isabella Fyvie Mayo. A few years older than Impey, Mayo was a successful novelist who wrote under the pen name Edward Garrett and took an interest in race relations. Unfortunately for Wells, the two women's collaboration collapsed not long after she arrived in Britain. Wells's trip brought the idealistic Catherine Impey into close contact with Mayo's South Asian protégé, a dentist named Dr. George Ferdinands, whom she fell in love with and wanted to marry. Nothing came of Impey's feelings, but when Mayo learned that Impey was interested in Ferdinands she was scandalized, and refused to continue to work with her. Whether Mayo was jealous of Impey, thought her feelings were unseemly for a woman of her age, or deplored Impey's interest in pursuing an interracial relationship with a South Asian man is not clear. But since Mayo was supposed to fund a visit to London in which Impey would introduce Wells to British reformers, Mayo's quarrel with Impey cut Wells's British trip short.

Wells was deeply disappointed. But she would return to Britain in 1894 (see chapter III), and even before then addressed an international audience that attended the Chicago World's Fair in the pamphlet *The Reason Why the Colored American Is Not in the World's Columbian Exposition*, which Wells and Frederick Douglass passed out to the fair's visitors.

Produced and edited in collaboration with Frederick Douglass, *The Reason Why* also contained chapters by newspaperman Irvine Garland Penn and Wells's Chicago lawyer, Ferdinand L. Barnett—whom she would meet for the first time at the World's Fair. The pamphlet was designed by its authors as a protest against the near exclusion of African Americans from the fair, as well as an analysis of the largely abysmal state of U.S. race relations. It contained an introduction by Frederick Douglass, followed by three Wells-authored chapters exposing the "Class Legislation" that segregated, disenfranchised, and disempowered black Southerners; "The Convict Lease System"; and "Lynch Law," which are all included in this volume. The pamphlet was largely ignored by the fair's visitors, but preparing it gave Wells a chance to get to know her coauthor, Ferdinand Barnett, who wrote a chapter detailing how black Chicagoans were systematically excluded from participation in the fair. Barnett, a widower in his early forties, hit it off with the vivacious young reformer. The couple had a great deal in common. In addition to practicing law, Barnett was a civil rights activist and the owner and editor of an African American newspaper, the *Chicago Conservator*. Wells married Barnett less than two years later, after a whirlwind courtship that took place as she continued to tour the United States and Britain giving anti-lynching lectures.

"AFRO-AMERICANS AND AFRICA"

Until the Memphis lynchings, Wells was at best ambivalent about the various migration movements contemplated by black Southerners. The 1880s and 1890s saw some black Southerners fleeing the post-Reconstruction South for new homes in western states such as Kansas, Oklahoma, and California, and also looking to Africa as a potential homeland. Wells moved to Visalia, California, to live with her aunt Fannie in 1886, but found it dull and dusty and returned after only a few months. She resettled in Memphis, and prior to 1892 remained optimistic about black Southerners' prospects for the South. After the Memphis lynchings, however, Wells became a fervent supporter of black migration. Although not inclined to travel to Africa herself, she did not rule it out as a possible destination for those who desired to go.

SOURCE: "Afro-Americans and Africa," *A.M.E. Church Review*, July 1892, 40–45.

AFRO-AMERICANS AND AFRICA

The April number of THE REVIEW, which had Bishop H. M. Turner's[5] letters on his recent visit to Africa, contained also a paper, "Will the Afro-American Return to Africa?" by that brilliant and forceful journalist, T. Thos. Fortune.

Mr. Fortune seems to think it is the white man only who wishes our race variety to return in a body to the home of its ancestors, whether the Afro-American himself will or no. Viewing the question from that standpoint the editor of the *Age* would not be the faithful watchman on the walls he is credited with being, if he had given any other reply than the emphatic and decided, "He will not!"

The Afro-American, as a race, would not return to Africa if he could, and could not if he would. We would not be true to the race if we conceded for a moment that any other race, the Anglo-Saxon not excepted, had more right to claim this country as home than the Afro-American race. The blood he has shed for liberty's sake, the toil he has given for improvement's sake, and the sacrifices he has made for the cause of progress, give him the supreme right of American citizenship. There will always be to the end of the chapter Afro-Americans here to enforce this claim and wrest from this government its tardy acknowledgment and concession of the same. Afro-Americans have no desire and cannot be forced to go to Africa.

But the entire race is not sanguine over our possessions in this country, and the object of this paper is to maintain that the right of those who wish to go to Africa should be as inviolate as that of those who wish to stay. That there are Afro-Americans who would return to Africa is proved by the presence in New York City last winter of three hundred who had managed to get that far on their journey. Somebody had told them they would be carried free if they got to New York. They were of course disappointed and returned to the South. The mistake these people made was not in wanting to go to Africa, but in being so poorly prepared in intelligence and finance. There are hundreds of others besides these poverty-stricken and ignorant people, all over the country, who chafe under the knowledge that what is the opportunity for the European and Chinese emigrant in this country is his disadvantage. In no other country but the vaunted "land of the free and home of the brave" is a man despised because of his color. As the Irish, Swede, Dutch, Italian and other foreigners find this the "sweet land of liberty," the Afro-American finds it the land of oppression, outrage and persecution. In the freest and most unprejudiced sections, in every walk of life, no matter how well dressed, courteous or intellectual, he never knows when he may not meet with and be humiliated by this distinctively American prejudice. He is becoming restless and discontented. He wishes to enjoy the full freedom of manhood and aspiration. Where shall he go?

Why should not they turn to Africa, the land of the forefathers, the most fertile of its kind, and the only one which the rapacious and ubiquitous Anglo-Saxon has not entirely gobbled—where they would be welcomed by their race, and given opportunities to assist in the development of Africa, such as are not possessed by any other nation waiting for a foothold?

That more Afro-Americans do not go to Africa is because the objectors say Africa is a death-trap, that we are not Africans, and that it is a country "without organized government, accepted religion or uniform language."

Everybody who goes to Africa does not die. Everybody knows of the African or acclimating fevers, and all travelers or explorers agree that with care and attention to diet, changes of weather and care of the system, the African fever is no more deadly than our Southern malaria; yet nobody thinks of staying away from the South because of it. The cause of death-rate is carelessness rather than the fever. All writers again agree that it is only along the low, marshy coast that this prevails. Back in the interior it is more healthy.

The recent contributions to African literature are instructive as to the obstacles to be met, the dangers to be overcome, and the way to accomplish it. No man who does not inform himself on any undertaking, and decide on the steps he will take, is a fit contribution to the citizenship of any country. He is not only liable, but will fall a victim to his own ignorance in any country.

The argument that Afro-Americans should not go to Africa because "it is a country without organized government, accepted religion or uniform language," is the very weakest that could be offered. No better reinforcement of the position of southern whites could be deduced than to concede the Afro-American incapable of self-government or the government of others. Children, or inherently weak persons, wait for the paths to be blazed out in which they should walk. The Romans who invaded Britain, nor yet the Puritans who came over in the "Mayflower," waited for "organized government, uniform language or established religion." They brought their own customs, language and religion with them, few in number though they were, and engrafted them into the warp and woof of the body politic. Is the Afro-American incapable of doing this?

It may be argued that it is not the intelligent class who wish to go to Africa. If this is true it is discreditable alike to their intelligence and desire for gain that they do not. The resources of Africa are boundless. White men of every nationality are braving "the white man's grave," and growing rich off the simple natives. They go home every three years to recover health, then go back to the work of making a fortune. They endure all things in their young manhood for the hope of affluence in their declining years. And if they die, as die they do, will not their children reap the benefit?

The Afro-American can better stand the climate than the European, because of his kinship with the natives; his opportunities would be better, because the Republic of Liberia is already a threshold from whence the enterprising and intelligent Afro-American could enter and possess the land. The need of Liberia is the development of her resources; for this it takes capital, skilled labor, and intelligent direction. Bishop Turner says, "A man with three hundred dollars could make a fortune in a few years." The captain of the ship which took him over to Africa, and which only made ten miles an hour, made this significant remark: "The colored people of the United States throw away enough money for whisky every year to build fifty ships that could run twenty miles an hour," and that he (Bishop Turner) "had better get them to save their money and build a faster ship. The United States had no steamers at all, fast or slow." A native African also said to him: "If our brethren will not come from America and make themselves immensely rich by traffic, as they might do in a few years, we natives will do it ourselves; white men shall not always be getting rich off us." Again, "If our rich colored men in the States would come here and open up the coal mines at Carrysburg they would be worth millions in a few years."

What a grand opportunity for the many wealthy colored men in our country! They could build ships and grow wealthy off the trade, or they could form a syndicate and transport and maintain those who will go, and whose brawn and muscle will assist in the development of the country and the greater increase of wealth to themselves. Our rich men are educating their sons in the best schools of the country every year, but furnish no outlet for the exercise of their talents. Is it any wonder that being thrown back on themselves they lose ambition and become anything else than an honor to their race?

The King of Belgium sent to this country for twenty young colored men, skilled in the different trades, to go to Africa and become instructors. Africa abounds in unskilled laborers. What is needed for her development and what she would welcome is the intelligence and skill of young Afro-America; the capacity for work and physical endurance which has drained the swamps, cleared the forests and cultivated the fields of the Southland. It is a cheering sign that there are those who wish to go, and so far from dissuading those who have physical strength, energy and strong common sense, the general government, or the race at large, should assist them to get there and maintain them till they get a foothold; for, after all, it is the sturdy yeomanry—the middle classes—who develop any country.

From what can be gleaned from current history, the great need of Liberia is a strong, intelligent citizenship, to develop her resources and evolve a government which shall command the attention and respect of the civilized world. For any fraction of our eight millions of Afro-Americans to devote its talents to the work with measurable success would be an example and inspiration for Afro-Americans the world over. The greater the obstacles the more pronounced the victory, and in the years to come their success would be the theme of song and story, as is to-day the perseverance of the Puritans, whose indomitable will and energy gave to the world the greatest country of the age. A handful of them, for no greater reason than have Afro-Americans to-day, and without ceding their rights as citizens of the countries whence they came, landed on what was then the bleak, barren and inhospitable coast of Massachusetts. Their effort then seemed a visionary and impracticable one; to-day their descendants, in song and story, laud them for it. They and the Virginia settlements were but little better prepared to meet the exigencies of a foreign country than the poor three hundred Afro-Americans who made such an ill-starred start.

Finally, I quote from a letter written to one who opposed the going of those men and women to Africa: "What though they are going from the white man's civilization? Surely, with what they have they can evolve and keep alive a civilization of their own! To argue that they cannot argues the inherent weakness of the race. That's the white man's argument.

"Encourage them to work for money to pay their passage and

have a little money over, if only to discover what is in them; we will never know otherwise. It is far better to die *trying* to live than drag along at such an uncertain rate, raising children under such restrictive and oppressive conditions; and these poor people show by their actions that they think so.

"I have never heard any but blessings poured out on the heads of the Puritans for their perseverance and endurance. Indeed, I think the hardships and trials brought out the energy and pluck which have been transmitted to their posterity and make the name of New England synonymous with thrift, advancement and prosperity. To me it seems an instructive effort in the right direction, and should be nurtured with hope."

MEMPHIS, TENN

"BISHOP TANNER'S 'RAY OF LIGHT' "

In the wake of the Memphis lynching, Wells published a series of anti-lynching editorials. In this article, Wells criticizes Bishop Benjamin Tucker Tanner's claim that a "ray of light" can be found in the recent lynching patterns. A prominent AM.E. minister, Tanner was opposed to lynching but also favored an accommodationist approach toward whites and therefore tended to downplay the problem of racial violence. Here, Wells disputes that African Americans would take some comfort in the fact that only "disreputable men" were lynched, and that the mob's victims included whites as well as blacks. She strongly disagreed, noting that blacks were far more likely than whites to be lynched, and that those murdered included highly respectable men such as Thomas Moss, Calvin McDowell, and Will Stewart.

SOURCE: "Bishop Tanner's 'Ray of Light,' " *Independent*, July 28, 1892.

BISHOP TANNER'S "RAY OF LIGHT"

BISHOP TANNER says, in THE INDEPENDENT of June 30th:
"What of the light? In answer to this query we beg to say first that the lynching is not confined to the blacks. The whites also are thus summarily dealt with. While it is true that within the past eight years 728 Negroes have been thus barbarously dealt

with, 878 whites met the same fate. Our first ray of light, then, is that it is not a question of race entirely, for the criminal classes of both races are treated alike, tho not in the same proportion. An additional ray of light is seen, and it is a good broad one, too, in the fact that it is only men of disreputable characters who suffer, or characters supposed to be disreputable. The Southern mob in its fury does not assail the good men of either race, but the supposed bad. We have already pronounced this a good broad ray of light, and how true. Suppose it were otherwise? Suppose it were the colored teacher that was lynched in any way the ingenuity of the barbarous mob could suggest. How different would the picture be! Or the colored preacher! We reiterate the hopefulness of this fact. In its blind and Satanic fury the Southern mob passes not only the colored teacher but by the schoolhouse in which he teaches; it not only passes by the colored preacher, but the church in which he preaches; it passes by the colored hall, whether Masonic or Odd Fellow; it passes by the goodly homestead of the well-to-do colored citizen—passes by all these and only makes for the miserable wretch who is supposed to be guilty of rape, murder, robbery and kindred crimes."

The things which Bishop Tanner calls a ray of light in regard to lynchings, in reality add to the Stygian darkness of the situation. His first ray is that 878 whites were lynched in eight years as against 728 blacks. The beast of prey which turns to destroy its own is not considered less, but more bloodthirsty and ferocious than when it preys on other animals. The taste for blood grows with indulgence, and when other means of satisfying it fail he turns to rend his own household. So far from being a broad ray of light, this murdering of each other, as well as the many cowardly lynchings of defenseless Afro-Americans by Southern white people, is a most shocking evidence of the depths of depravity to which they have sunk.

Do I speak strongly? How else can you term such instances as the lynching of Eph Grizzard in broad daylight in the classic city of Nashville? They took him from jail without resistance, dragged him through the streets, plunged knives into his body, and rained blows and kicks on him at every step; the militia and police, State and civil authorities looked on unmoved and inert. He was hung on the bridge in full view of all ages, sexes and colors, with hands cut to pieces, clothing torn off, and his lifeless, nude body filled with bullets. Some of the men who did this barbarous work, unchecked and without disguise, made up the coroner's jury, which found that the deceased had come to his death by the hands "of unknown parties." All this and the fury of the mob, which would have killed the policeman who killed a white man defending the prisoner the night before, and had to flee for his life, were condoned or upheld by the best citizens and newspapers. The spirit of mob rule thus set in motion and upheld by flaming headlines and minute accounts in leading Tennessee papers, where colored men are concerned, had so deadened conscience that the Shelbyville lynching of a white man two weeks ago is the natural sequence.

"An additional ray of light is seen, and it is a good broad one, in the fact that only men of disreputable character suffer, or characters supposed to be disreputable."

I need not dwell on the bishop's transparent inference that two wrongs make a right, or the intimation that so-called civilized people are justified in uprooting the foundations of that civilization on mere supposition, to subdue disreputable classes. I will simply ask the bishop, and those who believe with him, to remember who sits in judgment on the "supposed" character of the lynched. Is it not as easy to malign as to oppress and lynch? Who "supposes" the victims of lynch law are bad characters? Those who suppose they are justified in murdering them, and must have some excuse for their crimes. Dead men tell no tales, and living ones will not voluntarily do so when it means an exposure of their crimes. The press agents, telegraph wires and newspapers belong to the Southern whites—the colored man has no facilities if he has the courage to tell his side of the story. To accept the Southern white man's report that all the lynched are disreputable, or supposed disreputable characters, is to believe the race so criminal, ignorant and bestial it must be hunted with dogs and killed like wild beasts.

But it is not the criminal or supposed criminal class that is always lynched. The three young men who were lynched in Memphis, Tenn., March 9th, were some of the best representatives of the race and were highly respected. They were engaged in prosperous mercantile business a mile outside city limits or police protection, and rallied their forces for a threatened attack from a rival white grocer. When this grocer appeared at the back door of their premises after eleven o'clock Saturday night with a dozen men, these young men supposed it was the threatened attack, and fired, wounding three men who turned out to be deputy sheriffs. The presence of officers in citizens' clothes at that hour seemingly abetting the white grocer, was explained on the ground that they had a warrant for the arrest of a young man who could and would have been arrested by one man. The young men gave themselves up, declaring more than once they did not know it was officers upon whom they were firing. The papers denounced their act as cowardly and reiterated that there would be a lynching if the deputies died. They were pronounced out of danger the following Tuesday, and the friends of the prisoners breathed easier and relaxed their vigilance. The next morning their bodies were found in an old field north of the jail horribly shot to death.

The *Appeal-Avalanche*,[6] which goes to press at 3 A.M., had a "scoop" of all the horrid details in its morning edition. Its front page was covered with a description of how the jail was raided and how each of the victims acted. It was done between the hours of 2 and 3 A.M.—yet, according to their jury, it was done by "unknown parties."

It was given out to the world that these men were desperadoes and kept a low dive. In like manner the colored man lynched in Indianola, Miss., in May, was published as a black brute and fiend who had outraged the sheriff's eight-year-old daughter. The girl was eighteen years old and was found in the young man's room. He was a servant on her father's place. How many others of the "supposed disreputable class" have been made so by press reports there is no way of knowing.

If the race were really as degraded in every case as the South would have the world believe, every action of that section tends to make it more so. Little is being done by the whites to elevate, refine and ennoble. As a hewer of wood and a drawer of water— a menial—the Afro-American is welcomed everywhere. As a man—nowhere. The race teacher or preacher who tries to cultivate manhood and womanhood among his people is mobbed or run away.

The reason the mob passes by, so far as the world knows, the race teacher, editor or preacher, is because they get out of the way or are careful to give no offense. When they do, they suffer, and are promptly classed "disreputable." An editorial in the Memphis

Free Speech, defending the race against wholesale charges of rape, determined the mob according to the *Appeal-Avalanche* "to lynch whoever wrote it, whether it were man, woman or child." The owners had to flee, and our business was destroyed with as little compunction as was the flourishing grocery business of the young men lynched in that town. A young college professor in Rust University, Holly Springs, Miss., was chased out of town because he walked down the street one afternoon with the daughter of the president of the school. She was white. A. E. P. Albert, D. D., was chased out of a Louisiana town a year or so ago because he with the president of Straight University was soliciting pupils for the school. Prof. Edward D. Scott, of the Virginia Normal and Collegiate Institute, a State school, at Petersburg, recently lost his position because he delivered an address denouncing lynching and urging colored youth to think, write and talk of the "Negro Problem." Miss J. P. Moore, as saintly a white woman as ever lived, had a school at Baton Rouge, La., for colored women and girls. She went among the lowly and into the homes of the ignorant and taught the mothers how to read the Bible, tidy their homes and instruct their children. She edits a little paper called *Hope*, and was doing a world of good. The mob sent her a skull and crossbones letter, two years ago, ordering her away for teaching and associating with colored women. I am not sure but I think they burned up her schoolhouse. She left, but is continuing the same noble work in Little Rock, Ark. It is well known the white people of Port Gibson, Miss., refused to allow Miss Mary E. Holmes to establish her school for colored girls at that place. Only a few weeks ago a minister at Clarksdale, Miss., was waylaid and brutally beaten because it was thought he was advising his people to go to Oklahoma.

The dark cloud overhanging us may have a silver lining which reflects rays of light, but they cannot be seen from Bishop Tanner's point of view.

NEW YORK CITY

SOUTHERN HORRORS: LYNCH LAW IN ALL ITS PHASES

Wells's first pamphlet, *Southern Horrors*, contains an account of the Memphis lynchings that she first published under the title "Exiled" in the *New York Age* on June 25, 1892. A few months later, using money raised by her New York supporters, Wells expanded on this material to produce *Southern Horrors*, a pamphlet-length analysis of lynching. The New Yorkers who supported Wells's pamphlet included Victoria Earle Matthews (Manhattan) and Maritcha Lyons (Brooklyn), who were both influential members of the city's female black elite. Wells dedicated the pamphlet to Matthews and Lyons, and also included an introduction that she solicited from Frederick Douglass. Framed by these credentials, the pamphlet contains a detailed anti-lynching narrative that moves from an account of events in Memphis to a sweeping analysis of the role of violence in sustaining Jim Crow.

SOURCE: *Southern Horrors: Lynch Law in All Its Phases* (New York: New York Age, November 1892).

SOUTHERN HORRORS: LYNCH LAW IN ALL ITS PHASES

Preface

The greater part of what is contained in these pages was published in the New York *Age* June 25, 1892, in explanation of the editorial which the Memphis whites considered sufficiently infamous to justify the destruction of my paper, *The Free Speech*.

Since the appearance of that statement, requests have come from all parts of the country that "Exiled," (the name under which it then appeared) be issued in pamphlet form. Some donations were made, but not enough for that purpose. The noble efforts of the ladies of New York and Brooklyn Oct. 5 have enabled me to comply with this request and give the world a true, unvarnished account of the causes of lynch law in the South.

This statement is not a shield for the despoiler of virtue, nor altogether a defense for the poor blind Afro-American Sampsons[7] who suffer themselves to be betrayed by white Delilahs.[8] It is a contribution to truth, an array of facts, the perusal of which it is hoped will stimulate this great American Republic to demand that justice be done though the heavens fall.

It is with no pleasure I have dipped my hands in the corruption here exposed. Somebody must show that the Afro-American race is more sinned against than sinning, and it seems to have fallen upon me to do so. The awful death-roll that Judge Lynch is calling every week is appalling, not only because of the lives it takes, the rank cruelty and outrage to the victims, but because of the prejudice it fosters and the stain it places against the good name of a weak race.

The Afro-American is not a bestial race. If this work can contribute in any way toward proving this, and at the same time arouse the conscience of the American people to a demand for justice to every citizen, and punishment by law for the lawless, I shall feel I have done my race a service. Other considerations are of minor importance.

IDA B. WELLS.

NEW YORK CITY, OCT. 26, 1892.

To the Afro-American women of New York and Brooklyn, whose race love, earnest zeal and unselfish effort at Lyric Hall, in the City of New York, on the night of October 5th, 1892, made possible its publication, this pamphlet is gratefully dedicated by the author.

HON. FRED. DOUGLASS'S LETTER

Dear Miss Wells

Let me give you thanks for your faithful paper on the lynch abomination now generally practiced against colored people in the South. There has been no word equal to it in convincing power. I have spoken, but my word is feeble in comparison. You give us what you know and testify from actual knowledge. You have dealt with the facts with cool, painstaking fidelity and left those naked and uncontradicted facts to speak for themselves.

Brave woman! you have done your people and mine a service which can neither be weighed nor measured. If American conscience were only half alive, if the American church and clergy were only half christianized, if American moral sensibility were not hardened by persistent infliction of outrage and crime against colored people, a scream of horror, shame and indignation would rise to Heaven wherever your pamphlet shall be read.

But alas! even crime has power to reproduce itself and create conditions favorable to its own existence. It sometimes seems we are deserted by earth and Heaven—yet we must still think, speak and work, and trust in the power of a merciful God for final deliverance.

Very truly and gratefully yours,

FREDERICK DOUGLASS.

CEDAR HILL, ANACOSTIA, D. C., OCT. 25, 1892.

CHAPTER I

The Offense

Wednesday evening May 24th, 1892, the city of Memphis was filled with excitement. Editorials in the daily papers of that date caused a meeting to be held in the Cotton Exchange Building; a committee was sent for the editors of the "Free Speech" an Afro-American journal published in that city and the only reason the open threats of lynching that were made were not carried out was because they could not be found. The cause of all this commotion was the following editorial published in the "Free Speech" May 21st 1892, the Saturday previous.

"Eight negroes lynched since last issue of the "Free Speech" one at Little Rock, Ark., last Saturday morning where the citizens broke (?) into the penitentiary and got their man; three near Anniston, Ala., one near New Orleans; and three at Clarksville, Ga., the last three for killing a white man, and five on the same old racket—the new alarm about raping white women. The same programme of hanging, then shooting bullets into the lifeless bodies was carried out to the letter.

Nobody in this section of the country believes the old thread bare lie that Negro men rape white women. If Southern white men are not careful, they will over-reach themselves and public sentiment will have a reaction; a conclusion will then be reached which will be very damaging to the moral reputation of their women."

"The Daily Commercial" of Wednesday following, May 25th, contained the following leader:

"Those negroes who are attempting to make the lynchings of individuals of their race a means for arousing the worst passions of their kind are playing with a dangerous sentiment. The negroes may as well understand that there is no mercy for the negro rapist and little patience with his defenders. A negro organ printed in this city, in a recent issue publishes the following atrocious paragraph: 'Nobody in this section of the country believes the old thread bare lie that Negro men rape white women. If Southern white men are not careful, they will over-reach themselves and public sentiment will have a reaction; and a conclusion will be reached which will be very damaging to the moral reputation of their women.'

The fact that a black scoundrel is allowed to live and utter such loathsome and repulsive calumnies is a volume of evidence as to the wonderful patience of Southern whites. But we have had enough of it.

There are some things that the Southern white man will not tolerate, and the obscene intimations of the foregoing have brought the writer to the very outermost limit of public patience. We hope we have said enough."

The "Evening Scimitar" of same date, copied the "Commercial's" editorial with these words of comment: "Patience under such circumstances is not a virtue. If the negroes themselves do not apply the remedy without delay it will be the duty of those whom he has attacked to tie the wretch who utters these calumnies to a stake at the intersection of Main and Madison Sts., brand him in the forehead with a hot iron and perform upon him a surgical operation with a pair of tailor's shears."

Acting upon this advice, the leading citizens met in the Cotton Exchange Building the same evening, and threats of lynching were freely indulged, not by the lawless element upon which the deviltry of the South is usually saddled—but by the leading business men, in their leading business centre. Mr. Fleming, the business manager and owning a half interest in the Free Speech, had to leave town to escape the mob, and was afterwards ordered not to return; letters and telegrams sent me in New York where I was spending my vacation advised me that bodily harm awaited my return. Creditors took possession of the office and sold the outfit, and the "Free Speech" was as if it had never been.

The editorial in question was prompted by the many inhuman and fiendish lynchings of Afro-Americans which have recently taken place and was meant as a warning. Eight lynched in one week and five of them charged with rape! The thinking public will not easily believe freedom and education more brutalizing than slavery, and the world knows that the crime of rape was unknown during four years of civil war when the white women of the South were at the mercy of the race which is all at once charged with being a bestial one.

Since my business has been destroyed and I am an exile from home because of that editorial, the issue has been forced, and as the writer of it I feel that the race and the public generally should have a statement of the facts as they exist. They will serve at the same time as a defense for the Afro-American Sampsons who suffer themselves to be betrayed by white Delilahs.

The whites of Montgomery, Ala., knew J. C. Duke sounded the key-note of the situation—which they would gladly hide from the world, when he said in his paper, "The Herald," five years ago: "Why is it that white women attract negro men now more than in former days? There was a time when such a thing was unheard of. There is a secret to this thing, and we greatly suspect it is the growing appreciation of white Juliets for colored Romeos." Mr. Duke, like the "Free Speech" proprietors, was forced to leave the city for reflecting on the "honah" of white women and his paper suppressed; but the truth remains that Afro-American men do not always rape (?) white women without their consent.

Mr. Duke, before leaving Montgomery, signed a card disclaiming any intention of slandering Southern white women. The editor of the "Free Speech" has no disclaimer to enter, but asserts instead that there are many white women in the South who would marry colored men if such an act would not place them at once beyond the pale of society and within the clutches of the law. The miscegenation laws of the South only operate against the legitimate union of the races; they leave the white man free to seduce all the colored girls he can, but it is death to the colored man who yields to the force and advances of a similar attraction in white women. White men lynch the offending Afro American, not because he is a despoiler of virtue, but because he succumbs to the smiles of white women.

CHAPTER II

The Black and White of It

The "Cleveland Gazette" of January 16, 1892, publishes a case in point. Mrs. J. S. Underwood, the wife of a minister of Elyria, Ohio, accused an Afro-American of rape. She told her husband that during his absence in 1888, stumping the State for the Prohibition Party,[9] the man came to the kitchen door, forced his way in the house and insulted her. She tried to drive him out with a heavy poker, but he overpowered and chloroformed her, and when she revived her clothing was torn and she was in a horrible condition. She did not know the man but could identify him. She pointed out William Offett, a married man, who was arrested and, being in Ohio, was granted a trial.

The prisoner vehemently denied the charge of rape, but confessed he went to Mrs. Underwood's residence at her invitation and was criminally intimate with her at her request. This availed him nothing against the sworn testimony of a minister's wife, a lady of the highest respectability. He was found guilty, and entered the penitentiary, December 14, 1888, for fifteen years. Some time afterwards the woman's remorse led her to confess to her husband that the man was innocent.

These are her words. "I met Offett at the Post Office. It was raining. He was polite to me, and as I had several bundles in my arms he offered to carry them home for me, which he did. He had a strange fascination for me, and I invited him to call on me. He called, bringing chestnuts and candy for the children. By this means we got them to leave us alone in the room. Then I sat on his lap. He made a proposal to me and I readily consented. Why I did so, I do not know but that I did is true. He visited me several times after that and each time I was indiscreet. I did not care after the first time. In fact I could not have resisted, and had no desire to resist."

When asked by her husband why she told him she had been outraged, she said: "I had several reasons for telling you. One was the neighbors saw the fellow here, another was, I was afraid I had contracted a loathsome disease, and still another was that I feared I might give birth to a Negro baby. I hoped to save my reputation by telling you a deliberate lie." Her husband horrified by the confession had Offett, who had already served four years, released and secured a divorce.

There are thousands of such cases throughout the South, with the difference that the Southern white men in insatiate fury wreak their vengeance without intervention of law upon the Afro-Americans who consort with their women. A few instances to substantiate the assertion that some white women love the company of the Afro-American will not be out of place. Most of these cases were reported by the daily papers of the South.

In the winter of 1885-6 the wife of a practicing physician in Memphis in good social standing whose name has escaped me, left home husband and children and ran away with her black coachman. She was with him a month before her husband found and brought her home. The coachman could not be found. The doctor moved his family away from Memphis, and is living in another city under an assumed name.

In the same city last year a white girl in the dusk of evening screamed at the approach of some parties that a Negro had assaulted her on the street. He was captured, tried by a white judge and jury, that acquitted him of the charge. It is needless to add if there had been a scrap of evidence on which to convict him of so grave a charge he would have been convicted.

Sarah Clark of Memphis loved a black man and lived openly with him. When she was indicted last spring for miscegenation, she swore in court that she was *not* a white woman. This she did to escape the penitentiary and continued her illicit relation undisturbed. That she is of the lower class of whites, does not disturb the fact that she is a white woman. "The leading citizens" of Memphis are defending the "honor" of *all* white women, *demi-monde*[10] included.

Since the manager of the "Free Speech" has been run away from Memphis by the guardians of the honor of Southern white women, a young girl living on Poplar St., who was discovered in intimate relations with a handsome mulatto young colored man, Will Morgan by name, stole her father's money to send the young fellow away from that father's wrath. She has since joined him in Chicago.

The Memphis "Ledger" for June 8th has the following; "If Lillie Bailey, a rather pretty white girl seventeen years of age, who is now at the City Hospital, would be somewhat less reserved about her disgrace there would be some very nauseating details in the story of her life. She is the mother of a little coon. The truth might reveal fearful depravity or it might reveal the evidence of a rank outrage. She will not divulge the name of the man who has left such black evidence of her disgrace, and, in fact, says it is a matter in which there can be no interest to the outside world. She came to Memphis nearly three months ago and was taken in at the Woman's Refuge in the southern part of the city. She remained there until a few weeks ago, when the child was born. The ladies in charge of the Refuge were horrified. The girl was at once sent to the City Hospital, where she has been since May 30th. She is a country girl. She came to Memphis from her father's farm, a short distance from Hernando, Miss. Just when she left there she would not say. In fact she says she came to Memphis from Arkansas, and says her home is in that State. She is rather good looking, has blue eyes, a low forehead and dark red hair. The ladies at the Woman's Refuge do not know anything about the girl further than what they learned when she was an inmate of the institution; and she would not tell much. When the child was born an attempt was made to get the girl to reveal the name of the Negro who had disgraced her, she obstinately refused and it was impossible to elicit any information from her on the subject."

Note the wording. "The truth might reveal fearful depravity or rank outrage." If it had been a white child or Lillie Bailey had told a pitiful story of Negro outrage, it would have been a case of woman's weakness or assault and she could have remained at the Woman's Refuge. But a Negro child and to withhold its father's name and thus prevent the killing of another Negro "rapist." A case of "fearful depravity."

The very week the "leading citizens" of Memphis were making a spectacle of themselves in defense of all white women of every kind, an Afro-American, M. Stricklin, was found in a white woman's room in that city. Although she made no outcry of rape, he was jailed and would have been lynched, but the woman stated she bought curtains of him (he was a furniture dealer) and his business in her room that night was to put them up. A white woman's word was taken absolutely in this case as when the cry of rape is made, and he was freed.

What is true of Memphis is true of the entire South. The daily papers last year reported a farmer's wife in Alabama had given birth to a Negro child. When the Negro farm hand who was plowing the field heard it he took the mule from the plow and fled. The dispatches also told of a woman in South Carolina who gave birth to a Negro child and charged three men with being its father, *every one of whom has since disappeared.* In Tuscumbia, Ala., the colored boy who was lynched there last year for assaulting a white girl told her before his accusers that he had met her there in the woods often before.

Frank Weems of Chattanooga who was not lynched in May only because the prominent citizens became his body guard until

the doors of the penitentiary closed on him, had letters in his
pocket from the white woman in the case, making the appointment with him. Edward Coy who was burned alive in Texarkana,
January 1, 1892, died protesting his innocence. Investigation
since as given by the Bystander in the Chicago Inter-Ocean,
October 1, proves:

"1. The woman who was paraded as a victim of violence was
of bad character; her husband was a drunkard and a gambler.

2. She was publicly reported and generally known to have been
criminally intimate with Coy for more than a year previous.

3. She was compelled by threats, if not by violence, to make the
charge against the victim.

4. When she came to apply the match Coy asked if she would
burn him after they had 'been sweethearting' so long.

5. A large majority of the 'superior' white men prominent in
the affair are the reputed fathers of mulatto children.

These are not pleasant facts, but they are illustrative of the
vital phase of the so-called 'race question,' which should properly
be designated as earnest inquiry as to the best methods by which
religion, science, law and political power may be employed to
excuse injustice, barbarity and crime done to a people because of
race and color. There can be no possible belief that these people
were inspired by any consuming zeal to vindicate God's law
against miscegnationists of the most practical sort. The woman
was a willing partner in the victim's guilt, and being of the 'superior' race must naturally have been more guilty."

In Natchez, Miss., Mrs. Marshall, one of the *creme de la creme*
of the city, created a tremendous sensation several years ago. She
has a black coachman who was married, and had been in her
employ several years. During this time she gave birth to a child
whose color was remarked, but traced to some brunette ancestor,
and one of the fashionable dames of the city was its godmother.
Mrs. Marshall's social position was unquestioned, and wealth
showered every dainty on this child which was idolized with its
brothers and sisters by its white papa. In course of time another
child appeared on the scene, but it was unmistakably dark. All
were alarmed, and "rush of blood, strangulation" were the con-
jecture, but the doctor, when asked about the cause, grimly told
them it was a Negro child. There was a family conclave, the
coachman heard of it and leaving his own family went West, and

has never returned. As soon as Mrs. Marshall was able to travel she was sent away in deep disgrace. Her husband died within the year of a broken heart.

Ebenzer Fowler, the wealthiest colored man in Issaquena County, Miss., was shot down on the street in Mayersville, January 30, 1885, just before dark by an armed body of white men who filled his body with bullets. They charged him with writing a note to a white woman of the place, which they intercepted and which proved there was an intimacy existing between them.

Hundreds of such cases might be cited, but enough have been given to prove the assertion that there are white women in the South who love the Afro-American's company even as there are white men notorious for their preference for Afro-American women.

There is hardly a town in the South which has not an instance of the kind which is well-known, and hence the assertion is reiterated that "nobody in the South believes the old thread bare lie that negro men rape white women." Hence there is a growing demand among Afro-Americans that the guilt or innocence of parties accused of rape be fully established. They know the men of the section of the country who refuse this are not so desirous of punishing rapists as they pretend. The utterances of the leading white men show that with them it is not the crime but the *class*. Bishop Fitzgerald[11] has become apologist for lynchers of the rapists of *white* women only. Governor Tillman, of South Carolina, in the month of June, standing under the tree in Barnwell, S. C., on which eight Afro-Americans were hung last year, declared that he would lead a mob to lynch a *negro* who raped a *white* woman." So say the pulpits, officials and newspapers of the South. But when the victim is a colored woman it is different.

Last winter in Baltimore, Md., three white ruffians assaulted a Miss Camphor, a young Afro-American girl, while out walking with a young man of her own race. They held her escort and outraged the girl. It was a deed dastardly enough to arouse Southern blood which gives its horror of rape as excuse for lawlessness, but she was an Afro-American. The case went to the courts an Afro-American lawyer defended the men and they were acquitted.

In Nashville, Tenn., there is a white man, Pat Hanifan, who

outraged a little Afro-American girl, and, from the physical injuries received, she has been ruined for life. He was jailed for six
months discharged, and is now a detective in that city. In the
same city, last May, a white man outraged an Afro-American girl
in a drug store. He was arrested, and released on bail at the trial.
It was rumored that five hundred Afro-Americans had organized
to lynch him. Two hundred and fifty white citizens armed themselves with Winchesters[12] and guarded him. A cannon was placed
in front of his home, and the Buchanan Rifles (State Militia) ordered to the scene for his protection. The Afro-American mob
did not materialize. Only two weeks before Eph. Grizzard, who
had only been *charged* with rape upon a white woman, had been
taken from the jail, with Governor Buchanan and the police and
militia standing by, dragged through the streets in broad daylight, knives plunged into him at every step, and with every fiendish cruelty a frenzied mob could devise, he was at last swung out
on the bridge with hands cut to pieces as he tried to climb up the
stanchions. A naked, bloody example of the blood-thirstiness of
the nineteenth century civilization of the Athens of the South!
No cannon or military was called out in his defense. He dared to
visit a white woman.

At the very moment these civilized whites were announcing
their determination "to protect their wives and daughters," by
murdering Grizzard a white man was in the same jail for raping
eight-year-old Maggie Reeses, an Afro American girl. He was
not harmed. The "honor of grown women who were glad enough
to be supported by the Grizzard boys and Ed Coy, as long as the
liaison was not known needed protection, they were white. The
outrage upon helpless childhood needed no avenging in this case;
she was black.

A white man in Guthrie, Oklahoma Territory, two months ago
inflicted such injuries upon another Afro-American child that she
died. He was not punished, but an attempt was made in the same
town in the month of June to lynch an Afro-American who visited a white woman.

In Memphis, Tenn., in the month of June, Ellerton L. Dorr,
who is the husband of Russell Hancock's widow, was arrested for
attempted rape on Mattie Cole, a neighbor's cook; he was only
prevented from accomplishing his purpose, by the appearance of
Mattie's employer. Dorr's friends say he was drunk and not re-

sponsible for his actions. The grand jury refused to indict him and he was discharged.

CHAPTER III

The New Cry

The appeal of Southern whites to Northern sympathy and sanction, the adroit, insidious plea made by Bishop Fitzgerald for suspension of judgment because those "who condemn lynching express no sympathy for the *white* woman in the case," falls to the ground in the light of the foregoing.

From this exposition of the race issue in lynch law, the whole matter is explained by the well-known opposition growing out of slavery to the progress of the race. This is crystalized in the oft-repeated slogan: "This is a white man's country and the white man must rule." The South resented giving the Afro-American his freedom, the ballot box and the Civil Rights Law. The raids of the Ku-Klux and White Liners[13] to subvert reconstruction government, the Hamburg and Ellerton, S. C., the Copiah County Miss., and the Layfayette Parish, La., massacres were excused as the natural resentment of intelligence against government by ignorance.

Honest white men practically conceded the necessity of intelligence murdering ignorance to correct the mistake of the general government, and the race was left to the tender mercies of the solid South. Thoughtful Afro-Americans with the strong arm of the government withdrawn and with the hope to stop such wholesale massacres urged the race to sacrifice its political rights for the sake of peace. They honestly believed the race should fit itself for government, when that should be done, the objection to race participation in politics would be removed.

But the sacrifice did not remove the trouble, nor move the South to justice. One by one the Southern States have legally (?) disfranchised the Afro-American, and since the repeal of the Civil Rights Bill nearly every Southern State has passed separate car laws with a penalty against their infringement. The race regardless of advancement is penned into filthy, stifling partitions cut off from smoking cars. All this while, although the political cause has been removed, the butcheries of black men at Barnwell, S. C., Carrolton, Miss., Waycross, Ga., and Memphis, Tenn., has gone on; also the flaying alive of a man in Kentucky, the burning of one in Arkansas, the hanging of a fifteen year old girl in Louisiana, a woman in Jackson, Tenn., and one in Hollendale, Miss., until the dark and bloody record of the South shows 728 Afro-Americans lynched during the past 8 years. Not 50 of these were for political causes; the rest were for all manner of accusations from that of rape of white women, to the case of the boy Will Lewis who was hanged at Tullahoma, Tenn., last year for being drunk and "sassy" to white folks.

These statistics compiled by the Chicago "Tribune" were given the first of this year (1892). Since then, not less than one hundred and fifty have been known to have met violent death at the hands of cruel bloodthirsty mobs during the past nine months.

To palliate this record (which grows worse as the Afro American becomes intelligent) and excuse some of the more heinous crimes that ever stained the history of a country, the South is shielding itself behind the plausible screen of defending the honor of its women. This, too, in the face of the fact that only *one-third* of the 728 victims to mobs have been *charged* with rape, to say nothing of those of that one-third who were innocent of the charge. A white correspondent of the Baltimore Sun declares that the Afro-American who was lynched in Chestertown, Md., in May for assault on a white girl was innocent; that the deed was done by a white man who had since disappeared. The girl herself maintained that her assailant was a white man. When that poor Afro-American was murdered, the whites excused their refusal of a trial on the ground that they wished to spare the white girl the mortification of having to testify in court.

This cry has had its effect. It has closed the heart, stifled the conscience, warped the judgment and hushed the voice of press and pulpit on the subject of lynch law throughout this "land of liberty." Men who stand high in the esteem of the public for christian character, for moral and physical courage, for devotion to the principles of equal and exact justice to all, and for great sagacity, stand as cowards who fear to open their mouths before this great outrage. They do not see that by their tacit encouragement, their silent acquiescence, the black shadow of lawlessness in the form of lynch law is spreading its wings over the whole country.

Men who, like Governor Tillman, start the ball of lynch law rolling for a certain crime, are powerless to stop it when drunken or criminal white toughs feel like hanging an Afro-American on any pretext.

Even to the better class of Afro-Americans the crime of rape is so revolting they have too often taken the white man's word and given lynch law neither the investigation nor condemnation it deserved.

They forget that a concession of the right to lynch a man for a certain crime, not only concedes the right to lynch any person for any crime, but (so frequently is the cry of rape now raised) it is in a fair way to stamp us a race of rapists and desperadoes. They have gone on hoping and believing that general education and financial strength would solve the difficulty, and are devoting their energies to the accumulation of both.

The mob spirit has grown with the increasing intelligence of the Afro-American. It has left the out-of-the-way-places where ignorance prevails, has thrown off the mask and with this new cry stalks in broad daylight in large cities, the centres of civilization, and is encouraged by the "leading citizens" and the press.

CHAPTER IV

The Malicious and Untruthful White Press

The "Daily Commercial" and "Evening Scimitar" of Memphis, Tenn., are owned by leading business men of that city, and yet, in spite of the fact that there had been no white woman in Memphis outraged by an Afro-American, and that Memphis possessed a thrifty law abiding, property owning class of Afro-Americans the "Commercial" of May 17th, under the head of "More Rapes, More Lynchings" gave utterance to the following:

The lynching of three Negro scoundrels reported in our dispatches from Anniston, Ala., for a brutal outrage committed upon a white woman will be a text for much comment on "Southern barbarism" by Northern newspapers; but we fancy it will hardly prove effective for campaign purposes among intelligent people. The frequency of these lynchings calls attention to the frequency of the crimes which causes lynching. The "Southern barbarism" which deserves the serious attention of all people North and South, is the barbarism which preys upon weak and defenseless women. Nothing but the most prompt, speedy and extreme punishment can hold in check the horrible and bestial propensities of the Negro race. There is a strange similarity about a number of cases of this character which have lately occurred.

In each case the crime was deliberately planned and perpetrated by several Negroes. They watched for an opportunity when the women were left without a protector. It was not a sudden yielding to a fit of passion, but the consummation of a devilish purpose which has been seeking and waiting for the opportunity. This feature of the crime not only makes it the most fiendishly brutal, but it adds to the terror of the situation in the thinly settled country communities. No man can leave his family at night without the dread that some roving Negro ruffian is watching and waiting for this opportunity. The swift punishment which invariably follows these horrible crimes doubtless acts as a deterring effect upon the Negroes in that immediate neighborhood for a short time. But the lesson is not widely learned nor long remembered. Then such crimes, equally atrocious, have happened in quick succession, one in Tennessee, one in Arkansas, and one in Alabama. The facts of the crime appear to appeal more to the Negro's lustful imagination than the facts of the punishment do to his fears. He sets aside all fear of death in any form when opportunity is found for the gratification of his bestial desires.

There is small reason to hope for any change for the better. The commission of this crime grows more frequent every year. The generation of Negroes which have grown up since the war have lost in large measure the traditional and wholesome awe of the white race which kept the Negroes in subjection, even when their masters were in the army, and their families left unprotected except by the slaves themselves. There is no longer a restraint upon the brute passion of the Negro.

What is to be done? The crime of rape is always horrible, but for the Southern man there is nothing which so fills the soul with horror, loathing and fury as the outraging of a white woman by a Negro. It is the race question in the ugliest, vilest, most dangerous aspect. The Negro as a political factor can be controlled. But neither law nor lynchings can subdue his lusts. Sooner or later it will force a crisis. We do not know in what form it will come."

In its issue of June 4th, the Memphis "Evening Scimitar" gives the following excuse for lynch law:

"Aside from the violation of white women by Negroes, which is the outcropping of a bestial perversion of instinct, the chief cause of trouble between the races in the South is the Negro's lack of manners. In the state of slavery he learned politeness from association with white people, who took pains to teach him. Since the emancipation came and the tie of mutual interest and regard between master and servant was broken, the Negro has drifted away into a state which is neither freedom nor bondage. Lacking the proper inspiration of the one and the restraining force of the other he has taken up the idea that boorish insolence is independence and the exercise of a decent degree of breeding toward white people is identical with servile submission. In consequence of the prevalence of this notion there are many Negroes who use every opportunity to make themselves offensive, particularly when they think it can be done with impunity.

We have had too many instances right here in Memphis to doubt this, and our experience is not exceptional. *The white people won't stand this sort of thing, and whether they be insulted as individuals or as a race, the response will be prompt and effectual.* The bloody riot of 1866, in which so many Negroes perished, was brought on principally by the outrageous conduct of the blacks toward the whites on the streets. It is also a remarkable and discouraging fact that the majority of such scoundrels are Negroes who have received educational advantages at the hands of the white taxpayers. They have got just enough of learning to make them realize how hopelessly their race is behind the other in everything that makes a great people, and they attempt to "get even" by insolence, which is ever the resentment of inferiors. There are well-bred Negroes among us, and it is truly unfortunate that they should have to pay, even in part, the penalty of the offenses committed by the baser sort, but this is the way of the world. The innocent must suffer for the guilty. If the Negroes as a people possessed a hundredth part of the self-respect which is evidenced by the courteous bearing of some that the "Scimitar" could name, the friction between the races would be reduced to a minimum. It will not do to beg the question by pleading that many white men are also stirring up strife. The Caucasian blackguard simply obeys the promptings of a depraved disposition, and he is seldom deliberately rough or offensive toward strangers or unprotected women.

The Negro tough, on the contrary, is given to just that kind of offending, and he almost invariably singles out white people as his victims."

On March 9th, 1892, there were lynched in this same city three of the best specimens of young since the war Afro-American manhood. They were peaceful, law-abiding citizens and energetic business men.

They believed the problem was to be solved by eschewing politics and putting money in the purse. They owned a flourishing grocery business in a thickly populated suburb of Memphis, and a white man named Barrett had one on the opposite corner. After a personal difficulty which Barrett sought by going into the "People's Grocery" drawing a pistol and was thrashed by Calvin McDowell, he (Barrett) threatened to "clean them out." These men were a mile beyond the city limits and police protection; hearing that Barrett's crowd was coming to attack them Saturday night, they mustered forces and prepared to defend themselves against the attack.

When Barrett came he led a *posse* of officers, twelve in number, who afterward claimed to be hunting for a man for whom they had a warrant. That twelve men in citizen's clothes should think it necessary to go in the night to hunt one man who had never before been arrested, or made any record as a criminal has never been explained. When they entered the back door the young men thought the threatened attack was on, and fired into them. Three of the officers were wounded, and when the *defending* party found it was officers of the law upon whom they had fired, they ceased and got away.

Thirty-one men were arrested and thrown in jail as "conspirators," although they all declared more than once they did not know they were firing on officers. Excitement was at fever heat until the morning papers, two days after, announced that the wounded deputy sheriffs were out of danger. This hindered rather than helped the plans of the whites. There was no law on the statute books which would execute an Afro-American for wounding a white man, but the "unwritten law" did. Three of these men, the president, the manager and clerk of the grocery—"the leaders of the conspiracy"—were secretly taken from jail and lynched in a shockingly brutal manner. "The Negroes are getting too independent," they say, "we must teach them a lesson."

"What lesson? The lesson of subordination. "Kill the leaders and it will cow the Negro who dares to shoot a white man, even in self-defense."

Although the race was wild over the outrage, the mockery of law and justice which disarmed men and locked them up in jails where they could be easily and safely reached by the mob—the Afro-American ministers, newspapers and leaders counselled obedience to the law which did not protect them.

Their counsel was heeded and not a hand was uplifted to resent the outrage; following the advice of the "Free Speech," people left the city in great numbers.

The dailies and associated press reports heralded these men to the country as "toughs," and "Negro desperadoes who kept a low dive." This same press service printed that the Negro who was lynched at Indianola, Miss., in May, had outraged the sheriff's eight-year-old daughter. The girl was more than eighteen years old, and was found by her father in this man's room, who was a servant on the place.

Not content with misrepresenting the race the mob-spirit was not to be satisfied until the paper which was doing all it could to counteract this impression was silenced. The colored people were resenting their bad treatment in a way to make itself felt, yet gave the mob no excuse for further murder, until the appearance of the editorial which is construed as a reflection on the "honor" of the Southern white women. It is not half so libelous as that of the "Commercial" which appeared four days before, and which has been given in these pages. They would have lynched the manager of the "Free Speech" for exercising the right of free speech if they had found him as quickly as they would have hung a rapist, and glad of the excuse to do so. The owners were ordered not to return. "The Free Speech" was suspended with as little compunction as the business of the "People's Grocery" broken up and the proprietors murdered.

CHAPTER V

The South's Position

Henry W. Grady[14] in his well-remembered speeches in New England and New York pictured the Afro-American as incapable of self-government. Through him and other leading men the cry of the South to the country has been "Hands off. Leave us to solve our problem." To the Afro-American the South says, "the white man must and will rule." There is little difference between the Ante-bellum South and the New South.

Her white citizens are wedded to any method however revolting, any measure however extreme, for the subjugation of the young manhood of the race. They have cheated him out of his ballot, deprived him of civil rights or redress therefore in the civil courts, robbed him of the fruits of his labor, and are still murdering, burning and lynching him.

The result is a growing disregard of human life. Lynch law has spread its insidious influence till men in New York State, Pennsylvania and on the free Western plains feel they can take the law in their own hands with impunity, especially where an Afro-American is concerned. The South is brutalized to a degree not realized by its own inhabitants, and the very foundation of government, law and order, are imperiled.

Public sentiment has had a slight "reaction" though not sufficient to stop the crusade of lawlessness and lynching. The spirit of christianity of the great M. E. Church was aroused to the frequent and revolting crimes against a weak people, enough to pass strong condemnatory resolutions at its General Conference in Omaha last May. The spirit of justice of the grand old party asserted itself sufficiently to secure a denunciation of the wrongs, and a feeble declaration of the belief in human rights in the Republican platform at Minneapolis, June 7th. Some of the great dailies and weeklies have swung into line declaring that lynch law must go. The President of the United States issued a proclamation that it be not tolerated in the territories over which he has jurisdiction. Governor Northern and Chief Justice Bleckley of Georgia have proclaimed against it. The citizens of Chattanooga, Tenn., have set a worthy example in that they not only condemn lynch law, but her public men demanded a trial for Weems, the accused rapist, and guarded him while the trial was in progress. The trial only lasted ten minutes, and Weems chose to plead guilty and accept twenty-one years sentence, than invite certain death which awaited him outside that cordon of police if he had told the truth and shown the letters he had from the white woman in the case.

Col. A. S. Colyar, of Nashville, Tenn., is so overcome with the horrible state of affairs that he addressed the following earnest letter to the Nashville "American." "Nothing since I have been a reading man has so impressed me with the decay of manhood among the people of Tennessee as the dastardly submission to the mob reign. We have reached the unprecedented low level; the awful criminal depravity of substituting the mob for the court and jury, of giving up the jail keys to the mob whenever they are demanded. We do it in the largest cities and in the country towns; we do it in midday; we do it after full, not to say formal, notice, and so thoroughly and generally is it acquiesced in that the murderers have discarded the formula of masks. They go into the town where everybody knows them, sometimes under the gaze of the governor, in the presence of the courts, in the presence of the sheriff and his deputies, in the presence of the entire police force, take out the prisoner, take his life, often with fiendish glee, and often with acts of cruelty and barbarism which impress the reader with a degeneracy rapidly approaching savage life. That the State is disgraced but faintly expresses the humiliation which has settled upon the once proud people of Tennessee. The State, in its majesty, through its organized life, for which the people pay liberally, makes but one record, but one note, and that a criminal falsehood, 'was hung by persons to the jury unknown.' The murder at Shelbyville is only a verification of what every intelligent man knew would come, because with a mob a rumor is as good as proof."

These efforts brought forth apologies and a short halt, but the lynching mania has raged again through the past three months with unabated fury.

The strong arm of the law must be brought to bear upon lynchers in severe punishment, but this cannot and will not be done unless a healthy public sentiment demands and sustains such action.

The men and women in the South who disapprove of lynching

and remain silent on the perpetration of such outrages, are particeps criminis, accomplices, accessories before and after the fact, equally guilty with the actual law-breakers who would not persist if they did not know that neither the law nor militia would be employed against them.

CHAPTER VI

Self Help

In the creation of this healthier public sentiment, the Afro-American can do for himself what no one else can do for him. The world looks on with wonder that we have conceded so much and remain law-abiding under such great outrage and provocation.

To Northern capital and Afro-American labor the South owes its rehabilitation. If labor is withdrawn capital will not remain. The Afro-American is thus the backbone of the South. A thorough knowledge and judicious exercise of this power in lynching localities could many times effect a bloodless revolution. The white man's dollar is his god and to stop this will be to stop outrages in many localities.

The Afro-Americans of Memphis denounced the lynching of three of their best citizens and urged and waited for the authorities to act in the matter and bring the lynchers to justice. No attempt was made to do so, and the black men left the city by thousands, bringing about great stagnation in every branch of business. Those who remained so injured the business of the street car company by staying off the cars, that the superintendent, manager and treasurer called personally on the editor of the "Free Speech," asked them to urge our people to give them their patronage again. Other business men became alarmed over the situation and the "Free Speech" was run away that the colored people might be more easily controlled. A meeting of white citizens in June, three months after the lynching, passed resolutions for the first time, condemning it. *But they did not punish the lynchers.* Every one of them was known by name, because they had been selected to do the dirty work, by some of the very citizens who passed these resolutions. Memphis is fast losing her black population, who proclaim as they go that there is no protection for the life and property of any Afro-American citizen in Memphis who is not a slave.

The Afro-American citizens of Kentucky, whose intellectual and financial improvement has been phenomenal, have never had a separate car law until now. Delegations and petitions poured into the Legislature against it, yet the bill passed and the Jim Crow Car of Kentucky is a legalized institution. Will the great mass of Negroes continue to patronize the railroad? A special from Covington, Ky., says:

Covington, June 13th.—The railroads of the State are beginning to feel very markedly the effects of the separate coach bill recently passed by the Legislature. No class of people in the State have so many and so largely attended excursions as the blacks. All three have been abandoned, and regular travel is reduced to a minimum. A competent authority says the loss to the various roads will reach $1,000,000 this year.

A call to a State Conference in Lexington, Ky., last June had delegates from every county in the State. Those delegates, the ministers, teachers, heads of secret and other orders, and the head of every family should pass the word around for every member of the race in Kentucky to stay off railroads unless obliged to ride. If they did so, and their advice was followed persistently the convention would not need to petition the Legislature to repeal the law or raise money to file a suit. The railroad corporations would be so affected they would in self-defense lobby to have the separate car law repealed. On the other hand, as long as the railroads can get Afro-American excursions they will always have plenty of money to fight all the suits brought against them. They will be aided in so doing by the same partisan public sentiment which passed the law. White men passed the law, and white judges and juries would pass upon the suits against the law, and render judgment in line with their prejudices and in deference to the greater financial power.

The appeal to the white man's pocket has ever been more effectual than all the appeals ever made to his conscience. Nothing, absolutely nothing, is to be gained by a further sacrifice of manhood and self-respect. By the right exercise of his power as the industrial factor of the South, the Afro-American can demand and secure his rights, the punishment of lynchers, and a fair trial for accused rapists.

Of the many inhuman outrages of this present year, the only case where the proposed lynching did *not* occur, was where the men armed themselves in Jacksonville, Fla., and Paducah, Ky., and prevented it. The only times an Afro-American who was assaulted got away has been when he had a gun and used it in self-defense.

The lesson this teaches and which every Afro American should ponder well, is that a Winchester rifle should have a place of honor in every black home, and it should be used for that protection which the law refuses to give. When the white man who is always the aggressor knows he runs as great risk of biting the dust every time his Afro-American victim does, he will have greater respect for Afro-American life. The more the Afro-American yields and cringes and begs, the more he has to do so, the more he is insulted, outraged and lynched.

The assertion has been substantiated throughout these pages that the press contains unreliable and doctored reports of lynchings, and one of the most necessary things for the race to do is to get these facts before the public. The people must know before they can act, and there is no educator to compare with the press.

The Afro American papers are the only ones which will print the truth, and they lack means to employ agents and detectives to get at the facts. The race must rally a mighty host to the support of their journals, and thus enable them to do much in the way of investigation.

A lynching occurred at Port Jarvis, N.Y., the first week in June. A white and colored man were implicated in the assault upon a white girl. It was charged that the white man paid the colored boy to make the assault, which he did on the public highway in broad day time, and was lynched. This, too was done by "parties unknown." The white man in the case still lives. He was imprisoned and promises to fight the case on trial. At the preliminary examination, it developed that he had been a suitor of the girl's. She had repulsed and refused him, yet had given him money, and he had sent threatening letters demanding more.

The day before this examination she was so wrought up, she left home and wandered miles away. When found she said she did so because she was afraid of the man's testimony. Why should she be afraid of the prisoner? Why should she yield to his demands for money if not to prevent him exposing something he knew? It seems explainable only on the hypothesis that a *liaison* existed between the colored boy and the girl, and the white man knew of it. The press is singularly silent. Has it a motive? We owe it to ourselves to find out.

The story comes from Larned, Kansas, Oct. 1st, that a young white lady held at bay until daylight, without alarming any one in the house, "a burly Negro" who entered her room and bed. The "burly Negro" was promptly lynched without investigation or examination of inconsistent stories.

A house was found burned down near Montgomery, Ala., in Monroe County, Oct. 13th, a few weeks ago; also the burned bodies of the owners and melted piles of gold and silver.

These discoveries led to the conclusion that the awful crime was not prompted by motives of robbery. The suggestion of the whites was that "brutal lust was the incentive, and as there are nearly 200 Negroes living within a radius of five miles of the place the conclusion was inevitable that some of them were the perpetrators."

Upon this "suggestion" probably made by the real criminal, the mob acted upon the "conclusion" and arrested ten Afro-Americans, four of whom, they tell the world, confessed to the deed of murdering Richard L. Johnson and outraging his daughter, Jeanette. These four men, Berrell Jones, Moses Johnson, Jim and John Packer, none of them 25 years of age, upon this conclusion, were taken from jail, hanged, shot, and burned while yet alive the night of Oct. 12th. The same report says Mr. Johnson was on the best of terms with his Negro tenants.

The race thus outraged must find out the facts of this awful hurling of men into eternity on supposition, and give them to the indifferent and apathetic country. We feel this to be a garbled report, but how can we prove it?

Near Vicksburg, Miss., a murder was committed by a gang of burglars. Of course it must have been done by Negroes, and Negroes were arrested for it. It is believed that 2 men, Smith Tooley and John Adams belonged to a gang controlled by white men and, fearing exposure, on the night of July 4th, they were hanged in the Court House yard by those interested in silencing

82 THE LIGHT OF TRUTH

them. Robberies since committed in the same vicinity have been known to be by white men who had their faces blackened. We strongly believe in the innocence of these murdered men, but we have no proof. No other news goes out to the world save that which stamps us as a race of cut-throats, robbers and lustful wild beasts. So great is Southern hate and prejudice, they legally (?) hung poor little thirteen year old Mildrey Brown at Columbia, S. C., Oct. 7th, on the circumstantial evidence that she poisoned a white infant. If her guilt had been proven unmistakably, had she been white, Mildrey Brown would never have been hung.

The country would have been aroused and South Carolina disgraced forever for such a crime. The Afro American himself did not know as he should have known as his journals should be in a position to have him know and act.

Nothing is more definitely settled than he must act for himself. I have shown how he may employ the boycott, emigration and the press, and I feel that by a combination of all these agencies can be effectually stamped out lynch law, that last relic of barbarism and slavery. "The gods help those who help themselves."

"IOLA'S SOUTHERN FIELD"

Exiled from the South, Wells was hired by T. Thomas Fortune to write for the *New York Age*. In a column titled "Iola's Southern Field," she took on a number of topics in quick succession. She reiterated her opinion that African Americans should remain independent from the nation's political parties, urged blacks to save money, criticized segregated seating at a Columbus Day event, drew attention to white violence in Atlanta, and noted the success of a black streetcar boycott staged there.

SOURCE: "Iola's Southern Field," *New York Age*, November 19, 1892.

IOLA'S SOUTHERN FIELD

Save the Pennies—Outrages of Columbian Day— Southern Emigration—News From all Over the Field

Everybody is surprised at the result, and everybody is busy explaining the causes which brought about the result. The Republican party gave way to the South and submitted to a solid South when it had power to break its solidity, by reducing representation in Congress, or passing a law which would insure fair national elections by a free ballot and fair count; a Republican administration has stood by and confessed at home and abroad that the State is greater than the Union and it did not dare interfere to save the lives of its own citizens or those of foreign countries who were hanged, burned and shot within the borders of these several States; the Republican party instead of meeting the issues as drawn by the New York *Sun*, and boldly appealing to the country to sustain it in its efforts to protect the citizen—dodged and denied and relegated the Free Elections plan in their own platform—and tried to make the people believe protection and reciprocity of more value than human lives. In so doing they have ignored and alienated the larger part of the intelligent Afro-American vote of every one of the doubtful States—the balance of power in seven States—and this, together with the solid south, which the Republican party has fostered, largely brought about the defeat which is so richly deserved. A party which hasn't the courage of its convictions deserves to be taught a lesson, and I for one, am glad it has received this lesson. I am a Republican, but I was an Afro-American before I was a Republican, and the race cannot suffer more outrage, indignity and cruelty under a Democratic administration, than it has under a Republican administration, without any protest or effort on the part of the administration to stay it.

Let the Afro-American depend on no party, but on himself for his salvation. Let him continue to get education, character and above all, put money in his purse. When he has a dollar in his pocket and many more in the bank, he can move from injustice and oppression and no one to say him nay. When he has money, and plenty of it, parties and races will become his servants. The Afro-American for the next four years should bank every cent piece which does not have to go for the necessities of life, and at the end of that time he will be far more independent than any party can make him. The dimes which go for car rides, for cigars, for drinks, for bootblacks, for foolishness of all sorts, make others rich and keep us poor. A wasteful and spendthrift race or individual is always poor, is always the slave of the man who has money and will never be in a position to dictate to parties, or demand race rights. Let each one of us try saving a part of every day's earnings, for the next four years and see how much better off we will be.

It almost breaks my heart to have to go back to the four page Age, even for a time, when I have so long been proud of the eight page, and confident in the belief that the people would support it. But the support we looked for has not come, at least, not to the extent desired. Many have written and promised to renew themselves, and speak a word to a friend in its behalf, but few have kept their promises.

Eight millions of Afro-Americans, the intelligent classes of whom—the minister, lawyers, doctors, and teachers, and college bred and educated tradesmen,—excuse their failure to support race journals, on the plea "there is nothing in them." For four months we have given them the best paper of its kind, full of solid reading matter, live, helpful, interesting race news, which they could get nowhere else and we have not had four hundred new subscribers in all that time!

Eight million Afro-Americans without a national organ reaching in all quarters of this country, and representing every phase of race life, are without one of the strongest weapons of defense. To sustain such a journal is to sustain themselves and provide a champion to fight their battles. Here again, the doctrine of self-help must be practiced. The white journals will not give space to our defense and for lack of race support, our own cannot do so.

The colored people of several Southern cities so far forgot themselves as to permit their children to take part in a side show celebration of "Columbus Day" by the public schools. Of course they were treated to a "separate" place and hour for the exercises in which all school children were to take part. From McMenville, Tenn., comes the report of the most flagrant outrage to self-respect. The white children marched in one gate, and were seated on the northern side of the park,—and the exercises proceeded without waiting for the colored children. When they did arrive, prayer was being offered so the master of ceremonies rushed toward them, drove the colored band, which was playing "Hurrah for the Red, White and Blue" out of the procession and roughly ordered them to go by as they had not come at the appointed time. They were afterward seated at the back of the park, where they could neither see nor hear anything that was said; every speaker had his back to them. They marched there to sing "My Country 'Tis of Thee," and were not allowed to do even that. Those teachers and parents might have known what to expect and they knew where they were to sit, yet they went on and placed themselves where they were not wanted and where they were insulted. Will we ever learn self-respect?

The Southern Emigration Association of Chicago was organized for the purpose of finding work for and locating the colored people who wanted to leave the South. The association has no funds to pay the fare of those desiring to move. It only undertakes to find homes for those who are able to pay their own way. Yet many write for money to get away on, and because they do not receive it, express their belief that the Emigration Association is a humbug. It is an organization to aid those in finding work, who are enterprising to get together money to get away from the south.

Rev. D. M. Pinkard, an A. M. E. Zion minister, was brutally beaten in Georgia a few weeks ago by a white mob "for going about every day dressed up with shining shoes on." A white man called him out of his house four weeks ago, inviting him to go a short distance, as he wished to talk over a business matter. Rev. Pinkard went, and going a short distance was set upon by a mob that beat him into insensibility and ordered [illegible] to leave the community. After [illegible] hours he was able to drag himself back to the house where he lay for two weeks under medical treatment, then left his family [illegible] prosperity in obedience to the mob. He narrated his experiences to the North Georgia Conference, assembled at Altanta, Georgia last week, but beyond expressions of sympathy, I do not read that anything was done about it. The ministers will hardly make any mention of it to their people, and the people will go on living in and supporting the enterprises of communities which do these things. "The gods help those who help themselves."

The people of Atlanta are helping themselves right along in the street car matter. The ministers have taken hold of it. Elder L. Thomas, the pastor of Big Bethel, one of the largest churches in Atlanta and one other have put it to a vote to their congregations whether they would ride in the cars or stay on the ground. Both voted to stay on the ground. The Atlanta *Journal* announces that the street car company lost $700 during the month of October because the colored people refused to ride and now that the white man's pocket is feeling it, this paper condemns the unjust treatment of colored passengers. It never did so before, and if they keep on losing money, the whites will be the first to petition the legislation for the repeal of any such law. Let the good work go on. A colored lady who determined to ride any way was thrown off the cars two weeks ago, her head bruised, arm broken, and other injuries inflicted because she would not sit in the colored people's part of the street car. I only hope this notion will make others who refuse to unite with their race for a principle determine to stay off the street cars and keep their nickels to themselves.

The Cleveland *Gazette*'s Indianapolis correspondent says that Hon. B. K. Bruce went from Washington, D. C., to that city to vote during the late election. That ought to settle once for all Mr. Bruce's place of citizenship. Mississippi can no longer claim this distinguished son of her own, nor have him to represent her in national conventions.

"THE REQUIREMENTS OF SOUTHERN JOURNALISM"

A speech that Wells delivered to the National Press Association, an African American organization, "The Requirements of Journalism" was published in the *A.M.E. Zion Church Quarterly* in January 1893. In this essay, Wells challenges black journalists and editors to publicize racial injustices and violence against blacks even if such reporting proves dangerous.

SOURCE: "The Requirements of Southern Journalism," *A.M.E. Zion Church Quarterly*, January 1893, 189–96.

THE REQUIREMENTS OF SOUTHERN JOURNALISM

Mr. President, Members of the National Press Association, Ladies and Gentlemen:

The conditions which led to a memorial to Congress and a visit to the President of the United States by this body still obtain in this country since last you met, the outrages which prompted that memorial have increased; the lyncher has become so bold, he has discarded his mask and the secrecy of night, has left the out-of-the-way village and invaded the jails and penitentiaries of our largest cities, and hung and tortured his victims on the public streets. Not content with this, Arkansas furnishes the spectacle of a woman vindicating her honor (?) by setting fire to a living being, who, as the flames lick his burning flesh, dies protesting his innocence to the crowd of 5000 that looked on and applauded the act in ghoulish glee. A fifteen year old girl in Rayville, Louisiana, suspected of poisoning a white family is promptly hung on that suspicion; three reputable citizens of Memphis, Tenn., were taken from the jail and shot to death for prospering too well in business and defending themselves and property; one of the journals which was a member of your organization has been silenced by the edict of the mob which declared there shall be no such thing as "Free Speech" in the South. Within the past two weeks, honest, hardworking, land owning men and women of the race have been hung, shot, whipped and driven out of communities in Texas and Arkansas for no greater crime than that of too much prosperity. Indeed one almost fears to pick up the daily paper in which it is an unusual thing not to see recorded some tale of outrage or blood, with the Negro always the loser. The President of the United States announces himself unable to do anything to stay this "Reign of Terror," and the race in the localities in which these outrages occur are nearly always unable to protect themselves; the local authorities will not extend to them the protection they demand. The President and Congress have been petitioned, race indignation has vented itself in impassioned oratory and public meetings. But denouncing the flag as dirty and dishonored which does not protect its citizens, and repudiating the national hymn because it is a musical lie, has not stopped the outrages. Politics have been eschewed, civil rights given up, (rights which are dearer than life itself) and even life itself has been sacrificed on the altar of Southern hate, and still there is no peace. The assassin's bullet and ku-klux whip is still heard and the sight of the hangman's noose with an Afro-American dangling at the end, is becoming a familiar object to the eyes of young America.

If indeed "the pen is mightier than the sword," the time has come as never before that the wielders of the pen belonging to the race which is so tortured and outraged, should take serious thought and purposeful action. The blood, tears and groans of hundreds of the murdered cry to you for redress; the lamentations, distress and want, of numberless widows and orphans appeal to you to do the only thing which can be done—and which is the first step toward revolution of every kind—the creation of a healthy public sentiment.

In the creation of sentiment, the Southern newspaper can not do much, but it can do something. One of the first requirements then of Southern Journalism is to have, wherever practicable, an organ on the ground. Scattered throughout the South are journals which for lack of capital and good business management fail to do the good they might. Some have gone into the profession not always because of a love for it, or the desire to reach a high standard, but for personal aggrandizement or political preferment. Their weekly advent creates no ripples upon the body politic, disturbs no existing condition and if they can secure the wherewithal to feed the press—are permitted to exist, until they die a natural death. If it could be established, a fearlessly edited press is one of the crying necessities of the hour. Such a journal, edited in the midst of such conditions as exist in the South, can better give the facts, than out of it, or than the press dispatches will do. True, such a one might have to be on the hop, skip and jump but the seed planted even though the sower might not tarry to watch its growth, can never die. At present only one side of the atrocities against a defenceless people is given, and with all the smoothing over is a bad enough showing. The press dispatches of March 9, heralded to the country that "three negro toughs who kept a low dive, fired upon and wounded officers of the law who had gone to arrest one of their number, and as a consequence two nights afterward had been lynched." The *Free Speech* gave the facts in the case, exposing the rank injustice and connivance of the authorities with a white grocery keeper whose trade had been absorbed by these young colored men: how he set a trap into which they fell, and that although the wounded deputies were pronounced out of danger, these men were lynched in obedience to the unwritten law that an Afro-American should not shoot a white man, no matter what the provocation. Our paper showed the character of these men to be unblemished, gave the sketches and cuts of three as reputable and enterprising young men as the race afforded who were prospering in a legitimate grocery business; published a formal statement from our leading ministers addressed to the public; printed 2000 extra copies and mailed them to the leading dailies, public men and Congressmen of the United States. And so in part was counteracted the libel on these foully murdered men. How many such have gone down to a violent death without anything to chronicle the true facts in their case, will never be known. Besides, a respectful, yet firm demand for race rights is absolutely necessary among those whom they live, and through no agency can it so well be heard as the newspaper.

A prosecution of this work requires men and women who are willing to sacrifice time, pleasure and property to a realization of it; who are above bribes and demagoguery; who seek not political preferment nor personal aggrandizement; whose moral courage is strong enough to tell the race plainly yet kindly of its failings and maintain a stand for truth, honor and virtue.

This is the greatest need of all among the masses of the South— the need of the press as an educator. Children of a larger growth, the masses of our people have never been taught the first rudiments of an education, much less the science of civil government. The vast army who make the industrial wealth of the South to-day have had neither the experience of slavery nor the training of the school-room, to teach them some valuable lessons, yet they are citizens in name, making history every day for the race. Some of them are seemingly content with their lot, but it is the contentment of ignorance in which the white landlord strives to keep them, by pandering in all ways to the most depraved instincts, and especially by the aid of liquor can exert the influence.

The Afro-American needs to be taught the power of union, to realize his own strength; how to utilize that strength to secure to himself his inherent rights as did the plebeians of Rome.[15] He makes the money of the South, but has never been taught that a husbanding of resources will cease to enrich gigantic corporations at his own expense. Intelligently directed, by exercise of this power alone, the race can do much to bring about a change in race condition. The sudden withdrawal of the labor force of any one community, paralyzes the industry of that community. This is instanced in communities where preventive measures are used to keep the race, when outrages perpetrated have moved them to leave. The *Free Speech* advised the people of Memphis that if they could do nothing else, after the atrocious lynching there, they could save their money and get away from a city whose laws afforded no protection to a black man. They adhered so strictly to the advice that in six weeks the real estate dealers, rental agents, dry goods merchants complained—several firms went to the wall—and the superintendent, secretary and treasurer of the electric street railway company called on us at different times to know why colored people had stopped riding on the cars. They said they had recently spent half a million dollars to put in electricity, much of which had gone in colored people's pockets; that it was a matter of dollars and cents to them, because if they did not look after the company's income they would get somebody who would. "Then you acknowledge that the patronage of colored people keeps your business running?" "Yes, to a certain extent," was the reply, and then they voluntarily promised that there should be and was no discrimination on the cars; if such was reported it would be at once corrected, etc. For once in the history of Memphis, the colored people were united and the effect was wonderful. It was the silent forceful protest which was felt as nothing else had been felt.

The race as such must be taught the value of emigration, both to relieve the congested condition which obtains, and to better their own condition by coming in contact with newer ideas, higher standards and people who have the desire to be something. They must be led to go out in the boundless west where they will develop the manhood which lies dormant with nothing to call it into exercise. The Afro-American must be taught that there is one potent, never-failing method of dealing with prejudice; when you touch a white man's pocket, you touch his heart and his prejudices all melt away. Before the almighty dollar he worships as to no other deity, and through this weakness, a taking away of this idol, the Afro-American can effect a bloodless revolution. But he must be taught his power as an industrial and financial factor. He must be shown that the turning of his money into his own coffers strengthens himself; and that a religious staying off of the growing evil of the race—the excursion business—will do more to overthrow the odious Jim Crow laws of our statute books than all the railroad suits which are prosecuted. Who is to teach him this—line upon line, precept upon precept, example upon example? Neither the teacher whose work will not be discernable for years hence, nor the minister be he ever so able, for them it may be said as Franklin said of the Grecian and Roman orators—"they can only speak to the number of citizens capable of being assembled within reach of their voice—now by the press we can speak to the nations."

So great is the race need for instruction along the lines of education, of money-saving and character-making; of learning trades, cultivating self-dependence; of building good broad foundations upon which their citizenship is to stand; so imperative is the necessity for leading the race up to the clear heights of thought, then down into the valley of action, that if persecuted and driven from one place, we must set up the printing press in another and continue the great work till the evils we suffer are removed or the people better prepared to fight their own battles. Laboring to fill our columns with matter beneficial and calculated to stimulate thought, and cultivate race reading, the next move is to take all legitimate steps to circulate our journals among the people we hope to benefit. Many of our best journals adopt the first plan while ignoring the second. They do not seem to grasp the truth that they must not only champion race rights, but cultivate a taste for reading among the people whose champions they are.

As is well known, the requirements of Southern journalism make it impossible to always dwell in the section it hopes to represent, and show the true state of affairs. To read the white papers the Afro-American is a savage that is getting away from the restraint of the inherent fear of the white man which controlled his passions, and from whom women and children now flee as from a wild beast. This impression has gained ground from the white papers, and has blasted race reputation in many quarters. The Afro-American journal has not troubled itself to counteract that opinion—those of the South because they dare not in many cases, and those of other sections seeming to care not. But not only the reputation of individuals but that of the race is involved. The clearing of this odium attached to the race name is not only the duty of one section but belongs to all, and the National Press Association should no longer sit idly waiting for the garbled accounts of the Associated Press, which it in turn gives the world.

A white, not an Afro-American journal—the Chicago *Tribune*—kept sufficient tab of the lynchings of the past eight years, to be in position to say to the world that only one-third of the enormous lynching record of that time was for the crime of rape. Beyond a word or so of compliment to the writer, the exposure of the true inwardness of affairs in the South regarding this foul charge, which appeared in the *New York Age* of June 25, was almost unnoticed by race journals. Only one, the *Omaha Progress*, published the statement in full. It was not expected that Southern journals would, but there are many of them in other sections which could have done so. The writer thought until then that our journals only needed the facts to publish, and upon which to predicate a demand that public sentiment call a halt. That a matter of such vital race moment should be ignored by those whose duty it is to correct the growing impression so hurtful to the race's good name, was surprising, to say the least.

So frequent and serious has the grave charge of rape become, there should be full investigation of every such accusation which is considered sufficient excuse for the most diabolical outrage and torture. Afro-American Southern journalism cannot do it and hope to continue existence; but this united body as an association, can do something toward changing public opinion and moulding public sentiment in our favor. This is *the* work of the association, as such, and while I was only expected to speak of the requirements of Southern journalism, I trust I may be pardoned for deviating long enough to implore this convention here assembled not to adjourn until some practical, tangible step to that end shall have been taken. For years this association has met and concentrated itself with talking, and we returned to our respective homes with no tangible or practical work in hand—until the thinking portion of the race has classed press conventions with all other race conventions which meet, resolve and dissolve. If in face of daily occurrences we can still do only this, the charge against us is not without foundation. The time for *action* has come. Let the association tax itself to hire a detective, who shall go to the scene of each lynching, get the facts *as they exist* in each case of outrage—especially where the charge of rape is made— furnish them to the different papers of the association and those so situated shall publish them to the world. Money should be placed in the treasury at this session for that purpose, and a tax assessed by which it shall be kept up. It will pay from every point of view. You are thus in the position, despite the connivance of press agents, telegraph operators, and civil authorities to secure correct information, and vindicate the race from the charge of bestiality which stands before the world to-day practically unchallenged. A correspondent of *The Age* did it in Paris, Texas, in the month of September, and uncovered a tale of cruelty, outrage and murder against the race which would make sick the heart of a savage. Our race papers since have used that account extensively.

This could be done in every case, and for every garbled and slanderous dispatch sent out by the Associated Press, this association would be in position to match with the true account of these race disturbances and lynchings.

Sheridan exclaimed on one occasion: "Give me a tyrant king, give me a hostile House of Lords, give me a corrupt House of Commons,—give me the press and I will overturn them all." Gentlemen of the National Press Association, you *have* the press—what will you do with it? Upon your answer depends the future welfare of your race. Can you stand in comparative idleness, in purposeless wrangling, when there is earnest, practical, united work to be done?

"LYNCH LAW IN ALL ITS PHASES"

A speech delivered in Boston in February 1893, "Lynch Law in All Its Phases" was printed in the May 13 edition of *Our Day*, a Boston-based magazine that billed itself as "a Record and Review of Current Reform." Although much of the material it contains also appears in *Southern Horrors*, this article is important because it is the only surviving document that preserves the full text of any of the anti-lynching lectures that Wells delivered in the early 1890s.

SOURCE: "Lynch Law in All Its Phases," address at Tremont Temple in the Boston Monday Lectureship, February 13, 1893, *Our Day* (Boston: Our Day Publishing Co., 1893), 333–47.

LYNCH LAW IN ALL ITS PHASES

Address at Tremont Temple in the Boston Monday Lectureship. Feb. 13, 1893, by Miss Ida B. Wells, formerly editor of the *Free Speech*, Memphis, Tenn

I am before the American people to-day through no inclination of my own, but because of a deep-seated conviction that the country at large does not know the extent to which lynch law prevails in parts of the Republic, nor the conditions which force into exile those who speak the truth. I cannot believe that the apathy and indifference which so largely obtains regarding mob rule is other than the result of ignorance of the true situation.

And yet, the observing and thoughtful must know that in one section, at least, of our common country, a government of the people, by the people, and for the people, means a government by the mob; where the land of the free and home of the brave means a land of lawlessness, murder and outrage; and where liberty of speech means the license of might to destroy the business and drive from home those who exercise this privilege contrary to the will of the mob. Repeated attacks on the life, liberty and happiness of any citizen or class of citizens are attacks on distinctive American institutions; such attacks imperiling as they do the foundation of government, law and order, merit the thoughtful consideration of far-sighted Americans; not from a standpoint of sentiment, not even so much from a standpoint of justice to a weak race, as from a desire to preserve our institutions.

The race problem or negro question, as it has been called, has been omnipresent and all-pervading since long before the Afro-American was raised from the degradation of the slave to the dignity of the citizen. It has never been settled because the right methods have not been employed in the solution. It is the Banquo's ghost of politics, religion, and sociology which will not go down at the bidding of those who are tormented with its ubiquitous appearance on every occasion. Times without number, since invested with citizenship, the race has been indicted for ignorance, immorality and general worthlessness—declared guilty and executed by its self-constituted judges. The operations of law do not dispose of negroes fast enough, and lynching bees have become the favorite pastime of the South. As excuse for the same, a new cry, as fake as it is foul, is raised in an effort to blast race character, a cry which has proclaimed to the world that virtue and innocence are violated by Afro-Americans who must be killed like wild beasts to protect womanhood and childhood.

Born and reared in the South, I had never expected to live elsewhere. Until this past year I was one among those who believed the condition of the masses gave large excuse for the humiliations and proscriptions under which we labored: that when wealth, education and character became more general among us,—the cause being removed—the effect would cease, and justice be accorded to all alike. I shared the general belief that good newspapers entering regularly the houses of our people in every state could do more to bring about this result than any agency.

Preaching the doctrine of self-help, thrift and economy every week, they would be the teachers to those who had been deprived of school advantages, yet were making history every day—and train to think for themselves our mental children of a larger growth. And so, three years ago last June, I became editor and part owner of the *Memphis Free Speech*. As editor, I had occasion to criticize the city School Board's employment of inefficient teachers and poor school-building for Afro-American children. I was in the employ of that board at the time, and at the close of that school-term one year ago, was not re-elected to a position I had held in the city schools for seven years. Accepting the decision of the Board of Education, I set out to make a race newspaper pay—a thing which older and wiser heads said could not be done. But there were enough of our people in Memphis and surrounding territory to support a paper, and I believed they would do so. With nine months hard work the circulation increased from 1,500 to 3,500; in twelve months it was on a good paying basis. Throughout the Mississippi Valley in Arkansas, Tennessee and Mississippi—on plantations and in towns, the demand for and interest in the paper increased among the masses. The newsboys who would not sell it on the trains, voluntarily testified that they had never known colored people to demand a paper so eagerly.

To make the paper a paying business I became advertising agent, solicitor, as well as editor and was continually on the go. Wherever I went among the people, I gave them in church, school, public gatherings, and home, the benefit of my honest conviction that maintenance of character, money getting and education would finally solve our problem and that it depended on us to say how soon this would be brought about. This sentiment bore good fruit in Memphis. We had nice homes, representatives in almost every branch of business and profession, and refined society. We had learned that helping each other helped all, and every well-conducted business by Afro-Americans prospered. With all our proscriptions in theaters, hotels and on railroads, we never had a lynching and did not believe we could have one. There had been lynchings and brutal outrages of all sorts in our own state and those adjoining us, but we had confidence and pride in our city and the majesty of its laws. So far in advance of other Southern cities was ours, we were content to endure the evils we had, to labor and to wait.

But there was a rude awakening. On the morning of March 9, the bodies of three of our best young men were found in an old field horribly shot to pieces. These young men had owned and operated the People's Grocery, situated at what was known as the Curve—a suburb made up almost entirely of colored people—about a mile from the city limits. Thomas Moss, one of the oldest letter-carriers in the city, was president of the company, Calvin McDowell was manager and Will Stewart was a clerk. There were about ten other stockholders, all colored men. The young men were well known and popular and their businesses flourished, and that of Barrett, a white grocer who kept the store there before the "People's Grocery" was established, went down. One day an officer came to the "People's Grocery" and inquired for a colored man who lived in the neighborhood, and for whom the officer had a warrant. Barrett was with him and when McDowell said he knew nothing as to the whereabouts of the man for whom they were searching, Barrett, not the officer, then accused McDowell of harboring the man, and McDowell gave the lie. Barrett drew his pistol and struck McDowell with it; thereupon McDowell, who was a tall, fine-looking six-footer, took Barrett's pistol from him, knocked him down and gave him a good thrashing, while Will Stewart, the clerk, kept the special officer at bay. Barrett went to town, swore out a warrant for their arrest on a charge of assault and battery. McDowell went before the Criminal Court, immediately gave bond and returned to his store. Barrett then threatened to use his own words that he was going to clean out the whole store. Knowing how anxious he was to destroy their business, these young men consulted a lawyer who told them they were justified in defending themselves if attacked, as they were a mile beyond the city limits and police protection. They accordingly armed several of their friends—not to assail, but to resist the threatened Saturday night attack.

When they saw Barrett enter the front door and a half dozen men at the rear door at 11 o'clock that night, they supposed the attack was on and immediately fired into the crowd, wounding three men. These men, dressed in citizens' clothes, turned out to be deputies who claimed to be hunting another man for whom they had a warrant, and whom any one of them could have arrested without trouble. When these men found they had fired upon officers of the law, they threw away their firearms and

submitted to arrest, confident they should establish their innocence of intent to fire upon officers of the law. The daily papers
on flaming headlines roused the evil passion of the whites, denounced these poor boys in unmeasured terms, nor permitted
them a word in their own defense.

The neighborhood of the Curve was searched the next day,
and about thirty persons were thrown in jail, charged with conspiracy. No communication was to be had with friends any of
the three days these men were in jail; bail was refused and
Thomas Moss was not allowed to eat the food his wife prepared
for him. The judge is reported to have said, "Any one can see
them after three days." They were seen after three days, but they
were no longer able to respond to the greeting of friends. On
Tuesday following the shooting at the grocery, the papers which
had made much of the sufferings of the wounded deputies, and
promised it would go hard with those who did the shooting, if
they died, announced that the officers were all out of danger,
and would recover. The friends of the prisoners breathed more
easily and relaxed their vigilance. They felt that as the officers
would not die, there was no danger that in the heat of passion the
prisoners would meet violent death at the hands of the mob.
Besides, we had such confidence in the law. But the law did not
provide capital punishment for shooting which did not kill. So
the mob did what the law could not be made to do, as a lesson to
the Afro-American that he must not shoot a white man, no matter what the provocation. The same night after the announcement was made in the papers that the officers would get well, the
mob in obedience to a plan known to every prominent white
man in the city, went to the jail between two and three o'clock in
the morning, dragged out these young men, hatless and shoeless,
put them on the yard engine of the railroad which was in waiting just behind the jail, carried them a mile north of city limits
and horribly shot them to death while the locomotive at a given
signal let off steam and blew the whistle to deaden the sound of
firing.

"It was done by unknown men," said the jury, yet the *Appeal-
Avalanche*, which goes to press at 3 a.m., had a two-column account of the lynching. The papers also told how McDowell got
hold of the guns of the mob, and as his grasp could not be loos-
ened, his hand was shattered with a pistol ball and all the lower

part of his face was torn away. There were four pools of blood found and only three bodies. It was whispered that he, McDowell, killed one of the lynchers with his gun, and it is well known that a policeman who was seen on the street a few days previously to the lynching, died very suddenly the next day after.

"It was done by unknown parties," said the jury, yet the papers told how Tom Moss begged for his life, for the sake of his wife, his little daughter and his unborn infant. They also told us that his last words were, "If you will kill us, turn our faces to the West."

All this was learned too late to save these men, even if the law had not been in the hands of their murderers. When the colored people realized that the flower of our young manhood had been stolen away at night and murdered, there was a rush for firearms to avenge the wrong, but no house would sell a colored man a gun; the armory of Tennessee Rifles, our only colored military company, and of which McDowell was a member, was broken into by order of the Criminal Court judge, and its guns taken. One hundred men and irresponsible boys from fifteen years and up were armed by the order of the authorities and rushed out to the Curve, where it was reported that the colored people were massing, and at point of the bayonet dispersed these men who could do nothing but talk. The cigars, wines, etc., of the grocery stock were freely used by the mob, who possessed the place on pretense of dispersing the conspiracy. The money drawer was broken into and contents taken. The trunk of Calvin McDowell, who had a room in the store, was broken open, and his clothing, which was good enough to take away, was thrown out and trampled on the floor.

These men were murdered, their stock was attached by creditors and sold for less than one-eighth of its cost to the same man Barrett, who is to-day running his grocery in the same place. He had indeed kept his word, and by aid of the authorities destroyed the People's Grocery Company root and branch. The relatives of Will Stewart and Calvin McDowell are bereft of their protectors. The baby daughter of Tom Moss, too young to express how she misses her father, toddles to the wardrobe, seizes the legs of the trousers of his letter-carrier uniform, hugs and kisses them with evident delight and stretches up her little hands to be taken up into the arms which will nevermore clasp his daughter's form.

His wife holds Thomas Moss, Jr., in her arms, upon whose unconsciousness baby face the tears fall thick and fast when she is thinking of the sad fate of the father he will never see, and of the two helpless children who cling to her for support she cannot give. Although these men were peaceable, law-abiding citizens of this country, we are told there can be no punishment for their murderers nor indemnity for their relatives.

I have no power to describe the feeling of horror that possessed every member of the race in Memphis when the truth dawned upon us that the protection of the law which we had so long enjoyed was no longer ours; all this had been destroyed in a night, and the barriers of the law had been thrown down, and the guardians of the public peace and confidence scoffed away into the shadows, and all authority given into the hands of the mob, and innocent men cut down as if they were brutes—the first feeling was one of dismay, then intense indignation. Vengeance was whispered from ear to ear, but sober reflection brought the conviction that it would be extreme folly to seek vengeance when such action meant certain death for the men, and horrible slaughter for the women and children, as one of the evening papers took care to remind us. The power of the State, country and city, the civil authorities and the strong army of the military power were all on the side of the mob and of lawlessness. Few of our men possessed firearms, our only company guns were confiscated, and the only white man who would sell a colored man a gun, was himself jailed, and his store closed. We were helpless in our great strength. It was our first object lesson in the doctrine of white supremacy; and illustration of the South's cardinal principle that no matter what the attainments, character or standing of an Afro-American, the laws of the South will not protect him against a white man.

There was only one thing we could do, and a great determination seized upon the people to follow the advice of the martyred Moss and "turn our faces to the West," whose laws protect all alike. The *Free Speech* supported by our ministers and leading business men advised the people to leave a community whose laws did not protect them. Hundreds left on foot to walk four hundred miles between Memphis and Oklahoma. A Baptist minister went to the territory, built a church and took his entire congregation in less than a month. Another minister sold his church and took his flock to California, and still another has settled in Kansas. In two months, six thousand persons had left the city and every branch of business began to feel this silent resentment of the outrage, and failure of the authorities to punish the lynchers. There were a number of business failures and blocks of houses were for rent. The superintendent and treasurer of the street railway company called at the office of the *Free Speech* to have us urge the colored people to ride again on the street cars. A real estate dealer said to a colored man who returned some property he had been buying on the installment plan: "I don't see what you 'niggers' are cutting up about. You got off light. We first intended to kill every one of those thirty one 'niggers' in jail, but concluded to let all go but the 'leaders.'" They did let all go to the penitentiary. These so-called rioters have since been tried in the Criminal Court for the conspiracy of defending their property, and are now serving terms of three, eight, and fifteen each in the Tennessee State prison.

To restore the equilibrium and put a stop to the great financial loss, the next move was to get rid of the *Free Speech*,—the disturbing element which kept the waters troubled; which would not let the people forget, and in obedience to whose advice nearly six thousand persons had left the city. In casting about for an excuse, the mob found it in the following editorial which appeared in the Memphis *Free Speech*,—May 21, 1892: "Eight negroes lynched in one week. Since last issue of the *Free Speech* one was lynched at Little Rock, Ark., where the citizens broke into the penitentiary and got their man; three near Anniston, Ala., one near New Orleans, all on the same charge, the new alarm of assaulting white women—and three near Clarksville, Ga., for killing a white man. The same program of hanging—then shooting bullets into the lifeless bodies was carried out to the letter. Nobody in this section of the country believes the old threadbare lie that negro men rape white women. If southern white men are not careful they will overreach themselves, and public sentiment will have a reaction. A conclusion will then be reached which will be very damaging to the moral reputation of their women." Commenting on this, *The Daily Commercial* of Wednesday following said: "Those negroes who are attempting to make the lynchings of individuals of their race a means for arousing the worst passions of their kind, are playing with a dangerous sentiment. The negroes may as well understand that there is no mercy for the negro rapist, and little patience with his defenders. A negro organ printed in this city in a recent issue publishes the following atrocious paragraph: 'Nobody in this section of the country believes the old threadbare lie that negro men rape white women. If Southern white men are not careful they will overreach themselves and public sentiment will have a reaction. A conclusion will be reached which will be very damaging to the moral reputation of their women.' The fact that a black scoundrel is allowed to live and utter such loathsome and repulsive calumnies is a volume of evidence as to the wonderful patience of Southern whites. There are some things that the Southern white man will not tolerate, and the obscene intimations of the foregoing have brought the writer to the very outermost limit of public patience. We hope we have said enough."

The Evening *Scimitar* of the same day copied this leading editorial and added this comment: "Patience under such circumstances is not a virtue. If the negroes themselves do not apply the remedy without delay, it will be the duty of those he has attacked, to tie the wretch who utters these calumnies to a stake at the intersection of Main and Madison streets, brand him in the forehead with a hot iron and—"

Such open suggestions by the leading daily papers of the progressive city of Memphis were acted upon by the leading citizens and a meeting was held at the Cotton Exchange that evening. *The Commercial* two days later had the following account of it:

ATROCIOUS BLACKGUARDISM

There will be no Lynching and no Repetition of the Offense

In its issue of Wednesday *The Commercial* reproduced and commented on an editorial which appeared a day or two before in the negro organ known as the *Free Speech*. The article was so insufferably and indecently slanderous that the whole city awoke to a feeling of intense resentment which came within an ace of culminating in one of those occurrences whose details are so eagerly seized and so prominently published by Northern newspapers. Conservative counsels, however, prevailed, and no extreme measures were resorted to. On Wednesday afternoon a meeting of citizens was held. It was not an assemblage of hoodlums or irresponsible fire-eaters,[16] but solid, substantial business men who knew exactly what they were doing and who were far more indignant at the villainous insult to the women of the South than they would have been at any injury done themselves. This meeting appointed a committee to seek the author of the infamous editorial and warn him quietly that upon repetition of the offense he would find some other part of the country a good deal safer and pleasanter place of residence than this. The committee called on a negro preacher named Nightingale, but he disclaimed responsibility and convinced the gentlemen that he had really sold out his paper to a woman named Wells. This woman is not in Memphis at present. It was finally learned that one Fleming, a negro who was driven out of Crittenden Co. during the trouble there a few years ago, wrote the paragraph. He had, however, heard of the meeting, and fled from a fate which he feared was in store for him, and which he knew he deserved. His whereabouts could not be ascertained, and the committee so reported. Later on, a communication from Fleming to a prominent Republican politician, and that politician's reply were shown to one or two gentlemen. The former was an inquiry as to whether the writer might safely return to Memphis, the latter was an emphatic answer in the negative, and Fleming is still in hiding. Nothing further will be done in the matter. There will be no lynching, and it is very certain there will be no repetition of the outrage. If there should be—Friday, May 25.

The only reason there was no lynching of Mr. Fleming who was business manager and half owner of the *Free Speech*, and who did not write the editorial, was because this same white Republican told him the committee was coming, and warned him not to trust them, but get out of the way. The committee scoured the city hunting him, and had to be content with Mr. Nightingale who was dragged to the meeting, shamefully abused although it was known he had sold out his interest in the paper six months before. He was struck in the face and forced at the pistol's point to sign a letter which was written by them, in which he denied all knowledge of the editorial, denounced and condemned it as slander on white women. I do not censure Mr. Nightingale for his action because, having never been at the pistol's point myself, I do not feel that I am competent to sit in judgment on him, or say what I would do under such circumstances.

I had written that editorial with other matter for the week's paper before leaving home the Friday previous for the General Conference of the A. M. E. Church in Philadelphia. Conference adjourned Tuesday, and Thursday, May 25, at 3 p.m., I landed in New York City for a few days' stay before returning home, and there learned from the papers that my business manager had been driven away and the paper suspended. Telegraphing for news, I received telegrams and letters in return informing me that the trains were being watched, that I was to be dumped into the river and beaten, if not killed; it had been learned that I wrote the editorial and I was to be hanged in front of the court-house and my face bled if I returned, and I was implored by my friends to remain away. The creditors attacked the office in the meantime and the outfit was sold without more ado, thus destroying effectually that which it had taken years to build. One prominent insurance agent publicly declares he will make it his business to shoot me down on sight if I return to Memphis in twenty years, while a leading white lady has remarked that she was opposed to the lynching of those three men in March, but she did wish there was some way by which I could be gotten back and lynched.

I have been censured for writing that editorial, but when I think of the five men who were lynched that week for assault on white women and that not a week passes but some poor soul is violently ushered into eternity on this trumped-up charge, knowing the many things I do, and part of which I tried to tell in the *New York Age* of June 25, (and in the pamphlets I have with me) seeing that the whole race in the South was injured in the estimation of the world because of these false reports, I could no longer hold my peace, and I feel, yes, I am sure, that if it had to be done over again (provided no one else was the loser save myself) I would do and say the very same again.

The lawlessness here described is not confined to one locality. In the past ten years over a thousand colored men, women and children have been butchered, murdered and burnt in all parts of the South. The details of these horrible outrages seldom reach beyond the narrow world where they occur. Those who commit the murders write the reports, and hence these lasting blots upon the honor of a nation cause but a faint ripple on the outside world. They arouse no great indignation and call forth no adequate demand for justice. The victims were black, and the reports are so written as to make it appear that the helpless creatures deserved the fate which overtook them.

Not so with the Italian lynching of 1891. They were not black men, and three of them were not citizens of the Republic, but subjects of the King of Italy. The chief of police of New Orleans was shot and eleven Italians were arrested charged with the murder; they were tried and the jury disagreed; the good, law-abiding citizens of New Orleans thereupon took them from the jail and lynched them at high noon. A feeling of horror ran through the nation at this outrage. All Europe was amazed. The Italian government demanded thorough investigation and redress, and the Federal Government promised to give the matter the consideration which was its due. The diplomatic relations between the two countries became very much strained and for a while war talk was freely indulged. Here was a case where the power of the Federal Government to protect its own citizens and redeem its pledges to a friendly power was put to the test. When our State Department called upon the authorities of Louisiana for investigation of the crime and punishment of the criminals, the United States government was told that the crime was strictly within the authority of the State of Louisiana, and Louisiana would attend to it. After a farcical investigation, the usual verdict in such cases was rendered: "Death at the hands of parties unknown to the jury," the same verdict which has been pronounced over the bodies of over 1,000 colored persons. Our general government has thus admitted that it has no jurisdiction over the crimes committed at New Orleans upon citizens of the country, nor upon those citizens of a friendly power to whom the general government and not the State government has pledged protection. Not only has our general government made the confession that one of the states is greater than the Union, but the general government has paid $25,000 of the people's money to the King of Italy for the lynching of those three subjects, the evil doing of one State, over which it has no control, but for whose lawlessness the whole country must pay. The principle involved in the treaty power of the government has not yet been settled to the satisfaction of for-

eign powers; but the principle involved in the rights of State jurisdiction in such matters, settled long ago by the decision of the
United States Supreme Court.

I beg your patience while we look at another phase of the
lynching mania. We have turned heretofore to the pages of ancient and medieval history to Roman tyranny, the Jesuitical
Inquisition of Spain for the spectacle of a human being burnt to
death. In the past ten years three instances, at least, have been
furnished where men have literally been roasted to death to ap-
pease the fury of the Southern mobs. The Texarkana instance of
last year and the Paris, Texas, case of this month are the most
recent as they are the most shocking and repulsive. Both were
charged with crimes for which the laws provide adequate punishment. The Texarkana man, Ed Coy, was charged with assaulting
a white woman. A mob pronounced him guilty, strapped him to
a tree, chipped the flesh from his body, poured coal oil over him
and the woman in the case set fire to him. The country looked on
and in many cases applauded, because it was published that this
man had violated the honor of a white woman, although he protested his innocence to the last. Judge Tourjee[17] in the Chicago
Inter Ocean of recent date says investigation has shown that Ed
Coy had supported this woman, (who was known to be of bad
character.) and her drunken husband for over a year previous to
the burning.

The Paris, Texas, burning of Henry Smith, February 1st, has
exceeded all the others in its horrible details. The man was drawn
through the streets on a float, as the Roman generals used to pa-
rade their trophies of war, while the scaffold ten feet high, was
being built, and irons were heated in the fire. He was bound on
it, and red-hot irons began at his feet and slowly branded his
body, while the mob howled with delight at his shrieks. Red hot
irons were run down his throat and cooked his tongue; his eyes
were burned out, and when he was at last unconscious, cotton
seed hulls were placed under him, coal oil poured all over him,
and a torch applied to the mass. When the flames burned away
the ropes which bound Smith and scorched his flesh, he was
brought back to sensibility—and burned and maimed and sight-
less as he was, he rolled off the platform and away from the fire.
His half-cooked body was seized and trampled and thrown back
into the flames while the mob of twenty thousand persons who

came from all over the country howled with delight, and gathered up some buttons and ashes after all was over to preserve for relics. This man was charged with outraging and murdering a four-year-old white child, covering her body with brush, sleeping beside her through the night, then making his escape. If true, it was the deed of a madman, and should have been clearly proven so. The fact that no time for verification of the newspaper reports was given, is suspicious, especially when I remember that a negro was lynched in Indianola, Sharkey Co., Miss., last summer. The dispatches said it was because he had assaulted the sheriff's eight-year-old daughter. The girl was more than eighteen years old and was found by her father in this man's room, who was a servant on the place.

These incidents have been made the basis of this terrible story because they overshadow all others of a like nature in cruelty and represent the legal phases of the whole question. They could be multiplied without number—and each outrival the other in the fiendish cruelty exercised, and the frequent awful lawlessness exhibited. The following table shows the number of black men lynched from January 1, 1882, to January 1, 1892: In 1882, 52; 1883, 39; 1884, 53; 1885, 77; 1886, 73; 1887, 70; 1888, 72; 1889, 95; 1890, 100; 1891, 169. Of these 728 black men who were murdered, 269 were charged with rape, 253 with murder, 44 with robbery, 37 with incendiarism, 32 with reasons unstated (it was not necessary to have a reason), 27 with race prejudice, 13 with quarreling with white men, 10 with making threats, 7 with rioting, 5 with miscegenation, 4 with burglary. One of the men lynched in 1891 was Will Lewis, who was lynched because "he was drunk and saucy to white folks." A woman who was one of the 73 victims in 1886, was hung in Jackson, Tenn., because the white woman for whom she cooked, died suddenly of poisoning. An examination showed arsenical poisoning. A search in the cook's room found rat poison. She was thrown in jail, and when the mob had worked itself up to the lynching pitch, she was dragged out, every stitch of clothing torn from her body, and was hung in the public court house square in front of everybody. That white woman's husband has since died, in the insane asylum, a raving maniac, and his ravings have led to the conclusion that he, and not the cook, was the poisoner of his wife. A fifteen-year-old colored girl was lynched last spring, at Rayville, La., on the same charge of poisoning. A woman was also lynched at Hollendale, Miss., last spring, charged with being an accomplice in the murder of her white paramour who had abused her. These were only two of the 159 persons lynched in the South from January 1, 1892, to January 1, 1893. Over a dozen black men have been lynched already since the new year set in, and the year is not yet two months old.

It will thus be seen that neither age, sex nor decency are spared. Although the impression has gone abroad that most of the lynchings take place because of assaults on white women only one-third of the number lynched in the past ten years have been charged with that offense, to say nothing of those who were not guilty of the charge. And according to law none of them were guilty until proven so. But the unsupported word of any white person for any cause is sufficient to cause a lynching. So bold have the lynchers become, masks are laid aside, the temples of justice and strongholds of law are invaded in broad daylight and prisoners taken out and lynched, while governors of states and officers of law stand by and see the work well done.

And yet this Christian nation, the flower of the nineteenth century civilization, says it can do nothing to stop this inhuman slaughter. The general government is willingly powerless to send troops to protect the lives of its black citizens, but the state governments are free to use state troops to shoot them down like cattle, when in desperation the black men attempt to defend themselves, and then tell the world that it was necessary to put down a "race war."

Persons unfamiliar with the condition of affairs in the Southern States do not credit the truth when it is told them. They cannot conceive how such a condition of affairs prevails so near them with steam power, telegraph wires and printing presses in daily and hourly touch with the localities where such disorder reigns. In a former generation the ancestors of these same people refused to believe that slavery was the "league with death and the covenant with hell." Wm. Lloyd Garrison[18] declared it to be, until he was thrown into a dungeon in Baltimore, until the signal lights of Nat Turner[19] lit the dull skies of Northampton County, and until sturdy old John Brown[20] made his attack on Harper's Ferry. When freedom of speech was martyred in the person of Elijah Lovejoy[21] at Alton, when the liberty of free discussion in the Senate

of the Nation's Congress was struck down in the person of the
fearless Charles Sumner,[22] the Nation was at last convinced that
slavery was not only a monster but a tyrant. That same tyrant is
at work under a new name and guise. The lawlessness which has
been here described is like unto that which prevailed under slavery. *The very same forces are at work now as then.* The attempt
is being made to subject to a condition of civil and industrial de-
pendence, those whom the Constitution declares to be free men.
The events which have led up to the present wide-spread lawlessness in the South can be traced to the very first year Lee's[23] conquered veterans marched from Appomattox to their homes in the
Southland. They were conquered in war, but not in spirit. They
believed as firmly as ever that it was their right to rule black men
and dictate to the National Government. The Knights of White
Liners, and the Ku Klux Klans were composed of veterans of the
Confederate army who were determined to destroy the effect of
all the slave had gained by the war. They finally accomplished
their purpose in 1876. The right of the Afro-American to vote
and hold office remains in the Federal Constitution, but is destroyed in the constitution of the Southern states. Having destroyed the citizenship of the man, they are now trying to destroy
the manhood of the citizen. All their laws are shaped to this
end,—school laws, railroad car regulations, those governing
labor liens on crops,—every device is adopted to make slaves of
free men and rob them of their wages. Whenever a malicious law
is violated in any of its parts, any farmer, any railroad conductor,
or merchant can call together a posse of his neighbors and punish
even with death the black man who resists and the legal authorities sanction what is done by failing to prosecute and punish the
murderers. The Repeal of the Civil Rights Law removed their last
barrier and the black man's last bulwark and refuge. The rule of
the mob is absolute.

    Those who know this recital to be true, say there is nothing
they can do—they cannot interfere and vainly hope by further
concession to placate the imperious and dominating part of our
country in which this lawlessness prevails. Because this country
has been almost rent in twain by internal dissension, the other
sections seem virtually to have agreed that the best way to heal
the breach is to permit the taking away of civil, political, and
even human rights, to stand by in silence and utter indifference

while the South continues to wreak fiendish vengeance on the ir-responsible cause. They pretend to believe that with all the machinery of law and government in its hands; with the jails and penitentiaries and convict farms filled with petty race criminals; with the well-known fact that no negro has ever been known to escape conviction and punishment for any crime in the South—still there are those who try to justify and condone the lynching of over a thousand black men in less than ten years—an average of one hundred a year. The public sentiment of the country, by its silence in press, pulpit and in public meetings has encouraged this state of affairs, and public sentiment is stronger than law. With all the country's disposition to condone and temporize with the South and its methods; with its many instances of sacrificing principle to prejudice for the sake of making friends and healing the breach made by the late war; of going into this lawless country with capital to build up its waste places and remaining silent in the presence of outrage and wrong—the South is as vindictive and bitter as ever. She is willing to make friends as long as she is permitted to pursue unmolested and uncensored, her course of proscription, injustice, outrage and vituperation. The malignant misrepresentation of General Butler, the uniformly indecent and abusive assault of this dead man whose only crime was a defence of his country, is a recent proof that the South has lost none of its bitterness. The *Nashville American*, one of the leading papers of one of the leading southern cities, gleefully announced editorially that " 'The Beast is dead.' Early yesterday morning, acting under the devil's orders, the angel of Death took Ben Butler and landed him in the lowest depths of hell, and we pity even the devil the possession he has secured." The men who wrote these editorials are without exception young men who know nothing of slavery and scarcely anything of the war. The bitterness and hatred have been instilled in and taught them by their parents, and they are men who make and reflect the sentiment of their section. The South spares nobody else's feelings, and it seems a queer logic that when it comes to a question of right, involving the lives of citizens and the honor of the government, the South's feelings must be respected and spared.

Do you ask the remedy? A public sentiment strong against lawlessness must be aroused. Every individual can contribute to this awakening. When a sentiment against lynch law as strong, deep and mighty as that roused against slavery prevails, I have no fear of the result. It should be already established as a fact and not as a theory, that every human being must have a fair trial for his life and liberty, no matter what the charge against him. When a demand goes up from fearless and persistent reformers from press and pulpit, from industrial and moral associations that this shall be so from Maine to Texas and from ocean to ocean, a way will be found to make it so.

In deference to the few words of condemnation uttered at the M. E. General Conference last year, and by other organizations, Governors Hogg of Texas, Northern of Georgia, and Tillman of South Carolina, have issued proclamations offering rewards for the apprehension of lynchers. These rewards have never been claimed, and these governors knew they would not be when offered. In many cases they knew the ringleaders of the mobs. The prosecuting attorney of Shelby County, Tenn., wrote Governor Buchanan to offer a reward for the arrest of the lynchers of three young men murdered in Memphis. Everybody in that city and state knew well that the letter was written for the sake of effect and the governor did not even offer the reward. But the country at large deluded itself with the belief that the officials of the South and the leading citizens condemned lynching. The lynchings go on in spite of offered rewards, and in face of Governor Hogg's vigorous talk, the second man was burnt alive in his state with the utmost deliberation and publicity. Since he sent a message to the legislature the mob found and hung Henry Smith's stepson, because he refused to tell where Smith was when they were hunting for him. Public sentiment which shall denounce these crimes in season and out; public sentiments which turns capital and immigration from a section given over to lawlessness; public sentiment which insists on the punishment of criminals and lynchers by law must be aroused.

It is no wonder in my mind that the party which stood for thirty years as the champion of human liberty and human rights, the party of great moral ideas, should suffer overwhelming defeat when it has proven recreant to its professions and abandoned a position it created; when although its followers were being outraged in every sense, it was afraid to stand for the right, and appeal to the American people to sustain them in it. It put aside the question of a free ballot and fair count to every citizen and gave its voice and influence for the protection of the coat instead of the man who wore it, for the product of labor instead of the laborer; for the seal of citizenship rather than the citizen, and insisted upon the evils of free trade instead of the sacredness of free speech. I am no politician but I believe if the Republican party had met the issues squarely for human rights instead of the tariff, it would have occupied a different position to-day. The voice of the people is the voice of God, and I long with all the intensity of my soul for the Garrison, Douglas, Sumner, Whittier and Phillips who shall rouse this nation to a demand that from Greenland's icy mountains to the coral reefs of the Southern seas, mob rule shall be put down and equal and exact justice be accorded to every citizen of whatever race, who finds a home within the borders of the land of the free and the home of the brave.

Then no longer will our national hymns be sounding brass and a tinkling cymbal, but every member of this great composite nation will be a living, harmonious illustration of the words, and all can honestly and gladly join in singing:

> My country! 'tis of thee,
> Sweet land of liberty
>   Of thee I sing.
> Land where our fathers died,
> Land of the Pilgrim's pride,
> From every mountain side
>   Freedom does ring.[24]

"THE REIGN OF MOB LAW"

In this *New York Age* editorial, Wells offers her critique of those black men and women who supported the segregated "Afro-American Jubilee Day" at the World's Columbian Exposition in Chicago. African American representation at the World's Fair had been a controversial question from the start, and Wells, along with Frederick Douglass and others, opposed the fair organizers' attempts to encourage blacks who wished to attend the fair to come only on a special Jubilee Day, or "Colored People's Day," set aside for African American participants. Wells was particularly incensed that there were members of the black community who would donate time and money to promoting the Jubilee Day, which was to be held on August 25, 1893, rather than supporting her pamphlet.

SOURCE: "The Reign of Mob Law," *New York Age*, February 18, 1893.

THE REIGN OF MOB LAW

Iola's Opinion of Doings in the Southern Field

The lynching epidemic still rages in Texas. Gov. Hogg denounced the lynchers, who burned Henry Smith as murderers, telegraphed the District Attorney and sheriff of Lamar County, where the burning occurred, to discharge their duty and make complaint and report those known to have been engaged in the lynching. . . . The mob has so little fear and so great contempt of the Governor, the sheriff and the District Attorney that it went a few days later February 7th and lynched Will Butler.

Will Butler was a stepson of Henry Smith, the man who was burned alive, and made himself notorious during the search for Smith by claiming to know his whereabouts which he would not divulge—so said the dispatches. Hence, because Will Butler did not tell where his step-father was, he too was lynched. . . .

New Orleans, Jan. 21—A mob of masked men broke into the jail last night at Convent, St. Joseph Parish and forced the jailer to open the cells of Robert Landy and Pick George, who were incarcerated there, one for garroting and robbing a telegraph operator at Dehon Station and the other for murdering a man named Denhorst.

Both were taken to a shed and lynched. One race still sits and does nothing about it and say little except to doubt the expediency of or find fault with the remedy proposed. No plan of raising money by which the things can be investigated, the country abused and the temple of justice, the pulpit and the press besieged, lynch law and stake burning. No money and little support to give to this work, but some of our prominent men and women have put their names on a circular asking the race to give entertainments on March 9, to raise money to defray the expenses of a most comfortable day of praise at the World Fair August 17, to be known as "Afro American Jubilee Day." . . . Even if the condition of our race was not so serious in this country, the whole thing is lacking in dignity, self respect and judgment to say nothing of good taste.

March 9th is the anniversary of one of the most diabolical lynchings in this country. One year ago, on that day, three of our best young men were lynched in Memphis, and it could more appropriately be a day of mourning.

The idea of a separate day at the fair in which the race is to pose before the world in an attitude of worship and supplication, is a mockery on its face . . . So it seems to me, and though my judgment may be at fault, I decline to the use of my name and gave these reasons therefore.

Afro American Jubilee Committee:

I cannot permit the use of my name on the circular which has been sent out asking the race to give entertainments to pay the expenses of the contemplated Jubilee Day at the World's Fair in

Chicago. I see most of the exchanges, and feel sure had there been any movement of the race at large which appointed officials to speak for and represent us in making such appeal something would have been published concerning it. The eight persons who constitute this commission must have been unauthorized by the Afro Americans of Massachusetts as all of the officers and half of the members of this commission are Massachusetts men and women. If Massachusetts did this, it is too much for the Old Bay State to speak for the entire race in this matter.

Therefore the committee in issuing this circular has usurped an authority which does not belong to it and which will be repudiated by the Race in the United States. The world's Columbus Exposition Managers have persistently ignored and refused recognition in every department of the work. Not content with the slights and snubs we have received, some persons have begged for one day in which to exhibit the race to the world in a mockery of worship of the Most High. The World's Fair Joint Committee of Ceremonies has yielded to this prayer evidently on condition that the race defray the expenses of such wondrous concession on its part. I believe that the majority of the race is willing that the World Fair Columbus Exposition shall continue to the end the policy of ignoring the Afro Americans which has characterized its action.

They are far too self-respecting to seize the crumb thrown at the last moment. And will reject the action of those who not only are ready to grasp it, but under the cloak of religion pretend to illustrate the race's progress or believe it can be exhibited in one day by a few musicians.

"LYNCH LAW AND THE COLOR LINE"

Wells's brief trip to England in the spring of 1893 attracted largely negative notice in the mainstream U.S. press. In this letter to the editor of the *Washington Post*, Wells responds to the *Post*'s allegation that "mercenary motive[s]" inspired her to "misrepresent her native country." Such claims infuriated Wells, who never succeeded in making a living out of her anti-lynching work and was always short of money. Here, she responds to the *Post* by emphasizing that she traveled to Britain on the invitation of her British hosts, who covered only her expenses. She also notes that she took her anti-lynching campaign to Britain only after trying and failing to get a hearing in the United States, where newspapers such as the *Post* routinely failed to condemn even the most brutal lynchings.

SOURCE: "Lynch Law and the Color Line," *Washington Post*, July 7, 1893.

LYNCH LAW AND THE COLOR LINE

Reply of Miss Ida B. Wells to Editorial Comments in "The Post"

EDITOR POST: I have been shown the editorials of the daily papers of the country touching my recent visit to Great Britain and the addresses I delivered while there against "lynch law."

With Southern journals abuse has over answered for argument, and so the Southern press has outdone itself in vile abuse of me. But the people of Great Britain did not consider that calling me "adventuress," "slanderer," and "liar" was any rebuttal of my statements nor explanation of the fact that scarcely a week passes without a lynching in the civilized parts of our country.

In THE POST of May 31 an editorial on the same subject also accuses me of misrepresenting my native country from a mercenary motive. Permit me to say that I went to Great Britain in response to an invitation from British people themselves. This invitation came unsolicited and unexpected. They could not understand why such lawlessness prevailed in the "land of the free and the home of the brave," and volunteered to pay my expenses to have me come and tell how my friends had been lynched in Memphis and my newspaper destroyed there because I denounced lynching and lynchers. This I did gladly, and received not a cent for the forty public addresses I made in Scotland and England. I felt that as they were interested enough to pay expenses, amounting to $500, to learn the truth, I was no less interested to tell them.

Your editorial says: "If Miss Wells had cared to confine herself to a strict portrayal and denunciation of the evil results of mob violence, it would have not been necessary to go to Great Britain for an audience." For six months before the invitation came to me to go to Great Britain I tried to get a hearing in the white press and before white audiences in this country, because they could do something to check this evil. Boston was the only city in which I succeeded in doing this, and on three of the occasions I spoke to white audiences there. I paid my own expenses there and back from Washington. I was glad of this opportunity in any way to appeal to them to bestir themselves in behalf of their country's good name. On only one of these occasions, Rev. Joseph Cook's Monday lecture at Tremont Temple, was any action taken or resolutions of protest passed. In Washington city special efforts were made to get the whites to attend the lecture, but few responded.

Every white minister in the city was notified, and it was well advertised in the papers. Besides this, hundreds of neat invitations were printed at extra expense and mailed to all the Congressmen and prominent citizens of the District of Columbia. On the night of the lecture, there were not more than a dozen whites in the house, while the President, Benjamin Harrison, was so little concerned he forgot (?) to send the letter of regrets he promised Hon. Frederick Douglass he would. The report of that lecture in THE POST the following morning, February 2, said the recital was enough to cause a blush of shame, to think that such things could be in a civilized country. I told that very same story in Great Britain. If it were not a "misrepresentation" in Washington city, how could it be so in Birmingham and London? (!)

That same issue of your paper contained a full account of the awful barbarity in Texas—burning alive of Henry Smith.[25] If I misrepresented the case to my British audience THE POST also is guilty of the same offense, for the details of how Smith was tortured with red hot irons for fifty minutes, his tongue cooked, his eyes burned out, and his body thrown back into the flames when he crawled out, and how the mob fought over the ashes for buttons and bones as relics, were first taken from the columns of THE POST on the morning of February 22. It was when giving this account that English audiences cried "Shame," "Abominable," &c. THE POST editorial on this shocking affair the Sunday following, after denouncing alike the crime of Henry Smith and the Paris (Tex.) populace, says:

"Our correspondent, however, will find it very difficult to arouse any particularly strong feeling over the fate of Henry Smith. If he committed the unspeakable enormity of which he was accused, and it is just as easy to believe that as to accept the assertion that a collection of civilized men was temporarily transformed into a drove of pitiless wild beasts—if Henry Smith we say, were guilty as alleged, nobody is likely to concern himself very greatly as to what was done with him. Indeed, it is one of the worst effects of a frightful crime that it tends to dull men's minds to the almost equal enormity of its punishment.

"We hear a great deal nowadays of lynchings and the like, in truth, they are more frequent than any one could wish. But it is foolish, as well as untrue, to say that the negro is the especial victim of these extra judicial performances, and especially unwise of the colored people to think of it as a race affair. The vigilance committees of San Francisco, Vicksburg, New Orleans, and fifty other American towns in times gone by devoted themselves almost exclusively to white offenders. They sought to eradicate a special class of criminals, and that, no doubt is the object of the lynching parties to-day. The color of the victim is a mere incident. Neither is it fair to say that lynching belongs to any section more than another.

"Henry Smith would have been put to death in Ohio or New York or Massachusetts just as surely as he was in Texas, had he committed the same crime there and fallen into the hands of the populace. Human nature is very much the same all over this country, and in one part of it as much as in the other. You can argue from certain premises to their infallible results. No intelligent and observant person needs to be told that if lynching occurs oftener at the South than at the North it is because the crimes for which lynching is applied are committed oftener there, and for no other reason.

"Of course it would be better if the punishment of offense, no matter how heinous, were always left to the deliberate process of the law, but no one who lives in the District of Columbia should wonder at men's distrust of these processes elsewhere, or be too severe in their denunciation of people who at times, and under circumstances of peculiar enormity, refuse to wait upon their uncertain evolution."

The closing paragraph of this editorial destroys entirely the effect of the first third of it. If it were true that the law is uncertain in effect, the law makers and administrators should be punished for this. No law ever miscarries where a negro is concerned, and none others but negroes would have been or are being burned in this country. Since the appearance of the above condoning editorial in THE POST, the third negro was burned in the South April 24, and he was only charged with the murder of a white man, and, with no proof of guilt, was hurried away to a stake and burned.

The American press, with few exceptions, either by such editorials or silence, has encouraged mobs, and is responsible for the increasing wave of lawlessness which is sweeping over the States. Mobs may, and occasionally do, lynch white persons, but no white man has been burned alive by a white mob nor white woman hanged by one. The St. Louis Republic is authority for the statement that mobs draw the color line. In its issue the first week in February this year it says: "Of the nearly 7,000 homicides reported in 1892 236 were committed by mobs, this being an increase of 41 over the number reported for the previous year.*** Of the persons so murdered 231 were men and 5 were women; 80 were white and 135 were negroes, while only 1 Indian was reported."

Over fifty negroes have been lynched in this country since January 1, 1893, two of whom were burned at the stake with all the barbarity of savages. One man was under the protection of the governor of South Carolina, and he gave him up to the mob that promptly lynched him. A State senator was prominently mentioned in connection with the lynching. No concealment was attempted. One of these negroes was lynched almost in sight of Jackson Park the first of this month. In no case have the lynchers been punished, in few cases has the press said anything in favor of law and order, the religious and philanthropic bodies of the country utter no word of condemnation, nor demand the enforcement of the law, and still I am charged with misrepresenting my native country. If the pulpit and press of the country will inaugurate a crusade against this lawlessness, it will be no longer necessary to appeal to the Christian, moral, and humane forces of the outside world. And when they do so, not out of sympathy with criminals, but for the sake of their country's good name, they will have no more earnest helper than

IDA B. WELLS

"TO TOLE WITH WATERMELONS"

Wells promoted her pamphlet in the *Cleveland Gazette*, where one reader conceded only that it might be worth a dollar. Writing in response, Wells stressed that the pamphlet had become all the more necessary with the announcement that the fair would host a special Colored People's Day on August 25, 1893. Generally opposed to segregated events, Wells found this one especially objectionable, she explained in the following brief piece in the *Cleveland Gazette*. She saw the day as a cynical attempt by the fair's organizers to increase African American attendance at an event that provided very little recognition for their group. Moreover, she was additionally dismayed to find black entrepreneurs chartering special excursion trains to the fair, which she saw as a form of self-segregation. And finally, she was appalled to hear that the fair's Horticultural Department planned to pass out free watermelons on Colored People's Day.

SOURCE: "To Tole with Watermelons," *Cleveland Gazette*, July 22, 1893.

TO TOLE WITH WATERMELONS

A Novel Way to Increase the
World's Fair Attendance "Colored Folks' Day"

One of the important points in Mr. —'s letter is that he is in favor of the pamphlet one dollar's worth. It will be especially needed to offset the effect of "Colored Folks Day" at the world's fair, which will be August 25. Some colored men have promised to get two hundred thousand colored excursionists there that day, and the officials of the exposition have been published as highly in favor of the idea. The horticultural department has already pledged itself to put plenty of watermelons around on the grounds with permission to the brother in black to "appropriate" them. The secret of kindness (?) of the world's fair commissioners is that the attendance at the fair has been very poor all along, and the colored brother has been especially conspicuous by his absence. This "Colored Folks' Day" is to be an extra inducement to have him come. He has been shut out of any other participation in the fair except to spend his money there, and as he has not been doing that very freely, a cordial invitation to do so is given at the eleventh hour. Because the colored men are urging this scheme to put thousands of dollars into the pockets of the railroad corporations and the world's fair folks who thought no Negro good enough for an official position among them, it will succeed. The self-respect of the race is sold for a mess of pottage and the spectacle of the class of our people which will come on that excursion roaming around the grounds munching watermelons, will do more to lower the race in the estimation of the world than anything else. The sight of the horde that would be attracted there by the dazzling prospect of plenty of free watermelons to eat, will give our enemies all the illustration they wish as an excuse for not treating the Afro-American with the equality of other citizens.

—IDA B. WELLS' Chicago letter to the N. Y. Age

SELECTIONS FROM *THE REASON WHY THE COLORED AMERICAN IS NOT IN THE WORLD'S COLUMBIAN EXPOSITION*

The World Columbian Exposition was held in Chicago in 1893 to celebrate the four-hundredth anniversary of Columbus's arrival in the New World. Also known as the World's Fair, it was designed to celebrate the history and accomplishments of the people of the United States, and African Americans were eager to use the fair to document the progress of their race. But even though black leaders lobbied for African American representation, blacks ended up almost wholly excluded from the planning, staffing, and exhibits at the fair. As a result, when the fair opened in 1893, black protesters were divided as to how to get their message across. How could they represent the status of blacks in the United States at an event from which they were largely excluded? *The Reason Why the Colored American Is Not in the World's Columbian Exposition* was Ida B. Wells's and Frederick Douglass's attempt to address this issue. They published and distributed this pamphlet at the World's Columbian Exposition in Chicago in the hope that they could use it to air African American grievances to the international audience who would attend the event.

SOURCE: Ida B. Wells and Frederick Douglass, *The Reason Why the Colored American Is Not in the World's Columbian Exposition: The Afro-American's Contribution to Columbian Literature* (1893): preface; chapter III, "The Convict Lease System"; chapter IV, "Lynch Law."

THE REASON WHY THE COLORED AMERICAN IS NOT IN THE WORLD'S COLUMBIAN EXPOSITION

The Afro-American's Contribution to Columbian Literature

TO THE PUBLIC

This pamphlet is published by contribution from colored people of the United States. The haste necessary for the press, prevents the incorporation of interesting data showing the progress of the colored people in commercial lines.

Besides the cuts of a school and hospital it was desired to have a cut of the Capital Savings Bank, a flourishing institution conducted by the colored people of Washington, D. C. The cut, however, did not arrive in time for the press.

Twenty thousand copies of THE REASON WHY are now ready for gratuitous distribution. Applications by mail will enclose three cents for postage. All orders addressed to the undersigned will be promptly acknowledged.

IDA B. WELLS,
Room 9, 128 Clark St.,
Chicago, Ill.
AUGUST 30, 1893.

Preface

TO THE SEEKER AFTER TRUTH:

Columbia has bidden the civilized world to join with her in celebrating the four-hundredth anniversary of the discovery of America, and the invitation has been accepted. At Jackson Park are displayed exhibits of her natural resources, and her progress in the arts and sciences, but that which would best illustrate her moral grandeur has been ignored.

The exhibit of the progress made by a race in 25 years of freedom as against 250 years of slavery, would have been the greatest tribute to the greatness and progressiveness of American institutions which could have been shown the world. The colored people of this great Republic number eight millions—more than one-tenth the whole population of the United States. They were among the earliest settlers of this continent, landing at Jamestown, Virginia in 1619 in a slave ship, before the Puritans, who landed at Plymouth in 1620. They have contributed a large share to American prosperity and civilization. The labor of one-half of this country has always been, and is still being done by them. The first credit this country had in its commerce with foreign nations was created by productions resulting from their labor. The wealth created by their industry has afforded to the white people of this country the leisure essential to their great progress in education, art, science, industry and invention.

Those visitors to the World's Columbian Exposition who know these facts, especially foreigners will naturally ask: Why are not the colored people, who constitute so large an element of the American population, and who have contributed so large a share to American greatness—more visibly present and better represented in this World's Exposition? Why are they not taking part in this glorious celebration of the four-hundredth anniversary of the discovery of their country? Are they so dull and stupid as to feel no interest in this great event? It is to answer these questions and supply as far as possible our lack of representation at the Exposition that the Afro-American has published this volume.

CHAPTER III

The Convict Lease System

The Convict Lease System and Lynch Law are twin infamies which flourish hand in hand in many of the United States. They are two great outgrowths and results of the class legislation under which our people suffer to-day. Alabama, Arkansas, Florida,

Georgia, Kentucky, Louisiana, Mississippi, Nebraska, North Carolina, South Carolina, Tennessee and Washington claim to be too poor to maintain state convicts within prison walls. Hence the convicts are leased out to work for railway contractors, mining companies and those who farm large plantations. These companies assume charge of the convicts, work them as cheap labor and pay the states a handsome revenue for their labor. Nine-tenths of these convicts are Negroes. There are two reasons for this.

(1) The religious, moral and philanthropic forces of the country—all the agencies which tend to uplift and reclaim the degraded and ignorant, are in the hands of the Anglo-Saxon. Not only has very little effort been made by these forces to reclaim the Negro from the ignorance, immorality and shiftlessness with which he is charged, but he has always been and is now rigidly excluded from the enjoyment of those elevating influences toward which he felt voluntarily drawn. In communities where Negro population is largest and these counteracting influences most needed, the doors of churches, schools, concert halls, lecture rooms, Young men's Christian Associations, and Women's Christian Temperance Unions, have always been and are now closed to the Negro who enters on his own responsibility. Only as a servant or inferior being placed in one corner is he admitted. The white Christian and moral influences have not only done little to prevent the Negro becoming a criminal, but they have deliberately shut him out of everything which tends to make for good citizenship.

To have Negro blood in the veins makes one unworthy of consideration, a social outcast, a leper, even in the church. Two Negro Baptist Ministers, Rev. John Frank, the pastor of the largest colored church in Louisville, Ky., and Rev. C. H. Parish, President of Extein Norton University at Cane Spring, Ky., were in the city of Nashville, Tennessee, in May when the Southern Baptist Convention was in session. They visited the meeting and took seats in the body of the church. At the request of the Association, a policeman was called and escorted these men out because they would not take the seats set apart for colored persons in the back part of the Tabernacle. Both these men are scholarly, of good moral character, and members of the Baptist denomination. But they were Negroes, and that eclipsed everything else. This spirit is even more rampant in the more remote, densely populated plantation districts. The Negro is shut out and ignored—left to grow up in ignorance and vice. Only in the gambling dens and saloons does he meet any sort of welcome. What wonder that he falls into crime?

(2) The second reason our race furnishes so large a share of the convicts is that the judges, juries and other officials of the courts are white men who share these prejudices. They also make the laws. It is wholly in their power to extend clemency to white criminals and mete severe punishment to black criminals for the same or lesser crimes. The Negro criminals are mostly ignorant, poor and friendless. Possessing neither money to employ lawyers nor influential friends, they are sentenced in large numbers to long terms of imprisonment for petty crimes. The *People's Advocate*, a Negro journal, of Atlanta, Georgia, has the following observation on the prison showing of that state for 1892. "It is an astounding fact that 90 per cent of the state's convicts are colored. 194 white males and 2 white females; 1,710 colored males and 44 colored females. Is it possible that Georgia is so color prejudiced that she won't convict her white law-breakers. Yes, it is just so, but we hope for a better day."

George W. Cable, author of *The Grandissimes, Dr. Sevier*, etc., in a paper on "The Convict Lease System," read before a Prison Congress in Kentucky says: "In the Georgia penitentiary in 1880, in a total of nearly 1200 convicts, only 22 prisoners were serving as low a term as one year, only 52 others as low as two years, only 76 others as low a term as three years; while those who were under sentences of ten years and *over* numbered 538, although ten years, as the rolls show, is the *utmost* length of time that a convict can be expected to remain alive in a Georgia penitentiary. Six men were under sentence for simple assault and battery—mere fisticuffing—one of two years, two of five years, one of six years, one of seven and one of eight. For larceny, three men were serving under sentence of twenty years, five were sentenced each for fifteen years; one for fourteen years, six for twelve years; thirty-five for ten years, and 172 from one year up to nine years. In other words, a large majority of these 1200 convicts had for simple stealing, without breaking in or violence, been virtually condemned to be worked and misused to death. One man was under a twenty years' sentence for hog-stealing. Twelve men were sentenced to the South Carolina penitentiary on no other finding but a misdemeanor commonly atoned for by a fine of a few dollars, and which thousands of the state's inhabitants (white) are constantly committing with impunity—the carrying of concealed weapons. Fifteen others were sentenced for mere assault and battery. In Louisiana a man was sentenced to the penitentiary for 12 months for stealing five dollars worth of gunnysacks! Out of 2378 convicts in the Texas prison in 1882, only two were under sentence of less than two years length, and 509 of these were under twenty years of age. Mississippi's penitentiary roll for the same year showed 70 convicts between the ages of 12 and 18 years of age serving long terms. Tennessee showed 12 boys under 18 years of age under sentences of more than a year; and the North Carolina penitentiary had 234 convicts under 20 years of age serving long terms."

Mr. Cable goes on to say in another part of his admirable paper: "In the Georgia convict force only 15 were whites among 215 who were under sentences of more than ten years." What is true of Georgia is true of the convict lease system elsewhere. The details of vice, cruelty and death thus fostered by the states whose treasuries are enriched thereby, equals anything from Siberia. Men, women and children are herded together like cattle in the filthiest quarters and chained together while at work. The Chicago *Inter-Ocean* recently printed an interview with a young colored woman who was sentenced six months to the convict farm in Mississippi for fighting. The costs etc., lengthened the time to 18 months. During her imprisonment she gave birth to two children, but lost the first one from premature confinement, caused by being tied up by the thumbs and punished for failure to do a full day's work. She and other women testified that they were forced to criminal intimacy with the guards and cook to get food to eat.

Correspondence to the Washington D.C. *Evening Star* dated Sept. 27, 1892, on this same subject has the following:

"The fact that the system puts a large number of criminals afloat in the community from the numerous escapes is not its worst feature. The same report shows that the mortality is fearful in the camps. In one camp it is stated that the mortality is 10 per cent per month, and in another even more than that. In these camps men and women are found chained together, and from twenty to twenty-five children have been born in captivity in the convicts camps.

Some further facts are cited with reference to the system in use in Tennessee. The testimony of a guard at the Coal Creek prison in Tennessee shows that prisoners, black and dirty from their work in the mines, were put into their rooms in the stockades without an opportunity to change their clothing or sufficient opportunity for cleanliness. Convicts were whipped, a man standing at the head and another at the feet, while a third applied the lash with both hands. Men who failed to perform their task of mining from two to four tons of coal per day were fastened to planks by the feet, then bent over a barrel and fastened by the hands on the other side, stripped and beaten with a strap. Out of the fifty convicts worked in the mines from one to eight were whipped per day in this manner. There was scarcely a day, according to the testimony of the witness, James Frazier, in which one or more were not flogged in this manner for failure to perform their day's task. The work in the mines was difficult and the air sometimes so bad that the men fell insensible and had to be hauled out. Their beds he describes as "dirty, black and nasty looking." One of the convicts, testifying as to the kind of food given them, said that the pea soup was made from peas containing weevils and added: "I have got a spoonful of weevils off a cup of soup." In many cases convicts were forced to work in water six inches deep for weeks at a time getting out coal with one-fourth of the air necessary for a healthy man to live in, forced to drink water from stagnant pools when mountain springs were just outside of the stockades, and the reports of the prison officials showing large numbers killed in attempting to escape.

The defense of this prison is based wholly upon its economy to the state. It is argued that it would cost large sums of money to build penitentiaries in which to confine and work the prisoners as is done in the Northern States, while the lease system brings the state a revenue and relieves it of the cost of building and maintaining prisons. The fact that the convicts labor is in this way brought into direct competition with free labor does not seem to be taken into account. The contractors, who get these laborers for 30 or 40 cents per day, can drive out of the market the man who employs free labor at $1 a day.

This condition of affairs briefly alluded to in detail in Tennessee and Georgia exists in other Southern States. In North Carolina the same system exists, except that only able-bodied convicts are farmed out. The death rates among the convicts is reported as greater than the death rate of New Orleans in the greatest yellow fever epidemic ever known. In Alabama a new warden with his natural instincts unblunted by familiarity with the situation wrote of it: "The system is a better training school for criminals than any of the dens of iniquity in our large cities. The system is a disgrace to the state and the reproach of the civilization and Christian sentiment of the age."

Every Negro so sentenced not only means able-bodied men to swell the state's number of slaves, but every Negro so convicted is thereby *disfranchised*.

It has been shown that numbers of Negro youths are sentenced to these penitentiaries every year and there mingle with the hardened criminals of all ages and both sexes. The execution of law does not cease with the incarceration of those of tender years for petty crimes. In the state of South Carolina last year Mildred Brown, a little thirteen year old colored girl was found guilty of murder in the first degree on the charge of poisoning a little white infant that she nursed. She was sentenced to be hanged. The Governor refused to commute her sentence, and on October 7th, 1892, at Columbia, South Carolina, she was hanged on the gallows. This made the second colored female hanged in that state within one month. Although tried, and in rare cases convicted for murder and other crimes, no white girl in this country ever met the same fate. The state of Alabama in the same year hanged a ten year old Negro boy. He was charged with the murder of a peddler.

CHAPTER IV

Lynch Law

"Lynch Law," says the *Virginia Lancet*, "as known by that appellation, had its origin in 1780 in a combination of citizens of Pittsylvania County, Virginia, entered into for the purpose of suppressing a trained band of horse-thieves and counterfeiters whose well concocted schemes had bidden defiance to the ordinary laws of the land, and whose success encouraged and emboldened them in their outrages upon the community. Col. Wm. Lynch drafted the constitution for this combination of citizens, and hence "Lynch Law" has ever since been the name given to the summary infliction of punishment by private and unauthorized citizens."

This law continues in force to-day in some of the oldest states of the Union, where courts of justice have long been established, whose laws are executed by white Americans. It flourishes most largely in the states which foster the convict lease system, and is brought to bear mainly, against the Negro. The first fifteen years of his freedom he was murdered by masked mobs for trying to vote. Public opinion having made lynching for that cause unpopular, a new reason is given to justify the murders of the past 15 years. The Negro was first charged with attempting to rule white people, and hundreds were murdered on that pretended supposition. He is now charged with assaulting or attempting to assault white women. This charge, as false as it is foul, robs us of the sympathy of the world and is blasting the race's good name.

The men who make these charges encourage or lead the mobs which do the lynching. They belong to the race which holds Negro life cheap, which owns the telegraph wires, newspapers, and all other communication with the outside world. They write the reports which justify lynching by painting the Negro as black as possible, and those reports are accepted by the press association and the world without question or investigation. The mob spirit has increased with alarming frequency and violence. Over a thousand black men, women and children have been thus sacrificed the past ten years. Masks have long since been thrown aside and the lynchings of the present day take place in broad daylight. The sheriffs, police and state officials stand by and see the work well done. The coroner's jury is often formed among those who took part in the lynching and a verdict, "Death at the hands of parties unknown to the jury" is rendered. As the number of lynchings have increased, so has the cruelty and barbarism of the lynchers. Three human beings were burned alive in civilized America during the first six months of this year (1893). Over one hundred have been lynched in this half year. They were hanged, then cut, shot and burned.

The following table published by the Chicago *Tribune* January, 1892, is submitted for thoughtful consideration.

1882, 52 Negroes murdered by mobs
1883, 39   "   "   "   "
1884, 53   "   "   "   "
1885, 77   "   "   "   "
1886, 73   "   "   "   "
1887, 70   "   "   "   "
1888, 72   "   "   "   "
1889, 95   "   "   "   "
1890, 100   "   "   "   "
1891, 169   "   "   "   "

Of this number

269 were charged with rape.
253   "   "   "   murder.
 44   "   "   "   robbery.
 37   "   "   "   incendiarism.
  4   "   "   "   burglary.
 27   "   "   "   race prejudice.
 13   "   "   "   quarreling with white men
 10   "   "   "   making threats.
  7   "   "   "   rioting.
  5   "   "   "   miscegenation.
 32   "   "   "   no reasons given.

This table shows (1) that only one-third of nearly a thousand murdered black persons have been even charged with the crime of outrage. This crime is only so punished when white women accuse black men, which accusation is never proven. The same crime committed by Negroes against Negroes, or by white men against black women is ignored even in the law courts.

(2) That nearly as many were lynched for murder as for the above crime, which the world believes is the cause of all the lynchings. The world affects to believe that *white* womanhood and childhood, surrounded by their lawful protectors, are not safe in the neighborhood of the black man, who protected and cared for them during the four years of civil war. The husbands, fathers and brothers of those white women were away for four years, fighting to keep the Negro in slavery, yet not one case of assault has ever been reported!

(3) That "robbery, incendiarism, race prejudice, quarreling with white men, making threats, rioting, miscegenation (marrying a white person), and burglary," are capital offences punishable by death when committed by a black against a white person. Nearly as many blacks were lynched for these charges (and unproven) as for the crime of rape.

(4) That for nearly fifty of these lynchings no reason is given. There is not demand for reasons, or need of concealment for what no one is held responsible. The simple word of any white person against a Negro is sufficient to get a crowd of white men to lynch a Negro. Investigation as to the guilt or innocence of the accused is never made. Under these conditions, white men have only to blacken their faces, commit crimes against the peace of the community, accuse some Negro, nor rest till he is killed by a mob. Will Lewis, an 18 year old Negro youth was lynched at Tullahoma, Tennessee, August, 1891, for being "drunk and saucy to white folks."

The women of the race have not escaped the fury of the mob. In Jackson, Tennessee, in the summer of 1886, a white woman died of poisoning. Her black cook was suspected, and as a box of rat poison was found in her room, she was hurried away to jail. When the mob had worked itself to the lynching pitch, she was dragged out of jail, every stitch of clothing torn from her body, and she was hung in the public court-house square in sight of everybody. Jackson is one of the oldest towns in the State, and the State Supreme Court holds its sittings there; but no one was arrested for the deed—not even a protest was uttered. The husband of the poisoned woman has since died a raving maniac, and his ravings showed that he, and not the poor black cook, was the poisoner of his wife. A fifteen year old Negro girl was hanged in Rayville, Louisiana, in the spring of 1892, on the same charge of poisoning white persons. There was no more proof of investigation of this case than the one in Jackson. A Negro woman, Lou Stevens, was hanged from a railway bridge in Hollendale, Mississippi, in 1892. She was charged with being accessory to the murder of her white paramour, who had shamefully abused her.

In 1892 there were 241 persons lynched. The entire number is divided among the following states.

Alabama	22	Montana	4
Arkansas	25	New York	1
California	3	North Carolina	5
Florida	11	North Dakota	1
Georgia	17	Ohio	3
Idaho	8	South Carolina	28
Illinois	1	Tennessee	28
Kansas	3	Texas	15
Kentucky	9	Virginia	7
Louisiana	29	West Virginia	5
Maryland	1	Wyoming	9
Mississippi	16	Arizona Ter.	3
Missouri	6	Oklahoma	2

Of this number 160 were of Negro descent. Four of them were lynched in New York, Ohio and Kansas; the remainder were murdered in the south. Five of this number were females. The charges for which they were lynched cover a wide range. They are as follows:

Rape	46	Attempted Rape	11
Murder	58	Suspected Robbery	4
Rioting	3	Larceny	1
Race prejudice	6	Self-defense	1
No cause given	4	Insulting women	2
Incendiarism	6	Desperadoes	6
Robbery	6	Fraud	1
Assault and Battery	1	Attempted murder	2
		No offense stated, boy and girl.	2

In the case of the boy and girl above referred to, their father, named Hastings, was accused of the murder of a white man; his fourteen year old daughter and sixteen year old son were hanged and their bodies filled with bullets, then their father was also lynched. This was in November, 1892, at Jonesville, Louisiana.

A lynching equally as cold-blooded took place in Memphis, Tennessee, March, 1892. Three young colored men in an altercation at their place of business, fired on white men in self-defense. They were imprisoned for three days, then taken out by the mob and horribly shot to death. Thomas Moss, Will Stewart and

Calvin McDowell, were energetic business men who had built up a flourishing grocery business. This business had prospered and that of a rival white grocer named Barrett had declined. Barrett led the attack on their grocery which resulted in the wounding of three white men. For this cause were three innocent men barbarously lynched, and their families left without protectors. Memphis is one of the leading cities of Tennessee, a town of seventy-five thousand inhabitants! No effort whatever was made to punish the murderers of these three men. It counted for nothing that the victims of this outrage were three of the best known young men of a population of thirty thousand colored people of Memphis. They were the officers of the company which conducted the grocery. Moss being the President, Stewart the Secretary of the Company and McDowell the Manager. Moss was in the Civil Service of the United States as letter carrier, and all three were men of splendid reputation for honesty, integrity and sobriety. But their murderers, though well known, have never been indicted, were not even troubled with a preliminary examination.

With law held in such contempt, it is not a matter of surprise that the same city—one of the so-called queen cities of the South, should again give itself over to a display of almost indescribable barbarism. This time the mob made no attempt to conceal its identity, but reveled in the contemplation of its feast of crime. Lee Walker, a colored man was the victim. Two white women complained that while driving to town, a colored man jumped from a place of concealment and dragged one of the two women from the wagon, but their screams frightened him away. Alarm was given that a Negro had made an attempted assault upon the women and bands of men set out to run him down. They shot a colored man who refused to stop when called. It was fully ten days before Walker was caught. He admitted that he did attack the women, but that he made no attempt to assault them; that he offered them no indecency whatever, of which as a matter of fact, they never accused him. He said he was hungry and he was determined to have something to eat, but after throwing one of the women out of the wagon, became frightened and ran away. He was duly arrested and taken to the Memphis jail. The fact that he was in prison and could be promptly tried and punished did not prevent the good citizens of Memphis from taking the law into their own hands, and Walker was lynched.

The *Memphis Commercial* of Sunday, July 23, contains a full account of the tragedy from which the following extracts are made.

At 12 o'clock last night, Lee Walker, who attempted to outrage Miss Mollie McCadden, last Tuesday morning, was taken from the county jail and hanged to a telegraph pole just north of the prison. All day rumors were afloat that with nightfall an attack would be made upon the jail, and as everyone anticipated that a vigorous resistance would be made, a conflict between the mob and the authorities was feared.

At 10 o'clock Capt. O'Haver, Sergt. Horan and several patrol men were on hand, but they could do nothing with the crowd. An attack by the mob was made on the door in the south wall and it yielded. Sheriff McLendon and several of his men threw themselves into the breach, but two or three of the storming party shoved by. They were seized by the police but were not subdued, the officers refraining from using their clubs. The entire mob might at first have been dispersed by ten policemen who would use their clubs, but the sheriff insisted that no violence be done.

The mob got an iron rail and used it as a battering ram against the lobby doors. Sheriff McLendon tried to stop them, and some one of the mob knocked him down with a chair. Still he counseled moderation and would not order his deputies and the police to disperse the crowd by force. The pacific policy of the sheriff impressed the mob with the idea that the officers were afraid, or at least would do them no harm, and they redoubled their efforts, urged on by a big switchman. At 12 o'clock the door of the prison was broken in with a rail.

As soon as the rapist was brought out of the door, calls were heard for a rope; then someone shouted "Burn him!" But there was no time to make a fire. When Walker got into the lobby a dozen of the men began beating and stabbing him. He was half dragged, half carried to the corner of Front street and the alley between Sycamore and Mill, and hung to a telephone pole.

Walker made a desperate resistance. Two men entered his cell first and ordered him to come forth. He refused and they failing to drag him out, others entered. He scratched and bit his assailants, wounding several of them severely with his teeth. The mob retaliated by striking and cutting him with fists and knives. When he reached the steps leading down to the door he made another stand and was stabbed again and again. By the time he reached the lobby his power to resist was gone, and he was shoved along through the mob of yelling, cursing men and boys, who beat, spat upon and slashed the wretch-like demon. One of the leaders of the mob fell, and the crowd walked ruthlessly over him. He was badly hurt—a jawbone fractured and internal injuries inflicted. After the lynching friends took charge of him.

The mob proceeded north on Front street with the victim, stopping at Sycamore street to get a rope from a grocery. "Take him to the iron bridge on Main street," yelled several men. The men who had hold of the Negro were in a hurry to finish the job, however, and when they reached the telephone pole at the corner of Front street and the first alley north of Sycamore they stopped. A hastily improvised noose was slipped over the Negro's head and several young men mounted a pile of lumber near the pole and threw the rope over one of the iron stepping pins. The Negro was lifted up until his feet were three feet above the ground, the rope was made taut, and a corpse dangled in midair. A big fellow who helped lead the mob pulled the Negro's legs until his neck cracked. The wretch's clothes had been torn off, and, as he swung, the man who pulled his legs mutilated the corpse.

One or two knife cuts, more or less, made little difference in the appearance of the dead rapist, however, for before the rope was around his neck his skin was cut almost to ribbons. One pistol shot was fired while the corpse was hanging. A dozen voices protested against the use of firearms, and there was no more shooting. The body was permitted to hang for half an hour, then it was cut down and the rope divided among those who lingered around the scene of the tragedy. Then it was suggested that the corpse be burned, and it was done. The entire performance, from the assault on the jail to the burning of the dead Negro was witnessed by a score or so of policemen and as many deputy sheriffs, but not a hand was lifted to stop the proceedings after the jail door yielded.

As the body hung to the telegraph pole, blood streaming down from the knife wounds in his neck, his hips and lower part of his legs also slashed with knives, the crowd hurled expletives at him, swung the body so that it was dashed against the pole, and, so far from the ghastly sight proving trying to the nerves, the crowd looked on with complaisance, if not with real pleasure. The Negro died hard. The neck was not broken, as the body was drawn up without being given a fall, and death came by strangulation. For fully ten minutes after he was strung up the chest heaved occasionally and there were convulsive movements of the limbs. Finally he was pronounced dead, and a few minutes later Detective Richardson climbed on a pile of staves and cut the rope. The body fell in a ghastly heap, and the crowd laughed at the sound and crowded around the prostrate body, a few kicking the inanimate carcass.

Detective Richardson, who is also a deputy coroner, then proceeded to impanel the following jury of inquest J. S. Moody, A. O. Waldran, B. J. Childs, J. N. House, Nelson Bills, T. L. Smith, and A. Newhouse. After viewing the body the inquest was adjourned without any testimony being taken until 9 o'clock this morning. The jury will meet at the coroner's office, 51 Beale street, upstairs, and decide a verdict. If no witnesses are forthcoming, the jury will be able to arrive at a verdict just the same, as all members of it saw the lynching. Then some one missed the cry of, "Burn him!" It was quickly taken up and soon resounded from a hundred throats. Detective Richardson for a long time, single handed, stood the crowd off. He talked and begged the men not to bring disgrace on the city by burning the body, arguing that all the vengeance possible had been wrought.

While this was going on a small crowd was busy building a fire in the middle of the street. The material was handy. Some bundles of staves were taken from the adjoining lumber yard for kindling. Heavier wood was obtained from the same source, and coal oil from a neighboring grocery. Then the cries of "Burn him! Burn him!" were redoubled.

Half a dozen men seized the naked body. The crowd cheered. They marched to the fire, and giving the body a swing, it was landed in the middle of the fire. There was a cry for more wood, as the fire had begun to die owing to the long delay. Willing hands procured the wood, and it was piled up on the Negro, almost, for a time, obscuring him from view. The head was in plain view, as also were the limbs, and one arm which stood out high above the body, the elbow crooked, held in that position by a stick of wood. In a few moments the hands began to swell, then came great blisters over all the exposed parts of the body; then in places the flesh was burned away and the bones began to show through. It was a horrible sight, one which perhaps none there had ever witnessed before. It proved too much for a large part of the crowd and the majority of the mob left very shortly after the burning began.

But a large number stayed, and were not a bit set back by the sight of a human body being burned to ashes. Two or three white women, accompanied by their escorts, pushed to the front to obtain an unobstructed view, and looked on with astonishing coolness and nonchalance. One man and woman brought a little girl, not over 12 years old, apparently their daughter, to view a scene which was calculated to drive sleep from the child's eyes for many nights, if not to produce a permanent injury to her nervous system. The comments of the crowd were varied. Some remarked on the efficacy of this style of cure for rapists, others rejoiced that men's wives and daughters were now safe from this wretch. Some laughed as the flesh cracked and blistered, and while a large number pronounced the burning of a dead body as an useless episode, not in all that throng was a word of sympathy heard for the wretch himself.

The rope that was used to hang the Negro, and also that which was used to lead him from the jail, were eagerly sought by relic hunters. They almost fought for a chance to cut off a piece of rope, and in an incredibly short time both ropes had disappeared and were scattered in the pockets of the crowd in sections of from an inch to six inches long. Others of the relic hunters remained until the ashes cooled to obtain such ghastly relics as the teeth, nails and bits of charred skin of the immolated victim of his own lust. After burning the body the mob tied a rope around the charred trunk and dragged it down Main street to the court house, where it was hanged to a center pole. The rope broke and the corpse dropped with a thud, but it was again hoisted, the charred legs barely touching the ground. The teeth were knocked out and the finger nails cut off as souvenirs. The crowd made so much noise that the police interfered. Undertaker Walsh was telephoned for, who took charge of the body and carried it to his establishment, where it will be prepared for burial in the potter's field today.

A prelude to this exhibition of 19th century barbarism was the following telegram received by the Chicago *Inter-Ocean*, at 2 o'clock, Saturday afternoon—ten hours before the lynching:

"MEMPHIS, TENN, July 22, To *Inter-Ocean*, Chicago.

Lee Walker, colored man, accused of raping white women, in jail here, will be taken out and burned by whites to-night. Can you send Miss Ida Wells to write it up? Answer. R. M. Martin, with Public Ledger"

The *Public Ledger* is one of the oldest evening daily papers in Memphis, and this telegram shows that the intentions of the mob were well known long before they were executed. The personnel of the mob is given by the Memphis *Appeal-Avalanche*. It says, "At first it seemed as if a crowd of roughs were the principals, but as it increased in size, men in all walks of life figured as leaders, although the majority were young men."

This was the punishment meted out to a Negro, charged, not with rape, but attempted assault, and without any proof as to his guilt, for the women were not given a chance to identify him. It was only a little less horrible than the burning alive of Henry Smith, at Paris, Texas, February 1st, 1893, or that of Edward Coy, in Texarkana, Texas, February 20, 1892. Both were charged with assault on white women, and both were tied to the stake and burned while yet alive, in the presence of ten thousand persons. In the case of Coy, the white woman in the case, applied the match, even while the victim protested his innocence.

The cut which is here given is the exact reproduction of the photograph taken at the scene of the lynching at Clanton, Alabama, August, 1891. The cause for which the man was hanged is given in the words of the mob which were written on the back of the photograph, and they are also given. This photograph was sent to Judge A. W. Tourgee, of Mayville, N. Y.

In some of these cases the mob affects to believe in the Negro's guilt. The world is told that the white woman in the case identifies him, or the prisoner "confesses." But in the lynching which took place in Barnwell County, South Carolina, April 24, 1893, the mob's victim, John Peterson escaped and placed himself under Governor Tillman's protection; not only did he declare his innocence, but offered to prove an alibi, by white witnesses. Before his witnesses could be brought, the mob arrived at the Governor's mansion and demanded the prisoner. He was given up, and although the white woman in the case said he was *not* the man, he was hanged 24 hours after, and over a thousand bullets fired into his body, on the declaration that "a crime had been committed and some one had to hang for it."

The lynching of C. J. Miller, at Bardwell, Kentucky, July 7, 1893, was on the same principle. Two white girls were found murdered near their home on the morning of July 5th; their bodies were horribly mutilated. Although their father had been instrumental in the prosecution and conviction of one of his white neighbors for murder, that was not considered as a motive. A hue and cry was raised that some Negro had committed rape and murder, and a search was immediately begun for a Negro. A bloodhound was put on the trail which he followed to the river and into the boat of a fisherman named Gordon. This fisherman said he had rowed a white man, or a very fair mulatto across the river at six o'clock the evening before. The bloodhound was carried across the river, took up the trail on the Missouri side, and ran about two hundred yards to the cottage of a white farmer, and there lay down refusing to go further.

Meanwhile a strange Negro had been arrested in Sikestown, Missouri, and the authorities telegraphed that fact to Bardwell, Kentucky. The sheriff, without requisition, escorted the prisoner to the Kentucky side and turned him over to the authorities who accompanied the mob. The prisoner was a man with dark brown skin; he said his name was Miller and that he had never been in Kentucky. The fisherman who had said the man he rowed over was white, when told by the sheriff that he would be held responsible as knowing the guilty man, if he failed to identify the prisoner, said Miller was the man. The mob wished to burn him then, about ten o'clock in the morning, but Mr. Ray, the father of the girls, with great difficulty urged them to wait till three o'clock that afternoon. Confident of his innocence, Miller remained cool, while hundreds of drunken heavily armed men raged about him. He said: "My name is C. J. Miller, I am from Springfield, Ill., my wife lives at 716 North Second Street, I am here among you to-day looked upon as one of the most brutal men before the people. I stand here surrounded by men who are excited; men who are not willing to let the law take its course, and as far as the law is concerned, I have committed no crime, and certainly no crime gross enough to deprive me of my life and liberty to walk upon the green earth. I had some rings which I bought in Bismark of a Jew peddler. I paid him $4.50 for them. I left Springfield on the first day of July and came to Alton. From Alton I went to East St. Louis, from there to Jefferson Barracks, thence to Desoto, thence to Bismarck; and to Piedmont, thence to Poplar Bluff, thence to Hoxie, to Jonesboro, and then on a local freight to Malden, from there to Sikeston. On the 5th day of July, the day I was supposed to have committed the offense, I was at Bismarck."

Failing in any way to connect Miller with the crime, the mob decided to give him the benefit of the doubt and *hang, instead of burn him*, as was first intended. At 3 o'clock the hour set for the execution, the mob rushed to the jail, tore off Miller's clothing and tied his shirt around his loins. Some one said the rope was a "white man's death," and a log-chain nearly a hundred feet in length, weighing nearly a hundred pounds was placed about his neck. He was led through the street in that condition and hanged to a telegraph pole. After a photograph of him was taken as he hung, his fingers and toes cut off, and his body otherwise horribly mutilated, it was burned to ashes. This was done within twelve hours after Miller was taken prisoner. Since his death, his assertions regarding his movements have been proven true. But the mob refused the necessary time for investigation.

No more appropriate close for this chapter can be given than an editorial quotation from that most consistent and outspoken journal the *Inter-Ocean*. Commenting on the many barbarous lynchings of these two months (June and July) in its issue of August 5th, 1893, it says:

"So long as it is known that here is one charge against a man which calls for no investigation before taking his life there will be mean men seeking revenge ready to make that charge. Such a condition would soon destroy all law. It would not be tolerated for a day by white men. But the Negroes have been so patient under all their trials that men who no longer feel that they can safely shoot a Negro for attempting to exercise his right as a citizen at the polls are ready to trump up any other charge that will give them the excuse for their crime. It is a singular coincidence that as public sentiment has been hurled against political murders there has been a corresponding increase in lynchings on the charge of attacking white women. The lynchings are conducted in much the same way that they were by the Ku-Klux Klans when Negroes were mobbed for attempting to vote. The one great difference is in the cause which the mob assigns for its action.

The real need is for a public sentiment in favor of enforcing the law and giving every man, white and black, a fair hearing before the lawful tribunals. If the plan suggested by the Charleston *News and Courier* will do this let it be done at once. No one wants to shield a fiend guilty of these brutal attacks against unprotected women. But the Negro has as good a right to a fair trial as the white man, and the South will not be free from these horrible crimes of mob law so long as the better class of citizens try to find excuse for recognizing Judge Lynch."

CHAPTER III

Ida B. Wells Abroad

The beginning of 1894 found Wells planning another trip to England. The Society for the Recognition of the Brotherhood of Man (SRBM), an anti-lynching organization that had taken shape around Wells's first visit to England, had invited her to return, and British reformers Catherine Impey and Isabella Mayo seemed to have settled their differences. Moreover, Celestine Edwards, a black man from the British West Indian island of Dominica who had replaced Impey as the leader of the English SRBM at Mayo's insistence, was scheduled to manage Wells's trip, so she had every reason to hope that things would go smoothly this time. Still cautious, Wells negotiated the terms of her second visit in advance, asking for "expenses & 2 pound per week—as it was as little as I could come for that at a sacrifice to my business."[1]

Her planned three-month trip would force Wells to leave behind Ferdinand Barnett, who is the likely model for the suitor whose virtues Wells extols in "Two Christmas Days: A Holiday Story," which opens this chapter (much like the "model man" described by the story's protagonist, Emily Minton, Barnett was both a nondrinker and race man). He had proposed to Wells in the fall of 1893, and she had accepted and remained in Chicago rather than returning to New York at the end of the World's Fair. But Wells's engagement did not compromise her commitment to her anti-lynching cause: she continued to travel widely prior to her marriage in 1895.

Moreover, Wells was particularly eager to return to Britain. Having attracted large audiences and considerable attention from the British press during her abortive first trip, she hoped to make even more of an impact on her return trip. Her hopes would be fulfilled. But her second visit got off to a rocky start when she arrived in Britain to find Edwards gravely ill and preparing to return to the West Indies in hopes of recovering from a case of influenza that soon proved fatal. Moreover, the support for her trip had evaporated. Furious at Wells for not publicly denouncing Catherine Impey, Isabella Mayo had resigned from the SRBM, taking with her the funds that Wells had negotiated to cover her expenses.

This time Wells did not even consider leaving. "I have come abroad to give 3 months of my time to work," Wells wrote to Frederick Douglass as she scrambled to reorganize her plans, "and I am going to do it."[2] She had been invited to report on her visit in Chicago's *Daily Inter Ocean*, which gave her an unprecedented opportunity to chronicle her anti-lynching activities as a correspondent for a white newspaper. She also had plans to sell *Southern Horrors*—repackaged for a British audience under the title *American Atrocities*—and hoped to cover her expenses that way. Moreover, shortly after docking in Liverpool, she found a new supporter in Charles Aked, an energetic young Baptist minister who had built one of the largest congregations in that city. Scheduled to host Wells's first public lecture, Aked opened his family home to her as well, and worked with Catherine Impey to secure Wells's speaking invitations and coverage in the British press.

Wells chronicled her trip in her dispatches to the Chicago *Daily Inter Ocean*, most of which are included here.[3] In addition, this chapter reprints a handful of less well-known articles chronicling Wells's experiences abroad, starting with "Liverpool Slave Traditions and Present Practices." Published in the *Southwestern Advocate* in May 1894, this article contains Wells's fascinating meditation on her positive reception in Liverpool, a city once dedicated to the slave trade. In it, she praises the city's residents for hearing out the abolitionist Henry Ward Beecher, and proving likewise open to her anti-lynching message. She appealed still more directly to Britain's abolitionist heritage in "The Bitter Cry of Black America: A New 'Uncle Tom's Cabin,' " an interview with the *Westminster Gazette* that is also included here. In this interview, she sums up the point she sought to drive home with British audiences.

In "The English Speak" (1894), Wells expresses her appreciation for the modern-day Britons who supported her tour, most especially Charles Aked, whom she commended for giving "the

best speech I ever heard a white man give on the Negro's behalf."
Wells was also grateful to Aked for making her second trip to
Britain a success. In addition to hosting Wells and advancing an
anti-lynching resolution among British Baptists, Aked helped
mobilize support for Wells's work by attacking lynching in the
prominent British monthly the *Contemporary Review*. Writing
on "The Race Problem in America," he reiterated Wells's statistics and central arguments to explain: "The demand of the Negro
is for the most elementary justice. . . . Make your laws as terrible
as you like . . . but prove your criminal a criminal first. Hang,
shoot, roast him, if you will—if American civilization demands
this—but give a trial first."[4] Such arguments helped Wells make
an impact in Britain. By the time she left, she had inspired the
formation of an English Anti-Lynching Committee, designed to
carry on her work after her departure. Its members included
twenty liberal members of Parliament as well as several members
of the British nobility.

Although generally well received in Britain, Wells's speaking
tour received almost uniformly negative press in her home country's white newspapers, where the *New York Times* denounced
her as a "slanderous and nasty-minded mulatress," and the editors
of Southern newspapers issued new death threats against her.[5]
Wells's public response to some of these critiques is contained in
"Ida B. Wells, Her Reply to Governor Northen and Others," one
of her *Daily Inter Ocean* articles, which describes and refutes the
Memphis *Daily Commercial*'s account of her British tour.

In "The Scoundrel," an article published in the *Cleveland
Gazette*, she takes on a still more infuriating enemy in the form
of J. W. A. Shaw, a black man sent to Britain by the *Commercial
Appeal* to give speeches designed to undermine Wells's condem-
nations of the South. In his lectures, Shaw maintained that "the
Negro was not deprived of his vote and when lynched deserved it
for terrible crimes." Alarmed by this challenge to her credibil-
ity, Wells countered Shaw's claims with a letter from Frederick
Douglass supporting her work. Moreover, confronted with criticism from this self-appointed race leader, Wells also took the
time to identify individuals whom she thought of as the genuine
race leaders, naming Frederick Douglass, T. Thomas Fortune,
Booker T. Washington, and the African Methodist Episcopal
Church bishop Henry MacNeal Turner.

"TWO CHRISTMAS DAYS: A HOLIDAY STORY"

A rare piece of Wells's fiction writing and her only romantic work, this story was published in the *A.M.E. Zion Quarterly*. Written during her courtship with Ferdinand Barnett, it reveals the central place that Barnett had in Wells's thoughts. The semiautobiographical piece features a former schoolteacher who falls in love with a lawyer who proves himself more worthy than the teacher's other male suitors.

SOURCE: Ida B. Wells, "Two Christmas Days: A Holiday Story," *A.M.E Zion Church Quarterly*, 4:2, January 1894, 129–40.

TWO CHRISTMAS DAYS
A HOLIDAY STORY

"Going out to Wilson's this afternoon, George?"

"For what," asks George.

"To the croquet party. You surely haven't forgotten it."

"By George, Harry, I just had. It's too confoundedly hot to do what you have to much less play croquet. But Mrs. Wilson would never forgive me if I didn't go. This affair is in honor of her guest, I believe; Miss—what's her name?"

"Minton. Well if you are going, it's time you're getting a move on you. Its past five now," said Harry, rising.

"Guess I'll have to, as I haven't even called on the young lady yet. It's too bad to have to play the agreeable when you don't want to. Wait a minute, I'll go up with you." And George Harris leisurely put away his law papers and was soon on the way with his friend, Harry Brown.

Arriving at the home of Mrs. Wilson they found the spacious green lawn alive with young girls in cool summer dresses, who with obliging partners were playing at croquet.

Mrs. Wilson and her son, Clarence, rallied the young men on being late and introduced Harris, who knew of but had never met Miss Minton until now.

"What do you think of the visitor, George?" asked his friend as they rested on one of the rustic settees watching the players.

"Don't know," drawled George. "You can't tell much about girls at first sight. One thing she doesn't seem to put on airs. I take it also, that she goes in to win in everything she attempts. She is the only one of those girls who cares a pin about being beaten. See how hard she works in this heat, and with what precision she makes her shots. The other girls are so taken up flirting with their partners they neither know nor care when their turn comes to play."

"Ah, George, at your old professional habit of dissecting every character you meet in that cold analytic fashion. Don't you see anything to admire in the *woman*?"

"Yes, I see she is charmingly and becomingly dressed—a thing so few girls have the good taste to do."

Harry laughed. "You're a hard critic, my fastidious friend. You'll meet your match yet some day, old fellow; then you'll rave too, over your lady's charms without stopping to analyze her."

The conversation was ended, as with a peal of laughter Miss Minton and her partner won. Flushed with excitement and victory she seated herself in the place vacated by Harry Brown, who went to take a hand in another game just beginning. She and George exchanged a few words, and as she rested he looked at her more closely. She was a tall, slender, graceful girl, olive complexion, black hair and eyes. She was not strictly beautiful, but the features were regular and there was a nobility of expression which betokened the thinker; a clear open countenance, with wonderful eyes, a sweet yet dignified manner. Her dress of pink muslin fitted her figure to perfection and suited her complexion admirably. She was twenty-three years old and was a college graduate from one of the American Missionary Colleges in the

South. She had made so enviable a record that she was appointed a teacher in her Alma Mater—the first Afro-American teacher they had ever employed. She was in high spirits over her victory and her sallies of wit interested the young man beside her; he mentally decided to see more of her.

Meanwhile twilight had fallen and it was too dark to see the wickets. Mrs. Wilson called and the guests gathered round the dining room table, a laughing, happy group. While they discussed melons and ices, they chatted of everything in general and nothing in particular, as young folks will do.

"So you have decided to go to Oklahoma, Will," asked Mrs. Wilson, during a lull in the gay badinage.

"Yes, ma'am," replied Will Bramlette, a tall brown-skinned young fellow of twenty-five. "I leave next week."

"But I can't see what you want to go away out there for; you are doing well here at your trade. Mr. Wilson says you have all the work you can do."

"Yes, but I want to do better. I want to live where I can have something, and a man is as free as anybody else, once in my life. If Uncle Sam will give me one hundred and sixty acres of land to go and get it, I'm going after it sure."

"Oklahoma will never see me," laughed one of the young men. "Nor me," echoed another.

"I admire your spirit and determination, Mr. Bramlette," said Emily Minton, speaking very quickly.

"What, you an Oklahoma convert too?" chorused a number of voices.

"Yes, I am. I have long thought our young men have not enough ambition and get-up, or they couldn't be content to drift along here in the South the way things are going every day. For the last half dozen years, ever since I've been able to see clearly the causes of so much race trouble, everybody has said education would solve the problem. I have watched the young men who have left school when I was a pupil and since I became a teacher. They gave signs of the brightest promise, but the majority soon fall into a soft easy position which affords them a living and there they vegetate, until they lose all the manhood they ever possessed. If I could have my way with them, I'd transplant them all to Oklahoma or some place else where they would have to work and that would develop character and strengthen manhood in them."

"Thank you, Miss Emily, for your endorsement," said Will Bramlette. "It has given me a better determination, as the Methodist sisters say."

"Are you not rather hard on the young men, Miss Minton?" asked George Harris.

"I think not," answered she; "the race needs their services so much. Indeed, I think the most discouraging feature of it all, is the seeming contentment under conditions which ought to stir all the manhood's blood in them. So whenever I do meet one who thinks as I do and is ambitious to be somebody, I cannot help wishing him God-speed. If I were a man, I would join him only too quick."

"You might join some 'him' anyway Emily," said one of the young girls.

"Yes, indeed, and be far more acceptable as a companion—a helpmeet," Mrs. Wilson teasingly rejoined.

Everybody laughed, and even Emily, who had grown very earnest, was forced to smile at this clever turning of the tables on herself.

The party broke up, but George and Harry lingered in the moonlight on the verandah talking to the homefolks. George felt strangely attracted to this girl, and, walking over to where she sat, he said, watching her out of the corners of his eyes: "Bramlette was delighted with your approval of his course, Miss Minton. You have made a conquest of him already. That's the way with you girls—you have no mercy on a fellow's heart. How many scalps have you dangling at your belt already?"

Emily turned on him with a grieved, reproachful expression: "You do not mean to say you think me a flirt, Mr. Harris?"

"No, indeed," said he, quickly dropping his jesting tone, "I think you are too noble a girl for that." George spoke so gravely and respectfully that Emily knew he meant it.

"Thank you," she said simply. He bade them good-night and left shortly after.

"She is a remarkable girl," mused George as he went home. He called the next afternoon and the next. Very soon it so happened that there was no day after the Sun-god hid his face, that George did not "call by" on his way home, although it was several blocks out of his way. Sometimes it was a proposed walk, oftener a drive, a few flowers, or a few minutes conversation. Mrs. Wilson's niece was a brilliant musician, and George had a fine baritone voice, and they made splendid music these long summer evenings. Emily had the soul of a musician, with none of the musician's talent.

Those evenings with the moonlight, the music and the fragrance of the rose, the honeysuckle and the night-blooming jessamine, seemed the happiest of her life. She had become interested in this man as in no other, and she had met many in her short life. But this man with courtly manners, general culture and quiet, yet masterful and self-contained bearing, was unlike any she had ever met. If a day passed without his coming, she was conscious of a something lacking in its pleasure. Given to self-examination, she felt that she was falling in love, and she was sure the interest was mutual. She mentally determined before yielding herself to the fascination of her feelings, to know more about him. The opportunity came soon after.

While down town shopping one hot August day, they passed Harris's office. Mrs. Wilson teasingly asked Emily if she would like to call on him. She consented and they stepped into the office only to find him absent. The room was such a disagreeable surprise to her, that Emily was glad Harris was absent. It was a dingy apartment, with old and rickety furniture, and the atmosphere was musty with the fumes of tobacco smoke. There was absolutely nothing to harmonize with the careful, cleanly well-dressed man she had known for nearly two months. She gave no sign but was glad when Mrs. Wilson said they would not wait.

At tea-table that evening, the conversation turned on Harris, and Emily inquired of Mr. Wilson how long the young lawyer had been practicing, and was told about five years.

"Do our people patronize him very well? You know it seems our failing never to have the same confidence in our own ability that we have in the white man's," said she.

"I don't think it's our people's fault this time, Miss Emily. We've all known George ever since he was a baby and were proud of his record at school. When he came home and opened an office, I sent him several cases and gave him some of my own work to do. He attended to them all right enough, but he didn't get out and 'hustle' for other work. He's either too proud to do it, or lacks energy, one or the other. We all feel that he's no woman that we should be hunting work for. He gets work enough to do around these magistrate's courts and now and then a case in the Criminal Court, and manages to make a living out of these petty cases, but he's never had a case of any special merit that has demonstrated his real ability, like that young Johnson of your town."

The conversation drifted to other topics, but Emily thought she could understand some things more clearly than before.

A day or so after, in a talk with Harris about mutual friends who had gone out into the world, he was aroused at the trenchant criticism. "How merciless you are toward us poor fellows, Miss Emily," he exclaimed.

"Yes, indeed," she quickly replied. "I have no patience with dawdlers."

"But you find fault with all. Are there none who merit your ladyship's favor?"

"If not, it is because they do not measure up to their highest possibilities," said she.

"No? Well you shouldn't expect them do so at a bound."

"But so few seem to be even striving in that direction, Mr. Harris. That's the discouraging feature. Even Mr. Harris, who might achieve splendid success in his profession—and of course any distinction he might win, would redound to the credit of his race—does not seem ambitious to do so." She spoke gently yet regretfully.

George was silenced for a moment, but rallying immediately said: "Give us a picture of your model man, Miss Emily?"

"But where would I find a model to sit for the picture?" asked Emily playfully.

"Take me," said George, with double meaning in his tone and a tender light in his eyes.

"You?" asked Emily, striving hard to seem unconscious; "you wouldn't do at all—there's one great objection."

"What is it, Emily?" eagerly asked George. "Tell me please."

"Not to-night," said she, shaking her head, "some other time."

George's musings as he walked home that night were not of the most pleasant kind. It was not the first time since he knew this girl that he had left her presence with a faint feeling of discontent with himself and surroundings. He wondered what particular flaw this keen-eyed young woman had discovered in his make-up. The thought haunted him all next day and when wending his way homeward to dinner, he spied her in a hammock in the yard. With the liberty of a frequent visitor, he went in, and after a few words, asked her what was the fault she had found in him. She laughed musically, yet there was a tremor in her voice as she rallied him on his "woman's curiosity." He persisted, telling her he had thought of it all day.

"Have you not hit upon it yet?"

"I can think of only one thing," said he, "is it that I am not tall enough?"

Emily blushed as she saw he was thinking her objection a personal one. She felt he was on the eve of a proposal and she thought it her duty to spare him the refusal, if possible. She laughed again to cover her embarrassment and asked what height would have to do with the "model man."

"It's a question of deeds, not physical proportions, Mr. Harris," she remarked gravely.

He took her hand and in a voice trembling with emotion, besought her to tell him what it was. She thought a moment. "You promise not to be angry?"

"I promise."

"Well, Mr. Harris, I am almost sorry I spoke," said she, "but since you will have it, if I were asked the principal drawback to your becoming a model man I should say it is a love of—liquor."

He dropped her hand and turned away. After a moment he said in a constrained tone: "May I ask how Miss Minton has become so wise as to my habits?"

"I have detected the smell of it on your breath," answered Emily, flushing as she rapidly continued. "I hope you won't be angry, my friend, but I have wondered that you seem to have so much leisure. I was in your office one day and was struck with the general poverty of your surroundings. Mr. Johnson, of my own town, has as fine an office as there is in the city, and has made a name for successful practice in the Criminal and Chancery[6] courts. He has not your education, nor has he been practicing so long. For a man of such brilliant parts, I thought there must be a reason for such contentment, such a seeming lack of energy. I have concluded this is the reason, but I should not have risked your displeasure by saying so, if you had not urged me. The race needs the best service our young manhood can give it, my friend, and it seems so wrong to divert any part of it to the practice of a habit which can bring you no credit and gratify no noble ambition."

George's mind was in a conflicting whirl of emotions. He knew she spoke the truth; and yet with all his feelings of anger and mortification, he seemed to feel that this peerless girl was slipping away from him. He wanted her to think well of him and forgetful of the French proverb: "He who excuses, accuses," said eagerly:

"But this habit of mine never interferes with my business, Miss Emily. Indeed it rather helps me. I am the only Afro-American at this bar, and I must have some stimulus to help me through the difficulties the wall of prejudice throws in my way. Besides had I wished to appear other than I am, I might have kept this knowledge from you."

"But it isn't I, who is to be considered," said Emily, struggling for composure. "It is the race, Mr. Harris, and what you owe it. This habit may not have seriously interfered before, but it will if indulged, render you less ambitious to excel, if nothing more. For us as a race, in our present position, stagnation means death. The men who are best fitted for it, should be the leaders; those who lead others must be slaves to no unworthy passion or habit. The model man—*my* model man—is in deed and truth, in body and mind, master of himself."

As the low earnest tones ceased to vibrate, Emily extended her hand and George pressed it warmly, saying, "Thank you, Miss Emily. No girl ever talked to me that way before."

"I have paid your common sense a compliment in that I have risked your displeasure to be your friend, and you do not know how I appreciate your manner of taking it," said she. "You know I go away to-morrow, and as you have made the summer so pleasant for me, I should like us to part friends."

"You will let me write to you?" asked George. She gave her consent and on the morrow went home.

George wrote her before the week was out; throughout the fall he sent her letters regularly telling of his struggles. He understood as fully as if she had told him in so many words, that if he would win her he must make himself worthy, and he manfully withstood the jeers of his friends on his refusal to drink.

Emily answered promptly and rejoiced that the latent forces in him were at last roused to action. Her love for him and faith in him grew stronger with every letter. She looked forward to a promised visit during the holidays with much anticipation.

George arrived in the city New Year's Eve; was met by old friends who had arranged a "stag" for him at the home of the friend with whom he was to stop. He was tempted and yielded for the first time in four months, and drank the more for his past abstinence. In the early morning hours he was helped to bed by the "boys" who all voted him a jolly good fellow.

He arose late next day with a terrible headache and guilty conscience; he was to call on Emily that afternoon, and he knew she would discover his condition. With a mental comment on being soft enough to deter to a "woman's whim," he obeyed the craving for a "stimulant" and took several drinks during the day. When he presented himself at the house, Emily went forward to meet him with a beaming face and outstretched hand, and presented "My friend, Mr. Harris," to the several callers in the room. Catching the smell of liquor, she looked at him searchingly and as she realized his condition felt as if turned to stone. The heat and Emily's constraint, had their effect on George. He talked volubly and loudly, and the fumes of brandy were distilled throughout the room.

Emily maintained her composure till the other guests had gone; then without a word she broke down and wept convulsively. Shame, surprise, indignation and mortification each struggled for the mastery. No one had ever dared to come in her presence in such condition before, and to receive this humiliation at the hands of the man she loved; and in the presence of witnesses to whom she had spoken so highly of him. What must they think of her,—Miss Minton, the exclusive? To think that after all these years of choosing, her heart should go out to a—drunkard!

George came and stood before her. "Tears for me, my darling? I am not worthy of them. I came here to ask you to marry me, but after such a weak, miserable spectacle, I know it is useless. I do not deserve even your forgiveness. Farewell." He left the house, and the city that same evening. He wrote Emily a long letter of apology, telling her how dearly he loved her and that her influence could save him from his weakness and make a man of him. He told her how he came to yield to his weakness without sparing himself and cast himself on her mercy.

Emily wept over this letter. Her heart plead for the writer, but she could not get the consent of her judgment to risk her happi-

ness in the hands of a man whom she could not trust; who was
not master of himself. Though it cost her a great deal to say so,
she did it after a night of anguish.

Shortly after she heard that he had wound up his business suddenly and gone West, and then she heard no more for two years.

One day in November she found a letter on her return from
school, in a strange hand writing. It read as follows:

OKLAHOMA CITY, O. T., NOV. 15, 1892

DEAR MISS MINTON:

You may not remember me and you must pardon the liberty I
take. But for the sake of a friend one risks much. I am the one you
so generously encouraged when I declared my intention to come to
Oklahoma nearly three years ago. I came and have never regretted
it. Nearly two years ago, my friend George Harris joined me and
we have been together ever since. In our lonely hours he has talked
much of you and I know how dear you are to him. Since that fatal
New Year's Day, (you see he has told me all,) not a drop of liquor
has passed his lips. He says it lost him the only woman he ever
loved and he never wants to look at it again. He thinks you have
never forgiven him, and says he doesn't blame you. He has built up
a fine practice in the territory by hard work, and now he is very ill
with pneumonia. He has the best attention, but he does not care to
get well; he has lost all hope and says nothing when he is at himself
but when he is out of his mind he is always calling your name. He
does not know I have written this letter, but I know a word from
you would do him more good than medicine. Won't you write him
a word, Miss Emily, and save the best friend I have on earth,

And Oblige, Yours,

WILL BRAMLETTE

Emily was crying when she finished but they were happy tears.
Without a word she sat down at the desk and this is the letter she
sent him:

MY OWN DEAR LOVE:

A little bird has brought me the news that you are a very sick
man and that you do not get well because you do not seem to care
to live. If I tell you that I wish you to live for my sake, will you try
to get well? I have always loved you, and since you would neither

write to me nor ask me again to marry you, I am going to make use of my leap year prerogative and ask you to marry me. As the New Year is near at hand, and I have no gift to send, now that I know where you are, I have been wondering if you would accept me as a New Year's gift, and if you will be able to come for me by the New Year. I have a fancy I would like to give myself to you on that day. Will you come?

Yours, EMILY

When Bramlette read this letter to the sick man it was Thanksgiving Day, and tears of thankfulness stole down his wasted cheeks. "Can you pray Will," he asked. "Then kneel down here and thank God for my happiness." A look of great content spread over his face. "Write her a letter, Will, and tell her I'll be there on New Year's Day if God spares my life."

He called for food and with the precious letter pressed to his heart he fell asleep with the first smile Will had seen on his face. The letter which had been more than medicine, he had Will read every day until he was able to read it himself, and having something to live for, he gradually got better. Will wrote to Emily every day and she sent loving cheerful messages in return, urging him to be careful of his health. He had never been a demonstrative man, but when he was able to write, he poured out his soul to her and consecrated the life he said she had given back to him, to renewed effort for individual and race advancement. "With you by my side," he wrote, "to cheer life's pathway and strengthen my zeal, life which has been so dreary, will indeed be enriched and ennobled."

Emily handed in her resignation, to take effect with the holidays. On New Year's Day, directly after the service, these two,—George Harris and Emily Minton—stood before the altar and pronounced the words for "better or for worse" to unite them "until death do us part." Then hand in hand they went out to the boundless west to make a home together, in which love and confidence reign supreme.

"LIVERPOOL SLAVE TRADITIONS AND PRESENT PRACTICES"

An excellent example of the rhetorical strategy that Wells used in addressing British gatherings, this article appeals to her audience's abolitionist heritage to mobilize support for her anti-lynching movement. Wells opens with a brief history of Southern race relations since the Civil War before going on to outline the many racial injustices that contemporary black Americans faced in the South. She also addresses any doubts that Britons might have had about her testimony by outlining her personal history with Charles Aked, whose experience with firsthand accounts of lynchings in the United States had opened his mind to Wells's cause.

SOURCE: Ida B. Wells, "Liverpool Slave Traditions and Present Practices," *Independent*, May 17, 1894.

LIVERPOOL SLAVE TRADITIONS AND PRESENT PRACTICES

When deprived of the slave trade, Liverpool shipping merchants came gradually to deal with cotton. The profit which came by dealing directly in slaves was exchanged for that which came from slave labor. The cotton trade from the United States was the commercial feature which the traffic in human flesh had been. It was far more respectable to have cotton instead of slaves on their ships. The sights and sounds of slavery were removed to a distance; so the conscience of Liverpool was not troubled with a face to face acquaintance with the situation, and her citizens added to their wealth through the cotton trade.

In the year 1861 came our Civil War; the supply of cotton from the Southern States ceased, and the commercial and manufacturing interests in Liverpool and Manchester suffered greatly. Thousands of men were thrown out of employment in these districts, and great distress caused thereby; yet it is worthy of note that it was not these workingmen who suffered directly by the War who sympathized with the South, but the wealthy and cultured classes. The workingman's sympathy was for the slave. Blockade running became the favorite adventure, and stories are told of many of the fast steamships which made lucky hits running into Charleston, S. C., and bringing out cargoes of cotton upon which they realized a hundred per cent. But many of the ships lay rotting in the docks because there was no use to which they could be applied. The shipbuilders turned their attention to building gunboats for the Confederate service; and in April, 1862, the first one built on the Mersey River, sailed for a neutral port, and then became the armed cruiser "Florida." July 29th the celebrated "Alabama," which had been built in the Liverpool docks, made her escape from the Mersey under the title of "No. 290," before the order from the British Government to detain her was received. She did her part, as the world knows, together with other Liverpool ships, for the next two years in burning and sinking American war ships.

With such open and pronounced sympathy for the Confederacy it is no wonder that Henry Ward Beecher, on his visit to this country the following year, met with storms of opposition and that Manchester, Glasgow, Liverpool and London refused to hear him at first. The readers of The Independent are familiar with his victory over the mobs, and how he was heard in spite of howling, cushion throwing and hisses. But it was in Liverpool, the home of many Southern men that the opposition was greatest. I have been in Philharmonic Hall and tried to imagine that great man battling for nearly two hours with the mob in a determination to be heard. I have been told more than once how, after the first forty minutes, when the storms of yells, hisses and howls had nearly spent itself, he stooped over and asked a reporter in front of him a question; then another; curiosity got the better of the mob, which became quiet, and Mr. Beecher finished his speech. It was a triumph of will power which many Liverpudlians now living witnessed, and which they relate with pride.

Contrary to her former traditions, views and practices touching things American has been Liverpool's reception of the writer. Many things have had to do with that reception, but the strong moving force has been the Rev. C. F. Aked. When I accepted the invitation from England last year to discuss in Great Britain the question of lynching (an opportunity which had been denied me in my own home), I spoke in Liverpool, but did not meet Mr. Aked. Friends asked him to invite me to his church, but he could not see the good to accrue and had some doubts as to the veracity of my story. He visited the United States in July. He was at the World's Fair when the horrible story of the lynching of C. J. Miller at Bardswell, Ky., was reported at length through the newspapers. The injustice of the whole thing made his blood boil, especially as it became known before he left America that Miller was innocent of the crime for which he was hanged and that the mob refused him time to establish his innocence. Mr. Aked felt that if public sentiment against the enforcement of law was so deadened, it needed arousing through the Christian Churches.

When I came to Liverpool, the first week in March, I spoke first in his church to a crowded congregation of fifteen hundred persons. I told them the object of my visit to Great Britain was (1st) to disprove the falsehood against the good name of the colored American; and (2d), to secure the aid of the press and pulpit of this country in urging the Christian men and women of my own country to create a public sentiment which shall put down lynch law. It seems almost incredible to them over here that it is hard to get prominent individuals here and there to take hold of it and that our Christian bodies will not touch it, because it is an unpopular subject. Meanwhile, men, women and children are being lynched in America at an average of one a day. It is no pleasure to me to have to relate that "the South is in the saddle and rides men," if I may be allowed to paraphrase Emerson.[7] She rules in Washington and shapes legislation to her liking. For thirty years she has bided her time; and now—with Southern men on the bench of the Supreme Court of the United States, in the Cabinet, as Speaker of the House, Chairmen of the Committees,

and with a majority in both Houses of Congress—is it any wonder that she has secured the repeal of the Federal Elections Laws
and openly boasts that she will remove every vestige of War legislation from the statute books of the nation? The wonder is—
not that the South which has secured this power by means of
fraud and violence from the first days the Negro began to vote, is
doing this thing—the wonder is that the American people, who
gave so much blood and treasure to make such enactment possible, stand by so calmly and see the beginning of the end of the
undoing of it all. The Republican Party, long ago as 1876, gave
up any attempt to enforce the Fifteenth Amendment[8] in the
Southern States, thus yielding principle to prejudice, refusing to
demand its enforcement, submitted to a silencing of the Negro
vote and to the Solid South,[9] for fear of angering or hurting the
feelings of the South. Behold the result! The Federal Government
has even theoretically now no control of its own elections—
the only case of the kind in the civilized world. With Senator
Chandler,[10] I believe that an attack on the National Election Laws
is an index of attack on the Fifteenth Amendment. The Negro,
deprived of his vote for the past eighteen years, has no protection
whatever against mobs, and because of that first wrong step of
the Republican party, acquiesced in by the Northern press and
pulpit, these mobs have increased in number, frequence and violence. The latest dispatches from America announce that even
Pennsylvania has become inoculated with mob virus and a Negro
was lynched this month, and an innocent Negro at that.

I have explained the situation in many different meetings, averaging a thousand persons each. At Liverpool, Sir Edward Russell,
the editor of The Daily Post, presided. The Post is, outside of
London, the greatest English daily, and he is the most prominent
man in Liverpool life. Perhaps his example will stimulate some of
our own great journalists and ministers to take up the question
as Gen. Neal Dow took up that of the liquor traffic years ago.

LIVERPOOL, ENGLAND

"THE BITTER CRY OF BLACK AMERICA: A NEW 'UNCLE-TOM'S CABIN'"

An interview published in a British newspaper, this text exemplifies how Wells mobilized the British press to disseminate her message. British audiences were fascinated with Wells's appearance. Light-skinned and pretty, she did not strike them as wholly Negro, and was often described by British journalists as a mulatto. Wells used the simple fact of her appearance to drive home her point. Black Americans were not 100 percent black because the color line was often violated by predatory white men. White Southerners, she went on to argue, also denied black Americans their citizenship rights.

SOURCE: Ida B. Wells, "The Bitter Cry of Black America: A New 'Uncle-Tom's Cabin,'" *Westminster Gazette*, May 10, 1894.

THE BITTER CRY OF BLACK AMERICA

A NEW "UNCLE TOM'S CABIN"

"Taint, indeed! I tell you, if I have any taint to be ashamed of in myself, it is the taint of *white* blood!"

The speaker is a neatly dressed, energetic, brown-faced little woman, slightly American in accent, who bears strongly printed on her the partly negro origin of which she speaks so spiritedly, though one would not guess that there is also a Red Indian strain in the odd racial composition of which she is the outcome.

"If Christianity is to be the test," she goes on,—"and what is the Anglo-Saxon if not a Christian?—then I may well be prouder to belong to the dark race that is the most practically Christian known to history, than to the white race that in its dealings with us has for centuries shown every quality that is savage, treacherous, and un-Christian. Negro races have been all that, too, in some countries—yes, but not with the formulae of Christianity on their lips meanwhile!"

"Why do you call the negro the practical Christian, Miss Wells?"

"Who has ever shown himself 'meek in spirit' if not the negro? Who, if not he, has for centuries answered not again, turned the left cheek when smitten on the right, blessed them that persecuted him, prayed for those that despitefully used him? Talk of forbearance! Do you remember when the American negro had his great opportunity? When his master went into the field openly to fight against his—the negro's—freedom, and left his wife and children in the negro's charge? What wrongs those negroes had to avenge! And what a temptation to vengeance! Yet not a man of them betrayed his master's trust."

Miss Ida Wells—Ida B. Wells, as the American style runs—journalist and M.A. of a "colour" university, is in England on a mission on behalf of her black and mulatto kinsmen in the Southern States of the Union. She has come to voice the bitter cry of black America. She admits that there is nothing English people can do for her clients beyond sympathising with them; but she thinks that sympathy is worth much. If a tithe of the ghastly tales she tells are true, it is well-nigh incredible that this sympathy should be denied by any civilised human soul upon God's earth, in America or out of it. But that race-hatred, backed by power and utter licence, does carry men to incredible lengths is an integral part of Miss Wells's case. The middle ages are outdone. The inquisition fades into a merely medium horror.

The truth is, the plain, admitted facts about the fiendish saturnalia covered by the name "lynching" are so astounding to English ears that one must needs lead up to them by a few lines of explanation. Readers who do not see much of the American newspapers, and who may not have read the articles of the *Times* special correspondent a year or two back, might be picturing the negroes on whom these things are done as persons enjoying at any rate the forms of peaceable and decent citizenship among their former masters. Not so. True, they are not now slaves, and in the capacity of servants they are tolerated—indeed, preferred to whites. The *Times* correspondent's solution (Pack them all back to Africa) would be scouted by no one more than by these masters, who would lack decent servants, these farmers, who would whistle for cheap agricultural labourers. But the moment the liberated negro wants to exercise his liberty on his own account, the war might as well never have been fought. All the blood flowed in vain. Lincoln's words ring down history as a bad joke. For a matter of ten years, after the North's victory, while the Secessionist States were still held by Federal troops, the negro was a citizen. He voted for Congress, he even sat in it.[11] Then the Southern States came back into the Union. They agreed to those amendments to the Constitution which gave the negro his citizenship—and, with their hands thus freed, proceeded to make them a dead-letter. Since the Federal troops were removed, and the Southern States regained their autonomy, no negro can vote either in a State or National election. To-day, if Miss Wells is travelling by rail and attempts with a first-class ticket to use a first class carriage, the officials will forcibly remove her to third. That is good enough for "colour." She may be hungry, the journey may be long, but she must not enter a refreshment room. A tram-car, a hotel, a restaurant containing whites is closed to her. Should she or hers marry with a white in most Southern States they subject themselves to State penal laws. And in many places, if they are merely suspected of any sort of offence against a white person—an offence which from a white to a white would be only misdemeanor, and from a white to a black would not count— they need not look for justice, nor even for a trial, nor for any form of law at all; but may expect to be murdered in cold blood by an armed mob, perhaps with refinements of cruelty, no man saying nay, authority folding its hands, press and pulpit turning either a blind or an approving eye.

Most of what has just been said is familiar to everybody who knows America—familiar and undeniable. But the last sentences bring us to the controversy in which Miss Wells is engaged. We have all heard something of the lynching atrocities. To Miss Wells it seems a strange thing that we have read of them and yet sat silent, continuing to regard our American cousins as a civilised nation. Well, as I explained to Miss Wells, we are under certain impressions which account for this indifference. Lynching, we agree, is a barbarous and deplorable thing. But we did not know it was a thing specially practiced by whites on blacks. We thought it was the weapon of the community against crimes of special horror, by whomsoever committed, with which the ordinary machinery of the law had proved itself unable to cope.

But what is Miss Wells's answer?—

(1) *Four-fifths of the lynching is done on blacks. Last year, out of 200 victims, 158 were negroes, the balance being made up of half-breeds and whites.*

(2) *Out of these 158, only 30 were even* CHARGED *with any crime against women or children.*

(3) *In the case of the rest, any sort of offence against white property or white prejudice was good enough*

For instance: A negro step-son was hanged by a lynching party because when they were after his step-father he was "very officious" in declaring that he knew where the poor wretch was, but that he would not tell.

A negro lad was hanged for being "drunk and saucy to whites."

Three brothers of a negro who shot a judge (a white, of course) were hanged by the lynching party because they could not find the criminal, and they thought they might as well hang someone.

(4) *In bad cases* TORTURES ARE USED *so revolting as to degrade the executioners to the level of the horrible crime of which their victim may be accused.*

For instance: In Texas 15,000 stood by and watched a negro being branded for fifty minutes with red-hot irons all over his body, ending with the eyes and the tongue, and then burnt alive. Officials assisted, school-children got a holiday, special trains were run. The show was conducted on a platform elevated so that all the crowd could see; in the middle of the burning the victim writhed off the platform down to the crowd, and had to be held back in the flames till he was "finished."

(5) *In four cases the victims were negresses—women or girls, including one horrible torture case.*

A negro girl suspected of poisoning a white (not convicted) was put into a barrel with nails driven in and rolled down a hill. The body was dragged out in "rags."

(6) *It is certain that black victims are often innocent of the crimes for which they are lynched.*

This is obvious in some of the few cases already quoted. Sometimes it is clearly proved afterwards, but nobody is ever punished for the murder. The invariable inquest verdict talks of "some person or person unknown," though the whole town—men, and often women and children—has been present, grouping itself round the body in eagerness to be "taken" (as shown in the illustration given herewith from photograph). Photos, and scraps of the remains, sell merrily as *souvenirs*.

But there is one class of cases in which the truth is *never* admitted, not even afterwards, and it is for hinting at the facts in a paper which she then ran at Memphis that Miss Wells herself narrowly escaped lynching.

Dead men tell not tales. But according to Miss Wells—and nobody who knows human nature, and has studied race hatreds, will pronounce it incredible—many of the alleged rapes for which negroes are hurried out of existence are only so called to save, not so much the white woman's reputation, as the white man's ferocious pride of race.

"You see," Miss Wells explained, "the white man has never allowed his women to hold the sentiment 'black but comely,' on which he has always so freely acted himself. Libertinism apart, white men constantly express an open preference for the society of black women. But it is a sacred convention that white women can never feel passion of any sort, high or low, for a black man. Unfortunately, facts don't always square with the convention; and then, if the guilty pair are found out, the thing is christened an outrage at once, and the woman is practically forced to join in hounding down the partner of her shame. Sometimes she rebels, but oftener the overwhelming force of white prejudice is too much for her, and she must go through with the ghastly mockery. 'What!' cried out one poor negro at the stake, as the woman applied the torch, egged on by a furious mob, headed by her relatives, 'have you the heart to do that, when we have been sweethearting so long?' "

It was for breaking the conspiracy of silence on this point that Miss Wells was threatened with lynching, and found the South too hot to hold her ever since.

On the general question of miscegenation, when I admitted that, as a white, I was dead against it, the retort came like lightning:—

"Which race has sought it? Not ours. It is yours, who forced it upon our women when they were your slaves; and now, having created a mulatto population, you turn and curse it. Even to-day, whatever may be the truth about the white woman, you cannot deny that the white man is continually mixing his blood with black; it is only when he seeks to do it honourably that it becomes a crime."

And Miss Wells told a pathetic little story of a man who lived openly with a coloured mistress for nine years in all the odour of respectability, and was prosecuted by statute, and "cut" by the town, when at the end of the time he married the mother of his children.

One last point about the "confessions" of the lynched. According to Miss Wells these are often worth as much as those which were wrung out by the "question" in an earlier age. Once more her newspaper cuttings supplied an illustration. On July 7 last a negro was hanged for a murderous outrage on two white girls, with which there was so little to connect him that the dead children's father himself prevailed on the lynchers to put off their job from ten in the morning till the evening. They consented, but told their suspect that, if he did not confess, they would burn him. If he did, he would only be hanged. He continued, however, to declare his innocence; and at last, as no proof was forthcoming, they hanged him "as a compromise"!

"But, Miss Wells is there *never* found a preacher or an editor in the South strong enough to protest?"

"The few who ever dared have had to leave the South. For instance—"

"Well, then, in the North?"

"They have fought a war once; they are sick and hopeless, and shut their eyes."

"What, then, can *we* do?"

"Give us a hearing, and your sympathy, and say so. It will help, for the facts cannot be denied, and such facts cannot stand the light of day. Or am I to go back and tell my poor people that the only way to get the ear of the civilized world is to learn chemistry enough to make bombs?"

And at that Parthian shot we shook hands and parted. The handshake was possible—in England.

G.

"IDA B. WELLS ABROAD"

Wells's most sustained discussion of her experiences in England appeared in the following series of articles, written for Chicago's Republican newspaper, the *Daily Inter Ocean*. Written in an engaging first-person style, they show Wells rallying the British to join her anti-lynching campaign by appealing to them as Christians who had once rallied against American slavery and should now once again intervene to challenge racial violence. To underscore her message, Wells visits the elderly Quaker Ellen Richardson, who raised the money to purchase Frederick Douglass, and contrasts her heroism with the disrespect showed to Douglass by the white American Lady Managers of the World's Fair. Even though Douglass, who was the commissioner of the Haitian building at the fair, was on hand throughout the fair, the Lady Managers neglected to invite this prominent African American leader to any of their "numberless receptions, affairs, soirees." Indeed, he was the only one of the fair's commissioners who never appeared on their guest list. Meanwhile, the warm reception that Ida received in Britain dramatized the lack of similar color prejudices among the British. Her final dispatch addressed U.S. critics such as Georgia governor William J. Northen (1835–1913), who insisted that lynching was not a problem, and also addressed personal attacks against her published in the *Memphis Daily Commercial* and other white Southern newspapers. She noted that these attacks included the first interview with a colored man ever to appear in the *Police Gazette*, which featured a man named J. Thomas Turner, who claimed that "the respectable colored population of Memphis utterly repudiate Ida Wells and her statements." Wells did not dignify his statement with a reply, and noted that the information she presented was well documented. She concludes her article taking comfort from the British press's responses to her critics, which ran strongly in her favor.

SOURCE: "Ida B. Wells Abroad. Lectures in Bristol, England, on American Lynch Law," *Daily Inter Ocean*, May 19, 1894; "Ida B. Wells Abroad. Ellen Richardson, the Benefactress of Fred Douglass," *Daily Inter Ocean*, May 28, 1894; "Ida B. Wells Abroad. A Breakfast with Members of Parliament," *Daily Inter Ocean*, June 25, 1894; "Ida B. Wells, Her Reply to Governor Northen and Others," *Daily Inter Ocean*, July 7, 1894, reprinted in the *Cleveland Gazette*, July 14, 1894.

IDA B. WELLS ABROAD

Lectures in Bristol, England, on American Lynch Law

AUDIENCES ARE SHOCKED

Very Pleasant Afternoon with Lady Jeune

CORDIAL RECEPTIONS FROM CHURCHES OF ALL DENOMINATIONS—HORRIFIED AT CRUELTIES PERPETRATED

NEWCASTLE, April 23.—*Special Correspondence.*—Since my last letter from Manchester I have been so constantly traveling and speaking that I could not write. From Manchester I went to Southport and spoke to an audience of near 2,000 persons. Rev. J. J. Fitch presided and the three newspapers gave an extended report and the audience passed a strong resolution of condemnation of lynching in some strong speeches that were made. The resolution was seconded by Mrs. Callender Moss, a charming speaker and a prominent member of the British Women's Liberal Association.[12] I was the guest of an able English authoress, "Evan May." I could only stay the one night, so am to return in June and speak for the Women's Liberal Association and another meeting arranged by the Misses Ryley, the wealthiest women in the town, and whose guest I am to be. From Southport I went to Bristol,

that old historic town, and spent a week, speaking on an average
of twice a day.

HORRIFIED AT THE NEGRO LYNCHINGS

There were two drawing-room meetings at the homes of wealthy
and influential persons. In these drawing-rooms, in which there
were 100 persons each, were gathered the wealthiest and most
cultured classes of society who do not attend public meetings.
One was presided over by Dr. Miller Nicholson, the pastor of
the largest and most influential Presbyterian Church in the city
and the other by Mrs. Coote, president of the Women's Liberal
Association of Bristol. Their shock on being told the actual condition of things regarding lynching was painful to behold. Most
of them, as they said in their speeches, had imagined that since
emancipation the negroes were in the enjoyment of all their
rights. It is true they had read of lynchings, and while they
thought them dreadful had accepted the general belief that it was
for terrible crimes perpetrated by negro men upon white women.
I read the account of that poor woman who was boxed up in the
barrel into which nails had been driven and rolled down the hill
in Texas, and asked if that lynching could be excused on the same
ground.

THE TROUBLESOME QUESTION IGNORED

Again the question was asked where was all the legal and civil
authorities of the country, to say nothing of the Christian
churches, that they permitted such things to be. And I could only
say that, despite the axiom that there is a remedy for every wrong,
everybody in authority, from the President of the United States
down, had declared their inability to do anything, and that the
Christian bodies and moral associations would not touch the
question. It is the easiest way to get along with the South (and
those portions of the North where lynchings take place) to ignore
the question altogether, and it is done; they are too busy saving
the souls of white Christians from future burning in hell-fire to
save the lives of black ones from present burning in flames kin-

dled by the white Christians. The feelings of the people who do these acts must not be hurt by protesting against this sort of thing, and so the bodies of the victims of mob hate must be sacrificed, and the country disgraced, because of that fear to speak out.

NEGRO COMMUNICANTS REFUSED SEATS

It seems especially incredible to them that the Christian churches of the South refuse to admit negro communicants into their houses of worship save in the galleries or on the back seats. When I told of a young mulatto man named James Cotton, who was dragged out of one of the leading churches in Memphis, Tenn., by a policeman and shut up in the station-house all day Sunday for taking a seat in the church, one lady remarked that it was easy to believe anything after that. I was asked if the Northern churches knew of this discrimination and continued fellowship with the churches which practiced it. Truth compelled me to reply in the affirmative, and to give instances which showed that in every case the Northern churches, which do not practice these things themselves, tacitly agreed to them by the Southern churches; and that so far as I knew principle has always yielded to prejudice in the hope of gaining the good will of the South. I had especially in mind the national Baptist convention which met in Philadelphia June, 1892. An effort was made to have a resolution passed by that convention condemning lynching as the Methodist Episcopal general conference had done at Omaha in May. The committee on resolutions decided that it could not be done, as they had too many Southern delegates present and they did not wish to offend them.

THE Y. M. C. A. HAS NO COLORED DELEGATES

A clergyman of the Church of England who was present while was in America a few years ago, visiting at Mr. Moody's home, Northfield, Mass., he attended a national convention of the Y. M. C. A. and after it was over, being disappointed in seeing no colored delegates, asked if there were none who were members. He was told that there had been a few in previous meetings, but this particular year (I forget which one) special effort had been made to get the Southern delegates to be present, so no colored ones had been invited." These were the only terms upon which the Y. M. C. A. and the W. C. T. U. had obtained a foothold in the South, and they had consented to the arrangement which shut the negro out. They continually declared the negro degraded, intemperate, and wicked, and yet shut him out from all influences in which he might become better. The American press was little better. Now and then, when a particularly horrible case of lynching was reported, there were strong editorials against it, and then the subject died away. The New York *Independent* and the *Forum* had symposiums lately on the subject in which the Southern white man had vented his opinion fully and freely, and the *Independent* had been good enough to give the negro a voice in the discussion.

THE INTER OCEAN GIVES FAIR PLAY

Only THE INTER OCEAN among the dailies and Judge A. W. Tourgee[13] as an individual had given any systematic attention and discussion to the subject from the standpoint of equal and exact justice to all in the condemnation of lynching. On the behalf of my race I am glad of every opportunity to bear testimony to the work of these two powerful advocates, and especially the former for giving the negro a chance to be heard in his own behalf.

I spoke ten times in Bristol during my week's stay—at two Congregational, two Baptist, and two Wesleyan churches, and a large public meeting in the Y. M. C. A. Hall. This meeting was presided over by Rev. G. Arthur Sowter, rector of the largest parish in Bristol, a Church of England clergyman. Young, ardent, and enthusiastic, he made a most glowing speech after leading me on the platform. I spoke an hour and a half, and not a person in the vast audience moved.

WHITE-CAP OUTRAGES

I forgot time and place for again news had reached me of the work of the mob known as white caps on the negro, Alex Johnson, and of the lynching of the little 13-year-old negro boy who was charged with killing the sheriff. How long, oh, how long shall we have to suffer these things! The country owes something to the negro for his very forbearance. He has never given trouble, as the strikers and anarchists. The American dispatches in the British press tell how members of Congress, prominent citizens, women, and legal authorities are exercising themselves on behalf of the "Coxeyites" and other agitators. Nobody is moving a finger to stay these outrages upon negroes. No wonder the Liverpool *Daily Post* of April 19 devotes a column-and-a-half editorial to surprise at this apathy, and condemnation of the lynchings which take place with such regularity.

GREAT NATIONS SHAME EACH OTHER

Sir Edward Russell in that editorial said: "Certain fears seem to be entertained that if we as a nation rebuked the Americans too plainly for their tolerance of lynch law they might turn upon us with the retaliation that we still permit the sweating system to hold its sway. Let them. It is an essential part of the business of great nations to shame each other, and if sweating is a preventable evil—which does not quite appear—let the Americans shame us into preventing it. They are in the meanwhile horrifying the whole of the civilized world by allowing law to be ignored, justice to be disgraced, and humanity outraged by continuous exhibitions of reckless popular brutality, which to all appearance, in five cases out of ten do not even correspond with the rough justice of the case." Quoting Mr. Aked's article in the *Christian World* of last week, anent the C. J. Miller case, the *Post* continues: "Such things as these curdle the blood when read about in the books of adventure and sensation that have been written about the lawless West; but when one reflects that they still happen when we in this country are sending missions to the South Sea Islands and other places, they strike to our hearts much more forcibly, and we turn over in our minds whether it were not better to leave the heathen alone for a time and to send the gospel of common humanity across the Atlantic, which is now a five days' journey."

A MOVEMENT CONDEMNING LYNCHING

An effort is being made, seconded by the great Dr. Clifford, to pass a resolution before the National Baptist Union, which meets in London this week, condemning lynching. The *Christian World*, the leading religious journal of the kingdom, gives notice of the resolution and says editorially: "It is earnestly to be hoped that the voice of England will help the better feeling of America so to assert itself as to bring to a speedy end a state of things which, if the published reports be correct, would disgrace a nation of cannibals." The resolution at the British meeting was seconded by the great Dr. Culross, president of the Baptist College at that place, and a pulpit representative of every denomination in the city sat on the platform at that meeting. I spoke also before the Bristol Congregational Ministers' Union and the quarterly meeting of the Quakers from the two counties. That was a large gathering of 500, and as the men and women meet in separate rooms to transact their business, I was given an opportunity to speak after dinner in the long dining hall before they left the tables. They then decided to have a joint meeting, and in that meeting recommended me to the yearly meeting at London, and asked that mention be made in the yearly epistles to American Quakers urging them to take some steps to put down lynching, especially as one of the last lynchings was reported from Pennsylvania, the Quaker State.

From Bristol I went to Newbury, a small town of 11,000 inhabitants in Gloustershire, by invitation to hold two meetings. Here the meetings were presided over by the mayor of the town, Mr. Elliott, who feels most strongly on the lynching question. The meeting was characterized by the exhibition of strong feeling.

AFTERNOON TEA AT LADY JEUNE'S

Here through the good influences of the mayor, who drove me out to her ladyship's country seat, I met Lady Jeune, wife of Sir Francis Jeune, one of the most eminent jurists on the bench in the United Kingdom, and Mr. Elliott tells me that her ladyship is one

of the most influential and cultured women of the British aristoc-
racy. It was Saturday evening and Lord Randolph Churchill and
other nobles had just gone—having been Lady Jeune's guests for
the week. She had given orders that she was not at home, but
when the footman took in Mr. Elliott's card she came to the door
to welcome us, invited us to tea with herself and children, and
had me to tell her all about it. She, too, was glad to be enlightened on the lynching mania, and shocked for the sake of humanity. When I go up to London next week she will have a
drawing-room meeting of her friends, for she thinks they ought
to know that the negro race is not the degraded one she has been
led to believe.

From Newbury to Newcastle, in the north of England, is a
long journey, as English journeys go, of ten hours. But there are
important engagements which must be filled before I go to
London. Here again I meet the terrible impression that the negro
race is such a terribly degraded one that only burnings, etc., will
effect the result of striking terror to the hearts of the evil doers.
These people, too, are aghast that more than ten negro women
and children have been lynched during the past nine months, and
that two-thirds of the entire number lynched were not even
charged with this foul crime. They, too, are more than willing to
join with us in asking as a favor (what is our right as citizens (?)
of our free Republic) that we shall be given a trial by law for all
charges against us, full opportunity in which to prove our innocence, and punishment by law for all crimes of which the law
finds us guilty.

INTERVIEWED BY REPORTERS

It is not "carrying coals to Newcastle" to tell them these things,
for to them all the facts are received with the greatest surprise,
horror, and indignation. One woman said she blushed for her
race when thinking of these outrages. Rev. Walter Walsh, to
whose congregation of more than a thousand persons I spoke last
night, announced that a perusal of the facts contained in my
pamphlet had made him really ill with horror. There are five
daily newspapers in town, and every one of them has interviewed
me and given most extended accounts of the meetings. I have

been here for four days and have spoken four times, I shall address another meeting to-day and one at the Friends' meeting house tomorrow night, and in the afternoon a drawing-room meeting, cards for which have been issued by Mrs. Lockhart-Smith, one of the wealthiest ladies in town. Her husband is most enthusiastic over the meetings. When my own country men and women take hold of the matter in this vigorous way a means will be found to put down such lawlessness and free the country from disgrace.

"A NEGRO ADVENTURESS"

I see the Memphis *Daily Commercial* pays me the compliment of calling me a "negro adventuress," and violently abuses the English people for listening to me. If I am become an adventuress for simply stating facts when invited to do so, by what name must be characterized those who furnish these facts, and those who give the encouragement of their silence? However revolting these lynchings, I did not commit a single one of them, nor could the wildest effort of my imagination manufacture one to equal the reality. If the same zeal to excuse and conceal the facts were exercised to put a stop to these lynchings there would be no need for me to relate and none for the English people to give ear to these tales of barbarity. If the South would throw as much energy into an effort to secure justice to the negro as she has expended in preventing him from obtaining it all these years—if the North would spend as much time in unequivocal and unceasing demand for justice for him as it has in compromising and condoning wrong against him—the problem would soon be solved. Will it do so? Eight million of so-called free men and women await the answer, and England waits with them.

IDA B. WELLS

IDA B. WELLS ABROAD

Ellen Richardson, the Benefactress of Fred Douglass

CASTE BASED ON COLOR

Meeting of the National Baptist Union in London

DR. JOHN CLIFFORD AND REV. JOHN F. AKED ARE VEHEMENT IN THEIR DENUNCIATIONS OF LYNCH LAW

LONDON, April 26,—*Special Correspondence.*—In Newcastle there lives an old Quaker lady named Ellen Richardson, who was well known to the old Abolitionists for her sympathy and practical help to the cause. She was head mistress of a girls' school back in the 40s when Frederick Douglass first came to Newcastle a fugitive slave. Like most British people, her heart went out in intense sympathy for him away from wife and children, and fearing to return to free (?) America. The fugitive slave law[14] was in force by the consent of the nation, and he was an exile. All Britain sympathized with him, but it was through Ellen Richardson's inspiration that he became free. In a visit to her the day before I left Newcastle she told me how she came to do it. The privilege of an interview was a rare one, as Miss Richardson is nearly 85 years of age, her hearing is impaired, her health poor, and she rarely sees visitors at all, but I spent nearly the whole of the morning with her. She said that Mr. Douglass, her brother, and herself were at the seaside; that while sitting on the sand together, listening to the fugitive slave's talk, she suddenly asked him: "Frederic would you like to go back to America?" Of course his reply was in the affirmative. Like a flash the inspiration came to her, "Why not buy his freedom?"

JOHN BRIGHT[15] AIDED DOUGLASS

She said nothing of this thought to him, because she knew he belonged to the Garrisonian party, which refused to recognize man's right to barter in human flesh, and that dearly as he might wish to be free, he could not concede to the principle. But the idea had taken possession of her, and being entirely ignorant of how to proceed she consulted a lawyer friend, who told her that as a means to an end so noble he thought there could be no objection to buying a human being. Strengthened by this opinion, without saying a word to her relatives, she wrote letters to different influential persons throughout the kingdom and the responses were many and prompt. She was only a school mistress in moderate circumstances and was not able to advance the sum herself. A letter from John Bright, containing a check for £50, was especially reassuring. She thought what John Bright approved could not be wrong. Not until she had received many subscriptions did she venture to reveal the secret to her own sister and tell her of the difficulty. She knew no way of communicating with Mr. Douglass' whilom master, and she could not tell him her reasons for wishing to know even could he have told her. It so happened that her sister's husband was then in correspondence with a Philadelphia lawyer, and her sister not only approved the plan but entered into enthusiastic correspondence with him.

ELLEN RICHARDSON'S NOBLE WORK.

Mr. Hugh Auld was approached and found very willing to take English gold for the runaway slave, the sum was [illegible] ($800 I believe it was), paid over to him, the free papers were made out, sent to England, and Miss Richardson still preserves them.

Mr. Douglass had all along asserted his right to be free, which theoretically he was, but practically he was still liable to be dragged back into slavery once he left the freedom of Great Britain; so when the good news was told him that he was free indeed he was only told that it was through the generosity of English friends. He was also given some hundreds of pounds, which he used to establish *Fred Douglass' Paper*, which struck such hard blows against slavery for so long a time after. So modest was Miss Richardson that not until years after the emancipation, when Mr. Douglass was again on a visit to this country, did he know to whom he was most indebted for his freedom. In the same way she was instrumental in purchasing the freedom of Dr. William Wells Brown, who died some years ago in Boston. No mother could be prouder of her child than Miss Richardson is of Mr. Douglass and his achievements, and nearly her whole conversation was about him. She, like other British people who have talked over the matter, cannot understand how the American government could ignore such a man in the World's Fair commission.

DOUGLASS IGNORED
BY THE LADY MANAGERS

They take the ground that such a man, a product of American civilization, was a more wonderful tribute to America's greatness than all the material exhibits stored in the White City, and are perfectly amazed that, commissioner though he was, representing Hayti at the World's Fair, the Board of Lady Managers, at their numberless receptions, soirees, etc., made Mr. Douglass the single exception when inviting American and foreign commissions. This caste, based on color, is so entirely foreign to them, "and coming from America, which is always boasting so loudly of her democracy," said one, "it is especially absurd." The negro still hopes that some day the United States will become as great intellectually and morally as she is materially, to protect and honor all her citizens regardless of "race, color, or previous condition," and thus make her professions a living reality.

REV. CHARLES F. AKED'S SPEECH

The National Baptist Union holds its yearly meetings in London every year. This organization is composed of the leading Baptist ministers and laymen of the kingdom, and there were over 500 delegates to the meeting which has just closed. Notice had been published in all the papers that a resolution against lynching would be offered, and I was telegraphed to be present to reply to any questions which might be asked. This was done because at the Unitarian conference at Manchester two weeks ago a similar resolution was defeated because Dr. Brooke Herford[16] had said it was a "terrible misrepresentation" to say the press and pulpit of the South encouraged lynching. Owing to a previous engagement in Bristol I could not be at that conference, but it was thought better that I should cancel other engagements in the north of England and be in London to rebut similar influences. But I was not needed. There was not a single objection expressed or dissentient vote. Rev. Charles F. Aked, the mover of the resolution, had the utterances of Bishops Fitzgerald[17] and Haygood on the subject, in which they excused and condoned lynching on the ground of defending the honor of white women.

BISHOP HAYGOOD ON LYNCHINGS

No other construction can be placed on Bishop Haygood's article in the *Forum* of last October, in which he vigorously condemns lynching in one breath, and with the next, quotes Dr. Hoss' "belief" that 300 white women had been assaulted by colored men, and adds his "opinion" that "this is an underestimate." No mob would wish greater encouragement than this statement, based solely on beliefs and opinions. Mr. Aked also had the New York *Independent* of Feb. 1, containing Rev. J. C. Galloway's encouragement to the same effect, who is a South Carolina minister as well as that of Dr. Hoss, who has a similar statement in the same number of that excellent journal, and he is a Nashville doctor of divinity and editor of a great church organ.

Clippings from the daily papers of Memphis and Nashville, Tenn., Atlanta, Ga., New Orleans, Paris, and Dallas, Texas, where, in many cases, the mob was influenced by the editorials and reports to do these deeds of violence, he had in great number. It was only the rare exception that a Southern or Northern paper had taken an uncompromising stand for the exercise of law, no matter what the crime charged. Where they had failed to do this it was an encouragement to mobs; as for the churches, had there not been the above quotations to use, their very silence in the face of the hanging, shooting, and burning, which are of weekly occurrence, is an encouragement.

AN APPEAL TO THE AMERICAN CHURCH

Mr. Aked had also the published tabulated list of the Chicago *Tribune* for Jan. 1, 1894, where it was shown, despite Bishop Haygood's "opinion" to the contrary, that only forty of the 158 negroes lynched last year were even charged with outrage upon white women. Mr. Aked was received, with great applause, and in a thrilling, eager, impassioned voice, began with a statement of the negro's progress, then touched with regret upon the practices of the American people, whose genius he admired, and urged the necessity of the Christian church to do what it could in an appeal to the conscience of the American church to put down this great evil. It was an eloquent speech, a noble effort, and a brave thing to do to champion the cause of the weak and defenseless. He is, as I stated in a former letter, the young and popular minister of Pembroke Chapel, Liverpool, in whose church I made my first address on coming to this country. The shocking lynching of C. J. Miller, which occurred while he was in Chicago last year, made a lasting impression on his mind, and put the first check on his intense admiration for American institutions.

DR. JOHN CLIFFORD

Mr. Aked's speech carried weight with it and the effect might have been credited to his editorial powers and his impetuosity set down to the ardor and fire of youth; but the man who rose to second the resolution was his very opposite in all these aspects. Dr. John Clifford is 58 years of age, of magnificent scholarship, a judicial mind, and the strongest individual influence in London today. After Spurgeon, he was considered the greatest of living Baptists; now that Spurgeon is dead, he occupies first place in his love of his denomination, the people of London, and the country abroad. He has one of the largest and most active churches today at Westbourne Park Chapel, and he is the head of the Polytechnic Institute, which has a membership of over 15,000 young men and women. He is an M. A., L. L. B., and a D. D., all rolled into one, yet he is the most unassuming and lovable of men. The knowledge that Dr. Clifford approves a movement is an earnest of its success. When, therefore, he rose to second the resolution and in calm, dispassionate language pointed out the duties of the churches toward each other, and the conviction that their American brethren only needed encouragement to speak out on this great wrong, and continued speaking till it was put down, his endorsement was greeted with applause, and the resolution was unanimously carried.

RESOLUTION CONDEMNING LYNCHING PASSED

A feeble brother, who declared he traveled with Mr. Douglass through this country nearly fifty years ago, stayed the putting of the resolution to express his approval of the step taken by the Baptist Union and express the hope that the National Baptist Association of America would not only pass a similar resolution but work to have lynching become a thing of the past. There was a fervent amen to that from one person at least, who shall be nameless. All the London dailies published the resolution, together with the *Christian World Review of the Churches*, and the Baptist organ, the *Freeman*.

The *Daily Chronicle* had also an admirable reader in commendation of the union's action and has honored me with a lengthy interview which appears today.

I am to speak in Dr. Clifford's Church Sunday night, and hope to write next time of that great place and the great congregation of a great man and greater preacher.

IDA B. WELLS

IDA B. WELLS ABROAD

A Breakfast with Members of Parliament

AT SARAH GRAND'S

Attitude of the Author of "The Heavenly Twins"

THE CAMPAIGN AGAINST LYNCHING AND THE MEN AND WOMEN ENGAGED IN IT

LONDON, June 6.—*Special Correspondence.*—The thermometer has been at freezing point several times the past week in town and there has been frost in the country. Last May when I was here, everybody said there had not been such a mild and lovely spring for twenty years; this time it is said there has not been a time within memory of the oldest inhabitant when May was so cold and rainy as now. I fully agree with the American tourist who, when asked about the English climate, remarked that "they had no climate—only samples." The only other English thing I do not like is the railway carriage. They can change the one if they cannot the other. To me, the narrow railway compartments, with seats facing each other, knees rubbing against those of entire strangers, and being forced to stare into each other's faces for hours, are almost intolerable and would be quite so, were the English not uniformly so courteous as they are, and the journeys comparatively short. But primitive as are these railway carriages, I as a negro can ride in them free from insult or discrimination on account of color, and that's what I cannot do in many States of my own free (?) America. One other thing about English railways must strike the American traveler, the carefulness with which human life is guarded. The lines of railway are carefully inclosed on both sides by stone wall or hedge the entire length, and never cross a roadway through a tunnel or over it on a bridge. Passengers are never allowed to cross the track from one side of the station to the other—there is always a bridge or subway. As a consequence accidents to human life are most rare occurrences, and I begin to understand how aghast the Britisher was to see our railway and street car tracks laid through the heart of our towns and cities, and steam engines and cable cars dashing along at the rate of thirty miles per hour. Even in London the only rapid steam or cable locomotive is under ground.

THE STORY OF THE TRAM

They call the street cars here tramways, or tram cars, and I puzzled over it very much until I learned that a man named Outram first hit upon the experiment of rolling cars or trucks on tracks—this was before the invention of the steam engine—and all cars so propelled without the aid of steam were called Outram cars. This has since been shortened. The first syllable of the name of the inventor has been dropped, and they are known as trams. I have found many Englishmen who do not know the origin of the word, yet are surprised that the green American does not at first know what he means by trams.

London has been in the throes of a cab strike for two weeks, but beyond making it safe for pedestrians there seems little notice taken of it. The hansom is the only rapid means of general locomotion in London save the Underground Railway, and there were thousands plying every hour of the day and night. They never slacken the pace when crossing the street, because there are so many streets they would be always stopping. So that between the omnibuses[18] and cabs persons took almost as much risk in crossing the street as they do in Chicago from the cable cars. The strike has taken more than half the usual number of cabs off the streets, and the pedestrian is enjoying the result; for this two-wheeled friend of the weary—the hansom—has rubber tires, and as it rolls along the asphalt pavement there is only the sound of the horse's hoofs, and the cab is upon you before you know it.

London is a wonderful city, built as everybody knows in squares—the residence portion of it. The houses are erected generally on the four sides of a hollow square, in which are the trees, seats, grass, and walks of the typical English garden. Only the residents of the square have the entree to this railed-in garden. They have a key to this park in miniature, and walk, play tennis, etc., with their children, or sit under the trees enjoying the fresh air. The passer by has to content himself with the refreshing glimpse of the green grass and inviting shade of trees which make such a break in the monotony of long rows of brick and stone houses and pavements. The houses are generally ugly, oblong structures of mud-colored brick, perfectly plain and straight the entire height of the three or four stories. This exterior is broken only by the space for windows. The Englishman cares little for outside adornment—it is the interior of his home which he beautifies.

CHARMS OF ANTIQUITY

There is also the charm of antiquity and historic association about every part of the city. For instance, I am the guest of P. W. Clayden, Esq., editor of the London *Daily News*. His house is near Bloomsbury Square, in the shadow of St. Pancras Church, an old landmark, and from where I am now writing, I look out the windows of the breakfast-room across to Charles Dickens' London home. We are also only a few squares—five minutes' walk—from the British Museum.

I have been too engrossed in the work which brought me here to visit the British Museum (although I pass it every day), the Royal Academy, or Westminster Abbey, which every American tourist does visit. I have been to the houses of Parliament twice, and also to Cambridge University. My first visit to the British Parliament was under the escort of Mr. J. Keir Hardie, M. P. Mr. Hardie is a labor member and he outrages all the proprieties by wearing a workman's cap, a dark flannel shirt, and sack coat— the usual working-man's garb—to all the sittings. He is quite a marked contrast to the silk-hatted, frock-coated members by whom he is surrounded. The M. P.'s sit in Parliament with their hats on, and the sessions are held at night. A great deal of ceremony must be gone through to get a glimpse of the British law making body at work. A card of permit must be issued by a member for admission to the galleries, and it is a mark of honor to be conducted over the building by one. Mr. Hardie himself had to secure a card to permit me to enter the House of Lords and look upon a lot of real live lords, who, according to the trend of public opinion, should no longer be permitted to sit on their red-feathered sofas and obstruct legislation. There is a special gallery for women, and the night I stood outside the door and peered into the House of Commons I noticed above the speaking chair a wire netting which extended to the ceiling. Behind this were what I took to be gaily dressed waxed figures, presumably of historic personages. Imagine my surprise when I was told this was the ladies' gallery, and it was only behind this cage that they were allowed to appear at all in the scared precincts hitherto devoted to man.

LADIES IN PARLIAMENT

The question of removing the grille was again brought up in Parliament this year, as it had been for several years past, but nothing came of it. An amusing incident happened two weeks ago when two ladies, strangers, had applied for permission to visit the House. A member of Parliament left them, as he thought, at the door while he went into the chamber for the necessary card. Unaware that women were never permitted to enter, and the doorkeeper being for the moment off guard, they followed the member of Parliament up the aisle nearly half way to the speaker's chair, when they were discovered and hurriedly taken out. They are said to be the first ladies who were ever on the floor of the House during a sitting.

Mr. Hardie interviewed me for his paper, the *Labor Leader*, and explained much that was strange while we had tea on the beautiful terrace overlooking the Thames at 6 o'clock that evening. British M. P.'s are not paid to legislate and unless they are gentlemen of means they pursue their different avocations meanwhile. An M. P. does not necessarily reside in the district he represents; he may be, and most always is, an entire stranger to his constituents until he "stands" for elecion. M. P. Naoriji, a native of India, is representing a London constituency. He is the gentleman about whom Lord Salisbury said: "The time has not come yet for a British constituency to be represented in Parliament by a black man." The English people resented this attempt to draw a color line and promptly returned Naoriji to Parliament, and Lord Rosebery, the present Prime Minister, gave him a dinner on the eve of his election.

My second visit to the House of Commons was purely social,

and especially enjoyable, because I met again that staunch friend
of the colored people, Mr. H. H. Kohlsaat, of Chicago. Mr.
William Woodall, M. P., financial secretary to the War Department of her Majesty's government, was the host of the occasion
and tendered a delightful dinner party to Mr. and Mrs. Kohlsaat,
Miss Maud Hambleton, and your humble servant. Besides the
host and ourselves there were present Miss Florence Bulgarnie,
an English speaker and journalist; Mr. Byles, M. P., proprietor of
the Bradford *Observer*; Mr. G. W. E. Russell, M. P., a member of
the Duke of Bedford's family and an official in the office of the
House Secretary, and Mr. Edmund Robertson, M. P., Civil Lord
of the Admiralty. I have been told that we were specially honored to have as host and fellow guests three members of Queen
Victoria's Cabinet. Mr. and Mrs. Kohlsaat, their children, and
Miss Hambleton left London last week for Paris.

THE AGITATION AGAINST LYNCHING

The agitation against lynching has received fresh impetus from
the reports of the burning alive of the negro who had smallpox in
Arkansas and the shameless way it was confessed by the perpetrators, who have not yet been punished or even apprehended.
Resolutions against lynchings have been passed by the National
Baptist, Congregational, Unitarian, and temperance unions at
their annual meetings in this city. The Aborigines Protection
Society passed a similar resolution, with Lord Northbourne in
the chair. I have spoken before the Protestant Alliance, the
Women's Protestant Alliance, the Women's Protestant Union,
to the congregations of Bloombury Chapel, Belgravia Congregational Church, and several smaller congregations. These have all
passed strong resolutions and sent them to the American Minister, Mr. Bayard. I have addressed clubs, drawing-room meetings,
breakfast and dinner parties. I have spoken not less than thirty-five times at different gatherings of different sorts during my
six weeks' stay in London and find more and more invitations
than I can fill from people who are anxious to know the facts.
Again I cannot help wishing that our own people would give the
same opportunity for open discussion on the subject. In no other
way can it be conquered save to meet it fairly. At the Democratic

Club in this city a most interesting discussion of the subject pro and con took place. Mr. Herbert Burrows, who took part in the labor congress at Chicago last summer, presided and the resolution was passed unanimously after I replied to the objectors. The same thing happened at South Place Ethical Institute, where Moncure D. Conway presided. Mr. Conway is a Virginian, who was banished from his home fifty years ago because of his opposition to slavery. He called on me and arranged the details of the meeting at his chapel, and when the American objected to the passage of the resolution Mr. Conway asked his reasons. He produced the utterances of Henry W. Grady, which appeared in the *Century Magazine* some years ago in argument with George W. Cable, in which Mr. Brady was left *hors du combat*. I happened to know as much about those articles as the reader, and gave Mr. Cable's reply to Mr. Grady's specious arguments.

AT THE IDEAL CLUB

At the Ideal Club last Monday night a large and influential concourse gathered for my last London address. Lady Jeune bore the expenses of the meeting, and Mr. Percy Bunting, editor of the *Contemporary Review*, presided. He said that many good people who condemned lynching felt a delicacy about the public expression of that condemnation on the ground of interference. For his part the cry of humanity knew no such thing as boundary lines; the English people had expressed themselves about Bulgaria, the Siberian convicts, the Russian Jews, and the Armenian Christians. They could, with greater hope of success appeal to the conscience and humanity of the other great English speaking race, with which there was a greater bond of union. Miss Frances E. Willard, said he, has come over to teach us how to prosecute temperance work. We have welcomed her with open arms and have been glad of her vigorous blows against drunkenness than any other city in the world we would not call it interference. In the same way, he felt sure, there were hundreds of Americans who would not call their protest against hanging, shooting, and burning alive of human beings, interference. Even if they would it would still be the duty of the great nations to shame each other, and they were most kind when they pointed out the other's faults.

After an address of an hour and a quarter Mr. Alfred Webb, member of Parliament, moved the resolution. He also asked permission to arrange breakfast for me, to which members of Parliament would be invited, with the hope to hear me. I was only too glad to grant that permission, and this morning at 9:30 o'clock breakfast was served to sixteen members of Parliament and their wives, and one or two other friends.

A NOTABLE GATHERING

Sir Joseph W. Pease was chairman and he occupied himself during breakfast with questioning me as I sat at his right. After his introduction I gave an address of forty minutes and then the great temperance advocate, Sir Wilfrid Lawson, spoke for England, Mr. John Wilson for Scotland, and Mr. Alfred Webb for Ireland, expressing horror of lynching and promising to do all they could to bring influence to bear to have Americans move in this matter. The photograph of the lynching of C. J. Miller, which was reprinted in THE INTER OCEAN last summer and which I have in my possession, went around the beautifully decorated tables as I talked.

Besides the chairman there were four baronets and their wives present. They were filled with amazement and then amusement when I told them that such a gathering for any purpose tendered to a colored person could only happen in monarchical England—that it would be impossible in democratic America.

I am to speak at the Pioneer Club Thursday next and Mrs. Annie Besant will preside. The Pioneer is the first women's club ever established in London. It has outlived the days of ridicule, and most of the brainy women of London, belong to it. There is a membership of nearly 500, and the club occupies lovely suites of rooms in Burton street. They gave a swell reception a few weeks ago, and everybody and her husband, father, brother, or lover was there. The Writer's Club is another woman's organization, and the Princess Christian opened their building a few weeks ago. I spent a most pleasant afternoon there, and, as usual at these gatherings, was talked hoarse on America's lynching and race prejudice. The ubiquitous and (so far as I am concerned) almost invariably rude American was en evidence there. In a strident voice she pronounced my statements false. I found she had never been in the South and was a victim of her own imagination. I heard an English woman remark after the encounter was over that she had seen a side of Mrs.—'s character which she never knew before.

AT SARAH GRAND'S

Through the courtesy of a most cultured and charming member of these clubs I was bidden to visit the home of Sarah Grand on her reception day. The author of "The Heavenly Twins" welcomed me most cordially, and like, every one else, made me talk of myself and the treatment of my people when I wished to hear her talk and take observations of the distinguished persons in her drawing room. There was no chance to get any impressions about her, for she only listened silently and closely, with a quiet question now and again. She is coming to America next year.

But beyond all expectation has been the attention accorded to me by the London press. I have quite lost count of the number of times I have been interviewed. The *Daily Chronicle*, the *Daily News*, the *Westminster Gazette*, the *Sun*, the *Star*, and the London *Echo*, all dailies, have devoted columns of space to interviews and discussion of the subject. The *Labor Leader*, the *Methodist Times*, the *Christian World*, the *Independent*, the *Inquirer*, and the *Westminster Budget*, all weeklies, have interviews on the same line. The *Review of the Churches* for May, the *Contemporary Review* for June, and the *Review of Reviews* for June, all monthlies, have had trenchant articles about lynching. The *Economist* and the *Spectator* have each more than a column on the subject.

But the closing movement by the London people shows how real their interest, how anxious they are to help the agitation of this subject. At an evening party given by my host last night a committee, including the editors of the daily journals named above, has voluntarily concluded to form a nucleus to aid the work in any way. As an evidence that America is waking up an open letter sent me by the citizens of California, inviting me to come there and lay the subject before the town, was read. And much was said in praise of California's progressive spirit as compared with Boston, New York, and Philadelphia, which are older centers of law and order.

IDA B. WELLS.

IDA B. WELLS

Her Reply to Gov. Northen and Others

THE LYNCHING RECORD

Effect in England of Abuse by Memphis Papers

THE ENGLISH PAPERS AND PEOPLE RESENT THE ATTACK ON MISS WELLS

LONDON, Eng., June 23.—The seven weeks' agitation in this city against lynch law has waked up the south. Besides Gov. Northen's letter of general denial and request that the English people get their facts from a "reputable" source, the southern press has been very active along the same line. The Memphis Daily Commercial exceeds them all in the vigor, vulgarity and vileness of its attack, not upon lynching, but upon me personally. In its issue of May 20 it devoted nearly four columns to traduction of my personal character, in language more vulgar and obscene than anything the Police Gazette ever contained, and wound up all by giving space for the first time in its history to an interview with a colored man, J. Thomas Turner[19] who claimed that "the respectable colored population of Memphis utterly repudiate Ida Wells and her statements." This is the only reply the Commercial can make touching the statements that three respectable colored men were lynched in cold blood in Memphis March 9, 1892; that as the direct result of the Commercial's leader and the action of the leading citizens of Memphis, May 25, 1892, my newspaper business was destroyed, my business manager run out of town, and myself threatened with death should I ever return; that on July 22, 1893, a second lynching bee took place on the streets of Memphis with the full knowledge and connivance of the authorities; that the columns of the Commercial told how Lee Walker was hanged, half-burned, and then half-grown boys and men dragged his body up Main street and again hanged it before the court house, and that men, women and children stood by and saw the sight; that a telegram was sent from the office of the board of trade ten hours previous to the lynching apprising the Chicago Inter Ocean of the fact that the burning would take place and inviting that journal to send me down to write it up.

STATEMENTS NOT DISPROVED

The Commercial has not disproved a single one of these statements; it cannot do so. It mainly imagined that a foul tirade against me, and the "repudiation" of a negro sycophant who bent "the pliant hinges of the knee that thrift might follow fawning," would be a sufficient refutation of my narration of Memphis' terrible lynching record.

The editors of the Commercial have flooded England with copies of that issue, with more detriment to themselves than harm to me. The tone and style of that paper have shocked the English people far more than my own recital could do. It has given them an insight as to the low moral tone of a community that supports a journal which outrages all sense of public decency that no words of mine could have done. It has brought to the cause warmer friends and stronger supporters than perhaps it might have had.

Since the appearance of that paper in England the parliamentary breakfast was given me at the Westminster Palace hotel and the London anti-lynching committee has been formed. The object of this committee is to aid the ventilation and agitation of the subject, and bring all moral means to bear to assist America to put down lynch law. The Duke of Argyle, whose son is married to one of Queen Victoria's daughters, is a member of the committee. The editors of the Daily News, Echo, Chronicle and Westminster Gazette, Mr. Moncure D. Conway, Rev. C. F. Aked, Mrs. Helen Bright Clark,[20] Miss Kate Ryley[21] and Mr. Percy Banting, editor of the Contemporary Review, are also on the committee. Miss Florence Balgarnie is secretary.

FELL FLAT IN ENGLAND

The London papers would not touch the Commercial's articles
with a pair of tongs. So far as I have been able to learn only one
journal to which it was sent, the Liverpool Daily Post, has taken
any notice of the Commercial's foul attack. In its issue of June 13
the Post says:

We have received copies of the Memphis Commercial of May
20, containing references to Miss Ida B. Wells and her mission.
Both the articles are very coarse in tone, and some of the language is such as could not possibly be reproduced in an English
journal. Moreover, if we were to convey an idea of the things said
we should not only infringe the libel law, but have every reason
to believe that we would do a gross and grotesque injustice.
Happily it is not necessary for us to consider the element in the
Memphis Commercial's case to which we have just referred, because whatever that journal might prove against the champion of
the colored race would fail altogether to justify the existence of
lynch law.

The occurrence of lynching is freely admitted by the Memphis
Commercial, and is attributed to certain abundant misdemeanors of the black race in the south. We are not encouraged by experience to attach great importance to the accusations of superior
races; and we certainly have not been led to believe by history
that the men of the southern states have always proved in their
relations with the Negroes "the most chivalrous and gentle in the
world." A civilized community does not need lynch law, and it is
perfectly obvious that a country in which lynch law is resorted
to, with the approval of public opinion and the concurrence of
respectable citizens, as in the Commercial alleged, is one in which
any crimes committed by the black race could be effectually dealt
with by regular process of law. This is what has been demanded
by the large number of representative bodies in this country,
which have passed resolutions against the practice of lynching in
the southern states, and this is sufficient reason for their interpo-
sition, and the acknowledged existence of lynching is a sufficient
justification of the resolutions that have been passed. All else is
irrelevant, and we even include under this description a declaration quoted from a colored journalist named Thomas Turner.

THE CONDITIONS DO EXIST!

It is idle for me to say that the conditions which Miss Wells describes do not exist, when the Memphis Commercial admits the existence of lynching, which is the one material accusation of English journalists and English public meetings. Doubtless it is true that many Negroes realize that the welfare of the colored race depends almost entirely upon the amicable relations with the whites. Moreover, we can well believe "that the right thinking elements of the colored population do not believe that it is right to condone vice in the members of their race or justify crimes committed by them." The colored editor asserts that Miss Wells has preached that kind of doctrine. It is absolutely certain that she has not preached that kind of doctrine in this country.

The writer of this editorial, Sir Edward Russell, is one of the leading editors in the kingdom and presided at my Liverpool meeting.

The Liverpool Weekly Review adds "We have recounted the horrors and injustices common to the persecution of the blacks in their naked truth, gleaning from other authorities than Miss Wells. They constitute a lamentable, sickening list, at once a disgrace and a degradation to nineteenth century sense and feeling. Whites of America may not think so; British Christianity does, and happily, all the scurrility of the American press won't alter the fact."

It is particularly gratifying that denied any chance to get redress for these gross attacks on my good name at home, such powerful holders of public opinion on this side have come to my defense. I have sent a letter throughout Great Britain in reply, of which the following is an excerpt:

A WOMAN'S ANSWER

This is the third time the Commercial has so honored me. When a Boston newspaper gave me a ten-line leader on the occasion of my visit there, five months after my exile from Memphis, the Daily Commercial published a half-column leader of the vilest abuse of the Boston people and myself. When I spoke in

Scotland last year and sent the Commercial a marked copy of the
Aberdeen Daily Free Press containing an account of my address
there, again the Commercial and other Memphis papers broke
forth into foul language concerning me, and sent heavily marked
copies to those places. Now, as then, its only reply to my statements about lynching is not proof of their falsity, but detraction
of my personality. This the Commercial can safely do. There is
no court in the state in which the editor would be punished for
these gross libels and so hardened is the southern public mind
(white) that it does not object to the coarsest language and obscene vulgarity in its leading journals so long as it is directed
against the Negro.

No amount of abuse can alter the fact that three respectable
colored men were taken out of jail and horribly shot to death in
Memphis on March 9, 1892, for firing on white men in self-
defense that the Daily Commercial's inflammatory leaders were
greatly responsible for that lynching, and the authorities con-
nived at it. Not even the Commercial ever charged these men
with assaults on white women. The paper openly advised the
lynching of the editor of Free Speech for protesting against mobs
and the false charges brought against their Negro victims, and to
its utterances on that occasion I owe the destruction of my newspaper and my exile from home.

CAN'T CHANGE THE RECORD

All the vile epithets in the vocabulary of reckless statements cannot change the lynching record for 1893. There were lynched in
different parts of the state of Tennessee fourteen Negroes, three
were charged with "assaults on white women," one was lynched
"on suspicion," one "by mistake" at Gleason, eight for "murder,"
and one Charles Martin, near Memphis, no offense whatever. He
failed to stop when ordered to do so by a mob which was hunting
another Negro, and was shot dead in his tracks. One of the three
men who were lynched for nameless crime was only charged with
"attempted assault." He jumped in a wagon in which white girls
were driving and frightened them. He was caught, put in jail, and
the following was sent to the Inter Ocean ten hours before the

lynching took place: "Lee Walker, colored man, accused of raping white women in jail here. Will be taken out and burned by
whites tonight. Can you send Miss Ida Wells to write it up?
Answer. R. M. Martin, with Public Ledger."

The Commercial and other dailies told in detail on July 23,
1890, how the mob took him from jail, kicked and cut his flesh
with knives, hanged him to a telegraph pole, then placed his
corpse on a fire, and men, women and boys stood by to see it
burn; how these half-grown boys dragged the half-charred trunk
up the street, and after playing a game of football with it, hanged
it again in front of the courthouse, from whence the coroner cut
it down, and found the usual verdict.

A PROTEST

Even the Daily Commercial, which had previously incited mobs,
protested against this lynching in these words: "Already the press
and pulpit of Britain is thundering at us and Memphis has been
held up to them as an illustration of barbarism and savagery, and
such scenes as that of last night only tend to confirm such opinion." The editor went on to state that he had heard a young
white youth under 17 boast that he had assisted at three "nigger"
lynchings, and expected to take part in as many more. This in the
Daily Commercial of July 23, 1893, after my first tour in England.

The following is from a letter of mine published two weeks ago
in the Inter Ocean:

"I see the Memphis Daily Commercial pays me the compliment of calling me a 'Negro adventuress.' If I am become an
adventuress for simply stating facts, by what name must be characterized those who furnish these facts? However revolting these
lynchings, I did not commit a single one of them, nor could the
wildest effort of my imagination manufacture one to equal the
reality. If the same zeal to excuse and conceal the facts were exercised to put a stop to these lynchings, there would be no need for
me to relate, nor for the English people to give ear to these tales
of barbarity. Yours, etc.

                                                    "IDA B. WELLS
                                        "SOUTHPORT, JUNE 14, 1894"

CONVICTED BY THEIR OWN RECORD

In the same way the other defenders of lynching in the south have been convicted by their own record. The ink was hardly dry on Gov. Northen's letter in the Daily Chronicle before the cable brought news of the tarring and feathering of an Englishman in Virginia by a mob, and the hanging and flaying alive of a Negro in Gov. Northen's own state of Georgia. But there has been no report that Gov. Northen has taken steps to punish the perpetrators of that terrible deed. The London Daily News, in a ringing leader anent that lynching, pointed out in its issue of June 15 that "the north has not done its duty by its proteges. It freed them and gave them the vote, then failed to protect them in the exercise of their citizenship. Those states in which these terrible disorders are common, in which it seems an Englishman is not safe if he offends the mob, are appealing to the world for settlers and capital to develop their magnificent resources. So long as these outrages continue they will appeal in vain. The position of the great body of American people is one of direct responsibility. They are partners with these anarchic states in a great popular government which has hitherto been the admiration and envy of the world. Do they intend to stand by in consenting silence while their flag is dishonored and their government and its institutions disgraced by outrages which bring on all concerned in them the scorn and reprobation of mankind?" Surely with so strong and direct a challenge the American people will bestir themselves to find a remedy for this great wrong and outrage. The Review of Reviews for June prints a tabulated synopsis of the lynchings for 1893, and Mr. Stead tersely points out that every other day, except Sunday, last year, a Negro was lynched, and adds: "This is not civilization; it is savagery."

AT CAMBRIDGE

The seven weeks of constant speaking, writing, etc., have forced me to take a rest, and I visited Cambridge University for my sight-seeing trip. The old historic college buildings, the green trees, and greener meadows were a restful picture, and the visit to Newnham college, the girls' annex, was greatly enjoyed because we had tea with Miss Helen Gladstone, daughter of England's grand old man, who is one of the lady principals of the college. My next privilege was to be the guest of the eldest daughter of John Bright, Mrs. Helen Bright Clark, in her charming home in Somerset. From there I went to Southport, down by the sea, for a visit to Mrs. Thomas Cropper Ryley, the wealthy widow of a man whose name is well known in anti-slavery annals.

Mr. Ryley was one of the faithful few who stood at Harvey Ward Beecher's[22] side in 1863, when the mob in Liverpool tried to prevent his being heard on an anti-slavery lecture. In 1866, when Mr. Ryley knew that a testimonial was being raised in the United States for Wm. Lloyd Garrison, he undertook the English contribution to that testimonial and collected and forwarded to Jas. Russell Lowell nearly $1,000. Mrs. Ryley and her daughters exhibit, among their most precious relics, autograph letters from both Mr. Lowell and Mr. Garrison acknowledging receipt of this money; also a copy of the Liberator.[23] Having known and read of these brave anti-slavery workers it is so hard for the English people to believe that for the present emergency no Garrison, Lowell, Phillips or Beecher responds to the call of duty to rouse the nation. The nation and the race needs somebody to say now as Garrison said in August 1831, in that first copy of the Liberator: "I will not equivocate, I will not excuse, I will not retreat a single inch, *and I will be heard.*"

OLD ABOLITIONISTS IN FAVOR

It is remarkable that those men, who were so hated and persecuted by their own people for taking up an unpopular cause, are the only Americans of that era whose names are known and revered on this side. It is also remarkable that the parents of every American one meets abroad were abolitionists. It is a passport to favor and consideration which money will not give. Yet it is an especially galling thing to these "children of abolitionists" to meet the despised Negro wherever they turn and to be forced to be civil with him. The cloven foot shows almost invariably in persons who were never before known to be guilty of a breach of good manners, when the Negro question is introduced. A member of parliament, who took a prominent part in the parliamentary breakfast given me, told me the other day that he dined out that same evening, and took an American lady in to dinner. She was the "daughter of an abolitionist," and is known to be a woman of culture, refinement and broad sympathies. Thinking he was sure of his ground he hoped to be able to enlist her sympathies in the Negro's cry for justice. He said he was astounded at the bitterness she displayed. "She defended lynching," said he, "and declared that under no circumstances would she eat at a table with a Negro." He added that he could see more clearly than ever how hard it was for us to be heard in America, if the offspring of the abolitionists were like that. All this seems passing strange to John Bull, because the Americans have always boasted of their free country, where there is no class distinction. This crusade is revolutionizing entirely the standard by which American leaders, moral and philanthropic, are being judged, and many of them will be called on to prove their professions by their work against wrong and outrage upon the Negro. Meanwhile the time draws on apace when I shall cease to be a free human being with all their rights and privileges appertaining thereto, and become simply "a colored woman." I am returning to the United States, and in order to make sure I shall not be insulted en route, I must avoid taking passage in a ship which is likely to have any considerable number of my countrymen or women as passengers.

IDA B. WELLS

"THE ENGLISH SPEAK"

Written shortly before Wells left England, this article describes Wells's speaking engagements in Bristol, Newcastle, and London and summarizes an interview she conducted with Miss Ellen Richardson, "the lady who bought the freedom of Hon. Frederick Douglass and Dr. Wm. Wells Brown." In London, Wells notes, she was present at the National Baptist Union, where a resolution was made to condemn lynching. While she did not speak there, Charles Aked did, and Wells provides the account of his speech given in the London *Daily Chronicle*.

SOURCE: Ida B. Wells, "The English Speak," *Cleveland Gazette*, June 19, 1894.

THE ENGLISH SPEAK

Ida B. Wells Stirs Them Up and Has a Word to Say Relative to Afro-American Traitors

---

THE LONDON DAILY CHRONICLE AND THE BRITISH NATIONAL BAPTIST UNION DENOUNCE LYNCHING— THE LADY WHO YEARS AGO PURCHASED THE FREEDOM OF HON. FREDERICK DOUGLASS AND DR. WILLIAM WELLS BROWN STILL ALIVE.

LONDON, England—At last writing I was in Bristol. Here I found photographs of Dr. Price,[24] and met many persons who had most pleasant recollections of his visit twelve years ago. Mine host, Mr. Fox, was a most ardent admirer of his and was very grieved when I told him the doctor was dead. From Bristol, I went to Newcastle, away in the north, and held some very good meetings there. I spoke six times during the six days I was there and had interviews in all the Newcastle papers. This is the home of Miss Ellen Richardson, the lady who bought the freedom of Hon. Frederick Douglass and Dr. Wm. Wells Brown[25] nearly fifty years ago, when they were fugitive slaves in this country. She is very old and feeble and rarely seeks visitors, but she granted me an interview, which lasted near two hours. She talked nearly the whole time about Mr. Douglass, and how proud she was of him and his achievements.

From Newcastle I came to London to be present at the meeting of the National Baptist unions before which a resolution was introduced to condemn lynching. This is one of the largest unions in the kingdom and after much work the resolution was placed on the agenda. There was no opportunity or necessity for me to speak. Mr. Aked delivered a speech which far excelled anything I could have done and was the best speech I ever heard a white man deliver in the Negro's behalf. No Negro could have spoken for himself or the race better than Mr. Aked spoke for us. The account in the London Daily Chronicle, May 20, gives the synopsis of his address:

"The Rev. C. F. Aked (Liverpool) moved: "That this union, having learned with grief and horror of the wrongs done to the colored people of the southern states of America by lawless mobs, expresses the opinion that the perpetuation of such outrages, unchecked by the civil power, must necessarily reflect upon the administration of justice in the United States and upon the honor of its people. It, therefore, calls upon the lovers of justice, of freedom, and of brotherhood in the churches of the United States, to demand for every citizen of the republic accused of crime, a proper trial in the courts of law." He said that the scandal he referred to had no parallel in the history of the world, and it was their duty as Christians to do their best to put a stop to it. In the southern states of America there are 25,000 Negro teachers in elementary schools, 500 Negro preachers trained in the theological institutes of the people themselves, and 2,500 Negro preachers who had not received college training. The colored race had also produced 800 lawyers, 400 doctors, 200 newspapers, and they possessed property valued at 50,000,000 sterling. Yet these people are being whipped, scourged, hanged, flayed and roasted at the stake. There had been 1,000, lynchings within the last ten years, and the average now was from 150 to 200 every year. Some of these murders were foul beyond expression and such as to appall and disgrace humanity. Most of the lynchings were alleged to be assaults on women, but only a small portion of cases were really of that kind. The mobs who lynched these poor people were generally drunk and half insane and always bestial. The church must not keep silent while the press spoke out, and he was glad to see that the Daily Chronicle, who was doing splendid service in the cause of humanity (cheers), called attention to the subject that morning, and told them to give a moral nudge to their American brethren. It was the duties of great nations to shame each other, and if they could do any good he should be pleased. He appealed to them to prove by their action the solidarity of the human race and the brotherhood of man under the fatherhood of God, and thus to further the interest of the kingdom of Heaven." (Cheers)

The resolution was seconded by Dr. John Clifford, the great London preacher, who, since Spurgeon's[26] death, is called the greatest living Baptist, and carried with acclamation. The great Baptist denomination of England has thus put itself on record against lynching; perhaps the National Baptists of America will follow the example thus set. At their national meeting in Philadelphia, June, 1892, the committee refused to bring such a resolution before the body on the ground that there were too many southern delegates present and they didn't wish to offend them.

There was a colored man present at Bloomsbury chapel when the above resolution was passed the other day and I heard he wished to speak to the resolution. He said he was a journalist, but I didn't learn his name. Dr. Clifford told me next day that he sent up a card to the chairman asking permission to speak that he wished to show that the outrages were not as had been pictured! A speech like that from a Negro would have destroyed all that Dr. Clifford, Mr. Aked and I had done to overcome the scruples of the committee to permit the resolution to go on the agenda! I don't know where this Negro came from, nor could I learn his name, but I was speechless with rage. One is in a measure prepared to have white people, especially Americans, doubt and deny; but to have a Negro who can do so absolutely nothing to put a stop to these outrages, doing what he can to stop others, is monstrous! No wonder such little headway is made in our demand for justice, when the race has not only all the white race against them but must needs be cursed with such spawn calling themselves men. There are a few such in the United States who cringe and bow before the white man and call black white at his dictation. These Negroes who run when white men tell them to do so, and stand up and let the white man knock them down or kill them if it suits his pleasure, are the ones who see no good in "fire-eating speeches." Such Negroes do nothing themselves to stop lynching, and are too cowardly to do so, and too anxious to preserve a whole skin if they could, but never fail to raise their voices in depreciation of others who are trying to stop the infamy of killing Negroes at the rate of one a day.

I can never forget to my dying day that when I gave the world the true facts about lynching and the foul charge against the men of my race, it was three Negro men of Memphis who raised a protest. Not that what I said was not true, but that "it would do no good" to tell such things. The white men of Memphis and other towns could not gainsay my facts and have not done so to this day, but these Negro men, wishing to gain favor to the eyes of Mr. White Man, hastened to put a letter in the white man's paper condemning the exposure of the southern white man's methods. Thank God, the breed of this stamp of cowards is a small one, and it is not right to blame the whole race for the expressions of those who earn the contempt of the white men they would serve and the far-sighted men and women of our own race.

The warm, helpful, inspiring, grateful letters I receive, from the Atlantic to the Pacific, make me feel that the bulk of my people so far from "laying a straw in my path," know that my labors are for them, and they assure me of their prayers and support. While this holds true, the barking of a few curs cannot make me lose heart or hope.

—IDA B. WELLS. In N.Y. Age

"THE SCOUNDREL"

Writing for the *Cleveland Gazette*, Wells reveals a plot by editors of the Memphis *Daily Commercial* to discredit her character. Determined to sabotage her anti-lynching campaign, the *Daily Commercial* editors had hired a black man named J. W. A. Shaw to go to England to give speeches claiming that Wells was misrepresenting the South and that "the Negro was not deprived of his vote and when lynched deserved it for terrible crimes." To reinforce her own position, Wells cites a letter written by Frederick Douglass on her behalf.

SOURCE: Ida B. Wells, "The Scoundrel," *Cleveland Gazette*, August 8, 1894.

THE SCOUNDREL

A Traitorous Afro-American Employed by the South and Sent to England

___

TO OFFSET THE EFFECT OF MISS IDA B. WELLS' TELLING CRUSADE–DOUGLASS' RINGING LETTER– THE RIGHT KIND OF RACE LEADERS ACCORDING TO MISS WELLS

___

LONDON, Eng. June 22—Does any one in New York state know a brown skin Negro named J. W. A. Shaw? That is the name of the creature who wished to speak against the resolution at the Baptist Union condemning lynching. He has also been to the office of the

London Daily Chronicle trying to get them to take some notice of him and give him an interview denying my statements.

SOME OF THE MAN'S FALSEHOODS

At the Democratic club, after I had finished my address a man rose in the audience and asked if I knew that a Negro named Shaw was delivering speeches in Hyde park every Sunday which were the direct opposite of everything I said, *viz.*, that the Negro was not deprived of his vote and when lynched deserved it for terrible crimes? My interlocutor said in describing this Shaw, that he had no occupation, wore fine clothes, a lot of jewelry and displayed plenty of money, and that he drew large crowds because he was a black man. My reply was that I did not know these things and that it was a more terrible shock than I could express to know that a man of any race could sink so low as to traduce his race, "that thrift might follow fawning."

HIS SUPPLY OF MONEY

For if he "had plenty of money" he was more fortunate than I, who found it hard to secure the wherewithal to pay actual expenses. Clearly somebody was making it worth his while to do this. Dean Swift[27] said long ago that "when an Englishman wished to roast an Irishman, he would always find another Irishman to turn the spit:" and that as our Savior had his Judas, Caesar his Brutus, and America her Benedict Arnold, it should not surprise us that the Negro race was no exception to the rule in producing its cowards and traitors and leeches. This is what I said to them, but I was cut to the heart to hear that I owe it to the support, loyalty and trust of the white man of this country, whose race I am betraying, that my statements have not been discredited by this black man, whose race I am trying to defend.

HON. FREDERICK DOUGLASS' LETTER

Contrast this with a letter sent by the noblest Roman of them all, Frederick Douglass, to Dr. Clifford, the great London Baptist preacher, and printed in the London Daily News. His letter is as follows:

ANACOSTIA, D.C., MAY 22, 1894

Rev. Dr. Clifford—Dear Sir:—I take the liberty to write to you in the interest of Miss Ida B. Wells, now traveling and lecturing in England on the presentation and the lawless outrages to which colored people are now being subject in the United States. I wish to bear my testimony to the character of Miss Wells and to the truth of her statements. I think she is remarkably happy in the statement of the simple truth. She does not strain facts for effect. If asked why bring this matter before England, I answer because the judgment of England is a moral power and the cause of humanity has a right to that power. Humanity is as broad as the world. It is not limited by national boundaries. Besides where the side of the oppressor is heard, the voice of the oppressed should also be heard. It is meet that the Christianity of England should cry out against this terrible persecution. It is nearly fifty years ago when an exile and unable to return to the United States because I was a slave and was liable to be returned to bondage from which I had fled, I found shelter and sympathy in England and spoke to thousands in behalf of my enslaved people. Thanks to the Almighty, ruler of the hearts of men and nations, that old system of wrong no longer exists, and yet the spirit of bondage and of persecution is still here to afflict us, and we need the moral and religious influence of good men and women everywhere to assist in its banishment.

Sincerely and gratefully yours,

FREDERICK DOUGLASS

Could anything more clearly show the difference between the two men? One is the utterances of the demagogue, the politician: the other that of the statesman, the philanthropist and the true lover of his race. Nor is this the only occasion Mr. Douglass has taken to express to the English people his sympathy with and the great need of the work.

OTHER AID BY THE OLD MAN ELOQUENT

I have heard of letters he has written to four different persons in Great Britain on the same subject, all of which have been helpful and inspiring, the English love and revere Frederick Douglass as they do no other living American. Grand old man. When I think of how oft he has lifted his voice for his race, and how, though his duties were many, he made the round of the Chicago churches last summer with me until we had collected the $500 with which to publish the world's fair pamphlet, besides giving $50 and writing a chapter; how he risked censure for himself by distributing the books on the fair grounds, and how though bowed with weight of many winters he is still helping the crusade for his race—my eyes fill with tears that he cannot stay with us.

RACE LEADERS

It is men of this stamp whom the race should delight to know— and only those who are *doing* something for the race. If the colored people of the south have $50 to pay a race man to speak to them, let it be a man who is true to his race at all events. Brave John Mitchell,[28] who has waged such a relentless war against lynching in Virginia, and protected and helped many a Negro victim at real risk to himself; Booker T. Washington,[29] whose quiet, earnest work is a shining light in the Black Belt of Alabama, where it is so needed; Hon. Harry C. Smith,[30] who has always made a gallant fight for his race in THE GAZETTE, and now in the Ohio legislature; Peter H. Clark,[31] one of the ablest and most modest men living; T. Thomas Fortune, who has spent a modest fortune in trying to advance race interests and in the legal fight against discrimination in New York state, making it easier for the next Negro to win such fights; Bishop H. M. Turner,[32] than whom no man loves his race more, or has struck harder blows for it—these men (and many more like them) are the ones the race should delight to honor, because of the work they have done for the race.   —IDA B. WELLS, in N.Y. Age

CHAPTER IV

The Crusade Continues

After returning to the United States in the summer of 1894, Wells kept up her anti-lynching campaign, even as she planned her wedding to Ferdinand Barnett, and likewise continued campaigning after her marriage.

Her outspoken critique of U.S. race relations won her few friends among white Americans, who above all deplored that she had enlisted support from the British. Southern governors bristled when they received inquiries into racial violence in their states from members of the English Anti-Lynching Committee, who, following Wells's lead, made a point of investigating lynchings. Likewise, Northern journalists were almost equally hostile to the lecture tour that Wells embarked on after she returned from Britain, in which she crisscrossed the country, speaking in California and the Midwest as well as to audiences on the East Coast.

Wells had hoped to use the publicity generated by her second British tour to organize anti-lynching societies among whites as well as African Americans, but in the United States most of her supporters continued to be black. She won over a small number of white supporters, such as the liberal clergyman Lyman Abbott, the women's rights activist Susan B. Anthony, and William Lloyd Garrison Jr., the son of the famous abolitionist William Lloyd Garrison. But the funding for her American tour came almost wholly from black supporters.

After her tour, Wells returned to Chicago and married Ferdinand Barnett. She took over the *Chicago Conservator* offices, continued lecturing, served as president of the Ida B. Wells Club from 1894 to 1898, and campaigned for women's suffrage in Illinois for the Illinois Republican Women's Club in 1896. But after the arrival of her sons, Charles Aked Barnett, who was born in 1896, and Herman Barnett, who arrived just a year later, Wells decided that motherhood required her full-time attention, so she gave up her editorship duties at the *Chicago Conservator* and cut back her public speaking.

Although Wells-Barnett meant to stay at home with her children, the continued mob violence in the South at the turn of the century meant that she did not remain there for very long. Without the franchise and abandoned by the courts in the 1890s, black Americans had no national representation or protection of their civil rights. The late 1890s saw Wells-Barnett working with other black Americans to protest the failure of the federal government, and to protect civil rights at the national level. Wells-Barnett was among the founders of the Afro-American Council, a precursor to the NAACP, in 1898.

Moreover, although the Wells-Barnetts began a family shortly after their marriage, Wells continued to publish anti-lynching pamphlets. In the months leading up to her wedding in 1895, she wrote *A Red Record. Tabulated Statistics and Alleged Causes of Lynchings in the United States, 1892–1893–1894,* her longest and most detailed analysis of lynching, and published *Lynch Law in Georgia* in 1899. This pamphlet chronicled the lynching of Sam Hose, a black farmhand accused of murder and sexual assault in Atlanta in 1899. A nursing mother during these years, Wells was not able to investigate the events that led up to Hose's death, but she made ingenious use of information printed in the white press as well as the work of a private investigator to exonerate Hose.

"SHE PLEADS FOR HER RACE: MISS IDA B. WELLS TALKS ABOUT HER ANTI-LYNCHING CAMPAIGN"

This newspaper article about Wells's anti-lynching campaign transcribes the first speech she delivered after her return from her second tour in the United Kingdom. Speaking at the Bethel A.M.E. Church in New York, Wells addressed an audience of approximately three hundred black and white New Yorkers. In her speech Wells provides the rationale for her British speaking tour, her work in England, and the Anti-Lynching Committee that was founded just before she left. She also sought the support of black and white Americans across the country to help expose the real motive for lynchings—race prejudice.

SOURCE: Ida B. Wells, "She Pleads for Her Race. Miss Ida B. Wells Talks About Her Anti-Lynching Campaign," *New York Herald Tribune*, July 30, 1894.

SHE PLEADS FOR HER RACE

MISS IDA B. WELLS TALKS ABOUT HER ANTI-LYNCHING CRUSADE

SHE HOPES TO GET JUSTICE FOR THE NEGRO THROUGH THE MORAL SUPPORT OF THE NORTH AND WEST

Miss Ida B. Wells spoke to an audience of about 300 colored people last evening, at the Bethel Methodist Episcopal Church, in Sullvan-st., near Bleecker-st. She is the young colored woman who has been speaking in Great Britain against Southern lynch law. T. Thomas Fortune was scheduled to speak on the work done in England by Miss Wells, but Miss Wells returned unexpectedly, and she was invited to speak for herself. Mr. Fortune, however, made a speech before the evening was over. Miss Wells's enunciation and gestures last evening were those of a refined speaker. She is apparently about twenty-four years old, of medium height, and has a light complexion.

The Rev. John M. Henderson, pastor of the church, introduced Miss Wells. T. Thomas Fortune said that the white men of the South were not a civilized race. He said that in the South "a black man had no rights that a white man was bound to respect," and an evidence of this was the general disfranchisement, the miscegenation laws, and other unwritten laws which kept the black man down.

MISS WELLS BEGINS HER SPEECH

Miss Wells spoke on "The English Crusade Against Mob and Lynch Law in the United States." She said in part:

"Our work is only begun; our race—hereditary bondsmen—must strike the blow if they would be free. The negro is not free, in spite of the Emancipation Proclamation; that noble document has been a dead-letter in the south for the last thirty years. Protest after protest has been made to Congress and to the President, but

it has been of no use. We now ask the American people for justice. The negro vote in the South is as completely nullified as if
there were none, and every Southerner knows that one white vote
is equal to three negro votes. The North and West have tolerated
the barbarous conditions in the South because they are afraid to
hurt the South's feelings. We have tried to get a hearing from the
American press and people, without avail. The white people of
the North and West have believed the Southern reports of crimes
alleged to have been committed by our people; for the last two
years I have been endeavoring to tell the whole truth. I have been
banished from my home for this alone. An English lady who had
seen for herself the condition of our people in the South, and seeing the hopelessness of our ever arousing public opinion in the
North, asked me a few days after a colored man was burned alive
at Paris, Texas, in February, 1893, to come to England to arouse
a moral sentiment in England against these revolting cruelties
practiced by barbarous whites. The British people took with in-
credulity my statements that colored men were roasted or lynched
in broad daylight, very frequently with the sanction of the officers of the law; and looked askance at statements that half-grown
boys shot bullets into hanging bodies, and, after cutting off
toes and fingers of the dead or dying, carried them about as
trophies. They could easily have believed such atrocities of cannibals or heathens, but not the American people, and in the
'land of the free and the home of the brave.' But when I showed
them photographs of such scenes, the newspaper reports, and
the reports of searching investigations on the subject, they accepted the evidence of their own senses against their wills. As
soon as they were positively convinced resolutions were passed
asking the American people to put away from them such shame
and degradation."

HER WORK IN ENGLAND

Miss Wells spoke of her work in Liverpool, Bristol, Manchester
and in other places, making on an average ten addresses a week,
and while in London speaking once every day and twice on
Sunday.

"The resolutions," continued Miss Wells, "were not passed in the spirit of 'Holier than thou.' We told the British press that our reason for coming 3,000 miles was to win the moral force of Great Britain, the country whose opinion America held first. There were enough Americans in England who defended their country and flag; some loved the flag so well that they felt duty bound to support the spots on it as well as the stars and stripes. We asked for the lowest of our race the same protection by law that the highest white man receives. The British Nation recognized that no civilized nation could refuse such a request. We showed that the negro was not so black as he was painted. We did not ask for maudlin sympathy for criminals, but for common justice."

AN ANTI-LYNCHING COMMITTEE

Miss Wells spoke of "the unsuccessful effort" of the Southern newspapers to break down her testimony by publishing what the British press termed "cowardly, obscene and scurrilous" attacks. An Anti-Lynching Committee of which the editors of the London "Daily News" and "The Contemporary Review" were members, was formed as a result of Miss Wells's work, she said. Nothing since the days of "Uncle Tom's Cabin" had taken such a hold in England as the Anti-Lynching Crusade, was the comment of the Rev. Dr. Clifford, of London. The scene of the conflict "to put down later-day slavery" had been transferred to America. Dynamite, daggers and the torch were not necessary to accomplish the work. In spite of the centuries of slavery and oppression, the colored people never had been and never would be Anarchists. The colored man would appeal to the moral forces of the country. Lynching would cease when the elements for good combined. Miss Wells strongly urged all her race to unite all over the country. The charge of inhuman crime so frequently made against colored men was a mere cloak, Miss Wells said, to hide the real motive for lynching—race prejudice.

"Black women," she said, "have had to suffer far more at the hands of white men than white women at the hands of black men. Every single report which is published should be investigated by detectives, and let the negro witness ask that his statement be published side by side with that of the lynchers."

In closing, Miss Wells asked all to combine to vindicate the name of the race, and said: "Know ye not, hereditary bondsmen that they who would be free, themselves must strike the blow!"

Next Sunday evening the Woman's Loyal Union,[1] Miss Wells's society, will meet in Bethel Church to further agitate the anti-lynching crusade.

A RED RECORD

Wells's longest anti-lynching work, *A Red Record* (1895), listed all the known lynchings of black Americans that took place between 1892 and 1894. Using facts and figures from the *Chicago Tribune*'s annual compilation of statistics on lynching, Wells combated the common assumption that black men were lynched because of their assaults on women by documenting that most of the accused rapists who fell victim to lynch mobs had been participants in illicit relationships that were clandestine rather than nonconsensual.

A Red Record was a departure from Wells's earlier writings, and also from the writings of contemporary women reformers. Whereas women reformers traditionally wrote from a female moral authority they claimed came from within, Wells claimed authority by writing a social analysis according to the methodology of the emerging field of sociology, which required social analysis that was based on research and evidence. Indeed, in the opening lines of *A Red Record*, Wells states that she is writing for the "student of American sociology."[2]

A Red Record was also, in part, Wells's response to Frances Willard, a well-known white reformer who led the Woman's Christian Temperance Union. One of Wells's most influential critics, Willard routinely insisted that black rapists threatened the white womanhood of the South and that lynching was a necessary evil. *A Red Record* offers a forceful critique of Willard's views and addresses other critics who claimed that Wells offered only accounts of racial atrocities—without any form of remedy or cure. By way of an answer to that charge, Wells closes her pamphlet with a chapter entitled "The Remedy," in which she makes five recommendations to her readers: (1) she urges readers to bring the facts of the book to all their acquaintances, and to (2) have churches and civic groups pass anti-lynching resolutions and send copies whenever lynchings occur; (3) she calls on her readers to bring attention to the South's "refusal of capital to invest where lawlessness and mob violence hold sway"; and to (4) "think and act on independent lines in this behalf"; (5) and finally, she urges her readers to send resolutions to Congress to support the Blair Bill to create an investigatory commission on lynching (which eventually died in Congress).

SOURCE: Ida B. Wells-Barnett, *A Red Record. Tabulated Statistics and Alleged Causes of Lynchings in the United States, 1892–1893–1894. Respectfully Submitted to the Nineteenth Century Civilization in "the Land of the Free and the Home of the Brave"* (Chicago: Donohue and Henneberry, 1895).

A RED RECORD.
TABULATED STATISTICS AND ALLEGED CAUSES OF LYNCHINGS IN THE UNITED STATES, 1892–1893–1894

Preface

HON. FREDERICK DOUGLASS' LETTER

DEAR MISS WELLS:

Let me give you thanks for your faithful paper on the lynch abomination now generally practiced against colored people in the South. There has been no word equal to it in convincing power. I have spoken, but my word is feeble in comparison. You give us what you know and testify from actual knowledge. You have dealt with the facts with cool, painstaking fidelity, and left those naked and uncontradicted facts to speak for themselves.

Brave woman! you have done your people and mine a service which can neither be weighed nor measured. If the American conscience were only half alive, if the American church and clergy were only half Christianized if American moral sensibility were not hardened by persistent infliction of outrage and crime against colored people, a scream of horror, shame, and indignation would rise to Heaven wherever your pamphlet shall be read.

But alas! even crime has power to reproduce itself and create conditions favorable to its own existence. It sometimes seems we are deserted by earth and Heaven—yet we must think, speak and work, and trust in the power of a merciful God for final deliverance.

Very truly and gratefully yours,

FREDERICK DOUGLASS.

Cedar Hill, Anacostia, D. C.

CHAPTER I

The Case Stated

The student of American sociology will find the year 1894 marked by a pronounced awakening of the public conscience to a system of anarchy and outlawry which had grown during a series of ten years to be so common, that scenes of unusual brutality failed to have any visible effect upon the humane sentiments of the people of our land.

Beginning with the emancipation of the Negro, the inevitable result of unbridled power exercised for two and a half centuries, by the white man over the Negro, began to show itself in acts of conscienceless outlawry. During the slave regime, the Southern white man owned the Negro body and soul. It was to his interest to dwarf the soul and preserve the body. Vested with unlimited power over his slave, to subject him to any and all kinds of physical punishment, the white man was still restrained from such punishment as tended to injure the slave by abating his physical powers and thereby reducing his financial worth. While slaves were scourged mercilessly, and in countless cases inhumanly treated in other respects, still the white owner rarely permitted his anger to go so far as to take a life, which would entail upon him a loss of several hundred dollars. The slave was rarely killed, he was too valuable; it was easier and quite as effective, for discipline or revenge, to sell him "Down South."[3]

But Emancipation came and the vested interests of the white man in the Negro's body were lost. The white man had no right to scourge the emancipated Negro, still less has he a right to kill him. But the Southern white people had been educated so long in that school of practice, in which might makes right, that they disdained to draw strict lines of action in dealing with the Negro. In slave times the Negro was kept subservient and submissive by the frequency and severity of the scourging, but, with freedom, a new system of intimidation came into vogue the Negro was not only whipped and scourged; he was killed.

Not all nor nearly all of the murders done by white men, during the past thirty years in the South, have come to light, but the statistics as gathered and preserved by white men, and which have not been questioned, show that during these years more than ten thousand negroes have been killed in cold blood, without the formality of judicial trial and legal execution. And yet, as evidence of the absolute impunity with which the white man dares to kill a Negro, the same record shows that during all these years, and for all these murders only three white men have been tried, convicted, and executed. As no white man has been lynched for the murder of colored people, these three executions are the only instances of the death penalty being visited upon white men for murdering Negroes.

Naturally enough the commission of these crimes began to tell upon the public conscience, and the Southern white man, as a tribute to the nineteenth century civilization, was in a manner compelled to give excuses for his barbarism. His excuses have adapted themselves to the emergency, and are aptly outlined by that greatest of all Negroes, Frederick Douglass, in an article of recent date, in which he shows that there have been three distinct eras of Southern barbarism, to account for which three distinct excuses have been made.

The first excuse given to the civilized world for the murder of unoffending Negroes was the necessity of the white man to suppress and stamp out alleged "race riots." For years immediately succeeding the war there was an appalling slaughter of colored people, and the wires usually conveyed to northern people and the world the intelligence, first, that an insurrection was being planned by Negroes, which, a few hours later, would prove to have been vigorously resisted by white men, and controlled with a resulting loss of several killed and wounded. It was always a remarkable feature in these insurrections and riots that only Negroes were killed during the rioting, and that all the white men escaped unharmed.

From 1865 to 1872, hundreds of colored men and women were mercilessly murdered and the almost invariable reason assigned was that they met their death by being alleged participants in an insurrection or riot. But this story at last wore itself out. No insurrection ever materialized; no Negro rioter was ever apprehended and proven guilty, and no dynamite ever recorded the black man's protest against oppression and wrong. It was too much to ask thoughtful people to believe this transparent story, and the southern white people at last made up their minds that some other excuse must be had.

Then came the second excuse, which had its birth during the turbulent times of reconstruction. By an amendment to the Constitution the Negro was given the right of franchise, and, theoretically at least, his ballot became his invaluable emblem of citizenship. In a government "of the people, for the people, and by the people," the Negro's vote became an important factor in all matters of state and national politics. But this did not last long. The southern white man would not consider that the Negro had any right which a white man was bound to respect, and the idea of a republican form of government in the southern states grew into general contempt. It was maintained that "This is a white man's government," and regardless of numbers the white man should rule. "No Negro domination" became the new legend on the sanguinary banner of the sunny South, and under it rode the Ku Klux Klan, the Regulators, and the lawless mobs, which for any cause chose to murder one man or a dozen as suited their purpose best. It was a long, gory campaign; the blood chills and the heart almost loses faith in Christianity when one thinks of Yazoo, Hamburg, Edgefield, Copiah, and the countless massacres of defenseless Negroes, whose only crime was the attempt to exercise their right to vote.

But it was a bootless strife for colored people. The government which had made the Negro a citizen found itself unable to protect him. It gave him the right to vote, but denied him the protection which should have maintained that right. Scourged from his home; hunted through the swamps; hung by midnight raiders, and openly murdered in the light of day, the Negro clung to his right of franchise with a heroism which would have wrung admiration from the hearts of savages. He believed that in that small white ballot there was a subtle something which stood for manhood as well as citizenship, and thousands of brave black men went to their graves, exemplifying the one by dying for the other.

The white man's victory soon became complete by fraud, violence, intimidation and murder. The franchise vouchsafed to the Negro grew to be a "barren ideality," and regardless of numbers, the colored people found themselves voiceless in the councils of those whose duty it was to rule. With no longer the fear of "Negro Domination" before their eyes, the white man's second excuse became valueless. With the Southern governments all subverted and the Negro actually eliminated from all participation in state and national elections, there could be no longer an excuse for killing Negroes to prevent "Negro Domination."

Brutality still continued; Negroes were whipped, scourged, exiled, shot and hung whenever and wherever it pleased the white man so to treat them, and as the civilized world with increasing persistency held the white people of the South to account for its outlawry, the murderers invented the third excuse—that Negroes had to be killed to avenge their assaults upon women. There could be framed no possible excuse more harmful to the Negro and more unanswerable if true in its sufficiency for the white man.

Humanity abhors the assailant of womanhood, and this charge upon the Negro at once placed him beyond the pale of human sympathy. With such unanimity, earnestness and apparent candor was this charge made and reiterated that the world has accepted the story that the Negro is a monster which the Southern white man has painted him. And to-day, the Christian world feels that white lynching is a crime, and lawlessness and anarchy the certain precursors of a nation's fall, it can not by word or deed, extend sympathy or help to a race of outlaws, who might mistake their plea for justice and deem it an excuse for their continued wrongs.

The Negro has suffered much and is willing to suffer more. He recognizes that the wrongs of two centuries can not be righted in a day, and he tries to bear his burden with patience for to-day and be hopeful for to-morrow. But there comes a time when the veriest worm will turn, and the Negro feels to-day that after all the work he has done, all the sacrifices he has made, and all the suffering he has endured, if he did not, now, defend his name and manhood from this vile accusation, he would be unworthy even of the contempt of mankind. It is to this charge he now feels he must make answer.

If the Southern people in defense of their lawlessness would tell the truth and admit that colored men and women are lynched for almost any offense, from murder to a misdemeanor, there would not now be the necessity for this defense. But when they intentionally, maliciously and constantly belie the record and bolster up these falsehoods by the words of legislators, preachers, governors and bishops, then the Negro must give to the world his side of the awful story.

A word as to the charge itself. In considering the third reason assigned by the Southern white people for the butchery of blacks, the question must be asked, what the white man means when he charges the black man with rape. Does he mean the crime which the statutes of the civilized states describe as such? Not by any means. With the Southern white man any mesalliance[4] existing between a white woman and a colored man is a sufficient foundation for the charge of rape. The Southern white man says that it is impossible for a voluntary alliance to exist between a white woman and a colored man, and therefore, the fact of an alliance is a proof of force. In numerous instances where colored men have been lynched on the charge of rape, it was positively known at the time of the lynching, and indisputably proven after the victim's death, that the relationship sustained between the man and woman was voluntary and clandestine, and that in no court of law could even the charge of assault have been successfully maintained.

It was for the assertion of this fact, in the defense of her own race, that the writer hereof became an exile: her property destroyed and her return to her home forbidden under penalty of death, for writing the following editorial which was printed in her paper, the Free Speech, in Memphis, Tenn., May 21, 1892:

"Eight Negroes lynched since last issue of the Free Speech, one at Little Rock, Ark., last Saturday morning where the citizens broke (?) into the penitentiary and got their man; three near Anniston, Ala., one near New Orleans; and three at Clarksville, Ga., the last three for killing a white man, and five on the same old racket—the new alarm about raping white women. The same programme of hanging, then shooting bullets into the lifeless bodies was carried out to the letter. Nobody in this section of the country believes the old threadbare lie that Negro men rape white women. If Southern white men are not careful, they will over-reach themselves and public sentiment will have a reaction; a conclusion will then be reached which will be very damaging to the moral reputation of their women."

But threats cannot suppress the truth, and while the Negro suffers the soul of deformity, resultant from two and a half centuries of slavery, he is no more guilty of this vilest of all vile charges than the white man who would blacken his name.

During all the years of slavery, no such charge was ever made, not even during the dark days of the rebellion, when the white man, following the fortunes of war went to do battle for the maintenance of slavery. While the master was away fighting to forge the fetters upon the slave, he left his wife and children with no protectors save the Negroes themselves. And yet during those years of trust and peril, no Negro proved recreant to his trust and no white man returned to a home that had been despoiled.

Likewise during the period of alleged "insurrection," and alarming "race riots" it never occurred to the white man, that his wife and children were in danger of assault. Nor in the Reconstruction era, when the hue and cry was against "Negro Domination," was there ever a thought that the domination would ever contaminate a fireside or strike to death the virtue of womanhood. It must appear strange indeed, to every thoughtful and candid man that more than a quarter of a century elapsed before the Negro began to show signs of such infamous degeneration.

In his remarkable apology for lynching, Bishop Haygood, of Georgia, says: "No race, not the most savage, tolerates the rape of woman, but it may be said without reflection upon any other people that the Southern people are now and always have been most sensitive concerning the honor of their women—their mothers, wives, sisters and daughters." It is not the purpose of this defense to say one word against the white women of the South. Such need not be said, but it is their misfortune that the chivalrous white men of that section, in order to escape the deserved execration of the civilized world, should shield themselves by their cowardly and infamously false excuse, and call into question that very honor about which their distinguished priestly apologist claims they are most sensitive. To justify their own barbarism they assume a chivalry which they do not possess. True chivalry respects all womanhood, and no one who reads the record, as it is written in the faces of the million mulattoes in the South, will for a minute conceive that the southern white man had a very chivalrous regard for the honor due the women of his own race or respect for the womanhood which circumstances placed in his power. That chivalry which is "most sensitive concerning the honor of women" can hope for but little respect from the civilized world, when it confines itself entirely to the women who happen to be white. Virtue knows no color line, and the chivalry which depends upon complexion of skin and texture of hair can command no honest respect.

When emancipation came to the Negroes, there arose in the northern part of the United States an almost divine sentiment among the noblest, purest and best white women of the North, who felt called to a mission to educate and Christianize the millions of southern ex-slaves. From every nook and corner of the North, brave young white women answered that call and left their cultured homes, their happy associations and their lives of ease, and with heroic determination went to the South to carry light and truth to the benighted blacks. It was a heroism no less than that which calls for volunteers to India, Africa and the Isles of the sea. To educate their unfortunate charges; to teach them the Christian virtues and to inspire in them the moral sentiments manifest in their own lives, these young women braved dangers whose record reads more like fiction than fact. They became social outlaws in the South. The peculiar sensitiveness of the southern white men for women, never shed its protecting influence about them. No friendly word from their own race cheered them in their work; no hospitable doors gave them the companionship like that from which they had come. No chivalrous white man doffed his hat in honor or respect. They were "Nigger teachers," unpardonable offenders in the social ethics of the South, and were insulted, persecuted and ostracized, not by Negroes, but by the white manhood which boasts of its chivalry toward women.

And yet these northern women worked on, year after year, unselfishly, with a heroism which amounted almost to martyrdom. Threading their way through dense forests, working in schoolhouse, in the cabin and in the church, thrown at all times and in all places among the unfortunate and lowly Negroes, whom they had come to find and to serve, these northern women, thousands and thousands of them, have spent more than a quarter of a century in giving to the colored people their splendid lessons for home and heart and soul. Without protection, save that which innocence gives to every good woman, they went about their work, fearing no assault and suffering none. Their chivalrous protectors were hundreds of miles away in their northern homes, and yet they never feared any "great dark faced mobs," they dared night or day to "go beyond their own roof trees." They never complained of assaults, and no mob was ever called into existence to avenge crimes against them. Before the world adjudges the Negro a moral monster, a vicious assailant of womanhood and a menace to the sacred precincts of home, the colored people ask the consideration of the silent record of gratitude, respect, protection and devotion of the millions of the race in the South, to the thousands of northern white women who have served as teachers and missionaries since the war.

The Negro may not have known what chivalry was, but he knew enough to preserve inviolate the womanhood of the South which was entrusted to his hands during the war. The finer sensibilities of his soul may have been crushed out by years of slavery, but his heart was full of gratitude to the white women of the North, who blessed his home and inspired his soul in all these years of freedom. Faithful to his trust in both of these instances he should now have the impartial ear of the civilized world, when he dares to speak for himself as against the infamy wherewith he stands charged.

It is his regret, that, in his own defense, he must disclose to the world that degree of dehumanizing brutality which fixes upon America the blot of a national crime. Whatever faults and failings other nations may have in their dealings with their own subjects or with other people, no other civilized nation stands condemned before the world with a series of crimes so peculiarly national. It becomes a painful duty of the Negro to reproduce a record which shows that a large portion of the American people avow anarchy, condone murder and defy the contempt of civilization.

These pages are written in no spirit of vindictiveness, for all who give the subject consideration must concede that far too serious is the condition of that civilized government in which the spirit of unrestrained outlawry constantly increases in violence, and casts its blight over a continually growing area of territory. We plead not for the colored people alone, but for all victims of the terrible injustice which puts men and women to death without form of law. During the year 1894, there were 132 persons executed in the United States by due form of law, while in the same year, 197 persons were put to death by mobs who gave the victims no opportunity to make lawful defense. No comment need be made upon a condition of public sentiment responsible for such alarming results.

The purpose of the pages which follow shall be to give the record which has been made, not by colored men, but that which is the result of compilations made by white men, of reports sent over the civilized world by white men in the South. Out of their own mouths shall the murderers be condemned. For a number of years the Chicago Tribune, admittedly one of the leading journals of America, has made a specialty of the compilation of statistics touching upon lynching. The data compiled by that journal and published to the world January 1st, 1894, up to the present time has not been disputed. In order to be safe from the charge of exaggeration, the incidents hereinafter reported have been confined to those vouched for by the tribune.

CHAPTER II

Lynch Law Statistics

From the record published in the Chicago Tribune, January 1, 1894, the following computation of lynching statistics is made referring only to the colored victims of Lynch Law during the year 1893:

ARSON

Sept. 15, Paul Hill, Carrollton, Ala.; Sept. 15, Paul Archer, Carrollton, Ala.; Sept. 15, William Archer, Carrollton, Ala.; Sept. 15, Emma Fair, Carrollton, Ala.

SUSPECTED ROBBERY

Dec. 23, unknown negro, Fannin, Miss

ASSAULT

Dec. 25, Calvin Thomas, near Brainbridge, Ga.

ATTEMPTED ASSAULT

Dec. 28, Tillman Green, Columbia, La.

INCENDIARISM

Jan. 26, Patrick Wells, Quincy, Fla.; Feb. 9, Frank Harrell, Dickery, Miss.; Feb. 9, William Filder, Dickery, Miss.

ATTEMPTED RAPE

Feb. 21, Richard Mays, Springville, Mo.; Aug. 14, Dug Hazleton, Carrollton, Ga.; Sept. 1, Judge McNeil, Cadiz, Ky.; Sept. 11, Frank Smith, Newton, Miss.; Sept. 16, William Jackson, Nevada, Mo.; Sept. 19, Riley Gulley, Pine Apple, Ala.; Oct. 9, John Davis, Shorterville, Ala.; Nov. 8, Robert Kennedy, Spartansburg, S. C.

BURGLARY

Feb. 16, Richard Forman, Granada, Miss.

WIFE BEATING

Oct. 14, David Jackson, Covington, La.

ATTEMPTED MURDER

Sept. 21, Thomas Smith, Roanoke, Va.

ATTEMPTED ROBBERY

Dec. 12, four unknown negroes, near Selma, Ala.

RACE PREJUDICE

Jan. 30, Thomas Carr, Kosciusko, Miss.; Feb. 7, William Butler, Hickory Creek, Texas; Aug. 27, Charles Tart, Lyons Station,

Miss.; Dec. 7, Robert Greenwood, Cross county, Ark.; July 14, Allen Butler, Lawrenceville, Ill.

THIEVES

Oct. 24, two unknown negroes, Knox Point, La.

ALLEGED BARN BURNING

Nov. 4, Edward Wagner, Lynchburg, Va.; Nov. 4, William Wagner, Lynchburg, Va.; Nov. 4, Samuel Motlow, Lynchburg, Va.; Nov. 4, Eliza Motlow, Lynchburg, Va.

ALLEGED MURDER

Jan. 21, Robert Landry, St. James Parish, La.; Jan. 21, Chicken George, St. James Parish, La.; Jan 21, Richard Davis, St. James Parish, La.; Dec. 8, Benjamin Menter, Berlin, Ala.; Dec. 8, Robert Wilkins, Berlin, Ala.; Dec. 8, Joseph Gevhens, Berlin, Ala.

ALLEGED COMPLICITY IN MURDER

Sept. 16, Valsin Julian, Jefferson Parish, La.; Sept. 16, Basil Julian, Jefferson Parish, La.; Sept. 16, Paul Julian, Jefferson Parish, La.; Sept. 16, John Willis, Jefferson Parish, La.

MURDER

June 29, Samuel Thorp, Savannah, Ga.; June 29, George S. Riechen, Waynesboro, Ga.; June 30, Joseph Bird, Wilberton, I. T.; July 1, James Lamar, Darien, Ga.; July 28, Henry Miller, Dallas, Texas; July 28, Ada Hiers, Walterboro, S. C.; July 28, Alexander Brown, Bastrop, Texas; July 30, W. G. Jamison, Quincy, Ill.; Sept. 1, John Ferguson, Lawrens, S. C.; Sept. 1, Oscar Johnston, Berkeley, S. C.; Sept. 1, Henry Ewing, Berkeley, S. C.; Sept. 8,

William Smith, Camden, Ark.; Sept. 15, Staples Green, Livingston, Ala.; Sept. 29, Hiram Jacobs, Mount Vernon, Ga.; Sept. 29, Lucien Mannet, Mount Vernon, Ga.; Sept. 29, Hire Bevington, Mount Vernon, Ga.; Sept. 29, Weldon Gordon, Mount Vernon, Ga.; Sept. 29, Parse Stickland, Mount Vernon, Ga.; Oct. 20, William Dalton, Cartersville, Ga.; Oct. 27, M. B. Taylor, Wise Court House, Va.; Oct. 27, Isaac Williams, Madison, Ga.; Nov. 10, Miller Davis, Center Point, Ark.; Nov. 14, John Johnston, Auburn, N. Y.

Sept. 27, Calvin Stewart, Langley, S. C.; Sept. 29, Henry Coleman, Benton, La.; Oct. 18, William Richards, Summerfield, Ga.; Oct. 18, James Dickson, Summerfield, Ga.; Oct. 27, Edward Jenkins, Clayton county, Ga.; Nov. 9, Henry Boggs, Fort White, Fla.; Nov. 14, three unknown negroes, Lake City Junction, Fla.; Nov. 14, D. T. Nelson, Varney, Ark.; Nov. 29, Newton Jones, Baxley, Ga.; Dec. 2, Lucius Holt, Concord, Ga.; Dec. 10, two unknown negroes, Richmond, Ala.; July 12, Henry Fleming, Columbus, Miss.; July 17, unknown negro, Briar Field, Ala.; July 18, Meredith Lewis, Roseland, La.; July 29, Edward Bill, Dresden, Tenn.; Aug. 1, Henry Reynolds, Montgomery, Tenn.; Aug. 9, unknown negro, McCreery, Ark.; Aug. 12, unknown negro, Brantford, Fla.; Aug. 18, Charles Walton, Morganfeld, Ky.; Aug. 21, Charles Tait, near Memphis, Tenn.; Aug. 28, Leonard Taylor, New Castle, Ky.; Sept. 8, Benjamin Jackson, Quincy, Miss.; Sept. 14, John Williams, Jackson, Tenn.

SELF DEFENSE

July 30, unknown negro, Wingo, Ky.

POISONING WELLS

Aug. 18, two unknown negroes, Franklin Parish, La.

ALLEGED WELL POISONING

Sept. 15, Benjamin Jackson, Jackson, Miss.; Sept. 15, Mahala Jackson, Jackson, Miss.; Sept. 15, Louisa Carter, Jackson, Miss.;

Sept. 15, W. A. Haley, Jackson, Miss.; Sept. 15, Rufus Bigley, Jackson, Miss.

INSULTING WHITES

Feb. 18, John Hughes, Moberly, Mo.; June 2, Isaac Lincoln, Fort Madison, S. C.

MURDEROUS ASSAULT

April 20, Daniel Adams, Selina, Kan.

NO OFFENSE

July 21, Charles Martin, Shelby Co., Tenn.; July 30, William Steen, Paris, Miss.; August 31, unknown negro, Yarborough, Tex.; Sept. 30, unknown negro, Houston, Tex.; Dec. 28, Mack Segars, Brantley, Ala.

ALLEGED RAPE

July 7, Charles T. Miller, Bardwell, Ky.; Aug. 10, Daniel Lewis, Waycross, Ga.; Aug. 10, James Taylor, Waycross, Ga.; Aug. 10, John Chambers, Waycross, Ga.

ALLEGED STOCK POISONING

Dec. 16, Henry G. Givens, Nebro, Ky.

SUSPECTED MURDER

Dec. 23, Sloan Allen, West, Mississippi.

SUSPICION OF RAPE

Feb. 14, Andy Blount, Chattanooga, Tenn.

TURNING STATE'S EVIDENCE

Dec. 19, William Ferguson, Adele, Ga.

RAPE.

Jan. 19, James Williams, Pickens Co., Ala.; Feb. 11, unknown negro, Forest Hill, Tenn.; Feb. 26, Joseph Hayne, or Paine, Jellico, Tenn.; Nov. 1, Abner Anthony, Hot Springs, Va.; Nov. 1, Thomas Hill, Spring Place, Ga.; April 24, John Peterson, Denmark, S. C.; May 6, Samuel Gaillard, —, S. C.; May 10, Haywood Banks, or Marksdale, Columbia, S.C.; May 12, Israel Halliway, Napoleonville, La.; May 12, unknown negro, Wytheville, Va.; May 31, John Wallace, Jefferson Springs, Ark.; June 3, Samuel Bush, Decatur, Ill.; June 8, L. C. Dumas, Gleason, Tenn.; June 13, William Shorter, Winchester, Va.; June 14, George Williams, near Waco, Tex.; June 24, Daniel Edwards, Selina or Selma, Ala.; June 27, Ernest Murphy, Daleville, Ala.; July 6, unknown negro, Poplar Head, La.; July 6, unknown negro, Poplar Head, La.; July 12, Robert Larkin, Oscola, Tex.; July 17, Warren Dean, Stone Creek, Ga.; July 21, unknown negro, Brantford, Fla.; July 17, John Cotton, Connersville, Ark.; July 22, Lee Walker, New Albany, Miss.; July 26, — Handy, Suansea, S. C.; July 30, William Thompson, Columbia, S. C.; July 28, Isaac Harper, Calera, Ala.; July 30, Thomas Preston, Columbia, S. C.; July 30, Handy Kaigler, Columbia, S. C.; Aug. 13, Monroe Smith, Springfield, Ala.; Aug. 19, negro tramp, near Paducah, Ky.; Aug. 21, John Nilson, near Leavenworth, Kan.; Aug. 23, Jacob Davis, Green Wood, S. C.; Sept. 2, William Arkinson, McKenney, Ky.; Sept. 16, unknown negro, Centerville, Ala.; Sept. 16, Jessie Mitchell, Amelia C. H., Va.; Sept. 25, Perry Bratcher New Boston, Tex.; Oct. 9, William Lacey, Jasper, Ala.; Oct. 22, John Gamble, Pikesville, Tenn.

OFFENSES CHARGED ARE AS FOLLOWS

Rape, 39; attempted rape, 8; alleged rape, 4; suspicion of rape, 1; murder, 44; alleged murder, 6; alleged complicity in murder, 4; murderous assault, 1; attempted murder, 1; attempted robbery, 4; arson, 4; incendiarism, 3; alleged stock poisoning, 1; poisoning wells, 2; alleged poisoning wells, 5; burglary, 1; wife beating, 1; self defense, 1; suspected robbery, 1; assault and battery, 1; insulting whites, 2; malpractice, 1; alleged barn burning, 4; stealing, 2; unknown offense, 4; no offense, 1; race prejudice, 4; total, 159.

LYNCHINGS BY STATES

Alabama, 25; Arkansas, 7; Florida, 7; Georgia, 24; Indian Territory, 1; Illinois, 3; Kansas, 2; Kentucky, 8; Louisiana, 18; Mississippi, 17; Missouri, 3; New York, 1; South Carolina, 15; Tennessee, 10; Texas, 8; Virginia, 10.

RECORD FOR THE YEAR 1892

While it is intended that the record here presented shall include specially the lynchings of 1893, it will not be amiss to give the record for the year preceding. The facts contended for will always appear manifest—that not one-third of the victims lynched were charged with rape, and further that the charges made embraced a range of offenses from murders to misdemeanors.

In 1892 there were 241 persons lynched. The entire number is divided among the following states:

Alabama, 22; Arkansas, 25; California, 3; Florida, 11; Georgia, 17; Idaho, 8; Illinois, 1; Kansas, 3; Kentucky, 9; Louisiana, 29; Maryland, 1; Mississippi, 16; Missouri, 6; Montana, 4; New York, 1; North Carolina, 5; North Dakota, 1; Ohio, 3; South Carolina, 5; Tennessee, 28; Texas, 15; Virginia, 7; West Virginia, 5; Wyoming, 9; Arizona Territory, 3; Oklahoma, 2.

Of this number 160 were of Negro descent. Four of them were lynched in New York, Ohio and Kansas; the remainder were murdered in the South. Five of this number were females. The

charges for which they were lynched cover a wide range. They
are as follows:

Rape, 46; murder, 58; rioting, 3; race prejudice, 6; no cause
given, 4; incendiarism, 6; robbery, 6; assault and battery, 1; attempted rape, 11; suspected robbery, 4; larceny, 1; self defense, 1;
insulting women, 2; desperadoes, 6; fraud, 1; attempted murder,
2; no offense stated, boy and girl, 2.

In the case of the boy and girl above referred to, their father,
named Hastings, was accused of the murder of a white man; his
fourteen-year-old daughter and sixteen-year-old son were hanged
and their bodies filled with bullets, then the father was also
lynched. This was in November, 1892, at Jonesville, Louisiana.

CHAPTER III

Lynching Imbeciles

(AN ARKANSAS BUTCHERY)

The only excuse which capital punishment attempts to find is
upon the theory that the criminal is past the power of reforma-
tion and his life is a constant menace to the community. If, however, he is mentally unbalanced, irresponsible for his acts, there
can be no more inhuman act conceived of than the wilful sacrifice of his life. So thoroughly is that principle grounded in the
law, that all civilized society surrounds human life with a safeguard, which prevents the execution of a criminal who is insane,
even if sane at the time of his criminal act. Should he become insane after its commission the law steps in and protects him during
the period of his insanity. But Lynch Law has no such regard for
human life. Assuming for itself an absolute supremacy over the
law of the land, it has time and again dyed its hands in the blood
of men who were imbeciles. Two or three noteworthy cases will
suffice to show with what inhuman ferocity irresponsible men
have been put to death by this system of injustice.

An instance occurred during the year 1892 in Arkansas, a report of which is given in full in the Arkansas Democrat, published at Little Rock, in that state, on the 11th day of February of
that year. The paper mentioned is perhaps one of the leading

weeklies in that state and the account given in detail has every mark of a careful and conscientious investigation. The victims of this tragedy were a colored man, named Hamp Biscoe, his wife and a thirteen year-old son. Hamp Biscoe, it appears, was a hard working, thrifty farmer, who lived near England, Arkansas, upon a small farm with his family. The investigation of the tragedy was conducted by a resident of Arkansas named R. B. Carlee, a white man, who furnished the account to the Arkansas Democrat over his own signature. He says the original trouble which led to the lynching was a quarrel between Biscoe and a white man about a debt. About six years after Biscoe pre-empted his land, a white man made a demand of $100 upon him for services in showing him the land and making the sale. Biscoe denied the service and refused to pay the demand. The white man, however, brought suit, obtained judgment for the hundred dollars and Biscoe's farm was sold to pay the judgment.

The suit, judgment and subsequent legal proceedings appear to have driven Biscoe almost crazy and brooding over his wrongs he grew to be a confirmed imbecile. He would allow but a few men, white or colored, to come upon his place, as he suspected every stranger to be planning to steal his farm. A week preceding the tragedy, a white man named Venable, whose farm adjoined Biscoe's, let down the fence and proceeded to drive through Biscoe's field. The latter saw him; grew very excited, cursed him and drove him from his farm with bitter oaths and violent threats. Venable went away and secured a warrant for Biscoe's arrest. This warrant was placed in the hands of a constable named John Ford, who took a colored deputy and two white men out to Biscoe's farm to make the arrest. When they arrived at the house Biscoe refused to be arrested and warned them he would shoot if they persisted in their attempt to arrest him. The warning was unheeded by Ford, who entered upon the premises, when Biscoe, true to his word, fired upon him. The load tore a part of his clothes from his body, one shot going through his arm and entering his breast. After he had fallen, Ford drew his revolver and shot Biscoe in the head and his wife through the arm. The Negro deputy then began firing and struck Biscoe in the small of the back. Ford's wound was not dangerous and in a few days he was able to be around again. Biscoe, however, was so severely shot that he was unable to stand after the firing was over.

Two other white men hearing the exchange of shots went to the rescue of the officers, forced open the door of Biscoe's cabin and arrested him, his wife and thirteen-year-old son, and took them, together with a babe at the breast to a small frame house near the depot and put them under guard. The subsequent proceedings were briefly told by Mr. Carlee in the columns of the Arkansas Democrat above mentioned, from whose account the following excerpt is taken:

"It was rumored here that the Negroes were to be lynched that night, but I do not think it was generally credited, as it was not believed that Ford was greatly hurt and the Negro was held to be fatally injured and crazy at that. But that night, about 8 o'clock, a party of perhaps twelve or fifteen men, a number of whom were known to the guards, came to the house and told the Negro guards they would take care of the prisoners now, and for them to leave; as they did not obey at once they were persuaded to leave with words that did not admit of delay.

"The woman began to cry and said, 'You intend to kill us to get our money.' They told her to hush (she was heavy with child and had a child at her breast) as they intended to give her a nice present. The guards heard no more, but hastened to a Negro church near by and urged the preacher to go up and stop the mob. A few minutes after, the shooting began, perhaps about forty shots being fired. The white men then left rapidly and the Negroes went to the house. Hamp Biscoe and his wife were killed, the baby had a slight wound across the upper lip; the boy was still alive and lived until after midnight, talking rationally and telling who did the shooting.

"He said when they came in and shot his father, he attempted to run out of doors and a young man shot him in the bowels and that he fell. He saw another man shoot his mother and a taller young man, whom he did not know, shoot his father. After they had killed them, the young man who had shot his mother pulled off her stockings and took $220 in currency that she had hid there. The men then came to the door where the boy was lying and one of them turned him over and put his pistol to his breast and shot him again. This is the story the dying boy told as near as I can get it. It is quite singular that the guards and those who had conversed with him were not required to testify. The woman was known to have the money as she had exposed it that day. She also had $36 in silver, which the plunderer of the body did not get. The Negro was undoubtedly insane and had been for several years. The citizens of this community condemn the murder and have no sympathy with it. The Negro was a well to do farmer, but had become crazed because he was convinced some plot had been made to steal his land and only a few days ago declared that he expected to die in defense of his home in a short time and he did not care how soon. The killing of a woman with the child at her breast and in her condition, and also a young boy, was extremely brutal. As for Hamp Biscoe he was dangerous and should long have been confined in the insane asylum. Such were the facts as near as I can get them and you can use them as you see fit, but I would prefer you would suppress the names charged by the Negroes with the killing."

Perhaps the civilized world will think, that with all these facts laid before the public, by a writer who signs his name to his communication, in a land where grand juries are sworn to investigate, where judges and juries are sworn to administer the law and sheriffs are paid to execute the decrees of the courts, and where, in fact, every instrument of civilization is supposed to work for the common good of all citizens, that this matter was duly investigated, the criminals apprehended and the punishment meted out to the murderers. But this is a mistake; nothing of the kind was done or attempted. Six months after the publication, above referred to, an investigator, writing to find out what had been done in the matter, received the following reply:

OFFICE OF
S. S. GLOVER
SHERIFF AND COLLECTOR,
LONOKE COUNTY.

Lonoke, Ark., 9-12-1892.

Geo. Washington, Esq.,
Chicago, Ill.

DEAR SIR:—The parties who killed Hamp Briscoe February the 9th, have never been arrested. The parties are still in the county. It was done by some of the citizens, and those who know will not tell.

S. S. GLOVER, Sheriff.

Thus acts the mob with the victim of its fury, conscious that it will never be called to an account. Not only is this true, but the moral support of those who are chosen by the people to execute the law, is frequently given to the support of lawlessness and mob violence. The press and even the pulpit, in the main either by silence or open apology, have condoned and encouraged this state of anarchy.

TORTURED AND BURNED IN TEXAS

Never in the history of civilization has any Christian people stooped to such shocking brutality and indescribable barbarism as that which characterized the people of Paris, Texas, and adjacent communities on the 1st of February, 1893. The cause of this awful outbreak of human passion was the murder of a four year old child, daughter of a man named Vance. This man, Vance, had been a police officer in Paris for years, and was known to be a man of bad temper, overbearing manner and given to harshly treating the prisoners under his care. He had arrested Smith and, it is said, cruelly mistreated him. Whether or not the murder of his child was an act of fiendish revenge, it has not been shown, but many persons who know of the incident have suggested that the secret of the attack on the child lay in a desire for revenge against its father.

In the same town there lived a Negro, named Henry Smith, a well known character, a kind of roustabout, who was generally considered a harmless, weak-minded fellow, not capable of doing any important work, but sufficiently able to do chores and odd jobs around the houses of the white people who cared to employ him. A few days before the final tragedy, this man, Smith, was accused of murdering Myrtle Vance. The crime of murder was of itself bad enough, and to prove that against Smith would have been amply sufficient in Texas to have him committed to the gallows, but the finding of the child so exasperated the father and his friends, that they at once shamefully exaggerated the facts and declared that the babe had been ruthlessly assaulted and then killed. The truth was bad enough, but the white people of the community made it a point to exaggerate every detail of the awful affair, and to inflame the public mind so that nothing less than immediate and violent death would satisfy the populace. As a matter of fact, the child was not brutally assaulted as the world has been told of in excuse of the awful barbarism of that day. Persons who saw the child after its death, have stated, under the most solemn pledge to truth, that there was no evidence of such an assault as was published at that time, only a slight abrasion and discoloration was noticeable and that mostly about the neck. In spite of this fact, so eminent a man as Bishop Haygood deliberately and, it must also appear, maliciously falsified the fact by stating that the child was torn limb from limb, or to quote his own words, "First outraged with demonical cruelty and then taken by her heels and torn asunder in the mad wantonness of gorilla ferocity."

Nothing is farther from the truth than that statement. It is a cold blooded, deliberate, brutal falsehood which this Christian (?) Bishop uses to bolster up the infamous plea that the people of Paris were driven to insanity by learning that the little child had been viciously assaulted, choked to death, and then torn to pieces by a demon in human form. It was a brutal murder, but no more brutal than hundreds of murders which occur in this country, and which have been equaled every year in fiendishness and brutality, and for which the death penalty is prescribed by law and inflicted only after the person has been legally adjudged guilty of the crime. Those who knew Smith, believe that Vance had at some time given him cause to seek revenge and that this fearful crime was the outgrowth of his attempt to avenge himself of some real or fancied wrong. That the murderer was known as an imbecile, had no effect whatever upon the people who thirsted for his blood. They determined to make an example of him and proceeded to carry out their purpose with unspeakably greater ferocity than that which characterized the half crazy object of their revenge.

For a day or so after the child was found in the woods Smith remained in the vicinity as if nothing had happened, and when finally becoming aware that he was suspected, he made an attempt to escape. He was apprehended, however, not far from the scene of his crime and the news flashed across the country that the white Christian people of Paris, Texas and the communities thereabout had deliberately determined to lay aside all forms of law and inaugurate an entirely new form of punishment for the murder. They absolutely refused to make any inquiry as to the sanity or insanity of the prisoner, but set the day and the hour when in the presence of assembled thousands they put their helpless victim to the stake, tortured him, and then burned him to death for the declaration and satisfaction of Christian people.

Lest it might be charged that any description of the death that day are exaggerated, a white man's description which was published in the white journals of this country is used. The New York Sun of February 2d, 1893, contains an account, from which we make the following excerpt:

PARIS, Tex., Feb. 1, 1893.—Henry Smith, the negro ravisher of 4-year-old Myrtle Vance, has expiated in part his awful crime by death at the stake. Ever since the perpetuation of his awful crime this city and the entire surrounding country has been in a wild frenzy of excitement. When the news came last night that he had been captured at Hope, Ark., that he had been identified by B. B. Sturgeon, James T. Hicks, and many other of the Paris searching party, the city was wild with joy over the apprehension of the brute. Hundreds of people poured into the city from the adjoining country and the word passed from lip to lip that the punishment of the fiend should fit the crime—that death by fire was the penalty Smith should pay for the most atrocious murder and terrible outrage in Texas history. Curious and sympathizing alike, they came on train and wagons, on horse, and on foot to see if the frail mind of a man could think of a way to sufficiently punish the perpetrator of so terrible a crime. Whisky shops were closed, unruly mobs were dispersed, schools were dismissed by a proclamation from the mayor, and everything was done in a business-like manner.

MEETING OF CITIZENS

About 2 o'clock Friday a mass meeting was called at the courthouse and captains appointed to search for the child. She was found mangled beyond recognition, covered with leaves and brush as above mentioned. As soon as it was learned upon the recovery of the body that the crime was so atrocious the whole town turned out in the chase. The railroads put up bulletins offering free transportation to all who would join in the search.

Posses went in every direction, and not a stone was left unturned. Smith was tracked to Detroit on foot, where he jumped on a freight train and left for his old home in Hempstead county, Arkansas. To this county he was tracked and yesterday captured at Clow, a flag station on the Arkansas & Louisiana railway about twenty miles north of Hope. Upon being questioned the fiend denied everything, but upon being stripped for examination his undergarments were seen to be spattered with blood and a part of his shirt was torn off. He was kept under heavy guard at Hope last night, and later on confessed the crime.

BURNED AT THE STAKE

Arriving here at 12 o'clock the train was met by a surging mass of humanity 10,000 strong. The negro was placed upon a carnival float in mockery of a king upon his throne, and, followed by an immense crowd, was escorted through the city so that all might see the most inhuman monster known in current history. The line of march was up Main street to the square, around the square down Clarksville street to Church street, thence to the open prairies about 300 yards from the Texas and Pacific depot. Here Smith was placed upon a scaffold, six feet square and ten feet high, securely bound, within the view of all beholders. Here the victim was tortured for fifty minutes by red hot iron brands thrust against his quivering body. Commencing at the feet the brands were placed against him inch by inch until they were thrust against the face. Then, being apparently dead, kerosene was poured upon him, cottonseed hulls placed beneath him and set on fire. In less time than it takes to relate it, the tortured man was wafted beyond the grave to another fire, hotter and more terrible than the one just experienced.

Curiosity seekers have carried away already all that was left of the memorable event, even to pieces of charcoal. The cause of the crime was that Henry Vance when a deputy policeman, in the course of his duty was called to arrest Henry Smith for being drunk and disorderly. The Negro was unruly, and Vance was forced to use his club. The Negro swore vengeance, and several times assaulted Vance. In his greed for revenge, last Thursday, he grabbed up the little girl and committed the crime. The father is prostrated with grief and the mother now lies at death's door, but she has lived to see the slayer of her innocent babe suffer the most horrible death that could be conceived.

TORTURE BEYOND DESCRIPTION

Words to describe the awful torture inflicted upon Smith cannot be found. The Negro, for a long time after starting the journey to Paris, did not realize his plight. At last when he was told that he must die by slow torture he begged for protection. His agony was awful. He pleaded and writhed in bodily and mental pain. Scarcely had the train reached Paris than this torture commenced. His clothes were torn off piecemeal and scattered in the crowd, people catching the shreds and putting them away as mementos. The child's father, her brother, and two uncles then gathered about the Negro as he lay fastened to the torture platform and thrust hot irons into his quivering flesh. Every groan from the fiend, every contortion of his body was cheered by the thickly packed crowd of 10,000 persons. The mass of beings 600 yards in diameter, the scaffold being the center. After burning the feet and legs, hot irons—plenty of fresh ones being at hand—were rolled up and down Smith's stomach, back, and arms. Then the eyes were burned out and irons were thrust down his throat.

The men of the Vance family having wreaked vengeance, the crowd piled all kinds of combustible stuff around the scaffold, poured oil on it and set it afire. The Negro rolled and tossed out of the mass, only to be pushed back by the people nearest him. He tossed out again, and was roped and pulled back. Hundreds of people turned away, but the vast crowd still looked calmly on. People were here from every part of this section. They came from Dallas, Fort Worth, Sherman, Denison, Bonham, Texarkana, Fort Smith, Ark., and a party of fifteen came from Hempstead county, Arkansas, where he was captured. Every train that came in was loaded to its upmost capacity, and there were demands of many points for special trains to bring the people here to see the unparalleled punishment for an unparalleled crime. When the news of the burning went over the country like wildfire, at every country town anvils boomed forth the announcement.

SHOULD HAVE BEEN IN AN ASYLUM

It may not be amiss in connection with this awful affair, in proof of our assertion that Smith was an imbecile, to give the testimony of a well known colored minister, who lived in Paris, Texas, at the time of the lynching. He was a witness of the awful scenes there enacted, and attempted, in the name of God and humanity, to interfere in the programme. He barely escaped with his life, was driven out of the city and became an exile because of his actions. Reverend King was in New York about the middle of February, and he was there interviewed for a daily paper for that city, and we quote his account as an eye witness of the affair. Said he:

"I was ridden out of Paris on a rail because I was the only man in Lamar county to raise my voice against the lynching of Smith. I opposed the legal measures before the arrival of Henry Smith as a prisoner, and I was warned that I might meet his fate if I was not careful; but the sense of justice made me bold, and when I saw the poor wretch trembling with fear, and got so near him that I could hear his teeth chatter, I determined to stand by him to the last.

"I hated him for his crime, but two crimes do not make a virtue; and in the brief conversation I had with Smith I was more firmly convinced than ever that he was irresponsible.

"I had known Smith for years, and there were times when Smith was out of his head for weeks. Two years ago I made an effort to have him put in an asylum, but the white people were trying to fasten the murder of a young colored girl upon him, and would not listen. For days before the murder of the little Vance girl, Smith was out of his head and dangerous. He had just undergone an attack of delirium tremens and was in no condition to be allowed at large. He realized his condition, for I spoke with him not three weeks ago, and in answer to my exhortations, he promised to reform. The next time I saw him was on the day of his execution.

"'Drink did it! Drink did it' he sobbed. Then bowing his face in his hands, he asked: 'Is it true, did I kill her? Oh, my God, my God!' For a moment he seemed to forget the awful fate that awaited him, and his body swayed to and fro with grief. Some one seized me by the shoulder and hurled me back, and Smith fell writhing to the ground in terror as four men seized his arms to drag him to the float on which he was to be exhibited before he was finally burned at the stake.

"I followed the procession and wept aloud as I saw little children of my own race follow the unfortunate man and taunt him with jeers. Even at the stake, children of both sexes and colors gathered in groups, and when the father of the murdered child raised the hissing iron with which he was about to torture the helpless victim, the children became as frantic as the grown people and struggled forward to obtain places of advantage.

"It was terrible. One little tot scarcely older than little Myrtle Vance clapped her baby hands as her father held her on his shoulders above the heads of the people.

" 'For God's sake,' I shouted, 'send the children home.'

" 'No, no,' shouted a hundred maddened voices; 'let them learn a lesson.'

"I love children, but as I looked about the little faces distorted with passion and the bloodshot eyes of the cruel parents who held them high in their arms, I thanked God that I have none of my own.

"As the hot iron sank deep in to poor Henry's flesh a hideous yell rent the air, and, with a sound as terrible as the cry of lost souls on judgment day, 20,000 maddened people took up the victim's cry of agony and a prolonged howl of maddened glee rent the air.

"No one was himself now. Every man, woman and child in that awful crowd was worked up to a greater frenzy than that which actuated Smith's horrible crime. The people were capable of any new atrocity now, and as Smith's yells became more and more frequent, it was difficult to hold the crowd back, so anxious were the savages to participate in the sickening tortures.

"For half an hour I tried to pray as the beads of agony rolled down my forehead and bathed my face.

"For an instant a hush spread over the people. I could stand no more, and with a superhuman effort dashed through the compact mass of humanity and stood at the foot of the burning scaffold.

" 'In the name of God,' I cried, 'I command you to cease this torture.'

"The heavy butt of a Winchester rifle descended on my head and I fell to the ground. Rough hands seized me and angry men bore me away, and I was thankful.

"At the outskirts of the crowd I was attacked again, and then several men, no doubt glad to get away from the fearful place, escorted me to my home, where I was allowed to take a small amount of clothing. A jeering crowd gathered without, and when I appeared at the door ready hands seized me and I was placed on a rail, and, with curses and oaths, taken to the railway station and place upon a train. As the train moved out some one thrust a roll of bills into my hand and said, 'God bless you, but it was no use.'"

When asked if he should ever return to Paris, Mr. King said: "I shall never go south again. The impression of that awful day will stay with me forever."

CHAPTER IV

Lynching of Innocent Men

(LYNCHED ON ACCOUNT OF RELATIONSHIP)

If no other reason appealed to the sober sense of the American people to check the growth of the Lynch Law, the absolute unreliability and recklessness of the mob in inflicting punishment for crimes done, should do so. Several instances of this spirit have occurred in the year past. In Louisiana, near New Orleans, in July, 1893, Roselius Julian, a colored man, shot and killed a white judge, named Victor Estopinal. The cause of the shooting has never been definitely ascertained. It is claimed that the Negro resented an insult to his wife, and the killing of the white man was an act of a Negro (who dared) to defend his home. The judge was killed in the court house, and Julian, heavily armed, made his escape to the swamps near the city. He has never been apprehended nor has any information ever been gleaned as to his whereabouts. A mob determined to secure the fugitive murderer and burn him alive. The swamps were hunted through and through in vain, when, being unable to wreak their revenge upon the murderer, the mob turned its attention to his unfortunate relatives. Dispatches from New Orleans, dated September 19, 1893, described the affair as follows:

"Posses were immediately organized and the surrounding country was scoured, but the search was fruitless so far as the real criminal was concerned. The mother, three brothers and two sisters of the Negro were arrested yesterday at the Black Ridge in the rear of the city by the police and taken to the little jail on Judge Estopinal's place about Southport, because of the belief that they were succoring the fugitive.

"About 11 o'clock twenty-five men, some armed with rifles and shotguns, came up to the jail. They unlocked the door and held a conference among them as to what they should do. Some were in favor of hanging the five, while others insisted that only two of the brothers should be strung up. This was finally agreed to, and the two doomed negroes were hurried to a pasture one hundred yards distant, and there asked to take their last chance of saving their lives by making a confession, but the Negroes made no reply. They were told to kneel down and pray. One did so, the other remained standing, but both prayed fervently. The taller Negro was then hoisted up. The shorter Negro stood gazing at the horrible death of his brother without flinching. The mob decided to take the remaining brother out to Camp Parapet and hang him there. The other two were to be taken out and flogged, with an order to get out of the parish in less than half an hour. The third brother, Paul, was taken out to the camp, which is about a mile distant in the interior, and there he was hanged to a tree."

Another young man, who was in no way related to Julian, who perhaps did not even know the man and who was entirely innocent of any offense in connection therewith, was murdered by the same mob. The same paper says:

"During the search for Julian on Saturday one branch of the posse visited the house of a Negro family in the neighborhood of Camp Parapet, and failing to find the object of their search, tried to induce John Willis, a young Negro, to disclose the whereabouts of Julian. He refused to do so, or could not do so, and was kicked to death by the gang."

AN INDIANA CASE

Almost equal to the ferocity of the mob which killed the three brothers, Julian and the unoffending, John Willis, because of the murder of Judge Estopinal, was the action of a mob near Vincennes, Ind. In this case a wealthy colored man, named Allen Butler, who was well known in the community, and enjoyed the confidence and respect of the entire country, was made the victim of a mob and hung because his son had become unduly intimate with a white girl who was a servant around his house. There was no pretense that the facts were otherwise than as here stated. The woman lived at Butler's house as a servant, and she and Butler's son fell in love with each other, and later it was found that the girl was in a delicate condition. It was claimed, but with how much truth no one has ever been able to tell, that the father had procured an abortion, or himself had operated on the girl, and that she had left the house to go back to her home. It was never claimed that the father was in any way responsible for the action of his son, but the authorities procured the arrest of both father and son, and at the preliminary examination the father gave bail to appear before the Grand Jury when it should convene. On the same night, however, the mob took the matter in hand and with the intention of hanging the son. It assembled near Sumner, while the boy, who had been unable to give bail, was lodged in jail at Lawrenceville. As it was impossible to reach Lawrenceville and hang the son, the leaders of the mob concluded they would go to Butler's house and hang him. Butler was found at his home, taken out by the mob and hung to a tree. This was in the law-abiding state of Indiana, which furnished the United States its last president and which claims all the honor, pride and glory of northern civilization. None of the leaders of the mob were apprehended, and no steps whatever were taken to bring the murderers to justice.

KILLED FOR HIS STEPFATHER'S CRIME

An account has been given of the cremation of Henry Smith, at Paris, Texas, for the murder of the infant child of a man named Vance. It would appear that human ferocity was not sated, when it vented itself upon a human being by burning his eyes out, by thrusting a red hot iron down his throat, and then by burning his body to ashes. Henry Smith, the victim of these savage orgies, was beyond all the power of torture, but a few miles outside of

Paris, some members of the community concluded that it would be proper to kill a stepson named William Butler as a partial penalty for the original crime. This young man, against whom no word has ever been said, and who was in fact an orderly, peaceable boy, had been watched with the severest scrutiny by members of the mob who believed he knew something of the whereabouts of Smith. He declared from the very first that he did not know where his stepfather was, which statement was well proven to be a fact after the discovery of Smith in Arkansas, whence he had fled through swamps and woods and unfrequented places. Yet Butler was apprehended, placed under arrest, and on the night of February 6th, taken out on Hickory Creek, five miles southeast of Paris, and hung for his stepfather's crime. After his body was suspended in the air, the mob filled it with bullets.

LYNCHED BECAUSE THE JURY ACQUITTED HIM

The entire system of the judiciary of this country is in the hands of white people. To this add the fact of the inherent prejudice against colored people, and it will be clearly seen that a white jury is certain to find a Negro prisoner guilty if there is the least evidence to warrant such a finding.

Meredith Lewis was arrested in Roseland, La., in July of last year. A white jury found him not guilty of the crime of murder wherewith he stood charged. This did not suit the mob. A few nights after the verdict was rendered, and he declared to be innocent, a mob gathered in his vicinity and went to his house. He was called, and suspecting nothing, went outside. He was seized and hurried off to a convenient spot and hanged by the neck until he was dead for the murder of a woman of which the jury had said he was innocent.

LYNCHED AS A SCAPEGOAT

Wednesday, July 5th, about 10 o'clock in the morning, a terrible crime was committed within four miles of Wickliffe, Ky. Two girls, Mary and Ruby Ray, were found murdered a short distance from their home. The news of this terrible cowardly murder of two helpless young girls spread like wild fire, and searching parties scoured the territory surrounding Wickliffe and Bardwell. Two of the searching party, the Clark brothers, saw a man enter the Dupoyster cornfield; they got their guns and fired at the fleeing figure, but without effect; he got away, but they said he was a white man or nearly so. The search continued all day without effect, save the arrest of two or three strange Negroes. A bloodhound was brought from the penitentiary and put on the trail which he followed from the scene of the murder to the crime to the river and into the boat of a fisherman named Gordon. Gordon stated that he had ferried one man and only one across the river about half past six the evening of July 5th; that his passenger sat in front of him, and he was a white man or a very bright mulatto, who could not be told from a white man. The bloodhound was put across the river in the boat, and he struck a trail again at Bird's Point on the Missouri side, ran about three hundred yards to the cottage of a white farmer named Grant and there lay down refusing to go further.

Thursday morning a brakesman on a freight train going out of Sikeston, Mo., discovered a Negro stealing a ride; he ordered him off and had hot words which terminated in a fight. The brakesman had the Negro arrested. When arrested, between 11 and 12 o'clock, he had on a dark woolen shirt, light pants and coat, and no vest. He had twelve dollars in paper, two silver dollars and ninety-five cents in change; he had also four rings in his pockets, a knife and a razor which were rusted and stained. The Sikeston authorities immediately jumped to the conclusion that this man was the murderer for whom the Kentuckians across the river were searching. They telegraphed to Bardwell that their prisoner had on no coat, but wore a blue vest and pants which would perhaps correspond with the coat found at the scene of the murder, and that the names of the murdered girls were in the rings found in his possession.

As soon as this news was received, the sheriffs of Ballard and Carlisle counties and a posse (?) of thirty well armed and determined Kentuckians, who had pledged their word the prisoner should be taken back to the scene of the supposed crime, to be executed there if proved to be the guilty man, chartered a train and at nine o'clock Thursday night started for Sikeston. Arriving there two hours later, the sheriff at Sikeston, who had no warrant for the prisoner's arrest and detention, delivered him into the hands of the mob without authority for so doing, and accompanied them to Bird's Point. The prisoner gave his name as Miller, his home at Springfield, and said he had never been in Kentucky in his life, but the sheriff turned him over to the mob to be taken to Wickliffe, that Frank Gordon, the fisherman who had put a man across the river might identify him.

In other words, the protection of the law was withdrawn from C. J. Miller, and he was given to a mob by this sheriff at Sikeston, who knew that the prisoner's life depended on one man's word. After an altercation with the trainmen, who wanted another $50 for taking the train back to Bird's Point, the crowd arrived there at three o'clock, Friday morning. Here was anchored "The Three States," a ferry boat plying between Wickliffe, Ky., Cairo, Ill., and Bird's Point, Mo. This boat left Cairo at twelve o'clock, Thursday, with nearly three hundred of Cairo's best (?) citizens and thirty kegs of beer on board. This was consumed while the crowd and the bloodhound waited for the prisoner.

When the prisoner was on board "The Three States" the dog was turned loose, and after moving aimlessly around followed the crowd to where Miller sat handcuffed and there stopped. The crowd closed in on the pair and insisted that the brute had identified him because of that action. When the boat reached Wickliffe, Gordon, the fisherman was called on to say whether the prisoner was the man he ferried over the river the day of the murder.

The sheriff of Ballard county informed him, sternly that if the prisoner was not the man, he (the fisherman) would be held responsible as knowing who the guilty man was. Gordon stated before, that the man he ferried across was a white man or a bright colored man; Miller was a dark brown skinned man, with kinky hair, "neither yellow nor black," says the Cairo Evening Telegram of Friday, July 7th. The fisherman went up to Miller from behind, looked at him without speaking for fully five minutes, then slowly said, "Yes, that's the man I crossed over." This was about six o'clock, Friday morning, and the crowd wished to hang Miller then and there. But Mr. Ray, the father of the girls, insisted that he be taken to Bardwell, the county seat of Ballard, and twelve miles inland. He said he thought a white man committed the crime, and that he was not satisfied that was the man. They took him to Bardwell and at ten o'clock, this same excited, unauthorized mob undertook to determine Miller's guilt. One of the Clark brothers who shot at a fleeing man in the Dupoyster cornfield, said the prisoner was the same man; the other said he was not, but the testimony of the first was accepted. A colored woman who had said she gave breakfast to a colored man clad in a blue flannel suit the morning of the murder, said positively that she had never seen Miller before. The gold rings found in his possession had no names in them, as had been asserted, and Mr. Ray said they did not belong to his daughters. Meantime a funeral pyre for the purpose of burning Miller to death had been erected in the center of the village. While the crowd swayed by passion was clamoring that he be burnt, Miller stepped forward and made the following statement: "My name is C. J. Miller. I am from Springfield, Ill.; my wife lives at 716 N. 2d street. I am here among you today, looked upon as one of the most brutal men before the people. I stand here surrounded by men who are excited, men who are not willing to let the law take its course, and as far as the crime is concerned, I have committed no crime, and certainly no crime as gross enough to deprive me of my life and liberty to walk upon the green earth."

A telegram was sent to the chief of the police at Springfield, Ill., asking if one C. J. Miller lived there. An answer in the negative was returned. A few hours after, it was ascertained that a man named Miller, and his wife, did live at that number the prisoner gave in his speech, but the information came to Bardwell too late to do the prisoner any good. Miller was taken to jail, every stitch of clothing literally torn from his body and examined again. On the lower left side of the bosom of his shirt was found a dark reddish spot about the size of a dime. Miller said it was paint which he had gotten on him at Jefferson Barracks. This spot was only on the right side, and could not be seen from the under side at all, thus showing it had not gone through the cloth as blood or any liquid substance would do.

Chief-of-Police Mahaney, of Cairo, Ill., was with the prisoner, and he took his knife and scraped at the spot, particles of which came off in his hand. Miller told them to take his clothes to any expert, and if the spot was shown to be blood, they might do anything they wished with him. They took his clothes away and were gone some time. After a while they were brought back and thrown into the cell without a word. It is needless to say that if the spot had been found to be blood, that fact would have been announced, and the shirt retained as evidence. Meanwhile numbers of rough, drunken men crowded into the cell and tried to force a confession of the deed from the prisoner's lips. He refused to talk save to reiterate his innocence. To Mr. Mahaney, who talked seriously and kindly to him, telling him the mob meant to burn and torture him at three o'clock, Miller said: "Burning and torture here lasts but a little while, but if I die with a lie on my soul, I shall be tortured forever. I am innocent." For more than three hours, all sorts of pressure in the way of threats, abuse and urging, was brought to bear to force him to confess to the murder and thus justify the mob in its deed of murder. Miller remained firm; but as the hour drew near, and the crowd became more impatient, he asked for a priest. As none could be procured, he then asked for a Methodist minister, who came, prayed with the doomed man, baptized him and exhorted Miller to confess. To keep up the flagging spirits of the dense crowd around the jail, the rumor went out more than once, that Miller had confessed. But the solemn assurance of the minister, chief-of-police, and leading editor who were with Miller all along—is that this rumor is absolutely false.

At three o'clock the mob rushed to the jail to secure the prisoner. Mr. Ray had changed his mind about the promised burning; he was still in doubt as to the prisoner's guilt. He again addressed the crowd to that effect, urging them not to burn Miller, and the mob heeded him so far, that they compromised on hanging instead of burning, which was agreed to by Mr. Ray. There was a loud yell, and a rush was made for the prisoner. He was stripped naked, his clothing literally torn from his body, and his shirt was tied around his loins. Some one declared the rope was a "white man's death," and a log-chain, nearly a hundred feet in length, weighing over one hundred pounds, was placed round Miller's neck and body, and he was led and dragged through the streets of the village in that condition followed by thousands of people. He fainted from exhaustion several times, but was supported to the platform where they first intended burning him.

The chain was hooked around his neck, a man climbed the telegraph pole and the other end of the chain was passed up to him and made fast to the cross-arm. Others brought a long forked stick which Miller was made to straddle. By this means he was raised several feet from the ground and then let fall. The first fall broke his neck, but he was raised in this way and let fall a second time. Numberless shots were fired into the dangling body, for most of that crowd were heavily armed, and had been drinking all day.

Miller's body hung thus exposed from three to five o'clock, during which time, several photographs of him as he hung dangling at the end of the chain were taken, and his toes and fingers were cut off. His body was taken down, placed on the platform, the torch applied, and in a few moments there was nothing left of C. J. Miller save a few bones and ashes. Thus perished another of the many victims of Lynch Law, but it is the honest and sober belief of many who witnessed the scene that an innocent man has been barbarously and shockingly put to death in the glare of the 19th century civilization, by those who profess to believe in Christianity, law and order.

CHAPTER V

Lynched, or for Anything or Nothing

(LYNCHED FOR WIFE BEATING)

In nearly all communities wife beating is punishable with a fine, and in no community is it made a felony. Dave Jackson, of Abita, La., was a colored man who had beaten his wife. He had not killed her, nor seriously wounded her, but as Louisiana lynchers had not filled out their quota of crimes, his case was deemed of sufficient importance to apply the method of that barbarous people. He was in the custody of the officials, but the mob went to the jail and took him out in front of the prison and hanged him by the neck until he was dead. This was in Nov. 1893.

HANGED FOR STEALING HOGS

Details are very meagre of a lynching which occurred near Knox Point, La., on the 24th of October, 1893. Upon one point, however, there was not uncertainty, and that is, that the persons lynched were Negroes. It was claimed that they had been stealing hogs, but even this claim had not been subjected to the investigation of a court. That matter was not considered necessary. A few of the neighbors who had lost hogs suspected these men were responsible for their loss, and made up their minds to furnish an example for others to be warned by. The two men were secured by a mob and hanged.

LYNCHED FOR NO OFFENSE

Perhaps the most characteristic feature of this record of lynch law for the year 1893, is the remarkable fact that five human beings were lynched and that the matter was considered of so little importance that the powerful press bureaus of the country did not consider the matter of enough importance to ascertain the causes for which they were hanged. It tells the world, with perhaps greater emphasis than any other feature of the record, that Lynch Law has become so common in the United States that the finding of the dead body of a Negro, suspended between heaven and earth to the limb of a tree, is of so slight importance that neither the civil authorities nor press agencies consider the matter worth investigating. July 21st, in Shelby county, Tenn., a colored man by the name of Charles Martin was lynched. July 30th, at Paris, Mo., a colored man named William Steen shared the same fate. December 28th, Mack Segars was announced to have been lynched at Brantley, Alabama. August 31st, at Yarborough, Texas, and on September 19th, at Houston, a colored man was found lynched, but so little attention was paid to the matter that not only was no record made as to why these last two men were lynched, but even their names were not given. The dispatches simply stated that an unknown Negro was found lynched in each case.

There are friends of humanity who feel their souls shrink from any compromise with murder, but whose deep and abiding reverence for womanhood causes them to hesitate in giving their support to this crusade against Lynch Law, out of fear that they may encourage the miscreants whose deeds are worse than murder. But to these friends it must appear certain that these five men could not have been guilty of any terrible crime. They were simply lynched by parties of men who had it in their power to kill them, and who chose to avenge some fancied wrong by murder, rather than submit their grievances to court.

LYNCHED BECAUSE THEY WERE SAUCY

At Moberly, Mo., February 18th and at Fort Madison, S. C., June 2d, both in 1892, a record was made in the line of lynching which should certainly appeal to every humanitarian who has any regard for the sacredness of human life. John Hughes, of Moberly, and Isaac Lincoln, of Fort Madison, and Will Lewis in Tullahoma, Tenn., suffered death for no more serious charge than that they "were saucy to white people." In the days of slavery it was held to be a very serious matter for a colored person to fail to yield the sidewalk at the demand of a white person, and it will not be surprising to find some evidence of this intolerance existing in the days of freedom. But the most that could be expected as a penalty for acting or speaking saucily to a white person would be a slight physical chastisement to make the Negro "know his place" or an arrest and fine. But Missouri, Tennessee and South Carolina chose to make precedents in their cases and as a result both men, after being charged with their offense and apprehended were taken by a mob and lynched. The civil authorities, who in either case would have been very quick to satisfy the aggrieved white people had they complained and brought the prisoners to court, by imposing proper penalty upon them, did not feel it their duty to make any investigation after the Negroes were killed. They were dead and out of the way and as no one would be called upon to render an account for their taking off, the matter was dismissed from the public mind.

LYNCHED FOR A QUARREL

One of the most notable instances of lynching for the year 1893, occurred about the 20th of September. It was notable for the fact that the mayor of the city exerted every available power to protect the victim of the lynching from the mob. In his splendid endeavor to uphold the law, the mayor called out the troops, and the result was a deadly fight between the militia and mob, nine of the mob being killed.

The trouble occurred at Roanoke, Va. It is frequently claimed that lynchings occur only in sparsely settled districts, and, in fact, it is a favorite plea of governors and reverend apologists to couple two arrant falsehoods, stating that lynchings occur only because of assaults upon white women, and that these assaults occur and the lynchings follow in thinly inhabited districts where the power of the law is entirely inadequate to meet the emergency. This Roanoke case is a double refutation, for it not only disproves the alleged charge that the Negro assaulted a white woman, as was telegraphed all over the country at the time, but it also shows conclusively that even in one of the largest cities of the old state of Virginia, one of the original thirteen colonies, which prides itself on being the mother of presidents, it was possible for a lynching to occur in broad daylight under circumstances of revolting savagery.

When the news first came from Roanoke of the contemplated lynching, it was stated that a big burly Negro had assaulted a white woman, that he had been apprehended and that the citizens were determined to summarily dispose of his case. Mayor Trout was a man who believed in maintaining the majesty of the law, and who at once gave notice that no lynching would be permitted in Roanoke, and that the Negro, whose name was Smith, being in the custody of the law, should be dealt with according to law; but the mob did not pay any attention to the brave words of the mayor. It evidently thought that it was only another case of swagger, such as frequently characterizes lynching episodes. Mayor Trout, finding immense crowds gathering about the city, and fearing an attempt to lynch Smith, called out the militia and stationed them at the jail.

It was known that the woman refused to accuse Smith of assaulting her, and that his offense consisted in quarreling with her about the change of money in a transaction in which he bought something from her market booth. Both parties lost their temper, and the result was a row from which Smith had to make his escape. At once the old cry was sounded that the woman had been assaulted, and in a few hours all the town was wild with people thirsting for the assailant's blood. The further incidents of that day may well be told by a dispatch from Roanoke under the date of the 21st of September and published in the Chicago Record. It says:

"It is claimed by members of the military company that they frequently warned the mob to keep away from the jail, under penalty of being shot. Capt. Bird told them he was under orders to protect the prisoner whose life the mob so eagerly sought, and come what may he would not allow him to be taken by the mob. To this the crowd replied with hoots and derisive jeers. The rioters appeared to become frenzied at the determined stand taken by the men and Captain Bird, and finally a crowd of excited men made a rush for the side door of the jail. The captain directed his men to drive the would-be lynchers back.

"At this moment the mob opened fire on the soldiers. This appeared for a moment to startle the captain and his men. But it was only for a moment. Then he coolly gave the command: 'Ready! aim! fire!' The company obeyed to the instant, and poured a volley of bullets into that part of the mob which was trying to batter down the side door of the jail.

"The rioters fell back before the fire of the militia, leaving one man writhing in the agonies of death at the doorstep. There was a lull for a moment. Then the word was quickly passed through the throng in front of the jail and down the street that a man was killed. Then there was an awful rush toward the little band of soldiers. Excited men were yelling like demons.

"The fight became general, and ere it was ended nine men were dead and more than forty wounded."

This stubborn stand on behalf of law and order disconcerted the crowd and it fell back in disorder. It did not long remain inactive but assembled again for a second assault. Having only a small band of militia, and knowing they would be absolutely at the mercy of the thousands who were gathering to wreak vengeance upon them, the mayor ordered them to disperse and go to their homes, and he himself, having been wounded, was quietly conveyed out of the city.

The next day the mob grew in numbers and its rage increased in its intensity. There was no longer any doubt that Smith, innocent as he was of any crime, would be killed, for with the mayor out of the city and the governor of the state using no effort to control the mob, it was only a question of a few hours when the assault would be repeated and its victim put to death. All this happened as per programme. The description of that morning's carnival appeared in the paper above quoted and reads as follows:

"A squad of twenty men took the negro Smith from three policemen just before five o'clock this morning and hanged him to a hickory limb on Ninth avenue, in the residence section of the city. They riddled his body with bullets and put a placard on it saying: 'This is Mayor Trout's friend.' A coroner's jury of Bismel was summoned and viewed the body and rendered a verdict of death at the hands of unknown men. Thousands of persons visited the scene of the lynching between daylight and eight o'clock when the body was cut down. After the jury had completed its work the body was placed in the hands of officers, who were unable to keep back the mob. Three hundred men tried to drag the body through the streets of the town, but the Rev. Dr. Campbell of the First Presbyterian church and Capt. R. B. Moorman, with pleas and by force prevented them.

"Capt. Moorman hired a wagon and the body was put in it. It was then conveyed to the bank of the Roanoke, about two miles from the scene of the lynching. Here the body was dragged from the wagon by ropes for about 200 yards and burned. Piles of dry brushwood were brought, and the body was placed upon it, and more brushwood piled on the body, leaving only the head bare. The whole pile was then saturated with coal oil and a match was applied. The body was consumed within an hour. The cremation was witnessed by several thousand people. At one time the mob threatened to burn the Negro in Mayor Trout's yard."

Thus did the people of Roanoke, Va., add this measure of proof to maintain our contention that it is only necessary to charge a Negro with a crime in order to secure his certain death. It was well known in the city before he was killed that he had not assaulted the woman with whom he had had the trouble, but he dared to have an altercation with a white woman, and he must pay the penalty. For an offense which would not in any civilized community have brought upon him a punishment greater than a fine of a few dollars, this unfortunate Negro was hung, shot and burned.

SUSPECTED, INNOCENT AND LYNCHED

Five persons, Benjamin Jackson, his wife, Mahala Jackson, his mother-in-law, Lou Carter, Rufus Bigley, were lynched near Quincy, Miss., the charge against them being suspicion of poisoning. It appears from the newspaper dispatches at that time that a family by the name of Woodruff was taken ill in September of 1892. As a result of their illness one or more of the family are said to have died, though that matter is not stated definitely. It was suspected that the cause of their illness was the existence of poison in the water, some miscreant having placed poison in the well. Suspicion pointed to a colored man named Benjamin Jackson who was at once arrested. With him also were arrested his wife and mother-in-law and all were held on the same charge.

The matter came up for judicial investigation, but as might have been expected, the white people concluded it was unnecessary to wait the result of the investigation—that it was preferable to hang the accused first and try him afterward. By this method of procedure, the desired result was always obtained—the accused was hanged. Accordingly Benjamin Jackson was taken from the officers by a crowd of about two hundred people, while the inquest was being held, and hanged. After the killing of Jackson the inquest was continued to ascertain the possible connection of the other persons charged with the crime. Against the wife and mother-in-law of the unfortunate man there was not the slightest evidence and the coroner's jury was fair enough to give them their liberty. They were declared innocent and returned to their homes. But this did not protect the women from the demands of the Christian white people of that section of the country. In any other land and with any other people, the fact that these two accused persons were women would have pleaded in their favor for protection and fair play, but that had no weight with the Mississippi Christians nor the further fact that a jury of white men had declared them innocent. The hanging of one victim on an unproven charge did not begin to satisfy the mob in its bloodthirsty demands and the result was that even after the women had been discharged, they were at once taken in charge by the mob, which hung them by the neck until they were dead.

Still the mob was not satisfied. During the coroner's investigation the name of a fourth person, Rufus Bigley, was mentioned. He was acquainted with the Jacksons and that fact, together with some testimony adduced at the inquest, prompted the mob to decide that he should die also. Search was at once made for him and the next day he was apprehended. He was not given over into the hands of the civil authorities for trial nor did the coroner's inquest find that he was guilty, but the mob was quite sufficient in itself. After finding Bigley, he was strung up a tree and his body left hanging, where it was found the next day. It may be remarked here in passing that this instance of the moral degradation of the people of Mississippi did not excite any interest in the public at large. American Christianity heard of this awful affair and read of its details and neither press nor pulpit gave the matter more than a passing comment. Had it occurred in the wilds of interior Africa, there would have been an outcry from the humane people of this country against the savagery which would so mercilessly put men and women to death. But it was an evidence of American civilization to be passed by unnoticed, to be denied or condoned as the requirements of any future emergency might determine.

LYNCHED FOR AN ATTEMPTED ASSAULT

With only a little more aggravation than that of Smith who quarreled at Roanoke with the market woman, was the assault which operated as the incentive to a most brutal lynching in Memphis, Tenn. Memphis is one of the queen cities of the south, with a population of about seventy thousand souls—easily one of the twenty largest, most progressive and wealthiest cities of the United States. And yet in its streets there occurred a scene of shocking savagery which would have disgraced the Congo. No woman was harmed, no serious indignity suffered. Two women driving to town in a wagon, were suddenly accosted by Lee Walker. He claimed that he demanded something to eat. The women claimed that he attempted to assault them. They gave such an alarm that he ran away. At once the dispatches spread over the entire country that a big, burly Negro had brutally assaulted two women. Crowds began to search for the alleged fiend. While hunting him they shot another Negro dead in his tracks for refusing to stop when ordered to do so. After a few days Lee Walker was found, and put in jail in Memphis until the mob there was ready for him.

The Memphis Commercial of Sunday, July 23, contains a full account of the tragedy from which the following extracts are made:

At 12 o'clock last night, Lee Walker, who attempted to outrage Miss Mollie McCadden, last Tuesday morning, was taken from the county jail and hanged to a telegraph pole just north of the prison. All day rumors were afloat that with nightfall an attack would be made upon the jail, and as everyone anticipated that a vigorous resistance would be made, a conflict between the mob and the authorities was feared.

At 10 o'clock Capt. O'Haver, Sergt. Horan and several patrolmen were on hand, but they could do nothing with the crowd. An attack by the mob was made on the door in the south wall, and it yielded. Sheriff McLendon and several of his men threw themselves into the breach, but two or three of the storming party shoved by. They were seized by the police but were not subdued, the officers refraining from using their clubs. The entire mob might at first have been dispersed by ten policemen who would use their clubs, but the sheriff insisted that no violence be done.

The mob got an iron rail and used it as a battering ram against the lobby doors. Sheriff McLendon tried to stop them, and some one of the mob knocked him down with a chair. Still he counseled moderation and would not order his deputies and the police to disperse the crowd by force. The pacific policy of the sheriff impressed the mob with the idea that the officers were afraid, or at least would do them no harm, and they redoubled their efforts, urged on by a big switchman. At 12 o'clock the door of the prison was broken in with a rail.

As soon as the rapist was brought out of the door calls were heard for a rope; then some one shouted, "Burn him!" But there was no time to make a fire. When Walker got into the lobby a dozen of the men began beating and stabbing him. He was half dragged, half carried to the corner of Front street and the alley between Sycamore and Mill, and hung to a telegraph pole.

Walker made a desperate resistance. Two men entered his cell first and ordered him to come forth. He refused, and they failing to drag him out, others entered. He scratched and bit his assailants, wounding several of them severely with his teeth. The mob retaliated by striking and cutting him with fists and knives. When he reached the step leading down to the door he made another stand and was stabbed again and again. By the time he reached the lobby his power to resist was gone, and he was shoved along through the mob of yelling, cursing men and boys, who beat, spat upon and slashed the wretch-like demon. One of the leaders of the mob fell, and the crowd walked ruthlessly over him. He was badly hurt—a jawbone fractured and internal injuries inflicted. After the lynching friends took charge of him.

The mob proceeded north on Front street with the victim, stopping at Sycamore street to get a rope from a grocery. "Take him to the iron bridge on Main street," yelled several men. The men who had hold of the Negro were in a hurry to finish the job, however, and when they reached the telephone pole at the corner of Front street and the first alley north of Sycamore they stopped. A hastily improvised noose was slipped over the Negro's head, and several young men mounted a pile of lumber near the pole and threw the rope over one of the iron stepping pins. The Negro was lifted up until his feet were three feet above the ground, the rope was made taut, and a corpse dangled in midair. A big fellow who helped lead the mob pulled the Negro's legs until his neck cracked. The wretch's clothes had been torn off, and, as he swung, the man who pulled his legs mutilated the corpse.

One or two knife cuts, more or less, made little difference in the appearance of the dead rapist, however, for before the rope was around his neck his skin was cut almost to ribbons. One pistol shot was fired while the corpse was hanging. A dozen voices protested against the use of firearms, and there was no more shooting. The body was permitted to hang for half an hour, then it was cut down and the rope divided among those who lingered around the scene of the tragedy. Then it was suggested that the corpse be burned, and it was done. The entire performance, from the assault on the jail to the burning of the dead Negro was witnessed by a score or so of policemen and as many deputy sheriffs, but not a hand was lifted to stop the proceedings after the jail door yielded.

As the body hung to the telegraph pole, blood streaming down from the knife wounds in his neck, his hips and lower part of his legs also slashed with knives, the crowd hurled expletives at him, swung the body so that it was dashed against the pole, and, so far from the ghastly sight proving trying to the nerves, the crowd looked on with complaisance, if not real pleasure. The Negro died hard. The neck was not broken, as the body was drawn up without being given a fall, and death came by strangulation. For fully ten minutes after he was strung up the chest heaved occasionally, and there were convulsive movements of the limbs. Finally he was pronounced dead, and a few minutes later Detective Richardson climbed on a pile of staves and cut the rope. The body fell in a ghastly heap, and the crowd laughed at the sound and crowded around the prostrate body, a few kicking the inanimate carcass.

Detective Richardson, who is also a deputy coroner, then proceeded to impanel the following jury of inquest: J. S. Moody, A. C. Waldran, B. J. Childs, J. N. House, Nelson Bills, T. L. Smith, and A. Newhouse. After viewing the body the inquest was adjourned without any testimony being taken until 9 o'clock this morning. The jury will meet at the coroner's office, 51 Beale street, up stairs, and decide on a verdict. If no witnesses are forthcoming, the jury will be able to arrive at a verdict just the same, as all members of it saw the lynching. Then some one raised the cry of "Burn him!" It was quickly taken up and soon resounded from a hundred throats. Detective Richardson, for a long time, single-handed, stood the crowd off. He talked and begged the men not to bring disgrace on the city by burning the body, arguing that all the vengeance possible had been wrought.

While this was going on a small crowd was busy starting a fire in the middle of the street. The material was handy. Some bundles of staves were taken from the adjoining lumber yard for kindling. Heavier wood was obtained from the same source and coal oil from a neighboring grocery. Then the cries of "Burn him! Burn him!" were redoubled.

Half a dozen men seized the naked body. The crowd cheered. They marched to the fire, and giving the body a swing, it was landed in the middle of the fire. There was a cry for more wood, as the fire had begun to die owing to the long delay. Willing hands procured the wood, and it was piled up on the Negro, almost, for a time, obscuring him from view. The head was in plain view, as also were the limbs, and one arm which stood out high above the body, the elbow crooked, held in that position by a stick of wood. In a few moments the hands began to swell, then came great blisters over all the exposed parts of the body; then in places the flesh was burned away and the bones began to show through. It was a horrible sight, one which, perhaps, none there had ever witnessed before. It proved too much for a large part of the crowd and the majority of the mob left very shortly after the burning began.

But a large number stayed, and were not a bit set back by the sight of a human body being burned to ashes. Two or three white women, accompanied by their escorts, pushed to the front to obtain an unobstructed view, and looked on with astonishing coolness and nonchalance. One man and woman brought a little girl, not over 12 years old, apparently their daughter, to view a scene which was calculated to drive sleep from the child's eyes for many nights, if not to produce a permanent injury to her nervous system. The comments of the crowd were varied. Some remarked on the efficacy of this style of cure for rapists, others rejoiced that men's wives and daughters were now safe from this wretch. Some laughed as the flesh cracked and blistered, and while a large number pronounced the burning of a dead body as a useless episode, not in all that throng was a word of sympathy heard for the wretch himself.

The rope that was used to hang the Negro, and also that which was used to lead him from the jail, were eagerly sought by relic hunters.[5] They almost fought for a chance to cut off a piece of the rope, and in an incredibly short time both ropes had disappeared and were scattered in the pockets of the crowd in sections of from an inch to six inches long. Others of the relic hunters remained until the ashes cooled to obtain such ghastly relics as the teeth, nails, and bits of charred skin of the immolated victim of his own lust. After burning the body the mob tied a rope around the charred trunk and dragged it down Main street to the court house, where it was hanged to a center pole. The rope broke and the corpse dropped with a thud, but it was again hoisted, the charred legs barely touching the ground. The teeth were knocked out and the finger nails cut off as souvenirs. The crowd made so much noise that the police interfered. Undertaker Walsh was telephoned for, who took charge of the body and carried it to his establishment, where it will be prepared for burial in the potter's field today.

A prelude to this exhibition of 19th century barbarism was the following telegram received by the Chicago Inter Ocean, at 2 o'clock, Saturday afternoon—ten hours before the lynching.

"MEMPHIS, TENN., July 22, To Inter-Ocean, Chicago.

"Lee Walker, colored man, accused of raping white women, in jail here, will be taken out and burned by whites to-night. Can you send Miss Ida Wells to write it up? Answer. R. M. Martin, with Public Ledger."

The Public Ledger is one of the oldest evening daily papers in Memphis, and this telegram shows that the intentions of the mob were well known long before they were executed. The personnel of the mob is given by the Memphis Appeal-Avalanche. It says, "At first it seemed as if a crowd of roughs were the principals, but as it increased in size, men in all walks of life figured as leaders, although the majority were young men."

This was the punishment meted out to a Negro, charged not with rape, but attempted assault, and without any proof as to his guilt, for the women were not given a chance to identify him. It was only a little less horrible than the burning alive of Henry Smith, at Paris, Texas, February 1st, 1893, or that of Edward Coy, in Texarkana, Texas, February 20, 1892. Both were charged with assault on white women, and both were tied to the stake and burned while yet alive, in the presence of ten thousand persons. In the case of Coy, the white woman in the case, applied the match, even while the victim protested his innocence.

The cut which is here given is the exact reproduction of the photograph taken at the scene of the lynching at Clanton, Alabama, August, 1891. The cause for which the man was hanged is given in the words of the mob which were written on the back of the photograph, and they are also given. This photograph as sent to Judge A. W. Tourgee of Mayville, N. Y.

In some of these cases the mob affects to believe in the Negro's guilt. The world is told that the white woman in the case identifies him, or the prisoner "confesses." But in the lynching which took place in Barnwell County, South Carolina, April 24, 1893, the mob's victim, John Peterson, escaped and placed himself under Governor Tillman's protection; not only did he declare his innocence, but offered to provide an alibi, by white witnesses. Before his witnesses could be brought, the mob arrived at the Governor's mansion and demanded the prisoner. He was given up, and although the white woman in the case said he was not the man, he was hanged 24 hours after, and over a thousand bullets fired into his body, on the declaration that "a crime had been committed and some one had to hang for it."

CHAPTER VI

History of Some Cases of Rape

It has been claimed that the Southern white women have been slandered because, in defending the Negro race from the charge that all colored men, who are lynched, only pay penalty for assaulting women. It is certain that lynching mobs have not only refused to give the Negro a chance to defend himself, but have killed their victim with a full knowledge that the relationship of the alleged assailant with the woman who accused him, was voluntary and clandestine. As a matter of fact, one of the prime causes of the Lynch Law agitation has been a necessity for defending the Negro from this awful charge against him. This defense has been necessary because the apologists for outlawry insist that in no case has the accusing woman been a willing consort of her paramour, who is lynched because overtaken in wrong. It is well known, however, that such is the case. In July of this year, 1894, John Paul Bocock, a Southern white man living in New York, and assistant editor of the New York Tribune, took occasion to defy the publication of any instance where the lynched Negro was the victim of a white woman's falsehood. Such cases are not rare, but the press and people conversant with the facts almost invariably suppress them.

The New York Sun of July 30th, 1894, contained a synopsis of interviews with leading congressmen and editors in the South. Speaker Crisp, of the House of Representatives, who was recently a Judge of the Supreme Court of Georgia, led in declaring that lynching seldom or never took place, save for the vile crime against women and children. Dr. Hoss, editor of the leading organ of the Methodist Church South, published in its columns that it was his belief that more than three hundred women had been assaulted by Negro men within three months. When asked to prove his charges, or give a single case upon which his "belief" was founded, he said he could do so, but the details were unfit for publication. No other evidence but his "belief" could be adduced to substantiate this grave charge, yet Bishop Haygood, in the Forum of October 1893, quotes this "belief" in apology for lynching, and voluntarily adds: "It is my opinion that this is an underestimate." The "opinion" of this man, based upon a "belief," had greater weight coming from a man who had posed as a friend to "Our Brother in Black," and was accepted as authority. An interview of Miss Frances E. Willard, the great apostle of temperance, the daughter of abolitionists and a personal friend and helper of many individual colored people, has been quoted in support of the utterance of this calumny against a weak and defenseless race. In the New York Voice of October 23, 1890, after a tour in the South, where she was told all these things by the "best white people," she said: "The grogshop is the Negro's center of power. Better whisky and more of it is the rallying cry of great, dark-faced mobs. The colored race multiplies like the locusts of Egypt. The grogshop[6] is its center of power. The safety of woman, of childhood, the house, is menaced in a thousand localities at this moment, so that men dare not go beyond the sight of their own roof-tree."

These charges so often reiterated, have had the effect of fastening the odium upon the race of a peculiar propensity for this foul crime. The Negro is thus forced to a defense of his good name, and this chapter will be devoted to the history of some of the cases where assault upon white women by Negroes is charged. He is not the aggressor in this fight, but the situation demands that the facts be given, and they will speak for themselves. Of the 1,115 Negro men, women and children hanged, shot and roasted alive from January 1st, 1882, to January 1st, 1894, inclusive, only 348 of that number were charged with rape. Nearly 500 of these persons were lynched for any other reason which could be manufactured by a mob wishing to indulge in a lynching bee.

A WHITE WOMAN'S FALSEHOOD

The Cleveland, Ohio, Gazette, January 16, 1892, gives an account of one of these cases of "rape."

Mrs. J. C. Underwood, the wife of a minister of Elyria, Ohio, accused an Afro-American of rape. She told her husband that during his absence in 1888, stumping the state for the Prohibition Party, the man came to the kitchen door, forced his way in the house and insulted her. She tried to drive him out with a heavy poker, but he overpowered and chloroformed her, and when she revived her clothing was torn and she was in a horrible condition. She did not know the man, but could identify him. She subsequently pointed out William Offett, a married man, who was arrested, and, being in Ohio, was granted a trial.

The prisoner vehemently denied the charge of rape, but confessed he went to Mrs. Underwood's residence at her invitation and was criminally intimate with her at her request. This availed him nothing against the sworn testimony of a minister's wife, a lady of the highest respectability. He was found guilty, and entered the penitentiary, December 14, 1888, for fifteen years. Sometime afterwards the woman's remorse led her to confess to her husband that the man was innocent. These are her words: "I met Offett at the post office. It was raining. He was polite to me, and as I had several bundles in my arms he offered to carry them home for me, which he did. He had a strange fascination for me, and I invited him to call on me. He called, bringing chestnuts and candy for the children. By this means we got them to leave us alone in the room. Then I sat on his lap. He made a proposal to me and I readily consented. Why I did so I do not know, but that I did is true. He visited me several times after that and each time I was indiscreet. I did not care after the first time. In fact I could not have resisted, and had no desire to resist."

When asked by her husband why she told him she had been outraged, she said: "I had several reasons for telling you. One was the neighbors saw the fellow here, another was, I was afraid I had contracted a loathsome disease, and still another was that I feared I might give birth to a Negro baby. I hoped to save my reputation by telling you a deliberate lie." Her husband, horrified by the confession, had Offett, who had already served four years, released and secured a divorce.

There have been many such cases throughout the South, with the difference that the Southern white men in insensate fury wreak their vengeance without intervention of law upon the Negro who consorts with their women.

TRIED TO MANUFACTURE AN OUTRAGE

The Memphis (Tenn.) Ledger, of June 8, 1892, has the following: "If Lillie Bailey, a rather pretty white girl, seventeen years of age, who is now at the city hospital, would be somewhat less reserved about her disgrace there would be some very nauseating details in the story of her life. She is the mother of a little coon. The truth might reveal fearful depravity or the evidence of a rank outrage. She will not divulge the name of the man who has left such black evidence of her disgrace, and in fact says it is a matter in which there can be no interest to the outside world. She came to Memphis nearly three months ago, and was taken in at the Woman's Refuge in the southern part of the city. She remained there until a few weeks ago when the child was born. The ladies in charge of the Refuge were horrified. The girl was at once sent to the city hospital, where she has been since May 30th. She is a country girl. She came to Memphis from her father's farm, a short distance from Hernando, Miss. Just when she left there she would not say. In fact she says she came to Memphis from Arkansas, and says her home is in that state. She is rather good looking, has blue eyes, a low forehead and dark red hair. The ladies at the Woman's Refuge do not know anything about the girl further than what they learned when she was an inmate of the institution; and she would not tell much. When the child was born an attempt was made to get the girl to reveal the name of the Negro who had disgraced her, she obstinately refused and it was impossible to elicit any information from her on the subject."

Note the wording: "The truth might reveal fearful depravity or rank outrage." If it had been a white child or if Lillie Bailey had told a pitiful story of Negro outrage, it would have been a case of woman's weakness or assault and she could have remained at the Woman's Refuge. But a Negro child and to withhold its father's name and thus prevent the killing of another Negro "rapist" was a case of "fearful depravity." Had she revealed the father's name, he would have been lynched and his taking off charged to an assault upon a white woman.

BURNED ALIVE FOR ADULTERY

In Texarkana, Arkansas, Edward Coy was accused of assaulting a white woman. The press dispatches of February 18, 1892, told in detail how he was tied to a tree, the flesh cut from his body by men and boys, and after coal oil was poured over him, the woman he had assaulted gladly set fire to him, and 15,000 persons saw him burn to death. October 1st, the Chicago Inter Ocean contained the following account of that horror from the pen of the "Bystander"—Judge Albion W. Tourgee—as a result of his investigations:

> "1. The woman who was paraded as victim of violence was of bad character; her husband was a drunkard and a gambler.
> "2. She was publicly reported and generally known to have been criminally intimate with Coy for more than a year previous.
> "3. She was compelled by threats, if not by violence, to make the charge against the victim.
> "4. When she came to apply the match Coy asked her if she would burn him after they had 'been sweethearting' so long.
> "5. A large majority of the 'superior' white men prominent in the affair are the reputed fathers of mulatto children.

"These are not pleasant facts, but they are illustrative of the vital phase of the so-called 'race question,' which should properly be designated an earnest inquiry as to the best methods by white religion, science, law and political power may be employed to excuse injustice, barbarity and crime done to a people because of race and color. There can be no possible belief that these people were inspired by any consuming zeal to vindicate God's law against miscegenationists of the most practical sort. The woman was a willing partner in the victim's guilt, and being of the 'superior race' must naturally have been more guilty."

NOT IDENTIFIED BUT LYNCHED

February 11, 1893, there occurred in Shelby county, Tennessee, the fourth Negro lynching within fifteen months. The three first were lynched in the city of Memphis for firing on white men in self-defense. This Negro, Richard Neal, was lynched a few miles from the city limits, and the following is taken from the Memphis (Tenn.) Scimitar:

"As the Scimitar stated on Saturday the Negro, Richard Neal, who raped Mrs. Jack White near Forest Hill, in this county, was lynched by a mob of about 200 white citizens of the neighborhood. Sheriff McLendon, accompanied by Deputies Perkins, App, and Harvey and a Scimitar reporter, arrived on the scene of the execution about 3:30 in the afternoon. The body was suspended from the first limb of a post oak tree by a new quarter inch grass rope. A hangman's knot, evidently tied by an expert, and fitted snugly under the left ear of the corpse, and a new hame string pinioned the victim's arms behind him. His legs were not tied. The body was perfectly limber when the Sheriff's posse cut it down and retained enough heat to warm the feet of Deputy Perkins, whose road cart was converted into a hearse. On arriving with the body at Forest Hill the Sheriff made a bargain with a stalwart round man with a blonde moustache and deep blue eyes, who told the Scimitar reporter that he was the leader of the mob, to haul the body to Germantown for $3.

"When within half-a-mile of Germantown the Sheriff and posse were overtaken by Squire McDonald of Collierville, who had come down to hold the inquest. The Squire had his jury with him, and it was agreed for the convenience of all parties that he should proceed with the corpse to Germantown and conduct the inquiry as to the cause of death. He did so, and a verdict of death from hanging by parties unknown was returned in due form.

"The execution of Neal was done deliberately and by the best people of the Collierville, Germantown and Forest Hill neighborhoods, without passion or exhibition of anger.

"He was arrested on Friday about ten o'clock, by Constable Bob Cash, who carried him before Mrs. White. She said: "I think he is the man. I am almost certain of it. If he isn't the man he is exactly like him.'

"The Negro's coat was torn also, and there were other circum-

stances against him. The committee returned and made its report, and the chairman put the question of guilt or innocence to
a vote.

"All who thought the proof strong enough to warrant execution were invited to cross over to the other side of the road.
Everybody but four or five negroes crossed over.

"The committee then placed Neal on a mule with his arms tied
behind him, and proceeded to the scene of the crime, followed by
the mob. The rope, with a noose already prepared, was tied to the
limb nearest the spot where the unpardonable sin was committed,
and the doomed man's mule was brought to a standstill beneath it.

"Then Neal confessed. He said he was the right man, but denied that he used force or threats to accomplish his purpose. It
was a matter of purchase, he claimed, and said the price paid was
twenty-five cents. He warned the colored men present to beware
of white women and resist temptation, for to yield to their blan-
dishments or to the passions of men, meant death.

"While he was speaking, Mrs. White came from her home and
calling Constable Cash to one side, asked if he could not save the
Negro's life. The reply was, 'No,' and Mrs. White returned to the
house.

"When all was in readiness, the husband of Neal's victim
leaped upon the mule's back and adjusted the rope around the
Negro's neck. No cap was used, and Neal showed no fear, nor
did he beg for mercy. The mule was struck with a whip and
bounded out from under Neal, leaving him suspended in the air
with his feet about three feet from the ground."

DELIVERED TO THE MOB BY THE GOVERNOR OF THE STATE

John Peterson, near Denmark, S. C. was suspected of rape, but
escaped, went to Columbia, and placed himself under Gov.
Tillman's protection, declaring he too could prove an alibi by
white witnesses. A white reporter hearing his declaration volunteered to find these witnesses, and telegraphed the governor that
he would be in Columbia with them on Monday. In the meantime the mob at Denmark, learning Peterson's whereabouts, went
to the governor and demanded the prisoner. Gov. Tillman, who

had during his canvass for re-election the year before, declared that he would lead a mob to lynch a Negro that assaulted a white woman, gave Peterson up to the mob. He was taken back to Denmark, and the white girl in the case as positively declared that he was not the man. But the verdict of the mob was that "the crime had been committed and somebody had to hang for it, and if he, Peterson, was not guilty of that he was of some other crime," and he was hung, and his body riddled with 1,000 bullets.

LYNCHED AS A WARNING

Alabama furnishes a case in point. A colored man named Daniel Edwards lived near Selma, Alabama, and worked for a family of a farmer near that place. This resulted in an intimacy between the young man and a daughter of the householder, which finally developed in the disgrace of the girl. After the birth of the child, the mother disclosed the fact that Edwards was its father. The relationship had been sustained for more than a year, and yet this colored man was apprehended, thrown into jail from whence he was taken by a mob of one hundred neighbors and hung to a tree and his body riddled with bullets. A dispatch which describes the lynching, ends as follows. "Upon his back was found pinned this morning the following: 'Warning to all Negroes that are too intimate with white girls. This the work of one hundred best citizens of the South Side.'"

There can be no doubt from the announcement made by this "one hundred best citizens" that they understood full well the character of the relationship which existed between Edwards and the girl, but when the dispatches were sent, describing the affair, it was claimed that Edwards was lynched for rape.

SUPPRESSING THE TRUTH

In a county in Mississippi during the month of July the Associated Press dispatches sent out a report that the sheriff's eight year old daughter had been assaulted by a big, black, burly brute who had been promptly lynched. The facts which have since been investigated show that the girl was more than eighteen years old and that she was discovered by her father in this young man's room who was a servant on the place. But these facts the Associated Press has not given to the world, nor did the same agency acquaint the world with the fact that a Negro youth who was lynched in Tuscumbia, Ala., the same year on the same charge told the white girl who accused him before the mob, that he had met her in the woods often by appointment. There is a young mulatto in one of the State prisons of the South to-day who is there by charge of a young white woman to screen herself. He is a college graduate and had been corresponding with, and clandestinely visiting her until he was surprised and run out of her room en deshabille by her father. He was put in prison in another town to save his life from the mob and his lawyer advised that it were better to save his life by pleading guilty to charges made and being sentenced for years, than to attempt a defense by exhibiting the letters written him by this girl. In the latter event, the mob would surely murder him, while there was a chance for his life by adopting the former course. Names, places and dates are not given for the same reason.

The excuse has come to be so safe, it is not surprising that a Philadelphia girl, beautiful and well educated, and of good family, should make a confession published in all the daily papers of that city October, 1894, that she had been stealing for some time, and that to cover one of her thefts, she had said she had been bound and gagged in her father's house by a colored man, and money stolen therefrom by him. Had this been done in many localities, it would only have been necessary for her to "identify" the first Negro in that vicinity, to have brought about another lynching bee.

A VILE SLANDER WITH
SCANT RETRACTION

The following published in the Cleveland (Ohio) Leader of Oct. 23d, 1894, only emphasizes our demand that a fair trial shall be given those accused of crime, and the protection of the law be extended until time for a defense be granted.

"The sensational story sent out last night from Hicksville that a Negro had outraged a little four-year-old girl proves to be a base canard. The correspondents who went into the details should have taken the pains to investigate, and the officials should have known more of the matter before they gave out such grossly exaggerated information.

"The Negro, Charles O'Neil, had been working for a couple of women and, it seems, had worked all winter without being remunerated. There is a little girl, and the girl's mother and grandmother evidently started the story with the idea of frightening the Negro out of the country and thus balancing accounts. The town was considerably wrought up and for a time things looked serious. The accused had a preliminary hearing to-day and not an iota of evidence was produced to indicate that such a crime had been committed, or that he had even attempted such an outrage. The village marshal was frightened nearly out of his wits and did little to quiet the excitement last night.

'The affair was an outrage on the Negro, at the expense of innocent childhood, a brainless fabrication from start to finish.'"

The original story was sent throughout this country and England, but the Cleveland Leader, so far as known, is the only journal which has published these facts in refutation of the slander so often published against the race.

Not only is it true that many of the alleged cases of rape against the Negro, are like the foregoing, but the same crime committed by white men against Negro women and girls, is never punished by mob or the law. A leading journal in South Carolina openly said some months ago that "it is not the same thing for a white man to assault a colored woman as for a colored man to assault a white woman, because the colored woman had no finer feelings nor virtue to be outraged!" Yet colored women have always had far more reason to complain of white men in this respect than ever white women have had of Negroes.

ILLINOIS HAS A LYNCHING

In the month of June, 1893, the proud commonwealth of Illinois joined the ranks of Lynching States. Illinois, which gave to the world the immortal heroes, Lincoln, Grant and Logan, trailed its banner of justice in the dust—dyed its hands red in the blood of a man not proven guilty of crime.

June 3, 1893, the country about Decatur, one of the largest cities of the state was startled with a cry that a white woman had been assaulted by a colored tramp. Three days later a colored man named Samuel Bush was arrested and put in jail. A white man testified that Bush, on the day of the assault, asked him where he could get a drink and he pointed to the house where the farmer's wife was subsequently said to have been assaulted. Bush said he went to the well but did not go near the house, and did not assault the woman. After he was arrested the alleged victim did not see him to identify him—he was presumed to be guilty.

The citizens determined to kill him. The mob gathered, went to the jail, met with no resistance, took the suspected man, dragged him out tearing every stitch of clothing from his body, then hanged him to a telegraph pole. The grand jury refused to indict the lynchers though the names of over twenty persons who were leaders in the mob were well known. In fact twenty-two persons were indicted, but the grand jurors and the prosecuting attorney disagreed as to the form of the indictments, which caused the jurors to change their minds. All indictments were reconsidered and the matter was dropped. Not one of the dozens of men prominent in that murder have suffered a whit more inconvenience for the butchery of that man, than they would have suffered for shooting a dog.

COLOR LINE JUSTICE

In Baltimore, Maryland, a gang of white ruffians assaulted a respectable colored girl who was out walking with a young man of her own race. They held her escort and outraged the girl. It was a deed dastardly enough to arouse Southern blood, which gives its horror of rape as excuse for lawlessness, but she was a colored woman. The case went to the courts and they were acquitted.

In Nashville, Tennessee, there was a white man, Pat Hanifan, who outraged a little colored girl, and from the physical injuries received she was ruined for life. He was jailed for six months, discharged, and is now a detective in that city. In the same city, last May, a white man outraged a colored girl in a drug store. He was arrested and released on bail at the trial. It was rumored that five hundred colored men had organized to lynch him. Two hundred and fifty white citizens armed themselves with Winchesters and guarded him. A cannon was placed in front of his home, and the Buchanan Rifles (State Militia) ordered to the scene for his protection. The colored mob did not show up. Only two weeks before, Eph. Grizzard, who had only been charged with rape upon a white woman, had been taken from the jail, with Governor Buchanan and the police and militia standing by, dragged through the streets in broad daylight, knives plunged into him at every step—and with every fiendish cruelty that a frenzied mob could devise, he was at last swung out on the bridge with hands cut to pieces as he tried to climb up the stanchions. A naked, bloody example of the bloodthirstiness of the nineteenth century civilization of the Athens of the South![7] No cannon nor military were called out in his defense. He dared to visit a white woman.

At the very moment when these civilized whites were announcing their determination "to protect their wives and daughters," by murdering Grizzard, a white man was in the same jail for raping eight-year-old Maggie Reese, a colored girl. He was not harmed. The "honor" of grown women who were glad enough to be supported by the Grizzard boy and Ed Coy, as long as the liaison was not known, needed protection; they were white. The outrage upon helpless childhood needed no avenging in this case; she was black.

A white man in Guthrie, Oklahoma Territory, two months after inflicted such injuries upon another colored girl that she died. He was not punished, but an attempt was made in the same town in the month of June to lynch a colored man who visited a white woman.

In Memphis, Tennessee, in the month of June, Ellerton L. Dorr, who is the husband of Russell Hancock's widow, was arrested for attempted rape on Mattie Cole, a neighbor's cook; he was only prevented from accomplishing his purpose by the appearance of Mattie's employer. Dorr's friends say he was drunk and not responsible for his actions. The grand jury refused to indict him and he was discharged.

In Tallahassee, Florida, a colored girl, Charlotte Gilliam, was assaulted by white men. Her father went to have a warrant for their arrest issued, but the judge refused to issue it.

In Bowling Green, Virginia, Mosses Christopher, a colored lad, was charged with assault, September 10. He was indicted, tried, convicted and sentenced to death in one day. In the same state at Danville, two weeks before August 29, Thomas J. Penn a white man, committed a criminal assault upon Lina Hanna, a twelve-year-old colored girl, but he has not been tried, certainly not killed either by the law or the mob.

In Surrey county, Virginia, C. L. Brock, a white man, criminally assaulted a ten-year-old colored girl, and threatened to kill her if she told. Notwithstanding, she confessed to her aunt, Mrs. Alice Bates, and the white brute added further crime by killing Mrs. Bates when she upbraided him about his crime to her niece. He emptied the contents of his revolver into her body as she lay. Brock has never been apprehended, and no effort has been made to do so by the legal authorities.

But even when punishment is meted out by law to white villains for this horrible crime, it is seldom or never that capital punishment is invoked. Two cases just clipped from the daily papers will suffice to show how this crime is punished when committed by white offenders and black.

LOUISVILLE, KY., October 19.—Smith Young, colored, was to-day sentenced to be hanged. Young criminally assaulted a six-year-old child about six months ago.

Jacques Blucher, the Pontiac Frenchman who was arrested at that place for a criminal assault on his daughter Fanny on July 29 last, pleaded nolo contendere when placed on trial at East Greenwich, near Providence, R. I., Tuesday, and was sentenced to five years in State Prison.

Charles Wilson was convicted of assault upon seven-year-old Mamie Keys in Philadelphia, in October, and sentenced to ten years in prison. He was white. Indianapolis courts sentenced a white man in September to eight years in prison for assault upon a twelve-year old white girl.

April 24, 1893, a lynching was set for Denmark, S. C., on the charge of rape. A white girl accused a Negro of assault, and the mob was about to lynch him. A few hours before the lynching three reputable white men rode into the town and solemnly testified that the accused Negro was at work with them 25 miles away on the day and at the hour the crime had been committed. He was accordingly set free. A white person's word is taken as absolutely for as against a Negro.

CHAPTER VII

The Crusade Justified

(APPEAL FROM AMERICA
TO THE WORLD)

It has been urged in criticism of the movement appealing to the English people for sympathy and support in our crusade against Lynch Law that our action was unpatriotic, vindictive and useless. It is not a part of the plan of this pamphlet to make any defense for that crusade nor to indict any apology for the motives which led to the presentation of the facts of American lynchings to the world at large. To those who are not willfully blind and unjustly critical, the record of more than a thousand lynchings in ten years is enough to justify any peaceable movement tending to ameliorate the conditions which led to this unprecedented slaughter of human beings.

If America would not hear the cry of men, women and children whose dying groans ascended to heaven praying for relief, not only for them but for others who might soon be treated as they, then certainly no fair-minded person can charge disloyalty to those who make an appeal to the civilization of the world for such sympathy and help as it is possible to extend. If stating the facts of these lynchings, as they appeared from time to time in the white newspapers of America—the news gathered by white correspondents, compiled by white press bureaus and disseminated among white people—shows any vindictiveness, then the mind which so charges is not amenable to argument.

But it is the desire of this pamphlet to urge that the crusade started and thus far continued has not been useless, but has been blessed with the most salutary results. The many evidences of the good results can not here be mentioned, but the thoughtful student to the situation can himself find ample proof. There need not here be mentioned the fact that for the first time since lynching began, has there been any occasion for the governors of the several states to speak out in reference to these crimes against law and order.

No matter how heinous the act of lynchers may have been, it was discussed only for a day or so and then dismissed from the

attention of the public. In one or two instances the governor has
called attention to the crime, but the civil processes entirely failed
to bring the murderers to justice. Since the crusade against lynching was started, however, governors of states, newspapers, senators and representatives and bishops of churches have all been
compelled to take cognizance of the prevalence of this crime and
to speak in one way or another in the defense of the charge
against this barbarism in the United States. This has not been
because the entire American people now feel, both North and
South, that they are objects in the gaze of the civilized world and
that for every lynching humanity asks that America render its
account to civilization and itself.

AWFUL BARBARISM IGNORED

Much has been said during the months of September and October
of 1894 about the lynching of six colored men who on suspicion
of incendiarism were made the victims of a most barbarous massacre. They were arrested, one by one, by officers of the law; they
were handcuffed and chained together and by the officers of the
law loaded in a wagon and deliberately driven into an ambush
where a mob of lynchers awaited them. At the time and upon the
chosen spot, in the darkness of the night and far removed from
the habitation of any human soul, the wagon was halted and the
mob fired upon the six manacled men, shooting them to death as
no humane person would have shot dogs. Chained together as
they were, in their awful struggles after the first volley, the victims tumbled out of the wagon upon the ground and there in the
mud, struggling in their death throes, the victims were made the
target of the murderous shotguns, which fired into the writhing,
struggling, dying mass of humanity, until every spark of life was
gone. Then the officers of the law who had them in charge, drove
away to give the alarm and to tell the world that they had been
waylaid and their prisoners forcibly taken from them and killed.

It has been claimed that the prompt, vigorous and highly com-
mendable steps of the governor of the State of Tennessee and the
judge having jurisdiction over the crime, and of the citizens of
Memphis generally, was the natural revolt of the humane conscience in that section of the country, and the determination of

honest and honorable men to rid the community of such men as those who were guilty of this terrible massacre. It has further been claimed that this vigorous uprising of the people and this most commendably prompt action of the civil authorities, is ample proof that the American people will not tolerate the lynching of innocent men, and that in cases where brutal lynchings have not been promptly dealt with, the crimes on the part of the victims were such as to put them outside the pale of humanity and that the world considered their death a necessary sacrifice for the good of all.

But this line of argument can in no possible way be truthfully sustained. The lynching of the six men in 1894, barbarous as it was, was in no way more barbarous than took nothing more than a passing notice. It was only the other lynchings which preceded it, and of which the public fact that the attention of the civilized world has been called to lynching in America which made the people of Tennessee feel the absolute necessity for a prompt, vigorous and just arraignment of all the murderers connected with that crime. Lynching is no longer "Our Problem," it is the problem of the civilized world, and Tennessee could not afford to refuse the legal measures which Christianity demands shall be used for the punishment of crime.

MEMPHIS THEN AND NOW

Only two years prior to the massacre of the six men near Memphis, that same city took part in a massacre in every way as bloody and brutal as that of September last. It was the murder of three young colored men and who were known to be among the most honorable, reliable, worthy and peaceable colored citizens of the community. All of them were engaged in the mercantile business, being members of a corporation which conducted a large grocery store, and one of the three being a letter carrier in the employ of the government. These three men were arrested for resisting an attack of a mob upon their store, in which melee none of the assailants, who had armed themselves for their devilish deeds by securing court processes, were killed or even seriously injured. But these three men were put in jail, and on three or four nights after their incarceration a mob of less than a dozen men, by collusion with the civil authorities, entered the jail, took the three men from the custody of the law and shot them to death. Memphis knew of this awful crime, knew then and knows today who the men were who committed it, and yet not the first step was ever taken to apprehend the guilty wretches who walk the streets today with the brand of murder upon their foreheads, but as safe from harm as the most upright citizen of that community. Memphis would have been just as calm and complacent and self-satisfied over the murder of the six colored men in 1894 as it was over these three colored men in 1892, had it not recognized the fact that to escape the brand of barbarism it had not only to speak its denunciation but to act vigorously in vindication of its name.

AN ALABAMA HORROR IGNORED

A further instance of this absolute disregard of every principle of justice and the indifference to the barbarism of Lynch Law may be cited here, and is furnished by white residents in the city of Carrolton, Alabama. Several cases of arson had been discovered, and in their search for the guilty parties, suspicion was found to rest upon three men and a woman. The four suspects were Paul Hill, Paul Archer, William Archer, his brother, and a woman named Emma Fair. The prisoners were apprehended, earnestly asserted their innocence, but went to jail without making any resistance. They claimed that they could easily prove their innocence upon trial.

One would suspect that the civilization which defends itself against the barbarisms of the Lynch Law by stating that it lynches human beings only when they are guilty of awful attacks upon women and children, would have been careful to have given these four prisoners, who were simply charged with arson, a fair trial, to which they were entitled upon every principle of law and humanity. Especially would this seem to be the case when it is considered that one of the prisoners charged was a woman, and if the Nineteenth Century has shown any advancement upon any lines of human action, it is pre-eminently shown in its reverence, respect and protection of its womanhood. But the people of Alabama failed to have any regard for womanhood whatever.

The three men and the woman were put in jail to await trial. A few days later it was rumored that they were to be the subjects of Lynch Law, and sure enough, at night a mob of lynchers went to the jail, not to avenge any awful crime against womanhood, but to kill four people who had been suspected of setting a house on fire. They were caged in their cells, helpless and defenseless; they were at the mercy of civilized white Americans, who, armed with shotguns, were there to maintain the majesty of American law. And most effectively was their duty done by these splendid representatives of Governor Fishback's brave and honorable white southerners, who resent "outside interference." They line themselves up in the most effective manner and poured volley after volley into the bodies of their helpless, pleading victims, who in their bolted prison cells could do nothing but suffer and die. Then these lynchers went quietly away and the bodies of the woman and three men were taken out and buried with as little ceremony as men would bury hogs.

No one will say that the massacre near Memphis in 1894 was any worse than this bloody crime of Alabama in 1892. The details of this shocking affair were given to the public by the press, but public sentiment was not moved to action in the least; it was only a matter of a day's notice and then went to swell the list of murders which stand charged against the noble, Christian people of Alabama.

AMERICA AWAKENED

But there is now an awakened conscience throughout the land, and Lynch Law can not flourish in the future as it has in the past. The close of the year 1894 witnessed an aroused interest, an assertive humane principle which must tend to the extirpation of that crime. The awful butchery last mentioned failed to excite more than a passing comment in 1894, but far different is it today. Gov. Jones, of Alabama, in 1893 dared to speak out against the rule of the mob in no uncertain terms. His address indicated a most helpful result of the present agitation. In face of the many denials of the outrages on the one hand and apologies for lynchers on the other, Gov. Jones admits the awful lawlessness charged and refuses to join in the infamous plea made to

condone the crime. No stronger nor more effective words have
been said than those following from Gov. Jones.

"While the ability of the state to deal with open revolts against
the supremacy of its laws has been ably demonstrated, I regret
that deplorable acts of violence have been perpetrated, in at least
four instances, within the past two years by mobs, whose sudden
work and quick dispersions rendered it impossible to protect the
victims. Within the past two years nine prisoners, who were either in jail or in the custody of the officers, have been taken from
them without resistance, and put to death. There was doubt
of the guilt of the defendants in most of these cases, and few of
them were charged with capital offenses. None of them involved
the crime of rape. The largest rewards allowed by law were offered for the apprehension of the offenders, and officers were
charged to a vigilant performance of their duties, and aided in
some instances by the services of skilled detectives; but not a single arrest has been made and the grand juries in these counties
have returned no bills of indictment. This would indicate either
that local public sentiment approved these acts of violence or was
too weak to punish them, or that the officers charged with that
duty were in some way lacking in their performance. The evil cannot be cured or remedied by silence as to its existence. Unchecked,
it will continue until it becomes a reproach to our good name,
and a menace to our prosperity and peace; and it behooves you to
exhaust all remedies within your power to find better preventives
for such crimes."

A FRIENDLY WARNING

From England comes a friendly voice which must give to every
patriotic citizen food for earnest thought. Writing from London,
to the Chicago Inter Ocean, Nov. 25, 1894, the distinguished
compiler of our last census, Hon. Robert P. Porter, gives the
American people a most interesting review of the anti-lynching
crusade in England, submitting editorial opinions from all sections of England and Scotland, showing the consensus of British opinion on this subject. It hardly need be said, that without
exception, the current of English thought deprecates the rule
of mob law, and the conscience of England is shocked by the

revelation made during the present crusade. In his letter Mr. Porter says:

"While some English journals have joined certain American journals in ridiculing the well-meaning people who have formed the anti-lynching committee, there is a deep under current on this subject which is injuring the Southern States far more than those who have not been drawn into the question of English investment for the South as I can surmise. This feeling is by no means all sentiment. An Englishman whose word and active co-operation could send a million sterling to any legitimate Southern enterprise said the other day: "I will not invest a farthing in States where those horrors occur. I have no particular sympathy with the anti-lynching committee, but such outrages indicate to my mind that where life is held to be of such little value there is even less assurance that the laws will protect property. As I understand it the States, not the national government, control in such matters, and where those laws are strongest there is the best field for British capital.""

Probably the most bitter attack on the anti-lynching committee has come from the London Times. Those Southern Governors who had their bombastic letter published in the Times, with favorable editorial comment, may have had their laugh at the anti-lynchers here too soon. A few days ago, in commenting on an interesting communication from Richard H. Edmonds, editor of the Manufacturer's Record, setting forth the industrial advantages of the Southern States, which was published in its columns, the Times says: "Without in any way countenancing the impertinence of the 'anti-lynching' committee, we may say that a state of things in which the killing of Negroes by bloodthirsty mobs is an incident of not unfrequent occurrence is not conducive to success in industry. Its existence, however, is a serious obstacle to the success of the South in industry; for even now Negro labor, which means at best inefficient labor, must be largely relied on there, and its efficiency must be still further diminished by spasmodic terrorism.

"Those interested in the development of the resources of the Southern States, and no one in proportion to his means has shown more faith in the progress of the South than the writer of this article, must take hold of this matter earnestly and intelligently. Sneering at the anti-lynching committee will do no good.

Back of them, in fact, if not in form, is the public opinion of Great Britain. Even the Times cannot deny this. It may not be generally known in the United States, but while the Southern and some Northern newspapers are making a target of Miss Wells, the young colored woman who started this English movement, and cracking their jokes at the expense of Miss Florence Balgarnie, who, as honorable secretary, conducts the committee's correspondence, the strongest sort of sentiment is really at the back of the movement. Here we have crystallized every phase of political opinion. Extreme Unionists like the Duke of Argyll and advanced home rulers such as Justin McCarthy; Thomas Burt, the labor leader; Herbert Burrows, the Socialist, and Tom Mann, representing all phases of the Labor party, are co-operating with conservatives like Sir T. Eldon Gorst. But the real strength of this committee is not visible to the casual observer. As a matter of fact it represents many of the leading and most powerful British journals. A. E. Fletcher is editor of the London Daily Chronicle; P. W. Clayden is prominent in the counsels of the London Daily News; Professor James Stuart is Gladstone's great friend and editor of the London Star; William Byles is editor and proprietor of the Bradford Observer; Sir Hugh Gilzen Reid is a leading Birmingham editor; in short, this committee has secured if not the leading editors, certainly important and warm friends, representing the Manchester Guardian, the Leeds Mercury, the Plymouth Western News, Newcastle Leader, the London Daily Graphic, the Westminster Gazette, the London Echo, a host of minor papers all over the kingdom, and practically the entire religious press of the kingdom.

"The greatest victory for the anti-lynchers comes this morning in the publication in the London Times of William Lloyd Garrison's letter. This letter will have immense effect here. It may have been printed in full in the United States, but nevertheless I will quote a paragraph which will strengthen the anti-lynchers greatly in their crusade here:

"'A year ago the South derided and resented Northern protests; to-day it listens, explains and apologizes for its uncovered cruelties. Surely a great triumph for a little woman to accomplish! It is the power of truth simply and unreservedly spoken, for her language was inadequate to describe the horrors exposed.'

"If the Southern states are wise, and I say this with the earnestness of a friend and one who has built a home in the mountain regions of the South and thrown his lot in with them, they will not only listen, but stop lawlessness of all kinds. If they do, and thus secure the confidence of Englishmen, we may in the next decade realize some of the hopes for the new South we have so fondly cherished.

CHAPTER VIII

Miss Willard's Attitude

No class of American citizens stands in greater need of the humane and thoughtful consideration of all sections of our country than do the colored people, nor does any class exceed us in the measure of grateful regard for acts of kindly interest in our behalf. It is, therefore, to us, a matter of keen regret that a Christian organization so large and influential as the Woman's Christian Temperance Union, should refuse to give its sympathy and support to our oppressed people who ask no further favor than the promotion of public sentiment which shall guarantee to every person accused of crime the safeguard of a fair and impartial trial, and protection from butchery by brutal mobs. Accustomed as we are to the indifference and apathy of Christian people, we would bear this instance of ill fortune in silence had not Miss Willard gone out of her way to antagonize the cause so dear to our hearts by including in her Annual Address to the W. C. T. U. Convention at Cleveland, November 5, 1894, a studied, unjust and wholly unwarranted attack upon our work.

In her address Miss Willard said:

The zeal for her race of Miss Ida B. Wells, a bright young colored woman has, it seems to me, clouded her perception as to who were her friends and well-wishers in all high-minded and legitimate efforts to banish the abomination of lynching and torture from the land of the free and the home of the brave. It is my firm belief that in the statements made by Miss Wells concerning white women having taken the initiative in nameless acts between the races she has put an imputation upon half the white race in this country that is unjust, and, save in the rarest exceptional instances wholly without foundation. This is the unani-

mous opinion of the most disinterested and observant leaders of
opinion whom I have consulted on the subject, and I do not fear
to say that the laudable efforts she is making are greatly handi-
capped by statements of this kind, nor to urge her as a friend and
well-wisher to banish from her vocabulary all such allusions as a
source of weakness to the cause she has at heart.

This paragraph, brief as it is, contains two statements which
have not the slightest foundation in fact. At no time, nor in any
place, have I made statements "concerning white women having
taken the initiative in nameless acts between the races." Further,
at no time, or place nor under any circumstance, have I directly
or inferentially "put an imputation upon half the white race in
this country" and I challenge this "friend and well-wisher" to
give proof of the truth of her charge. Miss Willard protests
against lynching in one paragraph and then, in the next, deliberately misrepresents my position in order that she may criticize a
movement, whose only purpose is to protect our oppressed race
from vindictive slander and Lynch Law.

What I have said and what I now repeat—in answer to her first
charge—is, that colored men have been lynched for assault upon
women, when the facts were plain that the relationship between
the victim lynched and the alleged victim of his assault was voluntary, clandestine and illicit. For that very reason we maintain
that, in every section of our land, the accused should have a fair,
impartial trial, so that a man who is colored shall not be hanged
for an offense, which, if he were white, would not be adjudged a
crime. Facts cited in another chapter—"History of Some Cases of
Rape"—amply maintain this position. The publication of these
facts in defense of the good name of the race casts no "imputation upon half the white race in this country" and no such imputation can be inferred except by persons deliberately determined
to be unjust.

But this is not the only injury which this cause has suffered at
the hand of our "friend and well-wisher." It has been said that
the Woman's Christian Temperance Union, the most powerful
organization of women in America, was misrepresented by me
while I was in England. Miss Willard was in England at the time
and knowing that no such misrepresentation came to her notice,
she has permitted that impression to become fixed and widespread, when a word from her would have made the facts plain.

I never at any time or place or in any way misrepresented that organization. When asked what concerted action had been taken by churches and great moral agencies in America to put down Lynch Law, I was compelled in truth to say that no such action had occurred, that pulpit, press and moral agencies in the main were silent and for reasons known to themselves, ignored the awful conditions which to the English people appeared so abhorrent. Then the question was asked what the great moral reformers like Miss Frances Willard and Mr. Moody[8] had done to suppress Lynch Law and again I answered—nothing. That Mr. Moody had never said a word against lynching in any of his trips to the South, or in the North either, so far as was known, and that Miss Willard's only public utterances on the situation had condoned lynching and other unjust practices of the South against the Negro. When proof of these statements was demanded, I sent a letter containing a copy of the New York Voice, Oct. 23, 1890, in which appeared Miss Willard's own words of wholesale slander against the colored race and condonation of Southern white people's outrages against us. My letter in part reads as follows:

But Miss Willard, the great temperance leader, went even further in putting the seal of her approval upon the southerners' method of dealing with the Negro. In October, 1890, the Woman's Christian Temperance Union held its national meeting at Atlanta, Georgia. It was the first time in the history of the organization that it had gone south for a national meeting, and met the southerners in their own homes. They were welcomed with open arms. The governor of the state and the legislature gave special audiences in the halls of state legislation to the temperance workers. They set out to capture the northerners to their way of seeing things, and without troubling to hear the Negro side of the question, these temperance people accepted the white man's story of the problem with which he had to deal. State organizers were appointed that year, who had gone through the southern states since then, but in obedience to southern prejudices have confined their work to white persons only. It is only after Negroes are in prison for crimes that efforts of these temperance women are exerted without regard to "race, color, or previous condition." No "ounce of prevention" is used in their case; they are black, and if these women went among the

Negroes for this work, the whites would not receive them. Except here and there, are found no temperance workers of the Negro race; "the great dark-faced mobs" are left the easy prey of the saloonkeepers.

There was pending in the National Congress at this time a Federal Election Bill, the object being to give the National Government control of the national elections in the several states. Had this bill become a law, the Negro, whose vote has been systematically suppressed since 1875 in the southern states, would have had the protection of the National Government, and his vote counted. The South would have been no longer "solid;" the Southerners saw that the balance of power which they unlawfully held in the House of Representatives and the Electoral College based on the Negro population, would be wrested from them. So they nick-named the pending elections law the "Force Bill"—probably because it would force them to disgorge their ill-gotten political gains—and defeated it. While it was being discussed, the question was submitted to Miss Willard: "What do you think of the race problem and the Force Bill?"

Said Miss Willard: "Now, as to the 'race problem' in its minified, current meaning, I am a true lover of the southern people— have spoken and worked in, perhaps 200 of their towns and cities; have been taken into their love and confidence at scores of hospitable firesides; have heard them pour out their hearts in the splendid frankness of their impetuous natures. And I have said to them at such times: 'When I go North there will be wafted to you no word from pen or voice that is not loyal to what we are saying here and now.' Going South, a woman, a temperance woman, and a Northern temperance woman—three great barriers to their good will yonder—I was received by them with a confidence that was one of the most delightful surprises of my life. I think we have wronged the South, though we did not mean to do so. The reason was, in part, that we had irreparably wronged ourselves by putting no safeguards on the ballot box at the North that would sift out alien illiterates. They rule our cities today; the saloon is their palace, and the toddy stick their scepter. It is not fair that they should vote, nor is it fair that a plantation Negro, who can neither read nor write, whose ideas are bounded by the fence of his own field and the price of his own mule, should be entrusted with the ballot. We ought to have put an educa-

tional test upon that ballot from the first. The Anglo-Saxon race
will never submit to be dominated by the Negro so long as his
altitude reaches no higher than the personal liberty of the saloon,
and the power of appreciating the amount of liquor that a dollar
will buy. New England would no more submit to this than South
Carolina. 'Better whisky and more of it' has been the rallying
cry of great dark-faced mobs in the Southern localities where
local option was snowed under by the colored vote. Temperance
has no enemy like that, for it is unreasoning and unreasonable.
Tonight it promises in great congregation to vote for temperance
at the polls tomorrow; but tomorrow twenty-five cents changes
that vote in favor of the liquor-seller.

"I pity the southerners, and I believe the great mass of them are
as conscientious and kindly-intentioned toward the colored man
as an equal number of white church-members of the North.
Would-be demagogues lead the colored people to destruction.
Half-drunken white roughs murder them at the polls, or intimidate them so that they do not vote. But the better class of people
must not be blamed for this, and a more thoroughly American
population than the Christian people of the South does not exist.
They have the traditions, the kindness, the probity, the courage
of our forefathers. The problem on their hands is immeasurable.
The colored race multiplies like the locusts of Egypt. The grogshop is its center of power. 'The safety of woman, of childhood,
of the home, is menaced in a thousand localities at this moment,
so that the men dare not go beyond the sight of their own roof-
tree.' How little we know of all this, seated in our comfort and
affluence here at the North, descanting upon the rights of every
man to cast one vote and have it fairly counted; that well-worn
shibboleth invoked once more to dodge a living issue.

"The fact is that illiterate colored men will not vote at the South
until the white population chooses to have them do so; and under
similar conditions they would not at the North." Here we have
Miss Willard's words in full, condoning fraud, violence, murder, at
the ballot box; raping, shooting, hanging and burning; for all these
things are done and being done now by the Southern white people.
She does not stop there, but goes a step further to aid them in black-
ening the good name of an entire race, as shown by the sentences
quoted in the paragraph above. These utterances, for which the colored people have never forgiven Miss Willard, and which Frederick

Douglass has denounced as false, are to be found in full in the
Voice of October 23, 1890, a temperance organ published at New
York city.

This letter appeared in the May number of Fraternity, the organ
of the first Anti-Lynching society of Great Britain. When Lady
Henry Somerset learned through Miss Florence Balgarnie that
this letter had been published she informed me that if the interview was published she would take steps to let the public know
that my statements must be received with caution. As I had no
money to pay the printer to suppress the edition which was already published and these ladies did not care to do so, the May
number of Fraternity was sent to its subscribers as usual. Three
days later there appeared in the daily Westminster Gazette an
"interview" with Miss Willard, written by Lady Henry Somerset,
which was so subtly unjust in its wording that I was forced to
reply in my own defense. In that reply I made only statements
which, like those concerning Miss Willard's Voice interview,
have not been and cannot be denied. It was as follows:

LADY HENRY SOMERSET'S
INTERVIEW WITH MISS WILLARD

To the Editor of the Westminster Gazette: Sir—The interview published in your columns today hardly merits a reply, because of the
indifference to suffering manifested. Two ladies are represented
sitting under a tree at Relgate and, after some preliminary remarks
on the terrible subject of lynching, Miss Willard laughingly replies
by cracking a joke. And the concluding sentence of the interview
shows the object is not to determine how best they may help the
Negro who is being hanged, shot and burned, but "to guard Miss
Willard's reputation."

With me it is not myself nor my reputation, but the life of my
people, which is at stake, and I affirm that this is the first time to
my knowledge that Miss Willard has said a single word in denunciation of lynching or demand for law. The year 1890, the one in
which the interview appears, had a larger lynching record than
any previous year, and the number and territory have increased, to
say nothing of the human beings burnt alive.

If so earnest as she would have the English public believe her to be, why was she silent when five minutes were given me to speak last June at Princes' Hall, and in Holborn Town Hall this May? I should say it was as President of the Woman's Christian Temperance Union of America she is timid, because all these unions in the South emphasize the hatred of the Negro by excluding him. There is not a single colored woman admitted to the Southern W. C. T. U., but still Miss Willard blames the Negro for the defeat of Prohibition in the South. Miss Willard quotes from Fraternity, but forgets to add my immediate recognition of her presence on the platform at Holborn Town Hall, when, amidst many other resolutions on temperance and other subjects in which she is interested, time was granted to carry an anti-lynching resolution. I was so thankful for this crumb of her speechless presence that I hurried off to the editor of Fraternity and added a postscript to my article blazoning forth that fact.

Any statements I have made concerning Miss Willard are confirmed by the Hon. Frederick Douglass (late United States minister to Hayti[9]) in a speech delivered by him in Washington in January of this year, which has since been published in a pamphlet. The fact is, Miss Willard is no better or worse than the great bulk of white Americans on the Negro questions. They are all afraid to speak out, and it is only British public opinion which will move them, as I am thankful to see it has already begun to move Miss Willard. I am, etc.

May 21.   IDA B. WELLS.

Unable to deny the truth of these assertions, the charge has been made that I have attacked Miss Willard and misrepresented the W. C. T. U. If to state facts is misrepresentation, then I plead guilty to the charge.

I said then and repeat now, that in all the ten terrible years of shooting, hanging, and burning of men, women and children in America, the Women's Christian Temperance Union never suggested one plan or made one move to prevent those awful crimes. If this statement is untrue the records of that organization would disprove it before the ink is dry. It is clearly an issue of fact and in all fairness this charge of misrepresentation should either be substantiated or withdrawn.

It is not necessary, however, to make any representation concerning the W. C. T. U. and the lynching question. The record of that organization speaks for itself. During all the years prior to the agitation begun against Lynch Law, in which years men, women and children were scourged, hanged, shot and burned, the W. C. T. U. had no word, either of pity or protest; its great heart, which concerns itself about humanity the world over, was, toward our cause, pulseless as a stone. Let those who deny this speak by the record. Not until after the first British campaign, in 1893, was even a resolution passed by the body which is the self constituted guardian for "God, home and native land."

Nor need we go back to other years. The annual session of that organization held in Cleveland in November, 1891, made a record which confirms and emphasizes the silence charged against it. At that session, earnest efforts were made to secure the adoption of a resolution of protest against lynching. At that very time two men were being tried for the murder of six colored men who were arrested on charge of barn burning, chained together, and on pretense of being taken to jail, were driven into the woods where they were ambushed and all six shot to death. The six widows of the butchered men had just finished the most pathetic recital ever heard in any court room, and the mute appeal of twenty-seven orphans for justice touched the stoutest hearts. Only two weeks prior to the session, Gov. Jones of Alabama, in his last message to the retiring state legislature cited the fact that in the two years just past, nine colored men had been taken from the legal authorities by lynching mobs and butchered in cold blood—and not one of these victims was even charged with an assault upon womanhood.

It was thought that this great organization, in face of these facts, would not hesitate to place itself on record in a resolution of protest against this awful brutality towards colored people. Miss Willard gave assurance that such a resolution would be adopted, and that assurance was relied on. The record of the session shows in what good faith that assurance was kept. After recommending an expression against Lynch Law, the President attacked the anti-lynching movement, deliberately misrepresenting my position, and in her annual address, charging me with a statement I never made.

Further than that, when the committees on resolutions reported their work, not a word was said against lynching. In the interest of the cause I smothered the resentment I felt because of the unwarranted and unjust attack of the President, and labored with members to secure an expression of some kind, tending to abate the awful slaughter of my race. A resolution against lynching was introduced by Mrs. Fessenden and read, and then that great Christian body, which in its resolutions had expressed itself in opposition to the social amusement of card playing, athletic sports and promiscuous dancing; had protested against the licensing of saloons, inveighed against tobacco, pledged its allegiance to the Prohibition party; and thanked the Populist party[10] in Kansas, the Republican party in California and the Democratic party in the South, wholly ignored the seven millions of colored people of this country whose plea was for a word of sympathy and support for the movement in their behalf. The resolution was not adopted, and the convention adjourned.

In the Union Signal Dec. 6, 1894, among the resolutions is found this one:

> Resolved. That the National W. C. T. U., which has for years counted among its departments that of peace and arbitration, is utterly opposed to all lawless acts in any and all parts of our common lands and it urges these principles upon the public, praying that the time may speedily come when no human being shall be condemned without due process of law; and when the unspeakable outrages which have so often provoked such lawlessness shall be banished from the world, and childhood, maidenhood and womanhood shall no more be the victims of atrocities worse than death.

This is not the resolution offered by Mrs. Fessenden. She offered the one that passed last year by the W. C. T. U. which was strong unequivocal denunciation of lynching. But she was told by the chairman of the committee on resolutions, Mrs. Rounds, that there was already a lynching resolution in the hands of the committee. Mrs. Fessenden yielded the floor on that assurance, and no resolution of any kind against lynching was submitted and none was voted upon, not even the one above, taken from the columns of the Union Signal, the organ of the national W. C. T. U.

Even the wording of this resolution which was printed by the W. C. T. U., reiterates the false and unjust charge which has been so often made as an excuse for lynchers. Statistics show that less than one-third of the lynching victims are hanged, shot and burned alive for "unspeakable outrages against womanhood, maidenhood and childhood;" and that nearly a thousand, including women and children, have been lynched upon any pretext whatsoever; and that all have met death upon the unsupported word of white men and women. Despite these facts this resolution which was printed, cloaks an apology for lawlessness, in the same paragraph which affects to condemn it, where it speaks of "the unspeakable outrages which have so often provoked such lawlessness."

Miss Willard told me the other day before the resolutions were offered that the Southern women present had held a caucus that day. This was after I, as fraternal delegate from the Woman's Mite Missionary Society of the A. M. E. Church in Cleveland, O., had been introduced to tender its greetings. In so doing I expressed the hope of the colored women that the W. C. T. U. would place itself on record as opposed to lynching which robbed them of husbands, fathers, brothers and sons and in many cases of women as well. No note was made either in the daily papers or the Union Signal of that introduction and greeting, although every other incident of that morning was published. The failure to submit a lynching resolution and the wording of the one above appears to have been the result of that Southern caucus.

On the same day I had a private talk with Miss Willard and told her she had been unjust to me and the cause in her annual address, and asked that she correct the statement that I had misrepresented the W. C. T. U., or that I had "put an imputation on one-half the white race in this country." She said that somebody in England told her it was a pity that I attacked the white women of America. "Oh," said I, "then you went out of your way to prejudice me and my cause in your annual address, not upon what you had heard me say, but what somebody had told you I said?" Her reply was that I must not blame her for her rhetorical expressions—that I had my way of expressing things and she had hers. I told her I most assuredly did blame her when those expressions were calculated to do such harm. I waited for an honest and unequivocal retraction of her statements based on "hearsay." Not a word of retraction or explanation was said in the convention and I remained misrepresented before that body through her connivance and consent.

The editorial notes in the Union signal, Dec. 6, 1894, however, contains the following:

"In her repudiation of the charges brought by Miss Ida Wells against white women as having taken the initiative in nameless crimes between the races, Miss Willard said in her annual address that this statement 'put an unjust imputation upon half the white race.' But as this expression has been misunderstood she desires to declare that she did not intend a literal interpretation to be given to the language used, but employed it to express a tendency that might ensue in public thought as a result of utterances so sweeping as some that have been made by Miss Wells."

Because this explanation is as unjust as the original offense, I am forced in self-defense to submit this account of differences. I desire no quarrel with the W. C. T. U., but my love for the truth is greater than my regard for an alleged friend who, through ignorance or design misrepresents in the most harmful way the cause of a long suffering race, and then unable to maintain the truth of her attack excuses herself as it were by the wave of the hand, declaring that "she did not intend a literal interpretation to be given to the language used." When the lives of men, women and children are at stake, when the inhuman butchers of innocents attempt to justify their barbarism by fastening upon a whole race the oblique of the most infamous of crimes, it is little less than criminal to apologize for the butchers today and tomorrow repudiate the apology by declaring it a figure of speech.

CHAPTER IX

Lynching Record for 1894

The following tables are based on statistics taken from the columns of the Chicago Tribune, Jan. 1, 1895. They are a valuable appendix to the foregoing pages. They show, among other things, that in Louisiana, April 23-28, eight Negroes were lynched because one white man was killed by the Negro, the latter acting in self-defense. Only seven of them are given in the list.

Near Memphis, Tenn., six Negroes were lynched—this time charged with burning barns. A trial of the indicted resulted in an acquittal, although it was shown on trial that the lynching was prearranged for them. Six widows and twenty-seven orphans are indebted to this mob for their condition, and this lynching swells the number to eleven Negroes lynched in and about Memphis since March 9, 1892.

In Brooks county, Ga., Dec. 23rd, while this Christian country was preparing for Christmas celebration, seven Negroes were lynched in twenty-four hours because they refused, or were unable to tell the whereabouts of a colored man named Pike, who killed a white man. The wives and daughters of these lynched men were horribly and brutally outraged by the murderers of their husbands and fathers. But the mob has not been punished and again women and children are robbed of their protectors whose blood cries unavenged to Heaven and humanity. Georgia heads the list of lynching states.

MURDER

Jan. 9, Samuel Smith, Greenville, Ala.; Jan. 11, Sherman Wagoner, Mitchell, Ind.; Jan. 12, Roscoe Parker, West Union, Ohio; Feb. 7, Henry Bruce, Gulch Co., Ark.; March 5, Sylvester Rhodes, Collins, Ga.; March 15, Richard Puryea, Stroudsburg, Pa.; March 29, Oliver Jackson, Montgomery, Ala.; March 30, — Saybrick, Fisher's Ferry, Miss.; April 14, William Lewis, Lanison, Ala.; April 23, Jefferson Luggle, Cherokee, Kan.; April 23, Samuel Slaugate, Tallulah, La.; April 23, Thomas Claxton, Tallulah, La.; April 23, David Hawkins, Tallulah, La.; April 27, Thel Claxton, Tallulah, La.; April 27, Comp Claxton, Tallulah, La.; April 27, Scot Harvey, Tallulah, La.; April 27, Jerry McCly, Tallulah, La.; May 17, Henry Scott, Jefferson, Tex.; May 15, Coat Williams, Pine Grove, Fla.; June 2, Jefferson Crawford, Bethesda, S. C.; June 4, Thondo Underwood, Monroe, La.; June 8, Isaac Kemp, Cape Charles, Va.; June 13, Lon Hall, Sweethouse, Tex.; June 13, Bascom Cook, Sweethouse, Tex.; June 15, Luke Thomas, Biloxi, Miss.; June 29, John Williams, Sulphur, Tex.; June 29, Ulysses Hayden, Monett, Mo.; July 6, — Hood, Amite,

Miss.; July 7, James Bell, Charlotte, Tenn.; Sept. 2, Henderson Hollander, Elkhorn, W. Va.; Sept. 14, Robert Williams, Concordia Parish, La.; Sept. 22, Luke Washington, Meghee, Ark.; Sept. 22, Richard Washington, Meghee, Ark.; Sept. 22, Henry Crobyson, Meghee, Ark.; Nov. 10, Lawrence Younger, Lloyd, Va.; Dec. 17, unknown Negro, Williamston, S. C.; Dec. 23, Samuel Taylor, Brooks County, Ga.; Dec. 23, Charles Frazier, Brooks County, Ga.; Dec. 23, Samuel Pike, Brooks County, Ga.; Dec. 23, Harry Sherard, Brooks County, Ga.; Dec. 23, unknown Negro, Brooks County, Ga.; Dec. 23, unknown Negro, Brooks County, Ga.; Dec. 23, unknown Negro, Brooks County, Ga.; Dec. 26, Daniel McDonald, Winston County, Miss.; Dec. 26, William Carter, Winston County, Miss.

RAPE

Jan. 17, John Buckner, Valley Park, Mo.; Jan. 21, M. G. Cambell, Jellico Mines, Ky.; Jan. 27, unknown, Verona, Mo.; Feb. 11, Henry McCreeg, near Pioneer, Tenn.; April 6, Daniel Ahren, Greensboro, Ga.; April 15, Seymour Newland, Rushsylvania, Ohio; April 26, Robert Evarts, Jamaica, Ga.; April 27, James Robinson, Manassas, Va.; April 27, Benjamin White, Manassas, Va.; May 15, Nim Young, Ocala, Fla.; May 22, unknown, Miller County, Ga.; June 13, unknown, Blackshear, Ga.; June 18, Owen Opliltree, Forsyth, Ga.; June 22, Henry Capus, Magnolia, Ark.; June 26, Caleb Godly, Bowling Green, Ky.; June 28, Fayette Franklin, Mitchell, Ga.; July 2, Joseph Johnson, Hiller's Creek, Mo.; July 6, Lewis Bankhead, Cooper, Ala.; July 16, Marion Howard, Scottsville, Ky.; July 20, William Griffith, Woodville, Tex.; Aug. 12, William Nershbread, Rossville, Tenn.; Aug. 14, Marshall Boston, Frankfort, Ky.; Sept. 19, David Gooseby, Atlanta, Ga.; Oct. 15, Willis Griffey, Princeton, Ky.; Nov. 8, Lee Lawrence, Jasper County, Ga.; Nov. 10, Needham Smith, Tipton County, Tenn.; Nov. 14, Robert Mosely, Dolinite, Ala.; Dec. 4, William Jackson, Ocala, Fla.; Dec. 18, unknown, Marion County, Fla.

UNKNOWN OFFENSES

March 6, Lamsen Gregory, Bell's Depot, Tenn.; March 6, unknown woman, near Marche, Ark.; April 14, Alfred Brenn, Calhoun, Ga.; June 8, Harry Gill, West Lancaster, S. C.; Nov. 23, unknown, Landrum, S. C.; Dec. 5, Mrs. Teddy Arthur, Lincoln County, W. Va.

DESPERADO

Jan. 14, Charles Willis, Ocala, Fla.

SUSPECTED INCENDIARISM

Jan. 18, unknown, Bayou Sarah, La.

SUSPECTED ARSON

June 14, J. H. Dave, Monroe, La.

ENTICING SERVANT AWAY

Feb. 10, — Collins, Athens, Ga.

TRAIN WRECKING

Feb. 10, Jesse Dillingham, Smokeyville, Tex.

HIGHWAY ROBBERY

June 3, unknown, Dublin, Ga.

INCENDIARISM.

Nov. 8, Gabe Nalls, Blackford, Ky.; Nov. 8, Ulysses Nalls, Blackford, Ky.

ARSON

Dec. 20, James Allen, Brownsville, Tex.

ASSAULT

Dec. 23, George King, New Orleans, La.

NO OFFENSE

Dec. 28, Scott Sherman, Morehouse Parish, La.

BURGLARY

May 29, Henry Smith, Clinton, Miss.; May 29, William James, Clinton, Miss.

ALLEGED RAPE

June 4, Ready Murdock, Yazoo, Miss.

ATTEMPTED RAPE

July 14, unknown Negro, Biloxi, Miss.; July 26, Vance McClure, New Iberia, La.; July 26, William Tyler, Carlisle, Ky.; Sept. 14, James Smith, Stark, Fla.; Oct. 8, Henry Gibson, Fairfield, Tex.; Oct. 20, —Williams, Upper Marlboro, Md.; June 9, Lewis Williams, Hewett Springs, Miss.; June 28, George Linton,

Brookhaven, Miss.; June 28, Edward White, Hudson, Ala.; July 6, George Pond, Fulton, Miss.; July 7, Augustus Pond, Tupelo, Miss.

RACE PREJUDICE

June 10, Mark Jacobs, Blenville, La.; July 24, unknown woman, Sampson County, Miss.

INTRODUCING SMALLPOX

June 10, James Perry, Knoxville, Ark.

KIDNAPPING

March 2, Lentige, Harland County, Ky.

CONSPIRACY

May 29, J. T. Burgis, Palatka, Fla.

HORSE STEALING

June 20, Archie Haynes, Mason County, Ky.; June 20, Burt Haynes, Mason County, Ky.; June 20, William Haynes, Mason County, Ky.

WRITING LETTER TO WHITE WOMAN

May 9, unknown Negro, West Texas.

GIVING INFORMATION

July 12, James Nelson, Abbeyville, S. C.

STEALING

Jan. 5, Alfred Davis, Live Oak County, Ark.

LARCENY

April 18, Henry Montgomery, Lewisburg, Tenn.

POLITICAL CAUSES

July 19, John Brownlee, Oxford, Ala.

CONJURING

July 20, Allen Myers, Rankin County, Miss.

ATTEMPTED MURDER

June 1, Frank Ballard, Jackson, Tenn.

ALLEGED MURDER

April 5, Negro, near Selma, Ala.; April 5, Negro, near Selma, Ala.

WITHOUT CAUSE

May 17, Samuel Wood, Gates City, Va.

BARN BURNING

April 22, Thomas Black, Tuscumbia, Ala.; April 22, John Williams, Tuscumbia, Ala.; April 22, Toney Johnson, Tuscumbia, Ala.; July 14, William Bell, Dixon, Tenn.; Sept. 1, Daniel Hawkins,

Millington, Tenn.; Sept. 1, Robert Haynes, Millington, Tenn.;
Sept. 1, Warner Williams, Millington, Tenn.; Sept. 1, Edward
Hall, Millington, Tenn.; Sept. 1, John Haynes, Millington, Tenn.;
Sept. 1, Graham White, Millington, Tenn.

ASKING WHITE WOMAN TO MARRY HIM

May 23, William Brooks, Galesline, Ark.

OFFENSES CHARGED FOR LYNCHING

Suspected arson, 2; stealing, 1; political causes, 1; murder, 45;
rape, 29; desperado, 1; suspected incendiarism, 1; train wreck-
ing, 1; enticing servant away, 1; kidnapping, 1; unknown offense, 6; larceny, 1; barn burning, 10; writing letters to a white
woman, 1; without cause, 1; burglary, 1; asking white woman to
marry, 1; conspiracy, 1; attempted murder, 1; horse stealing, 3;
highway robbery, 1; alleged rape, 1; attempted rape, 11; race
prejudice, 2; introducing smallpox, 1; giving information, 1; con-
juring, 1; incendiarism, 2; arson, 1; assault, 1; no offense, 1; alleged murder, 2; total (colored), 134.

LYNCHING STATES

Mississippi, 15; Arkansas, 8; Virginia, 5; Tennessee, 15; Alabama,
12; Kentucky, 12; Texas, 9; Georgia, 19; South Carolina, 5;
Florida, 7; Louisiana, 15; Missouri, 4; Ohio, 2; Maryland, 1;
West Virginia, 2; Indiana, 1; Kansas, 1; Pennsylvania, 1.

LYNCHING BY THE MONTH

January, 11; February, 17; March, 8; April, 36; May, 16; June,
31; July, 24; August, 4; September, 17; October, 7; November, 9;
December, 20; total colored and white, 197.

WOMEN LYNCHED

July 24, unknown woman, race prejudice, Sampson County, Miss.;
March 6, unknown woman, unknown offense, Marche, Ark.; Dec.
5, Mrs. Teddy Arthur, unknown cause, Lincoln County, W. Va.

CHAPTER X

The Remedy

It is a well established principle of law that every wrong has a
remedy. Herein rests our respect for law. The Negro does not
claim that all of the one thousand black men women and children, who have been hanged, shot and burned alive during the
past ten years, were innocent of the charges made against them.
We have associated too long with the white man not to have copied his vices as well as his virtues. But we do insist that the punishment is not the same for both classes of criminals. In lynching,
opportunity is not given the Negro to defend himself against the
unsupported accusations of white men and women. The word of
the accuser is held to be true and the excited bloodthirsty mob
demands that the rule of law be reversed and instead of proving
the accused to be guilty, the victim of their hate and revenge must
prove himself innocent. No evidence he can offer will satisfy the
mob; he is bound hand and foot and swung into eternity. Then to
excuse its infamy, the mob almost invariably reports the monstrous falsehood that its victim made a full confession before he
was hanged.

With all military, legal and political power in their hands, only
two of the lynching States have attempted a check by exercising
the power which is theirs. Mayor Trout, of Roanoke, Virginia,
called out the militia in 1893, to protect a Negro prisoner, and in
so doing nine men were killed and a number wounded. Then the
mayor and militia withdrew, left the Negro to his fate and he was
promptly lynched. The business men realized the blow to the
town's were given light sentences, the highest being one of twelve
financial interests, called the mayor home, the grand jury indicted and prosecuted the ringleaders of the mob. They months

in State prison. The day he arrived at the penitentiary, he was
pardoned by the governor of the State.

The only other real attempt made by the authorities to protect
a prisoner of the law, and which was more successful, was that of
Gov. McKinley, of Ohio, who sent the militia to Washington
Courthouse, O., in October, 1894, and five men were killed and
twenty wounded in maintaining the principle that the law must
be upheld.

In South Carolina, in April, 1893, Gov. Tillman aided the mob
by yielding up to be killed, a prisoner of the law, who had voluntarily placed himself under the Governor's protection. Public sentiment by its representatives has encouraged Lynch Law, and
upon the revolution of this sentiment we must depend for its
abolition.

Therefore, we demand a fair trial by law for those accused of
the crime, and punishment by law after honest conviction. No
maudlin sympathy for criminals is solicited, but we do ask that the
law shall punish all alike. We earnestly desire those that control
the forces which make public sentiment to join with us in the
demand. Surely the humanitarian spirit of this country which
reaches out to denounce the treatment of the Russian Jews, the
Armenian Christians, the laboring poor of Europe, the Siberian
exiles and the native women of India—will not longer refuse to
lift its voice on this subject. If it were known that the cannibals
or the savage Indians had burned three human beings alive in the
past two years, the whole of Christendom would be roused, to
devise ways and means to put a stop to it. Can you remain silent
and inactive when such things are done in our own community
and country? Is your duty to humanity in the United States less
binding?

What can you do, reader, to prevent lynching, to thwart anarchy and promote law and order throughout our land?

1st. You can help disseminate the facts contained in this book
by bringing them to the knowledge of every one with whom
you come in contact, to the end that public sentiment may be
revolutionized. Let the facts speak for themselves, with you as a
medium.

2nd. You can be instrumental in having churches, missionary
societies, Y. M. C. A.'s W. C. T. U.'s and all Christian and moral
forces in connection with your religious and social life, pass res-

olutions of condemnation and protest every time a lynching takes place; and see that they are sent to the place where these outrages occur.

3d. Bring to the intelligent consideration of Southern people the refusal of capital to invest where lawlessness and mob violence hold sway. Many labor organizations have declared by resolution that they would avoid lynch infested localities as they would the pestilence when seeking new homes. If the South wishes to build up its waste places quickly, there is no better way than to uphold the majesty of the law by enforcing obedience to the same, and meting out the same punishment to all classes of criminals, white as well as black. "Equality before the law," must become a fact as well as a theory before America is truly the "land of the free and the home of the brave."

4th. Think and act on independent lines in this behalf, remembering that after all, it is the white man's civilization and the white man's government which are on trial. This crusade will determine whether that civilization can maintain itself by itself, or whether anarchy shall prevail; whether this Nation shall write itself down a success at self government, or in deepest humiliation admit its failure complete; whether the precepts and theories of Christianity are professed and practiced by American white people as Golden Rules of thought and action, or adopted as a system of morals to be preached to the heathen until they attain to the intelligence which needs the system of Lynch Law.

5th. Congressman Blair offered a resolution in the House of Representatives, August, 1894. The organized life of the country can speedily make this a law by sending resolutions to Congress indorsing Mr. Blair's bill and asking Congress to create the commission. In no better way can the question be settled, and the Negro does not fear the issue. The following is the resolution:

"Resolved, By the House of Representatives and Senate in congress assembled, That the committee on labor be instructed to investigate and report the number, location and date of all alleged assaults by males upon females throughout the country during the ten years last preceding the passing of this joint resolution, for or on account of which organized but unlawful violence has been inflicted or attempted to be inflicted. Also to ascertain and report all facts of organized but unlawful violence to the person, with the attendant facts and circumstances, which have been inflicted upon accused persons alleged to have been guilty of crimes punishable by due process of law which have taken place in any part of the country within the ten years last preceding the passage of this resolution. Such investigation shall be made by the usual methods and agencies of the Department of Labor, and report made to Congress as soon as the work can be satisfactorily done, and the sum of $25,000, or so much thereof as may be necessary, is hereby appropriated to pay the expenses out of any money in the treasury not otherwise appropriated."

The belief has been constantly expressed in England that in the United States, which has produced Wm. Lloyd Garrison, Henry Ward Beecher, James Russell Lowell, John G. Whittier and Abraham Lincoln there must be those of their descendants who would take hold of the work of inaugurating an era of law and order.[11] The colored people of this country who have been loyal to the flag believe the same, and strong in that belief have begun this crusade. To those who still feel they have no obligation in the matter, we commend the following lines of Lowell on "Freedom."

> Men! whose boast it is that ye
> Come of fathers brave and free,
> If there breathe on earth a slave,
> Are ye truly free and brave?
> If ye do not feel the chain,
> When it works a brother's pain,
> Are ye not base slaves indeed,
> Slaves unworthy to be freed?
>
> Women! who shall one day bear
> Sons to breathe New England air,
> If ye hear without a blush,
> Deeds to make the roused blood rush
> Like red lava through your veins,
> For your sisters now in chains,—
> Answer! are ye fit to be
> Mothers of the brave and free?
>
> Is true freedom but to break
> Fetters for our own dear sake,
> And, with leathern hearts, forget

That we owe mankind a debt?
No! true freedom is to share
All the chains our brothers wear,
And, with heart and hand, to be
Earnest to make others free!

There are slaves who fear to speak
For the fallen and the weak;
They are slaves who will not choose
Hatred, scoffing, and abuse,
Rather than in silence shrink
From the truth they needs must think;
They are slaves who dare not be
In the right with two or three.

A FIELD FOR PRACTICAL WORK

The very frequent inquiry made after my lectures by interested friends is, "What can I do to help the cause?" The answer always is, "Tell the world the facts." When the Christian world knows the alarming growth and extent of outlawry in our land, some means will be found to stop it.

The object of this publication is to tell the facts, and friends of the cause can lend a helping hand by aiding in the distribution of these books. When I present our cause to a minister, editor, lecturer, or representative of any moral agency, the first demand is for facts and figures. Plainly, I can not then hand out a book with a twenty-five cent tariff on the information contained. This would be only a new method in the book agents' art. In all such cases it is a pleasure to submit this book for investigation, with the certain assurance of gaining a friend to the cause.

There are many agencies which may be enlisted in our cause by the general circulation of the facts herein contained. The preachers, teachers, editors and humanitarians of the white race, at home and abroad, must have facts laid before them, and it is our duty to supply these facts. The Central Anti-Lynching League,[12] Room 9, 128 Clark st., Chicago, has established a Free Distribution Fund, the work of which can be promoted by all who are interested in this work.

Anti-lynching leagues, societies and individuals can order books from this fund at agents' rates. The books will be sent to their order, or, if desired, will be distributed by the League among those whose co-operative aid we so greatly need. The writer hereof assures prompt distribution of books according to order, and public acknowledgment of all orders through the public press.

LYNCH LAW IN GEORGIA

The lynching of Sam Hose in Georgia inspired Wells-Barnett to write this pamphlet, and also precipitated her final break with Booker T. Washington. A farmworker in southern Georgia, Sam Hose was murdered by a mob of more than two thousand people on April 23, 1899. Accused of murdering his employer, Alfred Crawford, and assaulting Crawford's wife and infant son, Hose was tortured by the mob, who severed his ears, fingers, and genitals before tying him to a tree and setting him on fire. Horrified by the savage violence, Wells-Barnett and other black activists protested Hose's death and were appalled when Booker T. Washington refused to make any public statement on the subject. They were even more disappointed by Washington's assumption that Hose had been guilty. Wells-Barnett and other black activists in Chicago questioned Hose's guilt and hired white private investigator Louis Levin to go to Georgia and investigate the circumstances that led to his death. Levin found that Hose had acted in self-defense. Hose was at work chopping wood when two men began a quarrel over wages, which ended with Crawford's leveling a gun on Hose and threatening to kill him. Afraid for his life, Hose responded by throwing his ax at Crawford, which struck and killed him. Moreover, Levin's research also revealed that charges that Hose had assaulted Mrs. Crawford and her infant son were fabricated. After killing Crawford, Hose had fled the scene immediately, without harming anyone else in the Crawford family. *Lynch Law in Georgia* was quickly published, the same month as the Hose lynching, and contained Levin's report. In addition to exposing the crime against Hose, Wells-Barnett also used material taken from the *Atlanta Journal* and the *Atlanta Constitution* to shed light on the lynching of eleven other men in Georgia between March and April 1899.

SOURCE: Ida B. Wells-Barnett, *Lynch Law in Georgia* (Chicago: Chicago Colored Citizens, 1899).

LYNCH LAW IN GEORGIA

A Six-Weeks' Record in the Center of Southern
Civilization, As Faithfully Chronicled by the "Atlanta
Journal" and the "Atlanta Constitution"

ALSO THE FULL REPORT OF LOUIS P. LE VIN

The Chicago Detective Sent to Investigate the Burning
of Samuel Hose, the Torture and Hanging of Elijah
Strickland, the Colored Preacher, and the Lynching
of Nine Men for Alleged Arson

CONSIDER THE FACTS

During six weeks of the months of March and April just past,
twelve colored men were lynched in Georgia, the reign of outlawry culminating in the torture and hanging of the colored
preacher, Elijah Strickland, and the burning alive of Samuel
Wilkes, alias Hose, Sunday April 23, 1899.

The real purpose of these savage demonstrations is to teach the
Negro that in the South he has no rights that the law will enforce. Samuel Hose was burned to teach the Negroes that no
matter what a white man does to them, they must not resist.
Hose, a servant, had killed Cranford, his employer. An example
must be made. Ordinary punishment was deemed inadequate.
This Negro must be burned alive. To make the burning a certainty the charge of outrage was invented, and added to the
charge of murder. The daily press offered reward for the capture
of Hose and then openly incited the people to burn him as soon
as caught. The mob carried out the plan in every savage detail.

Of the twelve men lynched during that reign of unspeakable
barbarism, only one was even charged with an assault upon a
woman. Yet Southern apologists justify their savagery on the
ground that Negroes are lynched only because of their crimes
against women.

The Southern press champions burning men alive, and says,
"Consider the facts." The colored people join issue and also say,

"Consider the facts." The colored people of Chicago employed a detective to go to Georgia, and his report in this pamphlet gives the fact. We give here the details of the lynching as they were reported in the Southern papers, then follows the report of the true facts as to the cause of the lynchings, as learned by the investigation. We submit all to the sober judgment of the Nation, confident that, in this cause, as well as all others, "Truth is mighty and will prevail."

IDA B. WELLS-BARNETT
2939 PRINCETON AVENUE, CHICAGO, JUNE 20, 1899.

CHAPTER I

Nine Men Lynched on Suspicion

In dealing with all vexed questions, the chief aim of every honest inquirer should be to ascertain the facts. No good purpose is subserved either by concealment on the one hand or exaggeration on the other. "The truth, the whole truth and nothing but the truth," is the only sure foundation for just judgment.

The purpose of this pamphlet is to give the public the facts, in the belief that there is still a sense of justice in the American people, and that it will yet assert itself in condemnation of outlawry and in defense of oppressed and persecuted humanity. In this firm belief the following pages will describe the lynching of nine colored men, who were arrested near Palmetto, Georgia, about the middle of March, upon suspicion that they were implicated in the burning of the three houses in February preceding.

The nine suspects were not criminals, they were hardworking, law-abiding citizens, men of families. They had assaulted no woman, and, after the lapse of nearly a month, it could not be claimed that the fury of an insane mob made their butchery excusable. They were in the custody of the law, unarmed, chained together and helpless, awaiting their trial. They had no money to employ learned counsel to invoke the aid of technicalities to defeat justice. They were in custody of a white Sheriff, to be prosecuted by a white State's Attorney, to be tried before a white judge, and by a white jury. Surely the guilty had no chance to escape.

Still they were lynched. That the awful story of their slaughter may not be considered overdrawn, the following description is taken from the columns of the Atlanta Journal, as it was written by Royal Daniel, a staff correspondent. The story of the lynching thus told is as follows:

Palmetto, Ga., March 16.—A mob of more than 100 desperate men, armed with Winchesters and shotguns and pistols and wearing masks, rode into Palmetto at 1 o'clock this morning and shot to death four Negro prisoners, desperately wounded another and with deliberate aim fired at four others, wounding two, believing the entire nine had been killed.

The boldness of the mob and the desperateness with which the murder was contemplated and executed, has torn the little town with excitement and anxiety.

All business has been suspended, and the town is under military patrol, and every male inhabitant is armed to the teeth, in anticipation of an outbreak which is expected to-night.

Last night nine Negroes were arrested and place in the warehouse near the depot. The Negroes were charged with the burning of the two business blocks here in February.

At 1 o'clock this morning the mob dashed into town while the people slept.

They rushed to the warehouse in which the nine Negroes were guarded by six white men.

The door was burst open and guards were ordered to hold up their hands.

Then the mob fired two volleys into the line of trembling, wretched and pleading prisoners, and to make sure of their work, placed pistols in the dying men's faces and emptied the chambers.

Citizens who were aroused by the shooting and ran out to investigate the cause were driven to their homes at the point of guns and pistols and then the mob mounted their horses and dashed out of town, back into the woods and home again.

None of the mob was recognized, as their faces were completely concealed by masks. The men did their work orderly and coolly and exhibited a determination seldom equaled under similar circumstances.

The nine Negroes were tied with ropes and were helpless.

The guard was held at the muzzle of guns and threatened with death if a man moved.

Then the firing was deliberately done, volley by volley.

The Negroes now dead are: Tip Hudson, Bud Cotton, Ed Wynn, Henry Bingham.

Fatally shot and now dying: John Bigby.

Shot but will recover: John Jameson.

Arm broken: George Tatum.

Escaped without injury: Ison Brown, Clem Watts.

The men who were guarding the Negroes are well known and prominent citizens of Palmetto, and were sworn in only yesterday as a special guard for the night.

The commitment trial of the Negroes was set for 9 o'clock this morning.

Bud Cotton, who was killed, had confessed to the burning of the stores in Palmetto, and had implicated all the others who had been arrested.

The military having been sent by Governor Candler arrived at 10:40 o'clock this morning on a special train under command of Colonel John S. Candler.

The Negro population of Palmetto has fled from town and it is believed the Negroes are now congregating on the outskirts and will make an assault upon the town to-night.

The place is in the wildest excitement and every citizen is armed, expecting an outbreak as soon as night shall fall.

The Negroes left the town in droves early this morning, weeping and screaming and dogged and revengeful.

Business has been entirely suspended and Palmetto, formerly a peaceful agricultural village, is running riot with intense excitement and anxiety is expressed by every one.

The lives and property of citizens will be protected at any cost, and the white people, while condemning the act of lawlessness of the mob, are determined to meet any attempt the Negroes may make for revenge.

It was just past the hour of midnight. The guards were sleepy and tired of the weary watch and the little city of Palmetto was sound asleep, with nothing to disturb the midnight hour or to interrupt the crime that was about to be committed.

Without the slightest noise the mob of lynchers approached the

318

THE LIGHT OF TRUTH

door to the warehouse. Not a false step was made, not a dead leaf was trod upon and not even the creaking of a shoe or the clearing of a throat broke the stillness.

With a noise that shook the buildings and threw every man to his feet the big fireproof door was suddenly struck as if with the force of a battering ram.

The guards sprang to their guns and the Negroes screamed for mercy.

But there were rifles, shotguns and pistols everywhere.

The little anteroom was packed full of armed men in an instant. The men seemed to come up through the floor and through the walls, so rapidly did they fill the room. And still others poured in at the door, and when the room was filled so that not another man could enter, the door was slammed to with awful noise and force.

The Negroes were screaming at the top of their voices.

"Hands up and don't move; if you move a foot or turn your hands I will blow your damned brains out," came the stern and rigid command of a man of small, thick stature, his face wholly concealed by a mask of white cloth and holding in his hands a couple of dangerous horse pistols.

The guards threw their hands up above their heads, all except one guard, James Hendricks, who lifted only one hand, while the other firmly grasped his revolver.

"I'll blow hell out of you in a minute if you don't put that hand up," came the warning, and the hand followed the other one.

The command was then given to move, and move quick.

"You guards, move, and move quick, if you don't want to get your brains blown out," cried the low man, who was the mob's leader.

The guards were then placed in line, six of them, and marched around the room and then marched to the front of the room, near the door through which the mob had entered.

They were placed in line against the front wall of the building and ordered not to move at the cost of their lives.

They did not speak, neither did they move, and not a word was said by the guard to the mob.

The men then walked around where they could get a good look at the trembling, pleading, terror-stricken Negroes, begging for life and declaring that they were innocent.

There was a moment's pause of deliberation. The Negroes

thought it meant that the assassins hesitated in their bloody deed, but the men hesitated only because they wanted deliberate action and a clear range for their bullets.

The Negroes, helpless, tied together with ropes, begged for mercy, for they saw the cold gun barrels, the angry and determined faces of the men, and they knew it meant death—instant death to them.

"Oh, God, have mercy!" cried one of the men in his agony. "Oh, give me a minute to live."

The cry for mercy and the prayer for life brought an oath from the leader and derisive laughter from the mob.

"Stand up in a line," said the man in command. "Stand up and we will see if we can't kill you out; if we can't, we'll turn out."

The Negroes faltered.

"Burn the devils," came a suggestion from the crowd.

"No, we'll shoot 'em like dogs," said the mob's leader.

"Stand up, every one of you and get up quick and march to the end of the room."

The Negroes slowly stood up. The mob came closer and pressed about the stacks of furniture that had been stored in the room.

The leader asked if everybody's gun was loaded and the men answered in the affirmative.

The Negroes pleaded and prayed for mercy.

They stood, trembling wretches, jerking at the long ropes that held them by the waist and about the wrists.

"Oh, give me a minute longer!" implored Bud Cotton.

"My men, are you ready?" asked the captain, still cool and composed and fearfully determined to execute the bloodiest deed that has ever stained Campbell County.

"Ready," came the unanimous response.

"One, two, three—fire!" was the command, given orderly, but hurriedly.

Every man in the room, and the number is estimated at from seventy-five to one hundred and fifty, fired point blank at the line of trembling and terror-stricken bound wretches.

The volley came as the fire from a gatling gun.

It filled the warehouse with smoke and flame and death and brought a wail of horror that chilled the helpless guard.

The volley awakened the peaceful town of Palmetto and from every house the excited citizens ran.

"Load and fire again," shouted the captain of the mob, and his voice was heard above the screaming and death cries of the wounded and dead.

The men rapidly loaded their guns, then fired at the given command.

"Now, before you leave, load and get ready for trouble," came the captain's order, and then men loaded their guns and got ready to leave the bloody room.

The guard was not relieved, however, until every man had left the building and all was safe for their hasty flight.

"I wonder if they are all dead," said one of the mob, when the order was given to leave the building.

"I reckon so," said one of the mob.

"But we had better see," said the captain coolly and assuming an air of business.

A detail of probably a half dozen men, probably a dozen and maybe more, the guard does not remember just how many, was sent forward into the blood and brains and into the twisting mass of dying men to examine if all were dead. They were given orders to finish those who were not dead.

The detail rushed forward.

The men jerked the fallen, twisting and writhing and bleeding bodies about.

The first man they reached was not dead. He was still groaning, and the breath was coming in great, quick gasps.

A pistol was placed at his breast and every chamber was emptied.

"He's dead now," laughed one of the crowd.

Other men, wounded, bleeding, moaning and begging, were caught, turned over and pistols emptied into their bodies.

But the shooting had made so much noise that the mob concluded its safety lay in flight.

The Negroes were quickly examined and with a parting shot and a volley of oaths of warning the mob left the warehouse and rushed to their horses.

The men ran from the warehouse to the little spot in the center of town, where horses are tied by countrymen and merchants.

They mounted quickly and began their ride for life.

With a sweeping of falling and echoing hoofs the cavalrymen dashed down the principal street at breakneck speed.

Mr. Henry Beckman, who lives a few hundred yards beyond the scene of the murders, heard the firing and ran from his house to the railroad tracks.

The horsemen, using the lash and urging their horses to their highest speed, dashed into view.

"Hello," said Beckman, "what does all this firing mean?"

Beckman was answered with an oath and told to get into his hole as quickly as possible. "If you don't, we'll kill you on the spot," was the warning.

Beckman flew for life, ran through the yard and entered the house as quickly as possible.

Dr. Hal L. Johnson saw a crowd of men on foot running down the sidewalk.

He hailed them, but there was no response.

"There must have been more than one hundred men on horses," said Mr. Beckman this morning, in telling the Journal of his wild night experience with the mob.

When the mob left, the guards, who had been held against the warehouse wall at the points of guns and pistols, turned their faces toward the scene of carnage and death.

The furniture in the room had been splattered and wrecked with bullets and the contortions of the Negroes.

On the floor, near the center of the room, were two Negroes, still tied with rope, locked in each other's embrace. Near their bodies streams of blood were dyeing red the floor and spreading out in pools.

Just beyond were two more bodies. These Negroes were dead, too.

Near the fireplace was John Bigby, twisting and writhing in his agony. Blood was spouting from a number of wounds.

Under the beds and tables and piles of furniture were other bodies, every prisoner apparently dead, except Bigby, who was fast regaining consciousness.

The guards opened the door cautiously, but there were no signs of the mob, save the echoing footfalls on the country road.

CHAPTER II

Tortured and Burned Alive

The burning of Samuel Hose, or, to give his right name, Samuel Wilkes, gave to the United States the distinction of having burned alive seven human beings during the past ten years. The details of this deed of unspeakable barbarism have shocked the civilized world, for it is conceded universally that no other nation on earth, civilized or savage, has put to death any human being with such atrocious cruelty as that inflicted upon Samuel Hose by the Christian white people of Georgia.

The charge is generally made that lynch law is condemned by the best white people of the South, and that lynching is the work of the lowest and lawless class. Those who seek the truth know the fact to be, that all classes are equally guilty, for what the one class does the other encourages, excuses and condones.

This was clearly shown in the burning of Hose. This awful deed was suggested, encouraged and made possible by the daily press of Atlanta, Georgia, until the burning actually occurred, and then it immediately condoned the burning by a hysterical plea to "consider the facts."

Samuel Hose killed Alfred Cranford Wednesday afternoon, April 12, 1899, in a dispute over wages due Hose. The dispatch which announced the killing of Cranford stated that Hose had assaulted Mrs. Cranford and that bloodhounds had been put on his track.

The next day the Atlanta Constitution, in glaring double headlines predicted a lynching and suggested burning at the stake. This is repeated in the body of the dispatch in the following language:

"When Hose is caught he will either be lynched and his body riddled with bullets or he will be burned at the stake." And further in the same issue the Constitution suggests torture in these words: "There have been whisperings of burning at the stake and of torturing the fellow, and so great is the excitement, and so high the indignation, that this is among the possibilities."

In the issue of the 15th, in another double-column display heading, the Constitution announces: "Negro will probably be burned," and in the body of the dispatch burning and torture is confidently predicted in these words:

"Several modes of death have been suggested for him, but it seems to be the universal opinion that he will be burned at the stake and probably tortured before burned."

The next day, April 16th, the double-column head still does its inflammatory work. Never a word for law and order, but daily encouragement for burning. The headlines read: "Excitement still continues intense, and it is openly declared that if Sam Hose is brought in alive he will be burned," and in the dispatch it said:

"The residents have shown no disposition to abandon the search in the immediate neighborhood of Palmetto; their ardor has in no degree cooled, and if Sam Hose is brought here by his captors he will be publicly burned at the stake as an example to members of his race who are said to have been causing the residents of this vicinity trouble for some time."

On the 19th the Constitution assures the public that interest in the pursuit of Hose does not lag, and in proof of the zeal of the pursuers said:

" 'If Hose is on earth I'll never rest easy until he's caught and burned alive. And that's the way all of us feel,' said one of them last night."

Clark Howell, editor, and W. A. Hemphill, business manager, of the Constitution, had offered through their paper a reward of five hundred dollars for the arrest of the fugitive. This reward, together with the persistent suggestion that the Negro be burned as soon as caught, make it plain as day that the purpose to burn Hose at the stake was formed by the leading citizens of Georgia. The Constitution offered the reward to capture him, and then day after day suggested and predicted that he be burned when caught. The Chicago anarchists[13] were hanged, not because they threw the bomb, but because they incited to that act the unknown man who did throw it. Pity that the same law cannot be carried into force in Georgia!

Hose was caught Saturday night, April 23, and let the Constitution tell the story of his torture and death.

From the issue of April 24th the following account is condensed:

Newman, Ga., April 23.—(Special.)—Sam Hose, the Negro murderer of Alfred Cranford and the assailant of Cranford's wife, was burned at the stake one mile and a quarter from this place this afternoon at 2:30 o'clock. Fully 2,000 people surrounded the small sapling to which he was fastened and watched the flames eat away his flesh, saw his body mutilated by knives and witnessed the contortions of his body in his extreme agony.

Such suffering has seldom been witnessed, and through it all the Negro uttered hardly a cry. During the contortions of his body several blood vessels bursted. The spot selected was an ideal one for such an affair, and the stake was in full view of those who stood about and with unfeigned satisfaction saw the Negro meet his death and saw him tortured before the flames killed him.

A few smoldering ashes scattered about the place, a blackened stake, are all that is left to tell the story. Not even the bones of the Negro were left in the place, but were eagerly snatched by a crowd of people drawn here from all directions, who almost fought over the burning body of the man, carving it with knives and seeking souvenirs of the occurrence.

Preparations for the execution were not necessarily elaborate, and it required only a few minutes to arrange to make Sam Hose pay the penalty of his crime. To the sapling Sam Hose was tied, and he watched the cool, determined men who went about arranging to burn him.

First he was made to remove his clothing, and when the flames began to eat into his body it was almost nude. Before the fire was lighted his left ear was severed from his body. Then his right ear was cut away. During this proceeding he uttered not a groan. Other portions of his body were mutilated by the knives of those who gathered about him, but he was not wounded to such an extent that he was not fully conscious and could feel the excruciating pain. Oil was poured over the wood that was placed about him and this was ignited.

The scene that followed is one that never will be forgotten by those who saw it, and while Sam Hose writhed and performed contortions in his agony, many of those present turned away from the sickening sight, and others could hardly look at it. Not a sound but the crackling of the flames broke the stillness of the place, and the situation grew more sickening as it proceeded.

The stake bent under the strains of the Negro in his agony and his sufferings cannot be described, although he uttered not a sound. After his ears had been cut off he was asked about the crime, and then it was he made a full confession. At one juncture, before the flames had begun to get in their work well, the fastenings that held him to the stake broke and he fell forward partially out of the fire.

He writhed in agony and his sufferings can be imagined when it is said that several blood vessels burst during the contortions of his body. When he fell from the stake he was kicked back and the flames renewed. Then it was that the flames consumed his body and in a few minutes only a few bones and a small part of the body was all that was left of Sam Hose.

One of the most sickening sights of the day was the eagerness with which the people grabbed after souvenirs, and they almost fought over the ashes of the dead criminal. Large pieces of his flesh were carried away, and persons were seen walking through the streets carrying bones in their hands.

When all the larger bones, together with the flesh, had been carried away by the early comers, others scraped in the ashes, and for a great length of time a crowd was about the place scraping in the ashes. Not even the stake to which the Negro was tied when burned was left but it was promptly chopped down and carried away as the largest souvenir of the burning.

CHAPTER III

Elijah Strickland, A Colored Preacher, Lynched

Sunday night, April 23d, a mob seized a well-known colored preacher, Elijah Strickland, and, after savage torture, slowly strangled him to death. The following account of the lynching is taken from the Atlanta Constitution:

Palmetto, Ga., April 24.—(Special.)—The body of Lige Strickland, the negro who was implicated in the Cranford murder by Sam Hose, was found this morning swinging to the limb of a persimmon tree within a mile and a quarter of this place, as told in the Constitution extra yesterday. Before death was allowed to end the sufferings of the Negro, his ears were cut off and the small finger of his left hand was severed at the second joint. One of these trophies was in Palmetto to-day.

On the chest of the Negro was a scrap of blood-stained paper, attached with an ordinary pin. On one side of this paper contained the following:

"N. Y. Journal. We must protect our Ladies. 23–99."

The other side of the paper contained a warning to the Negroes of the neighborhood. It reads as follows:

"Beware all darkies. You will be treated the same way."

Before being finally lynched, Lige Strickland was given a chance to confess to the misdeeds of which the mob supposed him to be guilty, but he protested his innocence until the end.

Three times the noose was placed around his neck and the Negro was drawn up off the ground; three times he was let down with warnings that death was in store for him should he fail to confess his complicity in the Cranford murder, and three times Strickland proclaimed his innocence, until, weary of useless torturing, the mob pulled on the rope and tied the end around the slender trunk of the persimmon tree.

Not a shot was fired by the mob. Strickland was strangled to death. He was lynched about 2:30 a.m.

The lynching of Strickland was not accomplished without a desperate effort on the part of his employer to save his life. The man who pleaded for the Negro is Major W. W. Thomas, an ex-State Senator, and one of the most distinguished citizens of Coweta County.

Sunday night, about 8:30 o'clock, about fifteen men went to the plantation of Major Thomas and took Lige Strickland from the little cabin in the woods that he called home, leaving his wife and five children to wail and weep over the fate they knew was in store for the Negro. Their cries aroused Major Thomas, and that sturdy old gentleman of the antebellum type followed the lynchers in his buggy, accompanied by his son, W. M. Thomas, determined to save, if possible, the life of his plantation darky.

He overtook the lynchers with their victim at Palmetto, and then ensued the weirdest and most dramatic scene this section has ever known, with only the moonlight to show the faces of the grim, determined men.

It had for its actors the Negro, apparently unconcerned even with the noose around his neck; the old white-haired gentleman, pleading for the life of his servant, and attempting to prove the innocence of the Negro to men who would not be convinced.

Lige Strickland was halted directly opposite the telegraph office. The noose was adjusted around his neck and the end of the rope was thrown over a tree. Strickland was told he had a chance before dying to confess his complicity in the crime. He replied:

"I have told you all I know, gentlemen. You can kill me if you wish, but I know nothing more to tell."

The Negro's life might have been ended then but for the arrival of Major Thomas, who leaped from his buggy and asked for a hearing. He asked the crowd to give the Negro a chance for his life here on the streets of Palmetto, and Major Thomas said he would speak in his defense. A short conference resulted in acquiescence to this, and Major Thomas spoke in substance as follows:

"Gentlemen, this Negro is innocent. Hose said Lige had promised to give him $20 to kill Cranford, and I believe Lige has not had $20 since he has been on my place. This is a law-abiding Negro you are about to hang. He has never done any of you any harm, and now I want you to promise me that you will turn him over either to the bailiff of this town or to some one who is entitled to receipt for him, in order that he may be given a hearing on his case. I do not ask that you liberate him. Hold him and if the courts adjudge him guilty, hang him."

There were some, however, who agreed with Major Thomas, and after a discussion a vote was taken, which was supposed to mean life or death to Lige Strickland. The vote to let him live was unanimous.

Major Thomas then retired some distance and the mob was preparing to send Strickland in a wagon to Newnan when a member of the mob said:

"We have got him here, let's keep him."

This again aroused the mob and a messenger was sent to advise Major Thomas to leave Palmetto for his own good, but the old gentleman was not frightened so easily. He drew himself up and said with all the emphasis he could summon:

"I have never before been ordered to leave a town and I am not going to leave this one." And then the Major, uplifting his hand to give his words force, said to the messenger:

"Tell them that the muscles in my legs are not trained to run-

ning; tell them that I have stood the fire and heard the whistle of
the minies from a thousand rifles and I am not frightened by this
crowd."

Major Thomas was not molested.

Then, with the understanding Lige Strickland was to be delivered to the jailer at Fairburn, Major Thomas saw the Negro he
had pleaded for led off to his death. This occurred at about 1
o'clock this morning.

Strickland was then taken in the rear of the home of Dr. W. S.
Zellars, to the persimmon tree upon which his lifeless body was
left hanging.

CHAPTER IV

Report of Detective Louis P. Le Vin

The colored citizens of Chicago sent a detective to Georgia, and
his report shows that Samuel Hose, who was brutally tortured at
Newnan, Ga., and then burned to death, never assaulted Mrs.
Cranford and that he killed Alfred Cranford in self-defense.

The full text of the report is as follows:

About three weeks ago I was asked to make an impartial and
thorough investigation of the lynchings which occurred near
Atlanta, Ga., not long since. I left Chicago for Atlanta, and spent
over a week in the investigation. The facts herein were gathered
from interviews with persons I met in Griffin, Newman, Atlanta
and in the vicinity of these places.

I found no difficulty in securing interviews from white people.
There was no disposition on their part to conceal any part they
took in the lynchings. They discussed the details of the burning of Sam Hose with the freedom which one would talk about
an afternoon's divertisement in which he had very pleasantly
participated.

Who was Sam Hose? His true name was Samuel Wilkes. He
was born in Macon, Ga., where he lived until his father died.
The family, then consisting of his mother, brother and sister,
moved to Marshall, where all worked and made the reputation of
hard-working, honest people. Sam studied and was soon able to
read and write, and was considered a bright, capable man. His

mother became an invalid, and as his brother was considered almost an imbecile, Sam was the mainstay of the family. He worked on different farms, and among the men he worked for was B. Jones, who afterward captured him and delivered him over to the mob at Newman.

Sam's mother partly recovered, and as his sister married, Sam left and went to Atlanta to better his condition. He secured work near Palmetto for a man named Alfred Cranford, and worked for him for about two years, up to the time of the tragedy. I will not call it a murder, for Samuel Wilkes killed Alfred Cranford in self-defense. The story you have read about a Negro stealing into the house and murdering the unfortunate man at his supper has no foundation in fact. Equally untrue is the charge that after murdering the husband he assaulted the wife. The reports indicated that the murderer was a stranger, who had to be identified. The fact is he had worked for Cranford for over a year.

Was there a murder? That Wilkes killed Cranford there is no doubt, but under what circumstances can never be proven. I asked many white people of Palmetto what was the motive. They considered it a useless question. A "nigger" had killed a white man, and that was enough. Some said it was because the young "niggers" did not know their places, others that they were getting too much education, while others declared that it was all due to the influence of the Northern "niggers." W. W. Jackson, of Newman said: "If I had my way about it I would lynch every Northern 'nigger' that comes this way. They are at the bottom of this." John Low, of Lincoln, Ala., said: "My negroes would die for me simply because I keep a strict hand on them and allow no Northern negroes to associate with them."

Upon the question of motive there is no answer except that which was made by Wilkes himself. The dispatches said that Wilkes confessed both to the murder and the alleged assault upon Mrs. Cranford. But neither of these reports is true. Wilkes did say that he killed Mr. Cranford, but he did not at any time admit that he assaulted Mrs. Cranford. This he denied as long as he had breath.

After the capture Wilkes told his story. He said that his trouble began with Mr. Cranford a week before. He said that he had word that his mother was much worse at home, and that he wanted to go home to visit his mother. He told Mr. Cranford and asked for some money. Cranford refused to pay Wilkes, and that provoked hard words. Cranford was known to be a man of quick temper, but nothing more occurred that day. The next day Cranford borrowed a revolver and said that if Sam started any more trouble he would kill him.

Sam, continuing his story, said that on the day Cranford was killed he (Sam) was out in the yard cutting up wood; that Cranford came out into the yard, and that he and Cranford began talking about the subject of their former trouble; that Cranford became enraged and drew his gun to shoot, and then Sam threw an ax at Cranford and ran. He knew the ax struck Cranford, but did not know that Cranford had been killed by the blow for several days. At the time of the encounter in the yard, Sam said that Mrs. Cranford was in the house, and that after he threw the ax at Cranford he never saw Mrs. Cranford, for he immediately went to the woods and kept in hiding until he reached the vicinity of his mother's home, where he was captured. During all the time Sam was on the train going to the scene of the burning, Sam is said by all I talked with to have been free from excitement or terror. He told his story in a straightforward way, said he was sorry he had killed Cranford and always denied that he had attacked Mrs. Cranford.

I did not see Mrs. Cranford. She was still suffering from the awful shock. As soon as her husband was killed she ran to the home of his father and told him that Sam had killed her husband. She did not then say that Sam had assaulted her. She was completely overcome and was soon unconscious and remained so for most of the next two days. So that at the time when the story was started that Sam had added the crime of outrage to murder, Mrs. Cranford, the only one who could have told about it, was lying either unconscious or delirious at the home of her father-in-law, G. E. Cranford.

The burning of Wilkes was fully premeditated. It was no sudden outburst of a furious maddened mob. It was known long before Wilkes was caught that he would be burned. The Cranfords are an old, wealthy and aristocratic family, and it was intended to make an example of the Negro who killed him. What exasperation the killing lacked was supplied by the report of the alleged attack on Mrs. Cranford. And it was not the irresponsible rabble that urged the burning, for it was openly advocated by some of the leading men of Palmetto. E. D. Sharkey, Superintendent Atlanta Bagging Mills, was one of the most persistent advocates of the burning. He claimed that he saw Mrs. Cranford the day after the killing and that she told him that she was assaulted. As a matter of fact, Mrs. Cranford was unconscious at that time. He persistently told the story and urged the burning of Sam as soon as caught.

John Haas, President of the Capitol Bank, was particularly prominent in advocating the burning. People doing business at his bank, and coming from Newman and Griffin, were urged to make an example of Sam by burning him.

W. A. Hemphill, President and business manager, and Clark Howell, editor of the Atlanta Constitution, contributed more to the burning than any other men and all other forces in Georgia. Through the columns of their paper they exaggerated every detail of the killing, invented and published inflammatory descriptions of a crime that was never committed, and by glaring head lines continually suggested the burning of the man when caught. They offered a reward of $500 blood money for the capture of the fugitive, and during all the time of the man-hunt they never made one suggestion that the law should have its course.

The Governor of the State acquiesced in the burning by refusing to prevent it. Sam Wilkes was captured at 9 o'clock Saturday night. He was in Griffin by 9 o'clock Sunday morning. It was first proposed to burn him in Griffin, but the program was changed, and it was decided to take him to Newman to burn him. Governor Candler had ordered that Wilkes should be taken to the Fulton county jail when caught. That would have placed him in Atlanta. When Wilkes reached Griffin he was in custody of J. B. Jones, J. L. Jones, R. A. Gordon, William Matthews, P. F. Phelps, Charles Thomas and A. Rogowski. They would not take the prisoner to Atlanta, where the Governor had ordered him to be taken, but arranged to take him to Newman, where they knew a mob of six thousand were waiting to burn him. It is nearer to Atlanta from Griffin than Newman. Besides, there was no train going to Newman that Sunday morning, so the captors of Wilkes were obliged to secure a special train to take the prisoner to the place of burning. This required over two hours' time to arrange, so that the special train did not leave Griffin for Newman until 11:40 a. m.

Meanwhile the news of the capture of Wilkes was known all over Georgia. It was known in Atlanta in the early morning that the prisoner would not be brought to Atlanta, but that he would be taken to Newman to be burned. As soon as this was settled, a special train was engaged as an excursion train, to take people to the burning. It was soon filled by the criers, who cried out. "Special train to Newman! All aboard for the burning!" After this special moved out, another was made up to accommodate the later comers and those who were at church. In this way more than two thousand citizens of Atlanta were taken to the burning, while the Governor, with all the power of the State at his command, allowed all preparations for the burning to be made during ten hours of daylight and did not turn his hand to prevent it.

I do not need to give the details of the burning. I mention only one fact, and that is the disappointment which the crowd felt when it could not make Wilkes beg for mercy. During all the time of his torture he never uttered one cry. They cut off both ears, skinned his face, cut off his fingers, gashed his legs, cut open his stomach and pulled out his entrails, then when his contortions broke the iron chain, they pushed his burning body back into the fire. But through it all Wilkes never once uttered a cry or beg for mercy. Only once in a particularly fiendish torture did he speak, then he simply groaned, "Oh, Lord Jesus."

Among the prominent men at the burning, and whose identity was disclosed to me, are William Pinton, Clair Owens and William Potts, of Palmetto; W. W. Jackson and H. W. Jackson of Newman; Peter Howson and T. Vaughn, of the same place; John Hazlett, Pierre St. Clair and Thomas Lightfoot, of Griffin, R. J. Williams, ticket agent at Griffin, made up the special Central Georgia Railroad train and advertised the burning at Griffin, while B. F. Wyly and George Smith, of Atlanta, made up two special Atlanta and West Point Railroad trains. All of these gentlemen of eminent respectability could give the authorities valuable information about the burning if called upon.

While Wilkes was being burned the colored people fled terror-stricken to the woods, for none knew where the fury would strike. I talked with many people, but all will understand why I can give no names.

The torture and hanging of the colored preacher is everywhere acknowledged to have been without a shadow of reason or excuse. I did not talk to one white man who believed that Strickland had anything to do with Wilkes. I could not find any person who heard Wilkes mention Strickland's name. I talked with men who heard Wilkes tell his story, but all agreed that he said he killed Cranford because Cranford was about to kill him, and that he did not mention Strickland's name. He did not mention it when he was being tortured because he did not speak to anybody. I could not find anybody who could tell me how the story started that Strickland hired Wilkes to kill Cranford.

On the other hand, I saw many who knew Strickland, and all spoke of him in the highest terms. I went to see Mr. Thomas, and he said that Strickland had been about his family for years, and that he never knew a more reliable and worthy man among the colored people. He said that he was always advising the colored people to live right, keep good friends with the white people and earn their respect. He said he was nearly sixty years old and had not had five dollars at one time in a year. He defended the poor old man against the mob for a long time, and the mob finally agreed to put him in jail for a trial, but as soon as they had Strickland in their control they proceeded to lynch him.

The torture of the innocent colored preacher was only a little less than that of Wilkes. His fingers and ears were cut off and the mob inflicted other tortures that cannot even be suggested. He was strung up three times and let down each time so he could confess. But he died protesting his innocence. He left a wife and five children, all of whom are still on Colonel Thomas' premises.

I spent some time in trying to find the facts about the shooting of the five colored men at Palmetto a few days before Cranford was killed. But no one seemed to be able to tell who accused the men, and as they were not given a trial, there was no way to get at any of the facts. It seems that one or two barns or houses had been burned, and it was reported that the Negroes were setting fire to the buildings. Nine colored men were arrested on suspicion. They were not men of bad character, but quite the reverse. They were intelligent, hard-working men, and all declared they could easily prove their innocence. They were taken to a warehouse to be kept until their trial next day. That night, about 12 o'clock, an armed mob marched to the place and fired three volleys into the line of chained prisoners. They then went away thinking all were dead. All the prisoners were shot. Of these five died. Nothing was done about the killing of these men but their families were afterward ordered to leave the place, and all have left. Five widows and seventeen fatherless children all driven from home, constitute one result of the lynching. I saw no one who thought much about the matter. The Negroes were dead, and while they did not know whether they were guilty or not, it was plain that nothing could be done about it. And so the matter ended. With these facts I made my way home, thoroughly convinced that a Negro's life is a very cheap thing in Georgia.

LOUIS P. LE VIN

CHAPTER V

Twentieth-Century
Journalism and Letters

The beginning of the twentieth century found Ida B. Wells-Barnett heading up the Afro-American Council's new Anti-Lynching Bureau, which was established by the council in 1899 to investigate lynchings and other forms of racial violence. The job was perfect for Wells, but the bureau received very little funding and limited support of any other kind from the Afro-American Council, which would itself collapse in 1907. Still, the first couple of years of the twentieth century would see Wells-Barnett attempting to capitalize on her position at the bureau with a flurry of publications. Writing on "Lynch Law in America" in the *Arena*, a national publication, she promoted the work of the Anti-Lynching Bureau, and described lynching as a "national crime" that all Americans must repudiate. She also made similar arguments in two articles published in the *Independent* the following year.

Thereafter, Wells's pace of publication slowed. By 1904 she had four children, having given birth to her daughter Ida in 1901, and her youngest child, Alfreda, in 1904. With four young children in the house, Wells-Barnett was no longer a regular contributor to any newspaper, but she remained deeply committed to reforming the world around her. Active in municipal and state politics, she also campaigned for women's suffrage, led a woman's club, worked as a parole officer, and founded a reform organization called the Negro Fellowship League (NFL), which was dedicated to serving the needs of the black Southern migrants who began migrating to Chicago in the years leading up to World War I. Moreover, even after the collapse of the Afro-American Council, she remained committed to creating a national civil rights

organization, and supported both the Niagara Movement of
1905—another short-lived attempt to create such a movement—
and its far more enduring successor, the NAACP, which was established in 1909. Her wide-ranging commitments are well
represented in the pamphlets and articles that she published between 1904 and her death in 1931.

These include "Booker T. Washington and His Critics" in the
World Today, an important critique of Booker T. Washington that
she wrote shortly after the birth of her youngest child. It appeared
alongside W. E. B. Du Bois's more well known "The Parting of
the Ways" and saw Wells-Barnett join Du Bois in decisively reject-
ing the accommodationist leadership of the nation's most famous
and powerful African American. A longtime critic of Washington,
Wells was most troubled by Washington's failure to denounce
antiblack violence and to support black civil rights, two subjects
she returned to in "How Enfranchisement Stops Lynching." This
essay originated as a speech that Wells-Barnett delivered at an
early meeting of the NAACP. Speaking before an organization
formed by people who largely rejected Booker T. Washington's
accommodationist politics, Wells-Barnett drew on her experience with activist politics in Illinois to show how blacks there
had made lynching a thing of the past by electing "one of their
own" to the state legislature, thereby securing "the passage of a
bill which provided for the suppression of mob violence, not only
by punishment of those who incited lynchings."

However, Northern blacks had problems of their own, as Wells-
Barnett emphasized in a variety of subsequent articles. "Northern
Negro Women" were excluded from many jobs and unwelcome
in many neighborhoods and recreational facilities, Wells-Barnett
noted in an article published in 1910. Moreover, the North was
often even less hospitable to black men, who inhabited Illinois's
prison system in increasing numbers.

Acutely aware that black men received no mercy once they fell
into the hands of the justice system, in 1910 Wells-Barnett sprang
to the defense of Steven Green, a fugitive from Arkansas whose
story she chronicled in the *Washington Post* under the headline
"Slayer, in Grip of Law Fights Return to South." Green had been
attacked by his employer, and ended up killing the other man in
self-defense, and then fled his home state rather than face a lynching. But Arkansas authorities located him in Chicago and had

him extradited and sent home. He was on the train south when Wells-Barnett finally managed to intervene, having secured the aid of two black attorneys who successfully challenged extradition before his train left Illinois. Likewise, in 1915, Wells-Barnett publicized and protested the mistreatment of "Chicken" Joe Campbell, a prisoner in Illinois's Joliet Correctional Center, who was accused of raping and murdering the prison warden's wife. Campbell had been held in a solitary, unlit cell and fed only bread and water for more than two days by the time Wells-Barnett heard about his plight. She protested his treatment in "The Ordeal of the Solitary," and hired a lawyer to represent him.

Even as Wells-Barnett became ever more involved in remedying legal injustices in Illinois, she never abandoned her campaign against lynching and racial violence in the South. She protested lynching yet again in "Our Country's Lynching Record" in 1913 in an article suggesting that the slow decline in the number of lynchings after 1892 should not be seen as a cause for celebration. There were sixty-five lynchings in 1912, she pointed out, which was still far too many.

Wells-Barnett's concerns about the persistence of racial violence in the United States were borne out during the World War I era, which saw a series of race riots. She was inspired to hit the road again, to investigate the causes of a 1917 riot in East St. Louis that killed between forty and two hundred people, and an equally deadly riot in Elaine, Arkansas, two years later that killed between one hundred and two hundred people. Chronicled by Wells-Barnett in *The East St. Louis Massacre: The Greatest Outrage of the Century* (1917), the first of these two riots took place during the war, making Wells-Barnett's investigation a matter of national security. The pamphlet she published on this event was censored by the War Department and disappeared for many years before being rediscovered by Wells biographer, Linda McMurray, who found it in the Military Intelligence Division's papers at the National Archives.[1] Read by government officials, if no one else, Wells-Barnett did help to inspire a congressional investigation into the events in East St. Louis.

By contrast, Wells-Barnett's pamphlet on *The Arkansas Race Riot*, which occurred in the fall of 1919 well after Armistice Day, was neither censored nor widely read outside Chicago. Even as Wells-Barnett rallied her energies to investigate these conflicts,

she could no longer mobilize the support she needed to draw national attention to her work. By 1916 the NAACP, an organization that Wells-Barnett found too cautious and moderate to work
with during its early years, had taken on racial violence as one of
its central causes and could sponsor far more widely publicized
responses to riots of the World War I era. Whereas Wells-Barnett
had to fund her own publications, and had limited influence outside Illinois, the NAACP, while far from wealthy, had the funds
to retain full-time staffers such as Walter White to investigate
racial violence, and could publish his findings in the NAACP's own
nationally circulated magazine, the *Crisis*. The NAACP's Chicago
branch was notably timorous and conservative, making Wells-
Barnett's efforts there far from redundant. But she had trouble
getting a hearing outside Illinois.

During the last decade of her life, Wells-Barnett focused her
reformist energies largely on her home state, drafted her autobiography, and published little on national events other than a series of articles on the Mississippi Flood of 1927. This catastrophic
natural disaster, which submerged twenty-seven thousand square
miles of land along the banks of the Mississippi River, was of
particular interest to blacks in Chicago, many of whom were
Southern migrants who worried about their friends and relatives.
Moreover, they had even greater cause for concern when it became evident that black refugees were being put to work shoring
up the levees at gunpoint, and starving in makeshift refugee
camps, where the Red Cross doled out unequal rations to black
and white flood victims. Three articles by Wells-Barnett protesting the conditions in the camps close out this volume and show
the sixty-five-year-old activist still pursuing her fearless crusade
for justice.

MOB RULE IN NEW ORLEANS: ROBERT CHARLES AND HIS FIGHT TO THE DEATH

Mob Rule in New Orleans chronicles the life and death of Robert Charles, a laborer who worked odd jobs and left behind a roomful of books documenting his attempts to improve himself through self-education. Charles triggered a race riot when he refused to allow the New Orleans police to arrest him for sitting on the front porch of the rooming house where he lived—for no other reason than that they found his presence there suspicious. Instead, he drew a gun, shot one of the officers, and fled. His actions triggered a manhunt in which Charles killed five police officers and wounded a dozen more, and inspired a mob of more than one thousand whites to join the police in their search for Charles, while also attacking other residents of black New Orleans at random. A total of twenty-eight people, most of them black, were killed in the conflict. Among them was Charles, who was cornered by the police and died in a hail of gunfire.

Wells-Barnett, who presided over the Afro-American Council's poorly funded Anti-Lynching Bureau, was deeply troubled by the events in New Orleans, and marshaled her meager resources to publish a pamphlet exploring Charles's life and death. In researching *Mob Rule in New Orleans*, Wells could not afford a private investigator but found out that she could, as she had in researching the Sam Hose lynching for *Lynch Law in Georgia* (1899), reconstruct much of what actually happened in New Orleans from a critical reading of the information contained in the city's white press—the *New Orleans Times-Democrat* and the *New Orleans Picayune*. She also wrote to Charles's friends to solicit additional information that might help her understand the actions of a man who had defied white authorities in New Orleans.

Mob Rule in New Orleans cannot fully explain Charles's actions. But it juxtaposes the white press's description of Charles as a "Negro desperado," a "ravisher," and a "fiend in human form" with the facts of his life as a quiet, law-abiding man with no criminal record. Charles owned a gun and proved willing to defend himself when attacked by the police, which made Wells-Barnett and many New Orleans black residents remember him as a hero.

SOURCE: Ida B. Wells-Barnett, *Mob Rule in New Orleans: Robert Charles and His Fight to the Death* (Chicago: Ida B. Wells-Barnett, 1900).

MOB RULE IN NEW ORLEANS: ROBERT CHARLES AND HIS FIGHT TO THE DEATH

INTRODUCTION

Immediately after the awful barbarism which disgraced the State of Georgia in April of last year, during which time more than a dozen colored people were put to death with unspeakable barbarity, I published a full report showing that Sam Hose, who was burned to death during that time, never committed a criminal assault, and that he killed his employer in self-defense.

Since that time I have been engaged on a work not yet finished, which I interrupt now to tell the story of the mob in New Orleans, which, despising all law, roamed the streets day and night, searching for colored men and women, whom they beat, shot and killed at will.

In the account of the New Orleans mob I have used freely the graphic reports of the New Orleans Times-Democrat and the New Orleans Picayune. Both papers gave the most minute details of the week's disorder. In their editorial comment they were at all times most urgent in their defense of law and in the strongest terms they condemned the infamous work of the mob.

It is no doubt owing to the determined stand for law and order taken by these great dailies and the courageous action taken by the best citizens of New Orleans, who rallied to the support of the civic authorities, that prevented a massacre of colored people awful to contemplate.

For the accounts and illustrations taken from the above named journals, sincere thanks are hereby expressed.

The publisher hereof does not attempt to moralize over the deplorable condition of affairs shown in this publication, but simply presents the facts in a plain, unvarnished, connected way, so that he who runs may read. We do not believe that the American people who have encouraged such scenes by their indifference will read unmoved these accounts of brutality, injustice and oppression. We do not believe that the moral conscience of the nation—that which is highest and best among us—will always remain silent in such outrages, for God is not dead, and His Spirit is not entirely driven from men's hearts.

When this conscience wakes and speaks out in thunder tones, as it must, it will need facts to use as a weapon against injustice, barbarism and wrong. It is for this reason that I carefully compile, print and send forth these facts. If the reader can do no more, he can pass this pamphlet on to another, or send to the bureau addresses of those to whom he can order copies mailed.

Besides the New Orleans case, a history of burnings in this country is given, together with a table of lynchings for the past eighteen years. Those who would like to assist in the work of disseminating these facts, can do so by ordering copies, which are furnished at greatly reduced rates for gratuitous distribution. The bureau has no funds and is entirely dependent upon contributions from friends and members in carrying on the work.

Chicago, Sept. 1, 1900

IDA B. WELLS-BARNETT

SHOT AN OFFICER

The bloodiest week which New Orleans has known since the massacre of the Italians in 1892 was ushered in Monday, July

24th, by the inexcusable and unprovoked assault upon two colored men by police officers of New Orleans. Fortified by the assurance born of long experience in the New Orleans service,
three policemen, Sergeant Aucoin, Officer Mora and Officer
Cantrelle, observing two colored men sitting on doorsteps on
Dryades street, between Washington avenue and 6th streets, determined, without a shadow of authority, to arrest them. One of
the colored men was named Robert Charles, the other was a lad
of nineteen named Leonard Pierce. The colored men had left
their homes, a few blocks distant, about an hour prior, and had
been sitting upon the doorsteps for a short time talking together.
They had not broken the peace in any way whatever, no warrant
was in the policemen's hands justifying their arrest, and no crime
had been committed of which they were the suspects. The policemen, however, secure in the firm belief that they could do anything to a Negro that they wished, approached the two men, and
in less than three minutes from the time they accosted them attempted to put both colored men under arrest. The younger of
the two men, Pierce, submitted to the arrest, for the officer,
Cantrelle, who accosted him, put his gun in the young man's face
ready to blow his brains out if he moved. The other colored man,
Charles, was made the victim of a savage attack by Officer Mora,
who used a billet[2] and then drew a gun and tried to kill Charles.
Charles drew his gun nearly as quickly as the policeman, and
began a duel in the street, in which both participants were shot.
The policeman got the worst of the duel, and fell helpless to the
sidewalk. Charles made his escape. Cantrelle took Pierce, his
captive, to the police station, to which place Mora, the wounded
officer, was also taken, and a man hunt at once instituted for
Charles, the wounded fugitive.

In any law-abiding community Charles would have been justified in delivering himself up immediately to the properly constituted authorities and asking for a trial by a jury of his peers. He
could have been certain that in resisting an unwarranted arrest
he had a right to defend his life, even to the point of taking one in
that defense, but Charles knew that his arrest in New Orleans,
even for defending his life, meant nothing short of a long term in
the penitentiary, and still more probable death by lynching at the
hands of a cowardly mob. He very bravely determined to protect
his life as long as he had the breath in his body and strength to

draw a hair trigger on his would-be murderers. How well he was justified in that belief is well shown by the newspaper accounts which were given of this transaction. Without a single line of evidence to justify the assertion, the New Orleans daily papers at once declared that both Pierce and Charles were desperadoes, that they were contemplating a burglary and that they began the assault upon the policemen. It is interesting to note how the leading papers of New Orleans, the Picayune and the Times-Democrat, exert themselves to justify the policemen in the absolutely unprovoked attack upon the two colored men. As these two papers did all in their power to give an excuse for the action of the policemen, it is interesting to note their versions. The Times-Democrat of Tuesday morning, the 25th, says:

"Two blacks, who are desperate men, and no doubt will be proven burglars, made it interesting and dangerous for three bluecoats on Dryades street, between Washington avenue and Sixth street, the Negroes using pistols first and dropping Patrolman Mora. But the desperate darkies did not go free, for the taller of the two, Robinson, is badly wounded and under cover, while Leonard Pierce is in jail.

"For a long time that particular neighborhood has been troubled with bad Negroes, and the neighbors were complaining to the Sixth Precinct police about them. But of late Pierce and Robinson had been camping on a door step on the street, and the people regarded their actions as suspicious. It got to such a point that some of the residents were afraid to go to bed, and last night this was told Sergeant Aucoin, who was rounding up his men. He had just picked up Officers Mora and Cantrell, on Washington avenue and Dryades street, and catching a glimpse of the blacks on the steps, he said he would go over and warn the men to get away from the street. So the patrolmen followed, and Sergeant Aucoin asked the smaller fellow, Pierce, if he lived there. The answer was short and impertinent, the black saying he did not, and with that both Pierce and Robinson drew up to their full height.

"For the moment the sergeant did not think that the Negroes meant fight, and he was on the point of ordering them away when Robinson slipped his pistol from his pocket. Pierce had his revolver out, too, and he fired twice, point blank at the sergeant, and just then Robinson began shooting at the patrolmen. In a second or so the policemen and blacks were fighting with their revolvers, the sergeant having a duel with Pierce, while Cantrell and Mora drew their line of fire on Robinson, who was working his revolver for all he was worth. One of his shots took Mora in the right hip, another caught his index finger on the right hand, and a third struck the small finger of the left hand. Poor Mora was done for; he could not fight any more, but Cantrell kept up his fire, being answered by the big black. Pierce's revolver broke down, the cartridges snapping, and he threw up his hands, begging for quarter.

"The sergeant lowered his pistol and some citizens ran over to where the shooting was going on. One of the bullets that went at Robinson caught him in the breast and he began running, turning out Sixth street, with Cantrell behind him, shooting every few steps. He was loading his revolver again, but did not use it after the start he took, and in a little while Officer Cantrell lost the man in the darkness.

"Pierce was made a prisoner and hurried to the Sixth Precinct police station, where he was charged with shooting and wounding. The sergeant sent for an ambulance, and Mora was taken to the hospital, the wound in the hip being serious.

"A search was made for Robinson, but he could not be found, and even at 2 o'clock this morning Captain Day, with Sergeant Aucoin and Corporals Perrier and Trenchard, with a good squad of men, were beating the weeds for the black."

The New Orleans Picayune of the same date described the occurrence, and from its account one would think it was an entirely different affair. Both of the two accounts cannot be true, and the unquestioned fact is that neither of them sets out the facts as they occurred. Both accounts attempt to fix the beginning of hostilities upon the colored men, but both were compelled to admit that the colored men were sitting on the doorsteps quietly conversing with one another when the three policemen went up and accosted them. The Times-Democrat unguardedly states that one of the two colored men tried to run away; that Mora seized him and then drew his billy and struck him on the head; that Charles broke away from him and started to run, after which the shooting began. The Picayune, however, declares that Pierce began the firing and that his two shots point blank at Aucoin were the first shots of the fight. As a matter of fact, Pierce never fired a single shot before he was covered by Aucoin's revolver. Charles and the officers did all the shooting. The Picayune's account is as follows:

"Patrolman Mora was shot in the right hip and dangerously wounded last night at 11:30 o'clock in Dryades street, between Washington and Sixth, by two Negroes, who were sitting on a door step in the neighborhood.

"The shooting of Patrolman Mora brings to memory the fact that he was one of the partners of Patrolman Trimp, who was shot by a Negro soldier of the United States government during the progress of the Spanish-American war. The shooting of Mora by the Negro last night is a very simple story. At the hour mentioned, three Negro women noticed two suspicious men sitting on a door step in the above locality. The women saw the two men making an apparent inspection of the building. As they told the story, they saw the men look over the fence and examine the window blinds, and they paid particular attention to the make-up of the building, which was a two-story affair. About that time Sergeant J. C. Aucoin and Officers Mora and J. D. Cantrell hove in sight. The women hailed them and described to them the suspicious actions of the two Negroes, who were still sitting on the step. The trio of bluecoats, on hearing the facts, at once crossed the street and accosted the men. The latter answered that they were waiting for a friend whom they were expecting. Not satisfied with this answer, the sergeant asked them where they lived, and they replied "down town," but could not designate the locality. To other questions put by the officers the larger of the two Negroes replied that they had been in town just three days.

"As this reply was made, the larger man sprang to his feet, and Patrolman Mora, seeing that he was about to run away, seized him. The Negro took a firm hold on the officer, and a scuffle ensued. Mora, noting that he was not being assisted by his brother officers, drew his billy and struck the Negro on the head. The blow had but little effect upon the man, for he broke away and started down the street. When about ten feet away, the Negro drew his revolver and opened fire on the officer, firing three or four shots. The third shot struck Mora in the right hip, and was subsequently found to have taken an upward course. Although badly wounded, Mora drew his pistol and returned the fire. At his third shot the

Negro was noticed to stagger, but he did not fall. He continued his flight. At this moment Sergeant Aucoin seized the other Negro, who proved to be a youth, Leon Pierce. As soon as Officer Mora was shot he sank to the sidewalk, and the other officer ran to the nearest telephone, and sent in a call for the ambulance. Upon its arrival the wounded officer was placed in it and conveyed to the hospital. An examination by the house surgeon revealed the fact that the bullet had taken an upward course. In the opinion of the surgeon the wound was a dangerous one."

But the best proof of the fact that the officers accosted the two colored men and without any warrant or other justification attempted to arrest them, and did actually seize and begin to club one of them, is shown by Officer Mora's own statement. The officer was wounded and had every reason in the world to make his side of the story as good as possible. His statement was made to a Picayune reporter and the same was published on the 25th inst., and is as follows:

"I was in the neighborhood of Dryades and Washington streets, with Sergeant Aucoin and Officer Cantrell, when three Negro women came up and told us that there were two suspicious-looking Negroes sitting on a step on Dryades street, between Washington and Sixth. We went to the place indicated and found two Negroes. We interrogated them as to who they were, what they were doing and how long they had been here. They replied that they were working for some one and had been in town three days. At about this stage the larger of the two Negroes got up and I grabbed him. The Negro pulled, but I held fast, and he finally pulled me into the street. Here I began using my billet, and the Negro jerked from my grasp and ran. He then pulled a gun and fired. I pulled my gun and returned the fire, each of us firing about three shots. I saw the Negro stumble several times, and I thought I had shot him, but he ran away and I don't know whether any of my shots took effect. Sergeant Aucoin in the meantime held the other man fast. The man was about ten feet from me when he fired, and the three Negresses who told us about the men stood away about twenty-five feet from the shooting."

Thus far in the proceeding the Monday night episode results in Officer Mora lying in the station wounded in the hip; Leonard

Pierce, one of the colored men, locked up in the station, and Robert Charles, the other colored man, a fugitive, wounded in the leg and sought for by the entire police force of New Orleans. Not sought for, however, to be placed under arrest and given a fair trial and punished if found guilty according to the law of the land, but sought for by a host of enraged, vindictive and fearless officers, who were coolly ordered to kill him on sight. This order is shown by the Picayune of the 26th inst., in which the following statement appears:

> "In talking to the sergeant about the case, the captain asked about the Negro's fighting ability, and the sergeant answered that Charles, though he called him Robinson then, was a desperate man, and it would be best to shoot him before he was given a chance to draw his pistol upon any of the officers."

This instruction was given before anybody had been killed, and the only evidence that Charles was a desperate man lay in the fact that he had refused to be beaten over the head by Officer Mora for sitting on a step quietly conversing with a friend. Charles resisted an absolutely unlawful attack, and a gun fight followed. Both Mora and Charles were shot, but because Mora was white and Charles was black, Charles was at once declared to be a desperado, made an outlaw, and subsequently a price put upon his head and the mob authorized to shoot him like a dog, on sight.

The New Orleans Picayune of Wednesday morning said:

> "But he has gone, perhaps to the swamps, and the disappointment of the bluecoats in not getting the murderer is expressed in their curses, each man swearing that the signal to halt that will be offered Charles will be a shot."

In that same column of the Picayune it was said:

> "Hundreds of policemen were about; each corner was guarded by a squad, commanded either by a sergeant or a corporal, and every man had the word to shoot the Negro as soon as he was sighted. He was a desperate black and would be given no chance to take more life."

Legal sanction was given to the mob or any man of the mob to kill Charles at sight by the Mayor of New Orleans, who publicly proclaimed a reward of two hundred and fifty dollars, not for the arrest of Charles, not at all, but the reward was offered for Charles's body, "dead or alive." The advertisement was as follows:

"$250 Reward.

"Under the authority vested in me by law, I hereby offer, in the name of the city of New Orleans, $250 reward for the capture and delivery, dead or alive, to the authorities of the city, the body of the Negro murderer,

"Robert Charles,

who, on Tuesday morning, July 24, shot and killed

"Police Captain John T. Day and Patrolman Peter J. Lamb, and wounded

"Patrolman August T. Mora.

"Paul Capdevielle, Mayor."

This authority, given by the sergeant to kill Charles on sight, would have been no news to Charles, nor to any colored man in New Orleans, who, for any purpose whatever, even to save his life, raised his hand against a white man. It is now, even as it was in the days of slavery, an unpardonable sin for a Negro to resist a white man, no matter how unjust or unprovoked the white man's attack may be. Charles knew this, and knowing to be captured meant to be killed, he resolved to sell his life as dearly as possible.

The next step in the terrible tragedy occurred between 2:30 and 5 o'clock Tuesday morning, about four hours after the affair on Dryades street. The man hunt, which had been inaugurated soon after Officer Mora had been carried to the station, succeeded in running down Robert Charles, the wounded fugitive, and located him at 2023 4th Street. It was nearly 2 o'clock in the morning when a large detail of police surrounded the block with the intent to kill Charles on sight. Capt. Day had charge of the squad of police. Charles, the wounded man, was in his house when the police arrived, fully prepared, as results afterward showed, to die in his own home. Capt. Day started for Charles' room. As soon as Charles got sight of him there was a flash, a report, and Day fell dead in his tracks. In another instant Charles was standing in the door, and seeing Patrolman Peter J. Lamb, he drew his gun, and Lamb fell dead. Two other officers, Sergeant Aucoin and Officer Trenchard, who were in the squad, seeing their comrades, Day and Lamb, fall dead, concluded to raise the siege, and both disappeared into an adjoining house, where they blew out their lights so that their cowardly carcasses could be safe from Charles' deadly aim. The calibre of their courage is well shown by the fact that they concluded to save themselves from any harm by remaining prisoners in that dark room until daybreak, out of reach of Charles' deadly rifle. Sergeant Aucoin, who had been so brave a few hours before when seeing the two colored men sitting on the steps talking together on Dryades street, and supposing that neither was armed, now showed his true calibre. Now he knew that Charles had a gun and was brave enough to use it, so he hid himself in a room two hours while Charles deliberately walked out of his room and into the street after killing both Lamb and Day. It is also shown, as further evidence of the bravery of some of New Orleans' "finest," that one of them, seeing Capt. Day fall, ran seven blocks before he stopped, afterwards giving the excuse that he was hunting for a patrol box.

At daybreak the officers felt safe to renew the attack upon Charles, so they broke into his room, only to find that—what they probably very well knew—he had gone. It appears that he made his escape by crawling through a hole in the ceiling to a little attic in his house. Here he found that he could not escape except by a window which led into an alley, which had no opening on 4th street. He scaled the fence and was soon out of reach.

It was now 5 o'clock Tuesday morning, and a general alarm was given. Sergeant Aucoin and Corporal Trenchard, having received a new supply of courage by returning daylight, renewed their effort to capture the man that they had allowed to escape in the darkness. Citizens were called upon to participate in the man hunt and New Orleans was soon the scene of terrible excitement. Officers were present everywhere, and colored men were arrested on all sides upon the pretext that they were impertinent and "game niggers." An instance is mentioned in the Times-Democrat of the 25th and shows the treatment which unoffending colored men received at the hands of some of the officers. This instance

shows Corporal Trenchard, who displayed such remarkable bravery on Monday night in dodging Charles' revolver, in his true
light. It shows how brave a white man is when he has a gun attacking a Negro who is a helpless prisoner. The account is as
follows:

"The police made some arrests in the neighborhood of the killing
of the two officers. Mobs of young darkies gathered everywhere.
These Negroes talked and joked about the affair, and many of
them were for starting a race war on the spot. It was not until several of these little gangs amalgamated and started demonstrations
that the police commenced to act. Nearly a dozen arrests were
made within an hour, and everybody in the vicinity was in a tremor
of excitement.

"It was about 1 o'clock that the Negroes on Fourth street became very noisy, and George Meyers, who lives on Sixth street,
near Rampart, appeared to be one of the prime movers in a little
riot that was rapidly developing. Policeman Exnicios and Sheridan
placed him under arrest, and owing to the fact that the patrol
wagon had just left with a number of prisoners, they walked him
toward St. Charles avenue in order to get a conveyance to take him
to the Sixth Precinct station.

"A huge crowd of Negroes followed the officers and their prisoners. Between Dryades and Baronne, on Sixth, Corporal Trenchard
met the trio. He had his pistol in his hand and he came on them
running. The Negroes in the wake of the officers and prisoner took
to flight immediately. Some disappeared through gates and some
over fences and into yards, for Trenchard, visibly excited, was waving his revolver in the air and was threatening to shoot. He joined
the officers in their walk toward St. Charles street, and the way he
acted led the white people who were witnessing the affair to believe
that his prisoner was the wanted Negro. At every step he would
punch him or hit him with the barrel of his pistol, and the onlook-
ers cried, "Lynch him!" "Kill him!" and other expressions until the
spectators were thoroughly wrought up. At St. Charles street
Trenchard desisted, and, calling an empty ice wagon, threw the
Negro into the body of the vehicle and ordered Officer Exnicios to
take him to the Sixth Precinct station.

"The ride to the station was a wild one. Exnicios had all he
could do to watch his prisoner. A gang climbed into the wagon and

administered a terrible thrashing to the black en route. It took a half hour to reach the police station, for the mule that was drawing the wagon was not overly fast. When the station was reached a mob of nearly 200 howling white youths was awaiting it. The noise they made was something terrible. Meyers was howling for mercy before he reached the ground. The mob dragged him from the wagon, the officer with him. Then began a torrent of abuse for the unfortunate prisoner.

"The station door was but thirty feet away, but it took Exnicios nearly five minutes to fight his way through the mob to the door.

There were no other officers present, and the station seemed to be deserted. Neither the doorman nor the clerk paid any attention to the noise on the outside. As the result, the maddened crowd wrought their vengeance on the Negro. He was punched, kicked, bruised and torn. The clothes were ripped from his back, while his face after that few minutes was unrecognizable."

This was the treatment accorded and permitted to a helpless prisoner because he was black. All day Wednesday the man hunt continued. The excitement caused by the deaths of Day and Lamb became intense. The officers of the law knew they were trailing a man whose aim was deadly and whose courage they had never seen surpassed. Commenting upon the marksmanship of the man which the paper styled a fiend, the Times-Democrat of Wednesday said:

"One of the extraordinary features of the tragedy was the marksmanship displayed by the Negro desperado. His aim was deadly and his coolness must have been something phenomenal. The two shots that killed Captain Day and Patrolman Lamb struck their victims in the head, a circumstance remarkable enough in itself, considering the suddenness and fury of the onslaught and the darkness that reigned in the alley way.

"Later on Charles fired at Corporal Perrier, who was standing at least seventy-five yards away. The murderer appeared at the gate, took lightning aim along the side of the house, and sent a bullet whizzing past the officer's ear. It was a close shave, and a few inches' deflection would no doubt have added a fourth victim to the list.

"At the time of the affray there is good reason to believe that Charles was seriously wounded, and at any event he had lost quantities of blood. His situation was as critical as it is possible to imagine, yet he shot like an expert in a target range. The circumstance shows the desperate character of the fiend, and his terrible dexterity with weapons makes him one of the most formidable monsters that has ever been loose upon the community."

Wednesday New Orleans was in the hands of a mob. Charles, still sought for and still defending himself, had killed four policemen, and everybody knew that he intended to die fighting. Unable to vent its vindictiveness and bloodthirsty vengeance upon Charles, the mob turned its attention to other colored men who happened to get in the path of its fury. Even colored women, as has happened many times before, were assaulted and beaten and killed by the brutal hoodlums who thronged the streets. The reign of absolute lawlessness began about 8 o'clock Wednesday night. The mob gathered near the Lee statue and was soon making its way to the place where the officers had been shot by Charles. Describing the mob, the Times-Democrat of Thursday morning says:

"The gathering in the square, which numbered about 700, eventually became in a measure quiet, and a large, lean individual, in poor attire and with unshaven face, leaped upon a box that had been brought for the purpose, and in a voice that under no circumstances could be heard at a very great distance, shouted: 'Gentlemen, I am the Mayor of Kenner.' He did not get a chance for some minutes to further declare himself, for the voice of the rabble swung over his like a huge wave over a sinking craft. He stood there, however, wildly waving his arms and demanded a hearing, which was given him when the uneasiness of the mob was quieted for a moment or so.

"'I am from Kenner, gentlemen, and I have come down to New Orleans to-night to assist you in teaching the blacks a lesson. I have killed a Negro before, and in revenge of the wrong wrought upon you and yours, I am willing to kill again. The only way that you can teach these Niggers a lesson and put them in their place is to go out and lynch a few of them as an object lesson. String up a few of them, and the others will trouble you no more. That is the only thing to do—kill them, string them up, lynch them! I will lead you, if you will but follow. On to the Parish Prison and lynch Pierce!'

"They bore down on the Parish Prison like an avalanche, but the avalanche split harmlessly on the blank walls of the jail, and Remy Klock sent out a brief message: 'You can't have Pierce, and you can't get in.' Up to that time the mob had had no opposition, but Klock's answer chilled them considerably. There was no deep-seated desperation in the crowd after all, only that wild lawlessness which leads to deeds of cruelty, but not to stubborn battle. Around the corner from the prison is a row of pawn and second-hand shops, and to these the mob took like the ducks to the proverbial mill-pond, and the devastation they wrought upon Mr. Fink's establishment was beautiful in its line.

"Everything from breast pins to horse pistols went into the pockets of the crowd, and in the melee a man was shot down, while just around the corner somebody planted a long knife in the body of a little newsboy for no reason as yet shown. Every now and then a Negro would be flushed somewhere in the outskirts of the crowd and left beaten to a pulp. Just how many were roughly handled will never be known, but the unlucky thirteen had been severely beaten and maltreated up to a late hour, a number of those being in the Charity Hospital under the bandages and courtplaster of the doctors."

The first colored man to meet death at the hands of the mob was a passenger on a street car. The mob had broken itself into fragments after its disappointment at the jail, each fragment looking for a Negro to kill. The bloodthirsty cruelty of one crowd is thus described by the Times-Democrat:

" 'We will get a Nigger down here, you bet!' was the yelling boast that went up from a thousand throats, and for the first time the march of the mob was directed toward the downtown sections. The words of the rioters were prophetic, for just as Canal street was reached a car on the Villere line came along.

" 'Stop that car!' cried half a hundred men. The advance guard, heeding the injunction, rushed up to the slowly moving car, and several, seizing the trolley, jerked it down.

" 'Here's a Negro!' said half a dozen men who sprang upon the car.

"The car was full of passengers at the time, among them several women. When the trolley was pulled down and the car thrown in total darkness, the latter began to scream, and for a moment or so it looked as if the life of every person in the car was in peril, for some of the crowd with demoniacal yells of 'There he goes!' began to fire their weapons indiscriminately. The passengers in the car hastily jumped to the ground and joined the crowd, as it was evidently the safest place to be.

" 'Where's that Nigger?' was the query passed along the line, and with that the search began in earnest. The Negro, after jumping off the car, lost himself for a few moments in the crowd, but after a brief search he was again located. The slight delay seemed, if possible, only to whet the desire of the bloodthirsty crowd, for the reappearance of the Negro was the signal for a chorus of screams and pistol shots directed at the fugitive. With the speed of a deer, the man ran straight from the corner of Canal and Villere to Customhouse street. The pursuers, closely following, kept up a running fire, but notwithstanding the fact that they were right at the Negro's heels their aim was poor and their bullets went wide of the mark.

"The Negro, on reaching Customhouse street, darted from the sidewalk out into the middle of the street. This was the worst maneuver that he could have made, as it brought him directly under the light from an arc lamp, located on a nearby corner. When the Negro came plainly in view of the foremost of the closely following mob they directed a volley at him. Half a dozen pistols flashed simultaneously, and one of the bullets evidently found its mark, for the Negro stopped short, threw up his hands, wavered for a moment, and then started to run again. This stop, slight as it was, proved fatal to the Negro's chances, for he had not gotten twenty steps farther when several of the men in advance of the others reached his side. A burly fellow, grabbing him with one hand, dealt him a terrible blow on the head with the other. The wounded man sank to the ground. The crowd pressed around him and began to beat him and stamp him. The men in the rear pressed forward and those beating the man were shoved forward. The half-dead Negro, when he was freed from his assailants, crawled over to the gutter. The men behind, however, stopped pushing when those in front yelled, 'We've got him,' and then it was that the attack on the bleeding Negro was resumed. A vicious kick directed at the Negro's head sent him into the gutter, and for a moment the body sank from view beneath the muddy, slimy water. 'Pull him out; don't let him drown,' was the cry, and instantly several of the men around the half-drowned Negro bent down and drew the body out. Twisting the body around they drew the head and shoulders up on the street, while from the waist down the Negro's body remained under the water. As soon as the crowd saw that the Negro was still alive they again began to beat and kick him. Every few moments they would stop and striking matches look into the man's face to see if he still lived. To better see if he was dead they would stick lighted matches to his eyes. Finally, believing he was dead, they left him and started out to look for other Negroes. Just about this time some one yelled, 'He ain't dead,' and the men came back and renewed the attack. While the men were beating and pounding the prostrate form with stones and sticks a man in the crowd ran up, and crying, 'I'll fix the d— Negro,' poked the muzzle of a pistol almost against the body and fired. This shot must have ended the man's life, for he lay like a stone, and realizing that they were wasting energy in further attacks, the men left their victim lying in the street."

The same paper, on the same day, July 26th, describes the brutal butchery of an aged colored man early in the morning:

"Baptiste Philo, a Negro, 75 years of age, was a victim of mob violence at Kerlerec and North Peters streets about 2:30 o'clock this morning. The old man is employed about the French Market, and was on his way there when he was met by a crowd and desperately shot. The old man found his way to the Third Precinct police station, where it was found that he had received a ghastly wound in the abdomen.

The ambulance was summoned and he was conveyed to the Charity Hospital. The students pronounced the wound fatal after a superficial examination."

Mob rule continued Thursday, its violence increasing every hour, until 2 P.M., when the climax seemed to be reached. The fact that colored men and women had been made the victims of brutal mobs, chased through the streets, killed upon the highways and butchered in their homes, did not call the best element in New Orleans to active exertion in behalf of law and order. The killing of a few Negroes more or less by irresponsible mobs does not cut much figure in Louisiana. But when the reign of mob law

exerts a depressing influence upon the stock market and city se-
curities begin to show unsteady standing in money centers, then
the strong arm of the good white people of the South asserts itself
and order is quickly brought out of chaos.

It was so with New Orleans on that Thursday. The better element of the white citizens began to realize that New Orleans in
the hands of a mob would not prove a promising investment for
Eastern capital, so the better element began to stir itself, not for
the purpose of punishing the brutality against the Negroes who
had been beaten, or bringing to justice the murderers of those
who had been killed, but for the purpose of saving the city's
credit. The Times-Democrat, upon this phase of the situation on
Friday morning says:

> "When it became known later in the day that State bonds had
> depreciated from a point to a point and a half on the New York
> market a new phase of seriousness was manifest to the business
> community. Thinking men realized that a continuance of un-
> checked disorder would strike a body blow to the credit of the city
> and in all probability would complicate the negotiation of the
> forthcoming improvement bonds. The bare thought that such a
> disaster might be brought about by a few irresponsible boys,
> tramps and ruffians, inflamed popular indignation to fever pitch.
> It was all that was needed to bring to the aid of the authorities the
> active personal cooperation of the entire better element."

With the financial credit of the city at stake, the good citizens
rushed to the rescue, and soon the Mayor was able to mobilize a
posse of 1,000 willing men to assist the police in maintaining
order, but rioting still continued in different sections of the city.
Colored men and women were beaten, chased and shot whenever
they made their appearance upon the street. Late in the night a
most despicable piece of villainy occurred on Rousseau street,
where an aged colored woman was killed by the mob. The Times-
Democrat thus describes the murder:

> "Hannah Mabry, an old Negress, was shot and desperately
> wounded shortly after midnight this morning while sleeping in her
> home at No. 1929 Rousseau street. It was the work of a mob, and
> was evidently well planned so far as escape was concerned, for the

place was reached by police officers and a squad of the volunteer police within a very short time after the reports of the shots, but not a prisoner was secured. The square was surrounded, but the mob had scattered in several directions, and, the darkness of the neighborhood aiding them, not one was taken.

"At the time the mob made the attack on the little house there were also in it David Mabry, the 62-year-old husband of the wounded woman; her son, Harry Mabry; his wife, Fannie, and an infant child. The young couple with their babe could not be found after the whole affair was over, and they either escaped or were hustled off by the mob. A careful search of the whole neighborhood was made, but no trace of them could be found.

"The little place occupied by the Mabry family is an old cottage on the swamp side of Rousseau street. It is furnished with slat shutters to both doors and windows. These shutters had been pulled off by the mob and the volleys fired through the glass doors. The younger Mabrys, father, mother and child, were asleep in the first room at the time. Hannah Mabry and her old husband were sleeping in the next room. The old couple occupied the same bed, and it is miraculous that the old man did not share the fate of his spouse.

"Officer Bitterwolf, who was one of the first on the scene, said that he was about a block and a half away with Officers Fordyce and Sweeney. There were about twenty shots fired, and the trio raced to the cottage. They saw twenty or thirty men running down Rousseau street. Chase was given and the crowd turned toward the river and scattered into several vacant lots in the neighborhood.

"The volunteer police stationed at the Sixth Precinct had about five blocks to run before they arrived. They also moved on the reports of the firing, and in a remarkably short time the square was surrounded, but no one could be taken. As they ran to the scene they were assailed on every hand with vile epithets and the accusation of 'Nigger lovers.'

"Rousseau street, where the cottage is situated, is a particularly dark spot, and no doubt the members of the mob were well acquainted with the neighborhood, for the officers said that they seemed to sink into the earth, so completely and quickly did they disappear after they had completed their work, which was complete with the firing of the volley.

"Hannah Mabry was taken to the Charity Hospital in the ambulance, where it was found on examination that she had been shot through the right lung, and that the wound was a particularly serious one.

"Her old husband was found in the little wrecked home well nigh distracted with fear and grief. It was he who informed the police that at the time of the assault the younger Mabrys occupied the front room. As he ran about the little home as well as his feeble condition would permit he severely lacerated his feet on the glass broken from the windows and door. He was escorted to the Sixth Precinct station, where he was properly cared for. He could not realize why his little family had been so murderously attacked, and was inconsolable when his wife was driven off in the ambulance piteously moaning in her pain.

"The search for the perpetrators of the outrage was thorough, but both police and armed force of citizens had only their own efforts to rely on. The residents of the neighborhood were aroused by the firing, but they would give no help in the search and did not appear in the least concerned over the affair. Groups were on almost every doorstep, and some of them even jeered in a quiet way at the men who were voluntarily attempting to capture the members of the mob. Absolutely no information could be had from any of them, and the whole affair had the appearance of being the work of roughs who either lived in the vicinity, or their friends."

DEATH OF CHARLES

Friday witnessed the final act in the bloody drama begun by the three police officers, Aucoin, Mora and Cantrelle. Betrayed into the hands of the police, Charles, who had already sent two of his would-be murderers to their death, made a last stand in a small building, 1210 Saratoga street, and, still defying his pursuers, fought a mob of twenty thousand people, single-handed and alone, killing three more men, mortally wounding two more and seriously wounding nine others. Unable to get to him in his stronghold, the besiegers set fire to his house of refuge. While the building was burning Charles was shooting, and every crack of his death-dealing rifle added another victim to the price which he had placed upon his own life. Finally, when fire and smoke became too much for flesh and blood to stand, the long sought for fugitive appeared in the door, rifle in hand, to charge the countless guns that were drawn upon him. With a courage which was indescribable, he raised his gun to fire again, but this time it failed, for a hundred shots riddled his body, and he fell dead face fronting to the mob. This last scene in the terrible drama is thus described in the Times-Democrat of July 26:

"Early yesterday afternoon, at 3 o'clock or thereabouts, Police Sergeant Gabriel Porteus was instructed by Chief Gaster to go to a house at No. 1210 Saratoga street, and search it for the fugitive murderer, Robert Charles. A private 'tip' had been received at the headquarters that the fiend was hiding somewhere on the premises.

"Sergeant Porteus took with him Corporal John R. Lally and Officers Zeigel and Essey. The house to which they were directed is a small, double frame cottage, standing flush with Saratoga street, near the corner of Clio. It has two street entrances and two rooms on each side, one in front and one in the rear. It belongs to the type of cheap little dwellings commonly tenanted by Negroes.

"Sergeant Porteus left Ziegel and Essey to guard the outside and went with Corporal Lally to the rear house, where he found Jackson and his wife in the large room on the left. What immediately ensued is only known by the Negroes. They say the sergeant began to question them about their lodgers and finally asked them whether they knew anything about Robert Charles. They strenuously denied all knowledge of his whereabouts.

"The Negroes lied. At that very moment the hunted and desperate murderer lay concealed not a dozen feet away. Near the rear, left-hand corner of the room is a closet or pantry, about three feet deep, and perhaps eight feet long. The door was open and Charles was crouching, Winchester in hand, in the dark further end.

"Near the closet door was a bucket of water, and Jackson says that Sergeant Porteous walked toward it to get a drink. At the next moment a shot rang out and the brave officer fell dead. Lally was shot directly afterward. Exactly how and where will never be known, but the probabilities are that the black fiend sent a bullet into him before he recovered from his surprise at the sudden onslaught. Then the murderer dashed out of the back door and disappeared.

"The neighborhood was already agog with the tragic events of the two preceding days, and the sound of the shots was a signal for wild and instant excitement. In a few moments a crowd had gathered and people were pouring in by the hundred from every point of the compass. Jackson and his wife had fled and at first nobody knew what had happened, but the surmise that Charles had recommenced his bloody work was on every tongue and soon some of the bolder found their way to the house in the rear. There the bleeding forms of the two policemen told the story.

"Lally was still breathing, and a priest was sent for to administer the last rites. Father Fitzgerald responded, and while he was bending over the dying man the outside throng was rushing wildly through the surrounding yards and passage-ways searching for the murderer. 'Where is he?' 'What has become of him?' were the questions on every lip.

"Suddenly the answer came in a shot from the room directly overhead. It was fired through a window facing Saratoga street, and the bullet struck down a young man named Alfred J. Bloomfield, who was standing in the narrow passage-way between the two houses. He fell on his knees and a second bullet stretched him dead.

"When he fled from the closet Charles took refuge in the upper story of the house. There are four windows on that floor, two facing toward Saratoga street and two toward Rampart. The murderer kicked several breaches in the frail central partition, so he could rush from side to side, and like a trapped beast, prepared to make his last stand.

"Nobody had dreamed that he was still in the house, and when Bloomfield was shot there was a headlong stampede. It was some minutes before the exact situation was understood. Then rifles and pistols began to speak, and a hail of bullets poured against the blind frontage of the old house. Every one hunted some coign of vantage, and many climbed to adjacent roofs. Soon the glass of the four upper windows was shattered by flying lead. The fusillade sounded like a battle, and the excitement upon the streets was indescribable.

"Throughout all this hideous uproar Charles seems to have retained a certain diabolical coolness. He kept himself mostly out of sight, but now and then he thrust the gleaming barrel of his rifle through one of the shattered window panes and fired at his besiegers. He worked the weapon with incredible rapidity, discharging from three to five cartridges each time before leaping back to a place of safety. These replies came from all four windows indiscriminately, and showed that he was keeping a close watch in every direction. His wonderful marksmanship never failed him for a moment, and when he missed it was always by the narrowest margin only.

"On the Rampart street side of the house there are several sheds, commanding an excellent range of the upper story. Detective Littleton, Andrew Van Kuren of the Workhouse force and several others climbed upon one of these and opened fire on the upper windows, shooting whenever they could catch a glimpse of the assassin. Charles responded with his rifle, and presently Van Kuren climbed down to find a better position. He was crossing the end of the shed when he was killed.

"Another of Charles' bullets found its billet in the body of Frank Evans, an ex-member of the police force. He was on the Rampart street side firing whenever he had an opportunity. Officer J. W. Bofill and A. S. Leclerc were also wounded in the fusillade.

"While the events thus briefly outlined were transpiring time was awing, and the cooler headed in the crowd began to realize that some quick and desperate expedient must be adopted to insure the capture of the fiend and to avert what might be a still greater tragedy than any yet enacted. For nearly two hours the desperate monster had held his besiegers at bay, darkness would soon be at hand and no one could predict what might occur if he made a dash for liberty in the dark.

"At this critical juncture it was suggested that the house be fired. The plan came as an inspiration, and was adopted as the only solution of the situation. The wretched old rookery counted for nothing against the possible continued sacrifice of human life, and steps were immediately taken to apply the torch. The fire department had been summoned to the scene soon after the shooting began; its officers were warned to be ready to prevent a spread of the conflagration, and several men rushed into the lower right-hand room and started a blaze in one corner.

"They first fired an old mattress, and soon smoke was pouring out in dense volumes. It filled the interior of the ramshackle structure, and it was evident that the upper story would soon become untenable. An interval of tense excitement followed, and all eyes were strained for a glimpse of the murderer when he emerged.

"Then came the thrilling climax. Smoked out of his den, the desperate fiend descended the stairs and entered the lower room. Some say he dashed into the yard, glaring around vainly for some avenue of escape; but, however that may be, he was soon a few moments later moving about behind the lower windows. A dozen shots were sent through the wall in the hope of reaching him, but he escaped unscathed. Then suddenly the door on the right was flung open and he dashed out. With head lowered and rifle raised ready to fire on the instant, Charles dashed straight for the rear door of the front cottage. To reach it he had to traverse a little walk shaded by a vine-clad arbor. In the back room, with a cocked revolver in his hand, was Dr. C. A. Noiret, a young medical student, who was aiding the citizens' posse. As he sprang through the door Charles fired a shot, and the bullet whizzed past the doctor's head. Before it could be repeated Noiret's pistol cracked and the murderer reeled, turned half around and fell on his back. The doctor sent another ball into his body as he struck the floor, and half a dozen men, swarming into the room from the front, riddled the corpse with bullets.

"Private Adolph Anderson of the Connell Rifles was the first man to announce the death of the wretch. He rushed to the street door, shouted the news to the crowd, and a moment later the bleeding body was dragged to the pavement and made the target of a score of pistols. It was shot, kicked and beaten almost out of semblance to humanity.

"The limp dead body was dropped at the edge of the sidewalk and from there dragged to the muddy roadway by half a hundred hands. There in the road more shots were fired into the body. Corporal Trenchard, a brother-in-law of Porteus, led the shooting into the inanimate clay. With each shot there was a cheer for the work that had been done and curses and imprecations on the inanimate mass of riddled flesh that was once Robert Charles.

"Cries of 'Burn him! Burn him!' were heard from Clio street all the way to Erato street, and it was with difficulty that the crowd was restrained from totally destroying the wretched dead body. Some of those who agitated burning even secured a large vessel of kerosene, which had previously been brought to the scene for the purpose of firing Charles' refuge, and for a time it looked as though this vengeance might be wreaked on the body. The officers, however, restrained this move, although they were powerless to prevent the stamping and kicking of the body by the enraged crowd.

"After the infuriated citizens had vented their spleen on the body of the dead Negro it was loaded into the patrol wagon. The police raised the body of the heavy black from the ground and literally chucked it into the space on the floor of the wagon between the seats. They threw it with a curse hissed more than uttered and born of the bitterness which was rankling in their breasts at the thought of Charles having taken so wantonly the lives of four of the best of their fellow-officers.

"When the murderer's body landed in the wagon it fell in such a position that the hideously mutilated head, kicked, stamped and crushed, hung over the end.

"As the wagon moved off, the followers, who were protesting against its being carried off, declaring that it should be burned, poked and struck it with sticks, beating it into such a condition that it was utterly impossible to tell what the man ever looked like.

"As the patrol wagon rushed through the rough street, jerking and swaying from one side of the thoroughfare to the other, the gory, mud-smeared head swayed and swung and jerked about in a sickening manner, the dark blood dripping on the steps and spattering the body of the wagon and the trousers of the policemen standing on the step.["]

MOB BRUTALITY

The brutality of the mob was further shown by the unspeakable cruelty with which it beat, shot and stabbed to death an unoffending colored man, name unknown, who happened to be walking on the street with no thought that he would be set upon and killed simply because he was a colored man. The Times-Democrat's description of the outrage is as follows:

"While the fight between the Negro desperado and the citizens was in progress yesterday afternoon at Clio and Saratoga streets another tragedy was being enacted downtown in the French quarter, but it was a very one-sided affair. The object of the white man's wrath was, of course, a Negro, but, unlike Charles, he showed no fight, but tried to escape from the furious mob which was pursuing him, and which finally put an end to his existence in a most cruel manner.

"The Negro, whom no one seemed to know—at any rate no one could be found in the vicinity of the killing who could tell who he was—was walking along the levee, as near as could be learned, when he was attacked by a number of white longshoremen or screwmen. For what reason, if there was any reason other than the fact that he was a Negro, could not be learned, and immediately they pounced upon him he broke ground and started on a desperate run for his life.

"The hunted Negro started off the levee toward the French Vegetable Market, changed his course out the sidewalk toward Gallatin street. The angry, yelling mob was close at his heels, and increasing steadily as each block was traversed. At Gallatin street he turned up that thoroughfare, doubled back into North Peters street and ran into the rear of No. 1216 of that street, which is occupied by Chris Reuter as a commission store and residence.

"He rushed frantically through the place and out on to the gallery on the Gallatin street side. From this gallery he jumped to the street and fell flat on his back on the sidewalk. Springing to his feet as soon as possible, with a leaden hail fired by the angry mob whistling about him, he turned to his merciless pursuers in an appealing way, and, throwing up one hand, told them not to shoot any more, that they could take him as he was.

"But the hail of lead continued, and the unfortunate Negro finally dropped to the sidewalk, mortally wounded. The mob then rushed upon him, still continuing the fusillade, and upon reaching his body a number of Italians, who had joined the howling mob, reached down and stabbed him in the back and buttock with big knives. Others fired shots into his head until his teeth were shot out, three shots having been fired into his mouth. There were bullet wounds all over his body.

"Others who witnessed the affair declared that the man was fired at as he was running up the stairs leading to the living apartments above the store, and that after jumping to the sidewalk and being knocked down by a bullet he jumped up and ran across the street, then ran back and tried to get back into the commission store. The Italians, it is said, were all drunk, and had been shooting firecrackers. Tiring of this, they began shooting at Negroes, and when the unfortunate man who was killed ran by they joined in the chase.

"No one was arrested for the shooting, the neighborhood having been deserted by the police, who were sent up to the place where Charles was fighting so desperately. No one could or would give the names of any of those who had participated in the chase and the killing, nor could any one be found who knew who the Negro was. The patrol wagon was called and the terribly muti-lated body sent to the morgue and the coroner notified.

"The murdered Negro was copper colored, about 5 feet 11 inches in height, about 35 years of age, and was dressed in blue overalls and a brown slouch hat. At 10:30 o'clock the vicinity of the French Market was very quiet. Squads of special officers were patrolling the neighborhood, and there did not seem to be any prospects of disorder."

During the entire time the mob held the city in its hands and went about holding up street cars and searching them, taking from them colored men to assault, shoot and kill, chasing colored men upon the public square, through alleys and into houses of any-body who would take them in, breaking into the homes of de-fenseless colored men and women and beating aged and decrepit men and women to death, the police and the legally-constituted authorities showed plainly where their sympathies were, for in no case reported through the daily papers does there appear the ar-rest, trial and conviction of one of the mob for any of the brutal-ities which occurred. The ringleaders of the mob were at no time disguised. Men were chased, beaten and killed by white brutes, who boasted of their crimes, and the murderers still walk the streets of New Orleans, well known and absolutely exempt from prosecution. Not only were they exempt from prosecution by the police while the town was in the hands of the mob, but even now that law and order is supposed to resume control, these men, well known, are not now, nor ever will be, called to account for the unspeakable brutalities of that terrible week. On the other hand, the colored men who were beaten by the police and dragged into the station for purposes of intimidation, were quickly called up before the courts and fined or sent to jail upon the statement of the police. Instances of Louisiana justice as it is dispensed in New Orleans are here quoted from the Times-Democrat of July 26th:

"Justice Dealt Out to Folk Who Talked Too Much

"All the Negroes and whites who were arrested in the vicinity of Tuesday's tragedy had a hard time before Recorder Hughes yesterday. Lee Jackson was the first prisoner, and the evidence established that he made his way to the vicinity of the crime and told his Negro friends that he thought a good many more policemen ought to be killed. Jackson said he was drunk when he made the remark. He was fined $25 or thirty days.

"John Kennedy was found wandering about the street Tuesday night with an open razor in his hand, and he was given $25 or thirty days.

"Edward McCarthy, a white man, who arrived only four days since from New York, went to the scene of the excitement at the corner of Third and Rampart streets, and told the Negroes that they were as good as any white man. This remark was made by McCarthy, as another white man said the Negroes should be lynched. McCarthy told the recorder that he considered a Negro as good as a white in body and soul. He was fined $25 or thirty days.

"James Martin, Simon Montegut, Eddie McCall, Alex Washington and Henry Turner were up for failing to move on. Martin proved that he was at the scene to assist the police and was discharged. Montegut, being a cripple, was also released, but the others were fined $25 or thirty days each.

"Eddie Williams for refusing to move on was given $25 or thirty days.

"Matilda Gamble was arrested by the police for saying that two officers were killed and it was a pity more were not shot. She was given $25 or thirty days.

INSOLENT BLACKS

"Recorder Hughes received Negroes in the first recorder's office yesterday morning in a way that they will remember for a long time, and all of them were before the magistrate for having caused trouble through incendiary remarks concerning the death of Captain Day and Patrolman Lamb."

"Lee Jackson was before the recorder and was fined $25 or thirty days. He was lippy around where the trouble happened Tuesday morning, and some white men punched him good and hard and the police took him. Then the recorder gave him a dose, and now he is in the parish prison."

"John Kennedy was another black who got into trouble. He said that the shooting of the police by Charles was a good thing, and for this he was pounded. Patrolman Lorenzo got him and saved him from being lynched, for the black had an open razor. He was fined $25 or thirty days."

"Edward McCarthy, a white man, mixed up with the crowd, and an expression of sympathy nearly cost him his head, for some whites about started for him, administering licks and blows with fists and umbrellas. The recorder fined him $25 or thirty days. He is from New York."

"Then James Martin, a white man, and Simon Montegut, Eddie Call, Henry Turner and Alex Washington were before the magistrate for having failed to move on when the police ordered them from the square where the bluecoats were Tuesday, waiting in the hope of catching Charles. All save Martin and Montegut were fined."

"Eddie Williams, a little Negro who was extremely fresh with the police, was fined $10 or ten days."

SHOCKING BRUTALITY

The whole city was at the mercy of the mob and the display of brutality was a disgrace to civilization. One instance is described in the Picayune as follows:

"A smaller party detached itself from the mob at Washington and Rampart streets, and started down the latter thoroughfare. One of the foremost spied a Negro, and immediately there was a rush for the unfortunate black man. With the sticks they had torn from fences on the line of march the young outlaws attacked the black and clubbed him unmercifully, acting more like demons than human beings. After being severely beaten over the head, the Negro started to run with the whole gang at his heels. Several revolvers were brought into play and pumped their lead at the refugee. The Negro made rapid progress and took refuge behind the blinds of a little cottage in Rampart street, but he had been seen, and the mob hauled him from his hiding place and again commenced beating him. There were more this time, some twenty or thirty, all armed with sticks and heavy clubs, and under their incessant blows the

Negro could not last long. He begged for mercy, and his cries were most pitiful, but a mob has no heart, and his cries were only answered with more blows.

"'For God's sake, boss, I ain't done nothin'. Don't kill me. I swear I ain't done nothin'.'

"The white brutes turned

"A DEAF EAR TO THE PITYING CRIES

of the black wretch and the drubbing continued. The cries subsided into moans, and soon the black swooned away into unconsciousness. Still not content with their heartless work, they pulled the Negro out and kicked him into the gutter. For the time those who had beaten the black seemed satisfied and left him groaning in the gutter, but others came up, and, regretting that they had not had a hand in the affair, they determined to evidence their bravery to their fellows and beat the man while he was in the gutter, hurling rocks and stones at his black form. One thoughtless white brute, worse even than the black slayer of the police officers, thought to make himself a hero in the eyes of his fellows and fired his revolver repeatedly into the helpless wretch. It was dark and the fellow probably aimed carelessly. After firing three or four shots he also left without knowing what extent of injury he inflicted on the black wretch who was left lying in the gutter."

MURDER ON THE LEVEE

One part of the crowd made a raid on the tenderloin district, hoping to find there some belated Negro for a sacrifice. They were urged on by the white prostitutes, who applauded their murderous mission. Says an account:

"The red light district was all excitement. Women—that is, the white women—were out on their stoops and peeping over their galleries and through their windows and doors, shouting to the crowd to go on with their work, and kill Negroes for them.

"'Our best wishes, boys,' they encouraged; and the mob answered with shouts, and whenever a Negro house was sighted a bombardment was started on the doors and windows."

No colored men were found on the streets until the mob reached Custom House place and Villiers streets. Here a victim was found and brutally put to death. The Picayune description is as follows:

"Some stragglers had run a Negro into a car at the corner of Bienville and Villere streets. He was seeking refuge in the conveyance, and he believed that the car would not be stopped and could speed along. But the mob determined to stop the car, and ordered the motorman to halt. He put on his brake. Some white men were in the car.

" 'Get out, fellows,' shouted several of the mob.

" 'All whites fall out,' was the second cry, and the poor Negro understood that it was meant that he should stay in the car.

"He wanted to save his life. The poor fellow crawled under the seats. But some one in the crowd saw him and yelled that he was hiding. Two or three men climbed through the windows with their pistols; others jumped over the motorman's board, and dozens tumbled into the rear of the car. Big, strong hands got the Negro by the shirt. He was dragged out of the conveyance, and was pushed to the street. Some fellow ran up and struck him with a club. The blow was heavy, but it did not fell him, and the Negro ran toward Canal street, stealing along the wall of the Tulane Medical Building. Fifty men ran after him, caught the poor fellow and hurried him back into the crowd. Fists were aimed at him, then clubs went upon his shoulders, and finally the black plunged into the gutter.

"A gun was fired, and the Negro, who had just gotten to his feet, dropped again. He tried to get up, but a volley was sent after him, and in a little while he was dead.

"The crowd looked on at the terrible work. Then the lights in the houses of ill-fame began to light up again, and women peeped out of the blinds. The motorman was given the order to go on. The gong clanged and the conveyance sped out of the way. For half an hour the crowd held their place at the corner, then the patrol wagon came and the body was picked up and hurried to the morgue.

"Coroner Richard held an autopsy on the body of the Negro who was forced out of car 98 of the Villere line and shot down. It was found that he was wounded four times, the most serious wound being that which struck him in the right side, passing through the lungs, and causing hemorrhages, which brought about death.

"Nobody tried to identify the poor fellow and his name is unknown."

A VICTIM IN THE MARKET

Soon after the murder of the man on the street car many of the same mob marched down to the market place. There they found a colored market man named Louis Taylor, who had gone to begin his early morning's work. He was at once set upon by the mob and killed. The Picayune account says:

"Between 1 and 2 o'clock this morning a mob of several hundred men and boys, made up of participants in many of the earlier affairs, marched on the French Market. Louis Taylor, a Negro vegetable carrier, who is about 30 years of age, was sitting at the soda water stand. As soon as the mob saw him fire was opened and the Negro took to his heels. He ran directly into another section of the mob and any number of shots were fired at him. He fell, face down, on the floor of the market.

"The police in the neighborhood rallied hurriedly and found the victim of mob violence seemingly lifeless. Before they arrived the Negro had been beaten severely about the head and body. The ambulance was summoned and Taylor was carried to the charity hospital, where it was found that he had been shot through the abdomen and arm. The examination was a hurried one, but it sufficed to show that Taylor was mortally wounded.

"After shooting Taylor the members of the mob were pluming themselves on their exploit. 'The Nigger was at the soda water stand and we commenced shooting him,' said one of the rioters. 'He put his hands up and ran, and we shot until he fell. I understand that he is still alive. If he is, he is a wonder. He was certainly shot enough to be killed.'

"The members of the mob readily admitted that they had taken part in the assaults which marked the earlier part of the evening.

" 'We were up on Jackson avenue and killed a Nigger on Villere street. We came down here, saw a nigger and killed him, too.' This was the way they told the story.

" 'Boys, we are out of ammunition,' said some one.

" 'Well, we will keep on like we are, and if we can't get some before morning, we will take it. We have got to keep this thing up, now we have started.'

"This declaration was greeted by a chorus of applauding yells, and the crowd started up the levee. Half of the men in the crowd, and they were all of them young, were drunk.

"Taylor, when seen at the charity hospital, was suffering greatly, and presented a pitiable spectacle. His clothing was covered with blood, and his face was beaten almost into a pulp. He said that he had gone to the market to work and was quietly sitting down when the mob came and began to fire on him. He was not aware at first that the crowd was after him. When he saw its purpose he tried to run, but fell. He didn't know any of the men in the crowd. There is hardly a chance that Taylor will recover.

"The police told the crowd to move on, but no attempt was made to arrest anyone."

A GRAY-HAIRED VICTIM

The bloodthirsty barbarians, having tasted blood, continued their hunt and soon ran across an old man of 75 years. His life had been spent in hard work about the French market, and he was well known as an unoffending, peaceable and industrious old man.

But that made no difference to the mob. He was a Negro, and with a fiendishness that was worse than that of cannibals they beat his life out. The report says:

"There was another gang of men parading the streets in the lower part of the city, looking for any stray Negro who might be on the streets. As they neared the corner of Dauphine and Kerlerec, a square below Esplanade avenue, they came upon Baptiste Thilo, an aged Negro, who works in the French Market.

"Thilo for years has been employed by the butchers and fish merchants to carry baskets from the stalls to the wagons, and unload the wagons as they arrive in the morning. He was on his way to the market, when the mob came upon him. One of the gang struck the old Negro, and as he fell, another in the crowd, supposed to be a young fellow, fired a shot. The bullet entered the body just below the right nipple.

"As the Negro fell the crowd looked into his face and they discovered then that the victim was very old. The young man who did the shooting said: 'Oh, he is an old Negro. I'm sorry that I shot him.'

"This is all the old Negro received in the way of consolation.

"He was left where he fell, but later staggered to his feet and made his way to the third precinct station. There the police summoned the ambulance and the students pronounced the wound very dangerous. He was carried to the hospital as rapidly as possible.

"There was no arrest."

Just before daybreak the mob found another victim. He, too, was on his way to market, driving a meat wagon. But little is told of his treatment, nothing more than the following brief statement:

"At nearly 3 o'clock this morning a report was sent to the Third Precinct station that a Negro was lying on the sidewalk at the corner of Decatur and St. Philip. The man had been pulled off of a meat wagon and riddled with bullets.

"When the police arrived he was insensible and apparently dying. The ambulance students attended the Negro and pronounced the wounds fatal.

"There was nothing found which would lead to the discovery of his identity."

FUN IN GRETNA

If there are any persons so deluded as to think that human life in the South is valued any more than the life of a brute, he will be speedily undeceived by reading the accounts of unspeakable barbarism committed by the mob in and around New Orleans. In no other civilized country in the world, nay, more, in no land of barbarians would it be possible to duplicate the scenes of brutality that are reported from New Orleans. In the heat of blind fury one might conceive how a mad mob might beat and kill a man taken red-handed in a brutal murder. But it is almost past belief to read that civilized white people, men who boast of their chivalry and blue blood, actually had fun in beating, chasing and shooting men who had no possible connection with any crime.

But this actually happened in Gretna, a few miles from New Orleans. In its description of the scenes of Tuesday night, the Picayune mentions the brutal chase of several colored men whom the mob sought to kill. In the instances mentioned, the paper said:

"Gretna had its full share of excitement between 8 and 11 o'clock last night, in connection with a report that spread through the town that a Negro resembling the slayer of Police Captain Day, of New Orleans, had been seen on the outskirts of the place.

"It is true that a suspicious-looking Negro was observed by the residents of Madison and Amelia streets lurking about the fences of that neighborhood just after dark, and shortly before 8 o'clock John Fist, a young white man, saw the Negro on Fourth street. He followed the darkey a short distance, and, coming upon Robert Moore, who is known about town as the 'black detective,' Fist pointed the Negro out and Moore at once made a move toward the stranger. The latter observed Moore making in his direction, and, without a word, he sped in the direction of the Brooklyn pasture, Moore following and firing several shots at him. In a few minutes a half hundred white men, including Chief of Police Miller, Constable Dannenhauer, Patrolman Keegan and several special officers, all well-armed, joined in the chase, but in the darkness the Negro escaped.

"Just as the pursuing party reached town again, two of the residents of Lafayette avenue, Peter Leson and Robert Henning, reported that they had just chased and shot at a Negro, who had been seen in the yard of the former's house. They were positive the Negro had not escaped from the square. Their report was enough to set the appetite of the crowd on edge, and the square was quickly surrounded, while several dozens of men, armed with lanterns and revolvers, made a search of every yard and under every house in the square. No Negro was found.

"The crowd of armed men was constantly swelling, and at 10 o'clock it had reached the proportions of a small army. At 10:30 o'clock an outbound freight train is due to pass through Gretna on the Texas and Pacific Road, and the crowd, believing that Captain Day's slayer might be aboard one of the cars attempting to leave the scene of his crime, resolved to inspect the train. As the train stopped at the Madison street crossing the engineer was requested to pull very slowly through the town, in order that the trucks of the cars might be examined. There was a string of armed men on each side of the railroad track and in a few moments a Negro was espied riding between two cars. A half dozen weapons were pointed at him and he was ordered to come out. He sprang out with alacrity and was pounced upon almost before he reached the ground. Robert Moore grabbed him and pushed an ugly looking Derringer[3] under his nose and the Negro threw up both hands. Constable Dannenhauer and Patrolman Keegan took charge of him and hustled him off to jail, where he was locked up. The Negro does not at all resemble Robert Charles, but it was best for his sake that he was placed under lock and key. The crowd was not in a humor to let any Negro pass muster last night. The prisoner gave his name as Luke Wallace.

"But now came the real excitement. The train had slowed down almost to a standstill, in the very heart of town. Somebody shouted: 'There he goes, on top of the train!' And sure enough, somebody was going. It was a Negro, too, and he was making a bee-line for the front end of the train. A veritable shower of bullets, shot and rifle balls greeted the flying form, but on it sped. The locomotive had stopped in the middle of the square between Lavoisier and Newton streets, and the Negro, flying with the speed of the wind along the top of the cars, reached the first car of the train and jumped to the tender and then into the cab. As he did several white men standing at the locomotive made a rush into the cab. The Negro sprang swiftly out of the other side, on to the sidewalk. But there were several more men, and as he realized that he was rushing right into their arms he made a spring to leap over the fence of Mrs. Linden's home, on the wood side of the track. Before the Negro got to the top one white man had hold of his legs, while another rushed up, pistol in hand. The man who was holding the darkey's legs was jostled out of the way and the man with the pistol, standing directly beneath the Negro, sent two bullets at him.

"There was a wild scramble, and the vision of a fleeing form in the Linden yard, but that was the last seen of the black man. The yard was entered and searched, and neighboring yards were also searched, but not even the trace of blood was found. It is almost impossible to believe that the Negro was not wounded, for the man who fired at him held the pistol almost against the Negro's body.

"The shots brought out almost everybody—white—in town, and though there was nothing to show for the exciting work, except the arrest of the Negro, who doesn't answer the description of the man wanted, Gretna's male population had its little fun and felt amply repaid for all the trouble it was put to, and all the ammunition it wasted."

BRUTALITY IN NEW ORLEANS

Mob rule reigned supreme Wednesday, and the scenes that were enacted challenge belief. How many colored men and women were abused and injured is not known, for those who escaped were glad to make a place of refuge and took no time to publish their troubles. The mob made no attempt to find Charles; its only purpose was to pursue, beat and kill any colored man or woman who happened to come in sight. Speaking editorially, the Picayune of Thursday, the 26th of July, said:

Escaped with Their Lives

At the Charity Hospital Wednesday night more than a score of people were treated for wounds received at the hands of the mob. Some were able to tell of their mistreatment, and their recitals are briefly given in the Picayune as follows:

"Alex Ruffin, who is quite seriously injured, is a Pullman car porter, a native of Chicago. He reached New Orleans at 9:20 o'clock last night, and after finishing his work, boarded a Henry Clay avenue car to go to Delachaise street, where he has a sick son.

" 'I hadn't ridden any way,' said he, 'when I saw a lot of white folks. They were shouting to 'Get the Niggers.' I didn't know they were after every colored man they saw, and sat still. Two or three men jumped on the car and started at me. One of them hit me over the head with a slingshot, and they started to shooting at me. I jumped out of the car and ran, although I had done nothing. They shot me in the arm and in the leg. I would certainly have been killed had not some gentleman taken my part. If I had known New Orleans was so excited I would never have left my car.'

"George Morris is the name of a Negro who was badly injured by a mob which went through the Poydras Market. Morris is employed as watchman there. He heard the noise of the passing crowd and looked out to see what the matter was. As soon as the mob saw him its members started after him.

" 'One man hit me over the head with a club,' said George, after his wounds had been dressed, 'and somebody cut me in the back. I didn't hardly think what was the matter at first, but when I saw they were after me I ran for my life. I ran to the coffee stand, where I work, for protection, but they were right after me, and somebody shot me in the back. At last the police got me away from the crowd. Just before I was hit a friend of mine, who was in the crowd, said, 'You had better go home, Nigger; they're after your kind.' I didn't know then what he meant. I found out pretty quick.'

"Morris is at the hospital. He is a perfect wreck, and while he will probably get well, he will have had a close call.

"Esther Fields is a Negro washerwoman who lives at South Claiborne and Toledano streets. She was at home when she heard a big noise and went out to investigate. She ran into the arms of the mob, and was beaten into insensibility in less time than it takes to tell it. Esther is being treated at the charity hospital, and should be able to get about in a few days. The majority of her bruises are about the head.

"T. P. Sanders fell at the hands of the Jackson avenue mob. He lives at 1927 Jackson avenue, and was sitting in front of his home when he saw the crowd marching out the street. He stayed to see what the excitement was all about, and was shot in the knee and thorax and horribly beaten about the head before the mob came to the conclusion that he had been done for, and passed on. The ambulance was called and he was picked up and carried to the charity hospital, where his wounds were dressed and pronounced serious.

"Oswald McMahon is nothing more than a boy. He was shot

in the leg and afterward carried to the hospital. His injuries are very slight.

"Dan White is another charity hospital patient. He is a Negro roustabout and was sitting in the bar room at Poydras and Franklin streets when a mob passed along and espied him. He was shot in the hand, and would have been roughly dealt with had some policeman not been luckily near and rescued him.

"In addition to the Negroes who suffered from the violence of the mob there were several patients treated at the hospital during the night who had been with the rioters and had been struck by stray bullets or injured in scuffles. None of this class were hurt to any extent. They got their wounds dressed and went out again."

WAS CHARLES A DESPERADO?

The press of the country has united in declaring that Robert Charles was a desperado. As usual, when dealing with a negro, he is assumed to be guilty because he is charged. Even the most conservative of journals refuse to ask evidence to prove that the dead man was a criminal, and that his life had been given over to law-breaking. The minute that the news was flashed across the country that he had shot a white man it was at once declared that he was a fiend incarnate, and that when he was killed the community would be ridden of a black-hearted desperado.

The reporters of the New Orleans papers, who were in the best position to trace the record of this man's life, made every possible effort to find evidence to prove that he was a villain unhung. With all the resources at their command, and inspired by intense interest to paint him as black a villain as possible, these reporters signally failed to disclose a single indictment which charged Robert Charles with a crime. Because they failed to find any legal evidence that Charles was a lawbreaker and desperado his accusers gave full license to their imagination and distorted the facts that they had obtained, in every way possible, to prove a course of criminality, which the records absolutely refuse to show.

Charles had his first encounter with the police Monday night, in which he was shot in the street duel which was begun by the police after Officer Mora had beaten Charles three or four times over the head with his billy in an attempt to make an illegal arrest. In defending himself against the combined attack of two officers with a billy and their guns upon him, Charles shot Officer Mora and escaped.

Early Tuesday morning Charles was traced to Dryades street by officers who were instructed to kill him on sight. There, again defending himself, he shot and killed two officers. This, of course, in the eyes of the American press, made him a desperado. The New Orleans press, in substantiating the charges that he was a desperado, make statements which will be interesting to examine.

In the first place the New Orleans Times-Democrat, of July 25th, calls Charles a "ravisher and a daredevil." It says that from all sources that could be searched "the testimony was cumulative that the character of the murderer, Robert Charles, is that of a daredevil and a fiend in human form." Then in the same article it says:

> "The belongings of Robert Charles which were found in his room were a complete index to the character of the man. Although the room and its contents were in a state of chaos on account of the frenzied search for clews by officers and citizens, an examination of his personal effects revealed the mental state of the murderer and the rancor in his heart toward the Caucasian race. Never was the adage, 'A little learning is a dangerous thing,' better exemplified than in the case of the negro who shot to death the two officers."

His room was searched, and the evidence upon which the charge that he was a desperado consisted of pamphlets in support of Negro emigration to Liberia. On his mantel-piece there was found a bullet mold and an outfit for reloading cartridges. There were also two pistol scabbards and a bottle of cocaine. The other evidences that Charles was a desperado the writer described as follows:

> "In his room were found negro periodicals and other 'race' propaganda, most of which was in the interest of the negro's emigration to Liberia. There were Police Gazettes strewn about his room and other papers of a similar character. Well-worn text-books, bearing

his name written in his own scrawling handwriting, and well-filled copybooks found in his trunk showed that he had burnt the midnight oil, and was desirous of improving himself intellectually in order that he might conquer the hated white race. Much of the literature found among his chattels was of a superlatively vituperative character, and attacked the white race in unstinted language and asserted the equal rights of the Negro.

"Charles was evidently the local agent of the 'Voice of Missions,' a 'religious' paper, published at Atlanta, as great bundles of that sheet were found. It is edited by one Bishop Turner, and seems to be the official organ of all haters of the white race. Its editorials are anarchistic in the extreme, and urge upon the negro that the sooner he realizes that he is as good as the white man the better it will be for him. The following verses were clipped from the journal; they were marked 'till forbidden,' and appeared in several successive numbers:

"OUR SENTIMENTS
"H. M. T.

"My country, 'tis of thee, Dear land of Africa, Of thee we sing. Land where our fathers died, Land of the Negro's pride, God's truth shall ring. "My native country, thee, Land of the black and free, Thy name I love; To see thy rocks and rills, Thy woods and matchless hills, Like that above.

"When all thy slanderous ghouls, In the bosom of sheol, Forgotten lie, Thy monumental name shall live, And suns thy royal brow shall gild, Upheaved to heaven high, O'ertopping thrones."

"There were no valuables in his room, and if he was a professional thief he had his headquarters for storing his plunder at some other place than his room on Fourth street. Nothing was found in his room that could lead to the belief that he was a thief, except fifty or more small bits of soap. The inference was that every place he visited he took all of the soap lying around, as all of the bits were well worn and had seen long service on the washstand.

"His wearing apparel was little more than rags, and financially he was evidently not in a flourishing condition. He was in no sense a skilled workman, and his room showed, in fact, that he was nothing more than a laborer.

"The 'philosopher in the garret' was a dirty wretch, and his room, his bedding and his clothing were nasty and filthy beyond belief. His object in life seemed to have been the discomfiture of the white race, and to this purpose he devoted himself with zeal. He declared himself to be a 'patriot,' and wished to be the Moses of his race."

Under the title of "The Making of a Monster," the reporter attempts to give "something of the personality of the arch-fiend, Charles." Giving his imagination full vent the writer says:

"It is only natural that the deepest interest should attach to the personality of Robert Charles. What manner of man was this fiend incarnate? What conditions developed him? Who were his preceptors? From what ancestral strain, if any, did he derive his ferocious hatred of the whites, his cunning, his brute courage, the apostolic zeal which he displayed in spreading the propaganda of African equality? These are questions involving one of the most remarkable psychological problems of modern times."

In answer to the questions which he propounds, the reporter proceeds to admit that he did not learn anything of a very desperate nature connected with Charles. He says:

"Although Charles was a familiar figure to scores of Negroes in New Orleans, and they had been more or less intimately acquainted with him for over two years, curiously little can be learned of his habits or mode of life. Since the perpetration of his terrible series of crimes it goes without saying that his former friends are inclined to be reticent, but it is reasonably certain that they have very little to tell. In regard to himself, Charles was singularly reticent for a Negro. He did not even indulge in the usual lying about his prowess and his adventures. This was possibly due to the knowledge that he was wanted for a couple of murders. The man had sense enough to know that it would be highly unwise to excite any curiosity about his past.

"When Charles first came to New Orleans he worked here and there as a day laborer. He was employed at different times in a sawmill, on the street gangs, as a roustabout on the levee, as a helper at the sugar works and as a coal shoveler in the engine room of the St. Charles Hotel. At each of the places where he worked he was known as a quiet, rather surly fellow, who had little to say to anybody, and generally performed his tasks in morose silence. He managed to convey the impression, however, of being a man of more than ordinary intelligence.

"A Negro named William Butts, who drives a team on the levee and lives on Washington street, near Baronne, told a Times-Democrat reporter yesterday that Charles got a job about a year ago as agent for a Liberian Immigration Society, which has headquarters at Birmingham, and was much elated at the prospect of making a living without hard labor."

According to the further investigations of this reporter, Charles was also agent for Bishop Turner's "Voice of Missions," the colored missionary organ of the African Methodist Church, edited by H. M. Turner, of Atlanta, Georgia. Concerning his service as agent for the "Voice of Missions," the reporter says:

"He secured a number of subscribers and visited them once a month to collect the installments. In order to insure regular payments it was necessary to keep up enthusiasm, which was prone to wane, and Charles consequently became an active and continual preacher of the propaganda of hatred. Whatever may have been his private sentiments at the outset, this constant harping on one string must eventually have had a powerful effect upon his own mind.

"Exactly how he received his remuneration is uncertain, but he told several of his friends that he got a 'big commission.' Incidentally he solicited subscribers for a Negro paper called the Voice of the Missions, and when he struck a negro who did not want to go to Africa himself, he begged contributions for the 'good of the cause.'

"In the course of time Charles developed into a fanatic on the subject of the Negro oppression and neglected business to indulge in wild tirades whenever he could find a listener. He became more anxious to make converts than to obtain subscribers, and the more conservative darkies began to get afraid of him. Meanwhile he got into touch with certain agitators in the North and made himself a distributing agent for their literature, a great deal of which he gave away. Making money was a secondary consideration to 'the cause.'

"One of the most enthusiastic advocates of the Liberian scheme

is the colored Bishop H. M. Turner, of Atlanta. Turner is a man of
unusual ability, has been over to Africa personally several times,
and has made himself conspicuous by denouncing laws which he
claimed discriminated against the blacks. Charles was one of the
bishop's disciples and evidence has been found that seems to indicate they were in correspondence."

This was all that the Times-Democrat's reporters could find
after the most diligent search to prove that Charles was the fiend
incarnate which the press of New Orleans and elsewhere declared
him to be.

The reporters of the New Orleans Picayune were no more successful than their brethren of the Times-Democrat. They, too,
were compelled to substitute fiction for facts in their attempt to
prove Charles a desperado. In the issue of the 26th of July it was
said that Charles was well-known in Vicksburg, and was there a
consort of thieves. They mentioned that a man named Benson
Blake was killed in 1894 or 1895, and that four Negroes were
captured, and two escaped. Of the two escaped they claim that
Charles was one. The four negroes who were captured were put
in jail, and as usual, in the high state of civilization which characterizes Mississippi, the right of the person accused of crime to
an indictment by legal process and a legal trial by jury was considered a useless formality if the accused happened to be black. A
mob went to the jail that night, the four colored men were delivered to the mob, and all four were hanged in the court-house
yard. The reporters evidently assumed that Charles was guilty, if,
in fact, he was ever there, because the other four men were
lynched. They did not consider it was a fact of any importance
that Charles was never indicted. They called him a murderer on
general principles.

DIED IN SELF-DEFENSE

The life, character and death of Robert Charles challenges the
thoughtful consideration of all fair-minded people. In the frenzy
of the moment, when nearly a dozen men lay dead, the victims of
his unerring and death-dealing aim, it was natural for a prejudiced press and for citizens in private life to denounce him as a

desperado and a murderer. But sea depths are not measured when the ocean rages, nor can absolute justice be determined while public opinion is lashed into fury. There must be calmness to insure correctness of judgment. The fury of the hour must abate before we can deal justly with any man or any cause.

That Charles was not a desperado is amply shown by the discussion in the preceding chapter. The darkest pictures which the reporters could paint of Charles were quoted freely, so that the public might find upon what grounds the press declared him to be a lawbreaker. Unquestionably the grounds are wholly insufficient. Not a line of evidence has been presented to prove that Charles was the fiend which the first reports of the New Orleans charge him to be.

Nothing more should be required to establish his good reputation, for the rule is universal that a reputation must be assumed to be good until it is proved bad. But that rule does not apply to the Negro, for as soon as he is suspected the public judgment immediately determines that he is guilty of whatever crime he stands charged. For this reason, as a matter of duty to the race, and the simple justice to the memory of Charles, an investigation has been made of the life and character of Charles before the fatal affray which led to his death.

Robert Charles was not an educated man. He was a student who faithfully investigated all the phases of oppression from which his race has suffered. That he was a student is amply shown by the Times-Democrat [r]eport of the 25th, which says:

"Well-worn text-books, bearing his name written in his own scrawling handwriting, and well-filled copy-books found in his trunk, showed that he had burned the midnight oil, and desired to improve himself intellectually in order that he might conquer the hated white race." From this quotation it will be seen that he spent the hours after days of hard toil in trying to improve himself, both in the study of text-books and in writing.

He knew that he was a student of a problem which required all the intelligence that a man could command, and he was burning his midnight oil gathering knowledge that he might better be able to come to an intelligent solution. To his aid in the study of this problem he sought the aid of a Christian newspaper, The Voice of Missions, the organ of the African Methodist Episcopal Church. He was in communication with its editor, who is a bishop, and is known all over this country as a man of learning, a lover of justice and the defender of law and order. Charles could receive from Bishop Turner not a word of encouragement to be other than an earnest, tireless and God-fearing student of the complex problems which affected the race.

For further help and assistance in his studies, Charles turned to an organization which has existed and flourished for many years, at all times managed by men of high Christian standing and absolute integrity. These men believe and preach a doctrine that the best interests of the Negro will be subserved by an emigration from America back to the Fatherland, and they do all they can to spread the doctrine of emigration and to give material assistance to those who desire to leave America and make their future homes in Africa. This organization is known as "The International Migration Society."[4] It has its headquarters in Birmingham, Alabama. From this place it issues pamphlets, some of which were found in the home of Robert Charles, and which pamphlets the reporters of the New Orleans papers declare to be incendiary and dangerous in their doctrine and teaching.

Nothing could be further from the truth. Copies of any and all of them may be secured by writing to D. J. Flummer, who is President and in charge of the home office in Birmingham, Alabama. Three of the pamphlets found in Charles' room are named respectively:

First, "Prospectus of the Liberian Colonization Society;" which pamphlet in a few brief pages tells of the work of the society, plans, prices and terms of transportation of colored people who choose to go to Africa. These pages are followed by a short, conservative discussion of the Negro question, and close with an argument that Africa furnishes the best asylum for the oppressed Negroes in this country.

The second pamphlet is entitled "Christian Civilization of Africa." This is a brief statement of the advantages of the Republic of Liberia, and an argument in support of the superior conditions which colored people may attain to by leaving the South and settling in Liberia.

The third pamphlet is entitled "The Negro and Liberia." This is a larger document than the other two, and treats more exhaustively the question of emigration, but from the first page to the last there is not an incendiary line or sentence. There is not even a suggestion of violence in all of its thirty-two pages, and not a word which could not be preached from every pulpit in the land.

If it is true that the workman is known by his tools, certainly no harm could ever come from the doctrines which were preached by Charles or the papers and pamphlets distributed by him. Nothing ever written in the "Voice of Missions," and nothing ever published in the pamphlets above alluded to in the remotest way suggest that a peaceable man should turn lawbreaker, or that any man should dye his hands in his brother's blood.

In order to secure as far as possible positive information about the life and character of Robert Charles, it was plain that the best course to pursue was to communicate with those with whom he had sustained business relations. Accordingly a letter was forwarded to Mr. D. J. Flummer, who is president of the colonization society, in which letter he was asked to state in reply what information he had of the life and character of Robert Charles. The result was a very prompt letter in response, the text of which is as follows:

Birmingham, Ala., Aug. 21, 1900.

Mrs. Ida B. Wells Barnett, Chicago, Ill.:

Dear Madam—Replying to your favor of recent date requesting me to write you giving such information as I may have concerning the life, habits and character of Robert Charles, who recently shot and killed police officers in New Orleans, I wish to say that my knowledge of him is only such as I have gained from his business connection with the International Migration Society during the past five or six years, during which time I was president of the society.

He having learned that the purpose of this society was to colonize the colored people in Liberia, West Africa, and thereby lessen or destroy the friction and prejudice existing in this country between the two races, set about earnestly and faithfully distributing the literature that we issued from time to time. He always appeared to be mild but earnest in his advocacy of emigration, and never to my knowledge used any method or means that would in the least appear unreasonable, and had always kept within the bounds of law and order in advocating emigration.

The work he performed for this society was all gratuitous, and apparently prompted from his love of humanity, and desires to be instrumental in building up a Negro Nationality in Africa.

If he ever violated a law before the killing of the policemen, I do not know of it. Yours very truly,

D. J. Flummer.

Besides this statement, Mr. Flummer enclosed a letter received by the Society two days before the tragedy at New Orleans. This letter was written by Robert Charles, and it attests his devotion to the cause of emigration which he had espoused. Memoranda on the margin of the letter show that the order was filled by mailing the pamphlets. It is very probable that these were the identical pamphlets which were found by the mob which broke into the room of Robert Charles and seized upon these harmless documents and declared they were sufficient evidence to prove Charles a desperado. In the light of subsequent events the letter of Charles, which follows, sounds like a voice from the tomb:

New Orleans, July 30, 1900.

Mr. D. J. Flummer:

Dear Sir—I received your last pamphlets and they are all given out. I want you to send me some more, and I enclose you the stamps. I think I will go over in Greenville, Miss., and give my people some pamphlets over there. Yours truly,

Robert Charles.

The latest word of information comes from New Orleans from a man who knew Charles intimately for six years. For obvious reasons, his name is withheld. In answer to a letter sent him he answers as follows:

New Orleans, Aug. 23, 1900.

Mrs. Ida B. Wells Barnett:

Dear Madam—It affords me great pleasure to inform you as far as I know of Robert Charles. I have been acquainted with him about six years in this city. He never has, as I know, given any trouble to anyone. He was quiet and a peaceful man and was very frank in speaking. He was too much of a hero to die; few can be found to equal him. I am very sorry to say that I do not know anything of his birthplace, nor his parents, but enclosed find letter from his uncle, from which you may find more information. You will also find one of the circulars in which Charles was in possession of which was styled as a crazy document. Let me say, until our preachers preach this document we will always be slaves. If you can help circulate this "crazy" doctrine I would be glad to have you do so, for I shall never rest until I get to that heaven on earth; that is, the west coast of Africa, in Liberia.

With best wishes to you I still remain, as always, for the good of the race,

By only those whose anger and vindictiveness warp their judgment is Robert Charles a desperado. Their word is not supported by the statement of a single fact which justifies their judgment and no criminal record shows that he was ever indicted for any offense, much less convicted of crime. On the contrary, his work for many years had been with Christian people, circulating emigration pamphlets and active as agent for a mission publication. Men who knew him say that he was a law-abiding, quiet, industrious, peaceable man. So he lived.

So he lived and so he would have died had not he raised his hand to resent unprovoked assault and unlawful arrest that fateful Monday night. That made him an outlaw, and being a man of courage he decided to die with his face to the foe. The white people of this country may charge that he was a desperado, but to the people of his own race Robert Charles will always be regarded as the hero of New Orleans.

BURNING HUMAN BEINGS ALIVE

Not only has life been taken by mobs in the past twenty years, but the ordinary procedure of hanging and shooting have been improved upon during the past ten years. Fifteen human beings have been burned to death in the different parts of the country by mobs. Men, women and children have gone to see the sight, and all have approved the barbarous deeds done in the high light of the civilization and Christianity of this country.

In 1891 Ed Coy was burned to death in Texarkana, Ark. He was charged with assaulting a white woman, and after the mob had securely tied him to a tree, the men and boys amused themselves for some time sticking knives into Coy's body and slicing off pieces of flesh. When they had amused themselves sufficiently, they poured coal oil over him and the woman in the case set fire to him. It is said that fifteen thousand people stood by and saw him burned. This was on a Sunday night, and press reports told how the people looked on while the Negro burned to death.

Feb. 1st, 1893, Henry Smith was burned to death in Paris, Texas. The entire county joined in that exhibition. The district attorney himself went for the prisoner and turned him over to the mob. He was placed upon a float and drawn by four white horses through the principal streets of the city. Men, women and children stood at their doors and waved their handkerchiefs and cheered the echoes. They knew that the man was to be burned to death because the newspaper had declared for three days previous that this would be so. Excursions were run by all the railroads, and the mayor of the town gave the children a holiday so that they might see the sight.

Henry Smith was charged with having assaulted and murdered a little white girl. He was an imbecile, and while he had killed the child, there was no proof that he had criminally assaulted her. He was tied to a stake on a platform which had been built ten feet high, so that everybody might see the sight. The father and brother and uncle of the little white girl that had been murdered were upon that platform about fifty minutes entertaining the crowd of ten thousand persons by burning the victim's flesh with red-hot irons. Their own newspapers told how they burned his eyes out and ran the red-hot iron down his throat, cooking his tongue, and how the crowd cheered with delight. At last, having declared themselves satisfied, coal oil was poured over him and he was burned to death, and the mob fought over the ashes for bones and pieces of his clothes.

July 7th, 1893, in Bardwell, Ky., C. J. Miller was burned to ashes. Since his death this man has been found to be absolutely innocent of the murder of the two white girls with which he was charged. But the mob would wait for no justification. They insisted that, as they were not sure he was the right man, they would compromise the matter by hanging him instead of burning. Not to be outdone, they took the body down and made a huge bonfire out of it.

July 22d, 1893, at Memphis, Tenn., the body of Lee Walker was dragged through the street and burned before the court house. Walker had frightened some girls in a wagon along a country road by asking them to let him ride in their wagon. They cried out; some men working in a field near by said it was an attempt of assault, and of course began to look for their prey. There was never any charge of rape; the women only declared that he attempted an assault. After he was apprehended and put in jail and perfectly helpless, the mob dragged him out, shot him, cut him, beat him with sticks, built a fire and burned the legs off, then took the trunk of the body down and dragged further up the street, and at last burned it before the court house.

Sept. 20th, 1893, at Roanoke, Va., the body of a Negro who had quarreled with a white woman was burned in the presence of several thousand persons. These people also wreaked their vengeance upon this helpless victim of the mob's wrath by sticking knives into him, kicking him and beating him with stones and otherwise mutilating him before life was extinct.

June 10th, 1898, at Knoxville, Ark., James Perry was shut up in a cabin because he had smallpox and burned to death. He had been quarantined in this cabin when it was declared that he had this disease and the doctor sent for. When the physician arrived he found only a few smoldering embers. Upon inquiry some railroad hands who were working near by revealed the fact that they had fastened the door of the cabin and set fire to the cabin and burned man and hut together.

Feb. 22d, 1898, at Lake City, S.C., Postmaster Baker and his infant child were burned to death by a mob that had set fire to his house. Mr. Baker's crime was that he had refused to give up the post office, to which he had been appointed by the National Government. The mob had tried to drive him away by persecution and intimidation. Finding that all else had failed, they went to his home in the dead of night and set fire to his house, and as the family rushed forth they were greeted by a volley of bullets. The father and his baby were shot through the open door and wounded so badly that they fell back in the fire and were burned to death. The remainder of the family, consisting of the wife and five children, escaped with their lives from the burning house, but all of them were shot, one of the number made a cripple for life.

Jan. 7th, 1898, two Indians were tied to a tree at Maud Post-office, Indian Territory, and burned to death by a white mob. They were charged with murdering a white woman. There was no proof of their guilt except the unsupported word of the mob. Yet they were tied to a tree and slowly roasted to death. Their names were Lewis McGeesy and Hond Martin. Since that time these boys have been found to be absolutely innocent of the charge. Of course that discovery is too late to be of any benefit to them, but because they were Indians the Indian Commissioner demanded and received from the United States Government an indemnity of $13,000.

April 23d, 1899, at Palmetto, Ga., Sam Hose was burned alive in the presence of a throng, on Sunday afternoon. He was charged with killing a man named Cranford, his employer, which he admitted he did because his employer was about to shoot him. To the fact of killing the employer was added the absolutely false charge that Hose assaulted the wife. Hose was arrested and no trial was given him. According to the code of reasoning of the mob, none was needed.

A white man had been killed and a white woman was said to have been assaulted. That was enough. When Hose was found he had to die.

The Atlanta Constitution, in speaking of the murder of Cranford, said that the Negro who was suspected would be burned alive. Not only this, but it offered $500 reward for his capture. After he had been apprehended, it was publicly announced that he would be burned alive. Excursion trains were run and bulletins were put up in the small towns. The Governor of Georgia was in Atlanta while excursion trains were being made up to take visitors to the burning. Many fair ladies drove out in their carriages on Sunday afternoon to witness the torture and burning of a human being. Hose's ears were cut off, then his toes and fingers, and passed round to the crowd. His eyes were put out, his tongue torn out and flesh cut in strips by knives. Finally they poured coal oil on him and burned him to death. They dragged his half-consumed trunk out of the flames, cut it open, extracted his heart and liver, and sold slices for ten cents each for souvenirs, all of which was published most promptly in the daily papers of Georgia and boasted over by the people of that section.

Oct. 19th, 1889, at Canton, Miss., Joseph Leflore was burned to death. A house had been entered and its occupants murdered during the absence of the husband and father. When the discovery was made, it was immediately supposed that the crime was the work of a Negro, and the motive that of assaulting white women.

Bloodhounds were procured and they made a round of the village and discovered only one colored man absent from his home. This was taken to be proof sufficient that he was the perpetrator of the deed. When he returned home he was apprehended, taken into the yard of the house that had been burned down, tied to a stake, and was slowly roasted to death.

Dec. 6th, 1899, at Maysville, Ky., Wm. Coleman also was burned to death. He was slowly roasted, first one foot and then the other, and dragged out of the fire so that the torture might be prolonged. All of this without a shadow of proof or scintilla of evidence that the man had committed the crime.

Thus have the mobs of this country taken the lives of their victims within the past ten years. In every single instance except one these burnings were witnessed by from two thousand to fifteen thousand people, and no one person in all these crowds throughout the country had the courage to raise his voice and speak out against the awful barbarism of burning human beings to death.

Men and women of America, are you proud of this record which the Anglo-Saxon race has made for itself? Your silence seems to say that you are. Your silence encourages a continuance of this sort of horror. Only by earnest, active, united endeavor to arouse public sentiment can we hope to put a stop to these demonstrations of American barbarism.

LYNCHING RECORD

The following table of lynchings has been kept year by year by the Chicago Tribune, beginning with 1882, and shows the list of Negroes that have been lynched during that time:

1882, Negroes murdered by mobs 52
1883, Negroes murdered by mobs 39
1884, Negroes murdered by mobs 53
1885, Negroes murdered by mobs 164
1886, Negroes murdered by mobs 136
1887, Negroes murdered by mobs 128
1888, Negroes murdered by mobs 143

1889, Negroes murdered by mobs 127
1890, Negroes murdered by mobs 176
1891, Negroes murdered by mobs 192
1892, Negroes murdered by mobs 241
1893, Negroes murdered by mobs 200
1894, Negroes murdered by mobs 190
1895, Negroes murdered by mobs 171
1896, Negroes murdered by mobs 131
1897, Negroes murdered by mobs 156
1898, Negroes murdered by mobs 127
1899, Negroes murdered by mobs 107

Of these thousands of men and women who have been put to death without judge or jury, less than one-third of them have been even accused of criminal assault. The world at large has accepted unquestionably the statement that Negroes are lynched only for assaults upon white women. Of those who were lynched from 1882 to 1891, the first ten years of the tabulated lynching record, the charges are as follows:

Two hundred and sixty-nine were charged with rape; 253 with murder; 44 with robbery; 37 with incendiarism; 4 with burglary; 27 with race prejudice; 13 quarreled with white men; 10 with making threats; 7 with rioting; 5 with miscegenation; in 32 cases no reasons were given, the victims were lynched on general principles.

During the past five years the record is as follows:

Of the 171 persons lynched in 1895 only 34 were charged with this crime. In 1896, out of 131 persons who were lynched, only 34 were said to have assaulted women. Of the 156 in 1897, only 32. In 1898, out of 127 persons lynched, 24 were charged with the alleged "usual crime." In 1899, of the 107 lynchings, 16 were said to be for crimes against women. These figures, of course, speak for themselves, and to the unprejudiced, fair-minded person it is only necessary to read and study them in order to show that the charge that the Negro is a moral outlaw is a false one, made for the purpose of injuring the Negro's good name and to create public sentiment against him.

If public sentiment were alive, as it should be upon the subject, it would refuse to be longer hoodwinked, and the voice of conscience would refuse to be stilled by these false statements. If the laws of the country were obeyed and respected by the white men of the country who charge that the Negro has no respect for law, these things could not be, for every individual, no matter what the charge, would have a fair trial and an opportunity to prove his guilt or innocence before a tribunal of law.

That is all the Negro asks—that is all the friends of law and order need to ask, for once the law of the land is supreme, no individual who commits crime will escape punishment.

Individual Negroes commit crimes the same as do white men, but that the Negro race is peculiarly given to assault upon women, is a falsehood of the deepest dye. The tables given above show that the Negro who is saucy to white men is lynched as well as the Negro who is charged with assault upon women. Less than one-sixth of the lynchings last year, 1899, were charged with rape.

The Negro points to his record during the war in rebuttal of this false slander. When the white women and children of the South had no protector save only these Negroes, not one instance is known where the trust was betrayed. It is remarkably strange that the Negro had more respect for womanhood with the white men of the South hundreds of miles away, than they have to-day, when surrounded by those who take their lives with impunity and burn and torture, even worse than the "unspeakable Turk."

Again, the white women of the North came South years ago, threaded the forests, visited the cabins, taught the schools and associated only with the Negroes whom they came to teach, and had no protectors near at hand. They had no charge or complaint to make of the danger to themselves after association with this class of human beings. Not once has the country been shocked by such recitals from them as come from the women who are surrounded by their husbands, brothers, lovers and friends. If the Negro's nature is bestial, it certainly should have proved itself in one of these two instances. The Negro asks only justice and an impartial consideration of these facts.

"LYNCH LAW IN AMERICA"

Written on behalf of the Anti-Lynching Bureau she chaired for the Afro-American Council, this article shows Wells-Barnett trying to capitalize on her new position by addressing a national audience. As the council's expert on lynching, Wells-Barnett was able to place her work in a number of mainstream publications. Here, she writes for the *Arena*, a liberal magazine published in Boston. In addressing the *Arena*'s largely white readership, she provides a comprehensive history of lynching, which she describes as America's "unwritten law." Challenging progressive reformers to join her protest against lynching, Wells-Barnett compares their current outrage over the anti-Semitic treatment of France's Captain Alfred Dreyfus, a Jewish military officer who was convicted of treason in the French courts, with their silence on the subject of mob violence in America.

SOURCE: Ida B. Wells-Barnett, "Lynch Law in America," *Arena*, January 1900, 15–24.

LYNCH LAW IN AMERICA

Our country's national crime is *lynching*. It is not the creature of an hour, the sudden outburst of uncontrolled fury, or the unspeakable brutality of an insane mob. It represents the cool, calculating deliberation of intelligent people who openly avow that there is an "unwritten law" that justifies them in putting human beings to death without complaint under oath, without trial by jury, without opportunity to make defense, and without right of appeal. The "unwritten law" first found excuse with the rough, rugged, and determined man who left the civilized centers of eastern States to seek for quick returns in the gold-fields of the far West. Following in uncertain pursuit of continually eluding fortune, they dared the savagery of the Indians, the hardships of mountain travel, and the constant terror of border State outlaws. Naturally, they felt slight toleration for traitors in their own ranks. It was enough to fight the enemies from without; woe to the foe within! Far removed from and entirely without protection of the courts of civilized life, these fortune-seekers made laws to meet their varying emergencies. The thief who stole a horse, the bully who "jumped" a claim, was a common enemy. If caught he was promptly tried, and if found guilty was hanged to the tree under which the court convened.

Those were busy days of busy men. They had no time to give the prisoner a bill of exception or stay of execution. The only way a man had to secure a stay of execution was to behave himself. Judge Lynch was original in methods but exceedingly effective in procedure. He made the charge, impaneled the jurors, and directed the execution. When the court adjourned, the prisoner was dead. Thus lynch law held sway in the far West until civilization spread into the Territories and the orderly processes of law took its place. The emergency no longer existing, lynching gradually disappeared from the West.

But the spirit of mob procedure seemed to have fastened itself upon the lawless classes, and the grim process that at first was invoked to declare justice was made the excuse to wreak vengeance and cover crime. It next appeared in the South, where centuries of Anglo-Saxon civilization had made effective all the safeguards of court procedure. No emergency called for lynch law. It asserted its sway in defiance of law and in favor of anarchy. There it has flourished ever since, marking the thirty years of its existence with the inhuman butchery of more than ten thousand men, women, and children by shooting, drowning, hanging, and burning them alive. Not only this, but so potent is the force of example that the lynching mania has spread throughout the North and middle West. It is now no uncommon thing to read of lynchings north of Mason and Dixon's line, and those most responsible for this fashion gleefully point to these instances and assert that the North is no better than the South.

This is the work of the "unwritten law" about which so much

is said, and in whose behest butchery is made a pastime and national savagery condoned. The first statute of this "unwritten law" was written in the blood of thousands of brave men who thought that a government that was good enough to create a citizenship was strong enough to protect it. Under the authority of a national law that gave every citizen the right to vote, the newly-made citizens chose to exercise their suffrage. But the reign of the national law was short-lived and illusionary. Hardly had the sentences dried upon the statute-books before one Southern State after another raised the cry against "negro domination" and proclaimed there was an "unwritten law" that justified any means to resist it.

The method then inaugurated was the outrages by the "red-shirt"[5] bands of Louisiana, South Carolina, and other Southern States, which were succeeded by the Ku-Klux Klans. These advocates of the "unwritten law" boldly avowed their purpose to intimidate, suppress, and nullify the negro's right to vote. In support of its plans the Ku-Klux Klans, the "red-shirt" and similar organizations proceeded to beat, exile, and kill negroes until the purpose of their organization was accomplished and the supremacy of the "unwritten law" was effected. Thus lynchings began in the South, rapidly spreading into the various States until the national law was nullified and the reign of the "unwritten law" was supreme. Men were taken from their homes by "red-shirt" bands and stripped, beaten, and exiled; others were assassinated when their political prominence made them obnoxious to their political opponents; while the Ku-Klux barbarism of election days, reveling in the butchery of thousands of colored voters, furnished records in Congressional investigations that are a disgrace to civilization.

The alleged menace of universal suffrage having been avoided by the absolute suppression of the negro vote, the spirit of mob murder should have been satisfied and the butchery of negroes should have ceased. But men, women, and children were the victims of murder by individuals and murder by mobs, just as they had been when killed at the demands of the "unwritten law" to prevent "negro domination." Negroes were killed for disputing over terms of contracts with their employers. If a few barns were burned some colored man was killed to stop it. If a colored man resented the imposition of a white man and the two came to blows, the colored man had to die, either at the hands of the white man then and there or later at the hands of a mob that speedily gathered. If he showed a spirit of courageous manhood he was hanged for his pains, and the killing was justified by the declaration that he was a "saucy nigger." Colored women have been murdered because they refused to tell the mobs where relatives could be found for "lynching bees." Boys of fourteen years have been lynched by white representatives of American civilization. In fact, for all kinds of offenses—and, for no offenses—from murders to misdemeanors, men and women are put to death without judge or jury; so that, although the political excuse was no longer necessary, the wholesale murder of human beings went on just the same. A new name was given to the killings and a new excuse was invented for so doing.

Again the aid of the "unwritten law" is invoked, and again it comes to the rescue. During the last ten years a new statute has been added to the "unwritten law." This statute proclaims that for certain crimes or alleged crimes no negro shall be allowed a trial; that no white woman shall be compelled to charge an assault under oath or to submit any such charge to the investigation of a court of law. The result is that many men have been put to death whose innocence was afterward established; and to-day, under this reign of the "unwritten law," no colored man, no matter what his reputation, is safe from lynching if a white woman, no matter what her standing or motive, cares to charge him with insult or assault.

It is considered a sufficient excuse and reasonable justification to put a prisoner to death under this "unwritten law" for the frequently repeated charge that these lynching horrors are necessary to prevent crimes against women. The sentiment of the country has been appealed to, in describing the isolated condition of white families in thickly populated negro districts; and the charge is made that these homes are in as great danger as if they were surrounded by wild beasts. And the world has accepted this theory without let or hindrance. In many cases there has been open expression that the fate meted out to the victim was only what he deserved. In many other instances there has been a silence that says more forcibly than words can proclaim it that it is right and proper that a human being should be seized by a mob and burned to death upon the unsworn and the uncorroborated charge of his accuser. No matter that our laws presume every man innocent until he is proved guilty; no matter that it leaves a certain class of individuals completely at the mercy of another class; no matter that it encourages those criminally disposed to blacken their faces and commit any crime in the calendar so long as they can throw suspicion on some negro, as is frequently done, and then lead a mob to take his life; no matter that mobs make a farce of the law and a mockery of justice; no matter that hundreds of boys are being hardened in crime and schooled in vice by the repetition of such scenes before their eyes—if a white woman declares herself insulted or assaulted, some life must pay the penalty, with all the horrors of the Spanish Inquisition and all the barbarism of the Middle Ages. The world looks on and says it is well.

Not only are two hundred men and women put to death annually, on the average, in this country by mobs, but these lives are taken with the greatest publicity. In many instances the leading citizens aid and abet by their presence when they do not participate, and the leading journals inflame the public mind to the lynching point with scare-head articles and offers of rewards. Whenever a burning is advertised to take place, the railroads run excursions, photographs are taken, and the same jubilee is indulged in that characterized the public hangings of one hundred years ago. There is, however, this difference: in those old days the multitude that stood by was permitted only to guy or jeer. The nineteenth century lynching mob cuts off ears, toes, and fingers, strips off flesh, and distributes portions of the body as souvenirs among the crowd. If the leaders of the mob are so minded, coal-oil is poured over the body and the victim is then roasted to death. This has been done in Texarkana and Paris, Tex., in Bardswell, Ky., and in Newman, Ga. In Paris the officers of the law delivered the prisoner to the mob. The mayor gave the school children a holiday and the railroads ran excursion trains so that the people might see a human being burned to death. In Texarkana, the year before, men and boys amused themselves by cutting off strips of flesh and thrusting knives into their helpless victim. At Newman, Ga., of the present year, the mob tried every conceivable torture to compel the victim to cry out and confess, before they set fire to the faggots that burned him. But their trouble was all in vain—he never uttered a cry, and they could not make him confess.

This condition of affairs were brutal enough and horrible enough if it were true that lynchings occurred only because of the commission of crimes against women—as is constantly declared by ministers, editors, lawyers, teachers, statesmen, and even by women themselves. It has been to the interest of those who did the lynching to blacken the good name of the helpless and defenseless victims of their hate. For this reason they publish at every possible opportunity this excuse for lynching, hoping thereby not only to palliate their own crime but at the same time to prove the negro a moral monster and unworthy of the respect and sympathy of the civilized world. But this alleged reason adds to the deliberate injustice of the mob's work. Instead of lynchings being caused by assaults upon women, the statistics show that not one-third of the victims of lynchings are even charged with such crimes. The Chicago *Tribune*, which publishes annually lynching statistics, is authority for the following:

In 1892, when lynching reached high-water mark, there were 241 persons lynched. The entire number is divided among the following States:

Alabama	22	Montana	4
Arkansas	25	New York	1
California	3	North Carolina	5
Florida	11	North Dakota	1
Georgia	17	Ohio	3
Idaho	8	South Carolina	5
Illinois	1	Tennessee	28
Kansas	3	Texas	15
Kentucky	9	Virginia	7
Louisiana	29	West Virginia	5
Maryland	1	Wyoming	9
Mississippi	16	Arizona Ter	3
Missouri	6	Oklahoma	2

Of this number, 160 were of negro descent. Four of them were lynched in New York, Ohio, and Kansas; the remainder were murdered in the South. Five of this number were females. The

charges for which they were lynched cover a wide range. They
are as follows:

Rape	46	Attempted rape	11
Murder	58	Suspected robbery	4
Rioting	3	Larceny	1
Race prejudice	6	Self-defense	1
No cause given	4	Insulting women	2
Incendiarism	6	Desperadoes	6
Robbery	6	Fraud	1
Assault and battery	1	Attempted murder	2
		No offense stated, boy and girl	2

In the case of the boy and girl above referred to, their father,
named Hastings, was accused of the murder of a white man. His
fourteen-year-old daughter and sixteen-year-old son were hanged
and their bodies filled with bullets; then the father was also
lynched. This occurred in November, 1892, at Jonesville, La.

Indeed, the record for the last twenty years shows exactly the
same or a smaller proportion who have been charged with this
horrible crime. Quite a number of the one-third alleged cases of
assault that have been personally investigated by the writer have
shown that there was no foundation in fact for the charges; yet the
claim is not made that there were no real culprits among them.
The negro has been too long associated with the white man not to
have copied his vices as well as his virtues. But the negro resents
and utterly repudiates the efforts to blacken his good name by
asserting that assaults upon women are peculiar to his race. The
negro has suffered far more from the commission of this crime
against the women of his race by white men than the white race
has ever suffered through *his* crimes. Very scant notice is taken of
the matter when this is the condition of affairs. What becomes a
crime deserving capital punishment when the tables are turned is
a matter of small moment when the negro woman is the accusing
party.

But since the world has accepted this false and unjust statement, and the burden of proof has been placed upon the negro to
vindicate his race, he is taking steps to do so. The Anti-Lynching
Bureau of the National Afro-American Council[6] is arranging to
have every lynching investigated and publish the facts to the

world, as has been done in the case of Sam Hose, who was burned alive last April at Newman, Ga. The detective's report showed that Hose killed Cranford, his employer, in self-defense, and that, while a mob was organizing to hunt Hose to punish him for killing a white man, not till twenty-four hours after the murder was the charge of rape, embellished with psychological and physical impossibilities, circulated. That gave an impetus to the hunt, and the Atlanta *Constitution's* reward of $500 keyed the mob to the necessary burning and roasting pitch. Of five hundred newspaper clippings of that horrible affair, nine-tenths of them assumed Hose's guilt—simply because his murderers said so, and because it is the fashion to believe the negro peculiarly addicted to this species of crime. All the negro asks is justice—a fair and impartial trial in the courts of the country. That given, he will abide the result.

But this question affects the entire American nation, and from several points of view: First, on the ground of consistency. Our watchword has been "the land of the free and the home of the brave." Brave men do not gather by thousands to torture and murder a single individual, so gagged and bound he cannot make even feeble resistance or defense. Neither do brave men or women stand by and see such things done without compunction of conscience, nor read of them without protest. Our nation has been active and outspoken in its endeavors to right the wrongs of the Armenian Christian, the Russian Jew, the Irish Home Ruler, the native women of India, the Siberian exile, and the Cuban patriot. Surely it should be the nation's duty to correct its own evils!

Second, on the ground of economy. To those who fail to be convinced from any other point of view touching this momentous question, a consideration of the economic phase might not be amiss. It is generally known that mobs in Louisiana, Colorado, Wyoming, and other States have lynched subjects of other countries. When their different governments demanded satisfaction, our country was forced to confess her inability to protect said subjects in the several States because of our State-rights doctrines, or in turn demand punishment of the lynchers. This confession, while humiliating in the extreme, was not satisfactory; and, while the United States cannot protect, she can pay. This she has done, and it is certain will have to do again in the case of the recent lynching of Italians in Louisiana. The United States already has paid in indemnities for lynching nearly a half million dollars, as follows:

Paid China for Rock Springs (Wyo.) massacre $147,748.74
Paid China for outrages on Pacific Coast 276,619.75
Paid Italy for massacre of Italian prisoners at
    New Orleans 24,330.90
Paid Italy for lynchings at Walsenburg, Col 10,000.00
Paid Great Britain for outrages on James Bain
    and Frederick Dawson 2,800.00

Third, for the honor of Anglo-Saxon civilization. No scoffer at our boasted American civilization could say anything more harsh of it than does the American white man himself who says he is unable to protect the honor of his women without resort to such brutal, inhuman, and degrading exhibitions as characterize "lynching bees." The cannibals of the South Sea Islands roast human beings alive to satisfy hunger. The red Indian of the Western plains tied his prisoner to the stake, tortured him, and danced in fiendish glee while his victim writhed in the flames. His savage, untutored mind suggested no better way than that of wreaking vengeance upon those who had wronged him. These people knew nothing about Christianity and did not profess to follow its teachings; but such primary laws as they had they lived up to. No nation, savage or civilized, save only the United States of America, has confessed its inability to protect its women save by hanging, shooting, and burning alleged offenders.

Finally, for love of country. No American travels abroad without blushing for shame for his country on this subject. And whatever the excuse that passes current in the United States, it avails nothing abroad. With all the powers of government in control; with all laws made by white men, administered by white judges, jurors, prosecuting attorneys, and sheriffs; with every office of the executive department filled by white men—no excuse can be offered for exchanging the orderly administration of justice for barbarous lynchings and "unwritten laws." Our country should be placed speedily above the plane of confessing herself a failure at self-government. This cannot be until Americans of every section, of broadest patriotism and best and wisest citizenship, not only see the defect in our country's armor but take the necessary steps to remedy it. Although lynchings have steadily increased in number and barbarity during the last twenty years, there has been no single effort put forth by the many moral and philanthropic forces of the country to put a stop to this wholesale slaughter. Indeed, the silence and seeming condonation grow more marked as the years go by.

A few months ago the conscience of this country was shocked because, after a two-weeks trial, a French judicial tribunal pronounced Captain Dreyfus[7] guilty. And yet, in our own land and under our own flag, the writer can give day and detail of one thousand men, women, and children who during the last six years were put to death without trial before any tribunal on earth. Humiliating indeed, but altogether unanswerable, was the reply of the French press to our protest: "Stop your lynchings at home before you send your protests abroad."

IDA B. WELLS-BARNETT
Chicago

"THE NEGRO'S CASE
IN EQUITY"

In this article, Wells-Barnett takes issue with an earlier publication by the *Independent* in which the author urged black leaders to tell their people not to take the law into their own hands. Wells-Barnett reminds readers that black Americans had consistently abided by the law yet were often murdered by officers of the law. She argues that self-defense was a proven method of deterring violence against blacks, and cites numerous examples proving her point. She also notes that that if white Americans obeyed the law, black self-defense would not be required.

SOURCE: Ida B. Wells-Barnett, "The Negro's Case in Equity," *Independent*, April 26, 1900, 1010–11.

THE NEGRO'S CASE IN EQUITY

[Mrs. Barnett was driven out of Tennessee at the time of the destruction by a mob of the colored paper of which she was an editor. She has since carried on a campaign in England and America against lynching, and is chairman of the Anti-lynching Bureau of the Afro-American Council.—Editors.]

The INDEPENDENT publishes an earnest appeal to negro editors, preachers and teachers "to tell their people to defend the laws and their own rights even to blood, but never, never to take guilty participation in lynching white man or black." This advice is given by way of comment on the double lynching in Virginia the other day. Theoretically the advice is all right, but viewed in the light of circumstances and conditions it seems like giving a stone when we ask for bread.

For twenty years past the negro has done nothing else but defend the law and appeal to public sentiment for defense *by* the law. He has seen hundreds of men of his race murdered in cold blood by connivance of officers of the law, from the governors of the States down to the sheriffs of counties, as in this Virginia case, and that upon the unsupported word of some white man or woman. He has seen his women and children stripped and strung up to trees or riddled with bullets for the gratification of spite as in the case of Postmaster Baker's family two years ago, and in that in Alabama a few weeks ago, when an entire family was wiped out of existence because a white man had been murdered.

The negro has seen scores of his race, absolutely innocent of any charge whatever, used as scapegoats for some white man's crime, as in the case of C. J. Miller, lynched in Bardwell, Ky., in 1893, and John Peterson, of Denmark, S. C., the same year. Miller was stripped, hung with a log chain to a telegraph pole, riddled with bullets, then burned, since which proceeding he was found to have suffered for a crime committed by a white man. Peterson had sought protection from Governor (now Senator) Tillman[8] but was given over to the mob, and altho the girl in the case said he was not the man, yet the lynchers, led by a State Senator, said a crime had been committed and somebody had to hang for it; so Peterson was swung up and five hundred bullets fired into his body. Such also was the case of a negro woman in Jackson, Tenn., who was stripped and hung in the court house yard by a mob led by the woman's employer. Her mistress had died suddenly of arsenical poisoning and the negro cook was accused because a box of rat poison was found in her room. The husband of the woman who was poisoned, and who led the mob, has since been confined in the insane asylum, and his ravings prove him to have been the poisoner of his wife.

All this and more the negro has seen and suffered without taking the law into his hands for, lo, these many years. There have been no Nat Turner[9] insurrections and San Domingan horrors[10] in retaliation for all the wrongs he has suffered. When the negro has appealed to the Christian and moral forces of the country—

asking them to create a sentiment against this lawlessness and unspeakable barbarism; demanding justice and protection of the law for every human being regardless of color—that demand has been met with general indifference or entirely ignored. Where this is not true he has been told that these same forces upon which he confidently depends refuse to make the demand for justice, because they believe the story of the mob that negroes are lynched because they commit unspeakable crimes against white women. For this reason the Christian and moral forces are silent in the presence of the horrible barbarities alleged to be done in the name of woman.

When the negro, confident in the justice of his cause and the sincerity of the aforesaid Christian and moral forces, seeks the opportunity to disprove this slander, he is refused, except in very rare instances. The columns of the powerful dailies, religious periodicals and thoughtful magazines have printed these charges wholesale until the civilized world has accepted them, but few wish to consider the refutation of them or give space for the possible other side. The leading pulpits of the country are open to stories of the negro's degradation and ignorance, but not to his defense from slander.

Again and again, during the present session of Congress, in both the House and Senate, the negro has been attacked and this foul slander against his good name made in several speeches and sent broadcast. Except a brief rejoinder by Congressman George White,[11] there was no attempt at refutation or rebuke in Congress or out by any of the champions of truth and justice.

Notwithstanding all this is true and has been true for twenty years past, while ten thousand men, women and children have been done to death in the same manner as in the late Virginia case; in spite of the fact that the governors of States, commanders of militia, sheriffs and police have taken part in these disgraceful exhibitions; and with absolute proof that the public sentiment of the country was with the mob—who, if not the negro preachers, editors and teachers, are to be credited with the fact that there are few, if any, instances of negroes who have had "guilty participation in lynching white men or black?"

And if all the negro preachers, editors and teachers should charge themselves with the responsibility of this one lapse after years of the greatest human provocation, should not all the white preachers, editors and teachers charge themselves with the thousands of lynchings by white men? Ought not they to tell their people over and over again that ten human beings have been burned alive in this country during the past seven years—three of them during the year 1899? For the seven years the negro has been agitating against lynching he has made this appeal to the leaders of thought and action among the white race. If they will do their duty in this respect the negroes will soon have no bad examples of the lynching kind set, which in their desperation they may be tempted to follow.

As matters now stand, the negroes down in Virginia the other day would have fared badly had they attempted to defend the law in either case. A band of negroes prevented a lynching in Jacksonville, Fla., in the summer of 1892 by guarding the jail, tho not a shot was fired. The man who led the band has been an exile from his home ever since. He was indicted for "conspiracy" and about to be sent to the penitentiary for preventing white men from lynching a negro, when he forfeited his bond by leaving home and sacrificing his property. Only last summer the same thing happened in Darien, Ga. A white woman gave birth to a negro child, and the mob prepared to lynch the father for the "usual crime." The negroes got wind of it, guarded the jail and prevented the lynching. They were all indicted for that "conspiracy" and lodged in jail. John Delegal, who helped guard his father when the mob was after him, lived in the country. The posse went after him as a "conspirator," broke open his house and entered firing. He returned the fire, killing the leader instantly. Those negroes have all been tried since by a jury of the kind of men who tried to lynch Delegal's father, found guilty of "conspiracy," and are now doing time in the penitentiary. John was sent up for life. In the present apathetic condition of public sentiment, North and South, this is what the negro gets who attempts to "defend the law and his rights." Not until the white editors, preachers and teachers of the country join with him in his fight for justice and protection by law can there be any hope of success.

CHICAGO, ILL.

"LYNCHING AND THE EXCUSE FOR IT"

Here, Wells-Barnett writes in direct response to an article by well-known Chicago reformer Jane Addams entitled "Respect for Law." In particular, she takes issue with Addams's assumption that only lower-class or poor blacks were lynched and that lynchings were often retaliations for rape, a falsehood that Wells-Barnett had spent more than a decade trying to put to rest. As she had many times before, she laid out the lynching statistics and made a note to include the five women who had also been lynched in the previous five years.

SOURCE: Ida B. Wells-Barnett, "Lynching and the Excuse for It," *Independent*, May 16, 1901, 1133–36.

LYNCHING AND THE EXCUSE FOR IT

It was eminently befitting that THE INDEPENDENT's first number in the new century should contain a strong protest against lynching. The deepest dyed infamy of the nineteenth century was that which, in its supreme contempt for law, defied all constitutional guarantees of citizenship, and during the last fifteen years of the century put to death two thousand men, women, and children, by shooting, hanging and burning alive. Well would it have been if every preacher in every pulpit in the land had made so earnest a plea as that which came from Miss Addams's[12] forceful pen.

Appreciating the helpful influences of such a dispassionate and logical argument as that made by the writer referred to, I earnestly desire to say nothing to lessen the force of the appeal. At the same time, an unfortunate presumption used as a basis for her argument works so serious, tho doubtless unintentional, an injury to the memory of thousands of victims of mob law that it is only fair to call attention to this phase of the writer's plea. It is unspeakably infamous to put thousands of people to death without a trial by jury; it adds to that infamy to charge that these victims were moral monsters, when, in fact, four-fifths of them were not so accused even by the fiends who murdered them.

Almost at the beginning of her discussion, the distinguished writer says:

"Let us assume that the Southern citizens who take part in and abet the lynching of Negroes honestly believe that that is the only successful method of dealing with a certain class of crimes."

It is this assumption, this absolutely unwarrantable assumption that vitiates every suggestion which it inspires Miss Addams to make. It is the same baseless assumption which influences ninety-nine out of every one hundred persons who discuss this question. Among many thousand editorial clippings I have received in the past five years, ninety-nine percent discuss the question upon the presumption that lynchings are the desperate effort of the Southern people to protect their women from black monsters, and, while the large majority condemn lynching, the condemnation is tempered with a plea for the lyncher—that human nature gives way under such awful provocation and that the mob, insane for the moment, must be pitied as well as condemned. It is strange that an intelligent, law-abiding, and fair minded people should so persistently shut their eyes to the facts in the discussion of what the civilized world now concedes to be America's national crime.

This almost universal tendency to accept as true the slander which the lynchers offer to civilization as an excuse for their crime might be explained if the true facts were difficult to obtain;

but not the slightest difficulty intervenes. The Associated Press dispatches, the press clipping bureau, frequent book publications, and the annual summary of a number of influential journals give the lynching record every year. This record, easily within the reach of everyone who wants it, makes inexcusable the statement and cruelly unwarranted the assumption that Negroes are lynched only because of their assaults upon womanhood.

For an example in point: For fifteen years past, on the first day of each year, the Chicago *Tribune* has given to the public a carefully compiled record of all the lynchings of the previous year. Space will not permit a *résumé* of these fifteen years, but as fairly representing the entire time, I desire to briefly tabulate here the record of the five years last past. The statistics of the ten years preceding do not vary; they simply emphasize the record here presented.

The record gives the name and nationality of the man or woman lynched, the alleged crime, the time and place of the lynching. With this is given a *résumé* of the offenses charged, with the number of persons lynched for the offenses named. That enables the reader to see at a glance the causes assigned for the lynchings, and leaves nothing to be assumed. The lynchers, at the time and place of the lynching, are the best authority for the causes which actuate them. Every presumption is in favor of this record, especially as it remains absolutely unimpeached. This record gives the following statement of the colored persons lynched and the causes of the lynchings for the years named:

1896.

Murder	24	Arson	2
Attempted murder	4	Assault	3
Rape	31	Unknown cause	1
Incendiarism	2	Slapping a child	1
No cause	2	Shooting at officer	1
Alleged rape	2	Alleged murder	2
Cattle stealing	1	Threats	1
Miscegenation	2	Passing counterfeit money	1
Attempted rape	4	Theft	1
Murderous assault	1		

1897.

Murder	55	Writing insulting letter	1
Attempted rape	8	Cattle Thief	1
Mistaken identity	1	Felony	1
Arson	3	Train wrecking	1
Murderous assault	2	Rape	22
Running quarantine	1	Race prejudice	1
Burglary	1	Alleged arson	1
Bad reputation	1	Robbery	5
Unknown offense	3	Assault	2
Killing white cap	1	Disobeying Fed. regulations	1
Insulting white woman	1	Theft	2
Suspected arson	1	Elopement	1
Giving evidence	2	Concealing murderer	1
Refusing to give evidence	1		

1898.

Murder	42	Theft	5
Rape	14	Miscegenation	1
Attempted rape	7	Unknown offense	2
Complicity in rape	1	Violation of contract	1
Highway robbery	1	Insults	2
Burglary	1	Race prejudice	3
Mistaken identity	1	Resisting arrest	1
Arson	1	Suspected murder	18
Murderous assault	1	Assaults upon whites	4

1899.

Murder	28	Arson	5
Robbery	6	Unknown offense	4
Inflammatory language	1	Resisting arrest	1
Desperado	1	Mistaken identity	3
Complicity in murder	3	Aiding escape of murderer	3
Rape	11	Attempted rape	8

1900.

Murder	30	No offense	1
Rape	16	Arson	2
Attempted assault	12	Suspicion of arson	1
Race prejudice	9	Aiding escape of murderer	1

Plot to kill whites	2	Unpopularity	1
Suspected robbery	1	Making threats	1
Giving testimony	1	Informer	1
Attacking white men	3	Robbery	2
Attempted murder	4	Burglary	4
Threats to kill	1	Assault	2
Suspected murder	2	Unknown offense	2

With this record in view there should be no difficulty in ascertaining the alleged offenses given as justification for lynchings during the last five years. If the Southern citizens lynch Negroes because "that is the only successful method of dealing with a certain class of crimes," then that class of crimes should be shown unmistakably by this record. Now consider the record.

It would be supposed that the record would show that all, or nearly all, lynchings were caused by outrageous assaults upon women; certainly that this particular offense would outnumber all other causes for putting human beings to death without a trial by jury and the other safeguards of our Constitution and laws.

But the record makes no such disclosure. Instead, it shows that five women have been lynched, put to death with unspeakable savagery, during the past five years. They certainly were not under the ban of the outlawing crime. It shows that men, not a few, but hundreds, have been lynched for misdemeanors, while others have suffered death for no offense known to the law, the causes assigned being "mistaken identity," "insult," "bad reputation," "unpopularity," "violating contract," "running quarantine," "giving evidence," "frightening child by shooting at rabbits," etc. Then, strangest of all, the record shows that the sum total of lynchings for these offenses—not crimes—and for the alleged offenses which are only misdemeanors greatly exceeds the lynchings for the very crime universally declared to be the cause of lynching.

A careful classification of the offenses which have caused lynchings during the past five years shows that contempt for law and race prejudice constitute the real cause of all lynching. During the past five years 147 white persons were lynched. It may be argued that fear of the "law's delays" was the cause of their being lynched. But this is not true. Not a single white victim of the mob was wealthy or had friends or influence to cause a miscarriage of justice. There was no such possibility—it was contempt for law which incited the mob to put so many white men to death without a complaint under oath, much less a trial.

In the case of the Negroes lynched the mobs' incentive was race prejudice. Few white men were lynched for any such trivial offenses as are detailed in the causes for lynching colored men. Negroes are lynched for "violating contracts," "unpopularity," "testifying in court," and "shooting at rabbits." As only Negroes are lynched for "no offense," "unknown offenses," offenses not criminal, misdemeanors, and crimes not capital, it must be admitted that the real cause of lynching in all such cases is race prejudice, and should be so classified. Grouping these lynchings under that classification and excluding rape, which in some states is made a capital offense, the record for the five years, so far as the Negro is concerned, reads as follows:

Year.	Race prejudice.	Murder.	Rape.	Total Lynchings.
1896	31	24	31	86
1897	46	55	22	123
1898	39	47	16	102
1899	56	28	11	90
1900	57	30	16	103
Total	229	179	96	504

This table tells its own story, and shows how false is the excuse which lynchers offer to justify their fiendishness. Instead of being the sole cause of lynching, the crime upon which lynchers build their defense furnishes the least victims for the mob. In 1896 less than thirty-nine per cent of the Negroes lynched were charged with this crime; in 1897, less than eighteen per cent; in 1898, less than sixteen per cent; in 1899, less than fourteen per cent; and in 1900, less than fifteen per cent were so charged.

No good result can come from any investigation which refuses to consider the facts. A conclusion that is based upon a presumption instead of the best evidence is unworthy of a moment's consideration. The lynching record, as it is compiled from day to day by unbiased, reliable, and responsible public journals, should be the basis of every investigation which seeks to discover the cause and suggest the remedy for lynching. The excuses of lynchers and the specious pleas of their apologists should be considered in the light of the record, which they invariably misrepresent or ignore. The Christian and moral forces of the nation should insist that misrepresentation should have no place in the discussion of this all important question, that the figures of the lynching record should be allowed to plead, trumpet tongued, in defense of the slandered dead, that the silence of concession be broken, and that truth, swift-winged and courageous, summon this nation to do its duty to exalt justice and preserve inviolate the sacredness of human life.

CHICAGO, ILL.

"BOOKER T. WASHINGTON AND HIS CRITICS"

In the spring of 1904, Wells-Barnett joined W. E. B. Du Bois in publicly denouncing Booker T. Washington at a symposium on "The Negro Problem from the Negro Point of View," sponsored by the *World Today*, where Washington was also in attendance. The essay she presented is included here and shows Wells-Barnett joining Du Bois in the critique that Washington's accommodationist leadership was among the main problems facing black Americans. In particular, Wells-Barnett was troubled by Washington's tendency to curry favor among whites as well as the humorous disdain with which he often spoke of rural black Southerners, the very people he claimed to represent. She also critiqued Washington for favoring industrial education for blacks rather than a liberal arts training when he, himself, was a product of the liberal arts tradition.

SOURCE: Ida B. Wells-Barnett, "Booker T. Washington and His Critics," *World Today*, April 1904, 518–21.

BOOKER T. WASHINGTON AND HIS CRITICS

Industrial education[13] for the Negro is Booker T. Washington's hobby. He believes that for the masses of the Negro race an elementary education of the brain and a continuation of the education of the hand is not only the best kind, but he knows it is the most popular with the white South. He knows also that the Negro is the butt of ridicule with the average white American, and that the aforesaid American enjoys nothing so much as a joke which portrays the Negro as illiterate and improvident; a petty thief or a happy-go-lucky inferior.

The average funny paragrapher knows no other class. Ignatius Donnelly,[14] with all his good intentions in writing "Dr. Huguet," could make no other disposition of his hero than to have him change places with a Negro chicken thief. The obvious moral was to portray a cultured white man's mental torture over the metamorphosis; and not, as the author intended, to show the mental, moral and physical anguish of the educated, Christian Negro gentleman, over the intolerable caste conditions which confront him at every step. There is no such type of Negro gentleman in Anglo-Saxon literature or art, and therefore the reader accepts, as a matter of course, the coarse swaggering Sam Johnsing of evil instinct, who is masquerading under the white skin of Dr. Huguet. That for white America is the typical Negro.

What Dr. Huguet did unintentionally Booker T. Washington has done deliberately. Yet he knows, as do all students of sociology, that the representatives which stand as the type for any race, are chosen not from the worst but from the best specimens of that race: the achievements of the few rather than the poverty, vice and ignorance of the many, are the standards of any given race's ability. There is a negro faculty at Tuskegee,[15] some of whom came from the masses, yet have crossed lances with the best intellect of the dominant race at their best colleges. Mr. Washington knows intimately the ablest members of the race in all sections of the country and could bear testimony as to what they accomplished before the rage for industrial schools began. The Business League[16] of which he is founder and president, is composed of some men who were master tradesmen and business men before Tuskegee was born. He therefore knows better than any man before the public to-day that the prevailing idea of the typical Negro is false.

But some will say Mr. Washington represents the masses and seeks only to depict the life and needs of the black belt. There is a feeling that he does not do that when he will tell a cultured body of women like the Chicago Woman's Club the following story:

"Well, John, I am glad to see you are raising your own hogs."

"Yes, Mr. Washington, ebber sence you done tole us bout rai-sin our own hogs, we niggers round here hab resolved to quit stealing hogs and gwinter raise our own." The inference is that the Negroes of the black belt as a rule were hog thieves until the coming of Tuskegee.

There are those who resent this picture as false and misleading in the name of the hundreds of Negros who bought land, raised hogs and accumulated those millions of which they were de-frauded by the Freedmen's Savings Bank,[17] long before Booker Washington was out of school. The men and women of to-day who are what they are by grace of the honest toil on the part of such parents, in the black belt and out, and who are following in their footsteps, resent also the criticism of Mr. Washington on the sort of education they received and on those who gave it.

They cherish most tender memories of the northern teachers who endured ostracism, insult and martyrdom, to bring the spelling-book and Bible to educate those who had been slaves. They know that the leaders of the race, including Mr. Washington himself, are the direct product of schools of the Freedmen's Aid Society,[18] the American Missionary Association[19] and other such agencies which gave the Negro his first and only opportunity to secure any kind of education which his intellect and ambition craved. Without these schools our case would have been more hopeless indeed than it is; with their aid the race has made more remarkable intellectual and material progress in forty years than any other race in history. They have given us thousands of teach-ers for our schools in the South, physicians to heal our ailments, druggists, lawyers and ministers.

They have given us 2,000 college graduates, over half of whom own property worth over $1,000 per capita. The Negro owes a debt of gratitude which he can never repay to the hundreds of self-sacrificing teachers who gave their lives to the work of Negro education, to the end that they brought the light of knowledge, the strength of educated manhood and the example of Christian culture to those who would otherwise have been without.

That one of the most noted of their own race should join with the enemies to their highest progress in condemning the educa-tion that they had received, has been to them a bitter pill. And so for a long while they keenly, though silently, resented the gibes against the college-bred youth which punctuate Mr. Washington's speeches. He proceeds to draw a moral therefrom for his entire race. The result is that the world which listens to him and which largely supports his educational institution, has almost unanimously decided that college education is a mistake for the Negro. They hail with acclaim the man who has made popular the unspoken thought of that part of the North which believes in the inherent inferiority of the Negro, and the always outspoken southern view to the same effect.

This gospel of work is no new one for the Negro. It is the South's old slavery practice in a new dress. It was the only education the South gave the Negro for two and half centuries she had absolute control of his body and soul. The Negro knows that now, as then, the South is strongly opposed to his learning anything else but how to work.

No human agency can tell how many black diamonds lie buried in the black belt of the South, and the opportunities for discovering them become rarer every day as the schools for thorough training become more cramped and no more are being established. The presidents of Atlanta University[20] and other such schools remain in the North the year round, using their personal influence to secure funds to keep those institutions running. Many are like the late Collis P. Huntington[21] who had given large amounts to Livingston College, Salisbury, North Carolina. Several years before his death he told the president of that institution that as he believed Booker Washington was educating Negroes in the only sensible way, henceforth his money for that purpose would go to Tuskegee. All the schools in the South have suffered as a consequence of this general attitude, and many of the oldest and best which have regarded themselves as fixtures now find it a struggle to maintain existence. As another result of this attitude of the philanthropic public, and this general acceptance of special educational standards for the Negro, Tuskegee is the only endowed institution for the Negro in the South.

Admitting for argument's sake that its system is the best, Tuskegee could not accommodate one-hundredth part of the Negro youth who need education. The Board of Education of New Orleans cut the curriculum in the public schools for Negro children down to the fifth grade, giving Mr. Washington's theory as an inspiration for so doing. Mr. Washington denied in a letter that he had ever advocated such a thing, but the main point is that this is the deduction the New Orleans school board made from his frequent statement that previous systems of education were a mistake and that the Negro should be taught to work. Governor Vardaman, of Mississippi, the other day in his inaugural address, after urging the legislature to abolish the Negro public school and substitute manual training therefore, concluded that address by saying that all other education was a curse to the Negro race.

This is the gospel Mr. Washington has preached for the past decade. The results from this teaching then would seem to be, first, a growing prejudice in northern institutions of learning against the admission of Negro students; second, a contracting of the number and influence of the schools of higher learning so judiciously scattered through all the southern states by the missionary associations for the Negro's benefit; third, lack of a corresponding growth of industrial schools to take their places; and fourth, a cutting down of the curriculum for the Negro in the public schools of the large cities of the South, few of which ever have provided high schools for the race.

Mr. Washington's reply to his critics is that he does not oppose the higher education, and offers in proof of this statement his Negro faculty. But the critics observe that nowhere does he speak for it, and they can remember dozens of instances when he has condemned every system of education save that which teaches the Negro how to work. They feel that the educational opportunities of the masses, always limited enough, are being threatened by this retrogression. And it is this feeling which prompts the criticism. They are beginning to feel that if they longer keep silent, Negro educational advantages will be even more restricted in all directions.

Does some one ask a solution of the lynching evil? Mr. Washington says in substance: Give me money to educate the Negro and when he is taught how to work, he will not commit the crime for which lynching is done. Mr. Washington knows when he says this that lynching is not invoked to punish crime but color, and not even industrial education will change that.

Again he sets up the dogma that when the race becomes taxpayers, producers of something the white man wants, land-owners, business, etc., the Anglo-Saxon will forget all about color and respect that race's manhood. One of the leading southern papers said editorially, in discussing the separate street car law which was to go into effect last winter in Memphis, Tennessee, that it was not the servant or working class of Negroes, who know their places, with whom the white people objected to riding, but the educated, property-owning Negro who thought himself the white man's equal.

There are many who can never be made to feel that it was a mistake thirty years ago to give the unfettered freedmen the franchise, their only weapon of defense, any more than it is a mistake to have fire for cooking and heating purposes in the home, because ignorant or careless servants sometimes burn themselves. The thinking Negro knows it is still less a mistake to-day when the race has had thirty years of training for citizenship. It is indeed a bitter pill to feel that much of the unanimity with which the nation to-day agrees to Negro disfranchisement comes from the general acceptance of Mr. Washington's theories.

Does this mean that the Negro objects to industrial education? By no means. It simply means that he knows by sad experience that industrial education will not stand him in place of political, civil and intellectual liberty, and he objects to being deprived of fundamental rights of American citizenship to the end that one school for industrial training shall flourish. To him it seems like selling a race's birthright for a mess of pottage.

They believe it is possible for Mr. Washington to make Tuskegee all it should become without sacrificing or advocating the sacrifice of race manhood to do it. They know he has the ear of the American nation as no other Negro of our day has, and he is therefore molding public sentiment and securing funds for his educational theories as no other can. They know that the white South has labored ever since reconstruction to establish and maintain throughout the country a color line in politics, in civil rights and in education, and they feel that with Mr. Washington's aid the South has largely succeeded in her aim.

The demand from this class of Negroes is growing that if Mr. Washington can not use his great abilities and influence to speak in defense of and demand for the rights withheld when discussing the Negro question, for fear of injury to his school by those who are intolerant of Negro manhood, then he should be just as unwilling to injure his race for the benefit of his school. They demand that he refrain from assuming to solve a problem which is too big to be settled within the narrow confines of a single system of education.

"HOW ENFRANCHISEMENT STOPS LYNCHINGS"

This article originated as a speech that Wells-Barnett delivered to the NAACP and showcases her argument for the importance of enfranchisement to anti-lynching initiatives. She focuses on events in Cairo, Illinois, where, she contends, the fact that blacks had the franchise helped make it possible to depose Cairo's sheriff, Frank Davis, after a lynching took place on his watch. In 1905 black votes had been influential in the passage of Illinois's first anti-lynching law, which held law enforcement officials responsible for the care and safety of prisoners. And when a man named Williams "Frog" James was lynched in Cairo, Wells-Barnett was able to press for the enforcement of that law. On hearing that Cairo's sheriff, Frank Davis, was likely to keep his job despite cooperating with the mob that lynched James, she traveled to Cairo and successfully lobbied for Davis's dismissal under the new law.

SOURCE: Ida B. Wells-Barnett, "How Enfranchisement Stops Lynchings," *Original Rights Magazine*, June 1910, 42–53.

HOW ENFRANCHISEMENT STOPS LYNCHINGS

The Negro question has been present with the American people in one form or another since the landing of the Dutch Slaveship[22] at Jamestown, Virginia, in 1619. For twelve years the founders of the English colony had indifferently succeeded in getting permanently established. The younger sons of the British were miserable failures as pioneers. They would not do the work necessary to wrest a livelihood from the bowels of the earth, and they could not make the Indian do it for them. One such colony perished from the face of the earth and succeeding ones lagged with indifferent success until the coming of those fourteen African slaves, who became the hewers of wood, drawers of water and tillers of the soil. They were submissive, and easily dominated, so they were harnessed to the plow and became the beasts of burden; then the Jamestown Colony began to thrive.

So successful was this first venture into slavery, that the shores of Africa were again invaded. Men, women and children were overpowered, captured, crowded into the holds of the slaveships, brought to this new country and made the slaves of the colonists. For two hundred and fifty years this condition obtained. The original fourteen slaves became four million. Their unrequited toil had made this country blossom as a rose, created vast wealth for the masters and made the United States one of the mighty nations of the earth, ere the American people harkened to the voice which commanded, "Let my people go." When the mighty upheaval came which almost rent the American nation in twain, it struck the shackles from the Negro slave, and did not stop until he was not only a free man, but a citizen.

The flower of the nineteenth century civilization for the American people was the abolition of slavery, and the enfranchisement of all manhood. Here at last was squaring of practice with precept, with true democracy, with the Declaration of Independence and with the Golden Rule. The reproach and disgrace of the twentieth century is that the whole of the American people have permitted a part, to nullify this glorious achievement, and make the fourteenth and fifteenth amendments to the Constitution playthings, a mockery and a byword; an absolute dead letter in the Constitution of the United States. One-third of the states of the union have made and enforced laws which abridge the rights of American citizens. Although the Constitution specially says, no state shall do so, they *do* deprive persons of life, liberty and property without due process of law, and *do* deny equal protection of the laws to persons of Negro descent. The right of citizens to vote is denied and abridged in these states, on account of race, color and previous condition of servitude, and has been so denied ever since the withdrawal of the United States troops from the South. This in spite of the fifteenth amendment, which declares that no state shall do this.

These rights were denied first by violence and bloodshed, by ku-klux klans, who during the first years after the Civil War murdered Negroes by wholesale, for attempting to exercise the rights given by these amendments, and for trusting the government which was powerful enough to give them the ballot, to be strong enough to protect them in its exercise. Senator Tillman told how it was done in a speech on the floor of the United States Senate, when he said, that he and the people of South Carolina shot Negroes to death to keep them from voting. This they did till Congressional investigation of Ku-Klux methods turned the limelight on the unspeakable barbarism of those wholesale murders.

The South changed its tactics after the investigation, but never once let up on its aim to nullify and finally abrogate these amendments, and rob the Negro of the only protection to his citizenship—his ballot. Again we have the testimony of this United States Senator, on the floor of the Senate, as to how this was further done, when Senator Tillman defiantly told how he and his compatriots stuffed ballot boxes and threw out those of that remnant of the black South, which still tried to register its gratitude at the polls.

When this bewildered race turned in dazed appeal to the Government which gave it freedom and the ballot, awaiting explanation and beseeching protection, it was told that the Government had made a mistake in enfranchising them; that it had offended the South by so doing, and was now busy repealing the civil rights bill, affirming Jim Crow legislation, upholding disfranchising state constitution, and removing in every way possible the constitutional guarantees to life, liberty and the pursuit of happiness, removing everything, in fact, which was offensive to those who had fired on the flag and tried to break up the union, and the Negro must now look out for himself.

This he has done for the past thirty years as best he could. He was advised that if he gave up trying to vote, minded his own business, acquired property and educated his children, he could get along in the South without molestation. But the more lands and houses he acquired, the more rapidly discriminating laws have been passed against him by those who control the ballot, and less protection is given by the law makers for his life, liberty and property. The Negro has been given separate and inferior schools, because he has no ballot. He therefore cannot protest against such legislation by choosing other law makers, or retiring to private life those who legislate against his interests. The more he sends his children to school the more restrictions are placed on Negro education, and he has absolutely no voice in the disposition of the school funds his taxes help to supply. His only weapon of defense has been taken from him by legal enactment in all the old confederacy—and the United States Government, a consenting Saul stands by holding the clothes of those who stone and burn him to death literally and politically.

With no sacredness of the ballot there can be no sacredness of human life itself. For if the strong can take the weak man's ballot, when it suits his purpose to do so, he will take his life also. Having successfully swept aside the constitutional safeguards to the ballot, it is the smallest of small matters for the South to sweep aside its own safeguards to human life. Thus "trial by jury" for the black man in that section has become a mockery, a plaything of the ruling classes and rabble alike. The mob says: "This people has no vote with which to punish us or the consenting officers of the law, therefore we indulge our brutal instincts, give free rein to race prejudice and lynch, hang, burn them when we please." Therefore, the more complete the disfranchisement, the more frequent and horrible have been the hangings, shootings, and burnings.

The records show that beginning with 1882, in which year there were fifty-two persons lynched, there was steady increase until 1892, when two hundred and fifty persons were lynched with the utmost cruelty, publicity and barbarism. Public sentiment condoned and approved this method of disposing of Negroes suspected or accused of misdemeanor or crime against white persons. The custom spread to the North, East and West and lynchings and burnings occurred in any community in which a crime was committed and suspicion put on the Negro. An effort made in 1893 to get these facts before the conscience of the world, proved by statistics based on charges made by the lynchers themselves, that less than one-fourth of the persons hanged, shot and burned by white Christians were even accused of the usual crime—that of assaulting white women.

From the year 1894 lynching decreased year by year for the next decade. The conscience of the nation was again lulled to sleep and the record of the past ten years shows a surprising increase in lynchings and riot even in the North. No Northern state has more frequently offended in this crime than Illinois, the State of Lincoln, Grant and Logan.[23] Since 1893 there have been sixteen lynchings within the State, including the Springfield riot. With each repetition there has been increased violence, rioting and barbarism. The last lynching, which took place November 11th of last year in Cairo, was one of the most inhuman spectacles ever witnessed in this country.

The Negroes of Illinois have taken counsel together for a number of years over Illinois' increased lynching record. They elected one of their number to the State Legislature in 1904, who secured the passage of a bill which provided for the suppression of mob violence, not only by punishment of those who incited lynchings, but provided for damages against the City and County permitting lynchings. The Bill goes further and provides that if any person shall be taken from the custody of the Sheriff or his deputy and lynched, it shall be prima facie evidence of failure on the part of the Sheriff to do his duty. And upon that fact being made to appear to the Governor, he shall publish a proclamation declaring the office of Sheriff vacant, and such Sheriff shall not therefore be eligible to either election or reappointment to the office. Provided, however, that such former Sheriff may within ten days after such lynching occurs file with the Governor his petition for reinstatement, and give ten days' notice of the filing of such petition. If the Governor upon hearing the evidence and argument, shall find that such Sheriff has done all within his power to protect the life of such prisoner then the Governor may reinstate the Sheriff and the decision of the Governor shall be final. This Bill passed both houses, was signed by Governor Deneen and became a law in 1905.

In the Springfield riot[24] and lynching two years later, the only parts of this law that were applicable were those providing punishment for the persons inciting rioting and lynching, and damages for the relatives of the victims of the mob. The men lynched were not prisoners in the custody of the Sheriff, but peaceable, law abiding citizens whom the mob lynched at their homes for the fun of it. Because of the dangerous public sentiment, which says it is all right to kill so long as the victim is a Negro, no jury has been found in Springfield to convict any of those who were tried for that lynching and murder.

On the morning of November 11th last year, a double lynching was reported from Cairo, Ill.—a white man and a Negro. A white girl had been found murdered two days before. The blood-hounds which were brought led to a Negro's house three blocks away. A Negro who had stayed in that house the night before was arrested and sweated for twenty-four hours. Although the only clew found was that the gag in the girl's mouth was of the same kind of cloth as the handkerchief of the prisoner, threats of lynching him became so frequent that the Sheriff took him away from the city, back in the woods twenty-five miles away. When the mob had increased its numbers, they chartered a train, went after the Sheriff, brought him and his prisoner back to Cairo. A rope was thrown over Will James' neck, he was dragged off the train to the main business corner of the town. The rope was thrown over a steel arch, which had a double row of electric lights. The lights were turned on and the body hauled up in view of the as-sembled thousands of men, women and children. The rope broke before James was strangled to death and before hundreds of waiting bullets could be fired into his body. However, as many as could crowd around, emptied their revolvers into the quivering mass of flesh as it lay on the ground. Then seizing the rope the mob dragged the corpse a mile up Washington Street, the princi-ple thoroughfare, to where the girl's body had been found. They were followed by a jeering, hooting, laughing throng of all ages and both sexes of white people. There they built a fire and placed this body on the flames. It was then dragged out of the fire, the head cut off and stuck on a nearby fence post. The trunk was cut open, the heart and other organs were cut out, sliced up and passed around as souvenirs of the ghastly orgy and our American civilization. Having tasted blood, a voice in the crowd said, "Let's get Salzner." Away went the mob to the county jail. Salzner, a white man, had been indicted for wife murder and was in jail awaiting trial. The suggestion is said to have come from the brother of Salzner's murdered wife. The mob demanded that the Sheriff, who had repaired to his office in the jail when Will

James had been taken from him an hour before—get Salzner for them. He begged them to go away, but when they began battering in the doors he telephoned the Governor for troops. The lynchers got Salzner, hanged him in the court yard in front of the jail, emptied their remaining bullets in his body and went away. When troops reached the scene six hours later, they found, as the leading morning paper said next day, that "the fireworks were all over."

In mass meeting assembled the Negro citizens of Chicago called on Governor Deneen to do his duty and suspend the Sheriff. Two days later the Sheriff's office was vacated. Ten days more and Sheriff Davis had filed his petition for reinstatement, and on December 1st, argument was had before Governor Deneen both for and against the Sheriff.

The Sheriff's counsel, an ex-state Senator, and one of the leading lawyers of Southern Illinois, presented the Sheriff's petition for reinstatement, which declared he had done all in his power to protect the prisoners in his charge. He read letters and telegrams from Judges, editors, lawyers, bankers, merchants, clergymen, the Mayor of the City, Captain of Company K, of the State Militia, his political opponents and even the temporary incumbent of the Sheriff's office himself—all wrote to urge Sheriff Davis' reinstatement. The petitions were signed by hundreds of citizens in all walks of life and the Catholic Priest of Sheriff Davis' Parish was present all day and sat at the Sheriff's side.

As representing the people who had sent me to Cairo to get the facts, I told of the lynching, of visiting the scenes thereof, of the three days' interview with the colored people of Cairo, and of reading the files of every newspaper in the city published during the lynching to find some account of the steps that had been taken to protect the prisoner. I told of the mass meeting of the Negroes of Cairo in which resolution was passed declaring that from Tuesday morning when Will James was arrested, until Thursday night when he was lynched—the Sheriff had neither sworn in deputies to aid him in defending the prisoners, nor called on the Governor for troops. We said that a reinstatement of the Sheriff would be an encouragement to mobs to hang, shoot, burn and pillage whenever they felt inclined in the future, as they had done in the past.

Governor Deneen rendered his decision a week later, removing the Sheriff. After reviewing the case he said: "The sole question presented is, does the evidence show that the said Frank E. Davis, as Sheriff of Alexander County, did all in his power to protect the life of the prisoners and perform the duties required of him by existing laws for the protection of prisoners? The measure of the duty of the Sheriff is to be determined from a consideration of his power. He is vested in his County with the whole executive power of the State. He wields within his jurisdiction all the power of the State for the preservation and protection of the public peace. In this capacity it is within his power to call to his aid when necessary any person or the power of the County. The law has made it a criminal offense for any person over the age of eighteen years to neglect or refuse to join the posse comitatus. In case the preservation of the peace and good order of society of any community shall require it, the Sheriff has the power to summon and enroll any number of special deputies. Such deputies when enrolled, have all the powers of deputy sheriffs and are subject absolutely to the orders of the Sheriff. It is made a criminal offense to decline to be enrolled as a special deputy. The Sheriff has the power to arm such force of special deputies to suppress riot. After having commanded the riotous persons to disperse, the Sheriff or his special deputies are justified in taking life should such riotous persons refuse to disperse.

The Sheriff is the keeper of the jail and has custody of all persons confined therein. In case of mob violence, which the Sheriff and his deputies are unable to suppress, the Sheriff may call upon the Governor for troops.

Such being the tremendous power vested in the Sheriff, what are his duties with respect to the protection of a prisoner who has been committed to his keeping?

Upon the question the Legislature has spoken in such terms as not to be misunderstood. It has cast upon the Sheriff the very highest degree of care. The Legislature in the mob violence Act of 1905, has said that in case a prisoner is taken from the Sheriff and lynched, the Sheriff after having been removed from office, must before reinstatement, show that he did all in his power to protect the life of such prisoner. The Legislature has in this Statute specifically defined the duty of the Sheriff. No part of his power can with safety be neglected. The very highest degree of care must be exercised for the protection of the prisoner. The

Sheriff must take every precaution that human foresight can reasonably anticipate. In fact under this Statute, the Sheriff is practically the insurer of the safety of the prisoner.

The law guarantees to the prisoner a fair and impartial trial, not by mob violence, but by the orderly proceedings of duly constituted courts. To this the personal presence of the prisoner is necessary. To await his trial the State has deprived the prisoner of his liberty. By the Statute in question, however, the whole power of the state surrounds the prisoner and guarantees to him the protection of his life.

Measured with these standards it does not appear that Frank E. Davis, as Sheriff of Alexander County, did all in his power for the protection of the prisoners. The crime was of such a nature to excite great public indignation. Ordinary prudence would indicate that at such a time riots, turmoils and breaches of the peace might be expected. No attempt was made then, nor at any time, to summon or enroll special deputies. Not the slightest preparation was made to resist the mob. No showing is made that the jail in Alexander County would not have been safe for the confinement of the prisoner William James. The Sheriff knew some hours before taking William James into custody that mob violence was threatened. Knowing this he neither enrolled special deputies nor communicated with the Governor advising him of the fact and requesting the aid of troops, although two companies of State Militia were stationed in the City of Cairo. In the face of this the Sheriff took his prisoner almost without protection, outside the County. When the Sheriff left the train at Dongola, no attempt was made to communicate either with the Governor or with the Sheriff of Union County. While the Sheriff had the prisoner William James in custody, it does not appear from the evidence in my judgment, that reasonable precaution was taken for his protection.

After the execution of James the mob repaired to the County jail. Although cognizant of the temper of the mob, no effort whatever was made to place additional guards about the jail. Neither the Sheriff nor his deputies made any showing of force. The most that was done was to ask for volunteers. Although it must have taken some time to beat down the cell door, yet the Sheriff is unable to identify a single person composing the mob, or to identify a single person whom he asked to aid him in suppressing the mob. After Salzner was taken from his cell, no effort was made to follow up the mob and rescue Salzner.

In view of these facts, only one conclusion can be reached, and that is that the Sheriff failed to take the necessary precaution for the protection of his prisoners. Mob violence has no place in Illinois. It is denounced in every line of the Constitution and in every Statute. Instead of breeding respect for the law it breeds contempt. For the suppression of mob violence our Legislature has spoken in no uncertain terms. When such mob violence threatens the life of a prisoner in the custody of the Sheriff, the law has charged the Sheriff, at the penalty of forfeiture of his office, to use the utmost human endeavor to protect the life of his prisoner. The law may be severe. Whether severe or not it must be enforced.

Believing as I do that Frank E. Davis, as Sheriff of Alexander County, did not do all within his power to protect the lives of William James and Henry Salzner, I must deny the petition of said Frank E. Davis for reinstatement as Sheriff of Alexander County, and the same is done accordingly."

Alexander County was one of the pivotal Counties, politically speaking, in the last election. Sheriff Davis belonged to the faction of the Republican party in Illinois, which gave Governor Deneen his re-election to the executive chair in 1908, by a smaller majority than four years before. It was believed that because of this the Governor was obligated to heed the wishes of Sheriff Davis' friends. But he had a higher obligation as Governor to protect the fair fame and uphold the Laws of Illinois. He had the highest obligation of protecting his friends from themselves, of enforcing their respect for the majesty of the law, and of aiding them to see beyond their passions and prejudices, "so they might rise on stepping stones of their dead selves to higher things."

It is believed that this decision with its slogan "Mob law can have no place in Illinois" has given lynching its death blow in this State. On three separate occasions since Sheriffs of other Counties in the State have checked the formation of mobs by calling at once on the Governor for troops, and in this way prevented the scheduled lynching.

But the people of Cairo were not convinced, besides they were in an ugly mood because of Sheriff Davis' retirement from office and they determined to try the metal of the new Sheriff, who had sworn to uphold the laws. During the first week in March, two months ago, two Negroes were in jail in Cairo, having been arrested on suspicion of pocket-book snatching. Sheriff Nellis, having heard threats of lynching, immediately swore in special deputies and strengthened his guard at the jail. When the mob appeared at eleven o'clock that night, the Sheriff warned them not to cross the threshold. The warning was unheeded—a volley rang out, and one man—the leader of the mob—lay dead on the steps, and several more were wounded. No lynching took place that night and Sheriff Nellis had done what the Grand Jury of Alexander County, sitting for the whole month of December, had failed to do—found the leaders of a mob. The dead man was John Halliday, the son of a former Mayor of Cairo, and his uncle owns the leading hotel in Cairo the Halliday House, which bears his name. The others who were wounded were men of like station. They have since been indicted by the Grand Jury and it rests with the local public sentiment whether a jury can be found to convict them of attempted murder, and make their punishment so severe that the lesson will not soon be forgotten.

In this work all may aid. Individuals, organizations, press and pulpit should unite in vigorous denunciation of all forms of lawlessness and earnest, constant demand for the rigid enforcement of the law of the land. Nay, more than this, there must spring up in all sections of the country vigilant, aggressive defenders of the Constitution of our beloved land. South Carolina and her section have dominated this country to its hurt and sorrow from the beginning. When Payne[25] wrote the Declaration of Independence, South Carolina refused to come into the Federation Colonies unless they struck out the clause abolishing slavery. She won, and slavery was fastened as an octopus upon the vitals of the land. She was responsible for the cringing, compromising, yielding attitude of Congress on the slavery question for the fifty years preceding the war. She fired on the flag of the United States and for the fifth time attempted to secede from the Union. She plunged the country into the most terrible Civil War the world has ever known. She has led in all the secession movements for the nullification of the constitution and for the abrogation of the 14th and 15th amendments. She has led in all butcheries on the helpless Negro which makes the United States appear a more cruel government than Russia, for her deeds are not done under the guise of democracy and in the name of liberty.

"THE NORTHERN NEGRO WOMAN'S SOCIAL AND MORAL CONDITION"

In this article, Wells-Barnett assesses the status of black women in the North. She emphasizes that both middle- and working-class black women were subject to racial prejudice and often unable to secure decent jobs, housing, or education, and were barred from many cultural and recreational spaces. She also addresses the negative stereotypes of black women and criticizes those who easily generalized all black women based on stereotypes.

SOURCE: Ida B. Wells-Barnett, "The Northern Negro Woman's Social and Moral Condition," *Original Rights Magazine* 1:2, April 1910, 83–87.

THE NORTHERN NEGRO WOMAN'S SOCIAL AND MORAL CONDITION

The social sphere of the Negro woman of the North, while not so restricted as that of her Southern sister, is also affected by caste influences. By law she is not denied the uplifting and refining influence of the theater, concert hall, lecture room, public park and library, woman's clubs, and church, with the peremptory refusal of the spoken word or printed placard of the South—which says, in many instances, "Negroes and dogs are not admitted"—but she is given to understand just as plainly by the frozen stare or chilly word that she is not wanted. The social as well as the industrial edict is: "Only as a menial—and not always that—will you be tolerated." The schoolroom seems to be the only American institution left in which the Negro woman of the North and her children may share equal opportunities; and as she reads the onslaughts being made on the mixed public schools of the North, and observes the growing disposition of public school teachers and their white pupils to make it hard for her boy and girl to remain in school, the deliberate effort made to shut them out of the social enjoyment of school life—she wonders how long before the doors of even the public schools of the North will be closed against them and they are told to flock by themselves. She has seen too many "revolutions go backward" in her case not to have an unsettled feeling about the whole of our vaunted democratic scheme of government.

This policy deters the presence of many Negro women or their families in places of public social gathering. It is the occasional Negro whose thirst for knowledge or culture overbalances her sensitiveness and for the attainment of her object schools herself to be deaf, dumb and blind to gibe, insult or hostility almost invariably displayed when she accepts public invitations. Hence, although Negroes reside by the thousands in all our Northern cities, very few are seen in public parks, colleges, libraries, lecture courses, art galleries, theaters or churches. In their own clubs, churches, literary and debating clubs they satisfy, as best they can, their craving for the larger social and intellectual life.

Within her own race ranks, the Negro woman finds classes, just as among other race varieties. There is a class composed mostly of the "old families," those who have lived in their different cities since before the war or immediately after. There is the professional class, composed mostly of representatives of the pulpit, the press, the lawyer, doctor, business man and woman, officeholder, trained nurse, school teacher, etc. And then there are the sectarian and secret society lines into which the masses group themselves socially in largest numbers. There is no money standard, because there are few who have amassed more than enough upon which to live decently, and no line of demarcation can be drawn, based upon occupation, outside the professions. This is because, as shown in the first article, too many of the best men and women of the race make their living in menial service. The race honors them for so doing, rather than be idlers or crooks. Just as the railroad porter who makes up your berth, shines your shoes, and waits on you in the diner and takes your tips, may be a well-read man of family whose social standing in his race may be second to none, so often the woman who does a day's laundry work for whites is herself the mistress and owner of a well-kept home in a good locality. In this home she presides and entertains her friends with as much grace and dignity as the Fifth or Michigan[26] avenue society leader for whom she has done a day's laundry or catering; whose hair she has dressed, or nails or corns she has manicured.

Like all members of the human family, these women have social instincts, which they gratify in whist, dancing, woman's and social clubs, and once in a great while they attempt what to them are big affairs. Mrs. Potter Palmer, the social queen of Chicago, arrived home from abroad in time to give the big charity ball of the winter at the Auditorium in December. This affair netted $40,000, which was divided among several worthy institutions in the city of Chicago, but none of it went this time to any Negro charity as heretofore. Therefore, Mrs. William Emanuel, sometimes called "the black Mrs. Potter Palmer," gave a charity ball by Negroes for a Negro orphan home, Old Folks' Home and Social Settlement, respectively, on New Year's night. Over two thousand Negroes paid fifty cents apiece admission fee, and the affair was a great financial and social success. The costumes and deportment of that throng compared favorably with that under the leadership of the real Mrs. Potter Palmer.

Mrs. Emanuel's husband and herself have made a small fortune in the business of chiropody,[27] which they started in Chicago a score of years ago in one room. They now have a large establishment, where chiropody, manicuring, shampooing and hairdressing are done. They have a beautiful home, have educated their children and cultivated all the graces and refinements of life while sticking to business. Mrs. Emanuel has a fine home, with every luxury heart could wish—an automobile which she manages herself with skill. She still goes to the office every day and works as hard as any of the dozen employees, attending to customers herself and superintending the force, thus leaving her husband free to give his whole time to the skilled work. This case is exceptional, but typical of the educated Negro woman of the North.

As to moral conditions, to them it seems a strange question to ask if they have the same love for husbands and children, the same ambitions for well-ordered families that white women have. In their study of human nature of all classes and conditions, going into the homes of the white women of this country in the menial capacity already mentioned, they find human nature to be the same under white as under dark skins. To the Negro woman herself this is such an axiomatic proposition, it is the strangest thing in the world that people of other race varieties in this country insist on differentiating her with the hopes and fears and ambitions, from all other classes of women God has made.

The reason is not far to seek. The lion in Aesop's fable, when asked why, if he were king of beasts, he was always worsted in his encounters with man, gave the same answer the red Indian gave when asked the same question about himself and the white man. It was because the white man wrote the stories. In all the literature extant touching Negro life, the stories are written by the white race. In every magazine those who have neither knowledge nor sympathy are attempting to depict Negro life and character and portray the Negro woman's hopes, fears and ideals. As a result, those representations are almost invariably caricatures, the writers forgetting or refusing to believe that "one swallow does not make a summer" with the Negro any more than any other race. Sketches from real life from the pens of Negroes offered to the magazines containing the libel, have invariably been "declined with thanks."

Mrs. Harriet Beecher Stowe[28] drew a character true to life even in slave days, when she endowed Eliza Harris with the passionate mother love that drove her across the Ohio River on the ice, at the peril of life itself, in the effort to be free and rear her child in freedom; that she might enjoy the love of husband and home, or die in the attempt; and Frederick Douglass, in his autobiography, gives pathetic testimony to the mother who toiled all day in the fields as the slave of a white man, and walked twelve miles after nightfall to spend a few stolen moments with her child living on another plantation; then walked the twelve miles back again in order to be in the fields again at sunrise. If slavery could not crush mother-love out of the hearts of Negro women, the race prejudice of the present cannot do it.

There are no statistics available in support of this contention, but in every city of the North, among the masses of the race, it is the toil of the women which keeps the family together after the men have grown discouraged over the odds against them and given up in despair. In the juvenile and county courts of Cook, Illinois, hundreds of such cases are passed upon yearly, with the result given above. The principal of one of the public schools of Chicago, which had a large number of Negro pupils, found that 50 per cent of the number were half orphans whose mothers worked out all day in order to provide food, shelter and clothing, that the children might attend school.

It has been demonstrated time and again that the reason there are so few Negro tramps, in the "bread line" or out, is that Negro women who know little else but hard work, labor with their husbands to keep the wolf from the door, to maintain their homes and keep up appearances. In the panic which followed the World's Fair in Chicago, in the winter of 1893–94,[29] hundreds of men were fed by the city to prevent starvation and freezing. Soup kitchens were established, and these men were permitted to sleep on the bare floors of police stations and in the City Hall. The marvel of that terrible winter was that, with so large a Negro population, so few Negro men presented themselves, begging for food or lodging. The same testimony is given by charity bureaus in all the large cities of the North: that of the many who seek help and sustenance, so few Negro applicants appear. One would expect the reverse of this to be true, when we consider that the grade of labor at which Negro men are employed, is of the most menial and poorly paid character. Again the credit largely belongs to Negro women, who can secure and willingly accept well-paid housework, which is always plentiful.

Only last month there came to the writer a delicate, refined woman, whose husband had always made a comfortable living for herself and four children. He has been ill with an incurable disease, for six months. She had never done other than her own housework, but when the necessity confronted her, she went out to do day's work, leaving a six-months'-old baby in the care of a ten-year-old daughter. She has earned money by washing, ironing and scrubbing this long, cold winter through, with which to pay for shelter, food and clothing for her loved ones.

Such cases are the rule among Negro women, wherever found. Those whose morals are low and lives are unclean, are the exceptions which prove the rule. Yes, like all races, this race has its bad women as well as good. With every other race, it is taken for granted that the vicious and immoral women found in its ranks are the exceptions, *and they are*. No one believes that because Evelyn Thaw made shameless confessions as to her revoltingly immoral life, on the witness stand, that all American white women live such lives. Nor that because Elsie Siegel was represented as consorting immorally with Chinamen that all girls of German descent are such characters. But everyone who comes across an immoral character among Negro women, or reads of one, like the naturalist who, finding a peculiar kind of beetle, knows that all beetles will be just like the specimen he dissects— so all white American readers or observers arrive at the conclusion that, having seen one immoral Negro woman, or a dozen, therefore the entire race of Negro women is immoral. Such logic confounds itself with all fair-minded persons.

"SLAYER, IN GRIP OF LAW, FIGHTS RETURN TO SOUTH"

An account of Wells-Barnett's successful effort to block the extradition of Steve Green, a fugitive from Arkansas, this piece shows her working with other black activists in Chicago to keep Green in Illinois. Aware that Green, who was charged with murdering his employer, was likely to be lynched if he returned to his home state, Wells-Barnett brought his case to black attorneys Edward H. Wright and W. G. Anderson, who were able to secure a writ of habeas corpus for Green just before the southbound train he had been forced to board left Illinois. Green returned to Chicago, where he was hosted by Wells-Barnett's Negro Fellowship League, and managed to avoid further extradition attempts until Arkansas finally abandoned his case.

SOURCE: Ida B. Wells-Barnett, "Slayer, in Grip of Law, Fights Return to South," *Washington Post*, October 21, 1910.

SLAYER, IN GRIP OF LAW, FIGHTS RETURN TO SOUTH

Negro, a Fugitive From Arkansas, Elicits Aid of Race in Chicago. Says He Shot White Man in Self-Defense, But Will Get No Justice at Home

Chicago Correspondence New York Evening Post.

Children of abolitionists of ante-bellum days have heard much of the underground railroad. Many stories have been told of the heroism of the people who hated slavery and were forced by the fugitive slave law to defy the government in an effort to make free those whom the law declared were slaves. It seems strange in this latter day that a condition exists in the South which would seem to make a revival of the underground railroad a necessity. Such, at any rate, is the conclusion of many who have heard the story of Steve Greene.

On August 15 Chicago newspapers announced that a negro by the name of Steve Greene had been arrested at the insistence of one George Chavis. Chavis told the police that a man named Greene was wanted in Arkansas for the murder of a white man whose name he had forgotten. Accordingly, Greene was arrested, locked up in the station, and within the next few days one paper announced that he had confessed to murder, that he had twice attempted suicide, and that he was then strapped to a chair in the station to prevent a third attempt. The same paper reported Greene as declaring he would rather die than be taken back to Arkansas. He said he had taken a life in self-defense, but he knew that fact would not weigh in his favor if once they got him back into Arkansas.

Chicago negroes sent a lawyer to inquire into the facts, and he proceeded to swear out a writ of habeas corpus in Greene's behalf. When an attempt was made to serve the writ it was found that Steve Greene had been taken away by an officer who had come from Arkansas for the purpose. The negroes, through their attorneys, Edward H. Wright and W. G. Anderson, immediately offered $100 to the sheriff of any county in the State of Illinois who would arrest Steve Greene, take him off the Illinois Central train on which he was speeding to the Southland, and bring him back to Chicago.

GREENE BROUGHT BACK

Telegrams and telephone messages were sent to every sheriff along the line, and when Sheriff Nellis, of Cairo, got the telephone message he demanded immediately to know on whose authority this was to be done. He was told by the sheriff of Cook county that the writ of habeas corpus superseded the governor's requisition. Accordingly, 24 hours after he had been spirited away, Greene was back in the city of Chicago. Sheriff Nellis, of Alexander county, who arrested him just as he was about to cross the State line of Illinois, is the sheriff who superseded Sheriff Davis, the man who let a mob take two men away from him and lynch them on the streets of Cairo last December.

After Gov. Deneen refused to reinstate Sheriff Davis, Nellis was appointed in his place. A few months after Nellis had become sheriff of Alexander county a mob tried him out in an effort to get two prisoners under his care, and he fired into the mob, killing one man and wounding many others. This was the man who took Steve Greene from the hands of the sheriff of Crittenden county, Ark., and brought him back to Chicago.

After a delay of some days the case was tried before Judge Tuthill, and the prisoner set free on the ground of a defect in the requisition papers. Greene went to work quietly as a laborer, his heart filled with thanksgiving that intervention had come in the nick of time. He says that while the train was waiting in the station at Cairo the deputy sheriff told the nephew of the planter who was killed, to send a telegram to Crittenden county to let the people know he was coming with his prisoner, and then turned to Greene and said, "Steve, you are the most important negro nigger in the United States today. Five thousand men are waiting in Jericho to burn you as soon as you get there."

A few minutes later Sheriff Nellis stepped up to him on the train and said: "I arrest this prisoner by virtue of authority vested in me as sheriff of Alexander county."

MAY STILL BE EXTRADITED

After Greene had been freed by the order of Judge Tuthill, he hoped that his troubles were over, but a few nights ago the news came from Springfield that the requisition papers had been amended and that the sheriff of Arkansas was again demanding that Gov. Deneen should deliver Steve Greene into his hands.

Greene's attorneys say they do not see how the governor can be prevented from delivering the prisoner up to Arkansas. They have consulted the best authorities and they say the only precedent they have is the case of Gov. Durbin of Indiana refusing the requisition of Gov. Beckham of Kentucky for the body of W. L. Taylor, accused of conspiracy in the murder of Gov. Goebel. Whether Gov. Deneen will do that in the case of Steve Greene remains to be seen.

The theory is that he will not wish to establish a precedent which will make Arkansas a refuge for criminals from Illinois or vice versa. In the event of an adverse decision, the Chicago negroes are asking themselves, will it be necessary to reestablish the underground railroad of antebellum days, for the protection of men who cannot get justice in the South? Steve Greene's story of the occurrence is as follows:

"I was born in Jackson, Tenn., during the war. My mother died shortly after and my father gave me to a white woman whose husband was a policeman, as well as a grocery store keeper. I nursed their children for six years, and got my board and clothes as wages, and then they took me to work in the store as porter. Although they promised me $3 a week, I got it very seldom. I was not permitted to go to school, so when I was 17 years of age, I ran away and came to Cairo and worked on the road at a dollar and a half a day for two years, then quit working on the railroad and worked for nine years at a boarding house there; then I went with a lumber company working in Arkansas, and married in Putnam county.

RENTED A FARM

"I rented a farm and worked on this farm six years and had no trouble. I was able to pay my rent and have something over for my wife and two children. The schools were so poor there that we moved to Crittenden county, where they could go to the schools in Jericho. At this place we signed with a farmer named Will Saddler, at $5 an acre for 25 acres of land. At the beginning of this year, 1910, I gave the place up, because Mr. Saddler wanted $9 instead of $5 an acre. He had four tenants beside myself, and they had all gathered their crops and moved before I did. We notified Mr. Saddler that we would not stay, and he sent for me to come over to his house during the Christmas week. He told me if I did not keep the place for this year that there would not be room in Crittenden county for him and me; but I told him that I would not do so. He went over into Tennessee for three weeks, and while he was gone I finished gathering my crop and had moved off before he got back.

SHOT BY OLD LANDLORD

"My mother-in-law had died before I moved, and my wife had been with her up to her death. Two days after I had moved away from Mr. Saddler's farm, my wife dropped dead of heart disease. I then went to work for J. H. Usher by the day. On the 17th day of February, three days after burying my wife, I was grinding an ax, getting ready to go down in the field, when Mr. Saddler rode up and called me; I went on down in the field, talking, my hand on his horse's neck. When we got down there, away from every-body, he stopped his horse and said: "Green, didn't I tell you if you didn't work my farm this year there would not be room enough in Crittenden county for you and me to live?"

"I said, 'Yes, sir, you told me so, but you would not try to hurt an old man like me because of that, would you?' He answered, 'I meant just what I said,' and drew his revolver. I broke and ran, but he shot me through the neck, in the fleshy part of my left arm, and in the calf of my right leg. No bones were broken, and I ran, keeping ahead of him on the horse. His nephew and a col-ored man, both of whom were armed, had joined him by this time, but I beat them to the house, ran in, and got my Winchester and ran out the back door. As I got out the door all three came running around the house on foot, but the nephew was the only one whose gun was loaded. He fired at me and the bullet plowed through my shoulder, again without breaking a bone.

"Although my arm was numb, I raised my Winchester and fired one shot into the group, then jumped into the lake, which was just behind the house. They say that shot killed Mr. Saddler, but I do not know, for I did not stop to see. This was 4 o'clock in the afternoon, and, although there was snow on the ground, it was not cold enough to freeze the lake, and I got across by wading and swimming, and climbed into a tree on the other side and stayed in that tree until 12 o'clock that night.

ON SANDBAR THREE WEEKS

"The doctor afterward told me that jumping into the lake was what saved my life, as the cold water stopped the flow of blood. I managed to get some cartridges, and by degrees got to the river some 30 miles away. I went across the river in a skiff to one of the many sandbar islands in the middle of the river, and stayed there three weeks, until I recovered from the effects of my wounds. High water was all through Arkansas at this time, and for fear of bloodhounds I waded and swam and traveled on logs for three weeks until I got to a town in Missouri, from there I took a boat to Cairo.

"I had not been in Cairo very long before I recognized some colored friends who knew me, and some Judas there wrote to Jericho to inquire about the reward offered for me. When I heard about that I left Cairo in June and worked my way by slow stages out of different towns until I landed in Chicago. I got here on Saturday night, August 13, and on Sunday morning, the 14th I was arrested. When the policeman took me to the Harrison street station and locked me up, and after a while took me upstairs and questioned me about Arkansas, I denied all knowledge of the place.

"Three times afterward they put me in a sweat box for a day and a night, and gave me neither food nor drink for four days. One policeman said while they were questioning me that he had a great mind to take a shot at me, but getting nothing out of me, they at last put me in a cell where I could see, then I took sick, and they put me in a hospital. After the doctor told them what was the matter with me they gave me something to eat; in the meantime they had sent down to Arkansas, and on the 25th Claude came.

Claude was the nephew of Mr. Saddler, whom they said I killed, and he is the one who fired the last shot into me. They took me back upstairs when he came, and had him identify me.

IDENTIFIED BY NEPHEW

"He said, 'Hello, Steve! If you deny me I will shoot you; you know who I am.' But still I declared that I knew nothing about the case. When they took me back downstairs, Inspector Wheeler told me if I would own up he would help me, but as I could not see my way out, I still stuck out that I knew nothing about the matter. At last they brought my photo, which they had got down there, and then I had to own up.

"When I got to thinking about what they had done to other colored men who had tried to defend themselves, and what I knew they would do to me, it seemed to me I would rather kill myself then wait to be burned, hanged, and shot by them. No matter what a white man does to a colored man down there he daren't resent it. On the other hand, white men kill negroes every day of the least little thing, and nobody does anything to them for it.

"I did not know what else to do, and I tried to kill myself by eating the heads off the matches. It did not kill me; it only made me sick. Then the police strapped me to a chair, and put a man as guard over me. It was two days after that, though, before any colored person came to see me. Both Mr. Anderson and the Rev. Mr. Carey said they were going to see what they could do to get me out, but on Sunday night Deputy Sheriff Monroe came from Arkansas, and on Monday morning we left.

"When the train stopped at Cairo to get water, Sheriff Monroe told Claude to go out and send a telegram to Jericho letting them know that we were coming. He then said to me: 'Steve, you are the most important nigger in the United States today: there will be a thousand men at the station when we get there, and they will have the rope and coal oil all ready to burn you alive.' Not until them did I give up hope, and I told the Lord that I would never again believe that there is any God if He did not help me. When Sheriff Nellis stepped up and arrested me it seemed to me that there was a direct answer to my prayers."

I.W.B.

"MRS. IDA WELLS BARNETT ON WHY MRS. JACK JOHNSON SUICIDED"

In this brief article, Wells-Barnett discusses the legal persecution of Jack Johnson, the first black boxer to hold the World Heavyweight Championship title. Johnson was also notorious for his high-profile relationships with white women, and in the fall of 1912, he became the first person to be charged with violating the Mann Act—a 1910 federal law prohibiting the interstate transport of females for "immoral purposes." A Chicago resident, Johnson was charged with violating the Mann Act on October 12, 1912, for having an interracial affair with Lucille Cameron, a white prostitute from Milwaukee whom he later married. The case fell apart after Cameron refused to testify against him, although Johnson was successfully prosecuted less than a month later for an earlier relationship with another white prostitute. His wife who "suicided" was not Cameron, but rather Brooklyn socialite Etta Duryea Johnson, a white woman he married in 1911, whose self-inflicted death preceded Johnson's legal troubles. But her suicide might have been inspired by an unhappiness brought on, at least in part, by Johnson's many infidelities. In this article, Wells-Barnett contends that Johnson's interracial relationships should not subject him to legal prosecution, while also sympathizing with the late Etta Johnson.

SOURCE: Ida B. Wells-Barnett, "Mrs. Ida Wells Barnett on Why Mrs. Jack Johnson Suicided," *Chicago Defender*, November 20, 1912.

MRS. IDA WELLS BARNETT ON WHY MRS. JACK JOHNSON SUICIDED

—Lucile Cameron Out on Bail—Jack Persecuted— Sane Resolutions.

CHICAGO, ILL., —Lucile Cameron, (white), whose association with Jack Johnson led to his original arrest for alleged violation of the Mann white slave act, was released from custody Nov. 25, in bonds of $1,000. The young woman has been held as a witness in the Johnson case for several weeks, most of the time in the Winnebago county jail in Rockford, Ill., where her mother was allowed to be with her. Recently, she has again refused to appear against Jack.

Gilchrist Stewart who came here recently from New York city to investigate the Johnson cases for the Constitution League, wrote it recently as follows: "I have found that there is not a scintilla of evidence upon which to base the prosecution much less the persecution of "Jack" Johnson, except that he has committed certain offenses against the established codes of morality—for which half of the men in New York or Chicago or elsewhere could just as well be indicted and railroaded to the penitentiary."

Representatives from nearly all of our organizations in Chicago have adopted the following resolutions:

"Whereas, Through the exploitation of the charges against Jack Johnson great injury has been done to the civic, industrial and business relations between Colored and white citizens of the entire country, leaving no means of defense for innocent victims of the intensified race hatred save an appeal to the public:

"Resolved, That we appeal to the public for the presumption of innocence which is every man's due, to the press for respite from this most harmful sensationalism, and to the government officials to subordinate prejudice to principle and to try their indictments in the courts."

Johnson's "cafe" has been an attraction and menace to the ignorant and unwary of both races and sexes who were looking for a "good time," ever since its opening, and the police knew it. One officer is quoted as saying that he knew that the place was open many times after closing hours. Had the law been enforced there would be no need now to suggest lynching or driving Jack Johnson away. Some of the things which are reported to have taken place in that saloon would have been prevented and perhaps Mrs. Jack Johnson would not have found life so intolerable as to be driven to suicide!

IDA B. WELLS-BARNETT

"OUR COUNTRY'S LYNCHING RECORD"

This article was published in the *Survey*, a national organ of professional social work, and discussed the steep drop in the number of lynchings after 1892. Whereas 1892 saw 241 lynchings, 1912 witnessed only 65. Wells-Barnett might have chosen to regard these numbers with some sense of satisfaction and accomplishment, but instead she was concerned that white authorities still defended lynching as a crime necessitated by rape. Despite the fact that there were now thirty years of data to show "no more than one-fourth of the persons hung, shot and burned to death [had] ever been charged with the crime" of rape, the rape myth was alive and well, and was mobilized by whites in both the North and the South.

SOURCE: Ida B. Wells-Barnett, "Our Country's Lynching Record," *Survey*, February 1, 1913, 573–74.

OUR COUNTRY'S LYNCHING RECORD

The closing month of the year 1912 witnessed an incident which probably could not happen in any other civilized country. The governor of one of the oldest states of the Union in an address before the Conference of Governors defended the practice of lynching, and declared that he would willingly lead a mob to lynch a Negro who had assaulted a white woman. Twenty years ago, another governor of the same state not only made a similar statement, but while he was in office actually delivered to a mob a Negro who had merely been charged with this offense—it was unproven—and who had taken refuge with the governor for protection.

It is gratifying to know that the governors' meeting formally condemned these expressions, and that a leading Georgia citizen has undertaken to refute the sentiment expressed by Governor Blease. However, while no other official has thus officially encouraged this form of lawlessness, yet, because of the widespread acquiescence in the practice, many governors have refused to deal sternly with the leaders of mobs or to enforce the law against lynchers.

To the civilized world, which has demanded an explanation as to why human beings have been put to death in this lawless fashion, the excuse given has been the same as that voiced by Governor Blease a short month ago. Yet statistics show that in none of the thirty years of lynching has more than one-fourth of the persons hung, shot and burned to death, been even charged with this crime. During 1912, sixty-five persons were lynched.

Up to November 15 the distribution among the states was as follows:

Alabama	5	Oregon	1
Arkansas	3	Oklahoma	1
Florida	3	South Carolina	5
Georgia	11	Tennessee	5
Louisiana	4	Texas	3
Mississippi	5	Virginia	1
Montana	1	West Virginia	1
North Carolina	1	Wyoming	1
North Dakota	1		

Fifty of these were Negroes; three were Negro women. They were charged with these offenses:

Murder	26	Insults to white women	3
Rape	10	Attempted rape	2
Murderous assault	2	Assault and robbery	1
Complicity in murder	3	Race prejudice	1
Arson	8	No cause assigned	1

Because the Negro has so little chance to be heard in his own defense and because those who have participated in the lynching have written most of the stories about them, the civilized world has accepted almost without question the excuse offered.

From this table it appears that less than a sixth of these persons were lynched because the mob believed them to be guilty of assaulting white women. In some cases the causes have been trivial. And it appears that the northern states have permitted this lawless practice to develop and the lives of hapless victims to be taken with as much brutality, if not as frequently, as those of the South—witness, Springfield, Ill., a few years ago, and Coatesville, Pa., only last year.

The lynching mania, so far as it affects Negroes, began in the South immediately after the Emancipation Proclamation fifty years ago. It manifested itself through what was known as the Klu Klux Klan, armed bodies of masked men, who during the period between 1865 and 1875, killed Negroes who tried to exercise the political rights conferred on them by the United States until by such terrorism the South regained political control. The aftermath of such practices is displayed in the following table giving the number of Negroes lynched in each year since 1885:

1885	184	1899	107
1886	138	1900	115
1887	122	1901	135
1888	142	1902	96
1889	176	1903	104
1890	127	1904	87
1891	192	1905	66
1892	235	1906	60
1893	200	1907	63
1894	190	1908	100
1895	171	1909	87
1896	131	1910	74
1897	106	1911	71
1898	127	1912	64

With the South in control of its political machinery, the new excuse was made that lynchings were necessary to protect the honor of white womanhood. Although black men had taken such good care of the white women of the South during the four years their masters were fighting to keep them in slavery, this calumny was published broadcast. The world believed it was necessary for white men in hundreds to lynch one defenseless Negro who had been accused of assaulting a white woman. In the thirty years in which lynching has been going on in the South, this falsehood has been universally accepted in all sections of our country, and has been offered by thousands as a reason why they do not speak out against these terrible outrages.

It is charged that a ceaseless propaganda has been going on in every northern state for years, with the result that not only is there no systematic denunciation of these horrible barbarisms, but northern cities and states have been known to follow the fashion of burning human beings alive. In no one thing is there more striking illustration of the North's surrender of its position on great moral ideas than in its lethargic attitude toward the lynching evil.

The belief is often expressed that if the North would stand as firmly for principle as the South does for prejudice, lynching and many other evils would be checked. It seems invariably true, however, that when principle and prejudice come into collision, principle retires and leaves prejudice the victor.

In the celebration of the fiftieth year of the Negro's freedom, does it seem too much to ask white civilization, Christianity and Democracy to be true to themselves on this as all other questions? They can not then be false to any man or race of men. Our democracy asserts that the people are fighting for the time when all men shall be brothers and the liberty of each shall be the concern of all. If this is true, the struggle is bound to take in the Negro. We cannot remain silent when the lives of men and women who are black are lawlessly taken, without imperiling the foundations of our government.

Civilization cannot burn human beings alive or justify others who do so; neither can it refuse a trial by jury for black men accused of crime, without making a mockery of the respect for law which is the safeguard of the liberties of white men. The nation cannot profess Christianity, which makes the golden rule its foundation stone, and continue to deny equal opportunity for life, liberty and the pursuit of happiness to the black race.

When our Christian and moral influences not only concede these principles theoretically but work for them practically, lynching will become a thing of the past, and no governor will again make a mockery of all the nation holds dear in the defense of lynching for any cause.

"THE ORDEAL OF
THE 'SOLITARY' "

Wells-Barnett was committed to defending the rights of even black prisoners, whom Chicago's other reformers tended to shun. Accordingly, in 1916, she took up the mistreatment of "Chicken" Joe Campbell, a prisoner in Illinois's Joliet Correctional Center, who was accused of the rape and murder of the prison warden's wife. The case against him was thin, and Wells-Barnett was appalled to find that he was being held in solitary confinement in a dark cell for days at a time, and was being forced to subsist on bread and water. She publicized Campbell's plight in the following letter to the *Chicago Defender*, and also drew on the resources of the Negro Fellowship League to provide Campbell with a lawyer. After several trials and appeals, Campbell was eventually convicted, but the NFL's lawyer did manage to get his sentence reduced from death to life in prison.

SOURCE: Ida B. Wells-Barnett, "The Ordeal of the 'Solitary': Mrs. Barnett Protests Against It," *Chicago Defender*, July 26, 1915.

THE ORDEAL OF THE "SOLITARY" MRS. BARNETT PROTESTS AGAINST IT

For more than fifty hours before he appeared before the coroner's jury Campbell had been in a "solitary" cell.

The "solitary" is this: There is a little whitewashed cell. It has two doors, the outer one of oak two inches thick, the inner of steel bars.

The man in "solitary" stands handcuffed to the steel door. The manacles are locked an inch or so higher than the arm extended from the shoulder. The prisoner looks directly in front of him at the blank oak door two feet ahead.

He stands in this way for two hours. A keeper then appears and the prisoner may rest for thirty minutes. Then he is shackled up again. From 6 o'clock in the morning until 8 at night this is kept up.

At night the man in "solitary" sleeps on a bare board six feet long and three wide.

Not a ray of light filters through to him day or night. He is in absolute darkness.

Bread and water is his fare three times a day.

Simpson, Cohn and George Edwards also have been undergoing this treatment. Several times they have been dragged at night from their fitful sleep to face inquisitors and volleys of sharp questions.

Back to their lonesome cells they go after each ordeal, there to be alone with their consciences.

Campbell has felt this grind more than the others, yet each time his stories have grown in strength.

Prison officials will not admit more stringent methods than the "solitary" have been used on "Chicken Joe." Physical force, they say, is taboo in the prison.

If Campbell has been physically mistreated his appearances belie it. Although pale from confinement in the dark, he appeared in good health. His answers, while given in an anxious manner, at times were almost defiant. Several times he started to take issue with his questioners.

MRS. BARNETT PROTESTS

Editor of the Herald: In common with thousands who have read of the horrible murder committed in Joliet penitentiary Sunday last, I have followed the testimony given at the inquest now being held in an effort to find the murderer.

All shudder to think so terrible a deed could be committed within prison walls, but I write to ask if one more terrible is not now taking place there in the name of justice, and if there is not enough decent human feeling in the state to put a stop to it and give "Chicken Joe" a chance to prove whether he is innocent or guilty.

The papers say he has been confined in solitary fifty hours, hands chained straight out before him and then brought in to the inquest, sweated and tortured to make him confess a crime that he may not have committed. Is this justice? Is it humanity? Would we stand to see a dog treated in such fashion without protest? I know we would not. Then why will not the justice-loving, law-abiding citizens put a stop to this barbarism?

The Negro Fellowship League will send a lawyer there tomorrow and we ask that your powerful journal help us to see that he gets a chance to defend "Chicken Joe" and give him an opportunity to prove whether he is innocent.

IDA B. WELLS-BARNETT,
Representing Negro Fellowship League.

THE EAST ST. LOUIS MASSACRE: THE GREATEST OUTRAGE OF THE CENTURY

The East St. Louis race riot was the first of a number of race riots that occurred during and immediately after World War I. The violence took place on July 2, 1917, and left thirty-nine blacks and nine whites dead. One of the most destructive race riots of the later teens, it also destroyed much of East St. Louis's downtown. Wells-Barnett traveled to East St. Louis to investigate the riot. Her pamphlet uses her research, along with testimony she collected from East St. Louis residents, to describe both the riot and the labor conflicts that inspired it. The pamphlet includes information about the National Guard and the East St. Louis police's participation in the violence that helped precipitate a congressional investigation into events in St. Louis, and captured the attention of the War Department's Division of Military Intelligence—which censored it for fear that it might foster "interracial antagonism."

SOURCE: Ida B. Wells-Barnett, *The East St. Louis Massacre: The Greatest Outrage of the Century* (Chicago: The Negro Fellowship Herald Press, 1917).

HISTORY OF THE EAST ST. LOUIS, ILLINOIS, RIOT

On Tuesday morning, July 3rd, 1917, the daily papers had big headlines announcing a riot which had been in progress in East St. Louis, Ill., for twenty-four hours previous. It stated that upwards of a hundred Negroes had been killed and that thousands had been driven from their homes; that more than sixty homes in Black Valley, the Negro district, had been burned and that nearly a half million dollars worth of property had been destroyed by fire.

The Negro Fellowship League immediately got out bills announcing a meeting to be held at the Reading Room, 3005 State Street, for that evening. Although the notice was short and the bills had been on the streets only two hours, the place was packed by 8:30 o'clock. At that meeting the following resolution was passed:

"RESOLVED, That we, the colored citizens of Chicago, in the shadow of the awful calamity at East St. Louis, hereby express our solemn conviction that the wholesale slaughter of colored men, women and children was the result of the reckless indifference of public officials, who, with the power of the police, sheriff and governor, could have prevented this massacre if they had discharged the duty which they law imposed upon them, and we call upon press, pulpit and moral forces to demand the punishment of the officials who failed to do their duty.

RESOLVED, That we insist upon the right of every American citizen to work in every field of honest labor, demanding the fullest protection of the law. We protest against the published recommendation of the state defense council as the peaceful exhibition of the same vindictive spirit which was expressed by the bloodthirsty riot at East St. Louis.

RESOLVED, that the situation which has just written the darkest pages in the annals of Illinois, calls for the most intelligent, courageous and conservative co-operation of all citizens, white or black, and we recommend a conference of white and colored citizens which should consider every phase of our present wrongs and strive to find a remedy."

Signed,

A. H. ROBERTS, Chairman.

B. W. FITTS

L. W. WASHINGTON

ATTY. F. L. BARNETT, Secretary.

These men all spoke to the resolution and the daily papers gave good reports of their expressions the following morning. L. W. Washington voiced the opinion that not only ought these resolutions be sent to Governor Lowden, but that the president of the Negro Fellowship League should be the one to carry them. The idea was unanimously adopted, but as chairman of the meeting, I expressed the hope that whoever was sent, should be the one to go to East St. Louis and get the facts and then take the same to the governor, with the resolutions.

The audience agreed and quickly raised $8.65 toward paying the expenses of the trip. Wednesday evening, July 4th, the writer took the train to East St. Louis, reaching there next morning. Against the advice of both the Pullman and the train conductors, I got off at East St. Louis. They told me that the porters had been locked in the cars while the train passed through the town. But I felt that if Governor Lowden had been on the scene, also Adjutant General Dickson, together with eleven companies of militia, they certainly ought to have been able to get control of the situation in forty-eight hours time.

I found that I was correct in my surmise. No one molested me in my walk from the station to City Hall, although I did not see a single colored person until I reached the City Hall building. I accosted the lone individual in soldier's uniform at the depot, a mere boy with a gun, and asked him if the governor was in town. When he said no, he had gone to Washington the night before, I asked how the situation was and he said, "bad." I asked what was the trouble and he said, "The Negroes won't let the whites alone. They killed seven yesterday and three already this morning." It was only 7 o'clock in the morning and I decided he was lying, so said nothing more on the score. I then asked him to show me where Adjutant General Dickson was, and he directed me to the City Hall. An interview with General Dickson followed and he told me that it was perfectly safe to go about and get the information that I had come in search of, and that he would be glad to send a guard with me whenever I got ready for it. He also promised to see that I had the opportunity to be present at the ten o'clock meeting of the Chamber of Commerce and to have an interview with Mayor Mollman.

While waiting at the City Hall for General Dickson, a number of colored women came in bareheaded and their clothing dirty. Hearing it was safe to do so, they had come back from St. Louis that morning where they had gone the day of the riot to get military escort to go to their homes and get some clothing. A Red Cross man offered one of Swift's biggest motor trucks, put a soldier with a loaded gun in front and one on the back of the truck, with thirty rounds of ammunition each, and told the women to get in and go to their homes and get what stuff they could.

I went with them and in that way went inside a dozen of their three and four room houses and saw the mob's work of destruction. In every case, the houses had been fired from the rear and as soon as the occupants came out, they were then shot at or beaten. In most of the homes in which I went, the inmates had gone before the mob got there. When these cottages were found to be empty, the mob went into them, threw the mattresses, quilts, blankets and wearing apparel that was not new, on the floor and then cut, tore and trampled these things under foot and set fire to them. Pictures, bric-a-brac, everything that they could destroy, they did.

Most of these houses had brass or iron bedsteads, and the mattresses were good, worth $4.00 or $5.00 a piece. In two of these homes I saw a piano. In one of them the woman found a few of her records, but her victrola and most of the records had been taken away. The windows were broken and doors had been split open, evidently with an ax. One woman found her pictures and some of her wearing apparel in a white neighbor's house, and when she accused the woman of taking them, this woman said that all the others were taking things and she did so too.

We crossed the bridge into St. Louis four different times that day, taking women with trunks of their wearing apparel which they were able to find. These women told me the following stories as we rode around the town.

MRS. BALLARD'S STORY

Mrs. Emma Ballard, with her husband George Ballard had lived in East St. Louis seven years. They had been married twenty-four years and came there from Jackson, Tenn. He worked in the Kansas City R. R. warehouse as a freighter and trucker, loading and unloading cars and boats. He got $2.25 a day. They had a six room house, nicely furnished. In this home was a piano. They had four children. She said the children heard the first of the mob between 12 and 1 o'clock Monday night. Men and boys were in the street hollering, "Come out, niggers" as they roamed up and down the Negro district. They shot and beat every Negro found on the streets Monday night. She saw fourteen men beaten and two killed. (In the excitement she and her children took their feather beds and pillows and some of their best wearing clothes across the alley to the barn of a white saloonkeeper.) She took her children and got away with what they had on, after trying to hide some of their best things. She did not come back to East St. Louis until the morning of the 5th when I went with her to her home in the auto truck. The windows were broken, bedding and clothing thrown on the floor, all wet and much of it scorched. After getting together a few wearing clothes, she went out and closed the door, leaving furniture and mattresses which must have cost five hundred dollars. After a day of uncertainty she found her husband who had already found a home in St. Louis and they were going to stay there.

MRS. LULU THOMAS' STORY

Mrs. Thomas has a husband and mother. She too had a very nice home. She is a nice looking stylish woman and had some very good clothing which she left in three rooms of handsome furniture. Her husband was a boiler washer on the Illinois Central railroad. He makes $80.00 a month. They have been living in East St. Louis six years. The Illinois Central yard officials kept her husband in the fire box of one of the engines from Monday night to Wednesday morning, afraid to let him go out on the street even to go to his home. It was this woman who saw some of her good clothes on one of her white women neighbors. Mrs.

Thomas' house had been set on fire, the mob had broken in the door, broken out the windows, dragged some of the mattresses out and set fire to them, and left others in the room, cut, torn and burned. Her pictures and bed clothes, wearing clothes, furniture, all broken and torn and thrown about. She too could only get a few wearing clothes together to enable her to have a change.

MRS. WILLIE FLAKE'S STORY

Mrs. Flake is a widow with three children, 11, 8, and 6 years old. She is a laundress who came to East St. Louis four years ago from Jackson, Tenn. She took care of her little family by taking in washing and she worked from Monday morning until Saturday night at the ironing board. She too had three rooms full of nice furniture. Both of the two front rooms having nice rugs on the floor, a brass bedstead and other furniture to correspond. She had about a hundred dollars worth of furniture ruined, fifty dollars worth of clothing and about fifty dollars more of bedding, mattresses, etc. The mob had taken a phonograph for which she had paid $15.00 and twenty-five records for which she had paid 75 cents and $1.00 each. She got away with her children before the mob reached her house and she too came back that morning to get some clothes for herself and children. The mob hadn't left much, but out of the debris, she was able to pack one trunk with some clothing and quilts for herself and children. It was in this house that I picked up one child's new shoe and although we looked the house over, we couldn't find the other. In its spasm of wanton destruction, the mob had doubtless carried it away. Mrs. Flake also had life insurance policies for herself and children, but she couldn't find any of the books. She too had already found a flat in St. Louis and was only too anxious to get away from the town where such awful things were transpiring, and where not even widows and children were safe from the fury of the mob bent on killing everything with black skins.

Mrs. Dolly Bruton, another widow, came to East St. Louis from Mississippi, December 8th, 1915. She had two trunks full of clothes at 513 Collinsville Ave., because she had been told that the worst of the riot was over and that it was alright for her to stay in East St. Louis. But on this very morning of July 5th, a soldier had come into this house and began to search for weapons. He found nobody there but Mrs. Mary Howard and three other women, one of whom was ill. When he could find no gun, he arrested every one of those women and brought them to the City Hall. They were bare headed and in the soiled clothing they had worn about their work at home. Mrs. Howard said, that she had lived in East St. Louis eighteen years. Her husband, Douglass Howard, was a grader, making $19.35 a week. They owned four houses in East St. Louis. She had seen a good part of the rioting Tuesday, but had not been disturbed herself. She thought it was because her house was right between the homes and stores of some of the white people. Just as she had thought the whole thing over, it both frightened and humiliated her to be subjected to this outrage at the hands of the soldiers at the time that General Dickson was in charge of the situation and everybody had been assured that the danger was over.

This was the last straw for her. She too wanted protection to go out to her home and get her things so she could leave town. She said that during the riot a young fellow whom she had sent to the grocery to get a chicken, was knocked off his wheel by the mob. Then the mob took his wheel and struck him on the side of his head with a brick and knocked a hole in it. His name was Jimmie Eckford, eighteen years old and roomed at her house. He ran into the nearest yard which happened to be that of white people. When the mob said they would burn the house down if they didn't make Eckford come out, the tenants picked him up and threw him out in the street to the mob where he was kicked and stamped on and beaten till they knocked his teeth from his head and killed him.

The street cars ran right along in front of her house, and she saw white women stop the street cars and pull colored women off and beat them. One woman's clothes they tore off entirely, and then took off their shoes and beat her over the face and head with their shoe heels. Another woman who got away, ran down the street, with every stitch of clothes torn off her back, leaving her with only her shoes and stockings on. Mrs. Howard saw two men beaten to death. She had escaped all excepting having rocks thrown at the house, until this soldier humiliated her by coming into her house and arresting her and the other women there, because they couldn't find any guns concealed. This happened on the morning of the 5th.

Mrs. Lizzie Holmes was another woman who was run out of her home by the mob and her household goods destroyed. She had six children, the youngest a sixteen months old baby. She too gathered up what she could save from the wreck and took it over to St. Louis where she had already placed her children. She said her husband C. A. Holmes is living at 1951 West Lake street Chicago, and that she had not heard from him during all this trouble. I promised to write him for her and give him her St. Louis address and tell him how badly she needed help for the care of those children. I have done so over two weeks and have had no word from him in response. As the letter did not come back, I am hoping that he has written to her or still better, has gone to look after his family.

Mrs. Ella Moss and husband John came from Pensacola, Florida, in March. He had been employed at once by the M. & O. Railroad Company, washing engines at $60.00 a month. Every bit of Mrs. Moss' furniture was brand new, and I was very glad to be able to help her save a brand new ice box, which she had stuffed full of clothes, two brand new mattresses, beside a trunk full of wearing apparel. This was on our last trip on the truck. As we had already carried two loads before, there was more room for Mrs. Moss' things than there would have been if there had been other women to look after. She too went over into St. Louis, Mo., and found a home there, because she felt more secure from mob violence there than she did in the state of Abraham Lincoln.

CLARISSA LOCKETT'S STORY

Mrs. Lockett lived in the house with her brother where she had been ever since both he and she came from Mississippi. Her brother worked nights, so that all during the rioting Monday night she was alone. They didn't get to set fire to her house that night, but she sat up all night long waiting. She was unwilling to leave her household goods until she had to. She went to work at the packing house Tuesday morning early, but quit at 9 A. M.

The soldiers who were guarding the plant took her and the other colored women home. Tuesday night the mob came to her number, 48 Third street, rear. After they had set fire to it and run her out, she ran into a Polish saloon not far away and the saloon-keeper and his wife agreed to let her stay there that night, although they knew the risk they ran in so doing. They told her to crouch down behind the piano and to stay there quietly all night. This she did, glad of the chance. She had been able only to bring her dog and her gun when she ran out of her home. After the saloonkeeper and his wife had gone upstairs to bed about 1 o'clock in the morning, the barkeeper and a man friend of his came back behind the piano and attempted to assault her. She drew her pistol and drove them off. When they found she had a gun, they left her in peace until morning. Early Wednesday morning, the day of our national independence, she found a man who hauled her trunk containing her own and her brother's clothes over into St. Louis, Missouri. She left two rooms filled with her new furniture. She saw soldiers take guns and knives from colored men, and then the mob would set on them and beat or murder them.

When I saw her at St. Louis, Missouri, she had not yet recovered from the shock. Her brother had come straight out of the packing plant for which he was working and went straight to the train in his working clothes and went to Meridian, Mississippi, his former home. She was very anxious until she got a card letting her know where he was.

Mrs. Josie Nixon whose husband Samuel and daughter Pearl had lived in their home in East St. Louis thirteen years. The family is well known and respected. Her husband is a carpenter and contractor. Her daughter has finished her third year in high school and she has been working at Swift's for nine months. The mob did not harm her or her husband at her home, but the excitement was so great, she was still suffering from the nervous strain. She said, that although they knew about the excitement and the burning of homes the night before, that on Tuesday morning at 5:30 o'clock, she and a man and his wife started to work that early, thinking that they would avoid the mob. They met a young fellow about nineteen or twenty years old, walking down the street with a soldier who had a gun. "This young fellow held up the man who was with us and searched him, and asked where he was going, told him not to come back this way and that he had better be out of town by night, if not, he, the white man, would get him if he had to set his house afire." All this while the soldier in Uncle Sam's uniform was standing by with his gun, and he said too, "Yes, you'd better get out of town."

She went back home and she and her daughter sat there nearly all day, fearing attack at any moment. She had not seen or heard of her husband since the day before. Fearing that some harm had come to him and having not a nickel in the house, she borrowed carfare from the druggist across from her home and leaving her comfortable home, went over into St. Louis. Late that evening, her husband came home and finding them gone, he hunted all over town, but nobody could tell him about her. He stayed in his house Tuesday night and saw two sons of a white neighbor set fire to his house. He ran and put out the fire himself, thus saving his home.

Mrs. Nixon saw a woman whose tongue was shot off when she was shot through the mouth, being taken to the hospital. She begged the police to go back for her son who was in the house. They found him lying behind a trunk shot dead. She said that woman was still in the hospital.

The mob went into one house near her, beat the man who was at home until he fainted. He begged them to spare him on account that his wife and new born baby who were in a rear room. When he revived he found both wife and baby dead in the bed where the mob had killed them. They only left him because they thought he was dead. She knew of another case, where as the mother came rushing out of the flames of her home, with her baby in her arms, the baby was shot through the head and thrown back into the fire. Many children were killed this way.

Mrs. Nixon had three gardens planted besides having this nice home and she felt that the mob would not harm her because she was so well known. After they told her that the excitement was all over, she went back to East St. Louis on Thursday morning and went again to her job. While she was at work that morning, a white man standing talking to a bunch of other men said, loud enough for her to hear, "If I have to leave here, and give my place to a nigger, I'll certainly kill me a lot of niggers before I go, to pay for it." All the white men in the crowd turned and glared at her in so menacing a fashion that she lost her nerve completely, threw up her job, went back to St. Louis, Missouri, and had rented her a house for the purpose of living over there.

Many of the women complained that the soldiers would not let them go into their homes except to get a few clothes. These and many other such stories all testify to the same thing, that the soldiers did not offer any protection to colored people, but did search them and take their fire arms from them and then stand aside and left them helpless before the mob.

CHAPTER II

When we made the last trip it was 5 o'clock in the afternoon. I had been so engrossed in the work of helping these poor women, that I had neither a drink of water nor a bite of food all day. The Red Cross man who was in charge seemed very glad to have my help. When I came back to the City Hall, the two colored men janitors whom I found there, told me that there was no place in East St. Louis where I could sleep that night, as all the colored people who lived there had gone in the country or over to St. Louis. With my bag in hand, after the man brought me a couple of sandwiches I went over the river, as so many thousands had done that day, to find a bed in St. Louis.

When I got over on the Missouri side, a policeman at the bridge told me to step in the room that the Red Cross people had established. I found that it was for the purpose of having me vaccinated. This was because of two cases of smallpox that had developed in the municipal lodging house that had been housing thousands of the unfortunates ever since Monday night. I was loaded into the patrol wagon with all the others who had been waiting in this room for the wagon to come, and ridden through the streets of St. Louis to the municipal lodging house about three or four miles away. While sitting there, I saw hundreds of men, women and children marched into the municipal lodging house and the physicians and the nurses working overtime vaccinating them. In spite of my objection to being vaccinated in this wholesale way, they said I couldn't leave the building until this had been done, but later on I did leave without having my arm scratched.

Every which way we turned there were women and children

and men, dazed over the thing that had come to them and unable to tell what it was all about. Most of them had left clothes and homes behind, thankful to have saved their lives and those of their families. Some of them had not located relatives and did not know whether the mob or fire had taken them. They lined the streets or were standing out on the grassy banks of the lawns that surrounded the City Hall, or stood in groups discussing their experiences. Red Cross and charitable workers gave them food to eat, and the city the place to sleep in the city lodging house, and some of them had clothing which they were issuing to these people who had suddenly been robbed of everything except what they stood in.

The invariable story was, that the rioting started on the morning of July 2nd, when the workers were coming off the 11 o'clock shift at the factories and packing plants. The cause was alleged to be the killing of two white police officers who had been shot by colored men when they went into the Negro district on the Denver side to quell a supposed riot. These colored men said that an automobile had gone through the neighborhood firing right and left into the windows of the houses and of the church. A bell was rung and the men rapidly came together at the church to plan for resisting other attacks of similar character. When a second automobile came on the scene very soon after, they thought it were the same parties, and fired into it after a parley, wounding two officers who afterwards died.

This seems to have been the signal for starting the blaze which had been smoldering ever since May 28th. At that time, members of the labor unions began to beat up colored men coming from the Aluminum Ore Packing Co. plant. At that time, one or two companies of militia were sent at the request of the sheriff, and the rioting seemed to have stopped. The colored people understood that the labor unions had gone on strike because of the employment of colored men, had made up their minds to drive out colored laborers who had come there in such large numbers from the south. Accordingly these Negro laborers made up their minds to sell their lives as dearly as possible, and to hold their ground in an effort to make a living for themselves and their families.

When the officers were killed in the unfortunate mixup of July 1st, it gave excuse for the breaking out of the mob composed largely of union workers and the Negro haters who gathered from small towns surrounding, and even from the South. Horrible stories were given both by eye witnesses as well as by others, the saddest part of them all being, that in every instance, as the mob set upon men coming from their work at 11 o'clock in the day, the soldiers or the police held up the black men, searched them and even took their pocket knives, then left them at the mercy of the mob. In all that disgraceful twenty-four hours of rioting, murder and arson, not a shot was fired by a single soldier in the effort to protect the lives of the helpless and innocent men, women and children! Jack Lait in the Chicago Herald of July 4th said, "As a matter of truth, just two shots had been fired by men in khaki, and each killed a man—a fleeing Negro both times."

Indeed, according to General Dickson, the state militia were given orders not to shoot white men and women, and they stood by and saw the most brutal savagery perpetrated without lifting a finger for protection or punishment for those who did murder, committed arson or burned up little children and old people. "Five hundred rioters, the ring leaders of the biggest mob, I am informed, are now under arrest," said General Dickson. "This was accomplished by surrounding the rioters and forcing them to submit without shooting or employing the bayonet." General Dickson said after the 500 were taken into custody, the disturbance at once took on a less serious aspect. "Eleven companies of Illinois troops are here with three more on the way. The troops already here are: Company I of Vandalia, G of Effingham, D of Newton, F of Benton, H of Shelbyville, L of Carbondale, all of the Fourth Illinois Infantry, and Company A Casey, C of Sullivan, L of Olney, also of the Fourth. These were two companies encamped in the city previous to the riot. Company F of Pontiac, numbering fifty-five men, and Company L of Paris, Fourth Infantry, fifty strong, are on the way here."

Col. Tripp could easily give orders to fire on Negro rescuers. "A report came to Col. Tripp that Negro inhabitants at Brooklyn, Ill., a city entirely populated by Negroes, were moving on East St. Louis, and he sent a commandeered truck full of guardsmen to the "black" bridge to meet any attack that might be attempted."

WHAT WHITE NEWSPAPERS SAID
ABOUT THE RIOT

From The Chicago Herald, July 4th, 1917

"Nobody seems able or willing to say when an inquest will be held, or over what or whom—any of the three that could be used as evidence for murder could have picked up this evening across the street from the public library, where three bodies were still being roasted in hot ashes of a completely devastated square block. **** Meanwhile three more victims of savage assaults died in the hospitals, and twenty-eight bodies in all had been recovered.

The guards were lax and cruelly good-natured. In one instance a corpulent Negress brought up in the rear of such a procession and for several blocks a boy, one of the gang of stone-throwing mischief-makers, who followed every squad, was beating her with an iron bar at intervals of a few yards. She did not dare to protest or to resist. She was even too frightened to scream. At last a white man, probably a nonresident of East St. Louis, called the attention of a guardsman to the outrage, and he laughingly drove the boy off.

The results so far have been almost unqualifiedly uncomplimentary to our Illinois state guard, or at least the portion of it that represented it in the first contingent sent here.

Hundreds of episodes are jocundly retailed here by spectators to the slaughter and rioting of Monday evening to evidence that the soldiers were toys in the hands of the determined and desperate mobs when they were not actually co-operating with them.

The square block from Broadway and Eighth streets was burned to an ash heap. On that corner stood a Negro commercial building containing a grocery and barber shop. The vanguard of the rioters invaded these stores and found a Negro crouching timorously in each. The armed invaders drove the two blacks out through the back doors and there they were shot down and left to be burned alive. The shots were fired from militia rifles by khaki-uniformed men. Dozens of men who saw it done today loudly proclaimed it so, slapped their thighs and said the Illinois National Guard was alright.

When the newly fired buildings were fired this morning the

militia men helped get property out of the homes of whites near by, but had done nothing to prevent the torching, for which they had been assigned.

When the tardy fire department vehicles came and two streams of water of the force of garden hose were turned, spurting and wheezing, toward the rising flames, the mob yelled: "Let 'em burn!" And at each fireman who tried to do his duty, "Nigger lover!"

Another newspaper says: "Saint Bartholomew's day did not outdo this massacre, when once it started. Indescribable barbarity was born on the moment and perpetrated with malicious deliberation not typical of the most depraved inhabitants of a western nation. Boys of 13, 14, 15 and 16 were in the forefront of every felonious butchery: girls and women, wielding bloody knives and clawing at the eyes of dying victims, sprang from the ranks of the mad thousands.

There was no attempt at avenging specific misdeeds upon selected individuals. A black skin was a death warrant. Wherever a Negro appeared he was stoned, beaten, shot, strung up—more than a dozen suffered all of these forms of savage onslaught. Fire came as an inspiration. A woman set the first blaze and was triumphantly carried on the shoulders of her brethren for it.

The outlying colored folks were shot and thrown into the river, the creek, down manholes—anywhere. Among them was a little girl, 2 years old, shot through the heart and flung into midroad.

Each man slain was frightfully abused, as a lesson to all others of his color. A murdered man wasn't allowed to die after he had been fatally pierced. He was kicked and beaten with fists, feet and clubs, hanged, shot some more, kicked and beaten again.

And his martyrdom was notice to the world in flame and blood, that East St. Louis would not tolerate a black man."

FROM THE DAILY NEWS, CHICAGO, JULY 10TH, 1917

Springfield, Ill., July 10. —"There is to be no passing of the buck and no evasion of responsibility on the part of the officials in St. Clair county in this race riot investigation," Attorney General

Brundage declared this morning before departing for East St. Louis to make a personal survey of the situation. It was intimated that the St. Clair county grand jury, sitting at Belleville, did not take up the riot cases at once because the proper officials had not prepared evidence on the basis of which indictment might be issued.

Mr. Brundage said lawless conditions had existed long enough in St. Clair county and that officials there would be forced either to correct the evils or get out.

"How could undesirable officials be eliminated?" the attorney-general was asked.

"Disbarment proceedings can be instituted against any attorney who is remiss or who fails to perform his duty," he replied.

Mrs. Brundage had been asked by the chamber of commerce of East St. Louis to take personal charge of the investigation and to direct the grand jury inquisition.

Mrs. Ida Wells Barnett of Chicago headed a delegation of colored residents of Chicago which waited upon Governor Lowden to ask relief for the large number of colored persons who were driven out of East St. Louis in the recent riots. Mrs. Barnett declared that it is the duty of the state to aid the colored persons who are now public charges of St. Louis. The delegation was named at a mass meeting held at Bethel Church, Chicago.

Following the conference with Governor Lowden, Mrs. Barnett departed for St. Louis to aid the Negroes now in public lodging houses in that city.

FROM THE ST. LOUIS POST DISPATCH, JULY 3RD, 1917

By Carlos F. Hurd, Staff Reporter

For an hour and a half last evening I saw the massacre of helpless Negroes at Broadway and Fourth street, in downtown East St. Louis, where a black skin was a death warrant.

I have read of St. Bartholomew's night.[30] I have heard stories of the latter-day crimes of the Turks in Armenia, and I have learned to loathe the German army for its barbarity in Belgium.[31] But I do not believe that Moslem fanaticism or Prussian frightfulness could perpetrate murders of more deliberate brutality than those which I saw committed in daylight by citizens of the State of Abraham Lincoln.

I saw man after man, with hands raised, pleading for his life, surrounded by groups of men—men who had never seen him before and knew nothing about him except that he was black—and saw them administer the historic sentence of intolerance, death by stoning. I saw one of those men almost dead from a savage shower of stones, hanged with a clothes line, and when it broke, hanged with a rope which held. Within a few spaces of the pole from which he was suspended, four other Negroes lay dead or dying, another had been removed, dead, a short time before. I saw the pockets of two of these Negroes searched, without the finding of any weapon.

I saw one of these men, covered with blood and half conscious, raise himself on his elbow, and look feebly about, when a young man, standing directly behind, lifted a flat stone and hurled it directly upon his neck. This young man was much better dressed than most of the others. He walked away unmolested.

I saw Negro women begging for mercy and pleading that they had harmed no one, set upon by white women of the baser sort, who laughed and answered the course sallies of men as they beat the Negresses' faces and breasts with fists, stones and sticks. I saw one of these furies fling herself at a militiaman who was trying to protect a Negress, and wrestle with him for his bayonetted gun, while other women attacked the refugee.

What I saw, in the 90 minutes between 6:30 P. M. and the lurid coming of darkness, was but one local scene of the drama of death. I am satisfied that, in spirit and method, it typified the whole. And I cannot somehow speak of what I saw as mob violence. It was not my idea of a mob.

A mob is passionate, a mob follows one man or a few men blindly; a mob sometimes take chances. The East St. Louis affair, as I saw it, was a man hunt, conducted on a sporting basis, though with anything but the fair play which is the principle of the sport. The East St. Louis men took no chances, except the chance from stray shots, which every spectator of their acts took. They went in small groups, there was little leadership, and there was a horribly cool deliberateness and a spirit of fun about it. I cannot allow even the doubtful excuse of drink. No man whom I saw showed the effect of liquor. It was no crowd of hot-headed

youths. Young men were in the greater number, but there were
the middle-aged, no less active in the task of destroying the life of
every discoverable black man. It was a shirt-sleeve gathering,[32]
and the men were mostly workingmen, except for some who had
the aspect of mere loafers. I have mentioned the peculiarly brutal
crime committed by the only man there who had the appearance
of being a business or professional man of any standing.

I would be more pessimistic about my fellow-Americans than I
am to-day, if I could not say that there were other workingmen
who protested against the senseless slaughter. I would be ashamed
of myself if I could not say that I forgot my place as a professional
observer and joined in such protests. But I do not think any ver-
bal objection had the slightest effect. Only a volley of lead would
have stopped these murderers.

"Get a nigger," was the slogan, and it was varied by the recur-
rent cry, "Get another!" It was like nothing so much as the holiday crowd, with thumbs turned down, in the Roman Coliseum,
except that here the shouters were their own gladiators, and their
own wild beasts.

When I got off a State street car on Broadway at 6:30, a fire
apparatus was on its way to the blaze in the rear of Fourth street,
south from Broadway. A moment's survey showed why this fire
had been set, and what it was meant to accomplish.

The sheds in the rear of Negroes' houses, which were themselves in the rear of the main buildings on Fourth street, had
been ignited to drive out the Negro occupants of the houses. And
the slayers were waiting for them to come out.

It was stay in and be roasted, or come out and be slaughtered.
A moment before I arrived, one Negro had taken the desperate
chance of coming out, and the rattle of revolver shots, which I
heard as I approached the corner, was followed by the cry,
"They've got him!"

And they had. He lay on the pavement, a bullet wound in his
head and his skull bare in two places. At every movement of pain
which showed that life still remained, there came a terrific kick in
the jaw or nose, or a crashing stone, from some of the men who
stood over him.

At the corner, a few steps away, were a Sergeant and several
guardsmen. The Sergeant approached the ring of men around the
prostrate Negro.

"This man is done for," he said. "You'd better get him away from here. No one made a move to lift the blood-covered form, and the Sergeant walked away, remarking, when I questioned him about an ambulance, that the ambulances had quit coming. However, an undertaker's ambulance did come 15 minutes later, and took away the lifeless Negro, who had in the meantime been further kicked and stoned.

By that time, the fire in the rear of the Negro houses had grown hotter, and men were standing in all the narrow spaces through which the Negroes might come to the street. There was talk of a Negro, in one of the houses, who had a Winchester, and the opinion was expressed that he had no ammunition left, but no one went too near, and the fire was depended on to drive him out. The firemen were at work on Broadway, some distance east, but the flames immediately in the rear of the Negro houses burned without hindrance.

A half-block to the south, there was a hue and a cry at a railroad crossing, and a fusillade of shots were heard. More militiamen than I have seen elsewhere, up to that time, were standing on a platform and near a string of freight cars, and trying to keep back men who had started to pursue Negroes along the track.

As I turned back toward Broadway, there was a shout at the alley, and a Negro ran out, apparently hoping to find protection. He paid no attention to the missiles thrown from behind, none of which had hurt him much, but he was stopped in the middle of the street by a smashing blow in the jaw, struck by a man he had not seen.

"Don't do that," he appealed. "I haven't hurt nobody." The answer was a blow from one side, a piece of curbstone from the other side, and a push which sent him on the brick pavement. He did not rise again, and the battering and the kicking of his skull continued until he lay still, his blood flowing half way across the street. Before he had been booted to the opposite curb, another Negro appeared, and the same deeds were repeated. I did not see any revolver shot fired at these men. Bullets and ammunition were used for use at longer range. It was the last Negro I have mentioned who was apparently finished by the stone hurled upon his neck by the noticeably well-dressed young man.

The butchering of the fire-trapped Negroes went on so rapidly that, when I walked back to the alley a few minutes later, one was lying dead in the alley on the west side of Fourth street and another on the east side.

And now women began to appear. One frightened black girl, probably 20 years old, got as far as Broadway with not worse treatment than jeers and thrusts. At Broadway, in view of militiamen, the white women, several of whom had been watching the massacre of the Negro men, pounced on the Negress. I do not wish to be understood as saying that these women were representatives of the womanhood of East St. Louis. Their faces showed, all too plainly, exactly who and what they were. But they were the heroines of the moment with that gathering of men, and when one man, sick of the brutality he had seen, seized one of the women by the arm to stop an impending blow, he was hustled away with fists under his nose, and with more show of actual anger than had been bestowed upon any of the Negroes. He was a stocky, nervy chap, and he stood his ground until a diversion elsewhere drew the menacing ring of men away.

"Let the girls have her," was the shout as the women attacked the young Negress. The victim's cry, "Please, please, I ain't done nothing," was stopped by a blow in the mouth with a broomstick, which one of the women swung like a base ball bat. Another woman seized the Negress' hands, and the blow was repeated as she struggled helplessly. Finger nails clawed her hair, and the sleeves were torn from her waist, when some of the men called, "Now let her see how fast she can run." The women did not really leave off beating her, but they stopped short of murder, and the crying, hysterical girl ran down the street.

An older Negress a few moments later came along with two or three militiamen, and the same women made for her. When one of the soldiers held his gun as a barrier, the woman with the broomstick seized it with both hands and struggled to wrest it from him, while the others, striking at the Negress, in spite of the other militiamen, frightened her thoroughly and hurt her somewhat.

From Negress baiting, the well-pleased procession turned to see a lynching. A Negro had his head laid open by a great stone-cut, had been dragged to the mouth of the alley on 4th Street and a small rope was being tied about his neck. It broke when it was pulled over a projecting cable, letting the Negro fall. A stouter rope was secured.

Right here I saw the most sickening sight of the evening. To put the rope around the Negro's neck, one of the lynchers stuck his fingers inside the gaping scalp and lifted the Negro's head by it, literally bathing his hand in the man's blood. "Get hold and pull for East St. Louis," called a man with a black coat and a new straw hat on as he seized the other end of the rope, and helped lift the body seven feet from the ground, and left hanging there.

A mob of white men formed and burned all the Negro houses on Bond Avenue between Tenth and Twelfth Streets, 43 houses being destroyed.

In the fire zone at Sixth and Broadway, two Negroes are reported to have burned to death. At Fifth and Railroad, another death by fire was reported. One of the mid-afternoon killings was at 4 o'clock, at Broadway and Main Street. A Negro was shot down. One of those firing on him being a boy in short trousers. The driver of the first ambulance that came was not permitted to remove this body, and it lay for an hour beside the street car tracks seen by the passengers in every passing car.

At 9:30 this morning a Negro, still living, but in a critical condition, was found in a sewer manhole at Sixth Street and Broadway. He was beaten by the mob with paving bricks 13 hours before and thrown in.

The 2-year old Negro child who was killed was the daughter of William Forest of 1118 Division Ave. A bullet fired into the house entered the body near the heart.

City Attorney Fekete is credited with having saved the life of a young Negro who was running from a crowd which had fired a number of shots at him while the Negro was plainly visible in the glare of the burning buildings. Fekete placed the Negro in his own automobile, and after arguing for several minutes with the group of men succeeded getting away with the rescued man.

CHAPTER III

On Sunday, July 8th, I returned to Chicago and made my report to the Negro Fellowship League that evening. This meeting passed resolutions which recommended:

1st, That a committee be sent to Governor Lowden, with the facts that I had collected, asking,

a) That a searching investigation be made into the reasons why not a single shot was fired by the militia for the protection of black men and women in all that forty-eight hours of rioting.

b) That in many instances, the soldiers combined with the police in searching black men, thus making it safe for the mob to beat and kill them.

c) Demanding that a court martial be instigated to find out the cause of this neglect of duty and to punish the offenders.

2nd, That the state of Illinois be requested to make provision for the care of the thousands of men, women and children who have been driven from their homes and were now being taken care of by the people of St. Louis, together with the Red Cross workers and the assistance of the colored citizens of St. Louis.

3rd, To inquire what action, if any, the state would take to restore order in East St. Louis to such an extent that the people might go back to their homes and their work, and demanding protection for those who do.

Acting on these recommendations, the Negro Fellowship League voted in a committee of five persons to wait upon the governor. The following committee was appointed. I. B. W. Barnett, chairman; Rev. J. W. Robinson, pastor St. Mark's A. M. E. Church; Professor R. T. Greener; B. W. Fitts and Mrs. William Farrow who had raised upwards of $6.00 in her effort to contribute toward the expenses of this trip.

At the meeting held at Bethel A. M. E. Church, Monday night, July 9th, through the courtesy of the pastor, Rev. W. D. Cooke and the trustees of Bethel, this committee was enlarged by the addition of two persons: Rev. W. D. Cooke, who was made chairman, and H. A. Watkins. The meeting gave $52.00 to pay the expenses of this committee to Springfield. They left on the midnight train, and had an interview with Governor Lowden Tuesday, July 10th, at which meeting were present besides the governor, Adjutant General Frank Dickson and Col. John R. Marshall, as well as our own committee.

The Governor listened attentively, and said the State would do everything it could to reestablish law and order, and that a court martial had been ordered to investigate the conduct of the state militia. He said that the state had no emergency fund from which to do anything for the refugees in St. Louis, Missouri, but he called up the Red Cross chairman, Mr. O'Connor, and asked him to take the matter up and see what might be done.

The interview was very satisfactory with the exception of the fact that Governor Lowden took occasion to advise us against incendiary talk. The writer told him that if he had seen women whose husbands had been beaten to death, whose children had been thrown into the flames and in the river, whose women had been burned to death, he would not say it was incendiary talk to denounce such outrages. In response to my statement that fifty persons whom I had interviewed, told me that the invariable customs of the soldier was to search the men and take from them even their pocket knives, thus leaving them at the mercy of the mob, or they would stand by and see the work well done, he told me to get him the names of the persons who would testify to the effect and see that they were placed in his hands. This terminated the interview.

Mrs. Farrow and I took this train at once for St. Louis and went immediately to the municipal lodging house. The papers had announced that this lodging house would be closed on Wednesday and the statement had also been made that Hon. Charles Nagel had made a complaint about Missouri taking care of Illinois' people. We expected to find the hundreds that we saw the Friday before, but in four days the thousands that were there had dispersed! Some had gone back South. Others had accepted the invitations of the Chamber of Commerce and gone back to the industrial plants to work by the day, but they came back every night to St. Louis to sleep. Hundreds had gone up to Pennsylvania and other centers of labor where they needed help. There were only 25 persons in the municipal lodging house and these 25 had already secured places to go. For this reason the lodging house was closing its doors; these people who had been beaten, persecuted, run out of their homes and robbed even of their wearing apparel, were taking up new courage, and utilizing the only capital they had, the labor in their hands.

Having been asked by Governor Lowden to get the names and addresses of people who made charges against the state militia for failure to do their duty or for assisting the mob, both Mrs. Farrow and I began as soon as we returned to St. Louis, to collect such stories.

The first person I talked with was a man named John Avant whose foot was so swollen he could not wear his shoes. He says he hurt his foot running; that he worked at the C., B. & Q.[33] He was with about twenty-five others who came out from their work on Tuesday morning. They were sitting or standing around the restaurant where they usually ate, when six soldiers and four or five policemen came upon them suddenly and shot into the crowd, wounding six. One of the number has since died. They also were searched and even their pocket knives taken from them.

One of the shots fired took off an arm of a woman who was working in this restaurant. A half dozen others told me that they went back over into East St. Louis to work, but that they came back to the Missouri side to sleep at night. The railroad companies for which they worked, gave carfare together with two meals a day, and paid them $3.00 and $4.00 a day, where previously they had only paid $2.00 and $2.50. They said they would do this as long as the soldiers remained.

One of the half dozen men standing around, told me that he saw a woman and two children killed, also her husband. That they were going across the bridge and the mob seized the baby out of her arms and threw it into the river.

Charles Perry, 19 years old, had been a year in East St. Louis from Jackson, Mississippi. He worked at Laden's Baking Powder Factory. On Tuesday, about 4:30 P. M., he saw a mob of about 50 on the bridge. He too has gone back to work, but he stays nights on the Missouri side.

Frank Brown was been in East St. Louis about a year, having come there from Salt Lake City, Utah. He saw a man hit a colored man with a piece of iron and shoot him four times in the stomach.

STORY OF MRS. MARY LEWIS

Saw the mob kill a man a few doors away. Became frightened and told husband she would have to leave. Man at house named Hugh McMurry told her she could come to his house in St. Louis, as she knew no one in St. Louis. "I put on my suit and clean dresses on four small children and then got on the car with them. The mob yelled, "There she goes," but did not fire, so she got away. While the house was still in sight, the mob had broken windows and set it on fire, shooting into it. Sister was in the house, but escaped, being shot, and was badly stoned. Husband, though shot, got up and ran about 40 feet before they finished him. Was heard to beg Mr. Warren not to let them kill him.

William Lues, an employee of the Wabash R. R. Co., was on his way home from work, sitting between his employer and his employer's son in the street car, when the mob grabbed him, shot him to pieces and then put a rope around his neck and dragged him in the streets.

James Frizzar, age 53 years, address where he worked. Lived in St. Louis since he was a child, having come there from Montgomery, Ala. When he was leaving his work Monday afternoon, July 2nd, five men attacked him, beat him and shot him through the chest. While he was helpless, some soldiers came and took him to St. Mary's hospital in East St. Louis. He stayed there three days, and then left and went to the County hospital, St. Louis. Bullet had not been extracted. Was married. Had no children. Wife lives in Cairo, Illinois.

STORY OF WILLIAM GOULD

Does not know the place of his birth. Has been in East St. Louis since he was a babe. Is 34 years old and a teamster. Worked for the Hill Thomas Lime and Cement Company at Sixth and Walnut. Riot started near City Hall July 2nd. The mob came to the plant and took all the horses up some place on Broadway, then came back and set the place on fire. There were six other Negro men in the place besides himself. The mob was composed of about 75 men, women and children. 50 feet away, the men in the burning building ran out, and the mob fired volleys, but none of the men were injured except Mr. Gould, who was shot in the right leg. He was being cared for in the City Hospital of St. Louis. Had no children. Was married. Wife escaped harm. Mr. Gould sought refuge from the mob by hiding in some large weeds near the old rolling mill. The next day the soldiers came and took him to the County hospital in St. Louis.

STORY OF JAMES TAYLOR

The mob started at 2:05 A. M. At 4:15 they hanged two Negroes who were coming from work, to a telegraph pole and shot them to pieces. Saw them rush to cars and pull women off and beat them to death, and before they were quite dead, stalwart men jumped on their stomachs and finished them by trampling them to death. This was at the corner of Broadway and Collinville. The cars were crowded and moving, yet they jumped and pulled them off. Others they stuck to death with hat pins, sometimes picking out their eyes with them before they were quite dead.

An old woman between 70 and 80 years old, who had returned to her house to get some things, was struck almost to death by women, then men stamped her to death.

A colored store keeper at 8th and Broadway with his family was shot and wounded. The store was set on fire and they burned to death.

George Launders and Robert Mosely were burned to death at the Library Flats at 8th and Walnut.

Rev. James Taylor's wife fled to the Broadway theatre with her five children, but left there in safety before it was burned. She said when she left there were about twenty-five white women in the basement of the theatre where they had sought safety.

There were 10 or 12 men with Rev. Taylor when he made a dash for safety, several of them armed. Doesn't know if any of them escaped.

He saw a soldier hand his gun to one of the mob.

Had narrow escape as there were men in autos and on motor cycles who shot into the grass and bushes everywhere they thought anyone might be hiding. Came across woman also hiding, who was frightened almost to death. Swam the Cahokia River with her.

Men had fingers cut off by mob, then heads split open with axes.

Colored people acted bravely in spite of handicaps.

Mr. Taylor said, he was searched 29 times for fire arms.

Colored men were frequently beaten while enroute to and from packing houses, with no protest from companies or police.

"The first and last shot fired at me was by a soldier in uniform."

Will Morgan, employed at the B. & O. roundhouse,[34] saw the mob make the Negroes swim into the Cahokia River, then shoot them, one being killed instantly. The other managed to struggle back to shore, only to be stoned to death by children.

Soldiers surrounded the home of William Bass. One of them went inside and drove husband, wife and 9 children out. Asked Mr. Bass if they had any guns. He replied, that he had one, but that it was no good. "Have you any money?" he asked. Receiving a negative reply, he cursed and walked out.

MR. BUCHANAN'S STORY

Mr. Buchanan says: He did not see a single soldier, excepting Col. Tripp, do anything to protect the Negroes. He formed a hollow square and made the first arrest of about 200, composed of women and men. He also took a rope from the neck of a Negro whom the mob had attempted to hang. Mr. Buchanan saw them beat men down with revolvers and clubs; white men knock Negro women down and then the white women would finish by beating them to death or nearly so.

Every Negro man that he saw get out of Black Valley alive, the soldiers would march them to the police station, badly beaten though they were, and scarcely able to walk, with their hands raised in front of them and afraid to turn their heads. The mob threw bricks at their heads and bodies, because the soldiers had their bayonets pointed at either side of them. They did the women in the same way, excepting their hands were not raised in front of them. They were dodging around the soldiers to keep the mob from hitting them with bricks, stones and sticks. Their clothing was badly torn.

A man who worked for the Hill Thomas Lime & Cement Co. on 6th and Walnut streets, after the building had caught fire and was surrounded by the mob, called the manager up and said, "The whole place is on fire, and if I stay it is death. I am going to stay. Good-bye."

Mr. Buchanan escaped death by hiding in the Southern Illinois Bank where he was employed as a messenger. C. Reeb, president of the bank, procured an automobile and took Mr. Buchanan and family, escorted by soldiers, to St. Louis. Mr. Buchanan still works at the bank but is undecided about the future. He said, they were almost sure one of the employees of the bank, a clerk, was one of the rioters and that the president was doing all in his power to obtain the facts about it, and had told him, if he was guilty he would see to it that his punishment fit the crime.

STORY OF RACHEL FRANCES INGRAHAM

Has lived in town 17 years and owned the home in which she lived. During that time there had never been an arrest. The soldiers came to her house Monday, July 2nd., or thereabouts, and asked the whites about the reputation of the Negroes in that same block. Then the soldiers came to Mrs. Ingraham and asked her about the white people across the street. She began by saying, "You have asked me about them and I will answer you. They disturb my peace; they curse and use indecent, vile language, and I saw one white woman take a pitch fork and run in front of a woman to kill her, and she slammed the door in her face. The white woman who had the pitch fork said the woman she was attacking said, "These houses where these niggers are living ought to be burned and the niggers killed."

The soldiers then told Mrs. Ingraham that the white woman living across the street gave her a good name. On the fourth, some cans were thrown back of her toilet off of thrifty garden. The white woman who lives just above Mrs. Ingraham on the same side of the street said, "Just look at that old s.. of b.... standing over there daring us. We are going to kill him if it is the last thing we do."

Dan Sullivan, owner of the Banner Ice Plant, Pennsylvania avenue, said, if it had not been for him, they would have burned that corner up.

Mrs. Ingraham's husband had started down town to attend to some business, and some one came and told him not to go; that they were killing people, Tuesday, July 3rd., so he returned. Later, Mrs. Ingraham tried to take a street car to go over to St. Louis. At the same time, another Negro, named Maggie Love, attempted to get a Collinsville car with five or six children, all small. The conductor pushed all the colored people back and said they couldn't get on. "You're not allowed on here." Then Mrs. Love went back home with her children. She left for St. Louis. Her place is for sale and white people are occupying it. Mrs. Ingraham and lots of other colored women tried to get on another car, and the conductor told them, "You can't get on this car, and I don't want to take you down town to get killed." Then all the women returned to their homes. The next day Mrs. Ingraham got a wagon and went to St. Louis and was housed in the Municipal Lodging place for two days and one night. Mr. Ingraham never left East St. Louis.

Tuesday about 7 A. M., two soldiers and another citizen came to their home and asked if he had any guns. Her husband said, "No." One said with an oath, "Now **** if you've got any guns in here, you know where you'll go." The next day, Wednesday, soldiers came just about dark, broke the fasteners off the screen door and came in. The occupants, seven families in all, had gone. Two families remained. Mr. Ingraham broke the door open and left them open. When they were leaving their wagon, containing Mr. and Mrs. Tally and their children, on 10th street, as they passed, they were jeered at, saying, "Here comes some niggers. We'll get 'em." They were carrying car pins, strung on a rope, about 10 or 20 men and children, and the soldiers saw them and circled around their wagon and kept the mob from attacking them. The soldiers guarded until they got off the bridge.

A huckster, David Lambart, white, told her, "There is a lot of these Red Cross women in here giving testimony. Governor Lowden was also present. As soon as the soldiers leave, they will kill them all up."

On the next day we made a visit to East St. Louis. We found that some of the citizens who had left their homes a week ago, had gone back and were again trying to take up the thread of life. Dr. M. B. Hunter, one of the leading physicians, was also one of the county physicians, had left his home with the intention of not returning. His office had been burned up. His operating table, his surgical instruments and his handsome office furniture had all gone up in smoke. He owned a handsome two-story residence, but had decided for the present to leave his home. The Board of Supervisors, which had six colored men on it, met the week previous and had taken his county office from him. They had met two weeks before that and deposed N. W. Parden as Assistant State's Attorney. They were said to be searching for Dr. N. A.

Bundy, a prominent Negro dentist, who was said to have encouraged colored men to purchase guns for the protection of their homes. Dr. Bundy was nowhere to be found. His wife had also left town. Mr. Parden, who had been a prominent feature in politics, had also disappeared.

Dr. W. A. Wallace, editor of the Western Star and a general officer of the Zion Church, had had his entire printing plant burned. He has a beautiful home and six lovely children. He had come back to his home, and his wife said she felt secure, because a company of soldiers were encamped in the church across the street from her home.

The feeling seems general that there is no safety or security for the colored people. That the people who figured in the mob were only held in abeyance by the presence of the soldiers, and that when they were gone, the colored people would be no longer safe. Many having openly stated on the railroad trains, the street cars and the industrial plants, that if Negroes took their jobs, they had already done some killing and they expected to do more. An Associated Press dispatch of July 10th, 1917, from East St. Louis had the following:

"A man arrested by Capt. O. C. Smith, F Company, 4th Illinois Infantry, was released by the police, ostensibly "on order of the state's attorney." Captain Smith asserted that he heard the man say:

'I've killed my share of Negroes today. I have killed so many I am tired and somebody else can finish them.'

When Capt. Smith went to the police station yesterday to prefer a formal charge he found that the prisoner had been released."

CHAPTER IV

Such is the present state of unrest at this writing. No one has any feeling of certainty that anything will be done, either to punish the rioters or to make the lives and property of Negroes more secure permanently. For this reason, on our second return, at the meeting held at Quinn Chapel, Tuesday evening, July 14th, the following resolution was passed, accompanied by a memorial to the federal government:

CITIZEN'S COMMITTEE REPORT

We, the undersigned Citizens Committee, chosen at the Mass Meetings held under the auspices of the Negro Fellowship League and Bethel A. M. E. Church and directed to confer with Governor Lowden over the situation caused by the riot at East St. Louis and to continue the investigation previously begun, beg leave to make the following report:

Your Committee arrived in Springfield July 10th, the morning following the Mass Meeting at Bethel Church, and by appointment met Governor Lowden in the Capital Building where our conference was held at eleven o'clock. There were present also Adj. Gen. Dickson who participated in the conference, also Col. John R. Marshall who had spent some time in East St. Louis soon after the riot.

The express purpose of the committee was:

First, to call the attention of the Governor to the fact that thousands of citizens of East St. Louis were exiled from their homes and were the beneficiaries of charity in St. Louis, Missouri, and to request that some provision be made by the Illinois authorities for their protection and maintenance. Governor Lowden took prompt action upon this matter. In our presence he called up the Red Cross officials at East St. Louis and directed that immediate attention be given to this situation and then assured the committee that the city of St. Louis would not be required further to take care of citizens of Illinois.

Second, to call to the attention of the Governor the manifest inefficiency and indifference of the Illinois militia, during the time of the mob—the possible connivance of members of the militia with the mob and to request that investigation be made of the work done by the militia to the end that a court martial be ordered if justified by the facts.

Upon these serious charges which the committee supported by newspaper reports and experiences related to members of the committee by victims of the mob the conference was frank and earnest; both sides desiring to determine upon the best way to fix responsibility upon all who aided and abetted the mob. So far as the militia was concerned the Governor gave his assurance that the charges would be fully investigated and if proper, a court martial would be ordered. Since the conference a court martial has been ordered, although we regret that no member of the Eighth Regiment was named thereon.

Third, to demand for the victims of East St. Louis, many of them refugees from home and work, the full protection of the law in the enjoyment of their lives, the protection of their property and the right to earn their living by honest toil. To the justice of this demand Governor Lowden gave his hearty assent and declared that all citizens of Illinois should have the fullest protection of the law if it required the exercise of all the power of the State. But your committee from the investigation believes that the same bitter vindictive spirit which manifests itself in the awful deeds of July 3rd still exists in a dangerous degree in East St. Louis today and that no earnest and effective measures will be taken by public officials to curb that spirit or prosecute known murderers who took part in the mob. Our belief is that security for life and property will come only through action of Federal authority by Congressional investigation and a Federal Grand Jury at East St. Louis. Believing this, your committee has prepared a Memorial which we respectfully submit for your consideration.

W. D. COOK, D. D., Chairman.
H. A. WATKINS.
L. W. WASHINGTON.
MRS. WM. FARROW.
IDA B. WELLS BARNETT, Secretary.

MEMORIAL

TO THE CONGRESS OF THE UNITED STATES, WASHINGTON, D.C.

The undersigned, a Citizens Committee, chosen at three Mass Meetings held by Chicago Colored Citizens interested in the protection of life and property of colored citizens of the State of Illinois, beg leave to submit this Memorial, praying for action on the part of the Federal Government in our behalf.

We plead for thousands of Colored Citizens of East St. Louis, who for more than six weeks prior to July 3rd last not only lived in immediate danger of mob violence, destruction of property and lynching, but later—many of them became the victims of the most deliberate, wanton and barbarous massacre that has blotted the pages of American history. It was a very orgy of inhuman butchery during which more than fifty colored men, women and children were beaten with bludgeons, stoned, shot, drowned, hanged or burned to death—all without any effective interference on the part of the police, sheriff or military authorities.

The riot was no sudden outburst of passion. It was a combination of a publicly declared determination on the part of white laborers to drive colored laborers from work or kill them. There was no provocation by acts of lawless blacks, no drunkenness on the part of the whites—nothing but the deadly vindictiveness of labor trouble accentuated by hatred toward the Negro.

The dangerous situation was well known to the Mayor and chief of police of East St. Louis; to the sheriff of St. Claire County, and on two separate occasions the impending danger was called to the attention of the Governor of the State. A brief outburst of fury on the 28th day of May was quelled, but the fires of race hatred smoldered and grew in intensity until July 3rd when mob frenzy sated itself by the burning of hundreds of humble homes and the unspeakable butchery of scores of victims whose only offense was their effort to earn their bread by honest toil. White men, white women and white children made the mob—laughing, jesting and gloating as they beat, tortured and burned their pleading victims to death.

An eye witness, Mr. Carlos F. Hurd of St. Louis, Mo., wrote and published a part of what he saw in The St. Louis Post-Dispatch; an excerpt from which account is appended hereto

> The victims of the mob in whose behalf Chicago Colored Citizens plead and for whom all humane people must plead—were citizens of the United States. Because Germany put to death American citizens upon the high seas—fewer in number than the mob killed in East St. Louis—the Nation entered into a world war that will cost billions of treasure and perhaps a million lives. Shall not the Stars and Stripes protect American citizens at home as well as upon the high seas?

We appeal through Congress to the Nation. The indifference and inefficiency of City, County and military authorities and their apparent connivance with the mob which made this awful tragedy possible, forbid our reliance upon our local authorities for security of life and property. One hundred and twenty-seven members of the mob, arrested while rioting, when brought into court were discharged, the State's Attorney publicly declaring there could be no successful prosecution. Justice can be meted out to the guilty and protection for the innocent can come only through a Federal Grand Jury impaneled by a Judge who knows his duty and dares to do it.

As American Citizens our lives are subject to the Nation's call, and at no call have we faltered or failed. As American Citizens we call to the Nation to save our lives; to that call will the Nation falter or fail?

In memory of the slaughtered dead and their bereaved ones—in behalf of the thousands made homeless and penniless by fire, and for the security of life and property—to exiled thousands of East St. Louis citizens we plead for Congressional investigation and appropriate action on the part of the Federal Government, and we bespeak for this Memorial the earnest consideration of the Congress of the United States.

This memorial was sent to Senators Lawrence Y. Sherman and James Hamilton Lewis, also to Congressman Martin B. Madden. As a result of which steps have already been taken to have the Department of Justice act.

CHAPTER V

East St. Louis, after the mischief had been done, through its Chamber of Commerce and committee of business men, took steps to bring back the thousands of Negro workmen who had been driven away by the brutalities described in these pages. Orders were given to let no more pass over the bridge and men had to get permits to go to their own homes or move their effects of Friday, the fourth day after the riot. The Post Dispatch of that day said:

"All except five of the twelve thousand refugees on the Missouri side declined today to accept the invitation of the East St. Louis Chamber of Commerce to return to work in the packing and manufacturing plants."

The Chicago Herald, July 6th, 1917, had the following article from the pen of Jack Lait, its well known correspondent:

East St. Louis, Ill., July 6—Mrs. Ida Wells Barnett of Chicago, one of the foremost colored women in America, left here tonight for her home.

"The Negroes and law-abiding Whites are in the hands of a conspiracy, unquestionably well financed and closely organized, a coalition of the labor unions of the North and the manufacturing and planters of the South," she declared.

"The South is almost bankrupt because the Negroes are leaving. In the North the control of labor unions is being torn away from the coming of competing, unorganized colored labor.

"Money is being spent like water to drive the Negro back where he came from and murder, arson, intimidation propaganda and scandal are being stirred up as the weapons of this infamous plot."

WILL NOT RETURN

Mrs. Barnett said that the Negroes will not return to East St. Louis, in spite of the sugar-coated invitation of the employers and the sincere promise of safety from the state authorities.

"When they hang at least one of the men who butchered our babies and strung up our decent men and bludgeoned our women and burned our homes and threw our wounded into the flames, then the Negroes might come back. But until some such symbol of lasting efficiency and sincerity on the part of the whites is revealed, our people will not return to this hotbed of hatred and crime."

Today's results verified her statement. Exactly five Negroes answered the call to return. Out of about 12,000 not half a dozen accepted the homecoming appeal.

ARMS BY ARMFUL

The work of disarming the remaining blacks went on. One after another the militia groups pulled up at the city hall and the soldiers lugged in armfuls of muskets, carbines, sixshooters, razors and bowie knives.

All the afternoon, the Chamber of Commerce and the Associated Merchants met in a mass at the council chambers and at the end signed a remarkable statement and set of resolutions, which Mayor Mollman was ordered to sign first.

He meekly drew his signature to the open, and thereby official, confession to the world of the city's shame, the guilt of its police, the inefficiency, inactivity and hostility of the first contingent of state troops.

The demand was incorporated that the police system be reorganized and that the guilty be fully punished.

All day long a star chamber inquest from which newspaper men and the public were rigidly barred went on.

Its purpose is not as secret as its methods—it is piling up an alibi for the white race as it is typified here, a record to back up the comfortable theory that the Negroes started the trouble willfully and are responsible for all the ghastly consequences.

Five white men and ten Negroes were fined $200 today on charges of carrying concealed weapons. Unable to pay the fines, they were locked up in the County jail.

East St. Louis has not been entirely idle in the effort to convince the public that there is a desire to punish the criminals.

Since this horrible thing took place, the Grand Jury of St. Clair county has brought indictments against 105 persons. It reported in the daily papers as follows:

Cornelius Hickey, lieutenant of police of East St. Louis, who was acting as chief the night of the massacre, is held on a charge of conspiracy.

Richard Brockway, an investigator for the Belleville and East St. Louis railroad, is indicted for conspiracy, riot and assault to kill.

Clark C. Fancher, known as "Tobe" Fancher, former policeman of East St. Louis, is held for assault with intent to kill. The indictment against him recites that he deliberately drew his revolver and fired four shots at a helpless Negro who was severely wounded and was thought to have only a few hours to live. The Negro is convalescing.

ONE WOMAN IS NAMED

One woman is indicted for assault with intent to kill. Her name is withheld for the present. The indictment charges that one of her favorite stunts that terrible night was stamping the heels of her French slippers in the faces of prostrate Negroes.

Several of those indicted are included in many different indictments, a few of the ringleaders, it is understood, being held for nearly all the crimes alleged to have been committed during the riots.

One man is being held for burning with the purpose to defraud, and out of this attempt to collect fire insurance he also is caught for arson.

SUMMARY OF JURY WORK

Summed up, the work of the Grand Jury follows:

Nine indictments for conspiracy naming thirty-three persons.

Eleven indictments for conspiracy, naming sixty-four persons.

Five indictments for arson, naming twenty-seven persons.

Thirteen indictments for rioting, naming sixty-nine persons.

Twenty-six indictments for assault to murder, naming sixty-three persons.

One indictment for malicious mischief, naming four persons.

Two indictments for burglary, naming four persons.

One indictment for burning for purpose of defrauding, naming one person.

One man has also been convicted and sentenced to five years imprisonment and it is asserted that all who are indicted will be punished.

Mayor Mollman has also been indicted on two counts. The test will come when these men are put on trial.

But up to date no punishment has been meted out to the militia who are responsible for the mob because they did not quell it. Carlos Hurd's account states that he found a corporal's guard of them who had just come from where the firemen were working and he told them of the lynching of the Negro. "I do not know that they could have done anything, but I do know they did not try. Most of the men in uniform were frankly fraternizing with the men in the street."

Thursday, July 5th, the following editorial appeared in the Post-Despatch of St. Louis.

THE EAST SIDE ATROCITIES

Gov. Lowden need not go far to find evidence of the utter failure of the major part of the forces of the Illinois National Guard to do their duty in stopping wholesale murder and arson in East St. Louis last Monday.

Carlos Hurd of the Post-Dispatch staff, who was an eyewitness of the atrocities on the East Side, told a plain circumstantial story of the outrage he witnessed. The assaults and murders were cold-blooded, deliberate and incredibly brutal. They were not the mob infuriated against particular offenders. They were the work of groups of men and women who sought out and burned out the Negroes and then shot, beat, kicked and hanged them. The work was done in a spirit of flippant, relentless barbarism. Mr. Hurd described it as a man-hunt.

Others who corroborated this testimony called it rabbit-hunting and rat-catching. Nothing like it in unmitigated cruelty has occurred before on American soil. It can be likened only to the fiendish atrocities of Turks in Armenia or in the pograms against the Jews incited by the Russian Black Hundred,[35] in which help-less Jews were smoked or dragged from their homes to be beaten, outraged or murdered on the streets. The black skin, without regard to age, sex or innocence, was the mark for slaughter.

All the impartial witnesses agree that the police were either indifferent or encouraged the barbarities, and that the major part of the National Guard was indifferent or inactive. No organized effort was made to protect the Negroes or disperse the murdering groups. The lack of frenzy and of a large infuriated mob made the task easy. Ten determined officers could have prevented most of the outrages. One hundred men acting with authority and vigor might have prevented any outrage.

The stain cannot be wiped from the record of Illinois, but the State may be vindicated by punishment of the officers responsible for the conduct of the guardsmen; and by the vigorous prosecution of the murder leaders.

East St. Louisans have a duty to perform in looking into the conduct of their own city government which permitted the trouble to culminate in these atrocities. They should find out the cause of the fatal weakness which encouraged the race riots and paralyzed the police while innocent men, women and children were shot, burned and tortured. The future of the city which in point of growth and prosperity is a marvel, should prompt thorough action by law-abiding citizens.

CHAPTER VI

Such is the history in part of one of the most dastardly crimes ever committed in the name of civilization, on defenseless black men, women and children. That the State of Lincoln, Logan and Grant[36]—three names made famous by their fight to give liberty to the black man—should furnish this black page for history, is the shame of all true American citizens. The world is at war because the race prejudice of one nation tries to dominate other nations. The race prejudice of the United States asks Americans of black skins to keep an inferior place and when these Negroes ask an equal opportunity for life, liberty and the pursuit of happiness, they are lynched, burned alive, disfranchised and massacred! Wherever a black man turns in this land of the free and home of the brave—in industry, in civic endeavor, in political councils in the ranks of Christians (?)—this hydra headed monster confronts him; dominates, oppresses and murders him!

This time it was done in the name of labor! The Negro accepted the opportunity made by the scarcity of labor in the North to leave the South, which has fattened on his labor and yet kept him in serfdom for fifty years of freedom. He was glad of the chance to get better wages, but even more glad to come where he could educate his children and be a man. But the labor unions which have this country by the throat, which paralyze its industries, dynamite its buildings and murder men at their own sweet will—refuse to let Negroes work with them and murder them if they work anyway, in what they call "white men's jobs."

In East St. Louis these labor forces had the aid of the civil authorities, the police and the state militia, in the work of murdering over two hundred Negroes and destroying three million dollars worth of property. Unless this outrage is punished, no American citizen's life, liberty or property is safe in any state.

In the present state of our National development, the only remedy, for the lynching and rioting evil of the American nation is to make it a federal crime. Public sentiment which has encouraged lynchings by silence or by sensational newspapers accounts must be aroused to see the evil to the whole American Nation. It is an awful commentary on our country's brand of Democracy—that aside from a few newspaper editorials—no persons in this country have spoken out against this black stain save Theodore Roosevelt and a minister of the gospel in a sermon preached in St. Louis, Mo., the Sunday following the massacre.

It rests then with the Negroes everywhere to stand their ground and sell their lives as dearly as possible when attacked; to work as a unit, demanding punishment for rioters, protection for workers, and liberty for all the citizens in our country. It is for the Negro to say whether they will unite their forces to make this country safe for the residence of any Negro anywhere he desires to live in it. It is for them to show whether we can bring sufficient influence to bear to see that the militia of Illinois, for whose maintenance we all pay taxes, will be courtmartialed for the wicked and wanton murder of hundreds of innocent men, women and children of our race, whom they failed to protect in that awful orgy of human butchery, which took place in East St. Louis, Illinois, on Monday, July 2nd, 1917.

THE ARKANSAS RACE RIOT

In this pamphlet Wells-Barnett explores the events behind the massacre of between 100 and 200 black sharecroppers in Elaine, Arkansas, on September 30, 1919. Local officials maintained that the armed posse of hundreds of white men who terrorized and killed African Americans in Elaine had been organized to quell a black uprising, and they went on to arrest 285 blacks in the aftermath of the violence. But the organization of a Progressive Farmers and Household Union among the sharecroppers seems to have been the major trigger for the conflict. The union members sought fair prices for their crops at a moment when cotton prices were at an all-time high—an initiative that local planters were determined to defeat. Wells-Barnett gathered information about the riot by traveling to Arkansas and sneaking into the state prison in Helena to visit the sharecroppers who were awaiting trial there. She accomplished this feat by going in with prisoners' wives and mothers—she posed as a visiting cousin from St. Louis. As a result, *The Arkansas Race Riot* includes the prisoners' testimony as well as lengthy excerpts from the trials of the accused. Ultimately, Wells-Barnett's investigation and protests helped lead to a Supreme Court decision to release the prisoners after they had spent years on death row (although the NAACP lawyers who defended the men played a far more important role in their eventual release than Wells-Barnett did).

SOURCE: Ida B. Wells-Barnett, *The Arkansas Race Riot* (Chicago: Ida B. Wells-Barnett, 1920).

THE ELAINE (ARK.) RIOT

The press dispatches of October 1, 1919, heralded the news that another race riot had taken place the night before in Elaine, Ark., and that it was started by Negroes who had killed some white officers in an altercation.

Later on the country was told that the white people of Phillips County had risen against the Negroes who started this riot and had killed many of them, and that this orgy of bloodshed was not stopped until United States soldiers from Camp Pike had been sent to the scene of the trouble.

Columns were printed telling of an organization among Negro farmers in this little burg who were banded together for the purpose of killing all the white people, the organization being known as the Farmers' Household Union.[37] As a result of these charges over one hundred Negro farmers and laborers, men and women, were arrested and jailed in Helena, Ark., the county seat of Phillips County. One month later they were indicted and tried for murder in the first degree and the jury found them guilty after six minutes of deliberation. Twelve were sentenced to die in the electric chair—six on December 27th and six on January 2nd, and seventy-five of them were sent to the penitentiary on sentences ranging from five to twenty-one years!

Several national bodies among colored people, notably the Equal Rights League, sent letters of protest to Governor Brough, but the press dispatches reported that the governor refused to interfere, because he believed the men had received justice. Thereupon, the Chicago branch of the Equal Rights League sent telegrams to Senators Medill McCormick and Curtis, chairmen on committee on race riots and Congressman Martin B. Madden asking the federal government to take some action to protect these men and see that they got justice.

The People's Movement, Chicago, Ill., on December 7th unanimously passed the following resolution offered by the writer and sent it to Governor Brough:

Whereas, The press dispatches bring the news that twelve Negroes have been condemned in Helena, Ark., to die in the electric chair for the alleged killing of five white men after deliberation of eight minutes by the jury which found them guilty, and

Whereas, It would appear that this riot arose over a determination of those Negroes to form a union for the protection of their cotton crop; therefore, be it

Resolved, That we demand of Governor Brough that he exert his influence to see that those men are given a new trial or chance to present their cases to the Supreme Court. Hundreds of Negroes have left Arkansas because of unjust treatment, and we pledge ourselves to use our influence to bring thousands away if those twelve men die in the electric chair. Arkansas needs our labor but we will never rest till every Negro leaves the state unless those men are given justice.

Very soon thereafter the governor of Arkansas called a conference of white and colored citizens in Little Rock, Ark. He learned from them that his own colored people were dissatisfied and wanted these men to have a chance in the Supreme Court. He promised to exert his influence to secure this and appointed an inter-racial committee to adjudicate matters between the races.

The Chicago Defender of that same week, December 13th, contained a letter of appeal by the writer to colored people throughout the country to raise funds to help these condemned men carry their cases to the Arkansas Supreme Court, also to the United States Supreme Court if necessary. Almost immediately following its appearance, donations were received by the writer from our people, and the tone of the letters was splendid in the expressed determination to help these poor men get justice. Other organizations to help were formed, lawyers were engaged, a stay of execution granted and proceedings begun for an appeal to the Supreme Court of Arkansas. Six of the men had been sentenced to be electrocuted December 27th and six on January 2nd.

During this time the following letter was received by the author of this pamphlet:

Little Rock, Ark., Dec. 30, 1919.

Dear Mrs. Wells-Barnett:

This is one of the 12 mens which is sentenced to death speaking to you on this day and thanking you for your great speech you made throughout the country in the Chicago Defender paper. So I am thanking you to the very highest and hope you will do all you can for your collord race. Because we are innercent men, we was not handle with justice at all in Phillips County Court. It is prejudice that the white people had agence we Negroes. So I thank God that thro you, our Negroes are looking into this truble, and thank the city of Chicago for what it did to start things and hopen to hear from you all soon. Now Mrs. Wells if you have any mail for us send it to ——————— if there be enny secret in it. So I will close with much love from all to Chicago, Ill. Please pray for us, I am a Christian man. Please Chicago let us hear from you at enny time.

In response to this cry from Macedonia, the writer took the train for Little Rock, Ark., went to the address given in the letter and talked with some of the wives of the twelve, then went to the penitentiary and spent the day interviewing those men. I wish every one whose contribution enabled me to make this investigation could have seen the light which came on the faces of these men when I told them who I was! Again they sent thanks to every one who had responded to my Defender letter of December 13, 1919. They had been in prison in Helena, Ark., since the first week in October; they had been beaten many times and left for dead while there, given electric shocks, suffocated with drugs, and suffered every cruelty and torment at the hands of their jailers to make them confess to a conspiracy to kill white people. Besides this a mob from the outside tried to lynch them. During all that two months of terrible treatment and farcical trial, no word of help had come from their own people until a copy of the Chicago Defender, December 13th, fell into their hands!

No wonder that during this time of terror they composed and sung in heart-breaking tones this song:

I Stand and Wring My Hands and Cry
By Ed Ware.

I used to have some loving friends to walk and talk with me,
But now I am in trouble, they have turned their backs on me;
They just laugh me to scorn and will not come nigh,
And I just stand and wring my hands and cry.

Chorus.

And I just stand and wring my hands and cry,
And I just stand and wring my hands and cry, Oh Lord!
Sometimes I feel like I ain't got no friends at all,
And I just stand and wring my hands and cry.

Sometimes I like to be in company and again I want to be alone,
With my enemies all crushing me and confusion in my home;
I then fold my arms and look to the skies,
And I just stand and wring my hands and cry. —Chorus.

My heart is overwhelmed with sorrow,
My eyes are melted down in tears;
But I have called to the God of Heaven,
And I know He always hears. —Chorus.

This they sang in the most mournful tones ever heard. Their wives and mothers and children were there spending Sunday with them, and talking through the bars, trying to encourage them. They sang and prayed together and were so grateful to the warden for his kind treatment of them. They exhorted each other to be faithful to the end, expressed their innocence of wrong-doing and readiness to die if it was God's will they should do so. I told them to pray to live and have faith to believe their God would open their prison doors as were those of Paul and Silas and to pray and believe that they would go free; that He would work on the hearts of those who held the scales of justice and to believe those prayers would be answered. Thousands of persons on the outside were praying for them and doing what they could to help, and for them to have faith to believe that the great state of Arkansas would undo the wrong that had been done to them. I said they should pray daily that God would give the authorities the wisdom to realize the wrong that had been done, and the courage to right that wrong. I earnestly believe such prayers will strengthen the hands of the white people of the state who want to do the right thing.

CHAPTER II

Their Crime

The terrible crime these men had committed was to organize their members into a union for the purpose of getting the market price for their cotton, to buy land of their own and to employ a lawyer to get settlements of their accounts with their white landlords. Cotton was selling for more than ever before in their lives. These Negroes believed their chance had come to make some money for themselves and get out from under the white landlord's thumb.

Phillips County got plenty Negro labor to till the land and they toiled with a will to raise the cotton crops of 1919, which would make them independent at last. Most of these men and their families had worked for years "on shares" and had come out every year in debt or just barely out. The price of cotton had been low, and the landlord who furnished the land and supplies saw to it that the Negro laborer remained in his clutches from year to year. Always the owner or agent who rents the land owns a general store or opens an account for the tenant where he must trade and pay the prices charged or get no food and supplies for himself family or hired hands. The season begins in March and lasts till the cotton is picked and ginned in October and November. So that for the period of nine months the cropper is dependent on the landlord for supplies. He receives no money until cotton is sold and settlements are made.

When cotton is ready to be marketed, the landlord simply tells the cropper what his bill for the year is and what he will allow him for his crop. As a rule the bill for supplies is almost always greater than the amount due the hardworking Negro and his family, and he has not been able to help himself. He must stay on the farm another year or be turned adrift to go to work on another farm under the same conditions. If he leaves in the debt the laws of the state make it a penal offense. Thousands of Negro farmers have worked under this economic slavery for years.

The colored men who went to war for this democracy returned home determined to emancipate themselves from the slavery which took all a man and his family could earn, left him in debt, gave him no freedom of action, no protection for his life or property, no education for his children, but did give him Jim Crow cars, lynching and disfranchisement. If they could get all the farmers in that neighborhood to join an organization they could employ a lawyer to look after settlements at the end of the year; they could create a treasury and buy a tract of land for themselves; they could get all the farmers to hold their cotton for higher prices.

Is it any wonder the idea spread like wild-fire? The Progressive Farmers and Household Union of America had been revived the year before, and when Robert L. Hill came among them with the plan the meetings were crowded with men and women bringing their money to join. There is not a word in the constitution and by-laws of this order about conspiracy to murder white people, as will be seen by the reader of this book.

It is most interesting to note that this union was first organized under Act of Congress in 1865, fifty-five years ago; was revised and reorganized in 1897; and revised and applied by Robert L. Hill and others in 1918. It was ratified and incorporated under orders of the Supreme Court of Arkansas in 1918 at Little Rock, Ark. The men who are now awaiting the verdict of the Supreme Court on their sentence of electrocution were working under a charter permitting them to organize granted by that same Supreme Court!

Robert Hill had organized under this constitution a lodge at Hoop Spur and one at Elaine, Ark. The white farmers, land owners and cotton brokers heard about those meetings and when the following circular was sent out by the union naturally they became uneasy and decided to take some action:

DON'T GET EXCITED

Hold your cotton until the World's Cotton Conference is over October 13, 14, 15, 16.

Let us see what Uncle Sam means. Uncle Sam can help you when nobody else can.

WORLD'S COTTON CONFERENCE

There will be more than 1,800 delegates to the World's Cotton Conference in New Orleans, October 13-16. Not only will there be delegates there from all parts of the south, but all parts of the world. Hundreds of delegates from twenty countries abroad are now on the way. There was a time that ginners begged the farmers to haul away cotton seed and get them out the way, but today the cotton seed industry has reached to more than $4,000,000,000 annually. This will enter largely into this conference showing the growing needs for cotton seed products. For the foreign delegates it is agreed that landing on American soil be made in New York and then trains made up to convey them to New Orleans from New York City.

That was all, but it was a Declaration on Economic Independence, and the first united blow for economic liberty struck by the Negroes of the South! That was their crime and it had to be avenged.

But why was this movement a crime? Because "cotton is king" of the agricultural products of the South. With cotton selling for 45 to 50 cents per pound—the highest price since the Civil War— it meant that Negroes were in a fair way to become independent and it was not to the interest of the white landowners to let them do so. Ed Ware, one of the most prosperous men there, had already offered two bales of cotton for sale. Ware was secretary of the Hoop Spur lodge, and he had already refused to sell for 24 cents per pound, or 33 cents. He was then refused a settlement of his account at the store. He had gone to Helena to give a lawyer his case. On his return home rumors were flying that the white people were going to lynch him for doing this. This was Saturday, three days before the riot.

The United States is the greatest cotton producing country in the world. Of the 17,410,000 bales of cotton produced in 1918 in the whole world 11,818,000 bales came from the United States. With the exception of the little grown in California, these twelve million bales—more than two-thirds of all the cotton raised in the world—were produced by the Negro labor of the South! Without the Negro there would be no cotton. The South wants the Negro to produce this cotton but not to share in its benefits.

With cotton selling at 45 and 50 cents a pound, a bale of cotton averaging 500 pounds would bring $250. Five bales of cotton would bring $1,250. No padding of accounts nor inflation of prices could use all that money for supplies and leave the Negro in debt and subjection. Another way must be found to do this, and keep the Negro's wealth from him.

CHAPTER III

The Riot

Tuesday, September 30th, the people gathered in their church at Hoop Spur to hold a meeting of the lodge. The place was crowded with men, women and children. Those who hadn't paid dues and become members were anxious to do so. A peaceful law-abiding hard-working group in their own church, attending strictly to their own business, about two hundred of them. Suddenly at 11 o'clock at night without warning a volley of shots are fired into this free assembly. The lights go out and those who are not killed or wounded get away as quickly as possible. One white man, W. A. Adkins, is killed out in front of this church, whether by the men he is with or the guards out front will probably never be known.

No one knows how many of these peaceable unoffending Negroes were killed by this volley as the persons who did this dastardly deed burned the church down the next day so no bullet holes in walls, broken windows or dead bodies of Negroes would show the conspiracy of whites to kill black people. Had this been a conspiracy of Negroes to kill whites, they would not have started in by killing their own members, break up their own meeting, nor burn their own church. They would have been in or near some white assembly hall or home working mischief. There would be more evidence of the conspiracy to kill whites than the single body of W. A. Adkins found dead beside the automobile which brought him to the Negro church to disturb a Negro meeting and commit murder. Some excuse was necessary for their action, and the persons capable of planning and executing such a terrible deed were not above furnishing that excuse for their action. Or Will Adkins may have been killed accidentally by the men he was with. One of the Negro guards at the church declares he heard one of the white men say, "We are killing our own men."

It is because that one white man was killed in front of the Negro church at 11 o'clock that night that Frank Moore and eleven other Negroes are in the Arkansas penitentiary condemned to die. Nothing in the record shows he had any business there; he was clearly a trespasser, for every Negro in that church agrees that without warning—while they were all in the church—a volley of bullets was fired in among them. Of those white men who were firing into the church without cause Will Adkins was one. If it had been clearly proven that he was killed by a bullet fired by the Negro guards on the outside, it was because of and in response to an attack made on the church they were there to guard. Nowhere in this land would an unprejudiced jury sentence a man to death for guarding and protecting his property and loved ones from unprovoked attack!

The other white man mentioned in the record, Clinton Lee, met his death next day while he and hundreds of other white men were chasing and murdering every Negro they could find, driving them from their homes and stalking them in the woods and fields as men hunt wild beasts. They were finishing up the job they began the night before. As a group of Negroes ran before the mob two shots were fired from a rifle one of them carried, and Clinton Lee fell dead. For his death five of the twelve men sentenced are awaiting death by electrocution. Yet no man in all this "land of the free and home of the brave" will say that a man is not justified in firing back on other men who are after him armed with shotguns to take his life!

Both these white men for whose death these men were found guilty of murder in the first degree and sentenced to death were in the attacking parties with crowds of other white men. If there was any conspiracy, it would seem to be among white men to kill and drive away Negroes.

Why? The Negroes had made their crop. Every one of the two hundred Negroes condemned and killed had picked or was gathering in his year's crop of cotton and corn! The labor needed to plow the ground, plant the seed chop the cotton and "lay it by" had been furnished by their toil. Some of the landlords drove the Negroes off the land after this had been done by refusing to feed them longer and forcing them to leave their crop before the cotton was ready to pick. But cotton was now ready to pick and some of it had been picked by October 1st. It had been ginned and was ready for market and the Negro due to get the reward of his toil and white men determined to reap the value of it. What they could not do lawfully they did unlawfully with the aid of public sentiment and the mob. They are now enjoying the result of these Negoes' labor, while the Negroes are condemned to die or stay in prison twenty-one years. The wives and children of the white men who committed this crime and robbed these Negroes are riding in automobiles, living in comfortable homes, enjoying good food and fine clothes. The wives and children of these Negroes are wandering from place to place, homeless, penniless, ragged and starving, depending on public charity.

CHAPTER IV

Their Case Stated

In this chapter is given the statements of these earnest, hard-working God-fearing men whose only ambition was to be good citizens and get on in the world. Ed Ware, who was secretary of the Progressive Farmers' Household Union, had 120 acres in cultivation. He owned a Ford car and while the crops were laid by, drove his car daily to Helena, thirty miles away, and made money carrying passengers. He says:

ED WARE'S STATEMENT

"On September 26, 1919, my merchants, Jackson & Longnecker, came to buy some cotton I had just ginned and offered me 24 cents and then 33 cents for it. I refused to take it, and they said they were going to take the cotton at that price. I rejected their offer and said I'd take my cotton to Helena to sell. They then said they were going to mob me, but I was warned about it. So when they tried to fool me into their store so they could get me I refused to go in and kept out of their way. On the 29th I went to Helena and gave my business over to an attorney so I would not have to deal with them. At the same time I went to see what cotton was selling at and found that Woolen & Davidson were paying 44½ cents for short cotton."

About the trouble which happened the next night Ed Ware says:

"On the 30th of September, 1919, we met in a regular meeting and while sitting attending to our business about 11 o'clock that night, some automobiles were heard to stop north of the church and in just a few minutes they began shooting in the church and did kill some people in the church (which they set afire and burned them up in it the next morning). Then about 150 armed men came over to my place and before they got over there the news reached us stating that they were coming over there to kill me and all of the other Negroes that belonged to that union and then I began to look out for myself. I went out in my field about 200 yards from my house, sitting there talking to two other men about the threats that I had just received. I happened to look up and I saw a Negro by the name of Kid Collins running down the road in front of my house and followed by a crowd of white men. The Negro and all of the white men were armed with guns and they almost surrounded my house when the old man, Charley Robinson, and Isaac Bird and myself began to run. The old man was crippled and could not run and they shot him down and took him up from there and carried him and put him in my wife's bed and let him stay there four days. Then they took the country broadcast and began to shoot down everything they saw like a Negro. I lost all of my household goods and 121 acres of cotton and corn, two mules, one horse, one Jersey cow and one farm wagon and all farming tools and harness and eight head of hogs, 135 chickens and one Ford car. This is a true report."

E. D. HICKS' STATEMENT

"On October 1, 1919, after the trouble the night before in the church, they were after all the colored people to kill them, so we ran into the swamp. I had 100 acres of land, rented from Stanley and Moore Bros. I had a good crop of cotton and corn on the whole place. My brother, Frank Hicks, worked about thirty acres of it in cotton and corn and I worked the rest. I bought four mules and wagon and farming tools and all of my wife's clothes and they took all that from me in that trouble. Now this is a true report from Frank and E. D. Hicks."

JOSEPH FOX'S AND ALBERT GILES' STATEMENT

"On October 1st we saw about 150 armed white men coming to our house and we left the house and ran on down into the woods and carried our sister down in the woods with us and they came and hunted us out and they shot at the women and killed three men and wounded Albert Giles and Alfred Banks and Joe Fox. They were so thick around us, they killed one white man, and we heard them say, "We are killing our own men," and they went to our house and took everything that was there. We do not know how the shooting started that night, because we were not there. We got the news the next day that they were going to kill every Negro they saw."

JOHN MARTIN'S STATEMENT

"I was at Hoop Spur Church that night to lodge meeting. I do know that four or five automobiles full of white men came about fifty yards from the church and put the lights out, then started shooting in the church with about 200 head of men, women and children. I was on the outside of the church and saw this for myself. Then I ran after they started firing in on the church. I don't know if anybody got killed at all. I went home and stayed home that night, then the white people was sending word that they was going to kill all the black people, then I run back in the woods and hid two days then the soldiers came then, I made it to them. I was carried to Elaine and put in the school house and I was there eight days. Then I was brought to Helena and put in jail and whipped near to death and was put in an electric chair to make me lie on other Negroes. It was not the union that brought this trouble; it was our crops. They took everything I had, twenty-two acres of cotton, three acres of corn. All that was taken from me and my people. Also all my household goods. Clothes and all. All my hogs, chickens and everything my people had. I was whipped twice in jail. These white people know that they started this trouble. This union was only for a blind. We were threatened before this union was there to make us leave our crops."

ALFRED BANKS' STATEMENT

"I was at Hoop Spur church on that night to union meeting and do know that the white people came about fifty yards of that church and got out of the cars and started to shoot in the church on the Negroes. It was four or five cars of white men. I was on the outside of the church when these white men stopped and put the car lights out, then started to shoot into the church. Then I ran with some of the rest of the people. I went home and stayed in the bushes until the soldiers came. Then I was taken to Elaine and put in the schoolhouse and I was there about six days. I was brought to Helena jail and whipped near to death to make me lie on myself and the others. I was whipped three times in jail, also was put in an electric chair in Helena jail and shocked. I have the scars on my body to show now. Now I am sentenced to death. I did not kill anybody. The white people started the trouble themselves. We all were driven from our crops before this trouble started. Nine families had been driven from the place I was on before this trouble started and several more were driven off other places. It was not the union made this trouble; it was for our crops. I was working thirty-two acres of cotton and eight acres of corn. All that was taken from me. Also one acre truck patch. All my hogs and all my household goods from us. All my clothes were taken and burned up. All I did in the time of this trouble was run to save my life and others. I saw when these white men came and started their dirt in that church."

WILLIAM WARDLOW'S STATEMENT

"I do know that it was four or five automobile loads of white men did come, about forty-five or fifty yards from Hoop Spur church on the night of September 30, 1919, where we were in union service that night and did shoot and kill some of the Negroes. I was out in front of the church in the road when these men came up in these cars and started shooting in the church on the other people both women, men and children. When the white men started that work I broke and ran away. I saw them when they made the first shot. I went in the woods and stayed all night. I stayed until the soldiers came, then I came to them. I had eight women and children with me to hide, keep them from getting killed. The white people sent word all through the county that they were coming to kill all the Negroes they could find. The soldiers took me to Elaine and I was put in the school-house and they kept me there seven days. Then they brought me on to Helena jail and we was whipped like dogs to make stories on each other. I did not kill no one. I did not have a gun. Then after my trial was over in six minutes, some of the white men came from Elaine to the jail and told me if I would put something on some more Negroes they would turn me free, if I would call just two or three men's names that they did call to me. I would not do so, because it would be a story and I will not lie on no one. I was whipped twice in jail. Near to death. While they were whipping me they put some kind of dope in my nose; also I was put in an electric chair and shocked to make me tell a story on other men.

"This is my crop. I was working sixteen acres of land, fifteen in cotton, one in corn. I was charged up for four months' groceries, $226.25, but I did not owe that much. So all that was taken from my wife and she was driven off the place. There was only three in the family. These white people of Phillips County want to say the union caused all this trouble. It's not so. The white people was threatened before this lodge organized in this county. They only put this to hold up their side. Just as fast as the Negroes lay their crops by they are driven from their homes and farms. When we were under arrest, the white people went and burned the church down to keep from showing up what they had done. We was not taught to kill no one. It was only for us to come into union to farm and to buy government land. Robert L. Hill did not tell us in no meeting whatever to harm the white man. They took it upon themselves to make this trouble. There was over eighty men, women and children killed and burned up by fire."

FRANK MOORE'S STATEMENT

"On the night of September 30th we Negroes was at Hoop Spur church at union meeting. Over 120 men, women and children were there in the lodge meeting and there was more than four or five automobiles of white people within about forty or fifty yards from the church and stopped and started shooting into the church on the Negroes and killed some of them. So I ran home that night and the next morning the whites sent us word that they was coming down there and 'kill every nigger they found.' So just as many of us could get together we did so. About 11:30 that day there was about 300 or 400 white men armed with guns walking and in automobiles at the railroad coming from Elaine to kill us. So we all ran back of the field and just as we got back of the field there was a big crowd of white men shooting and killing Jim Miller and his children and brother and setting them on fire. So when we saw them shooting and burning them we turned running and went to the railroad east from there, and the white people tried to cut us off. They were shooting at us all the time, so just as we crossed the railroad and the public road, it was only two shots was made from the colored people. It wasn't my rifle that was taken from the man who made the two shots. We all was running, I having made not a shot in the whole trouble. Then I slipped back through the field to save my mother and little children. About 5 o'clock that evening, there was near 300 more white people coming on with guns, shooting and killing men, women and children. So I took the children and women and went to the woods and stayed until the next morning when the soldiers' train came. I took the children and women and made it to the soldier men; then they took us and carried us to Elaine village and put us in the white school-house and I was there five days. Was carried to Helena County jail and whipped nearly to death to make me tell stories on the others, to say we killed the white people and colored people when at the church that night I did not have a gun whatever.

"The white people want to say that union was the cause of the trouble. It's not so; the white people were threatening to run us away from our crops before this trouble started. The Phillips County people know they started this trouble and they only got the army there to cover what they had done.

"I was working fourteen acres of cotton, five acres of corn and it was the best crop on that place where I was farming. Now after that they taken my old father and put him in jail after he had got his crops and taken everything from him. He was working thirty-eight acres of land, twenty-eight in cotton, ten acres in corn. Did not give him any of it, so he is still in Helena jail and I am sentenced to death. And all I made was taken from my wife and she was driven off the farm. Also took $678 worth of household goods from her. They did not give us a fair trial whatever and would not let us talk in court. Sentenced twelve men to death and put seventy-five other Negroes on the farm from one year to twenty-one years. Also they put my wife in jail and a great many other women. Also they was whipped as well as the men. Also while whipping us men, they put something in our nose to strangle us. Also we was put in an electric chair and shocked to make us lie on each other."

OLD MAN ED COLMAN, 79 YEARS OLD

"When this trouble started at Hoop Spur church, I was at home in bed asleep. I was living two and one-half miles from that trouble. By the Negroes running, I was awakened from my sleep and they told me about the white people shooting into the church on them. Then I was afraid to death near. When the morning had come, I saw about 200 white men in cars shooting down the Negroes and sent us word that they were going to "kill every nigger" they could find in the county. And at 11:30 that day we saw near 300 white armed white men coming and we all ran back of the field and when we got back of the field there was a big crowd of white men shooting and killing Jim Miller's family. We turned and went to the railroad. The white men tried to cut us off. When we got to the railroad, some of them was there shooting after us. It was only two shots made from we colored men. There was not any life taken whatever. We was still running and made it to the woods, where we were hid all night and all the next day. Then I came home to get my wife. She was about dead herself. When I got there, the white men had went and shot and killed some of the women and children. The next day I found her, then I taken her and went in the bushes and hid for all night and all the next day and part of the next night. The white people know they started this trouble. They did this to take our crops from us and run us away.

I was working eighteen acres of land, twelve in cotton, six in corn. All that was taken from me. All my hogs and everything was taken from me, then I am sentenced to die. Fifteen head of hogs was taken from me. Also my cotton and corn. The white people taken all that, then run my wife from home."

CHAPTER V

What White Folks Got from Riot

Billy Archdale, manager of Mrs. Jackson's farm at Elaine, Ark., was a leader in this movement against colored people. He had rented this farm for three years and then hired colored people to work it on shares. Last year he started with thirteen Negro families on the place. By the time the crops were "laid by" he had driven all but four of them off. This place is a mile and a half from Elaine. The way he did this was to refuse to feed the families longer, insist they were in his debt for supplies they got while planting, working and laying by the crop, and taking furniture, chickens, hogs and driving them away.

Four of these families determined not to be run away and made arrangements to get supplies without depending on Billy Archdale. They were Gilbert Jenkins, James and Frank Moore and Daisy Frazier. These worked and stood together, determined to stay and gather their crops, ignored the insults and threats of Archdale and were careful to give no offense. In May, 1919, Frank Moore, who was ill, asked Archdale for $10 to go to the hospital. Archdale refused, cursing and threatening to kill him. Moore got help from a friend and went to the hospital. While he was gone his wife hired help and laid by the crop first of all on the farm. Moore was one of the prime movers in organizing the union and was at the meeting the night of the riot. His wife wanted him to leave but he refused, saying he had "done nothing to leave for; that if he ran they would say he was guilty of something, he wasn't going to leave his crops." But when the mob came next day he took his mother and her children and all the women on the place down in the swamp and stayed with them till the soldiers came. His wife got away and was gone till she saw in the papers four weeks later that all was quiet and people could go back and gather crops. When she went back to her house, everything was gone! She went to the landlord's house and told his wife she had come to gather her crops and pay what she owed. She also asked Mrs. Archdale what had become of her furniture and clothes and where her husband was. Mrs. Archdale told her she would get nothing even though Mrs. Moore saw some of her furniture and clothes in Mrs. Archdale's house. She also told her her husband was in jail in Helena and they were going to have him put in the electric chair. Mrs. Moore asked why. "Did he kill anybody?" "No," she said, "but he had just come from the army and he was too bigoted."

Archdale himself demanded to know what she came back for. When she said she came back for her crop, her furniture and clothes, he told her if she didn't get out and stay out he would kill her, burn her up and no one would know where she was. So she had to leave with only the clothes she stood in, her whole year's work gone and her husband in jail. John Nelson, another landlord, arrested and took her to Helena to jail although she had gone back because the newspapers invited those who had gone away to return. She was kept in jail eight days and made to work from 3 o'clock in the morning to 9 or 10 o'clock at night; she and fifteen other colored women. This John Nelson who ran the farm of Wilford & White was recognized by some of the colored people as one of the leaders of the mob. A Dr. Parker was another of the leaders, also a Mr. Curtis who is a renter in the neighborhood.

Ed Ware told about the mob killing an old cripple named Charley Robinson and put him in his wife's bed. The two women were put in jail. Before doing this, however, they searched the house for Ed Ware. He was secretary of the hated union. They broke open trunks and drawers, took all of Ware's books, files, accounts with work people, secretary's minutes and Masonic lodge books away with him. They shot into the mirrors of the house and took fiendish delight in destroying things. They left the old man's body in the house for four days before they burned it. Longnecker and Jackson gave the Ware's three rooms of furniture to poor whites whom they afterwards moved on the place.

After keeping Mrs. Ware and the girl who was arrested with her in jail at hard labor for four weeks, sleeping sometimes on the concrete floor, they were discharged with seventeen others told to go back home and go to work as they had always done, "and never joining nothing more unless they got their lawyer's or landlord's consent." Mrs. Ware went back to get what she had left and found nothing. She saw her safe in a Mrs. Forsyth's house and a Mr. George had her chairs.

A woman named Lula Black, who with her four children were

working on a farm, was dragged out of her home by the mob and asked if she belonged to the union. She answered "Yes." They asked her why. She said, "Because it would better the condition of the colored people; when they worked it would help them to get what they worked for." When she said that they knocked her down, beat her over the head with their pistols, kicked her all over the body, almost killed her, then took her to jail.

The same mob went to Frank Hall's house and killed Frances Hall, a crazy old woman housekeeper, tied her clothes over her head, threw her body in the public road where it lay thus exposed till the soldiers came Thursday evening and took it up. Frank had gone to the gin with a load of cotton. He left horse, wagon and cotton to get away from the mob. His brother Paul had joined the union. He was shot in the foot, taken to jail and is now awaiting electrocution. He and his brother owned their forty acres which was in cultivation. His wife and aged father are still there.

James Moore, father of Frank Moore, although sixty-five years old, was farming twenty-five acres of land, he and his wife and four younger children. He also belonged to this union and got away when the mob came. He too went back on the assurance that trouble was over. They told him to go ahead and gather his crops which he did. Then he, too, was arrested and thrown in jail in Helena, where he is today. No charge against him and no trial. They have taken everything he had, every bit of the crops he gathered, and drove his wife and four small children off the place. They are now in Little Rock in want, while the father and husband is in prison.

Will Knox, his wife and three little children were working ten acres of land for two-thirds of the crop. They made six bales of cotton, the smallest bale weighing 550 pounds. When Knox was taken away Longnecker and Jackson said he owed them $606 for the year's supplies up to October 1st. Two bales were sold to them at their price, which left the balance due of $360. This meant that Mrs. Knox was allowed $246 for the two bales of cotton sold to Longnecker and Jackson when at the market price she should have received that for one bale. She had four bales left in the field and stayed to gather it. This too was turned over to the firm, and she was told nothing was coming to her because she was still $25 in debt! In other words six bales of cotton, the smallest one weighing 550 pounds at 45 cents per pound, should have paid the debt of $606 and left Mrs. Knox over $800 besides. They too are penniless and homeless.

Ed Hicks, president of the Elaine lodge, had 100 acres of land rented. His wife was the only woman to get any of her household goods when she went back after the trouble, also some of her hogs and chickens and a horse which she sold and realized a little money on. For the twenty-five acres of cotton and four in corn she received not a cent. All was taken from her.

After taking everything these people had, when these women went to Helena after the trial of their husbands they were permitted to see them only once and they had to pay a dollar each to the jailer for the privilege of doing that!

SUMMARY

Ed Ware, 100 acres cotton; 100 bales at $225 per bale	$22,500
Frank Hicks and Ed Hicks, 100 acres cotton; 100 bales at $225 per bale	22,500
Albert Giles, 20 acres cotton; 20 bales at $225 per bale	4,500
Joseph Fox, 20 acres cotton; 20 bales at $225 per bale	4,500
Alfred Banks, 32 acres of cotton; 32 bales at $225 per bale	7,200
John Martin, 22 acres of cotton; 22 bales at $225 per bale	4,950
William Wordlaw, 16 acres of cotton; 16 bales at $225 per bale	3,600
Frank Moore, 14 acres of cotton; 15 bales at $225 per bale	3,150
Ed Coleman, 12 acres cotton; 12 bales at $225 per bale	2,700
Will Knox, 10 acres cotton; 10 bales at $225 per bale	2,250
Paul Hall, 40 acres cotton; 40 bales at $225 per bale	9,000
Total	$86,050

This roughly estimates the yield of cotton at a bale to the acre, the average bale to weigh 500 pounds and the average price at 45 cents per pound. As a matter of fact the average was nearer 50 cents per pound. This does not include the cotton seed which has a high market value comparatively as cotton, nor does it include the 100 acres of corn raised by them, nor the stock, hogs and chicken raised by these men, all of which were stolen. It seems not too high as an estimate to say that these twelve men alone had $100,000 worth of cotton, corn and cattle stolen from them by the mob which stole their liberty and are in a fair way to steal their lives unless the nation intervenes!

The record for the seventy-five who are serving terms of imprisonment is not complete but a glance at the list secured shows:

Walter Guley, 23 acres of cotton and corn, farmed for B. B. Stanley, Elaine, Ark.

B. Earl, 30 acres cotton and corn, worked for Dick Howard, Wabash, Ark.

John and E. F. Foster, 40 acres cotton and corn, worked for Dr. Cruse, Elaine, Ark.

Will Hampton, 35 acres cotton and corn, worked for R. P. Alman, Elaine, Ark.

I. W. Swats, 20 acres cotton and corn, worked for George E. Blackburn, Melwood, Ark.

Andrew Goff, 20 acres cotton and corn, worked for Dr. Cruse, Elaine, Ark.

Gilmore Jenkins, 15 acres cotton and corn, worked for Billy Archdale, Elaine, Ark.

Ed Mitchell, 40 acres cotton and 5 in corn, worked for Dr. Cox, Elaine, Ark.

Dave Haas, 15 acres cotton and corn, worked for Longnecker & Jackson, Elaine, Ark.

Sykes Fox, 18 acres cotton and 7 in corn, worked for Deck Howard, Wabash, Ark.

Will Curry, 70 acres cotton and corn, worked for Wilford White, Hoop Spur, Ark.

Ed Baker, 25 acres cotton and corn, worked for C. L. Banard, Elaine, Ark.

Joe Leggens, 20 acres cotton and corn, worked for Deck Howard, Wabash, Ark.

Joe Meshane, 30 acres cotton and corn, worked for Deck Howard, Wabash, Ark.

S. J. Jackson, 58 acres cotton and corn, worked for J. L. Jones, Elaine, Ark.

Dan Rollins, 20 acres cotton and corn, worked for R. P. Alman, Elaine, Ark.

D. Paine, 22 acres cotton and corn, worked for S. S. Stokes, Elaine, Ark.

Charley Jones, 26 acres cotton and corn, worked for Dr. Richardson, Elaine, Ark.

C. C. Hubert, 20 acres cotton and corn, worked for Lambrook & Co., Elaine, Ark.

T. Dixon, 20 acres cotton and corn, worked for Lambrook & Co., Elaine, Ark.

James Moore, 35 acres cotton and corn, worked for Billy Archdale, Elaine, Ark.

Will Mack, 18 acres cotton and corn, worked for Key Plantation, Wabash, Ark.

Sam Barber, 22 acres cotton and corn, worked for S. S. Stokes, Elaine, Ark.

Abe Brown, 20 acres cotton and corn, worked for Dr. Cruse, Elaine, Ark.

Dave Reed, 20 acres cotton and corn, worked for Lambrook, Elaine, Ark.

Henry Avant, 58 acres cotton and corn, worked for Lambrook, Elaine, Ark.

Charley Hubbard, 58 acres cotton and corn, worked for Lambrook, Elaine, Ark.

John Thomas, 35 acres cotton and corn, worked for S. S. Stokes, Elaine, Ark.

John Jefferson, 35 acres cotton and corn, worked for R. P. Alman, Elaine, Ark.

Bob Jackson, 23 acres cotton and corn, worked for S. S. Stokes, Elaine, Ark.

Walter Ward, 20 acres cotton and corn, worked for Dr. Cruse, Elaine, Ark.

Will Steward, 50 acres cotton and corn, worked for R. P. Alman, Elaine, Ark.

Jim Smith, 48 acres cotton and corn, worked for Will Crege, Elaine, Ark.

Here are thirty-four of the seventy-five who are serving sentences ranging from five to twenty-one years. Less than half the whole number but this thirty-four had cultivated over a thousand acres of cotton and corn during the year of grace 1919! If the remaining forty-one did as well, those seventy-five Negroes are serving terms in the penitentiary for having nearly 2,000 acres of cotton and corn that the white men of Phillips County, Ark., could get away from them in no other way than by driving them away from their crops and preferring charges against them! It means that the white lynchers of Phillips County made a cool million dollars last year off the cotton crop of the twelve men who are sentenced to death, the seventy-five who are in the Arkansas penitentiary and the one hundred whom they lynched outright on that awful October 1, 1919! And that not one of them has ever been arrested for this wholesale conspiracy of murder, robbery and false imprisonment of these black men, nor for driving their wives and children out to suffer in rags and hunger and want!

CHAPTER VI

The Johnston Boys

The mob which killed Jim Miller, president of the Hoop Spur lodge of the Farmers' Union, and his family, then burned their bodies, also arrested and jailed other officers and members of this union and thus stamped it out of existence had no such excuse in the murder of the four Johnston brothers of Helena, Ark. Yet they too paid with their lives the penalty of being prosperous negroes in the neighborhood of the riot.

Dr. D. A. E. Johnston, a native of Pine Bluff, Ark., was married to the daughter of Mrs. E. A. Miller, one of Helena's most prosperous citizens, and owned a splendid practice there.

In the ten years of his practice as a dentist he had built up wealth for himself and family. He owned a building in which he also had a drug store on one of the main streets of the city and was doing well. His two younger brothers had been in the army. One of them, Leroy Johnston, was wounded in the trenches in France, and unable to come back with his regiment, the Fifteenth

New York Infantry, because he was suffering from his wounds in a hospital when they left for home. Nor had he entirely recovered from these wounds when he was murdered. The two younger brothers were running an automobile business and lived with Dr. D.A.E. Johnston. An older brother, Dr. L. H. Johnston, a physician living in Oklahoma, had come to visit the three brothers and a hunting trip to celebrate the reunion was planned. On October 2nd when on their way back to Helena with an auto loaded down with game, they were told of the riot and advised not to drive through Elaine. They went back to their starting point, left their auto, game and guns and boarded the train for Helena. Somebody was on the lookout for them for when the train came through Elaine members of the mob boarded it and took the Johnston boys off, handcuffed them with ropes and placed them in an auto driven by O. A. Lilly, a real estate dealer of Helena. As he started to drive the auto away, members of the mob blazed away at it, and killed the Johnston brothers, also the white driver, and filled the auto full of holes.

The bodies of these four brothers lay in the roadside where they fell from Thursday morning till Saturday afternoon in the hot sun just as if they had been so many dead dogs. At last permission was given the mother-in-law to move them and they were given burial. These prominent citizens, educated, cultured gentlemen, had committed no crime, nor were they even charged with belonging to the Farmers' Union or knowing anything about it. They were killed by Amos Jarman, county treasurer of Phillips County, who is also postmaster of Helena.

The Helena World of October 2, 1919, says in a bulletin: "The building on Walnut Street owned by Dr. D. A. E. Johnston, Negro dentist, killed by County Treasurer Amos Jarman today, after Johnston had shot and killed Alderman O. R. Lilly, was surrounded and searched this afternoon. More than a dozen high-power rifles and several cases of ammunition were found."

Another column in the same issue headed:

"IMPORTANT CORRECTION"

"In the excitement and uncertainty created by the events of yesterday it was stated that Clinton Lee was shot and killed accidentally.

The statement was made in absolute good faith, but investigation develops that young Lee was shot by a Negro with a high-power rifle. Other Helena boys who were with him bear witness to this fact. The sympathy of the entire city goes out to the bereaved family and that of James A. Tappen, who died from his injuries yesterday afternoon. They died in the line of duty and their memories will live forever in the hearts of the people of Phillips County."

What duty? That of leaving their home in Helena to go thirty miles away to hunt and shoot down Negroes who were peacefully minding their own business and exercising the rights of American citizens to organize to better their condition. The leading citizens of the towns nearby joined in the man hunt to kill Negroes as another article in this same paper states. It says:

"Parties of armed men who came to Helena from Clarendon, Marianna, Marvell and other points near Helena on the Arkansas side, and other parties from Lula, Tunica, Friars Point and Clarksdale, Miss. aided in patrolling the streets of Helena last night and assisted in preserving order in the trouble zone. Some of these visitors left for their homes this morning."

Another item states that:

"O. S. Bratton white, held on a charge of murder in connection with the killing of Special Officer Adkins Tuesday night, is said by the authorities to have been one of the instigators of the trouble at Elaine and Hoop Spur, was brought to Helena in chains last night. He is said to be a cousin of U. S. Bratton, attorney of Little Rock, and former postmaster of that city, and also a member of the law firm of Casey & Bratton with offices in Helena. Feeling against him is bitter, but there have been so far no indications of summary action. Bratton and nineteen Negroes, some of them women, arrested in connection with the race war, are held under strong guard in the county jail, and it is understood that they will be tried at the next term of the Phillips County Circuit Court which convenes two weeks hence."

The mayor of the city issues a proclamation which is also printed in black type and a two-column announcement reads:

"PROCLAMATION!
The funeral services of
JAMES TAPPAN

Will be held at 4 p. m. today and
The services of
CLINTON LEE
At 10:30 a. m., Friday, October 3rd.

Therefore, I, J. G. Knight, Mayor of the City of Helena, call on the citizens of Helena to close their places of business during the hour of the respective services in order that the respect due our citizens who sacrificed their lives at our call, can be shown.

J. G. KNIGHT, Mayor."

Neither of those men were officers of the law, yet "they sacrificed their lives at our call" says the mayor. The whole city did honor to the men who left their business, armed themselves and went out to murder black men like the Johnston brothers and others who had broken no law nor done them harm. The Johnston brothers were in chains and could do no harm; they were high-class citizens and successful professional men; yet their lives were taken and their bodies lay beside the roadside in the blistering heat of the summer sun until they putrified, while the city of Helena did honor to their murderers and those of their brothers in black.

CHAPTER VII

The Trial

When the Phillips County Circuit Court convened in Helena, Ark., the following indictment by the Grand Jury was made:

State of Arkansas⎫
      vs.   ⎪
John Martin   ⎬ Indictment.
Alf Banks, Jr.   ⎪
Will Wordlow   ⎭

The Grand Jury of Phillips County in the name of and by the authority of the State of Arkansas, accuse John Martin, Alf Banks and Will Wardlow of the crime of murder in the first degree committed as follows, to-wit.: The said John Martin, Alf Bank and Will Wordlow in the county and state aforesaid on the first day of October, A. D. 1919, did unlawfully, wilfully, feloniously and with malice aforethought and after deliberation and premeditation kill and murder one W. A. Adkins by shooting him, the said W. A. Adkins with a certain gun which the said John Martin, Alf Banks, Jr., and Will Wordlow then and there held in their hands, the said gun being then and there loaded with gunpowder and leaden balls, against the peace and dignity of the State of Arkansas.

JOHN E. MILLER,
No. 4482.   Prosecuting Attorney.
Indictment for murder in the first degree, 10-28-1919.

STATE'S TESTIMONY IN CASE OF ED WARE

Charley Pratt, having first been duly sworn, was called as a witness by the State and testified as follows:

My name is Charley Pratt and I am a deputy sheriff. I was sent down by the sheriff's office to the Hoop Spur church on October 1st, for the purpose of making an arrest at Elaine. I was with W. A. Adkins and the other Negro trusty, Kit Collins. We went in a car and stopped pretty near the Hoop Spur church, about fifty yards, I presume. A ridge or culvert was right in front of our car when we stopped.

While standing on the outside of my car with Mr. Adkins we were fired at by a crowd of Negroes, who came over from the church. I did not know the Negroes, but we were fired on by them and Mr. Adkins was killed. I knew Mr. Adkins. This occurred in Phillips County, State of Arkansas.

CROSS EXAMINATION

I do not know who killed Mr. Adkins. I did not know any of these defendants. I can't identify any of the defendants. I don't know where they came from. This was the last night of September, between 12:30 and 1:00 o'clock, nearly in the a. m. of October 1st.

REDIRECT EXAMINATION

I saw Mr. Adkins after he was shot. I presume seventy-five to one hundred and fifty shots were fired on the first occasion. We did not begin the shooting, because we did not have our guns out of the scabbards. The Negroes came from towards the church and began shooting. About ten or fifteen minutes elapsed between the first and second shooting. There were about one hundred and fifty shots fired in the second shooting. They came from all directions.

Witness excused.

Jones, having first been duly sworn, was called as witness by the State and testified as follows:

I am a special agent for the Iron Mountain Railroad. W. A. Adkins worked under me. I was called down to a Hoop Spur on the morning of October 1st, following some trouble that happened there and I got there about 4:30 or 5:00 a. m. The body of W. A. Adkins was lying on the west side of the road near the rear of the automobile, about seventy feet from Hoop Spur church where Mr. Adkins was dead.

Will Wordlow, having first been duly sworn, was called as a witness by the State and testified as follows:

My name is Will Wordlow and I belong to the Hoop Spur Lodge. I know Ed Ware; he was secretary of the Lodge. I was down there the last night in September, the night the shooting occurred. I went there about 7 or 8 o'clock. When I got there Ed Ware was on the outside talking. When we all got in church, he told me to go out there and help guard. I was a guard. He said if anybody came up to defend them on the inside. I presume that meant shooting. I had my gun with me, and he said if anybody came up there bothering us to shoot. I had a single barrel shot gun. There were about seven or eight of us out there on guard around the church.

I was under the trestle with John Martin and two other fellows. The balance of the crowd was on the right hand side of the church. The last time I saw Ed Ware was when he told me to go out with my gun and do guard duty. After the shooting that night, I went across the field. I went down in the woods and got lost back of the church; they caught me in the woods and I came on up to Dave Hay's house. Ed Ware passed Dave Hay's house; I says, Mr. Ed, what about the shooting. I says you think it is over and he says I don't know, I don't believe it is, and I says, who got killed and who won the fight and he says a white fellow got killed. He asked me about his wife, had I seen anything of his wife, he says she got away from him that night and he went out to defend her. He said he made three shots; he said he was shooting toward the car. That was the last time I saw Ed Ware. He told me he didn't think it was over yet and that he thought and said Albert Banks killed him. He said he fired three shots.

I have been found guilty by a jury of killing Mr. Adkins. The conversation I speak of the next morning, was in front of Dave Hays' house. Ed Ware had a gun, a long rifle, old gun, made sorter like soldiers' guns. It was between 7 or 8 or 9, or 8 or 9 o'clock in the morning. The first time I saw him was between 8 and 9 o'clock. At the time I saw him, we both had our guns. This conversation took place out in front of the church, telling me what to do, and I didn't want to go out there, and he says, this is Uncle Sam's law and we have to be ruled and governed under it. He says, you will have to go out, we can make you go out. He says, you are called a slacker now you ain't made a noise for two or three nights. He says he was going to put a fine on me and that is the reason I came out there that night. He says, if anybody came up there running over you to shoot.

REDIRECT EXAMINATION

Ed Ware had this rifle or gun, that I described to the jury over there at the church, that night and he had the same gun the next morning, the one he had with him over at Dave Hays the next morning. Witness excused.

Joe Mitchon testified to seeing Ed Ware with a gun and hearing him give orders to shoot white people. John Ratliff testified to seeing him behind a log with a gun on his shoulder and told him he had made three shots.

Frank Kitchens, having been first duly sworn, was called as witness by the State and testified as follows:

I am a sheriff of this county. I know the defendant, he was apprehended in New Orleans and brought back to Phillips County. I had a conversation with him about the charge now pending against him. He said he was at Hoop Spur on the 30th of September, 1919, the night Mr. Adkins was killed. He made these statements voluntarily. He said he was present at lodge that night as secretary, the night Mr. Adkins was killed. He said the next morning when the shooting began, that he had his gun in his grip, but that he lost both his gun and his grip getting away. And he remained out of the State until brought back.

CROSS EXAMINATION

Ed Ware said he did not have his gun at the church on the night of the shooting. I asked him did he have the authority in the lodge to give orders, he said he didn't know. He said Mr. McCullough told him a week before that happened, something was going on wrong there, and he intended to resign that night.

DEFENDANT'S TESTIMONY

Will McFarland, having first been duly sworn, was called as a witness and testified as follows:

My name is Will McFarland. I was a member of the Farmers' Progressive Union and belonged to the Hoop Spur Lodge. Ed Ware was secretary of the Hoop Spur Lodge. I was at church, on September 30th, the night Mr. Adkins was killed, I got there between 9 and 10 o'clock. Ed Ware and myself went together and his wife, my wife and some little ones. I was in the church at the time this shooting began. I didn't do anything when the shooting began, but get down on the floor and try to keep the bullets from hitting me. Just as soon as the first shooting was over and as quick as I could get a chance to get out of the church, I was gone. I didn't hear Ed Ware give any orders to any guards to do any shooting. I saw him next day about 9 o'clock.

CROSS EXAMINATION

I am thirty-seven years old. I came from Daniles, Miss., Hurds County. I stayed at 507 York Street. I am working for Mr. Lafe

Solomon. When I was not working for him I was working for the Chicago Lumber Company. I am a Baptist preacher. I have been preaching a year and six months. I don't know what Ed Ware carried in a little grip. It had secretary's books and papers in it. The lights went out when the shooting started. I couldn't see anything for a while. After the shooting, I went back in the woods with my wife and his and four other women. I did not see him until the next morning about 9 o'clock. When the lights went out and the shooting started, I got out and ran. He had a 41 Swiss gun. I left the place the next morning when I saw the white men coming up the road. I went in the woods back of the house, thence to Brickey, Arkansas. I stayed three weeks with a fellow named Fred Scott. He and I went on a train to New Orleans, where I stayed until I was captured and brought back. I left the country because I didn't want to get killed and Ed told me they were killing anybody that belonged to the union. I had planned to come back here Tuesday, but they captured me Sunday. I ran away because I was scared.

REDIRECT EXAMINATION

Ed Ware, having first been duly sworn, was called as a witness and in his own behalf and testified as follows:

My name is Ed Ware and I am the defendant in this case. I was a member of the Progressive Farmers' Union of America. I was secretary to the Hoop Spur Lodge prior to October 1st. This was my third meeting. I had belonged to the Union not quite a month. I was present September 30th, when Mr. Adkins was killed. I left home about 9:30 or 10 o'clock with my wife, McFarland and his wife and Lonzo Riley. I was sick. I went home and laid down and started not to go to the meeting and my wife insisted on me going because I had those books and papers. It is about a mile from my house over there. Neither my wife nor myself carried a gun or pistol. I had no orders to guard there that night. When I got to church that night, they was already in session, and the house was lit up and the light gleamed right out in the yard and I walked up in the light. I was sitting down at the secretary's table when the first shot was fired, filling out those blanks. I did not make the statement that if the guards couldn't handle it I would go out and handle it. When I got through, I was going to resign and turn the books over to them. I had told McFarland prior to this meeting, that I was going to resign. I had had a conversation with a white man about it prior to this time. I got in my car and went to the Elaine postoffice. Mr. McCollough came into the office and got his mail and he turned and says to me, "Ed, come here." We went out around the side of the office and he says, "Do you belong to the union?" and I says, "Yes, sir, I am secretary of it at Hoop Spur." "Well, tell me what is that thing?" I says, "You know as much about it as I do. It is called the Progressive Farmers' Household Union of America, as I understood it. It is to make better conditions among the farmers and that is why I belong to it. It is supposed to be a government agency, this fellow is, and they have affidavits to fill out to buy government blanks, homestead government lands; in other words he has questionnaire blanks. This little fellow Hill, that set up the institution that is what he presented to us. He said give him $10 a man and we would get 160 acres of land; he is supposed to have 1,600 acres located down at or below Mellwood and he wanted us to get him $200. Some people put in a dollar and some $1.25. I put in $10 myself and he written up an affidavit for me for 160 acres of land; that is why I belong to it to try to get some of that land. I never would have joined in the world if it hadn't been for that. I had no gun the night Mr. Adkins was shot. I went out when the shooting took place. I tried to get out the door and fellows was rushing in the door so fast I couldn't get out, so finally when I did get a chance to get outside, I went through an alfalfa patch to Henry Mason's house. It must have been somebody else Dave Hays testified to lying up behind a log about thirty rods from the point where this shooting occurred with a gun. I got home the next morning a little before the train run; I left Henry Mason's house that morning after the sun was up.

CROSS EXAMINATION

I joined the lodge in September at Hoop Spur. Joe Michon and an old fellow by the name of Charley Robinson, these two and Will Curry was the first man that brought them to me. They induced me to join the Hoop Spur lodge. I hadn't been to but two meetings when the trouble arose. Jim Miller was the president of the Hoop Spur Lodge, then I joined it and I got to be secretary. I had charge of the blanks and membership applications and the medical examination blanks and the books and all that, and the list of members. The last time I saw the books was Wednesday a. m., October 1st. It was in my hand, but when I broke and run, I don't know what became of it.

I know Robert L. Hill when I see him. I never have seen him but once or twice at Hoop Spur and at Elaine. The only speech he made was concerning government land. He made that speech at Elaine. I was at Elaine Thursday night prior to this killing the following Tuesday night, acting as secretary. I know Ed Hicks and Frank Moore, said to be the bravest man on the board. I knew all of the fellows that belonged to the board. I was not at Elaine lodge Thursday night prior to the killing Tuesday night. I was transferring people in my auto trying to make money.

I deny that I took charge of the secretary's office and posted those guards around there; that I sat at the table with Ed Hicks, Shelton Baker, Frank Moore and four or five others, and Knox the secretary at what you call this board meeting, and picked out certain men in the community that we were going to kill. I deny that prior to this killing Tuesday night, that Hicks Moore and Mr. Knox and myself and the officers of that lodge did select the names of Mr. Knox the postmaster to be killed, Charley Bernam, Jim Countias and Will Craighead, Mr. Crow, or pick these gentlemen out and consult about killing them provided the proper settlements were made and that these parties did submit that list to be for my approval. I deny that after discussing it openly for a few minutes and among the officers of the lodge, that we said we had better stop this conversation, that there are some white mouths here in the room that are liable to give us away, and that I did write the names down, one at a time, each one of us looked at is and voted that they were to be killed. I deny what old man Ratliff says is the truth and Wordlow. I deny I went over there with a gun and that I had a pistol in my grip and I deny everything that anyone has testified to in the case here against me. I didn't have but one gun, a little single barrel breech, and it wouldn't shoot and I got a new one that would shoot, a 41 Swiss A. P. Price, at Arkansas City. I had three or four shells at my home to fit this gun. This is not the gun I fired in the direction of Mr.

Adkins. I didn't have narry a gun with me that night. I went home the next morning and got it. I didn't have any talk with Will Wordlow in regard to the trouble. I ran away and went out in the woods and ran into this Negro preacher McFarland. We stayed with Fred Scott, a colored fellow that stayed on Hugh Piper's place. I met him on the 5th day of October on Crowley's Ridge. I stayed there two or three weeks. I didn't shoot anybody. I ran away to New Orleans because I was afraid, they was shooting everybody they said. After I got to Brickey's I got a letter from a man named Murray, he told me everything had quieted down and that the soldiers had gone. I had been at Brickey's about a week when I got that letter. I wrote Joe Murray a letter from Brickley, that is why he knew where I was. I was coming back as I got a pay day. I was at Algiers when I answered. I talked to the officers that arrested me about this charge against me and to the judge of the court also and I told them that I didn't want to come back here, that I would be lynched. I changed my name when I got to New Orleans and went under the name of Charley Hubbard. I did so because it was just foolish ignorance. I went by the name of Will Brown in Louisiana.

Suggas Bondman, having first been duly sworn, was called in the rebuttal by the State, etc.

I live at Elaine on M. K. Alderman's place. I having been living down there going on two years. I know Ed Ware. I belonged to the Elaine lodge down there. I went to it every time but once. I was down there at the meeting they had Thursday night before the trouble occurred next Tuesday. I heard a conversation between Ed Ware there that night and Ed Hicks, Baker and Knowles and Frank Moore and the other board members and officers that were running the lodge about killing people around there and who they were going to kill. Ed Ware when he come, he kinder took the meeting in charge, he thought he could handle it better than Ed Hicks and when he taken in it charge, he says, I will show you how I handle your people at Hoop Spur, and he goes to work then and sends out the guards outside and so on. They took out shot gun and Winchesters. Ed Ware took charge of the lodge in place of Ed Hicks. He advised them like this, he first says: There's Mr. Bernard and he specified Mr. Crow and Mr. Stokes and Mr. Moore and Mr. Counties and the postoffice man. He says that Mr. Moore gave him a lot of trouble about their mail;

they sure wanted to get him, too; he wanted the hooking cow, he said they sure wanted him and then E. W. told Ed Hicks he says, we will hold up this conversation right here, he says there is some white mouths and some niggers in here, and they gets close around the table and all the big men they just writes a name and asks how about this one and about the other one, and they would say he goes and some of the rest of them wrote and passed it round and says what about him and they said yes, we sure want to get him. Ed Ware and the others made those statements. Ed Ware was the one that told them to hold up this conversation, and they wrote to one another then around the table, he called the holding it up out of the snitchers' mouths, he said there was some white mouths and snitchers' mouths, he said for them to set clear of the windows and keep their eyes open, that some of the members may get shot and he said that every member in the house that has a gun if any white face poked his face in the window or door, everybody shoot right at it, and told the guards on the outside to go to every fork of the road, dog path and all not let nothing white pass. He said he wanted to show them how he handled his people up at Hoop Spur.

CROSS EXAMINATION

I was at the meeting last night. I got there about 6 or 7 o'clock. It was kinder getting dusk. Ed Ware was not there when I was there. It was an hour after dark or something like that when Ed Ware came. When he came in, they announced this Hill fellow, he goes to Robert Hill and shakes hands with him and had a new pump gun, looked like it might have been new, in his hands and they shook hands and Robert Hill asked him what was that he had and he says something to put in the racks. And he says it has not been shot more than just to try it, and he says when I do kill something it will be Ringard.

I was not a member of the board and held no official office but was just a bench member. The board did all this voting on this people. They planned to kill Mr. Bernard, Mr. Stokes, Mr. Moore, the postoffice man, and Mr. Countiss and Mr. Crow and Mr. Kreggs, and then they held up and just wrote one to another and might have pointed more than that but they done it themselves. I never knew Ed Ware, but I have seen him lots of times; I never knew him until he came to the meeting at Elaine. I knew him by being an active member then.

There were about three hundred present at the meeting. Ed Hicks, Frank Moore, Frank Hicks were there. Ed Ware had control of the meeting. He was a Hoop Spur man and he knew Ed Hicks, and I reckon he just took charge and I heard him tell them he wanted to show them how he handled his members at Hoop Spur. Ed Hicks was president of the Hoop Spur lodge and Ed Baker secretary.

This was all the testimony in the case.

THE STATE VS. FRANK HICKS—ABSTRACT OF RECORD

STATE'S TESTIMONY

R. L. Brooks, having first been duly sworn, was called as a witness by the State and testified as follows:

(DIRECT EXAMINATION BY P. R. ANDREWS)

My name is R. L. Brooks. I have lived at Helena for the past three years, excepting a couple of years in the army. I was in Helena on the 1st day of October, 1919, up until 9:15 that morning.

The first place I went that morning was Hoop Spur, with a posse of officers that went down to see about arresting some Negroes that were said to have killed a man. I was accompanied by Messrs. Nosby, J. D. Carlson, Meyers, Leo Markus.

I knew Clinton Lee. I saw him in the neighborhood of Hoop Spur and I was present on the morning of October 1st, when he was killed down there. He was seated in the rear seat, and I was standing on the running board holding to the left door. I didn't hear the report of the gun, I only heard the whistle of the bullets. I heard two bullets. They came in the back end of the car. Clinton Lee was struck by one bullet. The first thing he did, he got up from the seat and managed to get to the door; whether or not he opened the door I don't know, but he got to the running board and fell to the ground. He says, I am hit, take me in the house. We laid our guns on the ground and took him up and took him in Mr. McCoy's house. I stayed with him until he died which couldn't have been more than five minutes. This occurred in Phillips County, Arkansas, on the 1st day of October, 1919.

CROSS EXAMINATION

I heard only two bullets hissing near the car. There were six men in the car and I was on the running board. At the time the bullets came the car was in the process of turning around; the car pulled in from the road facing Mr. McCoy's house and we had pulled it out; in other words, the car had just gotten in motion, when the bullets came. Mr. Lee was sitting on the left side, rear seat, rear end. There were no curtains up; we were riding in a "Moon." Lee was exposed to the bullets from the direction the bullets came, I would say about half of his body. The bullet that hit him came through the car, his body wasn't exposed where the bullet hit him.

I heard shots discharged thirty minutes before that time. They were in the woods, it was kinder hard for me to pick out any direction. I was summoned to go down there by a member of the American Legion. I was sworn in as a member of the posse by some officer; Mr. Straub, I think it was; he was acting as sheriff.

This shooting occurred, as well as I can remember, between 12 and 12:30.

Witness excused.

L. R. Parmalee, having first been duly sworn, was called as a witness by the State and testified as follows:

I am a civil engineer. I assisted in the making of this plat, with W. K. Monroe. It is approximately a correct plat or diagram of the territory surrounding the town of Elaine, the Hoop Spur Church and Lorenzo Spur and other points down in that community. The names written in it are descriptive of the houses and the various people shown on this plat, and the points; Hoop Spur Church and the town of Elaine, and the railroad tracks, the public road and these bayous in the immediate neighborhood. I have been over this territory myself. I worked on this map in the office with Mr. Monroe. He didn't give me any data; from my knowledge and his knowledge of that territory down there he constructed the map; there was no accurate survey made of it; it is a general map showing the general location of those different points.

I did not go down there especially for the purpose of getting data to make this map. I was down there immediately after this trouble or during this trouble, and of course I worked there considerable, and from my general knowledge and from Mr. Monroe's particular knowledge this map was constructed by Mr. Monroe. I am not trying to testify as to the accuracy of this map, from the knowledge that Mr. Monroe has of it, but I do know from general knowledge and his particular knowledge, I do know those points are approximately correct. The supposed mark on the map where Frank Hicks was standing is accurate generally speaking; we do not know the spot but we do know the general position. This map is built according to scale. I didn't see Hicks standing there, but I would swear to the accuracy of this map. All of those points, those houses, etc., are correct, generally speaking. There has been no survey for the map so far as I know; I didn't see Mr. Monroe make the survey; it is what we call a sketch map. The scale on the map is 1,000 feet to the inch. I know it is accurate as the time has now come when all people it is accurate as mechanical skill—you can scale only to a certain degree of accuracy. If you are trying to make me say that we made an accurate survey, why I can't do it, but I say as a general layout that map is correct. I won't swear to the exact measurement, because I haven't taken them.

REDIRECT EXAMINATION

I made that from a map of the country, which shows the various subdivisions of land with respect to the land lines and the places where the houses and town of Elaine, which is shown on the country map—it is copied from the county map to this map. I got it from the county map. I say it is substantially correct.

Witness excused.

Dr. O. Parker, having been first duly sworn, was called as a witness by the State and testified as follows:

My name is Dr. O. Parker. I was present down at Mr. McCoy's

house on the morning of October 1st last when Clinton Lee was killed. I was in the house when he was shot. He was about forty feet from the automobile where he was killed. They brought him in the house at once. He was dying at the time. I had Mr. Tappan there; I was taking care of Mr. Tappan; I saw the boy was dying and I didn't make an examination. He died in my presence. The shot that entered his body just a short while before was the cause of his death.

George Green, having first been duly sworn, was called as a witness by the State, and testified as follows:

My name is George Green. I live on Mr. Stanley's place, down at Elaine. I was down at Elaine the first of October. I just came here three weeks before this happened. I joined the Farmers' Progressive Union immediately before this happened on Thursday night. I know Frank Hicks, the defendant. He was a member of the Lodge. He was at the meeting on Thursday night before this trouble came up on the following Tuesday. He had a gun on that night and everybody else in the church I seen.

I didn't hear about the shooting until Walter Ward came to my house and got me, a little before day, about 4 o'clock. I got up and put on my clothes and waited till he come back by there, and we went over to Frank Moore's. I carried with me a shot gun, and got to his house a little before day. Paul Hall's house is right close to Frank Moore's and Sweatman. When I got there, I found about thirty. They were sitting around Frank Moore's. All had guns. It was about 10 or 11 o'clock before we left that place. There were about seventy-five Negroes gathered at Paul Hall's and Sweatman's houses before we left there and Frank Hicks was there that morning. He got there about 8 o'clock. He had his gun; I never saw anyone with him. He was talking about first one thing and then another.

Frank Moore was in command of the army, when we all lined up and marched away about 11 o'clock.

They said they heard shooting over there. I didn't hear it, I was lying down on the gallery and they all said we hear some shooting over there. And they commenced hollering and whirling; and Frank Moore called them and says get in line two by two, Frank Moore and Ed Hicks and Joe Knox. I got in line about the middle. Frank Hicks kinder cut across the field. When he was in line, he was kinder in front.

Frank Moore was in command and he told us to march up and we marched in the direction of the shooting. And finally we came to the big road. When we got to the railroad all of them broke across the railroad, and before I got up on the railroad I heard a shot made. I was about twenty feet from the man that was doing the shooting.

Frank Hicks was doing the shooting. He did it with one of these here 70's, when he throwed up to shoot I throwed up my hands and said, Boys don't shoot; he says God damn it, I will shoot you. I never heard but one shot. I saw the shot he made and when he throwed up his gun, I throwed up my hand, and I says, Boys don't shoot.

Frank Hicks made that shot, he shot his gun right straight up the road. He shot toward Helena. It was a little after 12 o'clock I guess. Well, directly after that we seen a train coming and all of them hid, and after he shot, he came back up the railroad where I was; they seen the train coming and all of them hid, and when the train got by, I says I am going home and he says, I am too and the three of us went home. I couldn't see nothing but cars up the road in the direction in which he shot.

CROSS EXAMINATION

I heard two shots fired. Wasn't but just about the time he could shoot and unload and get his gun loaded. Frank Hicks had one of these here 70's. Rifle shoots these here long balls, it has one charge in it at a time. There were several people around there where Frank was. He did not hold an office in the lodge; he was just a common ordinary member. I joined the Thursday before and it was my first attendance at that meeting. I don't know what it organized for, the night I was there. Well, this fellow Hill, he was up talking and he spoke some big words about the white folks, he says I know you will tell them and I want them to know it; he says, we are liable to have trouble some time, but you all stand your ground. His order was to bring your gun. All of them went across the road together. When I saw Frank he was up in the road and the shot was made before I got up on the railroad.

Witness excused.

John Jefferson, having first been duly sworn, was called as a witness by the State and testified as follows:

I have been a member of that Order. I joined Friday night and the trouble started at Hoop Spur Tuesday. I got the orders to carry my gun the night I joined, because they was looking for trouble, looking for them to come down there and break the meeting up. This fellow Hill told me that he was there that night. I understood our union was for the good, to help us out; that is what they told me in the meeting. They were going to give us legal rights and everything. He says, we all was going to have our rights, we was going to be better; we was going to get along better in this world but it might cause trouble.

REDIRECT EXAMINATION

He said we was going to have trouble. They came after us to go and help fight whoever was in trouble over at Paul Hall's house. The place where Mr. Lee's body was, that was in Phillips County, Arkansas.

Witness excused.

Tom Faulkner testified as follows:

My name is Tom Faulkner. I was down at Hoop Spur on the 1st day of last October. We left about 8 o'clock in the morning. I knew Clinton Lee in this life. I saw him down there that day. He got down there about the same time I did.

I know where Mr. McCoy's house is on the public way down there. That is the correct location of his house on this map. The shot was from the south, on this map. I was present near Mr. McCoy's house about 12 or 1 o'clock, when Clinton Lee was shot. I was probably fifty or one hundred feet from him, when he was shot. He was in the car out there in front of the house. I heard the shots fired at the time Mr. Lee was shot. The shot was from the south. There were two shots fired at that time. The man who fired the shots was in a crouching position, on his knees. He was just off the public road. I had seen this man before the gun was fired. I saw three up there and I saw one of them fire. The other two seemed to be in the rear of the one who fired. The men that fired the shot was south of the car. This happened about noon time or afternoon.

Witness excused.

S. S. Stokes, having first been duly sworn, was called as a witness by the State and testified as follows:

My name is S. S. Stokes. I live at Elaine. I was at home on October 1st last when this trouble occurred at Hoop Spur and around Elaine. I know the defendant, Frank Hicks. I did, in the presence of other men, down at Elaine, some two or three days, after this trouble have a conversation with the defendant in which I asked him to state the facts to us about the fighting that occurred there and especially with reference to the killing of young Lee.

CROSS EXAMINATION

Those present were J. O. Crow, K. P. Alderman, Mr. Nelson, C. W. L. Armour and J. M. Countiss.

I asked him one or two questions and Mr. Crow. We were not armed. We asked him for a statement without putting him under duress or fear. He didn't answer the questions, he made a statement; when he got started he just told us the story right there, straight through; we didn't have to question him very much.

Frank Hicks said they had come and woke him up early that morning and had told him that they wanted him up at Paul Hall's house near Frank Moore's house, and he went up there. He told who it was that came after him; I don't remember who that was; and they went to Paul Hall's house where there was a big bunch of Negroes in the crowd there, and they stayed there until pretty nearly noon and Ed didn't come up until late and after he got there long before they heard the shots at Hoop Spur the firing up there, and he said that Frank Moore told them that there was Ed Ware up there that the time had come that they all had to go and fight, and they went toward Hoop Spur, towards the firing and he said they got pretty near to Hoop Spur and they stopped behind a bunch of bushes, and saw them firing on the house at Hoop Spur—it was Jim Miller's house, and they stopped and looked through the bushes a while; then Hicks and Moore, Frank Moore, told them that they would surround the bunch there and have the battle right there, that it didn't look like there was very many and they turned to the right and crossed the railroad track, went toward the railroad track, and when they got over there he said that Ed Hicks said that the white folks had better guns than they had and they better not go up there, and they crossed the tracks, and he said that he knelt in the road—Frank Hicks—and he said when he got to the road he thought he would just take a shot into the crowd and maybe get some of them; and he said he borrowed Sweat Coleman's rifle to make the shot, and he shot once, I am not positive whether he shot once or twice, he said he shot into the road and the crowd scattered, and Mr. Crow asked him what he said then and he says, I don't remember what I said, but after that we got up and went in the cornfield.

Witness excused.

It was on this testimony that Frank Hicks, Ed Ware and the other ten men were sentenced to die in the electric chair. After agitation by lovers of justice against this unjust finding, able counsel in Little Rock was engaged to make motion for a new trial and the following is the exact wording of that motion:

CHAPTER VIII

Motion for a New Trial

It was on this testimony that Frank Hicks, Ed Ware and the other ten men were sentenced to die in the electric chair. After agitation by lovers of justice against this unjust finding, able council in Little Rock was engaged to make motion for a new trial and the following is the exact wording of that motion:

Defendant, Frank Hicks, moves and prays the Court to set aside the verdict of the jury therein, and grant and give him a new trial herein, for the following reasons:

He is a Negro of the African race, and was at the time of the trial, and for a long time previous thereto a citizen of the United States and the State of Arkansas, and a resident of Phillips County;

That the deceased Clinton Lee, whom defendant is charged by the indictment with murdering, was killed on the 1st of October, 1919, by some person unknown to the defendant, in a deadly conflict following a disturbance between the white and black races of said county, on the night previous; for which he was in no way responsible;

That the excitement of the white residents and citizens of said county was intense, and their feelings against the blacks including the defendant, bitter, active and persistent;

That in the course of it, some four or five white men and a large number of Negroes were killed, from 50 to 100.

That on or about the said first day of October, 1919, defendant was, along with many other Negroes, 200 or more, taken into custody by said whites, carried to the county jail and there kept in close custody and confinement until he was indicted and put upon trial;

That at the time of the returning of said indictment and trial, said excitement and bitterness of feeling among the whites of said county, against the Negroes, especially against the defendant, was unabated and still at the height of intensity;

That this feeling among the whites was coextensive with the county;

That during his confinement he was frequently subjected to torture for the purpose of extracting from him admission of guilt—as were others then also in custody, to force them to testify against the defendant;

That he was given no opportunity to consult with friends, or to seek assistance for defense or relief, nor was he even informed of the charges against him until after his indictment;

That while he was thus confined, several hundred white men of said county, assembled at or near the court house and jail for the purpose of mobbing him, and were only prevented from doing so, as defendant is informed and believes, by the presence of United States soldiers;

That the indictment was returned on the 20th of October, 1919, by the grand jury composed wholly of white men;

That on the 30th of the same month subpoenas for the State's witnesses were issued, to appear and testify in his case on the 3rd of November following;

That on the said 3rd day of November, without ever having been permitted to see or talk with any attorney, or any person in reference to his defense, he was carried from the jail to the court room and put upon trial—the court appointed an attorney for him, before a jury composed of white men;

That the excitement and feeling against the defendant among the whites of the said county was such that it was impossible to obtain an unprejudiced jury of white men to try him—and that no white jury, being fairly disposed, would have had the courage to acquit him regardless of the testimony;

That the trial proceeded without consultation on his part, with any attorney, without witnesses in his behalf, and without an opportunity on his part to obtain witnesses or prepare for defense;

That no evidence was offered in his behalf;

That he had no knowledge or familiarity with Court procedure, had never been at a trial in Court before, and had no definite idea of his rights therein, and had no conception of what steps should be taken for his protection;

That the whole course of trial, from beginning to end, occupied about three-fourths of an hour;

That the jury after hearing State's evidence and the Court's charge retired and returned immediately; that is within about from three to six minutes with a verdict of guilty against the defendant.

Defendant, Frank Hicks, further says that no copy of the indictment was ever served upon him nor upon any attorney for him, and he says that he never consented to waive such service, nor requested nor consented to the trial without same. Defendant, therefore, says that he was convicted and sentenced to death without due process of law.

That under the law as it has existed for many years, the Circuit Courts of the state at each term appoint jury commissioners to select grand and petit jurors to serve at the succeeding term; and for more than thirty years it has been the unbroken practice of said courts to appoint only white men on such commissions, and of such commissions to select only white men for grand and petit jurors for the succeeding terms—constituting a discrimination in the administration of the law against the Negroes, on account of their color and of their being members of the African race; and that if in the course of the Court's proceedings it became or becomes necessary to issue a venire for talesmen, to the sheriff, the invariable course is, and has been, to summon only white men; this practice, with reference to the selection of grand and petit jurors, and the summoning of talesmen, prevails and has prevailed in the Circuit Court of Phillips County, with unbroken uniformity, to the extent that no Negro has been appointed on a jury commission, or selected to serve as a juror, either grand or petit, for more than thirty years, and that no Negro has been appointed to or has sat upon any jury in said Court at any time during such a period; that the Negro population of said county exceeds the whites at least five to one and that among them are a great many men, possessed of the intellectual, moral and legal qualification for jury commissioner, and for grand and petit jurors; and that they are excluded therefrom solely on account of their race or color.

That defendant has thus been, by said discriminating practices, and by said trial, deprived of his rights under the Constitution of the United States, and especially the Fourteenth Amendment thereto; and was in and by said trial and proceedings and still is, denied equal protection of the law.

Defendant further says, that while it is true, as he is now advised, that the proper and regular place and time to have objected to the grand jury, and to the indictment returned by it, would have been before the trial yet as before stated, he knew nothing about such proceeding or the proper order thereof; and was given no opportunity to object to the grand jury, or any member thereof, and knew nothing of his rights to raise any objections to either grand or petit jury; and nothing about how to challenge or object to either of them, and was not advised in that regard.

That the verdict is contrary to the law and the evidence, and is not supported by sufficient evidence.

FOURTH

That the Court erred in rendering judgment and sentence against defendant.

Defendant says that for the purpose of proving the statements in the first and second grounds of the motion, he has ascertained the names of the jury commissioners, at the various terms of this Court, from 1905 to 1919, inclusive, beginning with . . . ; and he now prays that they be summoned to testify on the hearing of this motion, and that he be permitted to prove said statements.

Defendant further prays that the verdict and judgment herein against him be set aside and that he be granted a fair and impartial hearing.

MURPHY & McHANEY,
SCIPIO JONES,
Attorneys for Defendant

Alf Banks, Jr., being first duly sworn, on his oath, says:

I am a Negro. I was living in Phillips County, Arkansas, up to the 1st of October, 1919, when I was arrested and thereafter kept in custody until after I was sentenced to death, on a charge of murdering W. A. Adkins. I was then sent to the State penitentiary for execution and I am now in the custody of the keeper of the penitentiary. I was never told of the charge against me, until I was indicted. I was put in the county jail at Helena and kept there in close confinement, with no opportunity to see or confer with anyone about my defense. A large number of Negroes, a hundred or more, were held in custody there with me during all that time. I was frequently whipped with great severity, and was also put into an electric chair and shocked, and strangling drugs would be put to my nose to make me tell things against others that they had killed or shot at some of the white people to force me to testify against them. I had not seen anything of the kind, and so told them, at first, but they kept on, and tortured me so that I finally told them falsely that what they wanted me to say was true and that I would testify it. They would have me blindfolded when torturing me. Once, they took me upstairs, put a rope around my neck, having me blindfolded, pulled on the rope, and one of them said, "Don't knock the trick out yet, we can make him tell," or words to that effect. That feeling that they would kill him, he agreed to tell what they wanted him to. That they would go over it and tell him that he knew that was so, and that he had to tell it. During the trials at one or two of them, they took me from the jail to the court room to testify against them. I think it was the trial of Joe Fox and Albert Giles, and I think also against one or two others. As they were taking me to the court room, they told me if I changed my testimony or did not testify as I had said, when they took me back they would skin me alive. I testified as I had told them, in the same way they had made me tell as near as I could. It was not true; it was false. This whipping and torturing was known generally among the Negroes there in custody, and it was known what it was for, to make them testify. I know that they so whipped and tortured a great many of them. But cannot say that they whipped them quite all. They used Negroes they had in or about the jail to do most of the whipping, but some white men would be present. One of the Negroes who saw part of the torture was Kid Collins, who seemed to be a trusty about the jail. Many of the scars from this torturing are still upon my body. I would never have testified falsely as I did if I had not been made to do it.

His
ALF X. BANKS.
Mark

Witness to mark:

  J. R. Booker.

Subscribed and sworn to before me this the 18th day of December, 1919.

  (SEAL) J. R. BOOKER, Notary Public.

My commission expires Jan. 31 1923.

Endorsed:

Filed December 20, 1919.

A. G. Burke, Clerk.

CHAPTER IX

The Progressive Farmers and Household Union of America

So much has been charged against this Union which those Negro farmers had organized among themselves, that a reprint of its constitution and bylaws ought to satisfy the most skeptical that the members were not organizing to kill white people. Every word and letter in this little volume is here given just as it appears in a copy which was given to each member. Special attention is called to the object of this organization.

"The object of this organization shall be to advance the interests of the Negro morally and intellectually and to **make him a better citizen and a better farmer.**"

Nothing could more clearly refute the slander of those who were interested in breaking up this organization among Negroes than that paragraph.

UNITED STATES CONSTITUTION AND BY-LAWS OF THE PROGRESSIVE FARMERS AND HOUSEHOLD UNION OF AMERICA

The Negro Business League

IN UNION IS STRENGTH

First organized under the act of Congress of 1865. Revised and organized by Robert L. Hill, Councillor. V. E. Powell, M. D., Knox Degraphenreed and Lewis Langroon in 1918, for the benefit of the Negro Race.

Organized at Winchester. Ratified and incorporated at Little Rock, Ark., under orders of the Supreme Court of Arkansas.

CONSTITUTION

This organization shall be known as THE PROGRESSIVE FARMERS AND HOUSEHOLD UNION OF AMERICA.

OBJECT

The object of this organization shall be to advance the interests of the Negro, morally and intellectually, and to make him a better citizen and a better farmer.

ARTICLE I

Officers

Section 1. —This organization shall have five (5) table officers; viz—President, Vice-President, Secretary, Treasurer and Chaplain.

ARTICLE II

Executive Board

There shall be an Executive Board consisting of nine members.

ARTICLE III

Election

The officers shall be elected to serve three months or until their successors shall be chosen and qualified.

A two-third vote of the membership of this order is necessary to elect any and all officers.

ARTICLE IV

This order shall have the power to enact any law for the protection and government of its members.

ARTICLE V

This order shall have a pass word, door words, grips and signs for its members. The same sign shall be changed every three months. Ritual shall be gotten out by the President, Secretary, and Chairman of the Executive Board. The President shall extend these pass words, signs, and grips to the members every three months. And if any of the signs or pass words should become exposed the President shall call the body together at once for the purpose of issuing new ones. Absence of the Secretary and Chairman of the Executive Board gives the President power to issue signs, pass words, etc., which shall remain in force until the next quarterly meeting.

ARTICLE VI

Any member known to expose any of the secrets of this order shall be tried by the order and upon conviction shall be fined and excluded.

ARTICLE VII

Any member excluded from this order as provided in Article VI shall not be allowed to rejoin within ninety-nine years.

Members are forbidden to associate with such excluded members, and for violation of this provision they shall themselves be excluded.

ARTICLE VIII

This Union shall organize among its members a joint Stock Company with a Capital Stock of One Thousand Dollars ($1000.00).

Section 1. —Each member shall purchase at least one share at five dollars ($5.00). Members may purchase as many shares as they can at five dollars ($5.00) each.

Section 2—When the Union shall have accumulated Two Thousand Dollars ($2000) they may invest the same in real estate for the Order.

Sec. 3—All money paid in the Union shall be deposited in the Bank of Winchester, Ark.

Sec. 4—No check shall be given on the Order, unless the bill be first presented to both the Supreme Commander and President. All checks must be signed by Supreme Commander, President and Secretary.

ARTICLE IX

A Grand Order meeting of this Union shall assemble semi-annually at the Court Houses of respective counties. The Order shall be composed of delegates from subordinate Lodges.

Sec. 1—Each subordinate Lodge shall elect at a regular meeting three delegates to represent them at the County seat twice a year.

ARTICLE X

The Grand Lodge shall have six officers: Grand President, Grand Vice-President, Grand Secretary, Grand Treasurer, Grand Chaplain and an Executive Board of 9 members. These Grand officers shall hold office for one year.

ARTICLE XI

The business of this Grand Lodge shall be to further advance the cause, uniting the race into a perfect Union in various counties. And to levy special taxes on subordinate Lodges for the purpose of purchasing land. Deeds and Titles to lands bought must be made in the name of the Order.

ARTICLE XII

Any member who shall fail to pay his dues after his arrears shall reach two months shall be suspended until same is paid.

ARTICLE XIII

Sec. 1—This Order shall elect a Deputy who shall hold office six months. He shall be a salaried officer and it shall be his duty to organize clubs in the county. He shall charge two two dollars ($2.00) per club organized, and the same shall be applied to his salary. He shall report monthly to the Order.

Sec. 2—If any Deputy be found guilty of collecting more than two dollars ($2.00) from any Lodge, he shall be removed by the Executive Board and his vacancy filled by appointment of the President, and the appointee shall serve for six months from the day of appointment.

ARTICLE XIV

Each Lodge shall have a door keeper, and each member must give to him the pass word before being allowed to enter the Lodge. Any member forgetting the pass word must remain outside until ordered admitted by the President.

BY LAWS

1. The Union shall be opened and closed with prayer by the Chaplain.
2. Reading of minutes.
3. Reports of Committees.
4. Appointment of Committees.
5. Report of Treasurer.
6. Consideration of applications.
7. Receiving members.
8. The president shall preside at all meetings of this order and in his absence the Vice-President shall preside.
9. The President shall rule on all points of order and shall appoint all committees not otherwise provided for.
10. No member shall speak more than twice on any question without consent of the body.

WE BATTLE FOR THE RIGHTS OF OUR RACE
"IN UNION IS STRENGTH"
We Champion the Moral, Material, Political and Intellectual
Interests of Our Race.

CHAPTER X

Summary and Contrast

Economic justice reached its awful climax in 1919 in the final answer to two appeals made by working men, both groups seeking through peaceful appeal to win better wage and working conditions; both presenting their grievances through chosen representatives, one to be rewarded by the President of the United States with patient hearing and final success, the other to suffer massacre at the hands of the mob and the death penalty by courts of law.

The first group of working men was composed of the coal miners whose appeal merged into a strike, the second group was composed of colored farmers, whose appeal was forestalled by a conspiracy against them, which, formed among white land owners, to perpetuate the peonage complained against, put to death by lynch law scores of colored farmers and then prostituted the process of courts to their purpose, sent seventy-five working men to the penitentiary for long terms of imprisonment, and doomed twelve to die in the electric chair.

The bare statement of these facts is so shocking to the sense of justice that it almost defies belief, but the statement finds its complete corroboration in the burnt and pillaged homes of the helpless colored farmers exiled or murdered and the ninety victims who in hopeless despair look through the penitentiary bars, twelve of them sentenced to death because they dared, in this democracy of ours, to ask relief from economic slavery.

The circumstances attending the two appeals were almost as remarkable as were the final and widely differing results. The miners made their appeals for higher wages accompanying them with the implied threat of a strike. That appeal was made to the Federal Government and was accorded a full and patient hearing. Representative labor leaders were heard by chosen representatives of the Government, who granted relief in some cases and denied it in others. The miners, dissatisfied, retired from the conference to determine further action.

Quick action by miners unions followed the report of the miner leaders. A strike vote was called, and in overwhelming numbers the miners decided to strike. The disastrous result of the proposed strike caused the government to counsel against the militant methods threatened by the miners and even the President of the United States from his sick bed sent his appeal to the strikers in the interest of peace.

But the miners turned deaf ears to that appeal, closed their eyes to the disastrous results of the impending strife, and boasting of their power to throttle the nation into submission, went on a nation-wide strike and for a period of ten days crippled transportation, deprived the public of food, shut off lights, banked fires, thus threatening to freeze the helpless public, and spread misery over every part of American soil. Court injunctions were ignored and the Government, helpless, yielded, and the President capitulated to the strikers. The strike leaders, triumphant, called off the strike and the miners' appeal was rewarded with success.

Shortly preceding these eventful days, another group of laborers decided to make their appeal for better wages and working conditions. They had suffered conditions which denied them freedom to make fair contracts, forced them to buy at exorbitant prices and sell their produce at rates amounting almost to confiscation. Land tilled on shares barely brought the farmers money enough to pay their "findings," supplied by the white land owner, leaving the toiler a pittance of his year's work, often leaving him in debt.

The Negro farmer hoped to share the increased price of cotton and the general prosperity of the Nation and all during 1919 looked forward to a bountiful reward at harvest time. Cotton, which in former years had sold for twelve and fourteen cents a pound, had gone to forty-five cents and higher. The sunshine of "Great Expectations" brightened the cabin homes. But when harvest time came, the farmers' dream failed, for profiteering land owners combined and no forty-five-cent prices were to be had. Farmers who would sell their cotton for twenty-five cents were paid the price. Those who demanded the market price were unable to sell. Naturally widespread unrest followed. The farmers resented the imposition of the cotton buyers, and the buyers denounced the "darkies" who dared to demand a square deal.

Meanwhile, the Negro farmers decided to combine their forces and employ a white lawyer to represent them in their plea for better systems of contract, better wages, and better working conditions. The result was an organization which was of the nature of a secret fraternal order.

The farmers joined the lodge rapidly and the section in and around Elaine was represented by nearly two hundred farmers. The meeting places were the colored churches at Elaine and Hoop Spur. Only three meetings had been held—two of them before the day of the "slaughter of innocents," which was the 30th day of September, 1919. The lodge employed Mr. Bratton, a white lawyer, to represent the members in their effort to secure the market price for their cotton, to arrange for better contracts, to adjust their accounts with the landowners and generally to safeguard their interests.

This labor movement among colored farmers did not please the white landowners and the proposal of the farmers to act through a white layer constituted a menace to the profiteering practices of the white people of the neighborhood. The dissatisfaction of the white people found expression at first in gentle hints that the Negroes were making a mistake; these were followed by warnings to colored people to let that lodge business alone. Colored men knew of the success of white men in labor movements, and, believing they would be protected by laws, continued their plans for presenting their claims.

Then came the tragedy such as no labor movement in this country has ever witnessed. On the night of September 30th, while the lodge was in session at the church in Elaine, about 150 men, women and children being present, five automobile loads of white men stopped in front of the church and immediately fired a volley of shots into the building. The people rushed out only to meet volley after volley from the white mob. Several persons were killed, the others ran to the woods or made their way home. One white man was shot, but whether he was killed accidentally by one of his fellow lynchers or was shot by some Negro during the fight is not known.

Next day white men from all over Phillips County and even from Mississippi set the church on fire, burning up several persons who were killed the night before, and then began a systematic man-hunt, killing colored men indiscriminately, driving others from their homes, and then taking from these abandoned homes the produce saved by the farmers for their winter use. Thousands of dollars worth of property was destroyed and stolen and cotton by the bale which the farmers had refused to sell was boldly carted away by members of the mob.

Next followed an even more deplorable act of this Arkansas tragedy. Upon pretense that the white man who was killed on the night of the riot, and also the two next day were the victims of a conspiracy formed by colored people to kill all the white people, over one hundred colored men were arrested and thrown into jail. While they were thus confined their homes were robbed of every bit of property, so that when those who were set at liberty, upon their promise not to join the lodge again returned, they were without food, shelter or clothes!

To contrast the result of the plea of the miners for better wages, with the results of the plea of the Arkansas colored farmers for identically the same thing, is to disclose to thinking people a phase of democracy not safe for the world or any part of it. The miners combined in unions, counseled together and chose representatives to present their pleas which carried the threat of a strike. Their demands were not granted and ignoring the President's appeal, they struck. Their strike menaced the lives, health, comfort and welfare of the entire nation. They defied the courts and brought the President to his knees. He yielded, the strike was won and the miners came into their own.

The colored farmers combined, counseled together, employed counsel to present their plea. They did not threaten to strike, did not strike, menaced nothing, injured nobody, and yet:

Hundreds of them today are penniless, "Refugees from pillaged homes";

More than a hundred were killed by white mobs, for which **not one white man has been arrested;**

Seventy-five men are serving life sentences in the penitentiary, and

Twelve men are sentenced to die.

If this is democracy, what is bolshevism?

CHAPTER XI

The Arkansas Supreme Court Acts

Since the foregoing was written, the Supreme Court of the State of Arkansas has acted on the appeal of the twelve men awaiting electrocution in the penitentiary at Little Rock. The decision against six of these men was reversed and their cases were remanded to Phillips County for trial. This decision was rendered on the indictments and not on the merits of the cases.

The cases of the six who were found guilty of murder in the first degree as charged in the indictment, were affirmed and they were thus left to be electrocuted according to the sentence of the lower court. The entire country awaits the result of the decision.

The six men who were sent back to Phillips County by the Supreme Courts decision have been tried again by the Circuit Court and again sentenced to death—the faulty wording of the indictment this time having been corrected. In sending out the reporter of the same the Associated Press dispatch made again the charge that those Negroes were organized to kill white people and *seize their property*.

The dispatch reads as follows:

TRY SIX COLORED MEN

Second Trial of Accused Rioters in Arkansas

"Helena Ark., May 3. —Six Negroes sentenced to death for alleged participation in the Phillips County race disturbance last October, faced retrial here today. Ben Helm, Negro recently arrested, also will be tried on a first degree murder charge. The retrial was ordered because of faulty wording of the verdict.

Seventy five Negroes have been convicted of participation in the disorder, which resulted in the death of five white persons and unknown number of Negroes, and which were not controlled until Federal troops were sent into the district.

Of those convicted, 12 received sentence of death and 53 prison terms ranging from one to 21 years.

The disturbance according to evidence adduced at the original trials, was the premature outbreak of an insurrection followed by the Progressive Farmers and Household Union of America, a Negro organization, the purpose of which it is said was the annihilation of all whites and the seizure of their property."

The American thinking public cannot bring back the dead but it can open the prison doors and let these poor defenseless men go free. There must be enough justice in Arkansas to never rest until this great wrong is righted. Not until this is done and the peonage system ended can Arkansas take her place among the brave and the free.

Governor Brough has started the movement. Let the Christian, moral and legal forces "carry on" until these black men are given their lives and their freedom and Arkansas clears her skirts of this awful disgrace. When black men can receive protection to life and liberty and property, they will gladly give their labor for the prosperity of the South. As long as this dastardly crime is condoned, shielded and encouraged by white men, black men whose labor is needed for its development will avoid the state and leave the South to ruin and desolation as they are doing every day.

Meanwhile this booklet goes into the greatest court in the world and before the bar of public opinion pleads the cases of these helpless men. Every reader a member of that bar and the white people of Arkansas—the honest, law-abiding Christian men and women of that state—are the judges and jury to whom this appeal is made. They are urged for the honor of the state and its material welfare to investigate the facts given in this book in an unprejudiced and impartial manner and if they are found to be true—these people will know what steps to take to right the great wrong done to these innocent hardworking men. If they are given freedom and opportunity, protection of the law for life and liberty—they will prove the greatest economic asset of the state. If not and this outrage is approved by the great Court of white public opinion in Arkansas, it will mean the loss of millions of dollars to the state, because Negroes will not remain in the state unless this great wrong is righted.

This is the answer to those who are honestly seeking a plan to stop Negro emigration from the farms of Arkansas. Put a stop to the plan of taking the fruit of the Negro's labor as was done at Elaine and Hoop Spur last October and is being done all over Arkansas where Negroes work the farms of white men.

Believing that under normal conditions with the black man's rights guaranteed him and the protection of law for his life, liberty, and property, the South is the best section of our country for the Negro, the writer (a native of the South) will be only too glad to cooperate with the progressive element of the white South in bringing about such a desideratum.

ARTICLES ON THE MISSISSIPPI FLOOD

Wells-Barnett's most ambitious publications from the 1920s are the following series of articles on the Mississippi Flood. One of the worst floods in U.S. history, the Mississippi Flood took place in the spring of 1927, and displaced 120,000 people living in the Yazoo-Mississippi Delta region—an area from which many of Chicago's black migrants had migrated. As the waters rose, rescue workers ferried white Mississippians out of the worst zones, but local planters forced many black sharecropping families to remain behind. They lived in terrible conditions and were put to work rebuilding the Mississippi River's levees under a pass system. Wells-Barnett sent letters to Herbert Hoover, who as secretary of commerce was managing the federal relief, and also published a series of articles in the *Chicago Defender* documenting conditions suffered by the black refugees and failures of the relief effort. As usual, Wells-Barnett spared no one in laying out the causes of the poor conditions among the delta's black refugees. The following is an example of Wells-Barnett's articles published in the *Chicago Defender* about the flood.

SOURCE: Ida B. Wells-Barnett, "Flood Refugees Are Held as Slaves in Mississippi Camp," *Chicago Defender*, July 30, 1927; "South Backs Down After Probe Looms," *Chicago Defender*, July 25, 1927; "Brand Ministers in Flood Areas Betrayers," *Chicago Defender*, July 16, 1927.

FLOOD REFUGEES ARE HELD AS SLAVES IN MISSISSIPPI CAMP

Men Who Escaped Death in Government Controlled Area Describe Viciousness of Southern Whites Ruling Workers

Last week's issue of the Defender had a letter from one of the men in Greenville, Miss., which claimed to tell of the conditions in the camps which are still being maintained only for our people in Greenville and Natchez and several other places. Naturally the question arose in the minds of thinking people: "Why are they Colored camps?" "Why are hundreds of thousands of our people herded in camps, instead of being provided for in houses, where they and their families can be helped as are the white refugees, and live together as families should do?" "Why must Colored people only be forced to work on the levees for $1 per day at the point of a gun before they can get rations?" "And why can't the Race, who are 90 per cent of the actual flood sufferers, share in the $14,000,000 relief fund which the country sent freely to the flooded district?"

All of these are pertinent questions which every one of the 12,000,000 people of our Race in this country should be asking themselves and using their brains to find answers for. Then, after they get the answers they should get busy in an effort to have the whole country know the facts and use their power to have these conditions changed.

ONLY RACE CAN ACT

Nobody else is going to do anything about it if we don't. So far the Defender is the only journal which is making any protest that I can see. Already some of our people have told Secretary Hoover and others who can correct these evils, that everything is all right; that Mrs. Barnett is a radical and that nobody pays any attention to her, as she is seeking notoriety. Even the "Colored committees' reports do not confirm the statements you mention," says Secretary Hoover, and the people of our race in Pine Bluff, Ark., are giving Mr. Hoover a loving cup in appreciation for his "good work" for them, while their own people are being treated like slaves.

I have had letters, phone calls and personal commendations for the things I have tried to tell in this column. But when I ask these persons if they have passed resolutions asking investigations of these camps and recommending better protection for our Race in their clubs, churches, lodges and fraternal societies and sent them to President Coolidge, Secretary Hoover, the National Red Cross, Senator Charles S. Deneen, Congressman Madden, they invariably say no. They do not seem to realize that it is their job to back up what the Defender and I have said about these intolerable conditions. The only way to bring public opinion to action is for those whose race is suffering to cry aloud, and keep on crying aloud until something is done. It will require the combined influence of all our people in the North, East and West, where our votes count, to put a stop to the slavery that is going on right now in the government camps in Arkansas, Mississippi and Louisiana. All the Defender and I can do is to tell the Race about these conditions. It is up to you who have the power of organizations to keep on with resolutions and demands until these helpless people of our Race down there are no longer held in captivity in the government camps, to be driven back to the plantations when the water goes down and delivered into the virtual slavery of the peonage system of the South.

The South needs, and is asking help in this, her time of trouble. It is the psychological moment for us to demand that the South do justice to our people before she receives help from the nation.

ESCAPED REFUGEES' STORIES

Meanwhile John Jones (that is not his name), 23 years old, came to my door last Friday evening. He was in his shirt sleeves and had a cotton blanket rolled up under his arm. He had just escaped from the government camp in Louisiana. He was born and reared in that state and when the high water came about 300 of them were taken to the camp.

All the men were put in one long tent and the women and children in another. He was there 15 days and was not permitted to associate with his wife and children in all that time. They had to lie on the floor with a piece of canvas only under them and no covering. Of course they slept in their clothes and had no change. He said: "The first thing they do is to line you up and give you a 'shot,' then they give you something to eat and tell you to lie down for a day. The 'shots' make you sick and sometimes are fatal. I saw one man drop dead as soon as he received the injection. He was about 40 years old. Over 25 people died in our camp from these 'shots.'"

"The next morning the gong rang at 5:30 o'clock and we got a breakfast of salty bacon, one egg, bread and some brownish water they called coffee with no sugar. Then the boss man arrived and told us that we were to go to work on the levee and would be given $1 a day and board. He has a gun and you know its useless to argue or refuse to go, so you say all right and take the shovel and go.

"At noontime they gave us navy beans, bread and more of the stuff they called coffee with no sugar. Then back to work until night, when we get potatoes, corn beef hash and more of that same so-called coffee.

"It was chilly without any cover so I asked for a blanket, but they wouldn't give me one. Then I said I would pay for one out of my wages and got it. I have it here. It is all I got for my 15 days' work.

REFUSED PAY, SHOT

"I was there 17 days and was worked like this every day and all day, except the two Sundays. Then I went to the boss man and told him I wanted to get my wages as I was going to leave. He said: 'Don't you go away, nigger. If you do I'll shoot you.' He had his gun pointed at me, so I said nothing, but went away. The next day I asked him again for my money. He said: 'Wait till I go down to the commissary and see how much time you have coming.' When he came back he said 'We don't pay till the first of the month. Nigger, you don't leave here; if you do I will shoot you.' I told him he might as well go ahead and shoot, because I was certainly going to leave there. He then pulled his gun out and shot me through the fleshy part of the leg. I fell and my wife ran out of the workman's tent and tied her handkerchief around my leg to stop blood. Another fellow helped me into the tent and laid me down."

"Didn't the other men say or do anything about it?" I asked.

"Not a thing," he said. "There were only three white men to the 300 Colored men, but they had guns and used them on anyone who dared to do anything. That night they beat four men because they refused to work hard all day and part of the night also.

HOW HE ESCAPED

"While I was lying there I wrote a note to my wife and told her I was going away, but for her to stay there until I sent for her. A friend took it over to her and she waved to let me know she had it. About 11 o'clock that night, when all were asleep, I rolled off the floor under the tent flap and hobbled away. My wound was a clean fresh wound, but my leg was very sore. (I saw the scars where the bullet went in and where it came out, in the fleshy part of the lower thigh.) I walked all night and next day till I reached Arkansas City. I rested four hours, then rode in a wagon for 20 miles. A truck carried me to Helena, Ark. Money for a ticket was given me and I rode to Memphis, Tenn. From there I rode on the Dixie highway to St. Louis in a man's car. From there I came to Springfield and stayed over night. I was brought from there to the Illinois Free Employment office on 35th St., in this city by a kind hearted white man in his car, arriving at 10 o'clock this morning. I waited there until 4 o'clock for work, which did not come, then went out on the street begging for something to eat and a place to sleep. A lady sent me to you, and here I am."

This was at 8 o'clock last Thursday night. Since then I have fed another escaped refugee from the Pine Bluff, Ark., camp. His story will be told in the next issue.

Have you readers here in the North no duty to perform for these, our suffering people?

SEE ATTEMPT TO HIDE FACTS AS COMMITTEE STARTS FLOOD PROBE

By IDA B. WELLS-BARNETT

Since the publication of Secretary Hoover's letter to the writer in the June 23 issue of the Defender, I have talked with Claude Barnett of the Associated Negro Press. Mr. Barnett (no relation, but of the same name) is one of Mr. Hoover's "Negro committee," and he very courteously furnished me with copies of his reports on the situation in the delta, relative to the treatment of the refugees of our Race.

These reports are very illuminating as to 90 per cent of the refugees, 580,000 in fact, being of our race; the food furnished, the assurance that the National Red Cross has been just and fair, "although local committees frequently have misinterpreted their policies," and especially that the Red Cross is mapping out a comprehensive program with the balance of the $14,000,000 a generous public contributed: that when congress convenes it is expected that additional provision will be made, also that Secretary Hoover, through the Red Cross, had already started an extensive campaign with public health doctors, nurses and social workers, to cover every swamp and bit of open water in the flood district, exterminate mosquitos, inspect and purify water in every well, so no epidemic may occur.

ASK ABOUT RATIONS

Mr. Barnett devotes much space in laudation of the good camps found in Baton Rouge and Lafayette, La., and Natchez, Miss. He tells of the three bad camps at Greenville, Miss., Crowley and Sicily Island, La., very briefly, with no assurance that these conditions which are bad, but they are touched upon very lightly. It does not seem enough to say that the National Red Cross is all right, "although local committees frequently have misinterpreted their policies." It is the actions of the local committees of which complaints are made. Nowhere does he tell whether the Red Cross has removed the W. A. Percys.

The public also wants to know if it is true that our women and children in the bad camps are still being refused food and clothing unless they have men in their families, who are forced to work on the levees at $1 per day, and that white men still have to certify to that fact before they can share in the relief which the people of the United States sent there for them, to be given freely to those who needed it.

NATIONAL RED CROSS ALL RIGHT

Unless the National Red Cross, which is responsible for the work of its local agents, has changed these conditions of which complaint has been made, the National Red Cross is encouraging and condoning a system of discrimination, of peonage and of robbery of funds sent to a helpless people. Black men ought not to hesitate to say so if these charges are true, since Mr. Hoover and the National Red Cross will depend on what they report. If they do not report the situation as it is, then they are to blame if the public is hoodwinked.

When a doctor visits a patient who has a bullet wound that is infected, he doesn't spend time admiring the part of the body which needs no attention nor draw attention to the symmetry of the patient's limbs. He gets busy at once on the infected wound and cleanses and disinfects the spot which needs it.

The public is dissatisfied with this "Colored committee's" report, and it has a right to be. That is why it was doubted whether a "Colored committee" could afford to tell the truth and still live down there. The public will never be satisfied that the National Red Cross is all right until it is definitely informed that the outrageous conditions at Greenville, Miss., and other points have been changed for the better and that the 90 per cent flood sufferers are sharing equally with the whites the relief sent for them.

TESTIMONY FROM A SUFFERER

Meanwhile the following letter comes to me:

Greenville, Miss.
June 27, 1927.

"Dear Mrs. Barnett: First, what I am giving you in this letter, whatever you do please do not publish my name, but I would like to see it appear in the Defenders next issue. I ask you to withhold my name because I am living here in Greenville, the gridiron of hell. Mr. Hoover states in last week's Defender that the Colored committees which were sent to make investigations in all the Colored camps in the flood area "do not confirm the statements you mention."

No, I guess not, just as you said below in the same column, it is due to where the Colored committeemen are living.

Had I had a chance to get to see one of them, he would have had something to tell, if he would have told it. The reason I didn't get a chance to see any of the committeemen was because I was hiding. I had to hide unless I wished to be made to work like a dog under a gun and club and tagged like a bale of cotton.

If there was no work for the men to do they were marched down to the river and made to sit in the hot sun on concrete, which was just like sitting on a hot griddle, and we had to sit there until night. No overseer would let any of our men go and scrub out some white woman's house and clean off her yard.

PROVISIONS DESTROYED

Not one Mexican, Italian, Greek or any other race but the Colored Race had to go to get just a little of the stale meat, meal, lard, etc., to eat. It was not much good.

Last week there were nearly two carloads of provisions thrown in the river which had spoiled. Why? Because they wouldn't let the Colored people have it when they went after it, and white people are not on the levees trying to get something to eat, because when they think the white people's supplies are about out trucks are loaded and sent around to their homes with the best of everything.

Up until now Colored men are not getting anything fit to eat unless they meet the boats and help unload them—then they get something. Any Colored woman who has no husband has to get some white man or woman's signature for clothes, bedding or anything else she needs. My people, not only here in Greenville, but throughout the South, are treated worse than convicts.

ACTIONS OF PREACHERS

Now, Mrs. Barnett, find enclosed clippings from the Greenville Democrat Times, the leading paper published in this town. H. H. Humes and A. B. Bolden and other Negro preachers like them are the only ones south of the Mason and Dixon line who meet the white people, who tell them to preach to their people that the white man in the South is our best friend and will do for them what the white man in the North will not do. Read the clippings, Mrs. Barnett. (The clipping is an editorial in the above named paper half a column long, which quotes Rev. Bolden as commending the white people of Greenville and thanking W. A. Percy and other whites, for their assistance and urging Colored people to remain in Greenville, where they had much property and four schools, which the white people had agreed to burden themselves with heavy taxation to maintain.)

PEOPLE IN SLAVERY

Mrs. Barnett, our people are in slavery. They are held in camps here on the levee. Lots of them would leave here and try to find something better for themselves but they are held here in these camps until some white man gets his plantation from under water. Then he comes to Greenville to get some "niggers." W. A. Percy consents to let a number of Colored men go to this plantation on the advice of E. D. Davis, who is chairman of the labor department. He has tagged all the Colored people when they go for something to eat. When they say they have no work and no money with which to buy, he tells the women Mr. so and so has cotton to chop. They can go out and make 50 or 60 cents a day chopping cotton. The men can make 75 cents a day plowing. If they want to eat they must take this offer.

This is only a part of what my people are undergoing in this hell hole. I can't tell the half of it on paper. I am afraid for what I have written, but I want you to know that the committee sent here by Mr. Moton did not see the people getting such treatment. If they did, they had no talk with them. Those who have homes or are teaching school or are doctors, are doing very well themselves and are being used as catspaws by the white people and could talk differently. We who are under the lash know better and pray God daily that the way may open for us to leave these terrible conditions. I am going to close by writing my name on a slip of paper. If you give this letter to Mr. Abbott, please tear my name off."

APPEALS FOR HELP

He asked before he closed if some of the organizations here which have raised money for flood sufferers would be willing to use some of it to help him get his family away, to please let him know through me. He gives the names of people in Chicago who will vouch for his character. If anyone is interested in helping him I will gladly show them the letter and give the names of the Chicago people whom he says know him. It certainly seems that they could not put their money to better use than to help deserving people escape from such conditions.

SOUTH BACKS DOWN AFTER PROBE LOOMS

"Colored Committee" to Be Catspaw

The letter to Secretary of Commerce Hoover, published in this paper June 11 from the Ida B. Wells club, the Race Welfare

committee and the Baptist Ministers' alliance, has been answered
by the secretary himself and is as follows:

> My dear Mrs. Wells-Barnett: I have your letter of June 6. As you are
> probably aware, I have appointed a committee of Colored leaders,
> under the chairmanship of Dr. Moton of Tuskegee institute, to make
> a complete investigation of conditions in all Colored camps in the
> flood area. In addition, we have set up Colored advisory committees
> in each of these camps, and the reports of these committees do not
> confirm the statements you mention.
>
>   In case you desire further information in this connection, I
> would suggest that you address Dr. Moton direct.
>
> Yours Faithfully,
HERBERT HOOVER

The "statements" mentioned in my letter contained the copy of
that infamous circular published by W. A. Percy of Greenville,
Miss., the local Red Cross official, which said "no Negro women
and children would receive any of the rations sent there by the
nation, unless there was a man in the family to work on the
levee," and that fact would have to be certified by a white man;
that "no Negro man" would receive these rations unless he
worked on the levee at $1 per day, and then only every three
days, and that fact must be certified to by a white man, and that
"no Negro" who was working for more than $1 per day would
receive rations.

GOVERNMENT INVESTIGATION

What was asked in that letter was a government investigation of
the outrageous treatment of men, women and children as indicated by that infamous circular and confirmed by letters received
from that district from Colored sufferers. What we get is this
shifting of responsibility onto the shoulders of "Colored committees" whose reports do not confirm the "statements you mention." We said in that letter, and we say now, that no Colored
man or men could get the facts, or if they got them they would
not dare publish them. Because they live in the South, or are at

the head of schools and businesses located in the South, they would make no report which would endanger their lives and property, and we could not expect them to do so. The Chicago branch of the Red Cross has refused to interfere in the disposal of money, food and clothing which has been given unstintedly by the nation for the benefit of all who suffered from the flood. Only the federal government, through Mr. Hoover, could intervene, and all he tells us is that the "Colored committee's" reports do not confirm the statements you mention!

Yet every mail has brought letters from members of our Race, telling of the terrible treatment they are receiving at the hands of the white men who are dispensing the thousands of dollars to white flood sufferers freely, and making Negroes work before they can share any of this bounty, and starving Negro women and children if they have no man to go to work on the levee! Colored people are harder hit than white, because more of them lived on the farms—they lost everything they had. They are herded in camps and in many places treated like dogs, say the letters which come to us.

Who knows better than the sufferers themselves how they are treated. Extracts from letters before me say: "I am getting along fairly well, as I work for big white folks, but my God! others are being treated like dogs by the whites, who carry guns and curse and kick around those who have no protection." "I have never in my life seen such suffering. We worked two nights and days in ——— after the levee broke, and with very little food. They took us for everything but human beings." "There is a burial every day. We buried five bodies in one common box yesterday. I have tried several times to get away, but there are no trains—only boats, and they carry only whites."

WHAT CAN WE DO?

It is as much as life is worth to write or speak of these things down there but we who can speak should send a united cry to the federal government for fuller investigation and better protection for these helpless people.

Let every Negro organization send resolutions to President

Coolidge and Secretary Hoover, and to Senator Deneen here in Chicago, demanding a thorough federal investigation of the terrible conditions by men clothed with the power of the government, to act for the protection of these poor people, and demand that the money, clothing and food sent by the nation through the Red Cross be given freely to those who need it.

Notes

INTRODUCTION

1. "A Lecture," an advertisement for one of Wells's speeches, *Washington Bee*, October 22, 1892.
2. Ida B. Wells, *Crusade for Justice: The Autobiography of Ida B. Wells*, ed. Alfreda M. Duster (Chicago: University of Chicago Press, 1991).
3. Ibid., 9.
4. Ibid.
5. Ibid., 16.
6. Ibid.
7. Ibid., 22.
8. Ibid., 24.
9. Robert T. Shannon, *Report of Cases Argued and Determined in the Supreme Court of Tennessee*, vol. 85 (Louisville, KY: Fetter Law Book Company, 1902), 616.
10. Wells, *Crusade*, 32.
11. Ibid., 64.
12. "The New Negro Crime," *Harper's Weekly* 48 (January 23,1904), 120–21.
13. Wells, *Crusade*, 66.
14. Ibid.
15. "Lynch Law in All Its Phases," address at Tremont Temple in the Boston Monday Lectureship, February 13, 1893, *Our Day* (Boston: Our Day Publishing Co., 1893), 333–47.
16. Ida B.Wells, *Southern Horrors: Lynch Law in All Its Phases* (New York: *New York Age*, 1892), 54.
17. Ibid., 10.
18. Quoted in Linda O. McMurray, *To Keep the Waters Troubled: The Life of Ida B. Wells* (New York: Oxford University Press, 1998), 244.
19. Booker T. Washington quoted in Louis R. Harlan, *Booker T.*

Washington: The Wizard of Tuskegee (New York: Oxford University Press), 265.

20. T. Thomas Fortune to Booker T. Washington, September 25, 1899, in *The Booker T. Washington Papers* (Urbana: University of Illinois Press, 1976), 5:220.

21. Paula J. Giddings, *Ida: A Sword Among Lions* (New York: Harper-Collins, 2008), 678.

NOTE ON THE TEXT

1. Ida B. Wells-Barnett, *The Memphis Diary of Ida B. Wells*, ed. Miriam DeCosta-Willis (Boston: Beacon Press, 1995).

CHAPTER I: "IOLA, THE PRINCESS OF THE PRESS"

1. Ida B. Wells, *Crusade for Justice* (Chicago: University of Chicago Press, 1991), 32.

2. Ibid., 36.

3. Ibid., 37.

4. Ibid., 39.

5. Ida B. Wells-Barnett, *The Memphis Diary of Ida B. Wells*, ed. Miriam DeCosta-Willis (Boston: Beacon Press, 1995), 78.

6. Quoted in Linda O. McMurray, *To Keep the Waters Troubled* (New York: Oxford University Press, 1998).

7. Thomas Fortune (1856–1928) was the part-owner and editor of a leading black newspaper, the *New York Freeman*, which he founded in 1884 and retitled the *New York Age* in 1888. One of the nation's most well-known black journalists, he would later employ Wells at the *New York Age*.

8. In speaking of the late political revolution, Wells is referring to the election of Grover Cleveland, the first Democratic president to be elected since the Civil War.

9. Banquo's ghost is a manifestation of Macbeth's guilt in the Shakespeare play *Macbeth*. Wells uses this reference here to present the South's guilt over racial injustice as a similarly powerful apparition.

10. The *Detroit Plaindealer* was that city's first successful black newspaper.

11. Pullman cars were railroad sleeping cars owned and operated by the Chicago-based Pullman Company. As an interstate business, the Pullman Company was subject to the Constitution's Interstate Commerce Clause and accommodated African American passen-

gers even in Jim Crow states until the 1890s, when the Southern states passed a series of sleeping-car laws that effectively forced the Pullman Company to exclude blacks.

12. The "Barter of '76" (also known as the Compromise of 1876) refers to the compromise that ultimately resolved the disputed presidential election of 1876. The election was close, and the electoral votes from Florida, Louisiana, and South Carolina could not be counted, as both the Republican and Democratic parties in each state reported that their candidate had won. A compromise was reached between Republicans and Democrats in Congress, wherein Republican Rutherford B. Hayes became president in exchange for the removal of all federal troops from the South.

13. John Sherman was the younger brother of the famous general William T. Sherman of the Union Army.

14. The phrase "Waving the bloody shirt" refers to the use of political rhetoric invoking the passions and hardships of the recent war, and was widely employed by politicians in the post–Civil War period.

15. The verse that Wells quotes here is from *The Pleasures of Hope* (1799), a popular romantic poem written by Scottish poet Thomas Campbell (1777–1844).

16. Written by Harriet Beecher Stowe, *Uncle Tom's Cabin* (1852) was a bestselling antislavery novel that helped mobilize support for the abolitionist cause.

17. This quote comes from William Wordsworth's "Perfect Woman."

18. Wells is paraphrasing Luke 2:14.

19. The lines are from a work by popular nineteenth-century author Emma Dorothy Eliza Nevitte Southworth, *Self Raised; or from the Depths* (Philadelphia: T. B. Peterson and Brother, 1876).

20. G. P. M. Turner was a former Union officer and the editor of the Memphis *Daily Scimitar.*

21. The Knights of Labor was the largest and most important American labor organization in the 1880s. Founded in 1869, it reached its peak membership in the mid-1880s.

22. The Masonic and Odd Fellows lodges were popular fraternal societies.

23. Frances E. Willard was a noted temperance reformer, women's suffragist, and educator who became president of the Woman's Christian Temperance Union (WCTU) in 1879 and held that position until 1889. Tolerant of segregation within the ranks of the WCTU, Willard consistently refused to support Wells's anti-lynching movement and was largely unresponsive to the concerns of African American temperance activists.

24. Convict camps were a prominent feature of the convict lease system that emerged in the U.S. South after the Civil War. The Southern

states leased out convicts to work for planters, mining companies, railroads, and other businesses, which typically housed these workers in dirty, overcrowded quarters known as convict camps.

25. Moloch is a biblical reference to the god of the Canaanites and Phoenicians. Featured in Leviticus 18:21, Leviticus 20:2–5, and several other texts, Moloch figures in the Bible as a false god who is closely associated with child sacrifice. Leviticus 18:21 warns: "Do not give any of your children to be sacrificed to Molek, for you must not profane the name of your God. I am the LORD."

26. The "League" to which Wells refers is the National Afro-American League, a civil rights organization established in 1887 by T. Thomas Fortune.

CHAPTER II: TO CALL A THING BY ITS TRUE NAME

1. Ida B. Wells, *Crusade for Justice* (Chicago: University of Chicago Press, 1991), 41.

2. Ibid., 52.

3. Ibid., 62, 54.

4. Ibid., 72.

5. Henry MacNeal Turner was a bishop in the A.M.E Church. Originally from South Carolina, he led congregations in St. Louis, Missouri; Baltimore; and Washington, DC. Turner was politically active in the Republican Party during Reconstruction. But by the 1890s he was pessimistic about African Americans' prospects in the United States and had begun to support black emigration to Africa.

6. Published under this name between 1890 and 1894, the *Appeal-Avalanche* was one of Memphis's daily newspapers.

7. "Afro-American Sampson" is a reference to the biblical hero Sampson, who was betrayed to the Philistines by a woman named Delilah in Judges, chapters 13–16.

8. The "white Delilah" Wells refers to is mistress and betrayer of Sampson in the Book of Judges.

9. The Prohibition Party was a political party founded in 1869 that opposed the sale and consumption of alcoholic beverages. Influential in U.S. politics during the late nineteenth and early twentieth centuries, it helped usher in Prohibition in 1919, and largely collapsed after the repeal of Prohibition.

10. *Demimonde* is a French term referring to a class of women on the fringe of respectable society, typically unmarried women kept by wealthy lovers.

11. Bishop (Oscar P.) Fitzgerald was a white Southern Methodist who maintained that Northern critics of lynching showed too little sympathy for the female victims of the "unspeakable crimes" avenged by lynching.

12. Winchesters are live-action repeating rifles.

13. Both the White Liners and the Ku Klux Klan were white paramilitary organizations that sought to oust Republicans from office, and used force to prevent freedmen from exercising their franchise.

14. Henry W. Grady, a well-known Democratic booster of the New South, was the editor of the *Atlanta Constitution*.

15. The plebeians were the common people of ancient Rome.

16. The Fire-Eaters were a group of extremist proslavery politicians from the South who advocated secession and were influential in the forming of the Confederate States of America.

17. "Judge Tourjee" refers to Albion W. Tourgee, who was a civil rights activist and outspoken supporter of black civil rights. Judge Tourgee, as he was called, was well known in the black press for his stance against lynching, segregation, disenfranchisement, and white supremacy. Tourgee litigated for the plaintiff in the famous segregation case *Plessy v. Ferguson* (1896).

18. A radical abolitionist, William Lloyd Garrison fought for the immediate emancipation of slaves and supported full civil and legal rights for blacks. He was the founder and editor of the *Liberator* and a founding member of the American Anti-Slavery Society.

19. Nat Turner was an enslaved Virginian who led a revolt in 1831 in Southampton County, Virginia. Turner and his approximately sixty followers killed fifty-five white men, women, and children before they were captured and executed.

20. Abolitionist John Brown and his followers (five black men and seventeen whites) raided the federal arsenal at Harpers Ferry, Virginia, on October 16, 1859, in an unsuccessful attempt to spearhead a large-scale revolt among Virginia slaves. The raid lasted thirty-six hours. Brown was ultimately tried, convicted, and executed for treason. Brown's raid is often seen as a key moment in the events leading to the Civil War.

21. Elijah Lovejoy was a Presbyterian minister, newspaper editor, and abolitionist who was murdered by a proslavery mob in Alton, Illinois, on November 7, 1937.

22. Massachusetts senator Charles Sumner was brutally beaten with a cane by proslavery congressman Preston Brooks of South Carolina on the Senate floor, May 22, 1856.

23. Robert E. Lee, general in the Confederate Army.

24. "My Country, 'Tis of Thee" (also known as "America") is a patriotic song written by Samuel Francis Smith in 1831. It served as the

national anthem before "The Star-Spangled Banner" was adopted as the official anthem.

25. Henry Smith was lynched on February 1, 1893, at the Paris Fairgrounds in Paris, Texas, before a crowd of ten thousand people, who tortured him for more than an hour before burning him alive.

CHAPTER III: IDA B. WELLS ABROAD

1. Isabella Mayo to Ida B. Wells, September 12, 1893, Frederick Douglass Papers.

2. Ida B. Wells to Frederick Douglass, March 13, 1894, Frederick Douglass Papers.

3. To date, two of her original dispatches to the *Daily Inter Ocean* are unavailable, and therefore not included in this book: "Ida B. Wells Abroad. Speaking in Liverpool Against Lynchers of Negroes," *Daily Inter Ocean*, April 9, 1894, 8; and "Ida B. Wells Abroad. The Bishop of Manchester on American Lynching," *Daily Inter Ocean*, April 28, 1894, 10. The material in both of these articles, however, and in her other dispatches as well can be found in Ida B. Wells, *Crusade for Justice* (Chicago: University of Chicago Press, 1991).

4. Charles F. Aked, "The Race Problem in America," *Contemporary Review* 65 (June 1894), 827.

5. *New York Times*, August 2, 1894; on the Southern press's response to Wells's anti-lynching campaign, see Floyd Crawford, "Ida B. Wells: Some Reactions to her Anti-Lynching Campaign in Britain," March 2, 1963, the Ida B. Wells Papers (Box 9, Folder 2), Special Collections Research Center, University of Chicago Library.

6. Chancery Courts are courts of equity designed to provide remedies not available under common law. Most common in England, they also exist in common-law jurisdictions in the United States, which include the states of Delaware, Mississippi, South Carolina, and Tennessee.

7. Ralph Waldo Emerson (1803–82) was an American essayist, poet, and lecturer. He is most well-known for leading the Transcendentalist movement of the mid-nineteenth century.

8. Ratified in February 1870, the Fifteenth Amendment to the United States Constitution prohibits the states from denying any citizen the right to vote based on that citizen's "race, color, or previous condition of servitude."

9. The term *the Solid South* refers to the one-party system (which supported the Democratic Party) that prevailed in the Southern United States between the 1890s and the civil rights movement.

10. Wells is referring to Zachariah Chandler (1813–79), an antislavery politician who served in the U.S. Senate from the state of Michigan

between 1857 and 1875. He was appointed secretary of the interior under Ulysses S. Grant in 1875 and served in that office until 1877.

11. The black congressmen in the Reconstruction era (to 1877) were Joseph Rainey (SC), Jefferson F. Long (GA), Robert C. De Large (SC), Robert B. Elliott (SC), Benjamin S. Turner (AL), Josiah T. Walls (FL), Richard H. Cain (SC), John R. Lynch (MS), James T. Rapier (AL), Alonzo J. Ransier (SC), Jeremiah Haralson (AL), John Adams Hyman (NC), Charles E. Nash (LA), and Robert Smalls (SC).

12. British Women's Liberal Association most likely refers to the Women's Liberal Federation, founded between 1886 and 1887.

13. Judge A. W. Tourgee refers to Albion W. Tourgee, see chapter 2, note 17.

14. Fugitive Slave Law, a controversial law passed by the United States Congress in 1850, declared that all runaway slaves must be returned to their masters.

15. John Bright (1811–99) was a British reform politician, Quaker, and outspoken opponent of the slaveholding South in the American Civil War.

16. Dr. Brooke Herford (1803–1903) was a British Unitarian minister who spent some time in the United States, most notably at Harvard University as one of the original members of the Board of Preachers. The university also awarded him an honorary degree of Doctor of Divinity.

17. Bishop Edward Mary Fitzgerald (1833–1907) was born in Ireland and moved to the United States during his childhood. Fitzgerald served the diocese of Little Rock, Arkansas, from 1867 to 1907. Bishop Atticus Green Haygood (1839–96) was a Georgia-born bishop of the Methodist Episcopal Church, South, and also served as president of Emory College (now Emory University). Haygood was a New South promoter and advocated reconciliation, reunion, and educational opportunities for African Americans.

18. Omnibuses were the precursors to the electric streetcar. The omnibus was an elongated horse-drawn carriage designed to carry passengers.

19. Unknown before and after his clash with Wells, J. Thomas Turner was a self-proclaimed representative of the respectable portion of the black population in Memphis who testified against her and claimed she was spreading falsehoods about the conditions of race relations in the South. His testimony was used by the *Daily Commercial* to discredit Wells.

20. British women's rights activist and suffragist Helen Bright Clark (1840–1927) was the daughter of John Bright (1811–89), a Quaker member of the British House of Commons. An abolitionist, John Bright supported the Union during the Civil War.

21. Little information exists on Thomas Cropper Ryley or his wife, but, like Helen Bright Clark, they seem to have been members of a British Quaker family once active in antislavery circles.

22. Harvey Ward Beecher is likely a misprinted reference to the abolitionist clergyman Henry Ward Beecher (1813–77), who was the brother of the author of *Uncle Tom's Cabin* (1852), Harriet Beecher Stowe.

23. The *Liberator* was an influential abolitionist newspaper published by William Lloyd Garrison.

24. Possibly Dr. Thomas Price, a British abolitionist.

25. William Wells Brown (1814–84) was born into slavery in Lexington, Kentucky. He escaped to the North in 1834. He was a prominent black abolitionist, writer, and historian. He lectured in England during the early 1850s to gather support for the abolitionist cause.

26. Charles H. Spurgeon (1834–92) was a popular Baptist minister who led a large congregation in London between 1854 and 1892.

27. Dean Swift refers to the Anglo-Irish satirist Jonathan Swift (1667–1745). Best known as the author of *Gulliver's Travels*, Swift also served as the dean of St. Patrick's Cathedral in Dublin.

28. John Mitchell Jr. (1863–1929) was the longtime editor of the African American newspaper the *Richmond Planet*, which was known for campaigning for black civil rights and against lynching.

29. The influential black leader Booker T. Washington (1856–1915) was an ex-slave educator who founded the Tuskegee Normal and Industrial Institute.

30. Harry C. Smith (1863–1941) was a black journalist, publisher, and member of the Ohio legislature. Along with several partners, Smith founded the *Cleveland Gazette* newspaper, which he used to advocate for civil rights and also as a platform to get into politics.

31. Peter H. Clark (1829–1925) was founder and principal of Ohio's first public high school for black students. He was a political activist in Ohio, and also an associate of Frederick Douglass.

32. H(enry) M(acNeal) Turner (see chapter 2, note 5).

CHAPTER IV: THE CRUSADE CONTINUES

1. The Woman's Loyal Union was an African American women's club established in New York and Brooklyn in 1892. The union was initially established to support the publication of *Southern Horrors*, but by 1894 its members were working to create a national antilynching organization. That year, they presented Congress with more than a dozen petitions calling for a congressional resolution to investigate lynching in the South from women's organizations in the United States and Canada.

2. Ida B. Wells-Barnett, *A Red Record. Tabulated Statistics and Alleged Causes of Lynchings in the United States, 1892–1893–1894. Respectfully Submitted to the Nineteenth Century Civilization in "the Land of the Free and the Home of the Brave"* (Chicago: Donohue and Henneberry, 1895), 5.

3. This reference to selling slaves "Down South" refers to the domestic slave trade. Most active during the antebellum era, this trade involved the sale of slaves from the more populous, well-established slave states of the upper South to newly settled states and territories in the lower South. Slaves were typically sold as individuals rather than in family units. Wells's mother lost most of her family to such sales.

4. *Mésalliance* is an old-fashioned term for marriage with a person of inferior social position.

5. The "relic hunters" who attended lynchings came home with the body parts and charred flesh that they collected from the corpses of lynching victims.

6. *Grogshop* was a common nineteenth-century term for an establishment that sold liquor.

7. The phrase the "Athens of the South" refers to Nashville, which was so known because it was home to multiple institutions of higher learning—for both blacks and whites. The city built a replica of the Parthenon.

8. Dwight C. Moody was a wildly popular American evangelist and publisher whom Wells was critical of for his failure to speak out against lynching.

9. Douglass was named minister to Haiti in 1889 and held the post until 1891.

10. Established in 1891, the Populist Party, or People's Party, was a political party formed by white farmers in the South and the Midwest. Hard-hit by the low agricultural prices of the 1890s, they also felt exploited by the railroads, merchants, and other business interests and organized to represent the interests of the small farmer. Most active during 1892 to 1896, some branches of the Populist Party allied with black farmers for brief periods of time, but they never succeeded in sustaining a biracial political alliance.

11. The abolitionist clergyman Henry Ward Beecher is discussed chapter 3, note 22. James Russell Lowell (1819–91) and John G. Whittier (1807–92) were American poets who supported abolition. Both hailed from Massachusetts and were members of a group known as the Fireside Poets, who were known for writing accessible poems that could be enjoyed by families around their firesides.

12. Founded by Wells-Barnett in 1895, the Central Anti-Lynching League worked alongside the Ida B. Wells Club to distribute *A Red Record* to humanitarian organizations.

13. The Chicago anarchists bombed Haymarket Square in Chicago on May 4, 1886, in an incident known as the Haymarket Affair. The violence took place at what was supposed be a peaceful rally to support workers who were striking for an eight-hour day.

CHAPTER V: TWENTIETH-CENTURY JOURNALISM AND LETTERS

1. Linda O. McMurray, *To Keep the Waters Troubled* (New York: Oxford University Press, 1998), 384, note 33.
2. A billet is a billy club.
3. A derringer is a pocket pistol.
4. Founded by a group of white businessmen in Birmingham, Alabama, in 1894, the International Migration Society was the brainchild of A.M.E. Church bishop Henry McNeal Turner, who by the 1890s had become a proponent of black emigration back to Africa. The IMS was founded to recruit prospective immigrants to Liberia, and arrange for their transportation there.
5. The Red Shirt bands were a Reconstruction-era white paramilitary group. Supporters of the Democratic Party who used force to help their candidates get elected, the Red Shirts originated in Mississippi and quickly spread to other states.
6. The National Afro-American Council was the nation's first national civil rights organization. A precursor to the NAACP, it was founded by newspaper editors T. Thomas Fortune and Bishop Alexander Walters at a meeting in Rochester, New York, in 1898. Wells-Barnett attended and was initially appointed as the council's secretary, but in 1899 she became the chairman of the council's newly formed Anti-Lynching Bureau.
7. The Dreyfus Affair was a political scandal in France in which Captain Alfred Dreyfus was accused of having sent French military secrets to the German Embassy in Paris. The treatment of Dreyfus raised questions of anti-Semitism in France.
8. Benjamin Ryan Tillman Jr., who was known as Pitchfork Ben Tillman (1847–1918), was the governor of South Carolina between 1890 and 1894 and a U.S. senator from 1895 to 1918. A Democrat, Tillman billed himself as the "Champion of White Men's Rule and Woman's Virtue" and maintained that he would "willingly lead a mob in lynching a Negro who had committed an assault upon a white woman." Quoted in Francis Butler Simkins, *Pitchfork Ben Tillman* (Baton Rouge: Louisiana State University Press, 1944), 86.
9. The Nat Turner Rebellion was a slave rebellion that took place in Southampton County, Virginia, in August 1831. The rebels killed

between 55 and 65 whites before they were subdued. In the aftermath of the revolt, 56 accused rebels were executed, and another 100 to 200 were killed by white mobs and militia members. The rebellion ignited widespread fear among whites and inspired a number of state legislatures across the South to pass new and more restrictive laws further limiting the rights of enslaved and free blacks.

10. "San Domingan Horrors" is a reference to the five-year struggle that transformed the French colony of Saint-Domingue to the Independent Republic of Haiti between 1791 and January 1804. Haiti's successful revolt resulted in the permanent elimination of slavery in the new nation.

11. Congressman George White was a Republican representative from North Carolina between 1897 and 1901. The last of a generation of black congressmen, White was the only remaining African American representative in Congress at the turn of the twentieth century.

12. Miss Addams is Chicago reformer Jane Addams (1860–1935). The founder of Hull House, a famous settlement house dedicated to educating and Americanizing Chicago's white immigrant population, Addams achieved international recognition for her work.

13. Industrial education was the form of education that Booker T. Washington advocated as most suited to African Americans. The founder of the Tuskegee Institute, Booker T. Washington rose to fame among white philanthropists by arguing that black Southerners would be best educated and uplifted by learning the practical skills needed for industrial labor rather than the more sophisticated subjects typically taught in institutions of higher education that served white students. French and Latin would be of no use to rural black Southerners, Washington insisted. However, his plan for industrial education did not acknowledge that Southern blacks were largely shut out of industrial jobs, or provide for the education of black teachers and leaders.

14. Ignatius Loyola Donnelly was a popular writer and amateur scientist who also served as a Republican congressman from Minnesota between 1863 and 1868.

15. Founded in 1881 by Booker T. Washington as a teacher's college, Tuskegee Institute quickly became one of the nation's premier institutions for industrial education for African Americans.

16. The Business League that Wells-Barnett refers to is the National Negro Business League, which was founded by Booker T. Washington in 1900.

17. The Freedman's Saving and Trust Company was founded by the U.S. government in 1865 and survived until 1874. The bank was created to provide financial services to black veterans of the Civil

War, as well as other freed slaves, and also provided loans for black community organizations. Its lending practices also helped black communities build hospitals, churches, and schools.

18. Founded in 1861 by the American Missionary Association, the Freedmen's Aid Society founded freedmen's schools for ex-slaves and sent teachers to the South during the Civil War and Reconstruction.

19. Established in 1846 and supported primarily by Congregationalist, Methodist, and Presbyterian churches, the American Missionary Association was a Protestant abolitionist group that went on to found and fund the Freedmen's Aid Society.

20. Founded in 1865 and operated by independent boards of Northern philanthropists, Atlanta University was and is a nondenominational black university. During Wells's lifetime it became known for promoting a liberal arts education for black students (as opposed to a Booker T. Washington–style industrial education).

21. Collis P. Huntington (1821–1900) was a railroad magnate who helped build the Central Pacific Railroad. He was also involved in the development of other interstate lines, including the Southern Pacific Railroad and the Chesapeake and Ohio Railway.

22. The Dutch slave ship (*White Lion*) that arrived in Jamestown, Virginia, in 1619 is widely known for bringing the first black Africans to British North America.

23. Abraham Lincoln, Ulysses S. Grant, and John A. Logan are Illinois's most famous nineteenth-century political leaders. Lincoln and Grant need no introduction; Logan was a Republican politician who served as an Illinois state senator, congressman, and U.S. senator. He is also known for founding Memorial Day.

24. The Springfield Riot took place on August 14, 1908. The violence began after a white mob formed to address reports that two black men were being held for alleged assaults against a white woman. The vigilantes hunted down the two men at the city jail, only to find that justice officials had secretly transported the prisoners out of town. When the mob discovered the prisoners were gone, they rioted, terrorizing their town's black community and lynching two other black men who had no connection to the crime. Black barber Scott Burton died while attempting to defend his shop, and William Donegan, who was between seventy-five and eighty-three years old, was hung in retaliation for his thirty-two-year marriage to a white woman. In addition to causing these senseless murders, the Springfield Riot was notable for having taken place in a Northern state, and in the town where Abraham Lincoln was born. It suggested that lynching was moving north, which horrified many progressives and thereby helped to inspire the creation of a new national civil rights organization: the NAACP.

25. In criticizing South Carolina for ignoring the principles that Payne laid down in the Declaration of Independence, Wells appears to mistake Thomas Paine, the author of *Common Sense*, with Thomas Jefferson, who penned the Declaration of Independence.

26. Here Wells refers to Fifth Avenue in New York City and Michigan Avenue in Chicago.

27. Chiropody is the treatment of the feet.

28. Harriet Beecher Stowe (1811–96) was a nineteenth-century novelist who is most famous for writing *Uncle Tom's Cabin*.

29. The Panic of 1893 was a nationwide economic depression.

30. "St. Bartholomew's Day" refers to the St. Bartholomew's Day Massacre, which took place in August 1752 during the French Wars of Religion, and resulted in deaths of thousands of French Huguenots. The violence was triggered by the French royal family, whose assassination of several important Huguenot leaders unleashed a wave of Roman Catholic mob violence against the Protestant sect.

31. "Turks in Armenia" is a reference to the Armenian genocide that took place in the years during and after World War I; and when Hurd notes the "German army for its barbarity in Belgium," he is referring to the crimes the German army perpetrated against the Belgian people during World War I. Germany invaded neutral Belgium in its effort to seize France as part of the Schlieffen Plan.

32. A shirtsleeve gathering is an informal gathering.

33. The C.B.&Q., or the Chicago, Burlington and Quincy Railroad, traversed the midwestern United States.

34. A B&O roundhouse is a building that is used to service locomotives. It is traditionally a large circular or semicircular structure.

35. The "Russian Black Hundred" is a reference to the ultranationalist, anti-Semitic groups that organized in Russia during the early twentieth century.

36. "The state of Lincoln, Logan and Grant" (see note 23).

37. The Farmer's Household Union is the Progressive Farmers and Household Union of America, an Arkansas-based African American organization that aimed "to advance the interests of the Negro, morally and intellectually, and to make him a better citizen and a better farmer."